MW00782360

# THE NEW AMERICAN COMMENTARY

An Exegetical and Theological
Exposition of Holy Scripture

**General Editor**
E. RAY CLENDENEN

**Assistant General Editor, OT**
KENNETH A. MATHEWS

**Assistant General Editor, NT**
DAVID S. DOCKERY

**Consulting Editors**

**Old Testament**
L. RUSS BUSH
DUANE A. GARRETT
LARRY L. WALKER

**New Testament**
RICHARD R. MELICK, JR.
PAIGE PATTERSON
CURTIS VAUGHAN

**Manuscript Editors**
LINDA L. SCOTT
MARC A. JOLLEY

# THE NEW AMERICAN COMMENTARY

Volume
17

EZEKIEL

Lamar Eugene Cooper, Sr.

BROADMAN
& HOLMAN
PUBLISHERS

© Copyright 1994 • Broadman & Holman Publishers
All rights reserved
4201-17
ISBN 0-8054-0117-2
Subject Heading: Bible. O.T. Ezekiel
Library of Congress Catalog Card Number: 93-48996
Printed in the United States of America

---

Unless otherwise indicated, Scripture quotations are from the Holy Bible, *New International Version* (NIV), copyright © 1973, 1978, 1984 by International Bible Society. Used by permission of Zondervan Bible Publishers. Quotations marked REB are from *The Revised English BIble.* Copyright © Oxford University Press and Cambridge University Press, 1989. Reprinted by permission. Quotations marked NEB are from *The New English Bible.* Copyright © The Delegates of the Oxford University Press and the Syndics of the Cambridge University Press, 1961, 1970. Used by permission. Scripture quotations marked GNB are from the Good News Bible, the Bible in Today's English Version. Old Testament: Copyright © American Bible Society 1976; New Testament: Copyright © American Bible Society 1966, 1971, 1976. Used by permission. Quotations marked NRSV are from the *New Revised Standard Version of the Bible,* copyright © 1989 by the Division of Christian Education of the National Council of Churches of Christ in the United States of America. Used by permission. All rights reserved. Quotations marked NASB are from the *New American Standard Bible.* © The Lockman Foundation, 1960, 1962, 1963, 1968, 1971, 1972, 1973, 1975, 1977. Used by permission. Quotations marked NKJV are from the *New King James Version.* Copyright © 1979, 1980, 1982, Thomas Nelson, Inc. Publishers. The map on p. 428 was adapted from THE EXPOSITOR'S BIBLE COMMENTARY, VOL. 6 edited by Frank E. Gaebelein. Copyright © 1986 by The Zondervan Corporation. Used by permission of Zondervan Publishing House.

**Library of Congress Cataloging-in-Publication Data**

Cooper, Lamar Eugene, 1942–
    Ezekiel / Lamar Eugene Cooper, Sr.
      p.  cm. — (The New American Commentary ; vol. 17)
    Includes index.
    ISBN 0-8054-0117-2
    1. Bible. O.T. Ezekiel—Commentaries.  I. Title.  II. Series:
New American commentary ; v. 17.
BS1545.3.C66
224'.407—dc20

*To My Family*

Barbara Ann
Lamar, Jr., Kristi, Elizabeth, & Sarah
Stephen Paul
Ruth Ann
Christopher David

with gratitude to our Lord
for your love and support

# Editors' Preface

God's Word does not change. God's world, however, changes in every generation. These changes, in addition to new findings by scholars and a new variety of challenges to the gospel message, call for the church in each generation to interpret and apply God's Word for God's people. Thus, THE NEW AMERICAN COMMENTARY is introduced to bridge the twentieth and twenty-first centuries. This new series has been designed primarily to enable pastors, teachers, and students to read the Bible with clarity and proclaim it with power.

In one sense THE NEW AMERICAN COMMENTARY is not new, for it represents the continuation of a heritage rich in biblical and theological exposition. The title of this forty-volume set points to the continuity of this series with an important commentary project published at the end of the nineteenth century called AN AMERICAN COMMENTARY, edited by Alvah Hovey. The older series included, among other significant contributions, the outstanding volume on Matthew by John A. Broadus, from whom the publisher of the new series, Broadman Press, partly derives its name. The former series was authored and edited by scholars committed to the infallibility of Scripture, making it a solid foundation for the present project. In line with this heritage, all NAC authors affirm the divine inspiration, inerrancy, complete truthfulness, and full authority of the Bible. The perspective of the NAC is unapologetically confessional and rooted in the evangelical tradition.

Since a commentary is a fundamental tool for the expositor or teacher who seeks to interpret and apply Scripture in the church or classroom, the NAC focuses on communicating the theological structure and content of each biblical book. The writers seek to illuminate both the historical meaning and contemporary significance of Holy Scripture.

In its attempt to make a unique contribution to the Christian community, the NAC focuses on two concerns. First, the commentary emphasizes how each section of a book fits together so that the reader becomes aware of the theological unity of each book and of Scripture as a whole. The writers, however, remain aware of the Bible's inherently rich variety. Second, the NAC is produced with the conviction that the Bible primarily belongs to the church. We believe that scholarship and the academy provide an indispensable foundation for biblical understanding and the service of Christ, but the editors and authors of this series have attempted to communicate the findings of their research in a manner that will build up the whole body of Christ. Thus, the commentary concentrates on theological exegesis while providing practical, applicable exposition.

THE NEW AMERICAN COMMENTARY's theological focus enables the reader to see the parts as well as the whole of Scripture. The biblical books vary in content, context, literary type, and style. In addition to this rich variety, the editors and authors recognize that the doctrinal emphasis and use of the biblical books differs in various places, contexts, and cultures among God's people. These factors, as well as other concerns, have led the editors to give freedom to the writers to wrestle with the issues raised by the scholarly community surrounding each book and to determine the appropriate shape and length of the introductory materials. Moreover, each writer has developed the structure of the commentary in a way best suited for expounding the basic structure and the meaning of the biblical books for our day. Generally, discussions relating to contemporary scholarship and technical points of grammar and syntax appear in the footnotes and not in the text of the commentary. This format allows pastors and interested laypersons, scholars and teachers, and serious college and seminary students to profit from the commentary at various levels. This approach has been employed because we believe that all Christians have the privilege and responsibility to read and seek to understand the Bible for themselves.

Consistent with the desire to produce a readable, up-to-date commentary, the editors selected the *New International Version* as the standard translation for the commentary series. The selection was made primarily because of the NIV's faithfulness to the original languages and its beautiful and readable style. The authors, however, have been given the liberty to differ at places from the NIV as they develop their own translations from the Greek and Hebrew texts.

The NAC reflects the vision and leadership of those who provide oversight for Broadman Press, who in 1987 called for a new commentary series that would evidence a commitment to the inerrancy of Scripture and a faithfulness to the classic Christian tradition. While the commentary adopts an "American" name, it should be noted some writers represent countries outside the United States, giving the commentary an international perspective. The diverse group of writers includes scholars, teachers, and administrators from almost twenty different colleges and seminaries, as well as pastors, missionaries, and a layperson.

The editors and writers hope that THE NEW AMERICAN COMMEN-

TARY will be helpful and instructive for pastors and teachers, scholars and students, for men and women in the churches who study and teach God's Word in various settings. We trust that for editors, authors, and readers alike, the commentary will be used to build up the church, encourage obedience, and bring renewal to God's people. Above all, we pray that the NAC will bring glory and honor to our Lord who has graciously redeemed us and faithfully revealed himself to us in his Holy Word.

SOLI DEO GLORIA
The Editors

# Author's Preface

Human interest in eschatology is perennial. This perhaps is one reason for the enduring interest in Ezekiel. But the Book of Ezekiel is much more than a book about end time events. It also is a book about present spiritual realities relevant for every age. Ezekiel was a man of unique abilities and calling well equipped to share those spiritual realities. He was a priest, a prophet, a captive in exile, a husband, and seer extraordinaire. God chose Ezekiel to be his watchman at one of the most crucial hours of the history of Israel/Judah.

Ezekiel had a unique consciousness about his role and relationship with those to whom he was to minister. He saw himself as a prophet "in the midst" of a time, place, and people who desperately needed a word from Yahweh. Ezekiel used the Hebrew word *bĕtôk,* translated "among" and "in the midst," 116 times, substantially more than any other Old Testament book and more than all others combined.[1] His consciousness of his place "in the midst" of crisis and "in the midst" of a ministry to people was unique to the prophets of the Old Testament. He had lived "in the midst" of a world religious, trade, and travel center in Jerusalem. This had afforded a great opportunity to learn about human needs.

He was taken captive and placed "in the midst" of a great world empire where he was called to be a spokesman for Yahweh to an unwelcome audience. Through these experiences he learned of human tragedy and sin, of impending judgment, the wrath of a holy God, and of divine love and compassion. Near the end of his ministry he was placed by vision "in the midst" of a coming ideal kingdom. There he added the perspective of God's ultimate plan and purpose for his people. His final vision placed him "in the midst" of the city called *Yahweh Shammah* (48:35), "The Lord is There." From this final vantage point he received an eternal perspective on God's plan for all who choose by faith to serve him.

In each concentric circle of prophetic perspective Ezekiel discovered life only has meaning and purpose when one experiences and shares a per-

---

[1] The use of the word בְּתוֹךְ in Ezekiel reveals the perspective of the prophet. He saw himself as one "in the midst" of a world encompassing ministry that would impact others until the end of time and beyond. See the use of this word in 1:1; 3:15; 5:5; see notes for each verse and BDB, 1063; *KHAT,* 1510-11.

sonal relationship with God. He discovered that "in the midst" of these concentric circles God must reign supreme. "In the midst" of the storms (1:1ff.) God is on his throne. "In the midst" of a sinful world God remains holy and righteous (8:1ff.; 10:1–11:25). "In the midst" of a world of nations who set themselves against God, he is a reprover and refiner (25:1–32:32). "In the midst" of shattered dreams he is the God who redeems and restores (33:1-39:29). "In the midst" of a world of sin and strife he is the hope of a coming reign of peace (40:1–46:24). "In the midst" of a world of sin and death he is our hope of eternal life (47:1–48:35).

So the message of Ezekiel is timeless. It speaks to us "in the midst" of our world despite our need. With God's message of love and hope is for *all* people and his plan and purpose for his *own* people.

One additional word of encouragement is offered to the reader. All the Scripture references cited throughout this volume as support for comments have been carefully selected. Unfortunately many readers ignore such references in considering the text. None included in the following pages are superfluous. Many additional ideas, summary studies, and biblical principles are contained in these references, which the limitations of this volume did not permit to be considered in depth. This volume should be read with a Bible in hand to add depth and insight into the message of Ezekiel, especially as it relates to the larger context of the biblical message of redemption. All translations and observations from the Hebrew text are based on the *BHS* text.

It would have not been possible to share the message of Ezekiel had it not been for the invaluable assistance of several people. My oldest son, Lamar Cooper, Jr., and his wife, Kristi, helped with the typing of most of the manuscript and offered valuable editorial advice. My wife, Barbara, was my best critic and number one proofreader. Mr. and Mrs. W. T. Henry helped in the typing and arrangement of some tables in the introduction and appendices. One friend who wishes to remain anonymous provided assistance without which this work would not have been completed on schedule. This work, in some sense, belongs to all these friends and encouragers who came to my assistance "in the midst" of need.

Lamar E. Cooper, Sr.
Nashville, TN

# Abbreviations

## Bible Books

| | | |
|---|---|---|
| Gen | Isa | Luke |
| Exod | Jer | John |
| Lev | Lam | Acts |
| Num | Ezek | Rom |
| Deut | Dan | 1,2 Cor |
| Josh | Hos | Gal |
| Judg | Joel | Eph |
| Ruth | Amos | Phil |
| 1,2 Sam | Obad | Col |
| 1,2 Kgs | Jonah | 1,2 Thess |
| 1,2 Chr | Mic | 1,2 Tim |
| Ezra | Nah | Titus |
| Neh | Hab | Phlm |
| Esth | Zeph | Heb |
| Job | Hag | Jas |
| Ps (pl. Pss) | Zech | 1,2, Pet |
| Prov | Mal | 1,2,3 John |
| Eccl | Matt | Jude |
| Song | Mark | Rev |

## Commonly Used Sources

| | |
|---|---|
| AB | Anchor Bible |
| *ABD* | *Anchor Bible Dictionary* |
| *AEL* | *Ancient Egyptian Literature,* M. Lichtheim |
| *AJSL* | *American Journal of Semitic Languages and Literatures* |
| *AnBib* | *Analecta Biblica* |
| *ANET* | *Ancient Near Eastern Texts,* ed. J. B. Pritchard |
| AOAT | Alter Orient und Altes Testament |
| *AOTS* | *Archaeology and Old Testament Study,* ed. D. W. Thomas |
| ATD | Das Alte Testament Deutsch |
| *BASOR* | *Bulletin of the American Schools of Oriental Research* |
| BDB | F. Brown, S. R. Driver, and C. A. Briggs, *Hebrew and English Lexicon of the Old Testament* |

| | |
|---|---|
| BHS | Biblia hebraica stuttgartensia |
| *Bib* | *Biblica* |
| BKAT | Biblischer Kommentar: Altes Testament |
| *BSac* | *Bibliotheca Sacra* |
| BSC | Bible Study Commentary |
| *BT* | *Bible Translator* |
| *BurH* | *Buried History* |
| BZAW | Beihefte zur ZAW |
| CAH | Cambridge Ancient History |
| CB | Cambridge Bible for Schools and Colleges |
| CBC | Cambridge Bible Commentary |
| *CBQ* | *Catholic Biblical Quarterly* |
| *CHAL* | *Concise Hebrew and Aramaic Lexicon,* ed. W. L. Holladay |
| *CTR* | *Criswell Theological Review* |
| *DOTT* | *Documents from Old Testament Times,* ed. D. W. Thomas |
| EBC | Expositor's Bible Commentary |
| *Ebib* | *Etudes bibliques* |
| FB | Forschung zur Bibel |
| FOTL | Forms of Old Testament Literature |
| GKC | Gesenius' Hebrew Grammar, ed. E. Kautzsch, tr. A. E. Cowley |
| HAT | Handbuch zum Alten Testament |
| HDR | Harvard Dissertations in Religion |
| Her | Hermeneia |
| HKAT | Handkommentar zum Alten Testament |
| HSM | Harvard Semitic Monographs |
| HT | Helps for Translators |
| *HUCA* | *Hebrew Union College Annual* |
| *IB* | *Interpreter's Bible* |
| IBC | Interpretation: A Bible Commentary for Teaching and Preaching |
| ICC | International Critical Commentary |
| *IDB* | *Interpreter's Dictionary of the Bible,* ed. G. A. Buttrick et al. |
| IDBSup | IDB Supplementary Volume |
| *IEJ* | *Israel Exploration Journal* |
| IES | Israel Exploration Society |
| *Int* | *Interpretation* |
| *ISBE* | *International Standard Bible Encyclopedia,* rev. ed. G. W. Bromiley |
| ITC | International Theological Commentary |

| | |
|---|---|
| *JAOS* | *Journal of the American Oriental Society* |
| *JBL* | *Journal of Biblical Literature* |
| *JEA* | *Journal of Egyptian Archaeology* |
| *JNES* | *Journal of Near Eastern Studies* |
| *JSOR* | *Journal of the Society for Oriental Research* |
| *JSOT* | *Journal for the Study of the Old Testament* |
| JSOTSup | JSOT—Supplement Series |
| *JSS* | *Journal of Semitic Studies* |
| *JTS* | *Journal of Theological Studies* |
| *JTSNS* | *Journal of Theological Studies, New Series* |
| KAT | Kommentar zum Alten Testament |
| KB | Koehler and W. Baumgartner, *Lexicon in Veteris Testamenti libros* |
| LCC | Library of Christian Classics |
| *LLAVT* | *Lexicon Linguae Aramaicae Veteris Testamenti* |
| NICOT | New International Commentary on the Old Testament |
| NJPS | New Jewish Publication Society Version |
| OTL | Old Testament Library |
| *PCB* | *Peake's Commentary on the Bible,* ed. M. Black and H. H. Rowley |
| *POTT* | *Peoples of Old Testament Times,* ed. D. J. Wiseman |
| *RB* | *Revue biblique* |
| RSR | Recherches de science religieuse |
| SBLDS | Society of Biblical Literature Dissertation Series |
| SBT | Studies in Biblical Theology |
| SR | Studies in Religion/Sciences religieuses |
| *TDOT* | *Theological Dictionary of the Old Testament,* ed. G. J. Botterweck and H. Ringgren |
| *TJ* | *Trinity Journal* |
| TOTC | Tyndale Old Testament Commentaries |
| *TWAT* | Theologisches Wörterbuch zum Alten Testament, ed. G. J. Botterweck and H. Ringgren |
| *TynBul* | *Tyndale Bulletin* |
| *VT* | *Vetus Testamentum* |
| WBC | Word Biblical Commentaries |
| WMANT | Wissenschaftliche Monographien zum Alten und Neuen Testament |
| *ZAW* | *Zeitschrift für die alttestamentliche Wissenschaft* |

# Contents

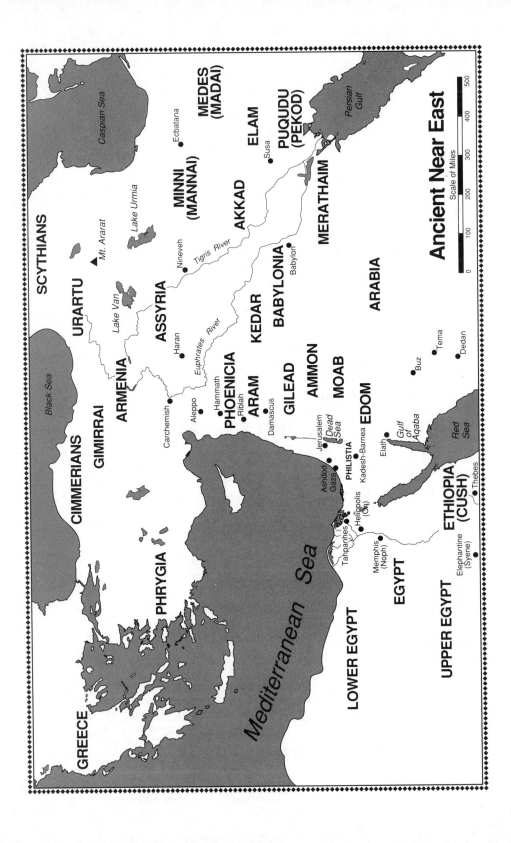

# Ezekiel

--------------------- **INTRODUCTION** ---------------------

In spite of the conquest of Judah by the Babylonians in 605 B.C., the Hebrew people were convinced of two things. First, they believed Jerusalem was inviolable. Though they had suffered the temporary setback of Babylonian domination, their city was still under Jewish administration. The city was the seat of Yahweh worship (Ps 48:1-14), and thus the people believed it would never be destroyed or fall to a pagan power. Second, they believed that those taken captive in 605 B.C. would be in Babylon only a short time. They were sure that friends, relatives, and leaders taken hostage to Babylon would be coming home soon.[1]

Nine years had elapsed since the day Nebuchadnezzar had come to

---

[1] W. Eichrodt, *Ezekiel,* OTL (Philadelphia: Westminster, 1970), 2-4; J. A. Thompson, *The Book of Jeremiah,* NICOT (Grand Rapids: Eerdmans, 1980), 22; H. L. Ellison, *Ezekiel: The Man and His Message* (Grand Rapids: Eerdmans, 1965), 20; P. R. Ackroyd, *Exile and Restoration,* OTL (Philadelphia: Westminster, 1968), 106-7.

Jerusalem and set up a provisional government with Eliakim, one of the sons of Josiah, as his vassal. He gave Eliakim the throne name of Jehoiakim. Unwise policies and unsound advisors led him to attempt a break with Babylon. Nebuchadnezzar quickly responded, and again the armies of Babylon returned to the streets of Jerusalem. Jehoiakim was taken hostage to Babylon with a second group of captives. His son Jehoiachin replaced him on the throne, and after only three months he also was supplanted by Zedekiah, who was another of the sons of Josiah.[2] Among those taken captive in 597 B.C. was a young priest named Ezekiel who fulfilled a crucial ministry to the exiles in Babylon and to the populace still in Jerusalem, a prophetic ministry that has affected God's people in every age since that time.

## 1. Historical Background

After the death of Solomon the years of the divided kingdoms of Israel and Judah were years of decline in every area of their national life.[3] Moral and spiritual decadence reached its zenith in the Northern Kingdom under Ahab and Jezebel (1 Kgs 17:1–22:40), who reigned from about 874 to 853 B.C. Although the Northern Kingdom continued for another hundred and thirty years, the fall of Samaria, its capital, finally came in 722 B.C. at the hands of the Assyrians. Assyria was in the waning years of its power when Samaria was overthrown, and it soon fell prey to the rising power of Babylon. With the end of Assyrian dominance and the captivity of the Northern Kingdom, there was a glimmer of hope for Judah. A new young king named Josiah ascended the throne in Judah who desired to see a spiritual-moral revival in his kingdom.[4]

Josiah became king ca. 640 B.C. The need for a spiritual renewal was evidenced by the social, moral, and spiritual decadence in the Southern Kingdom that exceeded the corruption of Samaria. The new young king set in motion many reforms he hoped would eradicate paganism and idolatry, return the people to Yahweh worship, and restore the spiritual and moral life of the nation (2 Kgs 23:1-30).

In spite of Josiah's sincerity, the people apparently regarded the re-

---

[2] P. P. Enns, *Ezekiel* (Grand Rapids: Zondervan, 1986), 13. Zedekiah was weak and yielded to a pro-Egyptian faction that encouraged revolt against Babylon (2 Kgs 24:20; Jer 27:1-11).

[3] W. Zimmerli (*Ezekiel 1*, Her [Philadelphia: Fortress, 1983], 9-16) traces the decline of Judah in his discussion of the historical background of the Book of Ezekiel.

[4] Ibid., 11; G. W. Anderson, *The History and Religion of Israel*, NClarBib (Oxford: Cambridge University Press, 1966), 140-49.

forms as the king's personal desires, but there was no strong public senti-
ment for their support. As a result the reforms were enacted but were
superficial. Jeremiah was the first prophet who spoke out against the failure of the reform movement to produce genuine spiritual revival. He condemned those who had not been sincere in promoting the spiritual and
moral goals of the reform (see, e.g., Jer 11; 22; 27–28).[5]

Josiah had good intentions in his desire to restore Yahweh worship. He
hoped to accomplish his aims by authorizing the remodeling of the temple and by reinstating the exclusive worship of Yahweh, including sacrifices and feast days (2 Kgs 22:4-7). The hope of success for this
movement was heightened further when during the temple remodeling
the scrolls of the Law were discovered in 622 B.C.[6] The fact that the
books of the Law, the Pentateuch, had fallen into disuse, were overlooked, and were forgotten underscores just how far the nation had drift-
ed away from true worship and commitment to God. The message of the
"Book of the Covenant" (2 Kgs 22:8-20) gave legitimacy to Josiah's
good intentions. He used the message of the law and attempted with the
help of Hilkiah the priest to eradicate Baal worship, destroy all the pagan
shrines (2 Kgs 23:4-20), and reinstate Yahweh worship as the only legitimate form of worship allowed in Judah.

When Nineveh fell in 612 B.C., the people of Judah interpreted this to
be a sign that the reforms of Josiah were working. They thought God was
about to restore the former glory of Judah to the splendor and power the
nation had enjoyed under David.[7] Jeremiah consistently warned of the
danger of listening to the false prophets, who predicted a peace and prosperity that would never come (see, e.g., Jer 27–28). Because of his failure
to acknowledge that Judah was on the verge of a great moral, spiritual,
social, and economic revival, Jeremiah was rebuffed and rejected.

With the sunset of Assyrian power and the rise of Babylon also came
an attempt from Egypt under Pharaoh Neco to reassert his influence in
regional affairs. But the might of the neo-Babylonian Empire under Nebuchadnezzar proved to be too much for Egypt. Forces from the two nations met in battle at Carchemish, located in what is today modern
Turkey; and in 605 B.C. Pharaoh Neco was defeated.[8] The real tragedy in

---

[5] The exact relation of Jeremiah to the reforms of Josiah as well as the nature of the
reform movement itself is a point of discussion. Some maintain that Jeremiah opposed the
reform from the beginning as futile and ineffective (see Thompson, *Jeremiah*, 56-67).

[6] Ibid., 98-99. Jeremiah did not criticize Josiah's reform movement but did warn that
external practices could not substitute for inward obedience.

[7] Ackroyd, *Exile and Restoration*, 68-69.

[8] E. H. Merrill, *Kingdom of Priests* (Grand Rapids: Baker, 1987), 441.

this engagement came four years earlier in 609 B.C. when Pharaoh Neco, coming to aid Assyria against Babylon, killed King Josiah in a skirmish at Megiddo. Details of this clash are unknown, but with the death of Josiah also came the end of the reforms he had championed.[9]

Josiah's son Jehoahaz replaced him on the throne. But after only three months Pharaoh Neco took him captive to Egypt (Jer 22:10-12; 2 Kgs 23:31-35) and placed another son of Josiah, Eliakim, on the throne in Judah, giving him the throne name Jehoiakim. For a time Jehoiakim cooperated with Egypt. He placed heavy taxation on the people, reinstituted pagan worship, and quickly eradicated the reforms of his father.[10] When Pharaoh Neco was defeated by Nebuchadnezzar, Jehoiakim was forced to become a vassal of the king of Babylon (2 Kgs 24:1ff.). No doubt he entertained hope that Babylon's power also would be short-lived and he would soon break away and reassert Judah's independence.

From 605 B.C. to 598 B.C., Jehoiakim remained publicly loyal to Nebuchadnezzar while privately plotting to break Babylon's hold on Judah. Nebuchadnezzar learned of these plans and in 598 B.C. once again returned to Jerusalem. The events surrounding the death of Jehoiakim are unclear. He died before the Babylonian armies reached Jerusalem. He may have been kidnapped and murdered, or he may have committed suicide.[11] Jehoiakim's successor was his eighteen-year-old son Jehoiachin, also called Coniah and Jeconiah (Jer 22:24,28; 1 Chr 3:16). He too had aspirations for breaking the stranglehold of Babylonian power. He hoped that Egypt would be the key to his plan and moved to form an alliance. But after only three months on the throne Jehoiachin was deposed. Upon learning of his treachery, Nebuchadnezzar immediately removed him and took him with a group of captives to Babylon.[12] Among those captives taken in 597 B.C. was Ezekiel (2 Kgs 24:14-17).

Jehoiachin was replaced by his father's brother Mattaniah (2 Kgs 24:17), who was given the throne name Zedekiah. Expectations were high that Zedekiah's reign would usher in a new era of peace, prosperity,

---

[9] Thompson, *Jeremiah,* 22-24.

[10] The complex political currents that led to the fall of Jerusalem are of vital importance to understanding the ministry and message of Ezekiel. Excellent detailed discussion of the period may be found in Zimmerli, *Ezekiel 1,* 9-16; J. Taylor, *Ezekiel,* TOTC (Downers Grove: InterVarsity, 1969), 29-39; and Thompson, *Jeremiah,* 9-27.

[11] Taylor, *Ezekiel,* 31.

[12] Texts unearthed in the palace vaults in Babylon refer to the capture of Jehoiachin of the land of Yahudu (see D. W. Thomas, ed., *Documents from Old Testament Times* [New York: Harper & Row, 1958], 84-86).

and better relations with Babylon (see Jer 28:1-9), but it soon became evident that this was not to be.

Clearly Ezekiel never shared the optimism of his fellow citizens, nor did he recognize the legitimacy of Zedekiah's reign.[13] Strong crosscurrents of rebellion continued to flow between Edom, Moab, Ammon, Tyre, Sidon, and Judah. Egypt, under Pharaoh Hophra (also called Apries),[14] led the revolt against Babylon. Zedekiah was eager to establish his independence and was easily persuaded to join the rebellion. Nebuchadnezzar moved swiftly to crush the insurrection and remove Zedekiah (2 Kgs 25:1-7). He laid siege to Jerusalem early in 588 B.C. Zedekiah attempted to flee but was captured, and Jerusalem fell in 587/586 B.C.[15]

The last thing Zedekiah saw was the execution of his sons. He was blinded and carried captive to Babylon, where he later died. Nebuchadnezzar destroyed Jerusalem and the temple and took the commercial, political, and military leaders to Babylon.[16] The city had earned a reputation as a seat of rebellion (Neh 2:19; 6:6) due to the consistent attempts of misguided leaders to assert their independence and break free from foreign dominance.

After the fall of Jerusalem, Judah was placed under the administration of a Babylonian-appointed governor named Gedaliah (2 Kgs 25:22-26; Jer 40:5).[17] Gedeliah's administration was short. He was murdered (Jer 41:1-10), and many of the remaining refugees in Judah fled to Egypt (2 Kgs 25:22-26).

Ezekiel's ministry spanned a large part of these troubled times. The

---

[13] Ezekiel never referred to Zedekiah as מֶלֶךְ ("king"; see Taylor, *Ezekiel*, 32. He instead dated all his messages by the exile of Jehoiachin.

[14] A. Cody, *Ezekiel* (Wilmington: Michael Glazier, 1984). When the new pharaoh ascended the throne in 589 B.C., Zedekiah entertained thoughts of an alliance with Egypt against Babylon.

[15] Thompson, *Jeremiah*, 24-25. Babylon responded swiftly by sending armies to Jerusalem in the fall of 589 B.C. The city was not immediately attacked, but the Babylonians first eliminated all surrounding fortified cities.

[16] Jerusalem was burned. The stones of the palace-temple complex were heated, causing them to disintegrate, and the city was reduced to rubble. The city was under siege at least three separate times beginning Jan. 15, 588 B.C. (see 24:1-27). The defeat of the city climaxed Aug. 25, 587 B.C., though the fighting continued until early in 586 B.C. See Zimmerli, *Ezekiel 1*, 15.

[17] A large group of bullae or clay seals affixed to official documents have been unearthed in Jerusalem in the Shiloh Excavations of the City of David, on the Hill Ophel just below the temple mount. Among the 255 seals found are those of Baruch, the son of Neriah, the scribe of Jeremiah, and Gedeliah, the son of Ahikam, appointed governor by Nebuchadnezzar. See N. Avigad, *Hebrew Bullae from the Time of Jeremiah*, 24-25, 28-29; T. Schneider, "Six Biblical Signatures," *BAR* 17.4 (1991): 26-33.

book that bears his name chronicles the flow of events with exact dates from his call in July 593 B.C. to his final vision in April of 571 B.C.[18] His ministry covered more than twenty of the most critical years in Judahite history. While his messages were filled with words of hope as well as judgment, he shared the pessimism of Jeremiah concerning hope for immediate restoration. Ezekiel was not taken seriously in the early years of his ministry because he, along with Jeremiah, forecasted the eventual fall and destruction of Jerusalem (Ezek 4:1-17; Jer 25:1-4; 29:1-9). Neither were optimistic about Judah's immediate future. Jeremiah prophesied that Judah and Jerusalem were to be judged and destroyed and that their inhabitants would remain captives in Babylon for seventy years (Jer 25:11; 29:10). Ezekiel foresaw a future resurrection of the nation (Ezek 37:1-28), reunification of the Northern and Southern kingdoms, rebuilding of the temple (Ezek 40:1–42:20), and restoration of sacrificial worship (Ezek 44–48).

While the lack of reference to Ezekiel in the Book of Jeremiah and to Jeremiah in the Book of Ezekiel is somewhat puzzling, Ezekiel's messages were consistent with the messages of Jeremiah.[19] One explanation for the absence of personal reference to Ezekiel in the Book of Jeremiah was that Ezekiel was called to his prophetic ministry while a captive in Babylon.[20] Jeremiah was still in Judah and was nearing the end of a ministry that began during the reign of Josiah. He already had completed most, if not all, of his written record prior to Ezekiel's call. By the time of Ezekiel's call, Jeremiah may already have joined the refugees who fled in fear of their lives after the assassination of Gedaliah.

## 2. Canaanite Religion

One hardly can comprehend all the implications of the message of Ezekiel, especially chaps. 6 and 8, without some consideration of Canaanite worship and theology.[21] Canaanite worship first became a problem for the Hebrews after the Egyptian bondage and years of wilderness wandering just prior to the conquest. As the Hebrews approached

---

[18] For a complete list of dated prophecies with discussion, see M. Greenberg, *Ezekiel 1–20*, AB (Garden City: Doubleday, 1986), 7-11. Also see Taylor, *Ezekiel*, 36-39, and the "Dated Prophecies of Ezekiel" in this introduction.

[19] Greenberg, *Ezekiel 1–20*, 14. The description of the mood and expectations of the exiles in Jer 29 provide an excellent setting for the Book of Ezekiel.

[20] S. Fisch, *Ezekiel* (London: Soncino, 1950), 1. Ezekiel was the first prophet both to live and to prophesy in exile.

[21] See "Canaanites, History and Religion of," *HBD*, 226-30.

the land after the forty years in the wilderness, they advanced toward Canaan on the east side of the Dead Sea. As they neared the land of Moab, Balak the king became concerned. He heard how God miraculously had protected and cared for the Hebrews in the wilderness. He also heard the stories of how God had driven out their enemies before them, and he wanted to avert a similar fate (Num 22:1ff.).[22]

Balak sent representatives to employ the services of a young man named Balaam, noted as a seer and well known for his ability to pronounce imprecations or curses (Num 22:5ff.). Balak employed the young man to ascend high places of Baal worship that overlooked the camp of the Israelites. From that vantage point he was to pronounce a curse on the Hebrews. But each time Balaam opened his mouth to curse Israel, he blessed them instead. He made seven such attempts, and each time the results were the same. Numbers 24 contains a lengthy blessing that angered Balak (24:10). But Balaam explained he could not go beyond the will of the Lord in this matter (24:13). So after finishing the blessing, he returned home (24:25).

Numbers 25 reports Balak's ultimate success. Having failed in his attempt to curse the Hebrews, Balak invited them to dwell among his people. Not until later do we learn the complete details. Numbers 31:16 says that Balaam advised the women to seduce the Hebrews and bring the judgment of God upon them. What Balaam failed to accomplish directly he almost succeeded at indirectly. The judgment of God fell upon Israel, and Balak was spared. The real tragedy of this story is that Israel took this tendency toward Baal worship with them when they entered the land of Canaan.

God originally intended that there be no Canaanites left in the land after the conquest (see Exod 23:31-33; 34:12-16; Num 32:20-23; 33:51-56; Deut 1:30-32; 6:16-19; 7:1-6; 8:11-20; 11:29–12:3). His motive was to preserve the spiritual integrity of the Hebrews. When the Hebrews entered the land, they were deceived into believing that the Canaanites were no threat. So rather than ridding the land of them as the Lord had instructed, Israel found ways to coexist with the Canaanites (Judg 1:27-36), for which they were punished.

Furthermore, the Canaanites would trouble them throughout their history (Judg 2:1-3,20-23). The combination of sexual immorality and the supposed benefits of worshiping an agricultural god like Baal proved a constant temptation once introduced to the people of Israel. From these early days in the history of Israel onward, Baal worship continued to

---

[22] G. J. Wenham, *Numbers,* TOTC (Downers Grove: InterVarsity, 1981), 184-85.

plague the nation until after the exile in Babylon.[23]

Baal is a Semitic word that literally means "lord," "ownership," "authority," or "control."[24] Local deities were called Baal and were associated with portions of land as the gods of the earth.[25] The attraction of Baal worship for the Hebrews went beyond immorality. It also included the promise of agricultural, animal, and human fertility. These fertility cults used sacred prostitutes, sexual activity, and imitative magic to insure fertility in every area of life.[26]

Three basic elements of the theology of Baal worship enhanced its attractiveness.

*Relation to Cycles of Nature.* Canaanite worship was closely linked with the cycle of the seasons. The people had observed that the seasons of the year followed a predictable pattern. In the fall vegetation became dormant and withered, then died in the winter months. Each spring vegetation revived, and in the summer it flourished. Also during the dormant winter months rains came and watered the earth. The rain was associated with the fertility of the land and the resurrection of vegetation in the spring. Rituals were performed to entreat Baal to send rain and restore the fertility of the land. These involved the dying and rising of their god with appropriate laments and rejoicing (cf. Ezek 8:14). Thus the fertility cult, with its sacred prostitutes, was employed to insure the fertility of the land for another year. Such foreign practices in the name of religion and worship appealed to the young Hebrew men when the Moabite girls first introduced them to it, and it continued when they entered Canaan.

*Immorality.* Baal worship not only approved of but also encouraged immorality. The rituals of Baal worship included sexual intercourse, considered an imitative act that invited the rain to fertilize the ground. The Book of Hosea is an example of the evils and tragedy of Baal worship. Hosea, a devout man, married Gomer, a woman from a background of Baal worship (Hos 1:1-11). Soon Gomer returned to her old ways and left Hosea and their children for a life of prostitution (Hos 3:1ff.).

Like Gomer, the people of Israel exhibited only a token commitment to Yahweh (Hos 4–7). They worshiped Baal, believing that sexual acts

---

[23] Merrill, *Kingdom of Priests,* 158-59.

[24] "Baal," *HBD,* 138; BDB, 127-28.

[25] See G. Fohrer, *History of Israelite Religion* (Nashville: Abingdon, 1972), 47-48; "Fertility Cult," *HBD,* 484; U. Cassuto, "Baal and Mot in the Ugaritic Texts," *IEJ* II (1962): 77-86; J. Gray, "Hunting for Baal," *JNES* X (1951): 46-55.

[26] See discussion of Baal as master of the land in Merrill, *Kingdom of Priests,* 160-61; Fohrer, *History of Israelite Religion,* 59-60; G. A. F. Knight, *Hosea* (London: SCM, 1972), 17-19; *ANET,* 129-35, 138-42.

with sacred prostitutes would insure fruitfulness and productivity. Israel, like Gomer, had forsaken its true lover and faithful husband. As a consequence of Israel's adultery, God promised judgment (Hos 8–11). Ezekiel soundly condemned the physical and spiritual adultery of his day (see Ezek 8:1–9:11; 22:1-31).

*Polytheism.* Israel's neighbors were polytheistic. This was a constant encouragement for the Hebrews to adopt a more syncretistic approach to religious faith and practice. Hosea stressed God's demand for exclusive worship: "I am the Lord your God, who brought you out of Egypt. You shall acknowledge no God but me, no Savior except me" (Hos 13:4). Ezekiel's emphasis on the exclusiveness of worshiping Yahweh and no other gods came in a constantly recurring phrase, "Then you shall know the LORD your God."[27] This phrase was used in association with judgment passages to warn that God would make himself known through the chastening and judgment of the exile.

Baal worship was popular and difficult to eradicate from Israel because it fed on the people's lust, fear, and the desire to conform to their neighbors. It was encouraged by natural concerns for food, farms, families, and flocks, believing that Baal could help them insure the best in each of these areas. By embracing polytheistic forms of worship, the Hebrews conformed to the standards and life-style of their neighbors and thus created the social, moral, and spiritual problems that brought about their judgment.[28]

## 3. Ezekiel, the Man

Considering the major role played by Ezekiel in the last days of Judah's history, we know relatively little about the prophet's personal life. He was a priest and son of a priest (1:1) and was called to his pro-

---

[27] This is attested to by the prolific use of the identification formula found more than seventy-two times in Ezekiel. See Zimmerli, *Ezekiel 1,* 37-38; R. M. Hals, *Ezekiel,* FOTL (Grand Rapids: Eerdmans, 1989), 362, where he defines the identification or "recognition" formula often used to express the purpose of Yahweh's actions.

[28] See Knight, *Hosea,* 19-20, who has suggested at least four problems this kind of worship produced for Israel. (1) Instead of restricting sex to marriage, the Baal cult led to the corruption of morals (Hos 4:13-14; Ezek 22:1-31). (2) Yahweh demanded worship and obedience while Baal demanded appeasement. Baal worship offered a way for persons to become masters of their fate by appeasing Baal (Ezek 8:1-18). (3) In Baal worship even the gods were captives of the cycle of years. Yahweh, by contrast, was the Lord of history, nature, the cycle of days, seasons, and years. History was his arena in which to accomplish his purposes and bless his people (Ezek 16:1-63). (4) Baal offered the promise of fruitful crops, fat cattle, and fine children, promises that only God could deliver (Ezek 23:1-49).

phetic ministry while a captive in Babylonian exile. This dual role of priest as well as prophet is evident in the detail and the viewpoint of the book.[29] Ezekiel was taken captive to Babylon with the second wave of hostages during the rebellion of Jehoiakim and Jehoiachin in 597 B.C.[30] He was well acquainted with the events and the human tragedies of the last days of Judah.

Although he was taken captive in 597 B.C., Ezekiel's prophetic call and ministry did not begin until 593 B.C. His name means "God Strengthens," an appropriate title for one called to serve his people in a time of crisis. His ministry continued until at least 573 B.C. (see 40:1), but we know nothing of how it ended or of his final fate.[31] His entire ministry was conducted in Babylon. Because of his return to Jerusalem in a vision as stated in 40:1-2, some have held that he actually visited the city. Yet there is no indication he ever physically returned to the city after his capture.[32]

The prophet also was acquainted with personal tragedy. Though we know little of his personal life, we do know that he was married. There is no mention of children, but he relates that his wife died suddenly; the impact of this misfortune on his ministry is described in Ezek 24:2,15-18.

## 4. Ezekiel, the Prophet

Ezekiel was one of more than twenty-five men and women called prophet or prophetess (i.e., preacher, seer, exhorter, servant of God) in Israel. W. VanGemeren has defined a prophet of God as "an Israelite, called by God, and empowered by the Spirit, who serves as God's spokesperson, who has received authority and a revelation from God, who is a good shepherd over God's flock, [and] who demonstrates God's Word and mission by signs."[33] This certainly fit Ezekiel. He was chosen to an-

---

[29] See G. A. Cooke, *The Book of Ezekiel*, ICC (Edinburgh: T & T Clark, 1936), xxvii; D. M. G. Stalker, *Ezekiel* (London: SCM, 1968), 25-26; J. W. Wevers, *Ezekiel*, NCB (Grand Rapids: Eerdmans, 1969), 23; J. T. Bunn, "Ezekiel," BBC (Nashville: Broadman, 1971), 225; L. J. Wood, *The Prophets of Israel* (Grand Rapids: Baker, 1979), 358-59; G. Van Groningen, *Messianic Revelation in the Old Testament* (Grand Rapids: Baker, 1990), 736-39.

[30] Wood, *Prophets of Israel,* 355. Ezekiel 33:21 speaks of Ezekiel's captivity as occurring in the twelfth year before the destruction of Jerusalem.

[31] Stalker, *Ezekiel,* 29. Jewish tradition says Ezekiel was put to death by fellow Israelites who disliked his preaching.

[32] The issue of whether the visions of Jerusalem and the description of the prophet's return as described in Ezek 8:11-18 were a literal physical return or a visionary spiritual return will be discussed more fully in relation to Ezek 8:3-10.

[33] W. A. VanGemeren, *Interpreting the Prophetic Word* (Grand Rapids: Zondervan, 1990), 32.

nounce the words of God to unwelcome ears as the nation faced imminent destruction and captivity at the hands of Nebuchadnezzar. Such a
task called for courage and strong will. Ezekiel stands in the tradition of
other great individuals who were called to similar assignments such as
Amos, Hosea, Isaiah, Micah, and his contemporary, Jeremiah. In the Old
Testament are several words associated with these prophets that describe
their unique characteristics. At least six specific names were used to
identify prophets, each of which suggest various aspects of their assignments and of their character: (1) *spokesman* (*nābî;* 1 Sam 9:9; 1 Kgs
1:8); (2) *seer* (*rōʾeh;* 1 Sam 9:9; 1 Chr 29:29; 2 Chr 16:7); (3) *visionary*
(*ḥōzeh;* 2 Sam 24:11; 2 Kgs 17:13; 2 Chr 33:18; Amos 7:12); (4) *man of
God* (*ʾîš ʾĕlōhîm;* 1 Kgs 13:1-2); (5) *servant of Yahweh* (*ʿebed-yhwh;*
Dan 9:11; Amos 3:7); and (6) *messenger of Yahweh* (*malʾak-yhwh;* Mal
2:7; 3:1).[34]

Visions figure more prominently in Ezekiel than in any other Old Testament prophet except Daniel. They are recounted in detail in chaps. 1–3;
8–11; 37; 40–48. These he received in what must have appeared to be a
semiconscious state and then reported to his audience once the vision
was over (11:25). This kind of prophetic experience is sometimes called
"ecstatic," but the term is problematic and perhaps best avoided. Another
distinctive of Ezekiel's prophetic activity is the amount of drama or symbolic portrayal he employed (see 2:8–3:3; 4:1-17; 5:1-17; 6:11-14; 12:3-
7,17-20; 21:6-7,12-23; 24:15-24; 37:15-23).

Ezekiel's ministry came near the end of the prophetic phenomenon in
the Old Testament. He was one of the last to fill a prophetic office. Both
he and Daniel were unique in that they received their call and exercised
their ministries as exiles in Babylon. Ezekiel viewed himself as a prophet
"in the midst" of the captives. Ezekiel used the word "in the midst" or
"among" 116 times, which is significantly more than that of any other
Old Testament writer.[35] The repeated use of this term revealed the unique
perspective he had of himself as a prophet in the midst of the captives
and the crucial events of the exile. As one in the midst of the captives he
was in the position to announce to the exiles the hope of future restoration and the resurrection of the life of the nation.

Other aspects of Ezekiel's position in the midst of his world gave

---

[34] See W. J. Beecher, *The Prophets and the Promise* (1905; reprint, Grand Rapids: Baker, 1975), 21-35.

[35] "In the midst" is the word תָּוֶךְ. See *KHAT,* 1510-11. It is first used in 1:1 to designate
his place "in the midst" of the captives in Babylon and in 3:15 as a term of identity signifying he was with them "in the midst" of their plight as captives.

breadth and depth to his ministry. He had been a citizen of Jerusalem, a city involved in the life and culture of the ancient Near East. It was a strategic crossroads of the ancient world. After being taken captive to Babylon, he found himself in the midst of a nation that was the political, economic, and military center of power for the world of his time. This gave his ministry a world perspective, a concept reflected in his prophecies against the nations (25:1–32:32). He saw himself as being in a world that needed God, a prophet to the nations as well as to Israel/Judah.

Ezekiel's perspective, however, went beyond these temporal relationships because he also saw himself as a prophet associated with of a coming new kingdom (40:1–47:23) and of its capital, the new Jerusalem (48:1-35, especially vv. 8,10,15,21-22), which was to be the center of God's eternal kingdom.

Ezekiel brought his unique insights and abilities to his assignment. But while his contribution was unique, he shared many characteristics with the other Old Testament prophets. (1) He experienced a *divine call* and received a *divine commission* to a specific assignment (cp. 1:1–3:27 with Isa 6:1-13; Jer 1:1-19; Amos 7:13-15; Hos 1:1-11; Jonah 1:2; and Zeph 1:1-6). (2) He received *visions* (cp. 3:22; 8:4; 11:24; 43:3 with Isa 6:1ff.; 21:2-3; Dan 2:19-20; 7:2-3; 8:1-2; 10:1-11; Mic 1:1; Zech 1:8ff.). (3) He used *preaching* to convey his message (cp. Ezek 16 with Jeremiah's temple sermon in Jer 26). (4) He made *predictions,* either of impending judgment or of restoration including the coming of Messiah (cp. Ezek 5; 7; 28:25-26; 34:20-31; 36:8-38; 37; etc. with Isa 24–27; Jer 25:11; 29:10; Dan 9:24-26). (5) He had a *theological view of history,* that is, like the other prophets Ezekiel saw God as the prime mover of history. Israel's prophets understood history to have a beginning and end that was in God's hands. This formed the basis for the idea of a future hope (cp. Ezek 40–48 with Isa 60–66; Amos 9:11-15). (6) His prophecies included *ethical teachings* (cp. Ezek 22:1-31 with Isa 5:1-30; Hos 8:1-14; Amos 5:1-27).

## 5. The Book

Although there are no specific claims to authorship in the Book of Ezekiel and Ezekiel's name is mentioned only twice (1:3; 24:24), there was little question about the genuineness and integrity of the book prior to the present century. S. R. Driver wrote: "No critical question arises in connection with the authorship of the book, the whole from beginning to end bearing unmistakably the stamp of a single mind."[36] Its canonicity,

---

[36] S. R. Driver, *Introduction to the Literature of the Old Testament* (New York: Scribner's, 1913), 279.

however, was debated in the first century A.D.[37] Those rabbis who opposed admission of Ezekiel did so on the ground that the book contradicted some of the teachings of the law. Rabbi Hannaniah ben Hezekiah is credited with carefully working through the book and reconciling every alleged difficulty so that it could be retained in the canonical list of prophetic books.[38]

## (1) Authorship and Textual Issues

There are at least six reasons the Book of Ezekiel was not widely challenged for so many centuries.[39] First, it is a well-organized unit that has a balanced structure.[40] There are no breaks in the flow of the messages and arrangement of the text of chaps. 1–48. Second, there is a uniformity of language and style that is characteristic of books with a single author. At least forty-seven phrases have been identified that recur throughout the book.[41] This phenomenon seems to suggest a unity of authorship. Third, the book is autobiographical throughout, written in first person singular (except 1:3; 24:24). Other prophets such as Jeremiah, Isaiah, Hosea, Amos, and Zechariah combine first and third person, which has been regarded by some as evidence of editorial compilation. Fourth, the consistent chronological sequence of messages in Ezekiel is unique, with at least fourteen dated prophecies.[42] No other prophet's book gives such careful and ordered chronological information. Fifth, the content of the book is consistent with its structural balance. For example, the first half of the book contains messages of judgment and concludes with the announcement of the fall of Jerusalem (24:21-24). The second half of the book contains messages of hope and encouragement and concludes with the establishment of the new Jerusalem (48:31-35). Sixth, both the character and the personality of the prophet remain constant throughout the book. The priestly character of Ezekiel, with his love for symbolism and his attention to detail, marks all the messages. His concern for the transcendence of God and for the sinfulness of the nation in

---

[37] Fisch, *Ezekiel,* xiii; P. C. Craigie, *Ezekiel* (Philadelphia: Westminster, 1983), 1.

[38] According to the Talmud (*Šabb.* 13b) he was given three hundred jars of oil for use as food and fuel while he completed his work (Fisch, *Ezekiel,* xiii-xiv).

[39] See R. H. Alexander, "Ezekiel," EBC 6 (Grand Rapids: Zondervan, 1986), 739-40; Stalker, *Ezekiel,* 19; Taylor, *Ezekiel,* 14-16.

[40] See R. M. Hals, *Ezekiel,* FOTL (Grand Rapids: Eerdmans, 1989), 3-4.

[41] H. G. May ("The Book of Ezekiel: Introduction and Exegesis," *IB* [Nashville: Abingdon, 1956], 6:50-51) lists all forty-seven references.

[42] See table "Dated Prophecies in Ezekiel" on p. 54.

general and of individuals in particular characterizes the book.[43]

Nevertheless, many attempts have been made, especially in this century, to identify and define the limits of editorial work on the book.[44] Baruch Spinoza (1632–1677), the seventeenth-century philosopher, was the first we know of to question whether the book came to us intact from Ezekiel. Spinoza's work was expanded a century later by G. L. Oeder.[45] Subsequently, doubts about single authorship were rare until 1900 when R. Kraetzschmar published a work that found twenty-three instances of duplicate passages (e.g., chap. 1 with 10:8-17; 3:16b-21 with 33:7-9). He explained these as the result of editorial compilation from parallel recensions.[46] Following Kraetzschmar, J. Hermann argued in works published in 1908 and 1924 that Ezekiel was primarily a preacher and that an editor produced the book, modifying the prophet's message to some degree.[47] G. Hölscher went further (also in 1924), arguing that Ezekiel himself only delivered the poetic messages of doom, sixteen in all (plus five brief prose passages), covering only 170 verses. The rest of the book's 1,273 verses he attributed to the hands of later editors.[48]

One of the most radical challenges to the genuineness of Ezekiel came in 1930. C. C. Torrey sought to demonstrate that the book was an example of Hellenistic pseudepigrapha. He claimed that a Hellenistic writer in Palestine, inspired by the account of the evil reign of Manasseh in 2 Kgs 21 and the mention of unnamed prophets through whom the Lord spoke (vv. 10-15), addressed the book to the people of Judah and Jerusalem as if it came from the pen of one of those prophets. "Both framework and

---

[43] Taylor (*Ezekiel,* 16) notes that only a handful of critics have ever been skeptical about the unity of Ezekiel.

[44] See especially Wevers, *Ezekiel,* 22-30; Zimmerli, *Ezekiel 1,* 68-74; G. R. Driver, "Linguistic and Textual Problems in Ezekiel," *Bib* 19 (1938): 60-69. Hals (*Ezekiel*) examines the "text," "structure," "genre," "setting," and "intention" of each passage and attempts to identify editorial influence. Taylor (*Ezekiel,* 13-20) gives an excellent summary of textual issues and includes six main reasons for ascribing the book to a single author, Ezekiel the prophet.

[45] May, "Ezekiel," 6:41-42; R. K. Harrison, *Introduction to the Old Testament* (Grand Rapids: Eerdmans, 1969), 823.

[46] See the discussion in Cooke (*Ezekiel,* xx), who asserts that "so many of the alleged parallels when examined turn out to be not parallel at all."

[47] Zimmerli (*Ezekiel 1,* 4) thinks that since Ezekiel was a preacher rather than a writer his lack of writing skill may have contributed to the supposed broken flow of the text.

[48] See discussion in Harrison, *Introduction,* 824-25. Cooke (*Ezekiel,* xxi) responded that while "every student of Ezekiel has much to learn from his critical handling of the text," Hölscher "exaggerates the contrast between the poetical passages and the prose," which actually agree in substance, personality, and idiom. Furthermore, "the general result of his method is to empty the book of all serious value."

fabric," he concluded, "are the product of imagination kindled by religious fervor."[49] A few years later a writer recast it in its present form as
the work of a prophet in exile in Babylon. But Torrey even regarded the
existence of a large community of Jewish exiles in Babylon to be a fic-
tion created by the Chronicler.[50]

Torrey's work, never widely accepted, was immediately answered in
detail by S. Spiegel.[51] Nevertheless, the idea that at least portions of
Ezekiel were written from Palestine rather than Babylon has found several proponents. Some proposed that Ezekiel prophesied both in Judah and
in Babylon (Spiegel,[52] Oesterly and Robinson,[53] Bertholet,[54] Pfeiffer,[55]
May,[56] Blenkinsopp[57]). Others confined his ministry to Judah (Berry,[58]
Herntrich[59]).

W. H. Brownlee argued more recently that Ezekiel ministered from his
home in Gilgal and that references to Gilgal were corrupted to *gôlâ*, "exile." From there Ezekiel delivered personally his prophecies against Ammon, Phoenicia, Edom, and Egypt (traveling there more than once). After
prophesying in Egypt in 568 B.C., he led a group of Jewish exiles there

---

[49] C. C. Torrey, *Pseudo-Ezekiel and the Original Prophecy*, Yale Oriental Series 18
(1930; reprint, New York: KTAV, 1970), 83. Torrey suggests (p. 99) ca. 230 B.C. as a more
precise date for the original work. A useful summary of Torrey's view and the response it
quickly received from the scholarly community may be found in the "Prolegomenon" to
that reprint, written by M. Greenberg (xiii-xxix).

[50] Torrey, *Pseudo-Ezekiel*, 31-33, 44, 102-13.

[51] S. Spiegel, "Ezekiel or Pseudo-Ezekiel?" *HTR* 24 (1931): 256-81, included in the
KTAV reprint of Torrey cited above (Torrey, *Pseudo-Ezekiel*, 123-99). Spiegel ("Ezekiel or
Pseudo Ezekiel?" 130) quotes favorably Kuenen's response (*Histor.-krit. Einleitung in die
Bücher des A. T.*, 1890) to earlier pseudepigraphal theories: "The book of Ezekiel . . . if
removed from Babylonia and the exilic era to Judea and a later century, becomes a purpose-
less and unintelligible piece of writing."

[52] S. Spiegel, "Toward Certainty in Ezekiel," *JBL* 54 (1935): 145-71.

[53] W. O. E. Oesterly and T. H. Robinson, *Introduction to the Books of the Old Testament*
(New York: Macmillan, 1955), 318-29. They believed that Ezekiel ministered in Jerusalem
before 597 and in Babylon after 597.

[54] A. Bertholet, *Hesekiel, mit einem Beitrag von Kurt Galling* (Tübingen: Mohr, 1936).

[55] R. H. Pfeiffer, *Introduction to the Old Testament,* 3d ed. (New York: Harper & Bros.,
1941), 534-43. He argued that Ezekiel ministered in Babylon, then in Palestine, then back
in Palestine.

[56] May ("Ezekiel," 52) agreed with Pfeiffer on Ezekiel's itineracy. The remarkable unity
of the book he thought to be the result of a single editor working in the early fifth century
B.C. (p. 45).

[57] J. Blenkinsopp, *A History of Prophecy in Israel* (Philadelphia: Westminster, 1983), 197.

[58] G. R. Berry, "Was Ezekiel in the Exile?" *JBL* 49 (1930): 83-93.

[59] V. Herntrich (*Ezechielprobleme*, BZAW 61 [Giessen: A. Töpelmann, 1932]) believed
Ezekiel prophesied in Palestine but that the book was edited in Babylon during the exile.

back to Gilgal, thus acting as a second Joshua.[60] Brownlee held that
Ezekiel's initial grouping of his prophecies was completed by a disciple
but that additions were made to the book as late as the time of Alexander.
Ezekiel's Babylonian setting was introduced by a major revision in the
late fourth century B.C. whose purpose was to defend the postexilic temple and the Jerusalemite priesthood.[61]

　　G. A. Cooke chose to accept the traditional view of date and authorship, maintaining that the book was a unity. Regarding the difficulty of
Ezekiel in Babylon addressing the inhabitants of Jerusalem, he appealed
to Ezekiel's temperament as more concerned with the unseen than the
seen and as totally consumed with how Israel had dishonored Yahweh
and their coming punishment.

> His words might reach only the ears that were listening, but his attention
> was fixed upon the nation at large. Mere distance does not count in the
> range of a prophet's message. Isaiah, Nahum, Zephaniah, Jeremiah could
> address nations far away from Jerusalem; why not Ezekiel, in the opposite
> direction? Tyre and Egypt came within his purview; why not the land of
> Judah? It is not for us to set limits to a prophet's vision.[62]

While recognizing evidence of editorial activity throughout, Cooke believed that the basic content and plan of the book came from Ezekiel the
prophet in exile.[63]

　　Most scholars since that time have favored the view that Ezekiel minis-
tered solely in Babylon before and after the exile (e.g., Y. Kaufmann,[64] C.
G. Howie,[65] Wevers,[66] Eichrodt,[67] Greenberg,[68] Boadt,[69] Vawter and
Hoppe[70]). Views have continued to differ, however, over Ezekiel's in-

---

[60] Brownlee, *Ezekiel 1–19*, xxiii-xxxiii.

[61] Ibid., xxxv-xli.

[62] Cooke, *Ezekiel*, xxiv.

[63] Ibid., xxiv-xxvii.

[64] Y. Kaufmann, *The Religion of Israel*, trans. M. Greenberg (Chicago: University of
Chicago Press, 1960), 401-9, 426-46.

[65] C. G. Howie (*The Date and Composition of Ezekiel*, SBLM 4 [Philadelphia: SBL,
1960], 100-102), in a 1950 doctoral dissertation directed by W. F. Albright, maintained that
there were fewer problems in accepting the traditional view than in trying to alter the text.

[66] Wevers, *Ezekiel*, 25.

[67] Eichrodt, *Ezekiel*, 7-9.

[68] Greenberg, *Ezekiel 1–20*, 12-17.

[69] L. Boadt, "Ezekiel, Book of," *ABD* 2:714-15.

[70] B. Vawter and L. J. Hoppe (*Ezekiel*, ITC [Grand Rapids: Eerdmans, 1991], 13), while
they consider Ezekiel to have been a prophet of the exile, believe the present form of the
book to be a product of editors and compilers (pp. 4-5ff.).

volvement in producing the book itself. Some have followed Cooke's basic assessment (e.g., R. K. Harrison,[71] J. B. Taylor[72]). Others have tended to regard the book as the product of later editors who compiled it from earlier collections of his sayings, some made by the prophet himself (e.g., G. Fohrer,[73] H. H. Rowley,[74] O. Eissfeldt[75]). W. Zimmerli argued in detail that the book contains original kernels of speeches and accounts of Ezekiel's actions (*Grundtext*) that may have been written and even edited by the prophet himself. Nevertheless, he rejects the possibility that Ezekiel composed the book. Rather, the Ezekiel material continued to be reworked and supplemented (*Nachinterpretation*) by a school of disciples that began in Ezekiel's house. They "edited the prophecies of Ezekiel, commented upon them, and gave them a fuller theological exposition."[76] Far from being haphazard, however, Zimmerli believes that the process by which the book grew is "an impressive witness to the painstaking care with which the extant material was arranged into a book."[77]

While recognizing the enormous contribution Zimmerli has made to Ezekiel studies, L. Boadt has expressed doubts about Zimmerli's reconstruction of Ezekiel's *Grundtext* versus the later *Nachinterpretation* of his disciples. Boadt thinks Zimmerli's method leads to "more atomizing of the text and a greater role for disciples and editors" than is reasonable.[78] He thinks that most of the book came from Ezekiel himself and was completed, including the often-disputed chaps. 40–48, by the end of the exile.[79]

M. Greenberg's approach is similar;[80] he observes in the Book of Ezekiel a unity of "patterns and ideas" from which emerge "a coherent world of vision . . . contemporary with the sixth-century prophet and de-

---

[71] Harrison, *Introduction*, 838-49.

[72] Taylor, *Ezekiel*, 20.

[73] G. Fohrer, *Die Hauptprobleme des Buches Ezechiel*, BZAW 72 (Leiden: Brill, 1952). See also E. Sellin and G. Fohrer, *Introduction to the Old Testament*, trans. D. E. Green (Nashville: Abingdon, 1968), 407-14.

[74] H. H. Rowley, "The Book of Ezekiel in Modern Study," *BJRL* 36 (1953-54): 140-90; reprinted in *Men of God* (New York: Nelson, 1963), 169-210.

[75] O. Eissfeldt, *The Old Testament: An Introduction*, trans. P. R. Ackroyd (New York: Harper & Row, 1965), 372-81.

[76] Zimmerli, *Ezekiel 1*, 70.

[77] Ibid., 74.

[78] Book review of vol. 1 in *CBQ* 43 (1981): 632-35. See also L. Boadt, "Rhetorical Strategies in Ezekiel's Oracles of Judgment," in *Ezekiel and His Book*, ed. J. Lust (Leuven: University Press, 1986), 182-84.

[79] *ABD* 2:718-20.

[80] L. Boadt ("Rhetorical Strategies," 182-85.) applauds Greenberg's "holistic interpretation" as a "new beginning" but thinks he has not sufficiently departed from a form-critical approach.

cisively shaped by him, if not the very words of Ezekiel himself."[81] Even chaps. 40–48, often judged to be a later addition, Greenberg concludes are "the product of a single mind (and hand) and that, as carrying forward ideas and values found in the preceding prophecies, it may reasonably be attributed to their author, the priest-prophet Ezekiel."[82] After a critique of the kind of form-critical studies that employ "minute literary analysis and the hyper-minute editorial stages conjectured both in the pentateuchal matter and in Ezekiel" which, he says, "taxes my credulity," Greenberg announces his verdict that "I could find nothing on[sic] the book of Ezekiel that necessitates supposing another hand than that of a prophet of the sixth century."[83]

H. L. Ellison summarized well the current state of affairs when he wrote in 1962: "It seems fair to say that the intensive critical studies of thirty-five years have largely canceled themselves out. They have led to a deeper understanding of many aspects of the book but have left the general position much as it was before 1924."[84] Another thirty years have elapsed since Ellison wrote these words, but the status of the book remains essentially unchanged.

More recently, the language of Ezekiel has undergone detailed analysis and has been shown to be a model of the transitional period in the development of the Hebrew language. This development was accelerated by the social upheaval of the last days of Judah and the exile. As we would expect of a book written in that period, Ezekiel possesses some characteristics of early biblical Hebrew and some of late biblical Hebrew including Aramaic.[85] The Aramaic influence was due to the impact of Assyro-Babylonian cultures and their use of Aramaic as the *lingua franca* of the seventh and sixth century B.C. The vocabulary, linguistic patterns, and style

---

[81] Greenberg, *Ezekiel 1–20,* 27.

[82] M. Greenberg, "The Design and Themes of Ezekiel's Program of Restoration," *Int* 38 (1984): 181-208.

[83] M. Greenberg, "What Are Valid Criteria for Determining Inauthentic Matter in Ezekiel?" in *Ezekiel and His Book,* ed. J. Lust (Leuven: University Press, 1986), 130,134. He also says (135), "I can see no demonstrable ground for supposing that the book underwent the extensive process many modern critics allege to account for its present shape."

[84] H. L. Ellison, "Ezekiel, Book of," *NBD,* 407. See also W. S. La Sor, D. A. Hubbard, and F. W. Bush, *Old Testament Survey* (Grand Rapids: Eerdmans, 1982), 465; A. E. Hill and J. H. Walton, *A Survey of the Old Testament* (Grand Rapids: Zondervan, 1991), 339-41. The latter suggests a time of authorship between 571 B.C., the last dated prophecy in Ezekiel, and 562 B.C., when King Jehoiachin was released from prison.

[85] M. F. Rooker's important work, *Biblical Hebrew in Transition: The Language of the Book of Ezekiel,* JSOTSup 90 (Sheffield, England: JSOT Press, 1990), shows that Ezekiel has seven out of fifteen characteristics in Chronicles of late biblical Hebrew (see p. 53). He cites thirty-seven examples of lexical and grammatical features, fifteen of which are Aramaisms, of late biblical Hebrew (pp. 177-81). See also Bunn, "Ezekiel," 227-28.

of the book suggest that it is a product of the sixth century B.C. when Ezekiel performed his ministry. This evidence confirms the position advanced by Cooke, Howie, Boadt, Greenberg, and others.

### (2) Apocalyptic Literature

The character of the book reflects the prophet's personality and his unique ministry. There is some disagreement over whether Ezekiel can be categorized as "apocalyptic literature." This is due largely to confusion over our use of the term "apocalyptic" to designate a literary form, a religious perspective, or a historical movement.[86] The so-called apocalyptic movement is considered a Jewish phenomenon of the intertestamental period. It was a movement of "the oppressed who saw no hope for the nation simply in terms of politics or on the plane of human history."[87] It expressed itself in writings such as 1 Enoch, the Book of Jubilees, and the Assumption of Moses. They explained their oppression as Satan's temporary domination of the world, which would end with a cataclysmic display of God's power, ushering in the new age of the kingdom of God. As a religious perspective this literature was characterized by a general abandonment of this world and a commitment to a future one instituted and managed wholly by God. Although this perspective has some features in common with biblical prophecy, in its instruction and encouragement regarding the future the Bible never loses its focus on the importance of godly living in the present. As long as there are believers in the world, those believers must not abandon this world but should work to affect it with the power of the gospel.

Although not part of apocalyptic as a historical movement and not completely at home with an apocalyptic dualistic perspective, the Book of Ezekiel does employ literary devices and forms generally associated with apocalyptic literature.[88] The extracanonical apocalyptic books bor-

---

[86] P. D. Hanson, *The Dawn of Apocalyptic* (Philadelphia: Fortress, 1979), 10-11, 430-31.

[87] D. S. Russell, *The Method and Message of Jewish Apocalyptic,* OTL (Philadelphia: Westminster, 1964), 17.

[88] See Russell, *Method and Message of Jewish Apocalyptic,* 104-39. He identifies Ezekiel as being in this prophetic tradition, though the book does not contain every element of apocalyptic. For further study see P. D. Hanson, "Apocalypses and Apocalyticism," *ABD* I (New York: Doubleday, 1992), 279-83; K. Koch, "What Is Apocalyptic? An Attempt at a Preliminary Definition," *Visionaries and Their Apocalypses* (Philadelphia: Fortress, 1983), 20-24; S. H. Travis, "The Value of Apocalyptic," *TB* 30 (1979): 53-69; J. J. Collins, "The Place of Apocalypticism in the Religion of Israel," in *Ancient Israelite Religion*, ed. P. D. Miller, Jr. et al. (Philadelphia: Fortress, 1987), 539-58; W. W. Gasque, "Apocalyptic Literature," *ZPEB* I (Grand Rapids: Zondervan, 1976), 200-204; G. E. Ladd, "Apocalyptic Literature," *ISBE* I (Grand Rapids: Eerdmans, 1979), 151-61.

rowed many of their forms and much of their perspective from the later canonical books such as Ezekiel, Daniel, and Zechariah. Later apocalypticists found easily adaptable the outlook of these exilic and postexilic prophets who wrote during a period of foreign domination. Judging from these biblical books, the use of dream visions and symbolic language that particularly characterized the intertestamental literature was apparently common by the sixth century in Israel (as well as elsewhere[89]). R. H. Alexander has defined biblical apocalyptic literature as "symbolic visionary prophetic literature, composed during oppressive conditions, consisting of visions whose events are recorded exactly as they were seen by the author and explained through a divine interpreter, and whose theological content is primarily eschatological."[90] Ezekiel, he says, employed the apocalyptic form as a literary device, for example, in 37:1-14 and chaps. 40–48. He also used "dream-visions," a device common in apocalyptic literature, in chaps. 1–3; 8–11. A. E. Hill has explained that by employing apocalyptic features (such as "strange visions and unusual symbols in combination with eschatological themes of judgment, divine intervention in human history, and the ultimate victory of God over the enemies of Israel"), Ezekiel "pointed to later Jewish apocalyptic writings."[91] Because of the symbolic language, imagery, visions, and special revelations characteristic of apocalyptic literature, biblical books where these features are common have been recognized as particularly difficult and have been somewhat neglected, as well as often misinterpreted.[92]

A note of caution seems appropriate here. The interpreter who seeks to understand apocalyptic must seek a balanced interpretation that avoids the extremes of claiming too much for the symbols and imagery on the one hand or too little on the other. Often there is a temptation to see much more than can be substantiated by the text, a practice that undermines the credibility both of the message and of the interpreter. Some have been sure, for example, that Gog in Ezek 38:1-23 is Russia. Maps have been drawn fixing the route the Russians will take in the launch of

---

[89] A. L. Oppenheim ("The Interpretation of Dreams in the Ancient Near East with a Translation of an Assyrian Dream-Book," *TAPS* 46 [1956]: 186-225) points out that apocalyptic dream visions such as those in Ezekiel were common in the seventh and sixth centuries B.C. More recently, see J. H. Walton, *Ancient Israelite Literature in its Cultural Context* (Grand Rapids: Zondervan, 1989), 217-226. Walton provides examples of "apocalyptic" literature in the ANE dating from the 12th century on.

[90] R. H. Alexander, "Ezekiel," EBC 6:745.

[91] A. E. Hill and J. H. Walton, *A Survey of the Old Testament* (Grand Rapids: Zondervan, 1991), 346.

[92] Craigie, *Ezekiel*, 1-2.

their invasion of Israel in the end time. Such liberty breaks the bounds of credible interpretation and becomes mere speculation (see comments at 38:1-3). With the demise of the Soviet Union in the last decade of the twentieth century, such interpretations have lost credibility. Guidelines for the interpretation of the symbols and visions of Ezekiel will be offered in the commentary section as passages are considered.

## (3) Contents

The book is arranged in four main divisions.[93] Chapters 1–3 present the call and commission of the prophet. Chapters 4–24 are prophetic messages concerning the judgment and fall of Judah, concluding with the announcement of the destruction of Jerusalem in chap. 24. Chapters 25–32 comprise an interlude of messages of judgment against foreign nations. Ezekiel wanted to declare that the Gentile nations also were accountable to God and would likewise receive judgment. Chapters 33–48 are messages of hope concerning the restoration of Israel and the reestablishment of the temple, sacrificial system, redistribution of the land, and the rebuilding of Jerusalem.

Another unique feature of the Book of Ezekiel is the ordered sequence of dated messages.[94] While these messages are not in strict chronological order, they do have a general chronological flow that makes the development of the book easy to follow. All but two of the messages begin with the year, month, and day the oracle was received (the two exceptions are 26:1 and 32:17, which contain only the day and year). Ezekiel's messages began with his call (1:1) in July of 593 B.C. and continued to his last dated message, which he received in either April or October 571 B.C. (29:17). While some see the use of dates in Ezekiel as evidence of editing,[95] the use of dating also may be taken as an indication that the messages were written personally by the prophet. In this case the precise dating was his way of keeping a diary of his ministry and messages. Jeremiah, on the other hand, who used an amanuensis, Baruch (Jer 36:4), did not give the same attention to chronological flow.

---

[93] See Wood, *Prophets of Israel,* 360; J. B. Payne, *Encyclopedia of Biblical Prophecy* (New York: Harper & Row, 1973), 350; Cooke, *Ezekiel,* xvii; and Hals, *Ezekiel,* 3-4.

[94] Taylor (*Ezekiel,* 36) identifies fourteen dated messages; Greenberg (*Ezekiel 1–20,* 8), fifteen; and Howie (*Ezekiel, Daniel* [London: SCM, 1961], 9), thirteen. The reason for the apparent discrepancy lies in the omission of the date in 29:17 by Howie and the omission by Taylor of the date in 3:16. The dated passages furnished by Greenberg are: 1:1; 1:2-3; 3:16; 8:1; 20:1; 24:1; 26:1; 29:1; 29:17; 30:20; 31:1; 32:1; 32:17; 33:21; and 40:1. See chart "Dated Prophecies of Ezekiel."

[95] Vawter and Hoppe, *Ezekiel,* 4-5.

Three of the messages of Ezekiel may be extensions of Jeremiah's prophecies. Ezekiel's visions of the cauldron in 11:1-12 and 24:3-14 are similar to Jer 1:13-15. The reference to the parable of the sour grapes in 18:1-32 is similar to Jer 31:29-30. Also the parable of the two sisters in 23:1-49 may be an extension of the message of backsliding Israel in Jer 3:6-11. This phenomenon perhaps may be due to direct influence of the ministry of Jeremiah on Ezekiel. Even if Ezekiel did not know or had never heard Jeremiah, he reflected the common mind of inspiration, the Holy Spirit, who was behind the written records of both prophets.

*Integrity of the Text.* Many of the critical attacks against the Book of Ezekiel have been based on the conclusion that the Hebrew text of Ezekiel has suffered greatly at the hands of editors and copyists. The text of Ezekiel sometimes has been identified as in one of the worst states of preservation of any book in the Old Testament.[96] Ezekiel used many hapax legomena, words that occur only once in the Bible, making their meaning uncertain. Many of them are technical terms related to measurements. Such rare words often are handled by interpreters through emendation, altering the vowels or even consonants, sometimes with no manuscript support, to produce a more common word or one that is believed to fit better in the context.[97] All too often the temptation to emend a difficult text is taken as the solution. Changes should never be made to the text unless they are clearly warranted, such as easily identifiable scribal errors. R. Alexander appropriately states that the textual evidence for most so-called corrections is sparse.[98]

Based on the status of studies that have generally sustained the integrity of authorship and date for the book, the Hebrew text should be interpreted as it stands. M. Rooker's work has further demonstrated that many of the textual eccentricities of the book may be due to its having been written at a time when the language was in transition and Aramaic was widely used.[99]

### (4) Theology of the Book

At least six significant theological themes can be identified in the Book of Ezekiel.

THE HOLINESS AND TRANSCENDENCE OF GOD. The book opens with an account of the call of the prophet. The majesty and transcendence of

---

[96] See May, "Ezekiel," *IB*, 63.

[97] Taylor (*Ezekiel*, 47-48) offers discussion of these concerns.

[98] Alexander ("Ezekiel," 746) maintains that the text of Ezekiel may be read and studied with confidence.

[99] Rooker, *Language of Ezekiel*, 177-81.

God are portrayed in the vision of Yahweh on his chariot-throne reigning as the Lord of creation (1:1-28).[100] The turmoil of the exile and the prediction of the imminent fall of Jerusalem (3:1-27) raised a serious theological issue. Where was Yahweh? Ezekiel saw him as the God who is still on his throne, still Lord of creation, transcendent yet caring and interactive with his creation.[101] Yahweh was portrayed as a holy God who transcends his creation but who also was concerned for the sinfulness of humanity (44:23). The concern for priestly regulations and the vision of the restored temple (40:1–42:20) denote a nonmystical view of the holiness of God that compliments Ezekiel's mystical vision of chap. 1.[102]

Divine justice is a theme in Ezekiel related to the holy character of Yahweh. Ezekiel's ministry and especially his role as a "watchman for the house of Israel" (3:17-21; 33:1-33) was considered by the rabbis as evidence of God's justice.[103] Various other aspects of God's holy character are evident such as divine jealousy (8:3; 23:25), concern for foreign nations (25:1–32:32), mercy (37:10), and wrath (7:1-8; 15:7; 24:24).[104]

THE SINFULNESS OF HUMANITY. The holiness and transcendence of God are presented in contrast to the sinfulness of humanity, especially of Judah.[105] Ezekiel used parables to illustrate his point. In chap. 16 he told the story of a child who was abandoned, rescued from certain death, cared for by a benevolent benefactor, and who grew to be a young woman of marriageable age. When she was betrothed and prepared for marriage, she decided instead to become a harlot (16:15). From this point Ezekiel clearly identified Israel/Judah as the harlot and the story of her life as an allegory of its history. Other passages that center on the sinfulness of the people in general are 8:1-18; 20:1-44; and 23:1-49. Prophets such as Amos had stressed the social sins of the nation, but Ezekiel took his message a step further and stressed the spiritual root of sin as the violation of

---

[100] Taylor (*Ezekiel,* 40-42) points out that because Ezekiel was from a priestly family, he undoubtedly felt deeply concerned about matters related to the holiness of God.

[101] See A. B. Davidson, *The Book of the Prophet Ezekiel,* CBSC (Cambridge: Cambridge University Press, 1906), xxxi-xliii.

[102] S. Fisch, *Ezekiel,* xv. The restored temple was a necessary and fundamental element in declaring the holiness of God.

[103] Ibid., xiv-xv.

[104] See W. Zimmerli, *I Am Yahweh* (Atlanta: John Knox, 1982), 29-98, especially pp. 42-98. Zimmerli traces the concept of "Knowledge of God" through its development and usage in the Book of Ezekiel especially in phrases such as "and they shall know that I Yahweh." The Book of Ezekiel is filled with the contrasting themes of God's wrath and judgment on the one hand and his love and mercy on the other, all of which are based on the concept of God's holiness (p. 96).

[105] Taylor, *Ezekiel,* 42-44; E. H. Merrill, "A Theology of Ezekiel and Daniel," in *A Biblical Theology of the Old Testament,* ed. R. B. Zuck (Chicago: Moody, 1991), 369-72. Ezekiel viewed Israel and Judah's disobedience as a violation of their covenant with God.

God's holiness presented in his character and Commandments.[106] The nation was so sinful that Ezekiel portrayed Yahweh reluctantly departing the temple (10:1ff.) and finally leaving Jerusalem (11:22-25).

THE INEVITABILITY OF JUDGMENT.   In spite of the loss of independence to Babylon in 605 B.C., the people had high expectations that the foreign intervention by Nebuchadnezzar was temporary.[107] Ezekiel condemned the false prophets in particular because they encouraged these ideas and thus made the people their prey instead of praying for the needs of the nation (13:1–14:23). They also predicted that Jerusalem would be spared. Ezekiel's indictment of these spurious prophets concluded with several ringing pronouncements of the doom of Jerusalem and the inevitability of the fall of Judah (14:12-23; 15:1-8; 16:1-63; 17:1-24). Ezekiel, like Jeremiah (e.g., Jer 25:1-14; 29:1-10), viewed coming judgment as a foregone conclusion.[108]

Ezekiel also teaches a concept developed more fully in the New Testament, that judgment is not reserved for the ungodly alone. God's own people are liable for judgment when they are disobedient (Ezek 6:8-10; 34:17-22; 36:31). They will be held accountable before him for their stewardship of life, talents, and possessions (Rom 14:10-12; 2 Cor 5:10-11). The New Testament teaching on rewards (1 Cor 3:11-15) and chastening (Heb 12:3-11) is based on an understanding of this accountability.

INDIVIDUAL RESPONSIBILITY.   Ezekiel, like a good pastor, took his message a step further. He applied the issue of sinfulness and judgment on a personal level. The people had sinned, and judgment was inevitable. A popular proverb both Ezekiel and Jeremiah recorded, "The fathers have eaten sour grapes, and the children's teeth are set on edge" (Jer 31:29; Ezek 18:1), was the people's way of complaining that their generation was suffering unjustly for the sins committed by previous generations.[109] The prophets' response was that whereas former generations had sinned and these sins affected future generations, the people of Ezekiel's and Jeremiah's day were being judged for their own sins; they were not innocent victims of their past.

---

[106] Taylor, *Ezekiel*, 44. Ezekiel scarcely mentioned the social sins Amos attacked.

[107] Eichrodt, *Ezekiel*, 4. The fact that the king of Israel was allowed to live in the palace in Babylon fueled these false hopes.

[108] See the discussion of Ezekiel's message of judgment in Merrill, "Theology of Ezekiel and Daniel," 372-76. Hananiah was a false prophet who predicted that the exile would end within two years. The incident occurred sometime in 594/593 B.C. Also see Thompson, *Jeremiah*, 537-38.

[109] Eichrodt, *Ezekiel*, 234-35. See also G. Matties, *Ezekiel 18 and the Rhetoric of Moral Discourse*, SBLD 126 (Atlanta: Scholars Press, 1990).

Ezekiel delivered his message of personal responsibility in which he stated that we all bear responsibility and are accountable to God for our own actions (18:4; 33:8-20).[110] His message helped to demonstrate the difference between guilt for sin and consequences of sin. We are guilty before God and accountable to him only for our own sins. But the consequences of our sins are more far-reaching and will affect others for generations to come (Exod 34:6-7).

HOPE OF RESTORATION. After Ezekiel's messages of judgment and individual responsibility for Judah (4:1–24:27) and foreign nations (25:1–32:32), he turned to messages of hope for future restoration in chaps. 33–48. He predicted not only the return from captivity (36:1-15) but also the spiritual renewal (36:16-38) of the people, the reunification of the nation (37:1-28), the rebuilding of the temple (40:1–42:20), the reinstitution of the sacrificial system (43:1–46:24), the reapportionment of the land (47:13–48:29), and the building of a new Jerusalem (48:30-35).[111]

His message was similar to that of Isaiah, whose messianic prophecies also were associated with the hope of restoration (cp. Isa 11:1-6 with Ezek 17:22; 34:25). Isaiah's hope focused on a general reign of peace in the world, whereas Ezekiel's hope focused on peace for the restored nation of Israel.[112] Ezekiel, like Jeremiah (Jer 31:31-34), based his hope for future restoration on a new covenant (Ezek 36:24-28). Although Jeremiah held forth some hope that judgment for Judah might be averted, Ezekiel clearly believed that the fall of Judah and the destruction of Jerusalem were inevitable.[113]

The future hope of restoration was a familiar theme among the prophets in the Old Testament. Many of them presented that hope in terms that refer to the return to the ideal circumstances and characteristics before the fall in the garden of Eden. The most direct reference, however, is found in Ezek 36:35.

GOD'S REDEMPTIVE PURPOSE. Ezekiel believed that God's actions in history had a singular purpose, namely, to bring the knowledge of his glory and greatness to all nations.[114] By sharing the knowledge of God, human accountability to God, and his clear warning of impending judg-

---

[110] See discussion in Howie, *Ezekiel, Daniel*, 46-47; Taylor, *Ezekiel*, 44-47; P. M. Joyce, "Individual Responsibility in Ezekiel 18?" *Studia Biblica 1978*, ed. E. A. Livingston, JSOT-Sup 11 (Sheffield: JSOT, 1979), 185-96.

[111] Ackroyd, *Exile and Restoration*, 110-17; Taylor, *Ezekiel*, 46-47.

[112] See brief discussion in Fisch, *Ezekiel*, xvi.

[113] Stalker, *Ezekiel*, 74-75. Jeremiah continued to mention hope of averting the coming judgment until Jerusalem was captured (Jer 7:5-7).

[114] Howie, *Ezekiel, Daniel*, 26-27.

ment, Ezekiel wanted to help the exiles understand God's redemptive purpose for all people. The motive for God's actions always was redemptive even when he brought acts of judgment against his own people. The God of Israel is not capricious. Nor does he bring acts of judgment on people to get even or for the joy of inflicting pain on the disobedient (18:31; 33:11). Whenever God acts in judgment, he does so with the desire that redemption will be the result (18:21-32; 33:11-20).[115]

This concept of the redemptive purpose behind judgment must be qualified as only applicable to judgment in this life. The final judgment at the end of human history will be purely and eternally punitive (Rev 20:10-15). Judgment in this life is based on God's desire for all people to share his redeeming grace. After this life all will be judged on whether they submitted to his lordship by faith. That faith was finally revealed in the person of the Messiah, who was the ultimate revelation of God's redeeming grace to humanity.

The Bible is replete with God's warnings of inevitable final judgment for all people. It is also replete with announcements of the availability of mercy and grace for the repentant who exercise faith (John 3:16; Rom 3:23; 6:23). The judgment of those at enmity with God (Ezek 38–39) and the resurrection and restoration of the faithful (Ezek 33–37; 40–48) are central themes in Ezekiel.

## 6. The Message of the Book

The Book of Ezekiel is not a random collection of messages from the prophet. Examination of the prophet's development of the themes indicates that the book was intended as a homogeneous unit. Ezekiel centered his message around four spiritual realities. These may be summarized as follows:

*The Reality of God (1:1–3:27).* These introductory chapters on Ezekiel's call center on a fresh vision of the character of God.

*The Reality of Judgment (4:1–32:32).* The first two-thirds of the book contains judgment messages that announce the fall of Judah and the destruction of Jerusalem (4:1–24:27). Ezekiel's prophecies against the nations follow (25:1–32:32), which show God's demands for righteousness to be universally applicable.

*The Reality of Restoration (33:1–46:24).* With the judgment mes-

---

[115] See J. B. Payne, *The Theology of the Older Testament* (Grand Rapids: Zondervan, 1971), 413-14; W. Zimmerli, *Old Testament Theology in Outline* (Atlanta: John Knox, 1978), 207-15; Eichrodt, *Ezekiel,* 91.

sages as a background, Ezekiel turned to the theme of restoration. He presented the promise of restoration (33:1–37:28), the power of restoration (38:1–39:29), and the prospect of restoration (40:1–46:24).

*The Reality of Redemption (47:1–48:35).* Ezekiel realized the promise of restoration in a prophetic vision as he saw the fulfillment of promises in the river of life (47:1-12), the land of the redeemed (47:13–48:29), and the city of God (48:30-35).

## 7. Ezekiel and the Millennium

The interpretation of the Book of Ezekiel must involve more than exegesis and text-critical analysis. It must involve relating the message of the book to biblical theology as a whole. Since Ezekiel's message is largely an eschatological one, this means relating Ezekiel to the Bible's teaching on eschatology.[116] The major questions in this regard are: Who are to be the recipients of the redemptive promises of Ezekiel? What is to be the nature of the fulfillment of those promises? Various answers to these questions largely distinguish four primary hermeneutical frameworks applied to biblical eschatology.[117]

DISPENSATIONAL PREMILLENNIALISM. Premillennialism is the teaching that Christ's second coming will inaugurate a visible kingdom of righteousness that will comprise the whole earth. The term "dispensationalism" refers to a system of scriptural interpretation that stresses literal fulfillment of prophecy as well as distinctions in God's administrative program historically, that is, "dispensations." The various dispensations (some of which may overlap) reflect different aspects of God's purposes in his plan for history.

The thousand years of Rev 20 are considered to be literal in fact and duration, fulfilling Old Testament promises of a Davidic messianic kingdom (distinct from the universal kingdom of God), including a restored national Israel and a redeemed earth. J. S. Feinberg has written, "While a

---

[116] The importance of one's eschatological approach is discussed in G. E. Ladd, "Historic Premillennialism," *The Meaning of the Millennium: Four Views,* ed. R. G. Clouse (Downers Grove: InterVarsity, 1977), 18; E. E. Johnson, "Premillennialism Introduced: Hermeneutics," in *A Case for Premillennialism: A New Consensus* (Chicago: Moody, 1992), 15-34; P. L. Tan, *The Interpretation of Prophecy* (Winona Lake, Ind.: Assurance, 1974), 201-36.

[117] Our concern here is only with those positions based on belief in "predictive prophecy" in the Bible and also in the personal visible return of Christ to the earth in glory. A careful yet succinct survey of the issues may be found in B. Hunt, *Redeemed! Eschatological Redemption and the Kingdom of God* (Nashville: Broadman & Holman, 1993), 240-304.

prophecy given unconditionally to Israel has a fulfillment for the church if the NT *applies* it to the church, it must also be fulfilled to Israel. Progress of revelation cannot cancel unconditional promises."[118] During the millennium Satan will be bound, signifying the elimination of his influence from the world. Most important, Jesus will reign as Messiah on earth, and believers will be his administrators. The millennial kingdom will entail blessings for all nations but will have a distinctive Jewish emphasis, including a form of worship involving a rebuilt Jewish temple and the reinstitution of certain sacrifices. There will be two resurrections, the first unto life before the millennium and the second unto judgment at the end of the millennium.[119]

Classic (or "essentialist") dispensationalists maintain a sharp distinction between the church and Israel. The church age is understood as a parenthesis in God's prophetic program, during which focus is on the salvation of Gentiles. God's program with Israel will be renewed after the church has been temporarily removed from the earth during the tribulation. Jesus' second coming to the earth with the church will begin the millennium, during which there will be two distinct peoples of God, the church and Israel.[120]

A contemporary variation known as "progressive dispensationism" places greater stress on ultimate fulfillment of divine purposes in the final eternal kingdom of the new heavens and earth. Also while maintaining the expectation of the restoration of national Israel in the millennium, they see the current church age as having inaugurated the Davidic kingdom in some sense and as having begun the fulfillment of Old Testament promises of spiritual blessing, including Gentile salvation. Thus this current age is not a parenthesis in God's prophetic program, and there is only one people of God united in Christ. In the millennium as well, although an ethnic distinction between Jew and Gentile will be recognized as "different dimensions of redeemed humanity," there will be only one

---

[118] J. S. Feinberg, "Systems of Discontinuity," in J. S. Feinberg, ed., *Continuity and Discontinuity* (Westchester, Ill.: Crossway, 1988), 76. Also see R. L. Saucy, "A Rationale for the Future of Israel," *JETS* 28 (1985): 433-42.

[119] The two resurrections are discussed in H. A. Hoyt, "Dispensational Premillennialism," in *The Meaning of the Millennium*, 92; J. P. Newport, *The Lion and the Lamb* (Nashville: Broadman, 1986), 94-102. For a thorough contemporary presentation of premillennialism see D. K. Campbell and J. L. Townsend, eds., *A Case for Premillennialism: A New Consensus* (Chicago: Moody, 1992.

[120] M. J. Erickson, *Contemporary Options in Eschatology* (Grand Rapids: Baker, 1977), 117-22; C. A. Blaising, "Dispensationism: The Search for Definition," in C. A. Blaising and D. L. Bock, eds., *Dispensationalism, Israel, and the Church* (Grand Rapids: Zondervan, 1992), 13-34; Feinberg, "Systems of Discontinuity," 67-86.

people of God.[121] Also stress is placed on fulfillment of prophecy not in Israel or in a Davidic kingdom but in Christ.[122]

HISTORIC PREMILLENNIALISM.  This hermeneutical approach is based upon a literal interpretation of New Testament prophecy and thus agrees with dispensational premillennialism that there will be two resurrections and that Jesus' second coming will inaugurate an earthly millennial kingdom (whether or not literally a thousand years).[123] Christ's messianic reign, however, is believed to have begun in an invisible form at his resurrection and ascension, so that the millennial kingdom is only part of Christ's reign.[124] More important to the distinctiveness of the view, Old Testament prophecies of the coming kingdom of righteousness are thought to be fulfilled in the New Testament church. G. E. Ladd explains that the "basic watershed between a dispensational and a nondispensational theology" is that dispensationalism "forms its eschatology by a literal interpretation of the Old Testament and fits the New Testament into it."[125] Nondispensational eschatology, however, follows the principle of the New Testament and reinterprets the Old Testament "in light of the Christ event."[126] Thus the church is identified as spiritual Israel, the people of God, although a future conversion of literal Israel is affirmed, perhaps in the millennium.[127] Nevertheless, the millennial kingdom is not interpreted as a Jewish kingdom involving temple and sacrifices but as a kingdom of Christ.[128]

POSTMILLENNIALISM.  This view, not widely held, while agreeing with premillennialism that there is a future earthly kingdom, asserts that the blessings promised to Israel in the Old Testament are in process of being fulfilled in the church. Initiated by the first coming of Christ, the kingdom of God is being extended through the work of the church with

---

[121] R. L. Saucy, "Israel and the Church: A Case for Discontinuity," in *Continuity and Discontinuity*, 239-40.

[122] See C. A. Blaising and D. L. Bock, "Dispensationalism, Israel, and the Church: Assessment and Dialogue," in *Dispensationalism, Israel, and the Church*, 377-94; V. S. Poythress, *Understanding Dispensationalists* (Grand Rapids: Zondervan, 1987), 19-38.

[123] Ladd, "Historic Premillennialism," 32-40; idem, *Crucial Questions about the Kingdom of God* (Grand Rapids: Eerdmans, 1952), 141-49; R. H. Mounce, *The Book of Revelation,* NICNT (Grand Rapids: Eerdmans, 1977), 356.

[124] Ladd, "Historic Premillennialism," 29-32; idem, *The Presence of the Future* (Grand Rapids: Eerdmans, 1974), 218.

[125] Ladd, "Historic Premillennialism," 27.

[126] Ibid., 21.

[127] D. J. Moo, "The Posttribulation Rapture Position," in *The Rapture: Pre-, Mid-, or Post-tribulational* (Grand Rapids: Zondervan, 1984), 207.

[128] Ladd, "Historic Premillennialism," 18-29.

the growth and power of the gospel. According to J. M. Kik, "The post-mill looks for a fulfillment of the Old Testament prophecies of the glorious age of the church upon the earth through the preaching of the gospel under the power of the Holy Spirit."[129] Those who hold this position expect the conversion of all nations prior to the second coming of Christ. The millennium is understood as a gradually beginning period of indeterminate length during which there will be unprecedented peace and righteousness on earth. It will be the final stage of the church age which will end with Christ's return and with one general resurrection of those who have lived in all previous ages of human history.[130]

AMILLENNIALISM.  The word "amillennial" means "no thousand years." This is the view, then, that there is to be no literal thousand year reign of Christ on earth. Rather, the millennium of Rev 20:1-10 is "not exclusively future but is now in process of realization."[131] In the sense of a present "inaugurated" reality it is most commonly considered to be a heavenly kingdom in which believers who have died reign with Christ. As such it extends from the first advent of Christ to just before the second.[132] An older view defines it more as symbolic of the reign of Christ in the church in the present age. Christian history since the ascension is the story of the conflict between good and evil, God and Satan. Many biblical passages regarding the millennium relate to this ongoing spiritual struggle which will intensify until a climactic conflict symbolized by the battle of Armageddon and the destruction of Gog and Magog (Ezek 38–39; Rev 16:16; 20:7-10) is ended by the return of Christ.[133] The binding of Satan (Rev 20:2-3) is frequently interpreted as his restriction from

---

[129] J. M. Kik, *An Eschatology of Victory* (Philadelphia: Presbyterian and Reformed, 1974), 4.

[130] Erickson, *Contemporary Options in Eschatology,* 55-58; S. J. Grenz, *The Millennial Maze* (Downers Grove: InterVarsity, 1992), 65-89. For recent expositions of postmillennialism by its proponents, see L. Boettner, "Postmillennialism," in *The Meaning of the Millennium: Four Views,* ed. R. G. Clouse (Downers Grove: InterVarsity, 1977), 117-41; D. Chilton, *Paradise Restored* (Tyler, Tex.: Reconstruction Press, 1985); J. J. Davis, *Christ's Victorious Kingdom* (Grand Rapids: Baker, 1986).

[131] A. A. Hoekema, "Amillennialism," in *The Meaning of the Millennium: Four Views,* 155-56.

[132] Hoekema, "Amillennialism," 164-72, 177-81; idem, *The Bible and the Future* (Grand Rapids: Eerdmans, 1979), 234-35; M. G. Kline, "The First Resurrection, *WTJ* 37 (1975): 372-75; J. A. Hughes, "Revelation 20:4-6 and the Question of the Millennium," *WTJ* 35 (1973): 288-302; V. S. Poythress, "Genre and Hermeneutics in Rev 20:1-6," *JETS* 36 (1993): 53-54.

[133] See, for example, G. C. Berkouwer, *The Return of Christ* (Grand Rapids: Eerdmans, 1972), 314-15; R. F. White, "Reexamining the Evidence for Recapitulation in Revelation 20:1-10," *WTJ* 51 (1989): 325-36.

deceiving the nations, making possible the evangelistic work of the church.[134] To an even greater degree than in historic premillennialism, the church is equated with spiritual Israel and is considered the direct recipient of Old Testament promises.[135] Christ's return and the final judgment will conclude the millennium, thus ending human history and inaugurating the final eternal state of believers and the new heavens and earth.[136] Many of the Old Testament prophecies commonly applied to the millennium by premillennialists are interpreted by amillennialists as referring to the new heavens and earth, which is understood to follow the church age as the second phase of the kingdom of God.[137] This approach advocates less literalness in the interpretation of prophecy and is less preoccupied with details and chronology of events related to the end of time since many eschatological events are expected to occur almost simultaneously.[138]

One's eschatological view will have a definite affect on the hermeneutical methodology employed in interpreting Scripture.[139] While there are capable scholars who favor each of the above approaches to the interpretation of end-time events, this commentary will follow the dispensational premillennial framework as that which best fits the exegesis of the text and which correlates with the theology of the rest of Scripture. A rationale for this orientation is presented in the next section.

## 8. Character of the Kingdom of God in Ezekiel

The kingdom of God has at least three manifestations. First is the uni-

---

[134] W. Hendricksen, *More Than Conquerors: An Interpretation of the Book of Revelation* (Grand Rapids: Baker, 1973), 226; Hoekema, "Amillennialism," 161-64.

[135] See T. R. Schreiner, "The Church as the New Israel and the Future of Ethnic Israel in Paul," *Studia Biblica et Theologica* 13 (1983): 17-38; M. W. Karlberg, "The Significance of Israel in Biblical Typology," *JETS* 31 (1988): 257-69; O. T. Allis, *Prophecy and the Church* (Grand Rapids: Baker, 1972), 134-59; W. Hendricksen, *Israel in Prophecy* (Grand Rapids: Baker, 1968), 16-57. While "all Israel" in Rom 11:26 usually has been understood by amillennialists as the elect from all the ages, many today interpret it as the remnant from literal Israel (see O. P. Robertson, "Is There a Distinctive Future for Ethnic Israel in Romans 11?" in *Perspectives on Evangelical Theology,* eds., K. S. Kantzer and S. N. Gundry (Grand Rapids: Baker, 1979), 217-27. Also see W. A. VanGemeren, "Israel as the Hermeneutical Crux in the Interpretation of Prophecy," *WTJ* 45 (1983): 143.

[136] Hoekema, "Amillennialism," 160, 181-86.

[137] M. W. Karlberg, "Legitimate Discontinuities Between the Testament," *JETS* 28 (1985): 18.

[138] Hoekema, "Amillennialism," 172-76; Erickson, *Contemporary Options in Eschatology,* 74-75; Newport, *The Lion and the Lamb,* 82-86; Grenz, *Millennial Maze,* 152.

[139] See Grenz, *Millennial Maze,* 181-84.

versal kingdom of God, which is his supreme rule over all creation in all time and eternity (Pss 10:16; 103:19). Second is the mediatorial kingdom of God, which is local, earthly, and future (Isa 24:23; Pss 2:4-6; 29:10; Zech 14:9). This kingdom will be initiated by Christ at his return. Third, the church is at present part of both the universal kingdom and the coming mediatorial kingdom. The church will reign with Christ during his earthly rule in the millennium (Col 1:3; 2 Tim 2:12; Heb 12:28; Rev 3:21; 5:10; 20:4,6,8). Likewise Israel will share in this coming earthly rule by receiving Jesus as the Messiah and reestablishing the Davidic kingdom under his administration.[140]

The promises made to Israel in Ezek 33–48 will have their fulfillment in a literal thousand-year reign of the Messiah. While the entire section comprises messages of hope and comfort concerning the future restoration of Israel, Ezek 36:16-38 is a key passage in understanding Ezekiel's contribution to biblical eschatology as well as his message. He demonstrates that 36:16-38 and chaps. 40–48 are best understood when interpreted according to dispensational premillennialism, as he discusses four aspects of the millennial reign of the Messiah according to Ezekiel:[141]

*The Return of Israel to the Land.* Ezekiel 36:16-38 promises a regathering of Israel from all the nations, a spiritual and numerical transformation of the people, and increased productivity of the land. This restoration will have the purpose of restoring Yahweh's reputation among the nations.[142]

*The Necessity of a Millennium* A millennial fulfillment of the promises of Ezek 36:16-38 is required for three reasons. First, the promises were not fulfilled in the postexilic restoration. Second, the fulfillment is yet future to the New Testament writers (cf. Rom 11:26-27).[143] Third, fulfillment in the eternal state does not do justice to God's purpose of vindicating himself among the nations of the earth.

*The Description of the Temple.* There are three reasons that the temple of Ezek 40–48 must be a future millennial temple. First, the temples of Solomon, Zerubbabel, and Herod do not meet Ezekiel's specifications. Second, symbolic fulfillment of the temple as the church or heaven fails to explain the intricate detail of Ezekiel's temple, such as the eight steps

---

[140] The role of the church is discussed by Hoyt, "Dispensational Premillennialism," 73-74.

[141] Rooker, "Evidence from Ezekiel," in *A Case for Premillennialism*, 119-34. He explains the overall theme of Ezek 36:16-38 as "God's reputation restored in the millennium."

[142] Ibid., 121-26.

[143] Ibid., 127.

leading to the inner courtyard (40:31).[144] Third, there is no temple in the eternal state (cf. Rev 21:22).

*The Nature of the Reinstated Sacrifices.* The sacrifices instituted in the millennial temple are compatible with the once-for-all sacrifice of Christ. They should be understood as (1) memorials, just as the Lord's Supper in the New Testament, (2) associated with ceremonial forgiveness or sanctification (cf. Heb 9:13), or (3) symbolic descriptions of worship in the millennium using terminology familiar to Ezekiel's readers.[145]

Dispensational premillennialism can accommodate all the details in Ezekiel's many prophecies by giving them their most literal and normal interpretation.[146] Chapters 33–48 are primarily eschatological and reveal a restoration for Israel/Judah that is future, final, purposeful, and preparatory for the advent of the final state of all creation.

Passages in Ezekiel and elsewhere reveal at least seven characteristics of the kingdom of God.[147] First, the kingdom is literal and will have Jerusalem as its capital (Ezek 36:33-38; Ps 48; Isa 2:1-4; Obad 12-21; Zech 14:1-21). The king will be a divine-human person who reigns as a descendant of David and has divine authority (37:24-28; Isa 11:1-9; 32:1-2; Jer 23:1-6).

Second, the government of the kingdom will be theocratic. The divine-human king will reign as God's personal representative (Ezek 34:11-24). He will have the government upon his shoulders (Isa 9:6) and receive dominion and glory (Dan 7:14). He will reign from God's holy hill called Zion (Ps 2:6; Isa 60:1-14) and will perform all legislative, judicial, and executive functions of government (Ezek 34:17-24; 37:24; Isa 33:17-24).

Third, the administration of the kingdom will be performed by a spiritual nobility made up of Old Testament believers (Ezek 37:24-25; Dan 7:18,22,27), the church (1 Cor 6:2; Rev 3:21; 20:6), and martyrs from the tribulation (Rev 20:4).

Fourth, while the kingdom will have a physical manifestation, its character is spiritual. It will be initiated, operated, and maintained by the

---

[144] Ibid., 129.

[145] Ibid., 131-34. Rooker, who seems to favor the third interpretation, explains that a symbolic understanding of the sacrifices is different from a symbolic fulfillment of the temple because unlike sacrifices (e.g., 1 Cor 5:7), there is no NT text that declares the temple promise to have been fulfilled by Christ.

[146] J. L. Townsend, "Premillennialism Summarized: Conclusion," in *A Case for Premillennialism: A New Consensus,* 266.

[147] See also ibid., 77-84.

Spirit of God (Ezek 36:24-28; Jer 23:5-6; 31:34; Rom 8:1-39). The Spirit will be in individuals to empower them and to grant knowledge, wisdom, and direction (Jer 31:31-34).

Fifth, the ethical conduct of the king, the rulers, and the citizens will give evidence of the spiritual character of this kingdom (Ezek 36:27,31; 37:24; Jer 33:14-16). God's law will go forth from Jerusalem, which will be the hub of a great worldwide administrative system (Isa 2:1-4; Zech 8:20-23). The spiritual character of the kingdom also will result in physical changes in and around Jerusalem, such as topography (Zech 14:3-4), climate (Isa 32:15-16; 35:7), agricultural productivity (Isa 35:1-5; Amos 9:13), radical improvements in human health (Isa 35:5-6; 34:23-31; 65:20-23; Zech 8:4), and even in animal behavior (Isa 11:6-9; 65:25).

Sixth, the ruler of the kingdom will unite the offices of prophet, priest, and king. He will be a priest after the order of Melchizedek (Ps 110; Zech 3:8-10; 6:9-15; Heb 7:1-27). He will set up a central sanctuary, and all nations will come to it (Ezek 37:26-28; Zech 8:9,21; 14:9,16). The glory of God in the sanctuary will signal his presence (Ezek 43:1-7), and sacrificial worship will be his memorial (Ezek 46:1-24).

Seventh, the water of life will flow freely from the rebuilt sanctuary (Ezek 47:1-12). This water will provide healing and produce the trees of healing and blessing for all nations (Rev 22:1-3) and signal the removal of the curse of sin.

Ezekiel's messages, style, and theological insights combine to rekindle hope today just as they did in the sixth century B.C. Ezekiel lived in a time that was marked by encroaching materialism (16:15-34), religious skepticism (13:1-14:11), religious syncretism (8:1-8) and moral decadence (22:1-31), a time not unlike our own. To these and other significant issues, the Book of Ezekiel speaks with clarity.

I. The Prophetic Call of Ezekiel (1:1-3:27)
   1. Introduction to the Call (1:1-3)
   2. Vision of the Glory of God (1:4-28)
   3. Call of the Prophet (2:1–3:15)
   4. Appointment as a Watchman (3:16-21)
   5. Reaction of the Prophet (3:22-27)
II. Prophetic Messages concerning Judah and Jerusalem (4:1–24:27)
   1. Prophecies of Destruction for Judah and Jerusalem (4:1–7:27)
   2. Prophetic Visions of Judgment for Polluting the Temple (8:1-11:25)
   3. Prophecies of Judgments to Befall Judah and Jerusalem (12:1–19:14)
   4. Prophecies concerning Judah (20:1–24:27)
III. Prophetic Messages concerning Foreign Nations (25:1–32:32)
   1. Prophecy against Ammon (25:1-7)
   2. Prophecy against Moab (25:8-11)
   3. Prophecy against Edom (25:12-14)
   4. Prophecy against Philistia (25:15-17)
   5. Prophecy against Tyre (26:1–28:19)
   6. Prophecy against Sidon (28:20-26)
   7. Prophecy against Egypt (29:1–32:32)
IV. Prophecies and Visions of the Restoration (33:1–48:35)
   1. Messages concerning the Restoration of Israel (33:1–39:29)
   2. Visions concerning the Restored Community (40:1–48:35)

## Table 1: Dated Prophecies in Ezekiel[1]

| PASSAGE | EVENT | EZEKIEL'S DATE | | | JULIAN CALENDAR |
|---|---|---|---|---|---|
| | | MONTH | DAY | YEAR | |
| 1:1-2 | Ezekiel's call to be a prophet | 4 | 5 | 30[5]* | July 593 B.C. |
| 3:16 | Ezekiel's commission in exile | 4 | 12 | 30[5]* | Aug. 593 B.C. |
| 8:1 | Visions of judgment for polluting the temple | 6 | 5 | 6 | Sept. 592 B.C. |
| 20:1 | Inquiry of the elders | 5 | 10 | 7 | Aug. 591 B.C. |
| 24:1 | Siege of Jerusalem begins | 10 | 10 | 9 | Jan. 588 B.C. |
| 26:1 | Prophecy of Tyre's destruction | ? | 1 | 11 | Feb. or Mar.(?) 586 B.C. |
| 29:1 | Prophecy of Egypt's destruction | 10 | 12 | 10 | Jan. 587 B.C. |
| 29:17 | Prophecy of Tyre and Egypt reinforced | 1 | 1 | 27 | Apr. 571 B.C. |
| 30:20 | Prophecy of Pharaoh's destruction | 1 | 7 | 11 | Apr. 587 B.C. |
| 31:1 | Prophecy of Pharaoh's destruction | 3 | 1 | 11 | June 587 B.C. |
| 32:1 | Lamentation of Pharaoh | 12 | 1 | 12 | Mar. 585 B.C. |
| 32:17 | Pharaoh in Sheol | 12 | 15 | 12 | Apr.(?) 585 B.C. |
| 33:21 | Lament over fall of Jerusalem | 10 | 5 | 12 | Jan. 585 B.C. |
| 40:1 | Vision of the new temple/ Jerusalem | 1 | 10 | 25 | Apr. or Oct. 573 B.C. |

*The thirtieth year probably refers to elapsed time since the discovery of the law in 622–21 B.C. and resulting reforms of Josiah (see comments on 1:1). Bracketed years and all years in this column refer to the years of captivity beginning with 598/597 B.C.

[1]All dates have been determined by comparison of tables in Greenberg, *Ezekiel 1–20,* 8-11; Taylor, *Ezekiel,* 36; Howie, *Ezekiel, Daniel,* 8-9; H. G. May, "Ezekiel," *IB* (Nashville: Abingdon, 1956), 59; see also K. S. Freedy and D. B. Redford, "The Dates of Ezekiel in Relation to Biblical, Babylonian, and Egyptian Sources," *JAOS* 90 (1970): 462-85.

**Table 2: Chronology of Exile and Restoration**

| | |
|---|---|
| 640 B.C. | Reign of Josiah begins over Judah (2 Kgs 22:1ff.). |
| 627 B.C. | Prophetic call of Jeremiah (Jer 1:1-3) |
| 626 B.C. | Babylonian independence from Assyria |
| 622 B.C. | Book of the law found in the temple; Josiah attempts religious reforms (2 Kgs 22:8-14). |
| 612 B.C. | Fall of Nineveh to Nebuchadnezzar of Babylon |
| 609 B.C. | Josiah killed at Megiddo by Pharaoh Neco (2 Kgs 23:28-30). |
| 605 B.C. | Battle of Charchemish established Babylon as world power; Jeremiah writes first scroll in fourth year of Jehoiakim; Nebuchadnezzar makes first attack on Jerusalem; first group of captives taken into exile; Daniel taken captive. |
| 601 B.C. | Jehoiakim rebelled against Nebuchadnezzar (2 Kgs 24:1-7). |
| 597 B.C. | Jehoiakim taken captive; Jehoiachin reigns three months. Zedekiah follows Jehoiachin as king of Judah; second group of captives (2 Kgs 24:8-20); Ezekiel taken captive with this group. |
| 589 B.C. | Zedekiah attempts an alliance with Egypt, provokes the anger of Nebuchadnezzar. |
| 587/586 B.C. | Siege and final destruction of Jerusalem by Nebuchadnezzar; third group of captives taken from Judah; Gedaliah appointed governor; Jeremiah goes to Egypt (2 Kgs 25:1-30). |
| 582 B.C. | Fourth group of captives taken from Judah to Babylon (Jer 52:30) |
| 539 B.C. | Fall of Babylon to Medo-Persians |
| 538 B.C. | Decree of Cyrus; first captives return, arriving ca. 535. |
| 535 B.C. | Foundation of the second temple laid (Ezra 3:8-13) |
| 520 B.C. | Completion of the temple work commenced (Ezra 5:1-17) |
| 516 B.C. | Second temple dedicated |

## Table 3: Rulers of Judah during Ezekiel's Lifetime

The following rulers led Judah during the fifty-four years from 640 B.C. to the final fall of Jerusalem in 586 B.C. Ezekiel was taken captive in 597 B.C. and lived under the ministry, rule, and misrule of these men.

| | |
|---|---|
| Josiah<br>640–609 B.C. | Josiah was a godly man who genuinely wanted to see a spiritual renewal in Judah. He instituted numerous religious reforms (2 Kgs 23:4-23; 2 Chr 34:3-34) in an attempt to suppress idolatry and restore true worship of Yahweh. The law found in the temple in 622 became the basis for his reform. He was killed in 609 at Megiddo by Pharaoh Neco. Jeremiah was called to be a prophet during Josiah's reign. |
| Jehoahaz<br>609 B.C | Jehoahaz was the son of Josiah. He reigned only three months (2 Kgs 23:31ff.). He was an evil king who immediately set out to undo the works of his father. He was captured by Pharaoh Neco, who replaced Jehoahaz with Jehoiakim. |
| Jehoiakim<br>609–597 B.C. | His real name was Eliakim. Pharaoh Neco made him his puppet by placing him on the throne of Judah and giving him the name Jehoiakim. When Pharaoh Neco was defeated in the Battle of Carchemish in 605, Jehoiakim declared his independence. It was short-lived because in the same year Nebuchadnezzar, who having defeated the Egyptians at Carchemish, controlled the whole ancient Near East. Jehoiakim was an evil king who burned the Word of God that had been written and delivered to him by Jeremiah (Jer 35:11-32). In 598/97 he rebelled against Nebuchadnezzar and along with his family was taken captive to Babylon where he died, was executed, or was assassinated (2 Kgs 24:1-7). He continued his wicked policies initiated after Josiah's death. |
| Jehoiachin<br>597 B.C. | He was an eighteen-year-old son of Jehoiakim. He ruled only three months after his father was deposed. Nebuchadnezzar dethroned the young king and took all the temple treasures from Jerusalem to Babylon (2 Kgs 24:8-17). Jehoiachin also was an evil ruler (24:9) who led the people away from God. Ezekiel probably was taken captive at this time. |
| Zedekiah<br>597–586 B.C. | His real name was Mattaniah. Jehoiakim was his brother (so he was Jehoiachin's uncle; 2 Kgs 24:17). He was the final wicked ruler over Judah. Jeremiah urged him to be submissive to Nebuchadnezzar, but in 587 he rebelled. Nebuchadnezzar reached his point of tolerance and came to Jerusalem, captured Zedekiah, blinded him, destroyed the city including the temple, and took him and the populace captive to Babylon (2 Kgs 25:1-21). |
| Gedaliah<br>586 B.C. | Gedaliah was appointed governor of Judah by Nebuchadnezzar (2 Kgs 25:22; Jer 40:5). He was assassinated by the leaders of those few who were left in Judah. The refugees fled to Egypt (2 Kgs 25:22-26). |

I. THE PROPHETIC CALL OF EZEKIEL (1:1–3:27)
  1. Introduction to the Call (1:1-3)
  2. Vision of the Glory of God (1:4-28)
    (1) The Windstorm (1:4)
    (2) The Four Living Creatures (1:5-14)
    (3) The Wheels (1:15-21)
    (4) The Platform (1:22-27)
    (5) The Response of the Prophet (1:28)
  3. Call of the Prophet (2:1–3:15)
    (1) The Prophet's Mission (2:1-7)
    (2) The Prophet's Motivation (2:8–3:3)
    (3) The Prophet's Divine Preparation (3:4-11)
    (4) The Conclusion of the Call (3:12-15)
  4. Appointment as a Watchman (3:16-21)
  5. Reaction of the Prophet (3:22-27)

## I. THE PROPHETIC CALL OF EZEKIEL (1:1–3:27)

A characteristic common to prophets of the Old Testament was a special call from God. Many prophets shared elements of their call in their written record.[1] Isaiah had a dramatic call as a prophet to Judah in the eighth century B.C. (see Isa 6:1-9). Amos reviewed elements of his call when he was challenged by the educated religious establishment of his day (Amos 7:13-15). No less sensational was the call of the young priest Ezekiel to his ministry as prophet among the exiles of Babylon.

There are five main segments of the call narrative in 1:1–3:27: (1) an introduction containing dating for the beginning of Ezekiel's ministry (1:1-3); (2) a vision of the glory of God providing the necessary context for his call (1:4-28); (3) the call itself, with specific directives (2:1–3:15); (4) his appointment as a "watchman," affirming his personal responsibility (3:16-21); and (5) the reaction of the prophet (3:22-27). H. Parunak has produced a more detailed structural analysis of 1:1–3:15 as a chiasm that

---

[1] See the comparative study in N. Habel, "The Form and Significance of the Call Narratives," *ZAW* 77 (1965): 297-323.

demonstrates the intricacy of its design:[2]

A   Circumstances of the Vision (1:1-3)
  B   Divine Confrontation: Chariot's Approach (1:4-28)
    C   Introductory Word (2:1-2)
      D   First Commission and Reassurance (2:3-8a)
        E   Confirmatory Sign (2:8b–3:3)
      D'   Second Commission and Reassurance (3:4-11)
    C'   Introductory Word (3:12)
  B'   Divine Confrontation: Chariot's Departure (3:13)
A'   Circumstances of the Vision (3:14-15)

## 1. Introduction to the Call (1:1-3)

**[1]In the thirtieth year, in the fourth month on the fifth day, while I was among the exiles by the Kebar River, the heavens were opened and I saw visions of God.**
**[2]On the fifth of the month—it was the fifth year of the exile of King Jehoiachin— [3]the word of the LORD came to Ezekiel the priest, the son of Buzi, by the Kebar River in the land of the Babylonians. There the hand of the LORD was upon him.**

The Book of Ezekiel is well documented throughout with exact dates of the major messages of the prophet.[3] Except for 1:2-3 and 24:24, the book is written in first person. The date, location, and situation of the young priest and a brief biographical and genealogical identification were recorded in vv. 1-3. These verses provide a preface to Ezekiel's call.

**1:1** Immediately betraying its narrative framework, the book begins with an introductory formula in the Hebrew text, "And it came to pass" (*wayhî*). This formula, typical of narrative, elsewhere introduces only the Books of Joshua, Judges, Ruth, Samuel, Esther, and Jonah. It focuses attention on the date and circumstances surrounding Ezekiel's call.

Beginning a written record about a person or event by marking the time of a message was a common practice.[4] The meaning of the "thirtieth

---

[2] H. Parunak, "The Literary Architecture of Ezekiel's *marʾôt ʾĕlōhîm*," *JBL* 99 (1980): 61-74. A chiasm (or chiasmus) is a literary device by which a set of items (words, phrases, themes, etc.) in the text is repeated in reverse order. Its function is often to call special attention to what is at the center.

[3] See "Dated Prophecies in Ezekiel" chart on p. 54 for list of dated oracles.

[4] M. Greenberg, *Ezekiel 1–20*, AB (New York: Doubleday, 1983), 39; G. A. Cooke, *Ezekiel*, 2 vols., ICC (Edinburgh: T & T Clark, 1936), 6-7; W. H. Brownlee, *Ezekiel 1–19*, WBC (Waco: Word, 1986), 5-6.

year" is unclear.[5] Several possibilities could explain the meaning of the thirtieth year. It may be a reference to the elapsed time since the beginning of the exilic period in 605 B.C.[6] But this explanation does not fit well into the chronology given in the remainder of the dated messages.[7] The rabbinic interpretation of the thirtieth year was that it referred to the elapsed time since the last observance of the Year of Jubilee, which Moses ordered to be observed after seven sabbatical years (Lev 25:8-17).[8]

The suggestion that the thirtieth year refers to Ezekiel's age at the time of his call seems unlikely.[9] Writers normally did not date material by their date of birth but used pivotal historical events (see, e.g., Isa 1:1; 6:1). The most likely possibility is that it refers to the date of the discovery of the law in the temple and the beginning of the reforms of Josiah (ca. 622–621 B.C.). Ezekiel was called to his ministry in the fifth year of the exile (v. 2), which would have been 593/592 B.C., thirty years after the discovery of the law and the reforms of Josiah. This explanation seems to fit best the context of the message and the chronology of the entire book.[10]

The thirtieth year generally is taken to be 593 B.C., and the fourth month, fifth day would be equivalent to July 31, 593 B.C.[11] At that time Ezekiel already was in exile by the river Kebar as a relocated captive. The Kebar River was a man-made canal used for irrigation.[12] This canal brought water from the Euphrates River for use in agricultural irrigation. Excavations at Babylon have revealed evidence of Jewish settlements along such a canal called *naru kabiri* or *nehar kebār*.[13]

Foreign countries were considered unclean habitations. The exiles probably would seek running water to use in ritual purification prior to

---

[5] W. Zimmerli (*Ezekiel 1,* Her [Philadelphia: Fortress, 1979], 114) adopts the position that the text was edited to provide a chronology for Ezekiel's ministry.

[6] C. G. Howie, *Ezekiel, Daniel* (London: SCM, 1961), 21-22.

[7] If the exile began in 605 B.C., then the thirtieth year would be 575 B.C. But other dated messages begin in 592 B.C.

[8] See S. Fisch, *Ezekiel,* Soncino Books of the Bible (London: Soncino, 1950), 1, for a brief discussion of the Year of Jubilee. He considered the reference to the Year of Jubilee as a signal of impending judgment on Jerusalem (cf. 2 Kgs 22:8-20).

[9] C. L. Feinberg, *The Prophecy of Ezekiel* (Chicago: Moody, 1969), 17. For a full summary of various interpretations of the thirtieth year, see J. Bewer, "The Text of Ezekiel 1:1-3," *AJSL* 50 (1933-34): 96-101.

[10] Brownlee, *Ezekiel 1–19,* 3. After discussing several options, he adopts this approach because it best satisfies the context, though none of the approaches answers all the questions.

[11] J. Taylor, *Ezekiel,* TOTC (Downers Grove: InterVarsity, 1969), 36; and R. H. Alexander, "Ezekiel," EBC (Grand Rapids: Zondervan, 1986), 755.

[12] Taylor, *Ezekiel,* 21-22; Fisch, *Ezekiel,* 2; Greenberg, *Ezekiel 1–20,* 40.

[13] Cooke, *Ezekiel,* 4-5. The term נְהַר כְּבָר means "the great river" and appears in tablets from both Babylon and Nippur.

prayer or other religious observances.[14] Ezekiel may have gone there for a time of personal prayer and devotion. It was there by the river that "the heavens were opened"[15] and he saw "visions of God" (cf. 8:3; 40:2). The picture created by Ezekiel's description is of the door being opened into the heavenly throne room of God.[16] The word "saw" may refer to physical sight but also was associated with spiritual insight.[17] It often was used of visionary experiences that characterized the messages of some prophets. Such revelations came in visions, dreams, or inspiration of words directly from God (see Isa 6:1ff.; Zech 1:18; 1 Sam 9:9).

**1:2** The year also was the fifth year of the exile of King Jehoiachin, whose reign ended in 598/97 B.C. Jehoiachin was placed on the throne of Judah by Nebuchadnezzar after he carried Jehoiakim captive in 598 B.C. Jehoiachin was only eighteen years old and proved to be an unwise and unstable ruler. After only three months he too was taken captive to Babylon. He was replaced by his uncle Mattaniah, who was given the throne name Zedekiah (2 Kgs 24:8-17). This was a crucial time in the history of Judah. There were patriots in both Babylon and Jerusalem who believed the exile was only a short-term event. They plotted against Babylon to restore independence to the Israelite state. Both Ezekiel and Jeremiah warned unheeding ears that the exile would last much longer and Jerusalem would be destroyed, not restored.[18]

**1:3** The frequently used formula "the word of the LORD came" is in this verse an emphatic form in Hebrew and could be translated "the word of the LORD indeed came." This emphatic statement was used here to mark a point of absolute beginning. It may have identified the point at which Ezekiel the priest became Ezekiel the prophet of Yahweh.[19] He was known as the son of Buzi, a Zadokite priest (see 44:15 and cf. 1 Kgs 1:32-35). The expression "hand of the LORD" occurs seven times in Ezekiel (cf. 3:14,22; 8:1 ["the hand of the Sovereign LORD"]; 33:22; 37:1; 40:1) and suggests a

---

[14] Greenberg, *Ezekiel 1–20*, 40-41; Zimmerli, *Ezekiel 1*, 115-16.

[15] Similar expressions are found in 2 Sam 22:10 and Isa 63:19, although the verbs are different.

[16] D. Block, "Text and Emotion: A Study in the 'Corruptions' in Ezekiel's Inaugural Vision (Ezekiel 1:4-28)," *CBQ* 50 (1988): 428. The expression מַרְאוֹת אֱלֹהִים, he says, translated "visions of God," refers more precisely to a vision of "heavenly realities." It was a "supernatural vision," i.e., one that is "inaccessible to ordinary mortals apart from the revelation of God."

[17] See discussion of the root רָאָה in BDB, 906-9.

[18] Fisch, *Ezekiel*, 2. Both Ezekiel and Jeremiah interpreted the revolt against Babylon as rebellion against the judgment God had announced for Jerusalem.

[19] Greenberg, *Ezekiel 1–20*, 41; Zimmerli, *Ezekiel 1*, 144-45. The emphatic expression הָיֹה הָיָה occurs only here.

state of divine possession in which the prophet received his supernatural revelation.[20] It also denotes the divine compulsion of the call of God on the prophet. D. Block has written that although others like Elijah had been gripped and energized by the hand of God (1 Kgs 18:46), "in Ezekiel the 'hand of Yahweh' gains complete mastery over his movements" so that he can be described as "a man seized by God." This, he says, "more than any other quality distinguishes him from the other prophets. It accounts for his mobility and immobility, the apparent lunacy of some his actions, and his stoic response to rejection, opposition and grief."[21]

## 2. Vision of the Glory of God (1:4-28)

Israel was constituted as a theocracy by the covenant at Mount Sinai under Moses' leadership (Exod 19:1-8). Ultimately the people rejected the theocratic state for a theocratic monarchy in the days of Samuel (1 Sam 8:4-22). During the years after the constitution of Israel at Sinai, an exclusive nationalism developed that viewed Yahweh as absolutely tied to Israel.

This elite nationalism can be observed in the ministry of Jonah. He refused God's specific command to go and preach a message of deliverance to the Ninevites because they were foreigners (Jonah 1:1-3). Jonah fled from Israel to get away from the presence of Yahweh, a clear indication of the perceived tie between Yahweh and the land.[22] Ezekiel and the exiles had been removed by force from the land and thus, they thought, in some sense from the presence of the Lord.

So where was God? Was he in Israel? If so, how could he allow pagan armies to occupy the land? Was he absent? The implications of Nebuchadnezzar's capture and control of Jerusalem raised serious theological problems. If the capture of Jerusalem was allowed to stand, it would mean that the gods of Babylon were mightier than Yahweh, God of Israel. This was one reason the exiles refused to accept the idea of a long-term captiv-

---

[20] Greenberg, *Ezekiel 1–20,* 41-42; and Fisch, *Ezekiel,* 2. Compare 2 Kgs 3:15; 1 Chr 28:19; Ezra 7:28; Prov 21:1; Isa 66:14. See also R. R. Wilson, "Prophecy and Ecstasy: A Reexamination," *JBL* 98 (1979: 325.

[21] D. Block, "The Prophet of the Spirit: The Use of *rwḥ* in Ezekiel," *JETS* 32 (1989): 33.

[22] R. A. Redford, *Studies in the Book of Jonah* (London: Hodder & Stoughton, 1883), 152-54; 191-99. The relationship of Yahweh to the land was one element of worship that Y. Aharoni sought to clarify in excavations at Beersheba. The border sanctuaries seem to have been tied to concepts of the limits of the land and therefore the limits of Yahweh's jurisdiction (Aharoni's *The Beersheba Excavations,* Institute of Archaeology [Israel: Tel Aviv University, 1970], 2.

ity. They could not believe God would use another nation as an instrument of judgment (Hab 1:5-11). Ezekiel declared Yahweh to be God of the whole world and that God cared for his people and was with his people even in the punishment of the exile.[23] He believed God was free to use whomever he chose, including pagan kings (cf. Isa 45:1), to accomplish his purposes.

The vision of the glory of Yahweh was comforting because it confirmed God's continued concern for his people. But it was also the foundation for the call of Ezekiel as the prophet of judgment.[24] This vision has five elements: (1) the windstorm (v. 4), (2) the four living creatures (vv. 5-14), (3) the wheels (vv. 15-21), (4) the platform (vv. 22-27), and (5) the prophet's response (v. 28).[25]

The text of chap. 1, especially vv. 4-28, is extremely difficult. The problems are frequently removed by attributing them to later scribes or editors, favoring in many cases the shorter text of the LXX. Wevers, for example, exclaimed with confidence, "One thing is certain: the original text was much shorter—and much clearer!" In vv. 4-14 he removes as secondary all but vv. 4-6,9a,11,13.[26] W. A. Lind, however, argued that in text criticism the shorter text is not always the earlier one. The seemingly superfluous or inconsistent descriptive phrases in Ezek 1, he says, were added by the author Ezekiel, "excited by his mental picture of the vision he was trying to describe."[27] His argument was extended by D. Block,

---

[23] Taylor, *Ezekiel,* 41-42; Howie, *Ezekiel, Daniel,* 22-23; R. W. Klein, *Ezekiel: The Prophet and His Message* (Columbia, S.C.: University of South Carolina Press, 1988), 23. Ezekiel's vision provided a historical perspective to the exile by providing evidence that God was still at work.

[24] Ackroyd, *Exile and Restoration,* 106-10. Ezekiel stressed the imminent judgment of God but also the fact that God offers life and hope to those who repent. Brownlee (*Ezekiel 1-19,* 18) presents the view, also argued by L. C. Allen ("The Structure and Intention of Ezekiel 1," *VT* 43 [1993]:145-61) that "the import of the vision . . . is that the cosmic Lord of the universe is intervening in history to judge Israel and to warn them through one man, Ezekiel."

[25] This paragraph division agrees with Block ("Text and Emotion," 424). Parunak ("Literary Architecture," 63) divides the last two paragraphs differently, with vv. 22-25 on the creatures' relation to the expanse/platform and vv. 26-28 on the "chariot rider," returning as an inclusio with v. 4 to the brightness of the chariot throne. He notes that כְּעֵין, "like the gleam of," occurs in each of these paragraphs (cf. vv. 4,7,16,22,27). Greenberg (*Ezekiel 1-20,* 51-52) considers vv. 27-28 a unit. For a survey of approaches as well as additional support for Parunak's approach, see Allen, "Structure and Intention of Ezekiel 1," 145-51.

[26] Wevers, *Ezekiel,* 40-41. He describes this as "one of the most difficult chapters in the OT," for which he blames primarily later additions.

[27] W. A. Lind ("A Text-Critical Note to Ezekiel 1: Are Shorter Readings Really Preferable to Longer?" *JETS* 27 [1984]: 138).

who surveys numerous grammatical, stylistic, and substantial problems in Ezek 1 and various redactional and scribal explanations. He then argues that such an "unusual, unprecedented, unexpected encounter with divinity" so affected Ezekiel that he found himself frustrated with the "inadequacy of human language and "grasping for appropriate forms of expression."[28] Thus "the reason the account of the inaugural vision appears so garbled and contains so many obscurities lies in the emotional state of the recipient, who by internal data is purported to have been the narrator of the experience as well."[29]

### (1) The Windstorm (1:4)

**4I looked, and I saw a windstorm coming out of the north—an immense cloud with flashing lightning and surrounded by brilliant light. The center of the fire looked like glowing metal,**

**1:4**   Great upheavals in nature, society, and in our personal lives have a way of redirecting attention to the things that are of prime importance. This remarkable vision introduced Ezekiel to a theophany, a visible manifestation of God.[30] When Ezekiel saw God, the revelation came in a great thunderstorm (cf. Job 38:1; 40:6; Ps 29:3-5; 1 Kgs 19:11-13). The flashing fire of lightning and the awesome display of nature arrested his attention just as the burning bush claimed Moses' curiosity (Exod 3:1-15). Many other references associate similar occurrences with a supernatural manifestation of Yahweh. In the wilderness the Hebrews were led by the pillar of fire and the pillar of the cloud (Exod 13:17-22). When God came down on Mount Sinai, he came in lightning, smoke, and fire (Exod 19:16-18). God is characterized elsewhere as a consuming fire (Deut 4:24; Heb 12:28-29), which was regarded as a symbol of his presence.

Fire not only represented the presence of God, but it also was a symbol of the refining and purifying elements of judgment (e.g., Mal 3:1-6). The captives had lost the sense of awe and majesty of Yahweh. Yahweh presented himself to the prophet in power, majesty, and holiness so that

---

[28] Block, "Text and Emotion," 429-30.

[29] Ibid., 433. A prophet's emotional response to divine revelation may be exemplified by Isa 21:3-4 and Hab 3:16. Block argues (p. 437) that Ezekiel's account of the vision was recorded by the time he experienced or at least recorded the vision described in chap. 10. Citing Isa 8:1,16-18; 30:8; Jer 22:30; 25:13; 30:2; 45:1; Hab 2:2; and Nah 1:1, he observes, "From other prophetic texts we learn that the recording of prophetic messages as soon as they were received was a common practice" (p. 438).

[30] Taylor, *Ezekiel,* 54. Ezekiel received this vision while he was alone, as 3:4ff. indicates.

Ezekiel could sense God's character as he communicated his message to the captives.

The storm vision has several significant features. It was described as "immense," a reference not only to its size but also to its intensity. Successive bursts of lightning came from this storm, creating an intense electrical display. The flashing fire was so intense that it illuminated the storm cloud like the brightness of molten metal (v. 4).

The storm came from the north, the direction from which the Babylonians invaded Judah.[31] The great storm from the north represented the coming invasion and destruction of Judah and Jerusalem by the Babylonian army (cf. Jer 1:14).[32]

### (2) The Four Living Creatures (1:5-14)

**5and in the fire was what looked like four living creatures. In appearance their form was that of a man, 6but each of them had four faces and four wings. 7Their legs were straight; their feet were like those of a calf and gleamed like burnished bronze. 8Under their wings on their four sides they had the hands of a man. All four of them had faces and wings, 9and their wings touched one another. Each one went straight ahead; they did not turn as they moved.**

**10Their faces looked like this: Each of the four had the face of a man, and on the right side each had the face of a lion, and on the left the face of an ox; each also had the face of an eagle. 11Such were their faces. Their wings were spread out upward; each had two wings, one touching the wing of another creature on either side, and two wings covering its body. 12Each one went straight ahead. Wherever the spirit would go, they would go, without turning as they went. 13The appearance of the living creatures was like burning coals of fire or like torches. Fire moved back and forth among the creatures; it was bright, and lightning flashed out of it. 14The creatures sped back and forth like flashes of lightning.**

**1:5-14** As the prophet watched the approaching storm, four living creatures emerged. But this was not their only appearance to the prophet. They also are introduced again in 10:5 and 10:20, where they are called "cherubim." These angelic creatures were divinely appointed guardians of the holiness of God. Their mission was to prevent anything unholy from coming into the presence of a holy God. They were indicators of the pres-

---

[31] Fisch, *Ezekiel*, 2-3.

[32] Greenberg, *Ezekiel 1–20*, 42-43. Storms were common in Babylon during the summer months, especially in July. The storm Ezekiel witnessed represented the invading armies of Babylon.

ence of Yahweh, the holy God of Israel, in the storm cloud.

After the fall of Adam, cherubim were stationed at the entrance of the garden in Eden to guard against reentry by sinful humans into the presence of God (Gen 3:22-24). Their likeness was embroidered on the curtain of the tabernacle to guard the holy of holies against unauthorized entry (Exod 26:31). Within the holy of holies their likeness was placed atop the ark bearing the tablets of covenant, and they affirmed God's presence there (Exod 25:18-22). In Ezekiel's vision they are indicators of God's presence and his concern for the exiles in Babylon (cf. also Rev 4:7-8).

These verses list ten characteristics of the cherubim. These servants of God were equipped uniquely to perform their assigned tasks. Every aspect of their appearance represented some characteristic related to the performance of those tasks.[33]

First, the four living beings had the form or appearance of a "man" (i.e., a human being, v. 5).[34] While their general appearance was human, they had some additional unique, nonhuman features. Although they were not human (vv. 6-7), their human qualities were a subtle reminder that mortals are the crown of God's creative work (Gen 1:26-28) and the central focus of his creation (Gen 2:8-25).

Second, every creature had four faces. The four faces, one each on four sides (v. 8), are described in detail in v. 10.[35] Each face represented the highest form of animal life in a general category. One face was a lion and represented wild, undomesticated animals. Another face was like an ox and represented domesticated animals. A third face was like an eagle, the most powerful and magnificent of God's winged creatures. Other categories of animals such as fish and creeping beings were not represented. These creatures show God as the Lord of his creation. Human beings were the crown of his creative work. They were to exercise dominion as

---

[33] S. Briscoe, *All Things Weird and Wonderful* (Wheaton: Victor, 1977), 15-16; Taylor, *Ezekiel*, 54-56; Greenberg, *Ezekiel 1–20*, 42-46. The characteristics identified vary among interpreters. The imagery used was part of the Babylonian culture and thus familiar to the exiles in Babylon.

[34] The word "form" is דְּמוּת, which is used in Gen 1:26 concerning humans who are created in the image of God. The notion that spirit beings including God have a form clearly is taught in the Bible. All spirit beings appearing to humans had a form like humans (see, e.g., Gen 18:1–19:29; Dan 10:5-6; Ezek 9:2-4; Acts 1:11; Heb 13:2). See also J. A. Motyer, "Old Testament Theology," NBC (Grand Rapids: Eerdmans, 1973), 27.

[35] Parunak ("Literary Architecture," 63) considers v. 10 the center of a chiasm that spans vv. 5-14. This accounts for the repetition of phrases in vv. 9,12 and perhaps for the seeming addition of וּפְנֵיהֶם, "and their faces," at the beginning of v. 11, which is followed here by וְכַנְפֵיהֶם as it is in v. 8 (contra Brownlee, *Ezekiel 1–19*, 8; Greenberg, *Ezekiel 1–20*, 45).

the chief steward of creation (Gen 1:28).[36]

Third, their legs were "straight" (v. 7) with gleaming hooves like a calf. The term "straight" refers to their unjointed structure.[37] The foot was like the hoof of a calf, rounded for ease in turning. This characteristic suggested the stability of these creatures in performing assigned tasks.[38]

Fourth, under their wings each creature had hands like a human being (v. 8). Each of the four wings touched those of the creature next to it. The wings of the cherubim in the holy of holies also touched (v. 11; cf. 1 Kgs 6:27).[39] Each was related closely to his neighbor and united as one in performing assigned tasks.

Fifth, when they moved, they went "straight" forward (vv. 9,12). Since there was a face on each of the four sides, any direction they moved could be forward; so the creatures did not turn to change direction of movement.[40] This suggests a sense of purpose, commitment, and availability for assignments.

Sixth, these cherubim were winged creatures, each having four wings (v. 11; cf. 8). Two wings were extended upward apparently to support the throne-platform and/or in praise to God on the throne. These two wings touched the wings of each neighboring creature (cf. vv. 9,23). The other two wings were used to cover the body of each creature as a sign of humility and modesty. Isaiah 6:2 and Rev 4:1-11 present similar visions in which the creatures each had six wings. The additional pair of wings was used to shield the faces of the creatures from the face of God. Brownlee suggests that the creatures of Ezekiel's vision had no need to cover their faces since they were under and supporting the platform (v. 22) and looked straight ahead (v. 9) and so they could not see the face of God.

Seventh, they followed the "spirit" in their movement (vv. 12,20). This

---

[36] The word "dominion" (רְדָה) in Gen 1:26 refers to rule, authority, or possession (BDB, 922-23). The context clearly makes God the creator and owner of the universe. Human beings have vested authority over the created order but are to be held accountable as stewards of the universe (1 Cor 4:1-2; Matt 25:14-30). The earth and all its creatures belong to God (Ps 24:1). The dominion given to the human family implies that it is to be exercised with accountability and stewardship in view.

[37] Fisch, *Ezekiel,* 3; Greenberg, *Ezekiel 1–20,* 44; Zimmerli, *Ezekiel 1,* 126. It also indicates that they moved by flight rather than walking.

[38] Briscoe, *All Things Wierd and Wonderful,* 16. Stability was an important and necessary quality of these creatures who were responsible for bearing the throne of God.

[39] Greenberg (*Ezekiel 1–20,* 44-45) believes the wings may have been joined at the tips, enabling them to give added support as pictured on the veil in the tabernacle and temple.

[40] Ibid., 45. The root סבב, when used as it is here in the *niphal* stem, may mean "to change position or status" as well as the usual meaning "turn." The reference in 10:16 also suggests that when the creatures moved, all directions were straight ahead.

refers to the divine Spirit of the one who sat on the throne above them, who was directing and enabling their movements. The Old Testament taught that the beings who surrounded Yahweh were there to perform his will, and in the New Testament the Spirit is the one who enables all created beings to perform the will of God (John 14:5-31; 16:1-15; Rom 8:1-8; Acts 2:1-38; Eph 1:13-14). D. Block has argued that the frequent use of *rûaḥ* ("spirit/wind/breath") in Ezekiel warrants calling him "the prophet of the spirit."[41] Although the term can have many senses (wind, direction, side, agency of conveyance, agency of animation, agency of inspiration, mind, sign of divine ownership),[42] the use here as an agency of animation is the most frequent in Ezekiel. That it further refers to "the vitalizing principle of life that comes from God himself" is indicated by the otherwise anomalous use of the article (*hārûaḥ,* "the spirit").[43] So the cherubim were divinely appointed and empowered to do the will and work of God.

Eighth, their appearance was like "burnished bronze" (v. 7) and "coals of fire" or "torches" (v. 13). This characteristic, mentioned again in 10:7, was associated with a theophany. The brightness of their appearance suggests their close relation and proximity to Yahweh. The skin of Moses' face was radiant with light after having been in the presence of God (Exod 34:29-35).

Ninth, the movement of the creatures was as quick as a flash of lightning (v. 14). This concept suggests instantaneous action that resulted in immediate implementation of the will of God activated by the power of the "spirit."

Tenth, the wings of the creatures made an awesome sound (vv. 23-25). "Rushing waters" (v. 24) was to Ezekiel like the voice of God. This language confirms that this is a theophany.

These spiritual beings who were part angel, part human, and part animal were fitting representatives of the whole created order. Their activity affirmed the relationship of God to his creation as Lord of all things. This idea was vital in helping Ezekiel and the captives in exile and the people in Judah understand that in the midst of the storms of life, God was still on his throne. He was not oblivious to their circumstances.

### (3) The Wheels (1:15-21)

---

[41] It is found fifty-two times, more than in any other prophet. The longer Book of Isaiah uses it fifty-one times; Jeremiah, only eighteen. See Block, "Prophet of the Spirit," 28.

[42] See the chart in Block, "Prophet of the Spirit," 29.

[43] Ibid., 34-36. See also Alexander, "Ezekiel," 757.

**15**As I looked at the living creatures, I saw a wheel on the ground beside each creature with its four faces. **16**This was the appearance and structure of the wheels: They sparkled like chrysolite, and all four looked alike. Each appeared to be made like a wheel intersecting a wheel. **17**As they moved, they would go in any one of the four directions the creatures faced; the wheels did not turn about as the creatures went. **18**Their rims were high and awesome, and all four rims were full of eyes all around.

**19**When the living creatures moved, the wheels beside them moved; and when the living creatures rose from the ground, the wheels also rose. **20**Wherever the spirit would go, they would go, and the wheels would rise along with them, because the spirit of the living creatures was in the wheels. **21**When the creatures moved, they also moved; when the creatures stood still, they also stood still; and when the creatures rose from the ground, the wheels rose along with them, because the spirit of the living creatures was in the wheels.

**1:15-21** Associated with each cherubim were wheels whose appearance was explained more in terms of function than of mechanical construction.[44] The wheels gave mobility to the chariot-throne of God.[45] God appeared to Ezekiel in imagery of movement and action that presented him as both transcendent and immanent.[46] The whole picture of the cherubim, the chariot, and the throne was associated intimately with an affirmation of the presence of God.

The ark of the covenant in the holy of holies was considered the throne of Yahweh or the stool of his feet (cf. 4:37, where the "place of my throne" was used to designate the place where the ark was kept in the holy of ho-

---

[44] Brownlee, *Ezekiel 1–19,* 12. Two wheels, an inner and an outer (each of which could flop over to the horizontal plane), gave them contact with the ground, allowing them to roll in any direction. Verses 15-21 often are considered a later addition (W. Eichrodt, *Ezekiel,* OTL [Philadelphia: Westminster, 1970], 118; Zimmerli, *Ezekiel 1,* 105). The problems with its inclusion, however, can be resolved by a structural analysis such as Parunak's ("Literary Architecture") coupled with Block's study ("Text and Emotion") of the inevitable effects on the text of Ezekiel's heightened emotional state. See also Allen, "Structure and Intention of Ezekiel 1," 150.

[45] Verses 25-28 make clear that this living vehicle with wheels represented the throne of the glory of God. Other prophets also speak of God sitting on a throne (see 1 Kgs 22:19; Dan 7:9; 1 Chr 28:18; Isa 6:1-9). The idea of a mobile throne was not unique to Ezekiel and the OT but appears elsewhere in ancient Near Eastern literature (see, e.g., Zimmerli, *Ezekiel 1,* 127-28). The vision in Ezek 1 gave rise to a whole body of Jewish thought known as *merkabah mysticism* (see "Merkabah Mysticism," *EncJud* [1972]: 11, 1386-87, and "Maaseh Merkavah," in D. Cohn-Sherbock, *The Blackwell Dictionary of Judaica* (Blackwell: Oxford, 1992), 333-34). See also Greenberg, *Ezekiel 1–20,* 205-6.

[46] B. S. Childs, *Old Testament Theology in a Canonical Context* (Philadelphia: Fortress, 1985), 41. God was never viewed as monolithic, so his transcendence did not suppress his immanence, a concept that formed the basis for trinitarian language.

lies).[47] Some representations of the ark have portrayed it as a box with wheels.[48] The wheels Ezekiel saw were the lowest part of the chariot-throne and sat on the ground below the cherubim (v. 15). Their appearance was like chrysolite, which may have been a topaz or other semiprecious stone. Each wheel was actually two in one, with one apparently set inside the other at right angles.

This arrangement allowed movement of the throne-platform in any direction.[49] The circumference or outer rim of the wheels was described as high and awesome with the outer edge of the rims inset with "eyes" (v. 18). When the cherubim moved, the wheels moved, activated by the Spirit. The Spirit gave direction to the wheels through direct knowledge and access to the will of God.[50] Verse 21 is a recap of vv. 19-20 and forms a conclusion to the section, emphasizing the unity and coordination between the cherubim, the wheels, the Spirit, and the throne-chariot.[51]

Ezekiel's imagery vividly represents the basic characteristics of the divine nature. Yahweh was seated above the cherubim on his throne-chariot as the Lord of creation. The mobility of the wheels suggests the omnipresence of God; the eyes, his omniscience; the elevated position, his omnipotence.[52]

### (4) The Platform (1:22-27)

**[22]Spread out above the heads of the living creatures was what looked like an expanse, sparkling like ice, and awesome. [23]Under the expanse their wings**

---

[47] W. Zimmerli, *Old Testament Theology in Outline* (Atlanta: John Knox, 1978), 80; see also "Throne of God," *EncJud* (1972): 15, 1126-27.

[48] S. Loffreda, *Recovering Capernaeum* (Gerusalemme: Edizioni Custodia Terra Santa, n.d.), 36. Excavations at Capernaeum yielded an ark with wheels on it that was etched in one of the stones of the synagogue.

[49] Greenberg, *Ezekiel 1–20,* 46-47. Wheels such as these were part of the chariot of Sargon depicted on seals that date to the third millennium B.C.

[50] Fisch, *Ezekiel,* 6. Parunak ("Literary Architecture," 63) points out that this united movement of Spirit, wheels, and cherubim is stressed by the repetition and climactic ordering of forms of the verbs הלך, "go," נשא, "rise," and עמד, "stand," in vv. 17-21. D. Block ("Prophet of the Spirit," 36-37) has argued recently that the phrase רוּחַ הַחַיָּה in vv. 20-21 should be translated "the spirit of life." The repetition, he says, "seems to emphasize that these normally inanimate objects appear to the prophet to be as alive as the 'living creatures' themselves. For him the unusual phenomenon may be attributed only to the presence of the life-giving spirit of God."

[51] A wooden translation of v. 20 is, "To where it was, the spirit going, they went, there the spirit going." This is usually cited as a case of dittography (see also vv. 16,23-26). See Lind, "A Text-Critical Note to Ezekiel 1," 137; Block, "Text and Emotion," 422-23.

[52] Greenberg, *Ezekiel 1–20,* 46-47; Wevers, *Ezekiel,* 48.

were stretched out one toward the other, and each had two wings covering its
body. ²⁴When the creatures moved, I heard the sound of their wings, like the
roar of rushing waters, like the voice of the Almighty, like the tumult of an
army. When they stood still, they lowered their wings.

²⁵Then there came a voice from above the expanse over their heads as they
stood with lowered wings. ²⁶Above the expanse over their heads was what
looked like a throne of sapphire, and high above on the throne was a figure
like that of a man. ²⁷I saw that from what appeared to be his waist up he
looked like glowing metal, as if full of fire, and that from there down he
looked like fire; and brilliant light surrounded him.

**1:22**    The word "expanse" is the same word used in Gen 1:6 to describe the creation of the heavens. Here it refers to some kind of platform
above the living creatures.⁵³ The texture and appearance of the platform
resembled ice and was the support for the throne of God.

**1:23-25**    Under the firmament the movement of the living creatures
produced an awesome noise that resembled the sound of rushing waters
like the voice of the Almighty (v. 24).⁵⁴ Parallel to that sound (note the
repetition at the end of vv. 24-25), the awesome voice itself came from
above the firmament.⁵⁵ The sound of God's voice was the same as John
described in his opening vision in Rev 1:15, which also was a theophany.

**1:26-27**    Positioned on the platform was a throne of *sappîr,* translated
"sapphire" but more likely referring to lapis lazuli, which was more common in the ancient world.⁵⁶ The vision of the throne is similar to the experience of Moses and the seventy elders in Exod 24:10. The throne also
is mentioned again in Ezek 10:1.

Upon the throne was seated a figure like that of a man.⁵⁷ The radiance

---

⁵³ רָקִיעַ has been associated with the dome shape of something made firm by hammer-
ing. This is based more on the Latin word *firmamentum* than on the Heb. word, which
makes no specific reference to shape (*TWOT,* 862). Some keep the idea of the dome shape
while most use the term "platform" or even "floor" (Fisch, *Ezekiel,* 7). This reference is
similar to the vision of John in Rev 4:6-8. See Alexander, "Ezekiel," 759; Taylor, *Ezekiel,*
58; Stalker, *Ezekiel,* 48; Wevers, *Ezekiel,* 48; Greenberg, *Ezekiel 1–20,* 48; BDB, 956.

⁵⁴ שַׁדַּי is one designation for God especially prominent in the poetic books (Stalker,
*Ezekiel,* 49) and generally is translated "Almighty." The word has been associated with the
Akkadian term *shaddu,* which means "mountain" (*TWOT,* 907; BDB, 994-95).

⁵⁵ Parunak, "Literary Architecture," 64.

⁵⁶ *TWOT,* 631.

⁵⁷ The idea of God with a human form sometimes has been dismissed as an anthropo-
morphic accommodation, God's way of trying to help us in comprehending deity. Yet the
discussion in Gen 1:26 concerning the human form as an image of the divine seems to suggest that God has a form. Spirit beings who appear in Scripture all have human form and
often are mistaken for human beings. See note on 1:5-14.

of his appearance was like fire described in other theophanies (see Exod 3:2-15; 24:17; Rev 4:1-4).[58] The striking elements of this vision communicated two important concepts. First, Yahweh is a God of splendor and great power. This was not a new idea but one that had been neglected in those days of spiritual decline prior to the fall of Jerusalem. Second, the God of Israel is not bound to the land of Israel, an idea that seemed revolutionary for the Israelites at that time.[59]

Another tension was presented by this and other theophanies. The idea that no mortal could see God and live was grounded in the experience of Moses in his request to see God in Exod 33:18 and the subsequent denial of that request in 33:20. The concept so permeated Hebrew thought that when Manoah, Samson's father, and his wife had an encounter with the angel of Yahweh, they felt that death was imminent and inevitable because they had seen God (Judg 13:22). Yet in Exod 24:9-18, as here in Ezek 1; 10, the Bible speaks about God on his throne. Because of the infiniteness of his being and his holiness, God could only reveal himself to humans in a limited way.[60]

Ezekiel saw the majesty of God, who came to Ezekiel and the people in the crisis of the exile and reminded them of his holiness and power as Lord of his creation. They were not forgotten or overlooked in the suffering of their exile. As terrifying as this vision must have been, it had a redemptive dimension. God uses and permits crisis circumstances to draw people to him (Rom 8:28).

### (5) The Response of the Prophet (1:28)

**[28]Like the appearance of a rainbow in the clouds on a rainy day, so was the radiance around him.**

---

[58] Note the repetition of וְנֹגַהּ לוֹ סָבִיב in vv. 4,27 and הַנֹּגַהּ סָבִיב in v. 28 that help to mark vv. 4-28 as a unit.

[59] See the introduction to 1:4-28 and Stalker, *Ezekiel*, 49.

[60] See B. S. Childs, *The Book of Exodus*, OTL (Philadelphia: Westminster, 1974), 595-96. Genesis 32:30; Exod 33:11; Num 12:8 refer to experiencing God face-to-face. The use of face-to-face refers to intimate knowledge. It is a figure of speech that need not mean literally one face before another but may also mean "in the presence of," or "directly," i.e., apart from intermediaries (cf. Num 12:8). While the elders and Moses saw the throne and the one on it, the face of God obviously was covered. It was the face of God that revealed his full glory, which no person could see and live. Therefore Moses was allowed to see the unveiled glory only from behind (Exod 33:22-23). The elders and Moses saw God on the throne, as did Ezekiel, but none saw his face. Ultimately, God did give a face-to-face encounter through Jesus (John 14:6; 2 Cor 4:6). The transfiguration of Jesus in Matt 17:1-13/ Mark 9:2-13 declares that Jesus was God in human flesh, which veiled the glory of God.

**This was the appearance of the likeness of the glory of the LORD. When I saw it, I fell facedown, and I heard the voice of one speaking.**

**1:28** When people are consumed by insurmountable problems and buffeted by the storms of life, they usually do not need another perspective on their problems. What they do need is a new perspective on God as Lord of life and larger than all its difficulties. Humanity in peril needs a sense of the awesome majesty of God. There needs to be an awareness that God is greater than adversity. He is with his people in the midst of their problems. This was a need of both Ezekiel and the people to whom he ministered. They needed a new vision of and commitment to the holiness and majesty of God. For this reason the opening vision was crucial as the first revelation in the call of Ezekiel to be a prophet to the exiles.

The cherubim, as protectors of God's holiness, were a reminder that humankind was sinful. People often want to blame the storms of life on God and forget that human sin brought chaos in the world. This lack of accord is evident in the storms of nature as well as the storms of human nature. The only hope for humanity is to recognize God in the midst of the storms as one who can restore them to calm (see Luke 8:22-25).

Like Isaiah (6:1-9), Ezekiel fell on his face in response to the awesome presence of God. Ezekiel, prostrate before God, must have wondered who could minister in such a place, to such people. The answer came in the voice that related the details of his call. The opening vision of Ezekiel's ministry affirmed three significant truths about God that are summarized in v. 28. First, the vision was a reaffirmation of the nature of God as holy, powerful, and majestic. Second, the rainbow was a reminder of God's promise-making and promise-keeping character (Gen 9:16). It was a re-kindler of hope that God could and would help. Third, it was an assurance that nothing, including geographic location, separated one from God (cf. Rom 8:38-39).[61]

Through this vision Ezekiel received a message of hope. God was still atworkamongtheexiles.Thismeantthathatheknewaboutthemandwasconcerned about their plight. People need a vision of hope, but such hope is always dependent on a willing response and a humble, repentant attitude.

## 3. Call of the Prophet (2:1–3:15)

Like the burning bush, which arrested Moses' attention (Exod 3:1-15), the awesome vision of God in chap. 1 captured Ezekiel's focus. God, the

---

[61] P. C. Craigie, *Ezekiel*, DSB (Philadelphia: Westminster, 1983), 12-14. The three truths in this vision indicate that the message extended beyond Ezekiel's time and place.

all-powerful Lord of creation, was in Babylon just as he was in Israel. He came to communicate a specific message to Ezekiel, details of which revealed the call of Ezekiel to a prophetic ministry.

This section has an introduction (2:1-2) and a conclusion (3:12-15). Described within is the prophet's mission, his motivation, and the divine fortification for the difficult task ahead. H. Parunak has argued that the considerable repetition in the two parallel paragraphs, 2:3-7 (which he concludes with v. 8a) and 3:4-11, is due to their interlaced structure. Furthermore, they flank the central paragraph (2:8–3:3, his 2:8b–3:3) of the entire call narrative, which contains the command to eat the scroll.[62] Ezekiel's call can be expounded in four parts: (1) the prophet's melancholy mission (2:1-7), (2) his motivation (2:8–3:3), (3) his divine preparation (3:4-11), and (4) the conclusion of the call (3:12-15).

While the specific details of this call were unique to Ezekiel, the special call was a common element in the experience of most, if not all, of the prophets of the Old Testament.[63] Each prophet brought to his ministry unique insights from his background. God called Ezekiel the priest to be a prophet and to undertake a most difficult and unpopular assignment as mediator to the people in exile.

## (1) The Prophet's Mission (2:1-7)

**[1]He said to me, "Son of man, stand up on your feet and I will speak to you." [2]As he spoke, the Spirit came into me and raised me to my feet, and I heard him speaking to me.**

**[3]He said: "Son of man, I am sending you to the Israelites, to a rebellious nation that has rebelled against me; they and their fathers have been in revolt against me to this very day. [4]The people to whom I am sending you are obstinate and stubborn. Say to them, 'This is what the Sovereign LORD says.' [5]And whether they listen or fail to listen—for they are a rebellious house— they will know that a prophet has been among them. [6]And you, son of man, do not be afraid of them or their words. Do not be afraid, though briers and thorns are all around you and you live among scorpions. Do not be afraid of what they say or terrified by them, though they are a rebellious house. [7]You must speak my words to them, whether they listen or fail to listen, for they are rebellious.**

---

[62] Parunak, "Literary Architecture," 64-66. See the chart in the introduction to 1:1–3:27. The parallel paragraphs are analyzed as comprising five subparagraphs each: 2:3-4a,4b-5,6,7,8a, and 3:4,5-7,8-9,10,11. The structural relationship between the two may be symbolically represented as $a\ b_1\ b_2\ b_3\ c\ //\ b_3'\ a'\ b_2'\ c'\ b_1'$.

[63] See Introduction, "Ezekiel, the Prophet."

Ezekiel's call opens with an explanation of the task God was assigning to him. After establishing a relationship with the prophet in the opening words in vv. 1-2, God explains in vv. 3-7 the nature and difficulties of his assignment.

**2:1-2**   God uses the designation "son of man" ninety-three times in the book to address the prophet, while he never calls him by his proper name (contrast Exod 3:4; 1 Sam 3:4,6,10; 1 Kgs 19:9,13; Jer 1:11; Amos 7:8; 8:2). The expression "son of" in Hebrew could mean "having the characteristics of," as in the phrases (literally) "son of a night" (Jonah 4:10), "son of death" (1 Sam 10:31), and "son of peace" (Luke 10:6). "Son of man," then, can mean simply "member of humanity."[64] But characteristic of humanity, and perhaps the focus in its use in Ezekiel, is frailty and mortality, in contrast to the eternality and awesome majesty of God (cf. 31:14).[65] While used as an equivalent to "man" (ʾîš) in Num 23:19, the focus is on human unreliability. In Job 25:6 it is associated with "maggot" and "worm." Emphasizing "human frailty and moral ineptitude," it is associated with terms that "symbolize a wretched, lowly existence" and that "have the smell of death about them."[66] It describes man's apparent insignificance in Ps 8:4[Heb., 5] (also Ps 144:3). But in Ps 80:17[Heb., 18] the reference is to the Davidic dynasty as God's appointed agent on the throne of Israel, also called "the man at your right hand." It would be through him that God would renew his favor toward his people.[67] Thus in addition to a reminder of his dependence upon God, the repeated address also may have reminded him of his responsibility as God's watchman and messenger of redemption. The same phrase was used of the messianic figure in Dan 7:13 who appeared before the Ancient of Days and of Daniel himself in 8:17. It was often used later in the New Testament by Jesus about himself (see Matt 8:20; 9:6; 11:19; Mark 2:28).[68] Thus G. Van Groningen probably is right that "when used of an individual person, who

---

[64] Cooke, *Ezekiel,* 31; Zimmerli, *Ezekiel 1,* 131.

[65] Brownlee (Ezekiel 1–19, 25-26), while acknowledging this possibility, nevertheless understands the main point of the address as to "nobody special, simply as a member of the human race." See Taylor, *Ezekiel,* 60; Alexander, "Ezekiel," 761; Eichrodt, *Ezekiel,* 61.

[66] J. E. Hartley, *The Book of Job,* NICOT (Grand Rapids: Eerdmans, 1988), 357. The phrase and its parallel אֱנוֹשׁ, he says, "bear the note of human weakness and earthiness," as אָדָם, "man," is related to אֲדָמָה, "ground."

[67] See W. A. VanGemeren, "Psalms," EBC, vol. 5 (Grand Rapids: Zondervan, 1991), 527.

[68] On the meaning of the expression in the Gospels, see C. L. Blomberg, *Matthew,* NAC (Nashville: Broadman, 1992), 146-47. On this and other connections between Ezekiel and the Messiah of the NT, see C. H. Bullock, "Ezekiel, Bridge Between the Testaments," *JETS* 25 (1982): 23-31.

is spoken of as Yahweh's agent, it points to humankind created royal, restored to a regal position, and called to serve as Yahweh's human representative on behalf of human beings."[69]

Ezekiel's response to the awesome vision was to fall prostrate in an act of worship and fearful reverence (v. 28). God commanded him to stand to receive the message of his call and commission (compare the experience of Daniel in Dan 10:11), indicating his acceptance of Ezekiel and this intention of calling tha tman into service. So the Spirit entered him and enabled him to obey God's command, as the indwelling Holy Spirit does today (see Rom 8:1-28).[70] The presence of the Spirit also enabled Ezekiel to speak with authority, confidence, and courage.

**2:3-5** Ezekiel was sent to the Israelites, including those captives in Babylon and those who remained in the homeland.[71] But he also was to address the rebellious nations (chaps. 25–32). The term "nation" in v. 3 is in fact plural in the Hebrew text and is the usual designation for non-Hebrew people or Gentiles.[72] While Ezekiel's message had specific reference to Israel, its truths also were universally applicable.

God also described to Ezekiel the character of those to whom he was sent. Four terms were used to define their character. First, previously they were called "rebellious" here and throughout the call narrative (2:3,5,6-8; 3:9,26-27).[73] Except for the use in v. 3, "rebellious" in Ezekiel translates the noun *mĕrî* ("rebellion").[74] It usually is found in the expression (literally) "house of rebellion" (2:5-6; 3:9,26-27; 12:2-3,9,25; 17:12; 24:3), although it also occurs independently (2:7-8; 44:6). The final clause in v. 7

---

[69] Van Groningen, *Messianic Revelation*, 739.

[70] D. Block argues: "The fact that the raising of the prophet occurs concurrently with the sound of the voice suggests a dynamic and enabling power in that voice. We should probably associate the *rwḥ* that vitalizes the wheels with the *rwḥ* that energizes the prophet" ("Prophet of the Spirit," 37).

[71] Fisch, *Ezekiel,* 9. The verb שׁלח ("send") helps link the subparagraphs 2:3-4a and 3:5-7.

[72] גּוֹיִם may be taken as a reference to foreign nations (Zimmerli, *Ezekiel 1,* 133) although some see the term as applicable to Judah and Benjamin (see Fisch, *Ezekiel,* 9-10).

[73] The phrase כִּי בֵּית מְרִי הֵמָּה occurs once in each of the subparagraphs Parunak labels $b_1$, $b_2$, and $b_3$, then again in $b_2'$.

[74] The word in v. 3 is מֹרֵד ("rebel"). It is used first as an active participle (because of the continuous nature of their rebellion), then as a finite verb. It could describe rebellion against either God (as here; cf. 20:38; Josh 22:16,18-19,29; the noun מֶרֶד ("rebellion") is used in Josh 22:22) or a human king (e.g., 11:15). The remaining occurrences of "rebellious" in Ezekiel (NIV) translate the noun מְרִי ("rebellion") from the root מרה, used almost always of rebellion against God. Outside Ezekiel מְרִי occurs only in Num 17:25[10]; Deut 31:27; 1 Sam 15:23; Neh 9:17; Prov 17:11; Isa 30:9. The verb is used in Ezek 5:6; 20:8,13,21 and several times in Numbers, Deuteronomy, Jeremiah-Lamentations, Isaiah, and Psalms (note especially 78:17,40,56).

is literally "for they are rebellion." The emphasis is on Israel's disloyalty to Yahweh their God. The history of the nation was replete with examples of their rebellion against God.[75] From their first episode with the golden calf in Exod 32:1-35 to the introduction of Baal worship in Num 25:1-18 and in later occurrences in 1 and 2 Kings, there was constant recurrence of idolatry. This behavior accelerated after the division of the kingdom in 1 Kgs 12.

In spite of the past history of the nation as a rebellious people, Ezekiel was not to let personal feelings or the hope of visible response from the people become the measure of his success as a prophet.

Second, the term "revolt" (*paša,* v. 3) was the word often translated "transgress," meaning to go beyond the bounds proscribed by the law of God, or to betray a trust.[76] Thus the term referred to an act of defiance against the will of God. The people were rebellious because they had revolted against the commands of God.

Third, the people were described as "obstinate" (v. 4) or literally "hard [*qěšê*] of face."[77] This referred to their stubborn selfish will, which totally disregarded the commands of God's Word. This stubbornness was further reinforced by the fact that even though the prophet brought a message from God, it made no difference in their behavior.

Fourth, the term "stubborn" reinforced the third characteristic and is literally "firm [*ḥizqê*, a synonym of *qěšê*] of heart." The word "heart" (*lev*) is most often used in the Old Testament to refer to the "will" or center of volition. Thus the people were described as motivated by a fixed, stubborn self-will that dismissed the will of God as irrelevant.[78]

With the message destined for such an unwelcome audience, there should be no surprise that God warned the prophet of the rejection he would face. His success would not be measured in terms of the people's response but in terms of his obedience. Though he was told that no one would welcome his messages from God, the prophet still was responsible for delivering them. Once delivered, the messages placed the burden of response on the people (v. 5).

---

[75] *TWOT,* 525.

[76] See E. A. Martens, *God's Design: A Focus on Old Testament Theology* (Grand Rapids: Baker, 1981), 49.

[77] קְשֵׁי פָנִים.

[78] Contrast is made between the obstinate, self-willed person and the person who yields to the divine will. King Saul was obstinate and disobedient (see 1 Sam 13:13; 15:11,22-23; 16:14); therefore God could not establish his dynasty. David, on the other hand, was sinful but not obstinate; thus he was responsive to God's own heart (BDB, 54; cf. 11:17-21, note; 1 Sam 13:14; Acts 13:22).

**2:6-7**   Like Joshua (Josh 1:9), Ezekiel was encouraged at the beginning of his mission not to fear opposition.[79] His congregation was described as "briers and thorns" and "scorpions" (v. 6), terms that allude to their stubborn rebellion and hardened disobedience. Ezekiel would not be held accountable for the people's lack of receptivity; he was responsible only to speak the words God gave him, "so that they will know that a prophet has been among them" (vv. 5,7). The measure of success in God's work is not always in terms of the amount and frequency of visible response. Success is to be measured in terms of our obedience to the words, commands, and will of God regardless of the visible results. So the mission of the prophet was to proclaim the word of God to a rebellious and unresponsive Israel.

### (2) The Prophet's Motivation (2:8–3:3)

[8]But you, son of man, listen to what I say to you. Do not rebel like that rebellious house; open your mouth and eat what I give you."
[9]Then I looked, and I saw a hand stretched out to me. In it was a scroll, [10]which he unrolled before me. On both sides of it were written words of lament and mourning and woe.

[1]And he said to me, "Son of man, eat what is before you, eat this scroll; then go and speak to the house of Israel." [2]So I opened my mouth, and he gave me the scroll to eat.
[3]Then he said to me, "Son of man, eat this scroll I am giving you and fill your stomach with it." So I ate it, and it tasted as sweet as honey in my mouth.

How could a person get highly motivated for a ministry that others are bound to reject? Motivation must come from a deep sense of commitment based on a divine call. Like the apostle Paul later (2 Cor 4–5), Ezekiel was certain that God had given him an assignment. He also was certain of his message of truth, the Word of God.[80]

**2:8-10**   After being warned about Israel's obstinacy he would experience, Ezekiel was instructed to submit to the will of God and to indicate

---

[79] Note the thrice repeated אַל־תִּירָא in v. 6 (Parunak's subparagraph $b_2$), also used once (with לֹא) in 3:9 (in Parunak's $b_2$'). In both cases it appears to be at the focal point of the paragraph. In v. 6 it is flanked on either side by commands to speak "whether they listen or fail to listen" (vv. 5,7).

[80] See the note on Ezek 1:28 in *The Believer's Study Bible* (Nashville: Nelson, 1991), 1104, which shows how the prophet fulfilled five essential characteristics of a good witness of God's message.

his obedience by eating what God offered to him.[81] If Parunak's analysis of 1:1–3:15 is correct, this paragraph (2:8–3:3), which contains ten commands, is at the center of the chiasm and is therefore the most prominent paragraph of the entire section. This is because of the critical importance to be played by the Word of God in Ezekiel's ministry.

Scrolls were papyrus or leather sheets specially prepared for writing. They were sewn or glued together, inscribed, then rolled. This was the standard form for books prior to the beginning of the second century when the codex or leaf book came into wide use.[82]

Some rabbis interpreted eating the scroll as part of the vision experience while others have interpreted it as an allegory.[83] The ideas of eating and drinking sometimes were used in a figurative sense to denote the operation of the mind in receiving, understanding, and applying doctrine or instruction of any kind.[84] Ezekiel was to assimilate the message and proclaim its contents.

When it was unrolled, Ezekiel saw that the scroll had an unusual feature. It had writing on both sides (v. 10). This may have been a way to present the idea of the fullness of coming judgment. It may also have been a way to suggest that there was no room for Ezekiel to add personal opinion; his message was to be God's alone.[85]

Three words were used to describe the character of the scroll's contents. The scroll was filled with "lament, mourning and woe" (v. 10). A lament (*qinah*) was a funeral song written in a specific meter in Hebrew poetry and sung in times of bereavement. "Mourning" (*hegeh*) referred to the words and moans uttered by a bereaved family and by professional mourners employed to mourn the death of a loved one. "Woe" (*hi*) was an exclamation of distress at a great loss of any kind.[86] Nevertheless, the meanings of the three terms overlapped, stressing that Ezekiel's message would contain bad news. It clearly would produce great "lament, mourning and woe." He would declare good news as well, but he did not need to

---

[81] Comparable, perhaps, is Moses' obedience to God's seemingly absurd command to grasp the serpent's tail in Exod 4:4. The command to eat a scroll also was given to John the apostle in a strikingly similar vision in Rev 10:8-11.

[82] Scrolls varied in length. The longest biblical Qumran scroll is 1QIsa$^a$, which is 7.34 m, but they could be much longer. See E. Tov, *Textual Criticism of the Hebrew Bible* (Minneapolis: Fortress, 1992), 201-7.

[83] Fisch, *Ezekiel*, 11.

[84] See E. W. Bullinger, *Figures of Speech Used in the Bible* (Grand Rapids: Baker, 1968), 826.

[85] Zimmerli, *Ezekiel 1*, 135; Taylor, *Ezekiel*, 63; Bunn, "Ezekiel," 241.

[86] The third term הִי is used only in Ezek 2:10 and may be an abbreviated form of הוֹי (see Zimmerli, *Ezekiel 1*, 91-92, and Alexander, "Ezekiel," 763).

be warned about that. The unpleasant part of a messenger's role, which one might like to avoid, is the communication of bad news. But faithfulness demands that the whole message of God be delivered.[87]

**3:1-3** Ezekiel was commanded four times to eat the scroll, then to go preach his message to the Israelites. These commands revealed that the message of the Old Testament prophets was external and originated with God. They did not discover the truths they preached through logic or deduction but through divine revelation. Nevertheless, God did not supplant the personality of the prophets through whom he spoke. Their messages also reflected their personalities, backgrounds, and individual character traits. Thus the truths that emerged were neither wholly from the prophets alone nor from God alone but from both.[88] Their messages were divine truths through human channels.

When Ezekiel obeyed the command to consume the scroll, he discovered that its taste was sweet though its message was stern (vv. 2-3). The subject of his message was judgment, a message that was just and right in light of Judah's rebellion and disobedience. When the apostle John ate the scroll of his vision (Rev 10:8-11), it tasted like honey but produced a bitter stomach. The sweetness of God's Word is a figure also used elsewhere in the Old Testament (Pss 19:10; 119:103). Bitterness was a contrasting characteristic of the message that contained severe judgment. Normally the Word of God was considered sweet, but in this case its truth was the declaration of coming bitterness of judgment that would be a bitter experience for an apostate people (Jer 2:19; 4:18).[89]

## (3) The Prophet's Divine Preparation (3:4-11)

**⁴He then said to me: "Son of man, go now to the house of Israel and speak my words to them. ⁵You are not being sent to a people of obscure speech and difficult language, but to the house of Israel— ⁶not to many peoples of obscure speech and difficult language, whose words you cannot understand. Surely if I had sent you to them, they would have listened to you. ⁷But the**

---

[87] D. Stuart, *Ezekiel,* CC (Dallas: Word, 1989), 41.

[88] See Cooke, *Ezekiel,* 38-39.

[89] Zimmerli (*Ezekiel 1,* 136-37) sees a parallel to the experience of Jeremiah and his scribe Baruch. They delivered the message of the prophet, written on a scroll, to King Jehoiakim. The king was angered by the stern words of judgment, so he had the scroll cut in pieces and burned (see Jer 36:1-32). God reissued the message as a testimony of the certainty of judgment (36:27-32). Ezekiel had a similar assignment. He had been a resident in Jerusalem in 603 B.C. when the events of Jer 36 took place. He was being asked to deliver a similar message. He, on the other hand, was commanded to consume the message so that it would be a part of him and his new ministry. See also Craigie, *Ezekiel,* 17-18.

house of Israel is not willing to listen to you because they are not willing to listen to me, for the whole house of Israel is hardened and obstinate. **8But I will make you as unyielding and hardened as they are. 9I will make your forehead like the hardest stone, harder than flint. Do not be afraid of them or terrified by them, though they are a rebellious house."**

**10And he said to me, "Son of man, listen carefully and take to heart all the words I speak to you. 11Go now to your countrymen in exile and speak to them. Say to them, 'This is what the Sovereign LORD says,' whether they listen or fail to listen."**

These verses reiterate the message of 2:3-7.[90] Their unity is confirmed by the parallel phrases at the beginning and end, "Go now to the house of Israel" in v. 4 and "Go now to your countrymen in exile" in v. 11. The focus is on the difficulty of the assigned task and the specific qualities with which God had endowed the prophet to enable him to face opposition. The irony in this passage is its observation that foreigners would have been more receptive to a message from God than were the Israelites. The difficulties of cross-cultural communication are nothing compared to the obstacle of spiritual blindness.[91]

**3:4-6** There was never any doubt that the Israelites were the primary audience of Ezekiel's ministry. Even the messages of judgment against the nations in 25:1–32:32 centered on the relationship of those countries to Israel and especially atrocities committed against Israel. Ezekiel was sent to the people of Judah, his people, who spoke his language but whose decadence had surpassed that of the foreign nations (v. 6; 5:6-12; 16:47-52).[92]

**3:7** Rejection of Ezekiel, his mission, and his message would not be a rebuff of the prophet so much as a renunciation of God. The people refused to listen to Ezekiel because he was God's spokesman. This situation was similar to the rejection of Samuel's leadership (1 Sam 8:4-7), when

---

[90] Note the parallels between 3:4 and 2:7; between 3:5-7 and 2:3-4a; between 3:8 and 2:6; between 3:10 and 2:8; and between 3:11 and 2:4b-5. See the comments introducing 2:1–3:15.

[91] The phrase "obscure speech and difficult language" literally means "deep lipped," עִמְקֵי שָׂפָה, and "heavy tongued," כִּבְדֵי לָשׁוֹן. The idea was a speech that sounded guttural and strange and therefore unintelligible (see Fisch, *Ezekiel*, 13; Cooke, *Ezekiel*, 39). The phrase "deep lipped" is also used in Isa 33:19. The phrase "heavy tongued" was used by Moses in Exod 4:10 as an excuse for rejecting God's call. There it may mean "slow speech" or even that he had a speech impediment; see J. Rabbinowitz, "The Book of Ezekiel" (London: Soncino, 1977), 337.

[92] Cooke, *Ezekiel*, 39. This revelation of Israel's rejections of God is a reaffirmation of their rebellious nature as revealed in 2:4.

the Israelites demanded a human king. Samuel was told that this was not a rejection of his leadership but a rejection of Yahweh, whom he represented (cf. Num 14:1-12). Whereas 2:4 described the people as (literally) "hard of face" and "firm of heart," they are described here as "firm of forehead" and "hard of heart." The hardness of Pharaoh's heart is given many times in Exodus (see especially chaps. 7–10) as the reason for his refusal to obey God. Using a similar expression of Israel would have been a serious indictment (cf. 2 Chr 36:13; Prov 28:14).

**3:8-9** Opposition was pictured as coming from people with hardened faces. This implied a hardened will set against the word and will of God. God responded by promising the prophet that he would harden the forehead of Ezekiel so that it was like "hardest stone." The word "hardest stone" (v. 9) probably was reference to a diamond, the hardest stone known, and has been rendered "diamond" in some translations (e.g., NCB, NJB). The same word appears in Jer 17:1, where it is translated "flint."[93] Ezekiel therefore was assured of divine protection for his assignment.

**3:10-11** The prophet was instructed (literally) to listen with his ears and receive with his heart all that God said. This verse implies a continuous relationship. Ezekiel was to keep on hearing as God kept on speaking to him. Receiving the words of God was not to be confined to the call experience alone but to the ongoing revelation throughout his entire ministry.[94] In these opening words of the final charge the prophet was exhorted to listen, understand, grasp, and apply the words of God.[95] He was called to be God's spokesman in exile to his fellow countrymen.

In this assignment he shared the same burden as his contemporary, Jeremiah. Both men were called to preach messages of severe judgment. But it is a mistake to conclude that either man was insensitive to the chilling weight of the message of destruction they announced. Ezekiel, unlike Jeremiah, repressed his feelings. But there are subtle hints in his book, such as this sad report of Judah's obstinacy in v. 11, which revealed that he too felt the pain of the coming destruction to befall Jerusalem.[96]

---

[93] The AV translates the word שָׁמִיר ("diamond") in Jer 17:1, and that translation is suggested here by Zimmerli (*Ezekiel 1*, 137) and Eichrodt (*Ezekiel*, 66).

[94] Zimmerli (*Ezekiel 1*, 138) alludes to the continuing process of receiving revelation in Ezekiel's experience. The dated messages of the book (see table in Introduction) and the repeated phrase "the word of the LORD came" (about fifty times) confirm the fact that the revelation of God's word did not come all at once to the prophet.

[95] Brownlee, *Ezekiel 1–19*, 34-35. Use of שָׁמַע with אֹזֶן was not simply to "hear with the ears" but also referred to grasping the words from God with the mind.

[96] Eichrodt, *Ezekiel*, 66. Jeremiah openly lamented the coming judgment of Judah. By contrast, Ezekiel concealed his feelings of pain over the coming fall of the city but was just as sensitive to the plight of the people.

## (4) The Conclusion of the Call (3:12-15)

**¹²Then the Spirit lifted me up, and I heard behind me a loud rumbling sound—May the glory of the LORD be praised in his dwelling place!— ¹³the sound of the wings of the living creatures brushing against each other and the sound of the wheels beside them, a loud rumbling sound. ¹⁴The Spirit then lifted me up and took me away, and I went in bitterness and in the anger of my spirit, with the strong hand of the LORD upon me. ¹⁵I came to the exiles who lived at Tel Abib near the Kebar River. And there, where they were living, I sat among them for seven days—overwhelmed.**

This initial vision closed with a mandate that again reaffirmed the warning of 2:5. Israel would be rebellious and unreceptive. But Ezekiel was instructed to proclaim the Word of God despite his reception.

**3:12-15** Ezekiel was lifted by the Spirit (v. 12), the same activating force of 2:2.[97] This was a subjective visionary experience like the one experienced in 8:3 when he returned in a vision to Jerusalem.[98] As he was "lifted," he also heard the sound of the wings of the creatures and the movement of the wheels, suggesting the movement of the chariot throne and the end of the vision (v. 13).[99] The Spirit took the prophet to his place among the captives by the River Kebar at Tel Abib (v. 15). This was the same location identified in 1:1, where only the river was mentioned. But here in v. 15 the name of one city of the exile appears. The name Tel Abib probably means "hill of ears." The location in Babylon is unknown, but the name is preserved in its modern version, Tel Aviv, one of the principal cities of Israel.[100]

When the Spirit took him, the prophet departed in great distress, compelled by "the strong hand of the LORD" (v. 14). The reason for his strong

---

[97] D. Block ("Prophet of the Spirit," 33-34) compares this to Ezekiel's being controlled by the hand of God (see on 1:3). He also argues for רוּחַ here referring to the divine Spirit.

[98] There is almost unanimous agreement that the experience was visionary rather than a levitation of some kind. See, e.g., Alexander, "Ezekiel," 764; Cooke, *Ezekiel*, 41; Ellison, *Ezekiel: The Man and His Message*, 28-29; Zimmerli, *Ezekiel 1*, 139; Taylor, *Ezekiel*, 66.

[99] Taylor, *Ezekiel*, 66. This refers to the same power of God that lifted the prophet in 2:2. The parenthetical doxology in v. 12 is commonly considered foreign to the context. The first word בָּרוּךְ ("blessed") usually is emended to בְּרוּם ("as [the glory of the LORD] arose") on the basis of the similarity of ב and מ phonetically and graphically in Old Hebrew. See NRSV, REB; Tov, *Textual Criticism*, 247, 358; Brownlee, *Ezekiel 1–19*, 36.

[100] The name תֵּל אָבִיב has been associated with the Akkadian *til abubi*, meaning "mound of the flood." It was a town mentioned in the Code of Hammurapi and the Assyrian Annals of Tiglath-pileser (see Wevers, *Ezekiel*, 55). It also has been called "Hill of Corn Ears" (Fisch, *Ezekiel*, 15) and "Hill of Spring Fruit" (Greenberg, *Ezekiel 1–20*, 71). The name in modern Hebrew means "Spring Hill."

reaction is not specified. He may have been overwhelmed by the weight and unpleasantness of his assignment, especially the knowledge that the people would be generally unresponsive (2:5-8; 3:7). Ezekiel was not the first prophet to have a negative reaction to the reality of his call.[101] Jonah rejected his call and fled until God turned him around (Jonah 1:1-17). Some interpreters believe that this was not negative but only a state of "anguish" over the assignment and exhilaration over the theophany (cf. 27:30-31). The subsequent experience of the prophet as he sat seven days overwhelmed confirms that this was a negative experience.[102] It took him, like Job (Job 2:13), seven days to overcome the initial shock and despair of the awesome judgment he had seen.

One other fact that contributed to the overwhelming weight of the moment was the prophet's declaration, "I sat among them seven days" (v. 15).[103] As a prophet in the midst of the people, he was able to identify their needs and feel the weight of impending judgment (see Introduction, "Ezekiel, the Prophet"). It is a reminder that we must identify with the needs of those who search for God. While we do not participate with them in a godless life-style, we must seek to understand their emptiness and alienation if we are to be effective communicators of the words of God.[104]

---

[101] מַר may mean "bitter" but includes the idea of "distress," "anguish," and "heavy heartedness." It is used in a context of mourning and anguish in 27:30-31. בַּחֲמַת רוּחִי literally means "in the heat of my spirit." D. Block ("Prophet of the Spirit," 44) notes that of the 32 occurrences of חֵמָה in Ezekiel, this is the only place it does not refer to divine anger (except 23:25, where it is the nations' anger); thus it may not refer to anger here at all. The LXX, he notes, translates it with ὁρμή, "impulse/passion." It is "the 'glow of his spirit,'" which arose as a consequence of seizure by the spirit/hand of Yahweh." The term מַר he prefers to take from the Ugaritic root *mrr*, "to be strengthened/empowered," thus producing for the clause, "I went forth strengthened in the fervor of my spirit."

[102] Ezekiel sat seven days, a fact that is similar to the horror of Ezra, who was appalled at the words of the people confessing their disobedience to God (Ezra 9:4) and Job's contemplation of his circumstances (Job 2:13). The word "overwhelmed" in v. 15 is the *hiphil* participle מַשְׁמִים, which means "to be in a state of horror and wonder." See C. F. Keil, *Biblical Commentary on Ezekiel* (Grand Rapids: Eerdmans, 1970), 58.

[103] Verse 15 appears to contain considerable repetition. Especially difficult is the clause translated, "And there, where they were living." There is an alternate reading for the first word. The NIV has followed the *kethiv* וָאֵשֵׁר ("and where"; similarly NASB, NJB). The *qere* is וָאֵשֵׁב ("and I sat"; cf. NKJV), which Cooke (*Ezekiel*, 43) judges "impossible." Greenberg (*Ezekiel 1–20*, 71) considers the previous clause ("who lived near the Kebar River") a doublet, added later to explain the location of Tel Abib. NRSV, REB apparently consider the second clause a gloss and translate only the first.

[104] For a discussion of the structure and themes in the call of Ezekiel in 1:28–3:15, see Greenberg, *Ezekiel 1–25*, 72-81, and Eichrodt, *Ezekiel*, 67-74.

## 4. Appointment as a Watchman (3:16-21)

**[16]At the end of seven days the word of the LORD came to me: [17]"Son of man, I have made you a watchman for the house of Israel; so hear the word I speak and give them warning from me. [18]When I say to a wicked man, 'You will surely die,' and you do not warn him or speak out to dissuade him from his evil ways in order to save his life, that wicked man will die for his sin, and I will hold you accountable for his blood. [19]But if you do warn the wicked man and he does not turn from his wickedness or from his evil ways, he will die for his sin; but you will have saved yourself.**

**[20]"Again, when a righteous man turns from his righteousness and does evil, and I put a stumbling block before him, he will die. Since you did not warn him, he will die for his sin. The righteous things he did will not be remembered, and I will hold you accountable for his blood. [21]But if you do warn the righteous man not to sin and he does not sin, he will surely live because he took warning, and you will have saved yourself."**

The Hebrew text has an unusual division in the middle of v. 16. The break has led several interpreters to conclude that the section 3:16b-21 is a later insertion in the text.[105] While there is no consensus on why the break occurs, it is also found elsewhere (e.g., Gen 35:22; 1 Sam 16:2; 1 Kgs 13:20). Greenberg suggests that its intent is to call to mind a parallel passage, in this case 33:1-9.[106] After his initial vision Ezekiel was silent and overcome with awe for seven days. The second appearance of God after the seven days was therefore a natural development. God appeared a second time to reaffirm Ezekiel's call, to remind him of his responsibility as a watchman, and to warn the Israelites of their need for repentance. The theme of individual responsibility also occurs in Ezek 18:1-32 and 33:1-20.

This section has two main divisions. The call for the prophet to be a watchman is found in vv. 16-17. The second division in vv. 18-21 focuses on the responsibilities and accountability of the watchman.

**3:16-17**   Seven-day periods were common in Israel. For example, mourning for the dead continued for seven days (Gen 50:10; Num 19:11).

---

[105] Cooke, *Ezekiel*, 44; Wevers, *Ezekiel*, 56; Stalker, *Ezekiel*, 55; Zimmerli, *Ezekiel 1*, 157; H. G. May, "The Book of Ezekiel," *IB* (Nashville: Abingdon, 1956), 6:49,82-83, all argue that vv. 16b-21 were a later editorial addition. G. Van Groningen (*Messianic Revelation in the Old Testament* [Grand Rapids: Baker, 1990], 737) says that "one must lament the efforts" of such critical scholars, since "there is no textual or material evidence to support this opinion."

[106] Greenberg (*Ezekiel 1–20*, 83); see also Alexander ("Ezekiel," 766). Both consider vv. 16b-21 as genuine. A sectional division in the middle of a verse is called a *pisqah bĕʾemṣaʿ pasuq* (see Tov, *Textual Criticism*, 53).

Perhaps Ezekiel was thinking about the death of his former life as a priest and his call to a new life as God's prophet. Seven days also was the time of consecration for a priest (Lev 8:1-33). Perhaps this was the consecration of Ezekiel the priest to his new ministry as priest-prophet.[107]

When seven days elapsed, God appeared and began giving Ezekiel the words he was to deliver to the people. In chaps. 2–3 God had told the prophet repeatedly that he was to deliver divine words (2:4,7; 3:4,11), but he had not yet given him those words. Here in v. 16 is the first occurrence of the phrase "the word of the LORD came to me." This phrase was to characterize Ezekiel's prophecy, occurring in forty-one verses. It is found elsewhere in the Old Testament only in Jeremiah (nine times) and Zechariah (twice). As P. C. Craigie wrote, "For no other prophet is there a record of such sustained contact with the divine word, the very essence of prophecy."[108]

God told the prophet he was sent as a "watchman" to Israel (v. 17). Although the concept is mentioned elsewhere (Isa 21:6; 52:8; 62:6; Jer 6:17; Hab 2:1) Ezekiel's divine appointment as watchman is unique, and only here are the duties and responsibilities specified.[109] A watchman was a city employee appointed to be a lookout from some high vantage point such as a tower or the city wall. Such an office was extremely important because the safety of the entire population rested with the watchman. If a watchman failed in his duty to warn inhabitants of the town of impending attack, he was held personally responsible for any loss. God appointed Ezekiel as his watchman to warn Judah and Jerusalem of impending destruction. He was to open their eyes to "profounder evils that encompassed them, . . . break the spell . . . of delusions and raise the cry of danger when none was suspected."[110] If he chose to remain silent, he would be held accountable.

**3:18-21** These verses focus on the prophet's responsibility and accountability as God's watchman.[111] He was to warn the wicked of their

---

[107] Ellison, *Ezekiel,* 29. The watchman terminology was a further clarification of Ezekiel's call. It is used in 33:1-9 as a part of his recommissioning. Van Groningen (*Messianic Revelation,* 736-39) ties together Ezekiel's ministry as priest, prophet, and watchman and argues that he functions as a type of Christ. A watchman, he notes, represented the city's ruler; thus the position had "a regal dimension."

[108] Craigie, *Ezekiel,* 22.

[109] Eichrodt, *Ezekiel,* 75.

[110] P. Fairbairn, *Exposition of Ezekiel* (Evansville: Sovereign Grace, 1960), 41-42, cited in Van Groningen, *Messianic Revelation,* 738. See also Alexander, "Ezekiel," 765-66.

[111] Brownlee, *Ezekiel 1–19,* 50; Bunn, "Ezekiel," 243. The concept of the prophet as "watchman" was not new. It also was used in Hos 9:8 and Isa 21:6; 62:6; Jer 6:17; Hab 2:1.

sin and of impending judgment (v. 18). The responsibility for the message was then upon the wicked person who was warned. If the prophet failed the assignment, the wicked would be judged and the prophet also held responsible for failing to exercise his duty (vv. 19-21). Indifference that fails to save a life is comparable to negligent homicide. The prophet would be guilty of murder by his failure to fulfill his calling. According to the law of retribution, he was liable for the loss of life payable by the forfeit of his own (Gen 9:5-7).[112] The responsibility of a believer in Christ today to share the word of life, salvation, and forgiveness is no less awesome. Once the message of salvation is entrusted to us, we are responsible and accountable to share with those who are lost.[113]

## 5. Reaction of the Prophet (3:22-27)

[22]**The hand of the LORD was upon me there, and he said to me, "Get up and go out to the plain, and there I will speak to you."** [23]**So I got up and went out to the plain. And the glory of the LORD was standing there, like the glory I had seen by the Kebar River, and I fell facedown.**

[24]**Then the Spirit came into me and raised me to my feet. He spoke to me and said: "Go, shut yourself inside your house.** [25]**And you, son of man, they will tie with ropes; you will be bound so that you cannot go out among the people.** [26]**I will make your tongue stick to the roof of your mouth so that you will be silent and unable to rebuke them, though they are a rebellious house.** [27]**But when I speak to you, I will open your mouth and you shall say to them, 'This is what the Sovereign LORD says.' Whoever will listen let him listen, and whoever will refuse let him refuse; for they are a rebellious house.**

Opinions differ over whether this passage should be understood as the introduction to Ezekiel's first prophetic assignment, connected more closely to 4:1–5:17,[114] or as the conclusion to the call and commission in 1:1–3:21.[115] There is no reason to assume that this was a later message than the call and commission. Although similar terms and phrases are used in 4:1–5:17, this visionary experience occurred seven days after his first

---

[112] Fisch, *Ezekiel*, 16; Taylor, *Ezekiel*, 71. A dying person unwarned would be regarded as a murder victim. The murderer would be the watchman who failed in his duty.

[113] For a discussion of individual responsibility as it appears in Ezek 3, see Taylor, *Ezekiel*, 69-72; Craigie, *Ezekiel*, 21-24; and Enns, *Ezekiel*, 42-43.

[114] Keil, *Ezekiel*, 61-62; Brownlee, *Ezekiel 1–19*, 51-52; Enns, *Ezekiel*, 43-44; Greenberg, *Ezekiel 1–20*, 101; Zimmerli, *Ezekiel 1*, 176-78.

[115] Craigie, *Ezekiel*, 24-25; Alexander, "Ezekiel," 766-67; Taylor, *Ezekiel*, 72. Hals (*Ezekiel*, 8, 26) identifies thirty-three units in chaps. 1–24, identifies 4:1–5:17 as a separate subcollection, and rules out the inclusion of 3:22-27 as grouped with the vocation account.

vision-call and was the conclusion of the commission of the prophet.[116]

**3:22-23** The hand of the Lord was "on" the prophet, suggesting receipt of a visionary experience (v. 22). This experience was a logical extension of Ezekiel's commission as a watchman. Like Paul after his call, Ezekiel was summoned to go into the desert to receive further instruction for his assignment (Gal 1:16-17).[117]

When Ezekiel obeyed and moved to the plain (v. 23), he again encountered the glory of the divine presence, which he had seen in 1:3-28. His response also was the same as in 1:28. He fell facedown in worship and awe at the presence of God.

**3:24-27** The prophet was empowered by the Spirit and set on his feet as he had been in his first vision (2:2). This was the same Spirit who was the moving force behind the creatures he saw by the River Kebar (1:12,19). Then Ezekiel was given three restrictions. First, he was instructed to shut himself in his house (v. 24). The second restriction apparently was closely associated with the first. The prophet was to be bound with ropes to insure his seclusion, "so that you cannot go out among the people" (v. 25). While some interpreters reject the idea of a literal binding of the prophet, there seems no reason to take it as figurative.[118] Like the first restriction it was to be self-imposed, perhaps with the help of family and friends.

But more than Ezekiel's movement was to be restricted. He also was to be unable to speak (cf. Job 29:10; Ps 137:6). Neither the purpose, the duration, nor the extent of these restrictions is here made clear. The only explicit limitation is given in v. 27, and that only limits Ezekiel's silence. ezekiel would be silent until or except when the Lord enabled him to speak.

The Lord's further instructions in 24:25-27 appear to indicate that Ezekiel's silence would last until the fall of Jerusalem in 587 B.C., that is, for six years. His silence would end at that time when he spoke with a fu-

---

[116] Semantic structural analysis allows for devices that identify the beginning and conclusion of larger units. See, e.g., J. Beckman and J. Callow, *Translating the Word of God* (Grand Rapids: Zondervan, 1974), 279-81 ("criteria for delineating larger units"); W. C. Kaiser, Jr., *Toward an Exegetical Theology* (Grand Rapids: Baker, 1981), 71-72. The phrase "hand of the LORD was upon him" (1:3) may be compared to the similar phrase in 3:22. While Ezekiel used the phrase six times (1:3; 3:14,22; 37:1; 40:1), it was not used to introduce every new unit in the book.

[117] The term בַּקְעָה (translated "plain") refers to a "cleft" or an "opening," meaning an open valley surrounded by hills, characteristic of the wide plain of the Euphrates River in Babylon (Greenberg, *Ezekiel 1–20*, 101; Alexander, "Ezekiel," 767).

[118] Enns, *Ezekiel*, 44; Fisch, *Ezekiel*, 18; Greenberg, *Ezekiel 1–20*, 102, all favor a symbolic binding. Wevers, *Ezekiel*, 58, and Taylor, *Ezekiel*, 73, take the events of v. 25 as literal.

gitive from Jerusalem. Thus he would "be a sign unto them, and they will know that I am the LORD."

The Lord actually ended Ezekiel's silence "the evening before the man arrived" (33:22), but the news did not come until six or even eighteen months after Jerusalem fell (see discussion at 33:21). Thus Ezekiel's silence lasted six and a half to seven and a half years. These facts may be put together in various ways. Ezekiel may have been confined to his house only until he began preaching or his confinement may have lasted the entire time except when directed by the Lord to go out and deliver his messages.[119] A third option is that his confinement was even more extensive and made it necessary for the people to come to him to receive his messages.[120] Whatever the duration and nature of Ezekiel's seclusion, its purpose may have been to emphasize that like the apostle Paul, he belonged to the Lord and was a man under orders (cf. Eph 3:1; 4:1). Since his message until Jerusalem's fall was primarily one of judgment, this would have been an important point to make. Ezekiel was to be a holy vessel, dedicated solely to the service of God for the benefit of God's people. When he spoke, it would be by God's command and with his authority.[121]

Some have suggested that Ezekiel's restriction from "rebuke" (v. 26) refers to his role of reprover. As a reprover he was forbidden from becoming an advocate for the people. His role as a reprover would have led to a natural desire to become a mediator or legal arbiter between God and Israel. He therefore was prohibited from speaking to the nation in reproof or even to God as their advocate.[122]

The call closed with a prototype of a favorite saying of Jesus, "Whoever will listen, let him listen." When Ezekiel was permitted to speak, it was with the reminder that his message was to the rebellious house of Israel/

---

[119] Stuart, *Ezekiel*, 51.

[120] Alexander, "Ezekiel," 767. He supposes that Ezekiel left his home, however, to perform the symbolic actions of 4:1–5:17. Surely Ezekiel was not tied up for six and a half years!

[121] Taylor, *Ezekiel*, 74; Zimmerli, *Ezekiel 1,* 160. Ezekiel was to be known as God's mouthpiece. When he spoke to the people, it was only because God had something to say. When God was silent, Ezekiel was silent.

[122] מוֹכִיחַ is a *hiphil* participle and means "one reproving." R. R. Wilson ("Interpretation of Ezekiel's Dumbness," *VT* 22 [1972]: 91-104) argues that Ezekiel was forbidden to act as a legal covenant mediator and intercessor. Greenberg (*Ezekiel 1–20,* 102) is correct that the term מוֹכִיחַ does not refer to an "intercessor," and thus he disagrees with Wilson's conclusion. Yet there is a fine line between an intercessor and an arbiter, and it is true that the prophet was prohibited from speaking on Israel's behalf or reproving Israel with the view of restoring covenant promises.

Judah. He was to deliver the message and let those who possessed spiritual discernment understand and make the application. Jesus used parables punctuated with "who has ears let him hear" (see Matt 13:10-17).

As the nation faced days of judgment, the needs of the people could not be met by offering a new perspective on their problems. What the nation needed was a new perspective on God. The call experience of Ezekiel supplied that new perspective by reinforcing the holiness and majesty of God. He was able to share that viewpoint with the certainty of judgment. That judgment included the fall of Jerusalem, which God declared through the symbolic actions and prophetic messages of Ezekiel.

## II. PROPHETIC MESSAGES CONCERNING JUDAH AND JERUSALEM (4:1–24:27)
1. Prophecies of Destruction for Judah and Jerusalem (4:1–7:27)
   (1) Prophetic Dramatization of the Fall of Jerusalem: The Clay Brick (4:1-8)
   (2) Prophetic Dramatization of the Completeness of Destruction: The Unclean Meal (4:9-17)
   (3) Prophetic Dramatization of the Severe Limits of Destruction: The Shaved Head and Beard (5:1-17)
   (4) Prophetic Dramatization of the End of False Worship: Message to the Mountains (6:1-14)
   (5) Prophetic Dramas of Judgment in Summary (7:1-27)

## II. PROPHETIC MESSAGES CONCERNING JUDAH AND JERUSALEM (4:1–24:27)

### 1. Prophecies of Destruction for Judah and Jerusalem (4:1–7:27)

The prophets were great preachers, and Ezekiel was no exception. God called him to "go . . . speak my words" (3:4) to the people of Israel. Ironically, at the close of the call narrative God told the prophet that he was not to speak to the people. God withheld his word because of the rebelliousness of Israel (3:26). The time would come when God would open Ezekiel's mouth, but in the early days of his ministry his messages were to be dramatic. Ezekiel was instructed to present his messages in symbolic actions before the people. These symbolic actions were God's way of communicating truth without words. Sometimes words are so familiar that people pay little attention to the depth of their content. The dramatic presentations gave Ezekiel's message an arresting character.[1]

Use of symbolic actions was not a new phenomenon that God employed in the ministry of Ezekiel. Earlier prophets had used this method of presenting the "word of God" (1 Sam 15:27-31; 1 Kgs 11:29-33; 22:11; 2 Kgs 13:14-19). Jeremiah, Ezekiel's contemporary, also used many symbolic

---

[1] A. Cody, *Ezekiel* (Wilmington, Del.: Michael Glazier, 1984), 35.

91

actions to present his messages. Some examples were the decayed girdle or belt (Jer 13:1-11), the filled bottles (13:12-27), the broken pot (19:1-13), wearing the ox yoke (27:1-22), and buying the field 1 (32:1-15).[2]

Some forms of pagan worship used a phenomenon known as imitative magic. An individual performed actions involving a model or a representative object in the belief that such objects would produce the effect the action symbolized.[3] An early example of imitative magic was writing the name of an enemy on a clay vessel, then smashing it against the wall to insure the defeat of the adversary.

Some interpreters believe that the similar imitative actions employed by the Old Testament prophets were vestiges of the primitive forms of magic the Hebrews borrowed from the Canaanite culture.[4] Such claims overlook an important difference between the earlier forms of imitative magic and the symbolic acts of Jeremiah and Ezekiel. Earlier forms of magic were attempts to influence the gods or the events of the future or both. The Old Testament prophets, by contrast, were acting out a message that was just as much inspired revelation as was the spoken or written word. They were not trying to influence God or the future but communicating their message through dramatic forms.[5]

The analysis of chaps. 4–7 presented here recognizes five divisions: four prophetic dramatizations (4:1-8; 4:9-17; 5:1-17; 6:1-14) and a summary drama (7:1-27). L. Boadt has presented an alternative analysis of the chapters as comprising three symbolic actions followed by three judgment oracles.[6] The symbolic actions involve a brick (4:1-8), a meal (4:9-17), and shaving (5:1-4). The judgment oracles are first against Jerusalem (5:5-17), then the mountains of Israel (6:1-14), and finally the whole land (7:1-27). Thus he sees them arranged climactically with increasing wrath. The symbolic actions introduce dramatically the judgments God was to bring against Israel and Judah (note "the sin of the house of Israel" three times, 4:4,5,6). The themes of siege, famine, and violent death introduced in the

---

[2] H. L. Ellison (*Ezekiel: The Man and His Message* [Grand Rapids: Eerdmans, 1965], 32) believes the use of symbolic acts was practiced from the early days of prophecy.

[3] See J. B. Taylor, *Ezekiel,* TOTC (Downers Grove: InterVarsity, 1969), 76-77, for a brief discussion of "sympathetic magic"; see also "Canaanite Religion" in the Introduction.

[4] D. M. G. Stalker (*Ezekiel* [London: SCM, 1968], 57-58).

[5] Taylor, *Ezekiel,* 77; see also W. Eichrodt (*Ezekiel,* OTL [Philadelphia: Westminster, 1970], 81), who points out that דָּבָר means both "word" and "thing." The spoken word was itself a symbol of reality. Whether communicated in written or spoken words or by symbolic acts, the truth of God was still the same; Stalker (*Ezekiel,* 59-60).

[6] L. Boadt, "Rhetorical Strategies in Ezekiel's Oracles of Judgment," in *Ezekiel and His Book*, ed. J. Lust (Leuven: University Press, 1986), 190-93.

instructions to the prophet also run through the judgment oracles. Most obvious is the occurrence of the terrible triplet "plague, famine, and sword" in each of the three oracles (5:12,17; 6:11-12; 7:15). Also the cause for judgment introduced generally as "sin" in chap. 4 is specified in chaps. 5–7 as idolatry, violence, and rebellion against God's laws. Finally, variations of the divine formula "you will know that I am the LORD" occur ten times in chaps. 5–7, stressing the purpose for God's judgments.

### (5) Prophetic Dramatization of the Fall of Jerusalem: The Brick Tile (4:1-8)

[1]"Now, son of man, take a clay tablet, put it in front of you and draw the city of Jerusalem on it. [2]Then lay siege to it: Erect siege works against it, build a ramp up to it, set up camps against it and put battering rams around it. [3]Then take an iron pan, place it as an iron wall between you and the city and turn your face toward it. It will be under siege, and you shall besiege it. This will be a sign to the house of Israel.

[4]"Then lie on your left side and put the sin of the house of Israel upon yourself. You are to bear their sin for the number of days you lie on your side. [5]I have assigned you the same number of days as the years of their sin. So for 390 days you will bear the sin of the house of Israel.

[6]"After you have finished this, lie down again, this time on your right side, and bear the sin of the house of Judah. I have assigned you 40 days, a day for each year. [7]Turn your face toward the siege of Jerusalem and with bared arm prophesy against her. [8]I will tie you up with ropes so that you cannot turn from one side to the other until you have finished the days of your siege.

This prophetic dramatization has two distinct parts. Verses 1-3 focus on the tile. The prophet makes the tile, and it is the object of his lessons. In vv. 4-8 the tile is still part of the drama, but Ezekiel is the focal point as he lies on the ground before the tile to communicate his message.

**4:1-3** In the first dramatic presentation, Ezekiel used a clay brick commonly used in building. Into the soft clay he drew the map of Jerusalem so that the completed object represented the city of Jerusalem (v. 1). Using the clay brick as his focal point, the prophet enacted a battle against it. He constructed a siege wall, a mound or rampart, set up military camps around it, and employed battering rams against it. Using an iron pan to represent an impenetrable barrier, he glared upon the city with the intensity and determination of a general leading an attack.[7]

---

[7] Distinctive military terminology was used to describe Ezekiel's actions. The city was placed under siege and a siege wall, דָּיֵק, rampart, סֹלְלָה, and camps, מַחֲנוֹת, set against it (see M. Greenberg, *Ezekiel 1–20,* AB [Garden City: Doubleday, 1986], 103-4).

Ezekiel's actions demonstrated that he had some knowledge of Assyro-Babylonian battle tactics.[8] Seven aspects of this drama illustrate his understanding of military operations. First, he laid siege to the city. The Assyrians would lay siege by surrounding a city to cut off water and supplies until the people surrendered. Second, he built a siege wall to surround the city, preventing escape of the inhabitants. Third, he constructed an earthen rampart to enable the walls to be easily scaled. Fourth, he established military camps strategically around the city. Fifth, he used battering rams against the walls and gates. Sixth, he set up an iron wall to represent the iron will of God's judgment and the impenetrable barrier of Babylon's army, which was God's chastening rod. Finally, he set his face against it to suggest God's firm resolve. These actions provided a "sign" of coming destruction for Jerusalem and Judah. What the people refused to accept by word they witnessed in the symbolic actions of the prophet.

**4:4-8**   Some interpreters take these verses as beginning a new section of separate symbolic actions of the prophet. Since they relate the chronology of the siege described in vv. 1-3, they are more likely an extension and further clarification of the first symbolic act depicting the siege of Jerusalem. Ezekiel was instructed to lie on his left side for 390 days (vv. 4-5), then on his right side for forty days (v. 6) to suggest the length of the time of iniquity of Israel and Judah. God also told him to turn his face toward the siege with "bared arm," perhaps shaking his fist as a prophecy against the city (v. 7).

His left side would have been toward the north. Directions usually were calculated by facing east, which placed north to the left, south to the right, and west to rear. Israel after the division of the kingdom in 931 B.C. was the Northern Kingdom while Judah was the Southern Kingdom. The right and left sides symbolically pointed to Israel and Judah.

The interpretation of the 390 days and forty days has led to much speculation. None of the proposed interpretations are without some difficulties. First, some take the entire section, including the numbers, as symbolic of indefinite periods of time.[9] Some interpreters favor a literal interpretation of the "years" due to the statement in v. 5. Attempts to work out a literal timetable for placement of 390 years and forty years prior to the destruction of either Israel or Judah have never succeeded in producing a workable chronology.[10]

---

[8] S. Fisch, *Ezekiel* (London: Soncino, 1950), 19; Greenberg, *Ezekiel 1–20,* 103. Ezekiel's use of Akkadian and Syriac military terminology also indicates this.

[9] Eichrodt, *Ezekiel,* 84.

[10] Ellison (*Ezekiel,* 33) alludes to some of these problems and concludes that all elements of the literal vanishes; see also Greenberg, *Ezekiel 1–20,* 105-6.

Further compounding the problem is the substitution by the Septuagint (LXX, the Greek edition of the OT) of 190 days (years) for 390 and insertion of 150 days after v. 4. Several interpreters believe this better fits the chronology,[11] although the reasons for these changes by the compilers of the LXX are unknown.

Although no workable solution to the problem of a literal chronology of the day-years has come to light, a literal interpretation in principle is still preferable to a symbolic one.[12] The basic principles of hermeneutics dictate that a passage be taken literally whenever possible. That the days represent years is clearly defined in v. 6. Since the text is about the siege and destruction of Jerusalem, the logical starting point for the 390 plus forty years would be the siege of the city in which Ezekiel was deported, namely 597 B.C. Calculating the 430 years from 597 B.C. would take the judgment of Judah down to the Maccabean revolt in 167 B.C. Caution should be exercised in drawing dogmatic conclusions from this fact.

Several additional facts also are definite regarding the passage. First, each day of Ezekiel's drama represented a year in the life of sinful Israel or Judah (v. 6) and signified a time of discipline. Second, God was aware of sin in the lives of his people, and he was going to bring sin and sinner to a time of judgment. Third, the siege of would initiate the judgment that would proceed until the fall of Jerusalem and exile in Babylon. Fourth, the consequences of God's judgment are binding and inescapable (v. 8). God's judgment of sin is inevitable. He is longsuffering (4:1-8) and may wait for years, but ultimately he will dispense judgment. This judgment will include his people. Judah is a universal and timeless example of this principle (see 5:15).

### (6) Prophetic Dramatization of the Completeness of Destruction: The Unclean Meal (4:9-17)

**[9]"Take wheat and barley, beans and lentils, millet and spelt; put them in a storage jar and use them to make bread for yourself. You are to eat it during the 390 days you lie on your side. [10]Weigh out twenty shekels of food to eat each day and eat it at set times. [11]Also measure out a sixth of a hin of water and drink it at set times. [12]Eat the food as you would a barley cake; bake it in the sight of the people, using human excrement for fuel." [13]The LORD said, "In this way the people of Israel will eat defiled food among the nations where I will drive them."**

---

[11] Taylor (*Ezekiel*, 80-82) discusses the LXX dates as a possible solution preferred by Cooke (*Ezekiel*, 53) and C. G. Howie (*Ezekiel, Daniel* [London: SCM, 1961], 25-26).

[12] See, e.g., C. F. Keil, *Ezekiel*, vol. 1 (Grand Rapids: Eerdmans, 1970), 72-73, and Alexander, "Ezekiel," 769-70.

**¹⁴Then I said, "Not so, Sovereign LORD! I have never defiled myself. From my youth until now I have never eaten anything found dead or torn by wild animals. No unclean meat has ever entered my mouth."**

**¹⁵"Very well," he said, "I will let you bake your bread over cow manure instead of human excrement."**

**¹⁶He then said to me: "Son of man, I will cut off the supply of food in Jerusalem. The people will eat rationed food in anxiety and drink rationed water in despair, ¹⁷for food and water will be scarce. They will be appalled at the sight of each other and will waste away because of their sin.**

The drama of the unclean meal has three parts. First, the prophet is told to prepare the food to be cooked (vv. 9-11). Second, the prophet is to cook the meal but is granted a request that he not violate the laws of cleanliness (vv. 12-15). Third, there is an interpretation of the drama (vv. 16-17).

**4:9-11** The extreme severity of conditions during the siege was enacted by the prophet during the 390 days he lay on his side. He prepared a cake made of a mixture of six kinds of grain (v. 9). The combination of wheat, barley, beans, lentils, millet, and spelt is unusual but not prohibited by the Torah or by the Mishna.[13] The final product was a grade of flour inferior to pure wheat or barley flours. The mixture seems to portray a circumstance in which the people would mix anything edible due to the scarcity of the food.[14]

The amount of this inferior flour was specified as twenty shekel weight (v. 10). Shekels were coins, but they were weighed rather than counted[15] (see examples of weighing money in Isa 46:6; Jer 32:9-10; Zech 11:12). An average shekel weight was 11.4 grams. Ezekiel allotted himself about 230 grams of the inferior grade flour per day for food, the equivalent of about eight ounces.[16]

---

[13] Taylor, *Ezekiel,* 82; Zimmerli, *Ezekiel 1,* Her (Philadelphia: Fortress, 1979), 169. OT law did not prohibit mixing grains as stated in Lev 19:19. Such reference suggests meals were to be made up of available scraps of food.

[14] "Wheat" (חִטִּין) and "barley" (שְׂעֹרִים) were the most important and widely used grains in the ancient Near East. "Beans" (פּוֹל) and "lentils" (עֲדָשִׁים) also were staple products usually not mixed with grain or used for flour. These four items, wheat and barley, beans and lentils, often are listed in pairs. "Millet" (דֹּחַן) is mentioned only here in the OT but was used in Mesopotamia. "Spelt" (כֻּסְּמִים) sometimes was planted as a border to wheat or barley (see Zimmerli, *Ezekiel 1,* 168-69, for discussion).

[15] Weighing coins was necessary because of a widespread practice of shaving some silver from shekels to make more shekels. If a little silver was shaved off each of two hundred shekels, for example, one could create an extra ten or twenty shekels. Weighing shekels was an attempt to stop this practice and standardize currency.

[16] After comparing all the possibilities, Zimmerli (*Ezekiel 1,* 169) concluded that Ezekiel had at least 1.1 liters of food per day. Eichrodt (*Ezekiel,* 86) concludes the eight ounces of bread and one and three-quarter pints of water per day meant there would still be an agonizingly small amount of food.

He also rationed his daily intake of water just as it would be during an actual siege (v. 11). The water supply for Jerusalem, like many cities of the ancient Near East, was outside the city walls. This made cities vulnerable during long periods of siege so water usually was rationed. A sixth of a hin would be between one-half and one liter per day.[17]

The portion of food and water Ezekiel allowed himself was little more than starvation rations. The picture enacted by Ezekiel represented conditions during an actual siege. These actions reinforced the message of the previous dramas, the siege of the clay brick and the laying on his side to portray the destruction of Jerusalem.

Ezekiel performed these dramatic acts at set times each day (v. 10). Although he did not specify the exact time he put on his public display, he likely chose a time when he would have been insured an audience in the street or marketplace.

**4:12-15** The manner in which this mixed grain and barley cake meal was prepared portrayed the austere conditions prevalent during the siege. Ezekiel was to bake his cake on a fire made with dried human dung. While the use of dried animal dung as fuel may seem unusual or even repulsive to Westerners, it was a common practice in the ancient Near East that continues to this day.[18] Animal waste was mixed with straw, sundried, then burned for fuel. Trees were scarce; thus such a practice was necessary. Wood was a commodity too precious to use as a fuel. The use of animal manure as a fuel did not violate the strict dietary laws of Israel. Human waste, however, was considered a defilement (Deut 23:9-14), and its use in such a manner was strictly prohibited. Having grown up in a priestly family and probably in training as a priest himself, Ezekiel was especially sensitive to this command to prepare a meal in such an unclean manner.[19]

Meager rations prepared in an unclean manner presented a double lesson concerning the crisis conditions during the siege of Jerusalem. God had provided manna in the days of wilderness wandering that he might teach them to trust him. They had to learn that "man does not live on bread alone but on every word that comes from the mouth of the LORD" (Deut 8:3). But the reverse also was true. Neglect of the word produced a famine (see Amos 8:11; Hos 4:6) both of food and of the knowledge of God and spiritual truths. Second, the reaction of the prophet came not because of his view of the defilement of sin but because of his training as a

---

[17] Taylor, *Ezekiel,* 82.

[18] Fisch, *Ezekiel,* 22-23; Stalker, *Ezekiel,* 67. The hot ashes were perfectly clean, and bread was cooked directly on them.

[19] Alexander, "Ezekiel," 770. Since eating unclean food was prohibited by Mosaic law (Lev 22:8; Deut 12:15-19; 14:21; Ezek 44:31), he requested and was granted an alternative.

priest. This was God's way of reminding Ezekiel and Israel that they were more sensitive to regulations than to the violation of their relationship with God.[20] God graciously allowed Ezekiel to prepare his food in a ceremonially clean manner (v. 15) upon the prophet's request.

**4:16-17** Interpretation of this sign was not left to speculation. God specifically told Ezekiel that the meaning of his actions related to the severity of judgment. The rationing represented the interruption of the food and water supply to Jerusalem. Anxiety and despair were the natural reactions of those who lived in a city under siege. Their reaction to the sight of each other as they suffered starvation would be appalling (v. 17). The lessons were clear. Jerusalem was headed for judgment, and it would bring horrible conditions. The people would be filled with fear and despair when the siege began, and they would slowly waste away through starvation. Drastically reduced rations would take its toll on the population. Finally, all the judgments were to be understood as a direct result of the sins of the people.[21] The interpretation of this text is not open to speculation. Sin pollutes the external environment and the lives of those who choose it. When God sends judgment, it affects the land as well as the people (4:9-17; 6:1ff.).

### (7) Prophetic Dramatization of the Severe Limits of Destruction: The Shaved Head and Beard (5:1-17)

¹"Now, son of man, take a sharp sword and use it as a barber's razor to shave your head and your beard. Then take a set of scales and divide up the hair. ²When the days of your siege come to an end, burn a third of the hair with fire inside the city. Take a third and strike it with the sword all around the city. And scatter a third to the wind. For I will pursue them with drawn sword. ³But take a few strands of hair and tuck them away in the folds of your garment. ⁴Again, take a few of these and throw them into the fire and burn them up. A fire will spread from there to the whole house of Israel.

⁵"This is what the Sovereign LORD says: This is Jerusalem, which I have set in the center of the nations, with countries all around her. ⁶Yet in her wickedness she has rebelled against my laws and decrees more than the nations and countries around her. She has rejected my laws and has not followed my decrees.

⁷"Therefore this is what the Sovereign LORD says: You have been more unruly than the nations around you and have not followed my decrees or kept

---

[20] Craigie, *Ezekiel,* 34-35. The diet and manner of preparation symbolized judgment even though God was showing his love to the people. His concession on the manner of preparation indicates God's kindness regarding the emotional needs of the messenger.

[21] Enns, *Ezekiel* (Grand Rapids: Zondervan, 1986), 49-50.

my laws. You have not even conformed to the standards of the nations around you.

[8]"Therefore this is what the Sovereign LORD says: I myself am against you, Jerusalem, and I will inflict punishment on you in the sight of the nations. [9]Because of all your detestable idols, I will do to you what I have never done before and will never do again. [10]Therefore in your midst fathers will eat their children, and children will eat their fathers. I will inflict punishment on you and will scatter all your survivors to the winds. [11]Therefore as surely as I live, declares the Sovereign LORD, because you have defiled my sanctuary with all your vile images and detestable practices, I myself will withdraw my favor; I will not look on you with pity or spare you. [12]A third of your people will die of the plague or perish by famine inside you; a third will fall by the sword outside your walls; and a third I will scatter to the winds and pursue with drawn sword.

[13]"Then my anger will cease and my wrath against them will subside, and I will be avenged. And when I have spent my wrath upon them, they will know that I the LORD have spoken in my zeal.

[14]"I will make you a ruin and a reproach among the nations around you, in the sight of all who pass by. [15]You will be a reproach and a taunt, a warning and an object of horror to the nations around you when I inflict punishment on you in anger and in wrath and with stinging rebuke. I the LORD have spoken. [16]When I shoot at you with my deadly and destructive arrows of famine, I will shoot to destroy you. I will bring more and more famine upon you and cut off your supply of food. [17]I will send famine and wild beasts against you, and they will leave you childless. Plague and bloodshed will sweep through you, and I will bring the sword against you. I the LORD have spoken."

There are two main parts to this drama. First, Ezekiel was commanded to shave his head and beard and given instructions about how to dispose of the hair (vv. 1-4). Second is an interpretation of the drama (vv. 5-17). This includes an application explaining the significance for Jerusalem and an explanation of the divine motive for the drama (vv. 13-17).

**5:1-4** This verse opens with an emphatic declaration to mark the next stage in the unfolding drama of the prophet's demonstrations of divine judgment.[22] Ezekiel was commanded to take a sword and use it for a barber's razor to shave both his head and beard.[23] Just as a razor cuts away hair from the face and head, so the invading armies would cut away the

---

[22] The sentence initial וְאַתָּה introduces the next development in the story: "Now you, son of man, you take for yourself a sword."

[23] W. H. Brownlee (*Ezekiel 1–19,* WBC [Waco: Word, 1986], 82) seems confused about whether Ezekiel used a sword, חֶרֶב, or a barber's razor, תַּעַר. The sword was an implement of warfare, which is just the point. He was to use the חֶרֶב as a barber's razor to convey a specific message of judgment.

population from the land.[24] Shaving the head was a serious matter for a priest (Lev 19:27; 21:5) or a Nazirite (Num 6:5) because hair was the sign of their consecration to God. For this reason the loss of Samson's hair (Judg 16:17) was a tragic sin. Shaving the head normally was regarded as a sign of humiliation (2 Sam 10:4-5) or mourning (Isa 15:2; Jer 41:5-6; 48:37; Ezek 9:3). It also was practiced in pagan rituals for the dead.[25]

Some interpreters question whether the whole sequence of dramatic demonstrations was part of the prophet's visionary experience and therefore seen only by Ezekiel or whether they were a public demonstration and therefore external. The symbolic actions take on greater significance if they were a public demonstration. Further, Ezekiel was told explicitly to remain silent (4:26-27) and to enact these dramatic demonstrations of destruction "inside the city" and "all around the city" (v. 2).[26] This particular symbolic act was a fulfillment of Moses' prophetic warning in Lev 26:33-40. Moses predicted five stages of discipline, the last of which was destruction and exile.[27]

This dramatic demonstration unfolded in three stages. First, the prophet cut his beard and his hair using a sword as a barber's razor (v. 1). As the sword removed the hair from his head, so the sword of the invaders would soon remove the Hebrews from their land. Second, the hair was weighed and separated into three equal parts. Weighing was a symbol of evaluation and impending judgment (Dan 5:27; Prov 21:2).[28] Third, Ezekiel disposed of the hair in three ways (v. 2). One-third was burned to symbolize those soon to perish in the destruction of the city. One-third was hacked with the sword to represent civilians soon to perish in battle. One-third was scattered in the wind to represent soldiers who would be dispersed among the nations.[29]

One final significant act was the placement of a few remaining hairs in the folds of his garment. This represented the remnant who were the hope of the future (vv. 3-4). This theme of a remnant was similar to that of

---

[24] Fisch (*Ezekiel*, 24) notes that the same imagery was used in Isa 7:20 as emblematic of the invasion of Babylon.

[25] See Feinberg, *Ezekiel*, 36; J. W. Wevers, *Ezekiel*, NCB (Grand Rapids: Eerdmans, 1969), 63; Alexander, "Ezekiel," 771; and Greenberg, *Ezekiel 1–20*, 126, for a discussion of its meaning.

[26] Craigie, *Ezekiel*, 36; see also Keil, *Ezekiel*, 86-87.

[27] While the similarities are striking between Lev 26 and Ezek 5:1-4, there are differences. Greenberg (*Ezekiel 1–20*, 109) concludes that there is no verbal link between the two passages but that the similarity lies in the common theme of deserved judgment.

[28] According to Brownlee (*Ezekiel 1–19*, 83), human destiny was thought to be weighed out each New Year's Day. Ezekiel believed that impending judgment was fixed.

[29] Taylor, *Ezekiel*, 84-85.

Amos when he saw the remnant of Israel like the remains of a sheep in the mouth of a lion (Amos 5:12). The theme of a remnant appears in other Old Testament prophets as well (Isa 6:13; 10:22; Jer 23:3; Zech 13:8-9) and after the exile became the dominant theme in prophecy.[30] The few hairs that were preserved, like the scarlet cord in Rahab's window (Josh 2:18,21; 6:22-25), were a sign of deliverance. They were like the fringes on the priests' garments (Num 15:37-39) that were to preserve the nation through a call to be obedient to the commands of God.[31]

**5:5-6** The phrase "this is Jerusalem" (v. 5) may be applied all the way back to 4:1, where the map of Jerusalem was drawn on the brick. We have known since the first symbolic action of 4:1-8 that the symbols pointed to the destruction of Jerusalem. But those who witnessed Ezekiel's unusual performances probably lived in the hope that the prophet was depicting the fall of Babylon, which they felt was so imminent. In order that there be no mistake he was predicting the fall of Jerusalem, he stated bluntly, "This is Jerusalem." Whether this was given immediately after the drama or sometime later we do not know.[32]

Jerusalem was set "in the center of the nations" (v. 5).[33] Some would argue that this was a reference to an archaic persuasion that Jerusalem was the geographical center of the earth. For those in Ezekiel's day this impression was true to some extent. Jerusalem lay in the center of various world empires that rose and fell in the northern Mediterranean, Asia, Asia Minor, Mesopotamia, and North Africa. The land of Israel often was the battleground of those warring groups. Also because of its geographic location it was a trade and travel center. Today it is a center for three of the world's great religions: Judaism, Christianity, and Islam. Israel and Jerusalem have been an amazing focal point theologically and politically for the last four thousand years.[34] From 38:12 some believe that Ezekiel was

---

[30] Feinberg, *Ezekiel,* 36-37.

[31] Brownlee (*Ezekiel 1–19,* 82-83) believes the reference to Rahab also may have been chosen as a reminder of the massacre of the guilty at Jericho as an act of divine judgment.

[32] Craigie, *Ezekiel,* 39; Taylor, *Ezekiel,* 86.

[33] The phrase "in the center" (בְּתוֹךְ, usually "in the midst") was a favorite one of Ezekiel (used 116 times). This seems unusual since only seven other prophets use the word: Isaiah (twelve times), Jeremiah (twenty-three times), Amos (twice), Micah (three times), Zephaniah (once), Haggai (once), Zechariah (eight times). This shows the perspective of Ezekiel, who was one of two prophets who were "in the midst" of the captives, Daniel being the other. Ezekiel had that unique perspective, from the "midst" of captivity (Ezek 3:15).

[34] Enns, *Ezekiel,* 50-51; Eichrodt, *Ezekiel,* 88; Keil, *Prophecies of Ezekiel,* 88. Whereas in other countries the idea of centrality in the world was one of self-realized national importance, as in Babylon, Greece, Rome, and China, Ezekiel saw Jerusalem's centrality because of its place in God's redemption for all people.

referring to Jerusalem's central place in world affairs, calling it the "navel of the earth."[35]

There is another aspect to the position of Jerusalem and Israel seen by Ezekiel. The phrase "in the center of the nations" (v. 5) is one that has overtones of God's elect purpose for Israel. Israel and especially Jerusalem was that "place which the LORD shall choose out of all your tribes to put his name there" (Deut 12:5; cf. Ps 48:1-14).[36] From the time they were constituted as a theocracy (Exod 19:1-8), there was a clear delineation of God's elect purpose for the nation (Exod 19:5-6) as the channel of his redemption. In this sense also Israel was set in the "midst" of the nations as a kingdom of priests, and thus they were supposed to be instruments of God's missionary purpose.[37] But the nation dwelt on the privilege of being God's chosen people rather than on their responsibilities. The nationalistic spirit created an isolationism that can be seen in the example of Jonah.[38] Eventually the New Testament church was endowed with the missionary assignment originally planned for Israel (Exod 19:1-8; Matt 28:18-20; 1 Pet 2:9-10). Instead of fulfilling this missionary purpose, the Israelites exceeded the wickedness of the idolatrous nations around them (v. 6). In a time when they should have been God's instrument to proclaim redemption, they were an example of rebellion against laws and ordinances.[39]

**5:7-12** The "shearing" of Jerusalem was described in graphic terms. The introductory word "therefore" (*lākēn*) that begins v. 7 was used four times in this section (vv. 7,8,10,11). In vv. 7-8 it introduces the phrase "this is what the Sovereign LORD says." A better translation of *lākēn* would be "assuredly," since it introduces a divine response to an evil or unwarranted situation.[40] Israel had been "more unruly" than the foreign

---

[35] Fisch, *Ezekiel*, 255. The phrase "navel of the earth" is also found in Judg 9:37.

[36] Zimmerli, *Ezekiel 1*, 175; Wevers, *Ezekiel*, 65.

[37] Craigie (*Ezekiel*), in his discussion of vv. 13-17, notes that the missionary purpose of God for Israel was expressed in the covenant with Abraham in Gen 12:1-3 and the Sinai covenant in Exod 19:1-8.

[38] T. D. Alexander, D. W. Baker, and B. K. Waltke, *Obadiah, Jonah, Micah*, TOTC (Downers Grove: InterVarsity, 1988), 85-88.

[39] Both terms מִשְׁפָּט and חֹק are used as synonyms to describe the seriousness of Israel's repeated rebellion (מָאָס). Generally מִשְׁפָּט refers to civil and criminal law while חֹק refers to ceremonial and moral law. The expression refers to both casuistic and apodictic law. See A. Alt, "The Origins of Israelite Law," in *Essays in Old Testament History and Religion* (Garden City: Doubleday, 1968), 101-71. See also Alexander, "Ezekiel," 773, and Greenberg, *Ezekiel 1–20*, 111.

[40] For further study on the introductory formula see Zimmerli, *Ezekiel 1*, 38; Greenberg, *Ezekiel 1–20*, 111; Alexander, "Ezekiel," 773; and "Laken: Its Functions and Meanings," in *Rhetorical Criticism: Essays in Honor of J. Muilenberg* (Pittsburgh: Pickwick, 1974), 256-86.

nations, a term found only here.[41] The necessity of this judgment was all the more reprehensible considering the Hebrews had the laws and ordinances of God and therefore knew better.

After the introductory formula v. 8 contains an emphatic statement of God's response to their excessive wickedness:[42] "I myself am against you." God also declared that indeed it would be carried out "in the sight of the nations" (v. 8). Since the people of God refused to be an example of righteousness and godliness, they would be an example of chastening. Because of their abominations and idolatry, God pledged to do what he had not done before nor would ever do again (v. 9). He promised the severest forms of judgment.[43] Abominations that are unprecedented call for extraordinary judgment.

Ezekiel further dramatized the severity of the prescribed judgment by the declaration of v. 10. Cannibalism raises an image of the horrible specter of war when cities were under siege. One military tactic used was to surround the city and cut off all supplies, food, and water. The siege army then had but to wait for surrender or starvation. Such a scene was described in association with Ben Hadad's siege of Samaria in 2 Kgs 6:24-33. This judgment was a fulfillment of Moses' prophetic warnings in Lev 26:29 and Deut 28:53 that the slow drift into idolatry would at the last produce unthinkable consequences.

Using another oath formula, "as surely as I live," God swore by his own life that he would judge Israel (v. 11).[44] Not only was Israel guilty of idolatry and its accompanying detestable practices, but they had brought this abominable worship into the temple of God in Jerusalem. This is the first reference in Ezekiel to the problem of the defilement of the temple, discussed more completely in 8:1-18. Their unparalleled sin was the basis for unprecedented judgment. One-third were to be destroyed by plague

---

[41] The word הֲמֻנְכֶם is a hapax legomenon, so its meaning is somewhat obscure. It has been associated with the noun הָמוֹן, "to make noise" or "to rage." The meaning would be "you are more turbulent than the nations" or "you are a worse crowd than the nations." The point of the argument is that they have emulated and exceeded all the vices of the heathen nations but none of their virtues. See Fisch, *Ezekiel*, 26.

[42] The use of גַּם־אָנִי makes this an emphatic statement, frequently used in threats (see Greenberg, *Ezekiel 1–20*, 113; Fisch, *Ezekiel*, 26).

[43] The use of תּוֹעֵבָה, "detestable idols," employs language used in polemics against idolatry especially in Deuteronomy (cf. Deut 7:25-26; 12:31; 13:14; 14:3; 17:1,4; 18:9,12; 20:18; 22:5; 23:18; 24:4; 25:16; 27:15; 32:16). The use of the term in Deuteronomy in interpersonal relations clearly suggests also that these practices were associated with idolatry (e.g., 22:5; 23:18; 24:4; 25:16). See also Greenberg, *Ezekiel 1–20*, 113.

[44] Hals (*Ezekiel*, FOTL (Grand Rapids: Eerdmans, 1989), 32) notes that this formula is a modified form of the oath as given in Judg 8:19 and was used to identify Yahweh as the speaker.

and famine, one-third by the sword, and one-third scattered in every direction at the destruction of the nation (v. 12).[45] These words of judgment are awesome when related to the declaration of v. 5, "This is Jerusalem," and v. 11, "I will not look on you with pity or spare you." The greatness of God's love for his people demands a firm and severe response whenever that love is ignored or violated.[46]

**5:13-17**   The closing verses of chap. 5 present one of the major themes of the book: the nature and character of God. Whether God acted in judgment or deliverance, his motive was redemptive and salvific.[47] Ezekiel used four expressions in v. 13 to suggest the fury of God that diminished with the exercise of his judgment. Ezekiel said his anger would "cease," his wrath would "subside," he would be "avenged," and his wrath would be "spent." Therefore God was zealous to judge the people and vindicate his holiness and righteousness. His zeal works two ways to promote redemption. It moves him to punish sin so people will know he is not indifferent to unrighteousness, and it moves him to redeem and restore a remnant lest the unbelieving nations should question his faithfulness.[48]

Verse 13 contains the first use of the recognition formula "I the LORD" often joined with "you should know," employed seventy-two times by Ezekiel.[49] God's actions were done that all may "know" him and his motives, his true character. Such knowledge always was associated with either his judgment or his grace. The reaction of the nations was a commentary on Israel's failure to fulfill their role as a covenant people.[50]

---

[45] Plague, famine, and sword (i.e., disease, starvation, and war) are familiar from the curses associated with the Mosaic covenant (Lev 26:14-39; Deut 28:15-68; cf. 2 Sam 24:13; Jer 27:13; 29:17). This triad of divine punishment, sometimes supplemented by wild beasts, also occurs in Ezekiel outside these chapters (12:16; 14:21; 28:23; 33:27; 38:22). D. Block has argued that the phrase לְכָל־רוּחַ (NIV "to the winds") in vv. 10,12 should be translated "in every direction" ("The Prophet of the Spirit: The Use of *rwḥ* in the Book of Ezekiel," *JETS* 32 [1989]: 32-33). He confirms this by noting the use of מֵאַרְבַּע רוּחוֹת ("from the four winds") in 37:9; see especially Jer 49:36.

[46] See Craigie, *Ezekiel,* 40-41, for an excellent discussion of the theological perspectives that emerge from this message of judgment against Jerusalem.

[47] Howie, *Ezekiel, Daniel,* 26-27.

[48] Cooke (*Ezekiel,* 61) identifies these two opposite actions as ones that reveal God's zeal to accomplish the redemption of the non-Hebrew nations.

[49] Hals, *Ezekiel,* 32; Zimmerli, *Ezekiel 1,* 37-39; and Ellison, *Ezekiel,* 37. Hals sees this as an important and characteristic part of the book. It reveals that knowledge of God was one of the primary goals of Ezekiel. God acts in history so people will "know" he is Yahweh. This is a legal declaration rendering proof of who God is. Zimmerli notes that the formula always is used in association with actions Yahweh has done.

[50] Craigie (*Ezekiel,* 42-43) notes the true tragedy of Ezekiel's day was not the fall of Jerusalem but rather Israel's failure to fulfill its missionary purpose.

Instead of being a witness—proclaiming God's love, holiness, righteousness, and desire to save all nations—they would be a "ruin" (v. 14), "reproach" (vv. 14-15), "taunt" (v. 15), "warning," and "an object of horror."[51]

Ezekiel emphasized the severity of judgment in order to show how God's purpose for salvation of the nation had been frustrated by Israel's rebellion. God's plan for the salvation of the nations was his motive for the election of Israel. This responsible role of the elect was a dominant theme in the preaching of the prophets. Jesus expressed the same idea in Luke 12:48, "From everyone who has been given much, much will be demanded." Election is also a prominent idea in the New Testament as Jesus was rejected by the Jewish establishment, and the church became the elect of God (see, e.g., Matt 21:33-46; Rom 9:1-33; 1 Pet 2:4-10).[52]

As a priest, Ezekiel would have been familiar with the warnings of Lev 26; Deut 28; 32. Sitting on the brink of the fulfillment of judgment described in those passages, he was able to warn Israel for the last time. A comparison of Ezek 5:16-17 with Lev 26:31-32 and Deut 32:23-24 suggests that the prophet understood the true nature and purpose of impending judgment.[53] Perhaps for this reason Ezekiel thought judgment was inevitable, unlike Jeremiah, who seemed to hope that judgment could somehow be averted if the people repented.[54] Judgment is often severe and unrelenting (5:1-17). Though God has a redemptive purpose for judgment in this life, retribution still brings destruction and death (Rom 6:23).

## (8) Prophetic Dramatization of the End of False Worship: Message to the Mountains (6:1-14)

**¹The word of the LORD came to me: ²"Son of man, set your face against the mountains of Israel; prophesy against them ³and say: 'O mountains of Israel, hear the word of the Sovereign LORD. This is what the Sovereign LORD**

---

[51] Greenberg, *Ezekiel 1–20,* 115-16. These words look back to Lev 26:31 and are also common to Jeremiah (see Jer 24:9; 29:18; cf. also Joel 2:19).

[52] Eichrodt, *Ezekiel,* 91.

[53] Greenberg (*Ezekiel 1–20,* 116-17) gives particular emphasis to the elements of the siege described by Ezekiel and their relation to "bearing iniquity" (4:6). He especially is concerned with the question of why these elements from the exile are placed here. His conclusion is that Lev 26:14-33 formed the model for Ezek 4–5 (p. 124), thus the exile symbols of forty days, eating unclean food, and shaving the head were reminders of the hardship of the exile in Egypt and the wilderness. When related to the prophetic warning of Moses in Lev 26:14-33, they form a powerful link to underscore God's elect purpose for Israel that included discipline (pp. 117-28); see also Cooke, *Ezekiel,* 63.

[54] J. G. McConville, "Jeremiah: Prophet and Book," *TynBul* 42.1 (1991): 80-95.

says to the mountains and hills, to the ravines and valleys: I am about to bring a sword against you, and I will destroy your high places. [4]Your altars will be demolished and your incense altars will be smashed; and I will slay your people in front of your idols. [5]I will lay the dead bodies of the Israelites in front of their idols, and I will scatter your bones around your altars. [6]Wherever you live, the towns will be laid waste and the high places demolished, so that your altars will be laid waste and devastated, your idols smashed and ruined, your incense altars broken down, and what you have made wiped out. [7]Your people will fall slain among you, and you will know that I am the LORD.

[8]"'But I will spare some, for some of you will escape the sword when you are scattered among the lands and nations. [9]Then in the nations where they have been carried captive, those who escape will remember me—how I have been grieved by their adulterous hearts, which have turned away from me, and by their eyes, which have lusted after their idols. They will loathe themselves for the evil they have done and for all their detestable practices. [10]And they will know that I am the LORD; I did not threaten in vain to bring this calamity on them.

[11]"'This is what the Sovereign LORD says: Strike your hands together and stamp your feet and cry out "Alas!" because of all the wicked and detestable practices of the house of Israel, for they will fall by the sword, famine and plague. [12]He that is far away will die of the plague, and he that is near will fall by the sword, and he that survives and is spared will die of famine. So will I spend my wrath upon them. [13]And they will know that I am the LORD, when their people lie slain among their idols around their altars, on every high hill and on all the mountaintops, under every spreading tree and every leafy oak—places where they offered fragrant incense to all their idols. [14]And I will stretch out my hand against them and make the land a desolate waste from the desert to Diblah—wherever they live. Then they will know that I am the LORD.'"

The message of Ezek 6 is transitional. It moves from the purely dramatic forms of the messages in Ezek 4 and 5, combines dramatic and vocal elements, and anticipates the visions and messages that follow. This message also contains a thematic transition from the sins of the nation in general (chaps. 4–5) to the mountains and high places and "detestable practices" (6:11), which were associated with pagan worship. Thus the focus of chap. 6 is on the individual responsibility of the people and prepares the way for the subsequent spoken messages.

This drama has four divisions. First, the prophet is commanded to preach to the mountains of Israel (vv. 1-2). Second is a warning of approaching destruction of places of idolatry (vv. 3-7). Third, there is a brief interlude of hope—a repentant remnant will be preserved in exile (vv. 8-

10). Fourth is a mocking lament of the devastation Israel's idolatry will have caused (vv. 11-14).

**6:1-2** Although this was a spoken message, it also was accompanied by the symbolic action of setting his face against the mountains of Israel.[55] After his first oracle of judgment addressed to Jerusalem (5:5-17), Ezekiel was directed to announce judgment on the "mountains of Israel," a phrase occurring sixteen times in Ezekiel and nowhere else (the singular occurs in Josh 11:16). He was instructed to prophesy against the mountains as though they were a ready audience to hear God's message (v. 2). On the one hand they represented figuratively the whole land of Israel, especially Jerusalem (33:28; 34:13-14; 35:12; 37:22; 38:8; 39:2,4,17; cf. 17:22-23; 20:40).[56] As the mountains received this message of condemnation here, they would receive a message of blessing later (36:1-15, especially v. 4) that would apply to all Israel.

On the other hand, the mountains were especially centers of idolatrous worship, representing Israel's apostasy and perversion of the good and holy things of God (cf. 6:13; 18:6,11; 22:9). Shrines dedicated to Canaanite deities were built in groves on the hills and mountains.[57] As Elijah (1 Kgs 18:1-40), Hosea (4:12-13), and Amos (7:9) affirmed,[58] the Hebrews tried to produce an amalgamation of elements of Canaanite worship and Yahweh worship.[59]

**6:3-7** The words of 6:3 were used in the later message of 36:4 to describe the devastation of Israel's pagan shrines. These high places, called *bāmôt* in Hebrew, characteristically consisted of several basic elements.[60]

---

[55] Hals, *Ezekiel,* 39-40. Setting one's face against another was a symbolic gesture of judgment (see 13:17; 21:2[Eng., 20:46],7[Eng., 21:2]; 25:2; 28:21; 29:2; 35:2; 38:2).

[56] Alexander, "Ezekiel," 775. Note the "ravines and valleys" were included (v. 3). L. Boadt ("Rhetorical Strategies," 190-93) argues that Ezekiel's characteristic avoidance of the name "Jerusalem" is due to his rejection of Israel's false theology that had confused city, ruler, temple, and divine presence, making the city inviolable (cf. Jer 7:1-15; 9:11; 13:9; 26:1-9).

[57] Taylor, *Ezekiel,* 89-90. Worship in the high places was considered innocuous prior to the establishment of the temple in Jerusalem. After the temple was built, formal worship elsewhere was prohibited.

[58] Stalker, *Ezekiel,* 77. Stalker sees this tradition condemning worship in high places as extending back to the ministry of Amos and Hosea. The actions of Elijah on Mount Carmel, even though earlier, lie in this prophetic tradition as well (see Introduction, "Canaanite Religion").

[59] See the discussion of the nature and temptation of idolatry in D. Stuart, *Ezekiel,* CC (Dallas: Word, 1989), 69-72.

[60] A בָּמָה was a projection of rock or a mountain ridge, but the word became associated with worship centers built on these promontories by the time of Ezekiel (see Zimmerli, *Ezekiel 1,* 136; Greenberg, *Ezekiel 1–20,* 131-32).

First, there was an altar for offering sacrifices. These usually were built of stone or mud brick. Second, there was a wooden pole to represent the female goddess of fertility called Asherah. Third, there was at least one stone pillar called a *maṣṣebâ* to represent the male deity Baal. Fourth, there was a smaller incense altar with a tent for use in eating sacrificial meals, practicing sacred prostitution (1 Kgs 14:24; 2 Kgs 21:3; Isa 57:3-12), and storage of cultic vessels.

Ezekiel forecasted the systematic destruction of these worship centers, which attempted to combine Yahweh worship with pagan practices. What they had made was to be "wiped out" (v. 6). This was significant because Ezekiel was not describing judgment of the heathen but judgment of God's own people. He rejected their pagan altars as idolatrous and unclean (cf. chap. 8). As a result they would know by experiencing judgment that he, Yahweh, is God and that he does not accept adulterated worship (v. 7).

This was a clear indication that the reform measures Josiah initiated in 621 B.C. had failed. After Josiah's death the people reverted to their former practice of worshiping idols. Ezekiel used his favorite word (thirty-nine times; nine times elsewhere) for idols, *gillûlîm* (v. 4), which may have been created to sound like *šiqqûṣîm*, "detestable things" (cf. Hos 9:10; Deut 29:17[Heb. 16]. It also has been associated with *gēl/gālāl* ("dung"; cf. Ezek 4:12,15).[61] This term indicates the derision in which he held idol worship.

Judgment was described in graphic terms depicting the destruction of the sacrificial altars, incense altars, and idols (vv. 4,6). Whereas these worship centers usually had animal bones scattered about, Ezekiel said, "Your bones" (v. 5) will be scattered around these pagan altars. Through the passage the emphasis shifted from the mountains, to the worship centers, and then to the people who were directly responsible. The message of judgment reaffirmed the sovereignty of God by his rejection of pagan worship.[62]

**6:8-10** A word of encouragement and hope followed the hopelessness and despair presented in vv. 3-7. Some people would be spared although they will be scattered among the nations (v. 8). This message, which came before the siege of 587 B.C., revealed that the final destruc-

---

[61] *TDOT* 3:1-5; Greenberg, *Ezekiel 1-20,* 132. On the failure of Josiah's reforms see Hals, *Ezekiel,* 40; and K. W. Carley, *The Book of the Prophet Ezekiel,* CBC (Cambridge: Cambridge University Press, 1974), 41.

[62] Cooke, *Ezekiel,* 69; Fisch, *Ezekiel,* 31. The formula "you shall know that I am the LORD" asserts the sovereignty of God in judgment of idolatry.

tion would leave a small remnant that would be the hope for the future.[63]

When the scattered remnant were among the nations, they would remember God in anticipation of their repentance (v. 9). Remembrance as used here was more than mental recall of the facts but also included the idea of a new openness to God.[64] Idolatry is spoken of elsewhere in the prophets (e.g., Hosea) as spiritual harlotry but was further developed in Ezekiel.[65] The prophet saw a future time when a repentant Israel would "know him" again, turn from idolatry, and return to Yahweh (v. 10). This idea is developed again in Ezek 16:59-63; 23:1-49; and 36:1-38.

**6:11-14** The three forms of judgment mentioned—the sword, famine, and plague—are repeated from Ezek 5:1-3,12. The prophet was told to clap his hands, stomp his feet, and cry, "Alas" as signs of excitement and emotion used to decry the abominations and idolatrous practices of the Jewish people (v. 11).[66] While some have attributed these actions to malicious delight of the prophet at the prospect of severe judgment, the use of the term "alas" would suggest otherwise since it is a word of lamentation and judgment.[67]

The three forms of judgment are restated in v. 12 with the message that judgment will be all-inclusive and therefore inescapable. No identification has been made of Diblah, which appears in Scripture only in v. 14. This probably was a reference to Riblah, which is not mentioned elsewhere in the book but was a border city in the time of Ezekiel. Zedekiah was captured by Nebuchadnezzar at Riblah, and there his eyes were blinded (see 2 Kgs 25:5,7; Jer 39:6-7; 52:8-11,26-27).[68]

The closing formula, "Then they will know I am the LORD" (v. 14), specified the aim of the judgment described. This phrase was used throughout the message of Ezek 6 in vv. 7,10,13-14 and illustrated the longing of the prophet for all people to "know" the God of Israel as the one true God. The point, of course, was that people will know him either

---

[63] Hals, *Ezekiel*, 40. Hals believes the message to be "pre-587 B.C."

[64] Eichrodt, *Ezekiel*, 96. See also Zimmerli, *Ezekiel 1*, 189, where he notes that the use of זָכַר involves more than a sentimental return to what once was but is a "genuine grasping of a reality, which then becomes a new living and present fact."

[65] Wevers, *Ezekiel*, 69-70; Stalker, *Ezekiel*, 80.

[66] Fisch, *Ezekiel*, 32.

[67] אָהּ is an interjection used to introduce lamentations expressing grief or sorrow. It is used in Ezek 21:15 in a context of judgment, where it is translated, "Oh!"

[68] The close similarity between the letters ד and ר in Hebrew make this word a candidate for an easily recognizable copyist's error (see discussion of this phenomenon in Brownlee, *Ezekiel 1–19*, 110). Riblah was a town in Hamath (2 Kgs 23:33) and marked the boundary of Israel in Ezekiel's day (see Greenberg, *Ezekiel 1–20*, 137; Fisch, *Ezekiel*, 33; and Enns, *Ezekiel*, 55).

through response to his loving attempts of salvation and fellowship or through judgment. God's preference, as that of the prophets, was the former.[69]

### (9) Prophetic Dramas of Judgment in Summary (7:1-27)

Chapter 7 is not a drama in the same sense of those in chaps. 4–6, but it serves to summarize in a highly emotional manner the same message of judgment that is the theme of these preceding chapters. There are six parts to this summary message. First, God's determination to bring judgment is announced (7:1-4). Second is the repeated call for judgment to come (7:5-9). Third, the imminence and certainty of judgment is announced (7:10-13). Fourth, the total destruction of the nation is announced (7:14-18). Fifth, the uselessness of all physical resources is declared (7:19-22). Sixth, the fall of Jerusalem is announced (7:23-27).

**¹The word of the LORD came to me: ²"Son of man, this is what the Sovereign LORD says to the land of Israel: The end! The end has come upon the four corners of the land. ³The end is now upon you and I will unleash my anger against you. I will judge you according to your conduct and repay you for all your detestable practices. ⁴I will not look on you with pity or spare you; I will surely repay you for your conduct and the detestable practices among you. Then you will know that I am the LORD.**

JUDGMENT ANNOUNCED (7:1-4).    **7:1-4**    Ezekiel announced that the "end has come," reaffirming in emphatic language the imminent judgment of the Day of Yahweh (vv. 1-2,7-10,19). Ezekiel used an idea that was prominent in Amos 8:2, where he developed the "end" theme. Ezekiel also combined this concept with the Day of Yahweh (Amos 5:18).[70] Ezekiel said (literally), "An end has come, the end upon you." He spoke as though it already had happened. This device was a way of proclaiming the absolute certainty of a future event.[71]

---

[69] Taylor, *Ezekiel,* 92. God's desire that they "know" him is expressed four times in this chapter (vv. 7,10,13,14).

[70] The use of קֵץ here as in Amos 8:2 describes the end of God's forbearance and the beginning of judgment. It is more than a definition of time; it is a word that connotes final and irreversible judgment (see Zimmerli, *Ezekiel 1,* 204). For a recent discussion of the Day of Yahweh, see Y. Hoffman, "The Day of the Lord as a Concept and a Term in Prophetic Literature," *ZAW* 93 (1981): 37-45; D. Block (*Ezekiel,* NICOT [Grand Rapids: Eerdmans, forthcoming]) notes that Amos's language suggests that the concept already was familiar to his readers, though perhaps not as a time of judgment.

[71] The verb used, בָּא, is a perfect tense, expressing the prophet's certainty that what he predicted would come to pass (see Stalker, *Ezekiel,* 84).

The "end" that Ezekiel announced with such certainty was to come upon all the land, that is, the "four corners," suggesting no city would be spared (v. 3).[72] So the idea of the end of Jerusalem was expanded to encompass the end of Judah. God promised to punish the whole nation because of their abominations, an idea that looked back to Ezek 6:2-7. Guilt carried with it the idea of punishment deserved and repaid (vv. 4,8-9).[73]

Ezekiel did not see any signs of true repentance; therefore the "abominations" of the people would run their course until consumed by judgment (v. 3). Again the purpose of this judgment was to bring a new knowledge of God (v. 4). He never judges people capriciously or for the enjoyment of judging. Always God's goal was redemptive. God is a God of mercy, but he also is a God of justice. He acted against Judah in judgment to produce a repentant heart and open the way for more mercy and grace.

**⁵"This is what the Sovereign LORD says: Disaster! An unheard-of disaster is coming. ⁶The end has come! The end has come! It has roused itself against you. It has come! ⁷Doom has come upon you—you who dwell in the land. The time has come, the day is near; there is panic, not joy, upon the mountains. ⁸I am about to pour out my wrath on you and spend my anger against you; I will judge you according to your conduct and repay you for all your detestable practices. ⁹I will not look on you with pity or spare you; I will repay you in accordance with your conduct and the detestable practices among you. Then you will know that it is I the LORD who strikes the blow.**

CALLS FOR JUDGMENT (7:5-9). **7:5-9** Ezekiel's affirmation of inevitable judgment continued with a staccato style difficult to reproduce in translation. The passage is punctuated by the repeated use of the word *bāʾ*, "come" (nine times in vv. 5-12).[74] This "unheard of" disaster was literally an "evil which is one" (Heb.), meaning a singular or unprecedented judgment. This was doubtless a reference to the destruction of the temple, which the Jews thought to be inviolable.[75] The phrase from v. 2, "the end, the end has come," is echoed in v. 6 for emphasis. The evil or judgment is pictured as awakening like a predatory animal, ready to stalk its prey.

The term "disaster" (v. 5) sometimes is translated "evil." But it often is associated with judgment and does not necessarily carry the idea of moral

---

[72] Greenberg, *Ezekiel 1–20,* 147. In Isa 11:12 the same phrase refers to the whole earth (cf. Job 38:13).

[73] Cooke, *Ezekiel,* 77; Zimmerli, *Ezekiel 1,* 204.

[74] Taylor, *Ezekiel,* 93. In addition to the staccato style there also is a play on words in v. 6 between הַקֵּץ, "the end," and הֵקִיץ, "it awakens." It is reminiscent of Amos's judgment vision of the summer fruit in 8:1ff., where he used a similar play on words.

[75] Fisch (*Ezekiel,* 34) interprets this phrase to mean "most disastrous evil."

evil but rather of calamity, misfortune, and discomfort.[76] The "doom"
mentioned in v. 7 and again in v. 10 represents the translation of a word
whose meaning is uncertain. Ezekiel used this word in vv. 7,10, and it
also appears in Isa 28:5 ("crown"). The root probably carries the meaning
"to twist" and suggests something that has come full circle, such as plait-
ing a "crown."[77] This "doom" results in the loss of joy on the mountains.
At those high places where the fertility rites and harvest celebrations of
joy took place, there would be cries of anguish and pain.[78]

Verses 8-9 repeat the ideas expressed in vv. 3-4. The fruit of judgment
had ripened. The fact that this idea was repeated several times with no response from the people bears testimony to the deadening power of sin. It
is amazing how easily messages of judgment are forgotten. These messages constantly must be reinforced.[79] God stressed the redemptive purpose of judgment at the close this section with the words "then you will
know it is I the LORD" (v. 9). Judgment often brings renewed interest in
spiritual things. The tragedy is that this usually happens after judgment
has befallen a nation or an individual. Tragedy usually rekindles an interest in God.

**[10]"The day is here! It has come! Doom has burst forth, the rod has bud-
ded, arrogance has blossomed! [11]Violence has grown into a rod to punish**

---

[76] The use of רָעָה is often associated with God's activity of judgment. The word does
not necessarily carry the idea of moral evils but when referring to judgment stresses the calamity, confusion, and unwelcome circumstances associated with judgment. The play on
words associated with this "evil" is between the use of קֵץ and קִיץ. It is the same found in
the vision of the basket of summer fruit found in Amos 8:2. See note on v. 6 above for discussion of the play on words there, and see also Taylor, *Ezekiel,* 93; Fisch, *Ezekiel,* 34;
Greenberg, *Ezekiel 1–20,* 148.

[77] צְפִירָה is an obscure term that may mean "a circle," "a crown," or "twist" as in plait-
ing. It may be used in a figurative way to describe the dawn of a new day, i.e., judgment.
The translation "doom" is a guess based on its use in the context of this passage. It may be
equivalent to our modern phrase "what goes around, comes around," or "a new twist,"
which was judgment from God (see Fisch, *Ezekiel,* 34-35; Greenberg, *Ezekiel 1–20,* 148;
Wevers, *Ezekiel,* 73; Keil, *Ezekiel,* 101). The forthcoming commentary by D. Block (*Ezekiel*) suggests that it refers to a rope around the neck.

[78] Brownlee, *Ezekiel 1–19,* 109. He further notes that "doom" was not the primary
meaning of צְפִירָה but one that by connotation Ezekiel used in such a way as an "innova-
tive allusion" to the fact that Israel had come full circle. The landless people who celebrated
the conquest of Gilgal and Jericho were to be landless once more.

[79] On the recurrence in vv. 5-9 of words and themes from vv. 2-4, see the forthcoming
commentary by Block (*Ezekiel,* NICOT). He includes an excellent discussion of the many
textual problems in the chapter, explaining that, like chap. 1, they are the result of Ezekiel's
agitated state of mind.

wickedness; none of the people will be left, none of that crowd—no wealth, nothing of value. [12]The time has come, the day has arrived. Let not the buyer rejoice nor the seller grieve, for wrath is upon the whole crowd. [13]The seller will not recover the land he has sold as long as both of them live, for the vision concerning the whole crowd will not be reversed. Because of their sins, not one of them will preserve his life.

CERTAINTY OF JUDGMENT (7:10-13). **7:10-13** After announcing the end had come in vv. 1-4 and stressing the unprecedented nature of this judgment, Ezekiel pointed out that the judgment was imminent, permanent, fixed, and irreversible. God would use the Babylonians as the rod of his anger to judge Israel (cf. Isa 10:5; Jer 50:31). The rod that blossomed (v. 10) may be a reference to Aaron's rod in Num 17:8. The almond rod that budded suggested God's choice of Aaron as high priest but also was a sign of his displeasure with the arrogance of the people (Num 17:10-11), who had just witnessed the awesome judgment of Korah (Num 16:1ff.).

Buying and selling, like rejoicing and grieving, suggest activities of normal business, social, and personal life. Ezekiel announced the cessation of those normal activities (v. 11). Divine wrath wiped away all the regular elements of human stability. There also are overtones of the law of the Sabbath Year (Deut 15:1-2) and the Jubilee Year (Lev 25:1-6) in the passage. In the Sabbatical Year all slaves were set free, and in the Jubilee Year all property was restored to its original owner. Land was a sacred trust from God that the Hebrews had received at the conquest under Joshua. Therefore property was sold only in cases of extreme need. Such sales were regarded as temporary and redeemable transactions (v. 12). In the day of judgment envisioned by Ezekiel the seller would not recover his land, and the individual judgment of the coming bondage of the exile would not be reversed (v. 13).[80] Material things will be of no value in a time of divine judgment. Unbridled materialism and secularism that divorces God from human society tends only to intensify judgment.

[14]Though they blow the trumpet and get everything ready, no one will go into battle, for my wrath is upon the whole crowd.
[15]"Outside is the sword, inside are plague and famine; those in the country will die by the sword, and those in the city will be devoured by famine and plague. [16]All who survive and escape will be in the mountains, moaning like doves of the valleys, each because of his sins. [17]Every hand will go limp, and every knee will become as weak as water. [18]They will put on sackcloth and be

---

[80] Zimmerli, *Ezekiel 1*, 208; Stalker, *Ezekiel*, 87; Hals, *Ezekiel*, 45; Wevers, *Ezekiel*, 74; Alexander, "Ezekiel," 777-78.

clothed with terror. Their faces will be covered with shame and their heads will be shaved.

DESTRUCTION ANNOUNCED (7:14-18).   **7:14-18**   The concluding verses of this summary message contain three elements to underscore the picture of the total destruction of the nation. The first element is the approach of the invading army in vv. 14-18. The alarm would be sounded, but defense was useless since the knowledge of the invasion would paralyze and terrorize the populace (v. 14). The three scourges of war previously mentioned were the sword, plague, and famine (cf. Ezek 5:12; 6:11-12). They were divided between the city and country (v. 15). This was not so much to specify the location of each scourge as to make the point that the entire nation would be affected.[81] The people would respond like doves moaning in the valleys (v. 16). They also would seek remote hiding places to escape the invading armies. They would be overwhelmed with the terror, suffering, and shame brought upon them because of their inequities. "Limp" hands and "weak" knees describe a complete paralysis of strength and ability to resist the invading army (v. 17).

Sackcloth and shaved heads were traditional elements of mourning and appropriate to the context of judgment (v. 18). These were not signs of mourning that resulted from true repentance, however, but mourning over the catastrophe of destruction and the resulting famine and plague. The people were not sorry for their sin so much as they were sorry they were having to cope with the discomforts and horrors of the invasion.[82]

**[19]They will throw their silver into the streets, and their gold will be an unclean thing. Their silver and gold will not be able to save them in the day of the LORD's wrath. They will not satisfy their hunger or fill their stomachs with it, for it has made them stumble into sin. [20]They were proud of their beautiful jewelry and used it to make their detestable idols and vile images. Therefore I will turn these into an unclean thing for them. [21]I will hand it all over as plunder to foreigners and as loot to the wicked of the earth, and they will defile it. [22]I will turn my face away from them, and they will desecrate my treasured place; robbers will enter it and desecrate it.**

USELESSNESS OF PHYSICAL RESOURCES (7:19-22).   **7:19-22**   The second element of the destruction of the nation focused on their useless material resources. The silver and gold was worthless for averting judgment (v. 19). This was a sobering reality for a materialistic society. When

---

[81] Greenberg, *Ezekiel 1–20*, 151; Wevers, *Ezekiel*, 74-75.
[82] Zimmerli, *Ezekiel 1*, 208; Wevers, *Ezekiel*, 75; Cooke, *Ezekiel*, 81.

the invading armies came to the villages and towns, their silver and gold would be abandoned like an unclean object, thus signifying the repulsiveness of materialism.[83]

The phrase "They were proud of their beautiful jewelry" may also be translated, "And as for their beautiful adornments," a reference to the use of gold and silver to decorate places of worship (v. 20).[84] Personal jewelry that was once given to adorn the tabernacle and the temple was being used to beautify pagan shrines. This wealth would be given to foreigners, a reference to the invading army who would take it as spoils of war.

Verse 21 supports this idea with its reference to objects of plunder usually taken and profaned by the enemy. Nebuchadnezzar destroyed the temple and took the golden and silver vessels to Babylon, where they were profaned in the temple of his pagan gods. These same objects also were used by Belshazzar as objects of pagan worship and as a means of ridicule for the Hebrews and their God.[85] Verse 22 also seems to anticipate the departure of God's Spirit from the temple in Jerusalem and the temple's desecration and destruction at the hands of the Babylonians.[86] Ezekiel carefully chronicled all the basic elements of the sins of the people to show that they deserved the impending judgment of God on the nation. These elements included pride (7:10,20,24), self-confidence (7:14), materialism (7:19), and superficial worship (7:20-22).[87]

---

[23]"**Prepare chains, because the land is full of bloodshed and the city is full of violence. [24]I will bring the most wicked of the nations to take possession of their houses; I will put an end to the pride of the mighty, and their sanctuaries will be desecrated. [25]When terror comes, they will seek peace, but there will be none. [26]Calamity upon calamity will come, and rumor upon rumor. They will try to get a vision from the prophet; the teaching of the law by the priest will be lost, as will the counsel of the elders. [27]The king will mourn, the prince will be clothed with despair, and the hands of the people of the land will tremble. I will deal with them according to their conduct, and by their own standards I will judge them. Then they will know that I am the LORD."**

---

[83] The word נִדָּה ("unclean," Lev 15:19; 18:19; Isa 30:22) denotes any severe uncleanness that should be unconditionally avoided (see Zimmerli, *Ezekiel 1,* 208-9; Taylor, *Ezekiel,* 94; Alexander, "Ezekiel," 780; Greenberg, *Ezekiel 1–20,* 152).

[84] For a discussion of "jewelry" as the adornment of the temple, see Alexander, "Ezekiel," 779; Taylor, *Ezekiel,* 94. The construction of the tabernacle seems to support this possibility (see Exod 35:22).

[85] Fisch, *Ezekiel,* 38-39. See Dan 1:2; 5:3-4.

[86] Wevers, *Ezekiel,* 76; Fisch, *Ezekiel,* 39; Davidson, *Ezekiel,* 50.

[87] Craigie, *Ezekiel,* 53-55.

FALL OF JERUSALEM ANNOUNCED (7:23-27). **7:23-27** The third element of judgment in this summary is the fall of Jerusalem. Ezekiel depicted the violent overthrow of the city with its inhabitants taken captive. Chains were a sign of captivity (v. 23). The kind of chain mentioned by Ezekiel was used as a fetter for captives in transport to Babylon (cf. 1 Kgs 6:21; Isa 40:19).[88] The word for "bloodshed" was literally "judgment of bloodshed" (v. 23), signifying that the captives were guilty of crimes punishable by death.[89] Violence often characterizes a sinful society as a manifestation of self-inflicted judgment (7:23).

Capture of houses was part of the warning given by Moses as he described the penalties of disobedience (see Lev 26:31-32).[90] The search for comfort and guidance in the midst of the destruction of the nation would be futile, like Saul's attempt to seek counsel from the deceased prophet Samuel (1 Sam 28:1-5). Instead of the peace, prosperity, and solidarity that should have characterized Hebrew society, the exile brought pain, loss, and confusion (vv. 24-27).[91] Neither the prophets, priests, nor elders would be able to make sense of the situation, leaving the people with no direction from their national leaders (cf. Jer 18:18). Ezekiel envisioned a time of desperation in which people would return to the usual methods of revelation. They would seek a vision from a prophet, a teaching of the law from the priests, and counsel from the elders, all to no avail (v. 26).

Finally, according to v. 27 such desperation would be the experience of all, even those ("king"/"prince")[92] at the top of society (cf. "the pride of the mighty" in v. 4). By judging Judah in accordance with the standards and punishments declared to them from the beginning in the Mosaic covenant, the Lord would cause them to recognize him as different from the gods of the nations, a God not to be manipulated or taken for granted, but rather obeyed and trusted wholeheartedly.[93]

---

[88] The word רַתּוֹק is a hapax legomenon and is a special word for chains used to bind captives for the journey to Babylon (see Alexander, "Ezekiel," 779; Fisch, *Ezekiel,* 39).

[89] Fisch (*Ezekiel,* 39) points out that the rise of מִשְׁפַּט דָּמִים ("judgment of bloodshed") makes the point that the people had been guilty of crimes punishable by death.

[90] Greenberg, *Ezekiel 1–20,* 154. The occupation of the land was not a common theme in covenant curses, but it does occur in Lev 26:32.

[91] Wevers, *Ezekiel,* 76-77.

[92] The term מֶלֶךְ, "king," is not used elsewhere in Ezekiel of kings of Judah other than Jehoiachin (see comments at 28:11-12). Therefore the reference here probably is of a general nature. Otherwise "king" may refer to the mourning of Jehoiachin and "prince" of Zedekiah. See Alexander, "Ezekiel," 780; Greenberg, *Ezekiel 1–20,* 156-57.

[93] Alexander, "Ezekiel," 780.

2. Prophetic Visions of Judgment for Polluting the Temple
   (8:1–11:25)
   (1) Vision of the Abominations in the Temple of Jerusalem
       (8:1-18)
   (2) Vision of the Death of the Guilty (9:1-11)
   (3) Vision of the Departure of God's Glory (10:1-22)
   (4) Vision of Judgment, Restoration, and Departure of God's
       Glory from Jerusalem (11:1-25)

## 2. Prophetic Visions of Judgment for Polluting the Temple (8:1–11:25)

Ezekiel received a series of four visions and messages on the theme of
the desecration of the temple in Jerusalem. These messages came just a
year and two months after the first dated prophecy of the book in 3:16.
Although the nation was under Babylonian control, worship continued,
and the priests still performed their duties in the temple complex. Being
from a priestly family, Ezekiel was sensitive to the need for ritual purity.
His reaction to the appalling degeneration in worship was evident
throughout the four visions.[1]

The four visions correspond to the four chapters in this section: (1) the
abominations in the temple of Jerusalem (8:1-18), including four scenes
of apostate worship; (2) the death of the guilty (9:1-11), a vision of divine
judgment of the apostate worshipers; (3) the departure of God's glory
from the temple (10:1-22); (4) judgment of evil princes (11:1-25), departure of God's glory from Jerusalem, and a promise of restoration. The unity of the visions is suggested by the repetition in reverse order in 11:22-25
of three elements from 8:1-4—Ezekiel's audience (the exiles or elders),
the Spirit lifting the prophet, and "the glory of the God of Israel."

---

[1] For an argument against the unity of this section, see B. Vawter and L. J. Hoppe, *A
True Heart: Ezekiel,* ITC (Grand Rapids: Eerdmans, 1991), 63. Both Greenberg and
Parunak also have seen a chiastic arrangement of the visions centering around the chariot
vision in chap. 10. For Greenberg, however, the center consists only of vv. 8-22. See H.
Parunak, "The Literary Architecture of Ezekiel's *marʾôt ʾelōhîm,*" *JBL* 99 (1980): 66-69;
M. Greenberg, *Ezekiel 1–20* (New York: Doubleday, 1983), 192-205.

### *(1)  Vision of the Abominations in the Temple of Jerusalem (8:1-18)*

After the introduction to the visions (8:1-4) are scenes of idolatry: (1) the image of jealousy (8:5-6), (2) cultic worship of animals (8:7-13), (3) weeping for Tammuz (8:14-15), and (4) the worship of the sun (8:16-18).[2] These four pagan cults bear testimony to the pervasiveness of syncretistic worship in Israel in the time of Ezekiel.[3] In the years prior to the fall of Jerusalem in 587/586 B.C., there was a rise in syncretistic worship that abounded in the pagan practices of Judah's neighbors.[4] This increased the external pressure to be like the nations (1 Sam 8:5).

**[1]In the sixth year, in the sixth month on the fifth day, while I was sitting in my house and the elders of Judah were sitting before me, the hand of the Sovereign LORD came upon me there. [2]I looked, and I saw a figure like that of a man. From what appeared to be his waist down he was like fire, and from there up his appearance was as bright as glowing metal. [3]He stretched out what looked like a hand and took me by the hair of my head. The Spirit lifted me up between earth and heaven and in visions of God he took me to Jerusalem, to the entrance to the north gate of the inner court, where the idol that provokes to jealousy stood. [4]And there before me was the glory of the God of Israel, as in the vision I had seen in the plain.**

INTRODUCTION TO THE VISIONS (8:1-4).    In the days of the kingdom of Israel spiritual decline began with the construction of temples to pagan gods on the sacred temple mount area during Solomon's reign. Solomon married many pagan wives and allowed each who wished to do so to build a temple and altar to her god (1 Kgs 11:1-8). This spiritual decline led to a resurrection of Baal worship (1 Kgs 16:31-34; 17:1-17) and resulted in the division of the nation into northern and southern kingdoms at the death of Solomon (1 Kgs 11:41–12:33). The decline continued until the Northern Kingdom was taken captive by the Assyrians in 722 B.C. (2 Kgs 17:5-41) and the fall of the Southern Kingdom, which began in 605 B.C.

---

[2] A. B. Davidson, *The Book of the Prophet Ezekiel* (Cambridge: Cambridge University Press, 1892), 52.

[3] Polytheistic worship can be traced to the earliest cultures in the region, e.g., Sumer, Akkad, Egypt, and the Old Babylonian Empires. See S. N. Kramer, *History Begins at Sumer* (Garden City: Doubleday, 1959), 201; W. F. Albright, *Archaeology and the Religion of Israel* (Garden City: Anchor, 1969), 159.

[4] According to Gen 10–11, the story of the Tower of Babel, apostate worship may have started in the Old Babylonian Empire under Nimrod. See "The Babylonians and Assyrians," *The Bible Almanac,* 136; J. Wellard, *Babylon* (New York: Schoken, 1972), 158; W. F. Albright, *From the Stone Age to Christianity* (Garden City: Doubleday, 1957), 156; "Babylon, History and Religion of," *HBD,* 141-44).

when Nebuchadnezzar took the first group of captives and made Jehoiakim a puppet king. Nebuchadnezzar later replaced Jehoiakim with Jehoiachin, then Zedekiah, and finally destroyed Jerusalem in 587/586 B.C. when he took captive all the remaining leaders and merchants.

**8:1-4** Fourteen months had elapsed since the previous dated vision in 3:16. The date of this vision was September 17, 592 B.C.[5] Ezekiel was in his exile residence where the elders had assembled to await a word from God (cf. 14:1; 20:1; 33:31). Mention of elders suggests that even in exile there was some kind of organized structure to community life and corporate worship.[6] As the elders sat with Ezekiel, the "hand of the LORD" fell upon him. This phrase described the beginning of a visionary experience (1:3; 3:14,22; 33:22).

Ezekiel saw a glowing humanlike figure (v. 2) similar in appearance to the one he reported in his first vision in 1:26-28.[7] The angel put forth his hand, lifted the prophet by a lock of his hair, and brought him to Jerusalem (v. 3). Did Ezekiel return bodily to Jerusalem, or was this a visionary experience?

**5Then he said to me, "Son of man, look toward the north." So I looked, and in the entrance north of the gate of the altar I saw this idol of jealousy. 6And he said to me, "Son of man, do you see what they are doing—the utterly detestable things the house of Israel is doing here, things that will drive me far from my sanctuary? But you will see things that are even more detestable."**

IMAGE OF JEALOUSY (8:5-6). **8:5-6** Ezekiel stated that the figure brought him "in visions of God" (cf. 1:1) to Jerusalem, indicating that the trip to Jerusalem was a visionary experience in which his body remained in Babylon seated before the elders (v. 1). Upon his "arrival" at the temple in Jerusalem, the prophet saw the first of the four forms of apostate worship. He saw an image called an "idol of jealousy" (v. 5) or "the idol that provokes to jealousy" (v. 3). There was no physical description of this image that provoked jealousy. It is obvious from vv. 3-4 that God was the one provoked to jealousy against the image. Ezekiel looked toward the

---

[5] J. B. Taylor (*Ezekiel,* TOTC [Downers Grove: InterVarsity, 1969], 36) and Zimmerli (*Ezekiel 1,* Her (Philadelphia: Fortress, 1979), 236). M. Greenberg (*Ezekiel 1–20,* AB [Garden City: Doubleday, 1986], 166) places it on Sept. 18.

[6] S. Fisch, *Ezekiel* (London: Soncino, 1950), 40.

[7] Note that "the appearance of the likeness of the glory of the LORD" in 1:28 is now "the glory of the God of Israel" in 8:4. Note also that 8:4 connects this vision back to 3:22-23, which echoes the vision of chap. 1. Ezekiel connected his vision in chap. 10, however, directly to chap. 1 (see 10:15,20,22). Thus chaps. 8–10 echo chaps. 1–3 in reverse order.

north, the direction of the temple sanctuary, and saw the image of jealousy in the gate of the altar (v. 5).

The image was located near the sacrificial altar or perhaps a pagan altar was a part of the shrine of this idol (v. 5). The worship Ezekiel described suggested a developed program of regular pagan worship in the sanctuary that was to be exclusively for the worship of Yahweh.

Some have suggested that this image may have been the one of Asherah set up in the temple by Manasseh (2 Kgs 21:7; 2 Chr 33:7,15). This conclusion is not mere speculation but was suggested by the use of the same word (sēmel) for Manasseh's idol in 2 Chr 33:7,15. These are the only occurrences of the term except in the prohibition against idol worship in Deut 4:16-18.[8] After Manasseh, Josiah had purged Judah and Jerusalem of such things (2 Chr 34), but his work was reversed after his death (2 Chr 36:5,9; Jer 3:10).[9] Whatever the details are, the significant fact is that the people had violated God's prohibition and brought an idol into the temple area dedicated to worship of Yahweh alone (cf. Exod 20:4).

In addition to the image, Ezekiel also saw the glory of God that had appeared in the vision of chap. 1. The glory of God's visible self-revelation was in the form of a bright light. The light of God's glory appeared to Moses and the seventy elders on Mount Sinai (Exod 24:16). It also appeared at the dedication of the tabernacle (Exod 40:34) and later of the temple (1 Kgs 8:4). The New Testament records similar manifestations at the birth of Jesus (Luke 2:8-11) and at the conversion of Saul (Acts 9:3-9).

The things Ezekiel saw were "utterly detestable" to God (v. 6; cf. vv. 9-10,13,15,17). The use of first person by the voice and the reference to "my sanctuary" suggest that the speaker was God. A more serious or devastating evaluation is unimaginable than to have one's behavior judged "detestable" by the Lord of life. Yahweh was alienated from his house of worship by the inclusion of objects and elements of worship that strictly were forbidden. Such pagan practices in the temple complex were antithetical to the purity of worship God demanded.[10] God is a jealous God who accepts no rival (Exod 20:5). To allow idolatry to continue in the temple area was a direct challenge to his authority and the veracity of his word.

---

[8] If this was the same image, it was moved from the "house of God" (2 Chr 33:7) to the gate area (v. 5) on the north side of the complex where Ezekiel saw it. If it were still in the "house of God," it could not have been seen by looking north.

[9] Greenberg (Ezekiel 1–20, 201) suggests that what Ezekiel shows is "a montage of whatever pagan rites ever were conducted at the Jerusalem temple rather than a representation of what occurred there in the summer of the sixth year of Jehoiachin's exile."

[10] See discussion of "Canaanite Religion" in the Introduction.

⁷Then he brought me to the entrance to the court. I looked, and I saw a hole in the wall. ⁸He said to me, "Son of man, now dig into the wall." So I dug into the wall and saw a doorway there.

⁹And he said to me, "Go in and see the wicked and detestable things they are doing here." ¹⁰So I went in and looked, and I saw portrayed all over the walls all kinds of crawling things and detestable animals and all the idols of the house of Israel. ¹¹In front of them stood seventy elders of the house of Israel, and Jaazaniah son of Shaphan was standing among them. Each had a censer in his hand, and a fragrant cloud of incense was rising.

¹²He said to me, "Son of man, have you seen what the elders of the house of Israel are doing in the darkness, each at the shrine of his own idol? They say, 'The LORD does not see us; the LORD has forsaken the land.'" ¹³Again, he said, "You will see them doing things that are even more detestable."

WORSHIP OF ANIMALS (8:7-13). **8:7-13** The divine guide brought Ezekiel to the entrance of the court, where he saw a hole in the wall. Ezekiel dug in the wall and enlarged the hole. Behind it he discovered the door to a secret chamber (v. 8). The guide told him to enter and see what was happening inside (v. 9). To his shock and surprise the men inside were worshiping idols in various kinds of animal forms (v. 10). The terminology used was very much like the prohibitions against idolatry (cf. Deut 4:16-19; Lev 11:40-42).

There was no apparent reason for the secrecy of this group of worshipers. Some interpreters suggest that these practices resembled Egyptian worship rather than Babylonian cults. If so, the group would have had to worship in secret because the gods of the Egyptian pantheon would have been offensive, perhaps even illegal under Babylonian rule.[11] All public altars would have had to conform to required standards of Babylonian worship.

Seventy men identified as leaders in Jerusalem perhaps were secretly seeking deliverance from Babylonian domination by worshiping the gods of Egypt.[12] The fact that they were involved in such an apostate form of worship bears sober testimony to just how far the people had fallen spiritually.

In the midst of the group was Jaazaniah, the son of Shaphan (v. 11). Shaphan may have been the same person who was Josiah's secretary of

---

[11] The tension between Egypt and Babylon on the political front certainly would have spilled over into religious areas. See P. C. Craigie, *Ezekiel* (Philadelphia: Westminster, 1983), 60-61; Eichrodt, *Ezekiel*, 124; and Albright, *Archaeology*, 160-61.

[12] Craigie, *Ezekiel*, 61. This is ironic in light of the fact that seventy leaders confirmed the Mosaic Covenant, which delivered the Hebrews from bondage to the gods of Egypt (Exod 24:1,9). Threatened again with slavery, they appealed to Egypt's gods for help.

state (see 2 Kgs 22:8-14; 2 Chr 34:15-21; Jer 26:24; 29:3; 36:10; 40:5,9,11; 41:2; 43:6).[13] If so, his brother Ahikam also defended Jeremiah (Jer 26:24). For such a one to be found leading this apostate group bears testimony to the rapid degeneration of worship in Israel after Josiah's death.[14]

With this kind of corrupt spiritual leadership one can imagine the severe decline of spiritual purity and faithfulness to Yahweh among the general populace. Everyone was participating in worship of these false gods (v. 11). Leaders who were supposed to guide the people faithfully to serve Yahweh led them instead into apostate idolatrous worship.[15]

These leaders had lost faith in Yahweh and concluded that because Judah had been overthrown God had forsaken them. The words of v. 10 are very revealing about the true nature of human character. The guide said, "Son of man, have you seen what the elders of the house of Israel are doing in the darkness?" (v. 12). What people do when they think no one else can see them reveals their true character.

What a contrast between these people of the dark days of Judah and Jesus' challenge for his followers to be the "light of the world" (Matt 5:13-16). They concluded that since God had forsaken them, he was not around to see what they did. The words of v. 12 reflect a popular saying of the Jews in Babylon as well as in Jerusalem that reflected their attitude: "The LORD does not see us; the LORD has forsaken the land" (cf. 9:9).[16]

**[14]Then he brought me to the entrance to the north gate of the house of the LORD, and I saw women sitting there, mourning for Tammuz. [15]He said to me, "Do you see this, son of man? You will see things that are even more detestable than this."**

WEEPING FOR TAMMUZ (8:14-15).    **8:14-15**    During the seventh century B.C. there was a clear move toward religious syncretism in Israel and Judah. Second Kings, which recorded the prophetic perspective of the political, social, economic, and spiritual decline of Israel and Judah, clearly reflected this religious amalgamation. Albright has said, "Chapter 8 of

---

[13] N. Avigad, *Hebrew Bullae from the Time of Jeremiah*, 102. The name Jaazaniah has been found on seals of government officials of the period. See also R. H. Alexander, "Ezekiel," EBC 6 (Grand Rapids: Zondervan, 1986), 783.

[14] See Stuart, *Ezekiel*, 89-90.

[15] Greenberg, *Ezekiel 1–20*, 170; Zimmerli, *Ezekiel 1*, 240. The institution of seventy elders was an ancient tradition of Yahweh worship. These men stood before pagan altars to implore the help of pagan gods in violation of the covenant made by their predecessors.

[16] G. A. Cooke, *The Book of Ezekiel*, ICC (Edinburgh: T & T Clark, 1986), 95-96. Ezekiel quoted popular sayings of the people as convicting evidence of their lack of faithfulness.

Ezekiel is a valuable description of Syro-Mesopotamian syncretism in the priestly and noble circles of Jerusalem."[17]

Ezekiel then saw the third "detestable" form of idolatry, which was worship of Tammuz. At the door of the north gate of the temple[18] Ezekiel saw women weeping for Tammuz, the Babylonian equivalent of the Sumerian god of vegetation, Dumuzi, known also as Duzu. The name Dumuzi means "true son," "faithful son," or "proper son" and has been compared with Adonis in the Greek pantheon. Tammuz/Dumuzi was the male consort of Inanna, also called Ishtar, and was known as the "shepherd god."[19]

The seasons were thought by some to depict the death and resurrection of this nature god. The summer heat scorched, burned, and dried the vegetation. It gave way to the winter when the vegetation died. But the people observed that in spring when the rains returned, the vegetation came to life again, and the cycle again was repeated. In the rites of Tammuz women wept for him the fourth month. The text gives no explanation why Ezekiel saw these women weeping for him in the sixth month. As a visionary experience, the timing probably had no significance.[20]

The worship of Tammuz continued in the Middle East until the fourteenth century A.D. and developed into a month-long celebration in North Mesopotamia.[21] After the exile the Hebrew calendar included a month called Tammuz, the fourth month (June-July). This was the time for grapes to be harvested. The preservation of the name Tammuz in the calendar suggests the impact this form of pagan worship had on Jewish life and worship, both during and after the exile. Again Ezekiel's guide closed, as if to say, "You haven't seen anything yet!" He told Ezekiel, "You will see things more detestable than this" (v. 15).

**[16]He then brought me into the inner court of the house of the LORD, and there at the entrance to the temple, between the portico and the altar, were about twenty-five men. With their backs toward the temple of the LORD and**

---

[17] See Albright, *Archaeology and Religion of Israel,* 159.

[18] D. Stuart notes that of the three gates into the inner court (north, south, and east) this may have been the most prominent since it would have been the one used by the king (*Ezekiel* Dallas: Word, 1989], 89).

[19] For further discussion of Tammuz see J. Finegan, *Myth and Mystery;* Zimmerli, *Ezekiel 1,* 242; Taylor, *Ezekiel,* 99; *HBD,* "Fertility Cults," 484; "Tammuz," 1321.

[20] See brief discussion in Greenberg, *Ezekiel 1–20,* 171, 201-2; also see Fisch, *Ezekiel,* 44-45, who also offers a concise description of the Tammuz cult.

[21] This is the only place in the Bible that mentions worship of Tammuz although it was a part of ancient Near Eastern worship back to the Old Babylonian Empire ca. 3000 B.C. See E. M. Yamauchi, "Tammuz and the Bible," *JBL* 84 (1965): 283-90; O. R. Gurney, "Tammuz Rediscovered: Some Recent Developments," *JSS* 7 (1962): 147-60.

their faces toward the east, they were bowing down to the sun in the east.

[17]He said to me, "Have you seen this, son of man? Is it a trivial matter for the house of Judah to do the detestable things they are doing here? Must they also fill the land with violence and continually provoke me to anger? Look at them putting the branch to their nose! [18]Therefore I will deal with them in anger; I will not look on them with pity or spare them. Although they shout in my ears, I will not listen to them."

WORSHIP OF THE SUN (8:16-18).  **8:16-18**  The final scene of detestable worship practices occurred in the inner court, the holiest area for worship in the temple. Only the priests could go into this area of the sanctuary. Here Ezekiel saw twenty-five men facing east worshiping the sun and turning their backs on the temple of Yahweh. What a tragic commentary on the sinful obstinacy of a hardened, rebellious sinner who arrogantly turns away from God. These men are not identified as priests in v. 16, which may mean they were not. If they were not priests, then they had doubly desecrated the inner court of the sanctuary. First, if these men were not priests, they had violated a holy area restricted to the priesthood.[22] If they were priests, then their sin was all the more reprehensible because they were responsible for guarding the temple against defilement. Second, they were practicing idolatrous sun worship in one of the holiest precincts of the temple complex. Their location between the porch and the altar would have placed them directly in front of the entrance of the temple sanctuary (v. 16). Worship of the sun was one of the evil practices introduced by Manasseh (2 Kgs 21:5).[23]

According to v. 17, God was angered not only by the idolatries in the temple but also by the violence that was rampant in Judah (cf. 9:9). We may suppose, in fact, that violence always brings him grief (cf. Gen 6:11). God does not consider insignificant these violations of his holiness. These people provoked his anger and invited his judgment by their highly repugnant behavior. The phrase "putting the branch to their nose!" (v. 17) probably was a popular saying that meant their actions were an insult to God. While some have tried to interpret this phrase in light of some obscure cultic practice, it probably has more to do with a failure to follow God's commands, the equivalent of thumbing their noses at God.[24]

---

[22] Zimmerli (*Ezekiel 1,* 243) believes they were priests based on their number, twenty-five; see also Greenberg, *Ezekiel 1–20,* 171; Alexander, "Ezekiel," 784.

[23] See H. G. May, "Some Aspects of Solar Worship at Jerusalem," *ZAW* LV (1937): 269-81.

[24] For an interpretation in terms of ritual practice see H. W. F. Saggs, "Notes and Studies: The Branch to the Nose," *JTS* 11 (1980): 61-74. For a survey of interpretations see Greenberg, *Ezekiel 1–20,* 172-73. Also cf. Zimmerli, *Ezekiel 1,* 222, 244-45; Taylor, *Ezekiel,* 100; R. Gordis, "The Branch to the Nose," *JTS* 37 (1936): 284-85.

The justice of God demands chastening for such a breach of faith. Therefore God declared that he would deal with Judah in severe judgment and would show no mercy (v. 18). Thus chap. 8 opened the way for the somber picture of judgment that unfolds in the second vision in 9:1-11 and the subsequent departure of God's glory from the temple and city in 10:1–11:25.

God is not found in every religious experience. "There is some good in *all* religions" is a false axiom. The New Age movement popular in the last decade of the twentieth century illustrates such false religious philosophy. Many erroneously believe there are many valid religions and many ways to approach God. Idolatry is still an abomination to God, and Acts 4:12 is still true today. Jesus is the one and only way to salvation.

### (2) Vision of the Death of the Guilty (9:1-11)

[1]Then I heard him call out in a loud voice, "Bring the guards of the city here, each with a weapon in his hand." [2]And I saw six men coming from the direction of the upper gate, which faces north, each with a deadly weapon in his hand. With them was a man clothed in linen who had a writing kit at his side. They came in and stood beside the bronze altar.

[3]Now the glory of the God of Israel went up from above the cherubim, where it had been, and moved to the threshold of the temple. Then the LORD called to the man clothed in linen who had the writing kit at his side [4]and said to him, "Go throughout the city of Jerusalem and put a mark on the foreheads of those who grieve and lament over all the detestable things that are done in it."

[5]As I listened, he said to the others, "Follow him through the city and kill, without showing pity or compassion. [6]Slaughter old men, young men and maidens, women and children, but do not touch anyone who has the mark. Begin at my sanctuary." So they began with the elders who were in front of the temple.

[7]Then he said to them, "Defile the temple and fill the courts with the slain. Go!" So they went out and began killing throughout the city. [8]While they were killing and I was left alone, I fell facedown, crying out, "Ah, Sovereign LORD! Are you going to destroy the entire remnant of Israel in this outpouring of your wrath on Jerusalem?"

[9]He answered me, "The sin of the house of Israel and Judah is exceedingly great; the land is full of bloodshed and the city is full of injustice. They say, 'The LORD has forsaken the land; the LORD does not see.' [10]So I will not look on them with pity or spare them, but I will bring down on their own heads what they have done."

[11]Then the man in linen with the writing kit at his side brought back word, saying, "I have done as you commanded."

The vision of the detestable, idolatrous practices in chap. 8 closes with an announcement of judgment in 8:18 that is partially repeated at the end of this vision in 9:10. Chapter 9 details the coming judgment. First the primary agents are introduced—the guards who would carry out the slaughter and the man in linen who would protect the faithful (9:1-2). Then there is a parenthetical statement foreshadowing the departure of God's glory in chap. 10 (9:3a) followed by instructions to the man in linen to mark the innocent (9:3b-4) and the guards to slaughter the guilty (9:5-7a). Their obedience is noted in reverse order—the guards in vv. 7b-10 (interrupted by the prophet's intercession and the lad's response in vv. 8-10) followed by the man in linen in v. 11. Second is the marking of the guilty (9:4-6). Third is the execution of the guilty (9:7-10). Fourth is the announcement of a completed assignment (9:11).

**9:1-2**    Ezekiel heard a voice, evidently the voice of God, which called for the "guards" of the city to come forth with their weapons (v. 1). The word "guards" refers to those in charge of the city of Jerusalem who sometimes had authority to administer discipline.[25] While they were called "men" in v. 2, it becomes clear in subsequent verses that they were more than human and were divine messengers or angels. It was not uncommon for angels to be called "men" in Scripture (see, e.g., Gen 18:2; 32:24; Dan 10:5). God personally summoned these messengers to chasten his people as he had promised (8:18). These angels came to dispense judgment and divine wrath.[26]

At the command of the Lord six "men" came forth by way of the upper gate, which was built by Jotham (2 Kgs 15:35) and was located at the northeast corner of the temple complex (Ezek 9:2). This was the same area where Ezekiel had seen the sun worshipers (8:16) and the image of jealousy (8:5). Each of the "men" had a "deadly weapon" (v. 2) or battle ax in his hand.[27] Accompanying these executioners was a seventh "man" dressed in the white linen of a priest (v. 2; cf., Exod 28:29-42). He had a scribe's writing kit at his side. This writing kit usually was made from an animal horn. It had a palette with a slot for pens and a hollow place for

---

[25] Fisch, *Ezekiel*, 47; Taylor, *Ezekiel*, 101. The word פְּקֻדּוֹת may mean "to be in charge of appointments and administration of punishment."

[26] God brings irrevocable judgment on sin (9:1-11). But he never does so without first giving ample, clear warning of impending wrath. He had done so repeatedly through the ministry of his prophets (see Introduction, "Ezekiel the Prophet," and 2 Chr 36:15-17). Judgment is always a last resort with God. He never dispenses punishment because he enjoys it (cf. Ezek 18:21-32); see Greenberg, *Ezekiel 1–20*, 175.

[27] The word comes from the root שָׁחַת, which means "to ruin" (see BDB, 1007); see also Fisch, *Ezekiel*, 47; Wevers, *Ezekiel*, 84.

two kinds of ink, usually black and red. Professional scribes usually carried this kind of equipment.[28]

Upon their entry, these seven emissaries of judgment took up their station by the brazen altar in the inner court (Ezek 9:2). Seven was the number symbolic of completeness in Jewish apocalyptic and suggested that their actions would be conclusive.

**9:3-6** As they stood in place, the glory of God that rested above the cherubim[29] on the mercy seat in the holy of holies (Num 7:89) rose and moved to the threshold of the sanctuary (Ezek 9:3). This was the first stage of the departure of God's presence from his sanctuary, which concluded in 10:22.[30]

Before the executions commenced, the messenger in white linen was instructed to go through the city and place a mark on the forehead of those who "grieve and lament" over the detestable things done in the temple (v. 4). The "mark" was therefore to distinguish the righteous from the guilty. There was special significance to the "mark" used for the purpose. The word "mark" is the Hebrew word *taw,* which is the name of the last letter in the Hebrew alphabet. It may have been understood as an abbreviation for *tām,* "blameless."[31] In the seventh and sixth centuries B.C. the *taw* of Paleo-Hebrew script was written like an *X* or sloped cross. Its use here was to identify the righteous and exempt them from judgment. The "man" in white linen was to place the *taw* on the forehead of every righteous person. The significance of this sign to Christian interpreters obviously goes beyond what Ezekiel understood. As H. L. Ellison observed, the prophets often spoke more than they understood.[32] God's judgment always was tempered with mercy. The "man" in white linen marked those who were grieved over the sins of Judah. These were spared and became a small remnant of hope for future restoration. They were spared by receiving the sign of the cross (*X*), as would be those sealed for deliverance in Rev 7:3-4 and 14:1.

---

[28] Greenberg, *Ezekiel 1–20,* 176; Cooke, *Ezekiel,* 104. The word קֶסֶת, "writing kit," is an Egyptian loan word (see Eichrodt, *Ezekiel,* 130, and Taylor, *Ezekiel,* 101).

[29] The use of the singular כְּרוּב instead of the plural is unusual, but the reference is doubtless to the two כְּרוּבִים that sat atop the ark and formed the mercy seat (Exod 37:6-7; see Zimmerli, *Ezekiel 1,* 254).

[30] See both Fisch, *Ezekiel,* 47-48, and Greenberg, *Ezekiel 1–20,* 176, 194-98, where they address in detail the enigma of the movements of God's glory; see also Taylor, *Ezekiel,* 102.

[31] For various interpretations of the *X* (*taw*) in 9:4, compare Fisch, *Ezekiel,* 48; Craigie, *Ezekiel,* 68; Taylor, *Ezekiel,* 102; Carley, *Ezekiel,* 59; Wevers, *Ezekiel,* 85; Cooke, *Ezekiel,* 106; Feinberg, *Ezekiel,* 56.

[32] See Ellison, *Ezekiel,* 44.

The men with the slaughter weapons were told to follow the man in white and to slay all those who had no mark (v. 5). This is much like the Passover story, where the household was spared if the blood of the sacrificial lamb was placed over the lintel of the door (Exod 12:7,13), and the judgment of Jericho, where the faithful household of Rahab was marked by the scarlet cord (Josh 2). Those judged by the executioners were from five all-inclusive groups: the old men, the young men, the maidens, the women, and the children (Ezek 9:6). Judgment of the guilty was indiscriminate. God plays no favorites and gives no exemptions. Divine justice is served by the fact that no one who is guilty will be spared (9:5-6). Judgment not only included God's own people; it began in his sanctuary (9:6).[33] Those who are leaders are not exempt from the holy standard of God's Word. They are even more responsible and will incur more severe punishment for leading others astray (cf. Matt 18:6; Mark 9:42; Luke 17:2; Heb 13:17).

**9:7-11**    Normally a corpse was not allowed in the sanctuary because a dead body was considered unclean. Since the temple already had been defiled by the worshipers seen in Ezek 8, the angel-executioners were told to "defile the temple" and to "fill the courts with the slain" (v. 7).[34] Justice was more important than ritual purity.

From the sanctuary the executions spread throughout the remainder of the city (Ezek 9:7) so that Ezekiel was the only one left in the temple. His plea for mercy (v. 8) showed how deeply he felt the needs of the people. Although he was tough and outspoken (3:9), he had a compassionate heart (9:8). This vision of judgment and death aroused the pathos of the prophet.

In response to Ezekiel's plea for mercy, God reminded him that there was a just and equitable basis for the punishment he had witnessed. Their sin (v. 9), literally "wickedness,"[35] was great, the land was filled with violence and bloodshed, and the city was filled with injustice. Therefore there would be no relaxation of judgment (v. 10).

The final phase of the vision of judgment and departure of God from the temple did include a message of hope that promised a restored remnant (11:13-25). The second vision of the judgment of apostate worshipers also closed with the announcement from the "man" in white, "I have

---

[33] This idea appears in 1 Pet 4:17, where judgment begins at the "house of God" (AV) or "family of God" (NIV). See also Fisch, *Ezekiel*, 49; Cooke, *Ezekiel*, 107.

[34] God's command expressed the total unfitness of the temple for his presence. See Zimmerli, *Ezekiel 1*, 248; Greenberg, *Ezekiel 1–20*, 177-78.

[35] The word עָוֹן denotes perverseness and crookedness. It is the prominent word for wicked conduct in the OT. See Fisch, *Ezekiel*, 49-50.

done as you commanded," that is, a remnant had been preserved.

### (3) Vision of the Departure of God's Glory (10:1-22)

Chapter 10 has many words, phrases, and ideas that parallel the vision of the glory of God in chap. 1 and some that parallel passages in chap. 8.[36] Chapter 10 is an expansion of the theme of the departure of God's glory introduced in 9:3. It also presents additional insights into the role of the cherubim in transporting and/or accompanying the glory of God. These creatures also helped the man in white in dispensing judgment on Jerusalem. This information moves beyond that of the vision of the "living creatures" of chap. 1.

Chapter 10 has four scenes. First, the man in white was commanded to take coals from between the cherubim (10:1-2). Second, the glory of God moved to the threshold and paused while fire purged the city (10:3-8). Third, the cherubim were described (10:9-17). Fourth, the glory of God moved to a position above the cherubim and with them to the east gate (10:18-22). H. Parunak has argued that the two-stage movement of the glory of God is the focus of two chiasms (see introductory comments to chap. 1) in chap. 10. The first stage is the center of a chiasm comprising vv. 1-7, marked by the repeated references to taking fire "from among the cherubim" in vv. 2 and 6-7. The second stage is the center of a chiasm comprising vv. 8-22, marked by descriptions of the cherubim in vv. 8-17 and 20-22.[37]

**[1]I looked, and I saw the likeness of a throne of sapphire above the expanse that was over the heads of the cherubim. [2]The LORD said to the man clothed in linen, "Go in among the wheels beneath the cherubim. Fill your hands with burning coals from among the cherubim and scatter them over the city." And as I watched, he went in.**

THE MAN IN WHITE (10:1-2). **10:1-2** Ezekiel reported that these creatures were the same he had seen in his first vision in 1:1-28 (cf.

---

[36] See, e.g., C. B. Houk ("The Final Redaction of Ezekiel 10," *JBL* [1990]: 42-47) for a chart of parallels. The differences, however, he explains by positing different authors. H. Parunak ("Literary Architecture" 66-67) counters that the differences result from different themes—chap. 1 of prophetic call and chap. 10 of judgment. For other comparisons of the two chapters, see D. Block, "Text and Emotion: A Study in the 'Corruptions' in Ezekiel's Inaugural Vision (Ezekiel 1:4-28)" *CBQ* 50 (1988): 440-42; Greenberg, *Ezekiel 1–20,* 198-99. There is no evidence that these chapters are not compositions of a single hand, even that of Ezekiel.

[37] Parunak, "Literary Architecture," 68-69.

10:15,20,22). There is, in fact, no introduction to the vision of chap. 10. Rather, v. 1 assumes the first vision by referring simply to "the expanse that was over the heads of the cherubim" (see 1:22-26), and v. 2 refers to "the wheels beneath the cherubim" as if they have been introduced before. The "living creatures" of that vision are identified here as "cherubim." Verses 9-17 give the details of their appearance.

The name "cherub" probably is from an Akkadian root, *karabu,* which means "intercede," "be gracious," or "bless."[38] The cherubim appear at various places in the Old Testament as servant/worshipers of God and guardians of his holiness. Their first appearance in Scripture was in Gen 3:24 guarding the way to the tree of life and presence of God in the garden of Eden. Second, cherubim were embroidered on the veil that separated the holy place from the holy of holies (Exod 36:35) in the tabernacle and later in the temple (1 Kgs 6:23-29). Thus the suitability of the heavenly chariot as "a surrogate dwelling place for the Lord during his absence from the temple."[39] Third, cherubim appeared inside the holy of holies. They were placed atop the ark (Exod 25:18-22; 37:7-9) as the guardians of God's throne (1 Sam 4:4; 2 Sam 6:2; Isa 37:16). Fourth, they were associated with the movement of God (1 Chr 28:18; Ps 104:3; Ezek 10:19). These same creatures also will appear in the new temple envisioned by Ezekiel in 41:18-20.[40] The creatures moved about with the aid of "wheels" with which they were closely associated. These wheels also are described in 1:15-21 in Ezekiel's opening vision.[41]

There were burning coals of fire between the cherubim (v. 2), a fact not mentioned in chap. 1. Ezekiel heard a voice instructing the man in white linen to take coals from between the cherubim and scatter them over Jerusalem. Some see this as a rite of purification; others see it as an act of judgment.[42] Both ideas are appropriate. Judgment from God is redemptive in its purpose, not purely punitive. His ultimate goal was the restora-

---

[38] See Cooke, *Ezekiel,* 112-14, for an extensive note on cherubim.

[39] Parunak, "Literary Architecture," 67.

[40] For details of the role of cherubim, see Cooke, *Ezekiel,* 113-14; Taylor, *Ezekiel,* 105; Wevers, *Ezekiel,* 87.

[41] Fisch, *Ezekiel,* 51; May, "Ezekiel," 114; the אוֹפַנִּים of 1:16 are here called גַּלְגַּל, "rotating wheels." This suggests that the wheels may have been in constant motion. The whole picture suggests a vehicle that floats above the ground since we are told that the cherubim and the wheels "rose upward" (v. 15). If this is true, the "rotating" or "whirling" wheels (v. 13) may have been more like gyroscopes in constant motion than wheels for traversing the surface of the ground.

[42] Greenberg, *Ezekiel 1-20,* 181; see also Introduction, "God's Redemptive Purpose." The word זָרַק, "scatter," is used mostly in priestly lustrations although it does appear in nonsacramental texts as well.

tion of the nation through a purified remnant.

**³Now the cherubim were standing on the south side of the temple when the man went in, and a cloud filled the inner court. ⁴Then the glory of the Lord rose from above the cherubim and moved to the threshold of the temple. The cloud filled the temple, and the court was full of the radiance of the glory of the Lord. ⁵The sound of the wings of the cherubim could be heard as far away as the outer court, like the voice of God Almighty when he speaks.**

**⁶When the Lord commanded the man in linen, "Take fire from among the wheels, from among the cherubim," the man went in and stood beside a wheel. ⁷Then one of the cherubim reached out his hand to the fire that was among them. He took up some of it and put it into the hands of the man in linen, who took it and went out. ⁸(Under the wings of the cherubim could be seen what looked like the hands of a man.)**

THE GLORY OF GOD (10:3-8).   **10:3-8**   The "man" in white linen was first introduced in 9:2. He was an angel associated with the judgment of Jerusalem. The cherubim were stationed on the south side of the temple, which would be to the left when facing the sanctuary. When the "man" in white entered, the glory of God rose and moved over the cherubim. At that point their wings made a loud sound and a cloud filled the sanctuary. One cherub gave live coals to the "man," who then departed. Craigie sees two new perspectives added by these verses. First, the judgment of God cannot be distinguished from the glory of God. The presence of the glory of God demands purity and purging to produce holiness. Fire represented this twofold character of purification and purging by God. The same fire from God that purified the mouth of Isaiah (Isa 6:6) and brought destruction to Sodom and Gomorrah (Gen 19:24) would now purge the city in judgment. Second, judgment of the temple and Jerusalem was marked by the departure of God. The most severe aspect of God's judgment was his absence from among his people. Of course, God's presence had never been confined to the temple. Rather, the temple was where he made himself known in blessing and received the worship of his people (see 1 Kgs 8:27-53).⁴³

---

⁴³ "Glory" is the Heb. כָּבוֹד, which is from the root כָּבֵד, "to be heavy." Its meaning is "to give weight to" or "to honor" and was therefore associated with giving God the honor due him. The word also was used to denote the shining presence of God as in Exod 33:18. The departure of the glory meant the removal of God's visible presence. His glory was the manifestation of his presence, which allowed a human response of confession, worship, and praise. To remove God's glory was an act of judgment signaling the loss of blessings. See "Glory," *HBD*, 557, and Craigie, *Ezekiel*, 70-71.

⁹I looked, and I saw beside the cherubim four wheels, one beside each of the cherubim; the wheels sparkled like chrysolite. ¹⁰As for their appearance, the four of them looked alike; each was like a wheel intersecting a wheel. ¹¹As they moved, they would go in any one of the four directions the cherubim faced; the wheels did not turn about as the cherubim went. The cherubim went in whatever direction the head faced, without turning as they went. ¹²Their entire bodies, including their backs, their hands and their wings, were completely full of eyes, as were their four wheels. ¹³I heard the wheels being called "the whirling wheels." ¹⁴Each of the cherubim had four faces: One face was that of a cherub, the second the face of a man, the third the face of a lion, and the fourth the face of an eagle.

¹⁵Then the cherubim rose upward. These were the living creatures I had seen by the Kebar River. ¹⁶When the cherubim moved, the wheels beside them moved; and when the cherubim spread their wings to rise from the ground, the wheels did not leave their side. ¹⁷When the cherubim stood still, they also stood still; and when the cherubim rose, they rose with them, because the spirit of the living creatures was in them.

THE CHERUBIM (10:9-17).   **10:9-17**   Comparison of the first description of the living creatures in 1:5-25 and the cherubim of 10:1-20 confirms that they were the same spirit beings.[44] Yet there are several differences in the two visions. The most obvious one is the new designation "cherubim" for the "living creatures" of chap. 1 (cp. 10:1 and 1:22). Also, according to 10:2 the cherubim had burning coals of fire between them, a fact not stated in chap. 1 (but see 1:13). Chapter 10 contains a vision of judgment, and the coals represent the purging, purifying fire of judgment.[45]

Furthermore, the sound of the wings was compared to "rushing waters" in the earlier vision (1:24), but here the comparison is only to God's voice (10:5). It is also identified as coming from the inner court, heard by Ezekiel in the outer court. The sound of the wings suggested readiness to move with the glory of God, since the theme of the chapter is the departure of the glory from the temple. This is also stressed by the constant motion of the "wheels" (1:15-16), called "whirling wheels" in 10:13.[46]

A more striking difference in the two visions is that in 1:18 only the wheels were to be "full of eyes all around," whereas in 10:12 he saw that the creatures themselves also were "completely full of eyes" (the Heb. in

---

[44] Fisch, *Ezekiel*, 50. On the features of the cherubim, see Ezek 1.

[45] Greenberg, *Ezekiel 1–20*, 181; cf. Gen 19:24.

[46] A new word for "wheels" occurs in chap. 10. In chap. 1 it was אוֹפַן/אוֹפַנִּים (1:15-16,19-21; 3:13); in 10:2,6a,13b they are גַּלְגַּל (see also 23:24; 26:10), meaning "wheelworks" or "rotating/whirling wheels." אוֹפַן/אוֹפַנִּים occurs again in 10:6b,9,10,12,13a,16.

the two phrases is almost identical[47]). The close connection, however, between the cherubim and the wheels (10:16-17; 1:19-21) makes such variation less significant than it appears at first. The "eyes" were a reminder of the omniscience of God. Judgment, which was to include the removal of God's glory by the wheels, was based on his omniscience. He sees all things and knows all things.

The omniscience and omnipresence of God are divine characteristics that should be remembered in the face of judgment. One day every individual will stand before a holy and righteous God who sees and knows all things. Everyone will give an account for all of life (cf. Rom 14:10-12; 2 Cor 5:10). God also is omnipotent. Because he is all-powerful, there is no court of higher appeal. When he evaluates our lives both now and in the final judgment, his word is final. This should be a motivation for righteousness.

A marked addition to the vision in chap. 10 is the man in white linen who received from one of the cherubim the coals that were to be scattered over Jerusalem (10:2,6). He is thus associated with judgment, which was not in view in chap. 1. In chap. 9 he was associated with judgment by marking those who were exempt from destruction (9:4).

None of these differences contradict information given in chap. 1. All involve only added information related to the purpose of their assignment in chap. 10, which centered on judgment. D. Block also argues that the grammar of chap. 10, which is much tamer than that of chap. 1, suggests that Ezekiel was not as startled and overcome by this second exposure to the chariot vision, which occurred over a year after the first. This factor also allowed his description here to be more precise.[48]

The difference in the identity of the four faces is one for which there is no conclusive explanation. In 1:10 the faces were those of a man, a lion, an ox, and an eagle. In 10:14 the ox face is replaced by that of a cherub, which is listed first. One of Ezekiel's observations about the creatures in the first vision, their legs/feet being like those of a calf, also is not found in chap. 10. Nevertheless, chap. 10 makes clear that the creatures in the two visions were the same. Rabbinic interpreters explained that the ox face was removed at Ezekiel's request because he associated it with the golden calf of Exod 32.[49] H. Parunak, however, suggests that in the vision shown to Ezekiel by the Kebar River the cherubim took the form of the Mesopotamian winged bull rather than the winged lion more common in

---

[47] Ezek 1:18 has מְלֵאֹת עֵינַיִם סָבִיב; 10:12 has מְלֵאִים עֵינַיִם סָבִיב.

[48] Block, "Text and Emotion," 431-33.

[49] Fisch, *Ezekiel*, 54.

the west Semitic world. "The substitution of an ox-cherub for the expected sphinx-cherub may be one more way of emphasizing that though the Lord has sent his people into captivity, he follows them there—even adopting Mesopotamian motifs for his chariot!" In chap. 10 the concern is rather to connect the vision with the motifs of the temple.[50]

**[18]Then the glory of the Lord departed from over the threshold of the temple and stopped above the cherubim. [19]While I watched, the cherubim spread their wings and rose from the ground, and as they went, the wheels went with them. They stopped at the entrance to the east gate of the Lord's house, and the glory of the God of Israel was above them.**

**[20]These were the living creatures I had seen beneath the God of Israel by the Kebar River, and I realized that they were cherubim. [21]Each had four faces and four wings, and under their wings was what looked like the hands of a man. [22]Their faces had the same appearance as those I had seen by the Kebar River. Each one went straight ahead.**

THE GLORY OF GOD AND THE CHERUBIM (10:18-22). **10:18-22** The glory, having moved from above the ark of the covenant to the threshold of the temple in 10:4, now moved from the threshold to the cherubim and then to the east gate (vv. 18-19). This would have been the entrance directly in front of the temple that went out into the Kidron Valley. This valley separated the temple mount from the Mount of Olives. This move to the east gate anticipated the departure from the temple complex and from the city that followed in 11:22-23.[51]

God withdraws from unholy worship. We cannot come before the Lord any time and any way we choose. God demands holiness of those who would approach him (Lev 10:1-7; 20:3-7; Ps 15:1-5). God is long-suffering with us as he was with Israel, but he ultimately withdraws when his call for righteousness is ignored (Ezek 11:4-12).

---

[50] Parunak, "Literary Architecture," 66-67.

[51] The east gate, today called the Golden Gate, is a significant site in the eschatology of Judaism, Islam, and Christianity. It is the site of final judgment for Jews (Zech 14:1-9) and Moslems; for Christians and Jews it is where the Messiah will enter the city (Ezek 44:1-3). Jesus went to the mountain east of the city, the Mount of Olives, and ascended to the Father (Acts 1:9-12). At the second coming he will return to the same place. When Ezekiel saw the cherubim rise and moved to the east gate, it was apparently at this point that he realized they were the same creatures he had seen in his first vision by the river Kebar (vv. 15,20-22).

## VISIONS OF EZEKIEL 1; 8–10 COMPARED

| EZEKIEL 8–10 | EZEKIEL 1 |
|---|---|
| 8:1   In the sixth year, in the sixth month on the fifth day, while I was sitting in my house and the elders of Judah were sitting before me, the hand of the Sovereign LORD came upon me there. | 1:2   On the fifth of the month—it was the fifth year of the exile of King Jehoiachin—<br>1:3   the word of the LORD came to Ezekiel the priest, the son of Buzi, by the Kebar River in the land of the Babylonians. There the hand of the LORD was upon him. |
| | 1:4   I looked, and I saw a windstorm coming out of the north—an immense cloud with flashing lightning and surrounded by brilliant light. The center of the fire looked like glowing metal,<br>1:5   and in the fire was what looked like four living creatures. In appearance their form was that of a man, |
| 8:2   I looked, and I saw a figure like that of a man. From what appeared to be his waist down he was like fire, and from there up his appearance was as bright as glowing metal. | 1:26b   and high above on the throne was a figure like that of a man.<br>1:27   I saw that from what appeared to be his waist up he looked like glowing metal, as if full of fire, and that from there down he looked like fire; and brilliant light surrounded him. |
| 8:3   He stretched out what looked like a hand and took me by the hair of my head. The Spirit lifted me up between earth and heaven and in visions of God he took me to Jerusalem, to the entrance to the north gate of the inner court, where the idol that provokes to jealousy stood. | |
| 8:4   And there before me was the glory of the God of Israel, as in the vision I had seen in the plain. | 1:28   Like the appearance of a rainbow in the clouds on a rainy day, so was the radiance around him. This was the appearance of the likeness of the glory of the LORD. When I saw it, I fell facedown, and I heard the voice of one speaking. |
| 10:1   I looked, and I saw the likeness of a throne of sapphire above the expanse that was over the heads of the cherubim. | 1:22   Spread out above the heads of the living creatures was what looked like an expanse, sparkling like ice, and awesome.<br>1:26a Above the expanse over their heads was what looked like a throne of sapphire, |
| | 1:25   Then there came a voice from above the expanse over their heads as they stood with lowered wings. |

| EZEKIEL 8–10 | EZEKIEL 1 |
|---|---|
| 10:2   The LORD said to the man clothed in linen, "Go in among the wheels beneath the cherubim. Fill your hands with burning coals from among the cherubim and scatter them over the city." And as I watched, he went in. | 1:13   The appearance of the living creatures was like burning coals of fire or like torches. Fire moved back and forth among the creatures; it was bright, and lightning flashed out of it.<br>1:14   The creatures sped back and forth like flashes of lightning. |
| 10:3   Now the cherubim were standing on the south side of the temple when the man went in, and a cloud filled the inner court.<br>10:4   Then the glory of the LORD rose from above the cherubim and moved to the threshold of the temple. The cloud filled the temple, and the court was full of the radiance of the glory of the LORD. | |
| 10:5   The sound of the wings of the cherubim could be heard as far away as the outer court, like the voice of God Almighty when he speaks. | 1:23   Under the expanse their wings were stretched out one toward the other, and each had two wings covering its body.<br>1:24   When the creatures moved, I heard the sound of their wings, like the roar of rushing waters, like the voice of the Almighty, like the tumult of an army. When they stood still, they lowered their wings. |
| 10:6   When the LORD commanded the man in linen, "Take fire from among the wheels, from among the cherubim," the man went in and stood beside a wheel.<br>10:7   Then one of the cherubim reached out his hand to the fire that was among them. He took up some of it and put it into the hands of the man in linen, who took it and went out. | |
| | 1:7   Their legs were straight; their feet were like those of a calf and gleamed like burnished bronze. |
| 10:8   (Under the wings of the cherubim could be seen what looked like the hands of a man.) | 1:8   Under their wings on their four sides they had the hands of a man. All four of them had faces and wings, |
| 10:9   I looked, and I saw beside the cherubim four wheels, one beside each of the cherubim; the wheels sparkled like chrysolite.<br>10:10   As for their appearance, the four of them looked alike; each was like a wheel intersecting a wheel. | 1:15   As I looked at the living creatures, I saw a wheel on the ground beside each creature with its four faces.<br>1:16   This was the appearance and structure of the wheels: They sparkled like chrysolite, and all four looked alike. Each appeared to be made like a wheel intersecting a wheel. |

| EZEKIEL 8–10 | EZEKIEL 1 |
|---|---|
| 10:11 As they moved, they would go in any one of the four directions the cherubim faced; the wheels did not turn about as the cherubim went. The cherubim went in whatever direction the head faced, without turning as they went.<br>10:12 Their entire bodies, including their backs, their hands and their wings, were completely full of eyes, as were their four wheels. | 1:17 As they moved, they would go in any one of the four directions the creatures faced; the wheels did not turn about as the creatures went.<br>1:18 Their rims were high and awesome, and all four rims were full of eyes all around. |
| 10:13 I heard the wheels being called "the whirling wheels." | |
| 10:14 Each of the cherubim had four faces: One face was that of a cherub, the second the face of a man, the third the face of a lion, and the fourth the face of an eagle. | 1:6 but each of them had four faces and four wings.<br>1:10 Their faces looked like this: Each of the four had the face of a man, and on the right side each had the face of a lion, and on the left the face of an ox; each also had the face of an eagle. |
| | 1:11 Such were their faces. Their wings were spread out upward; each had two wings, one touching the wing of another creature on either side, and two wings covering its body.<br>1:12 Each one went straight ahead. Wherever the spirit would go, they would go, without turning as they went. |
| 10:15 Then the cherubim rose upward. These were the living creatures I had seen by the Kebar River. | |
| 10:16 When the cherubim moved, the wheels beside them moved; and when the cherubim spread their wings to rise from the ground, the wheels did not leave their side. | 1:19 When the living creatures moved, the wheels beside them moved; and when the living creatures rose from the ground, the wheels also rose. |
| 10:17 When the cherubim stood still, they also stood still; and when the cherubim rose, they rose with them, because the spirit of the living creatures was in them. | 1:20 Wherever the spirit would go, they would go, and the wheels would rise along with them, because the spirit of the living creatures was in the wheels.<br>1:21 When the creatures moved, they also moved; when the creatures stood still, they also stood still; and when the creatures rose from the ground, the wheels rose along with them, because the spirit of the living creatures was in the wheels. |

| EZEKIEL 8–10 | EZEKIEL 1 |
|---|---|
| 10:18   Then the glory of the LORD departed from over the threshold of the temple and stopped above the cherubim.<br>10:19   While I watched, the cherubim spread their wings and rose from the ground, and as they went, the wheels went with them. They stopped at the entrance to the east gate of the LORD'S house, and the glory of the God of Israel was above them.<br>10:20   These were the living creatures I had seen beneath the God of Israel by the Kebar River, and I realized that they were cherubim. | |
| 10:21   Each had four faces and four wings, and under their wings was what looked like the hands of a man. | 1:6   but each of them had four faces and four wings.<br>1:8   Under their wings on their four sides they had the hands of a man. All four of them had faces and wings, |
| 10:22   Their faces had the same appearance as those I had seen by the Kebar River. Each one went straight ahead. | 1:9   and their wings touched one another. Each one went straight ahead; they did not turn as they moved. |

### (4) *Vision of Judgment, Restoration, and Departure of God's Glory from Jerusalem (11:1-25)*

The vision of the pollution of the temple that began in chap. 8 concluded with a final view of judgment, a glimmer of hope, and the departure of God from his sanctuary, the city, and the land. Verse 5 of this section contains one of the most explicit statements of Ezekiel's divine inspiration (cf. 2:2; 3:24; 13:1-3). This concluding vision may be divided into three parts. First is the judgment of Jerusalem, its leaders, and inhabitants (11:1-13). Second is a glimmer of hope in the darkest hour (11:14-21). Third, the glory of God departs (11:22-25).

[1]Then the Spirit lifted me up and brought me to the gate of the house of the LORD that faces east. There at the entrance to the gate were twenty-five men, and I saw among them Jaazaniah son of Azzur and Pelatiah son of Benaiah, leaders of the people. [2]The LORD said to me, "Son of man, these are the men who are plotting evil and giving wicked advice in this city. [3]They say, 'Will it not soon be time to build houses? This city is a cooking pot, and we are the meat.' [4]Therefore prophesy against them; prophesy, son of man."

[5]Then the Spirit of the LORD came upon me, and he told me to say: "This is what the LORD says: That is what you are saying, O house of Israel, but I

know what is going through your mind. ⁶You have killed many people in this city and filled its streets with the dead.

⁷"Therefore this is what the Sovereign LORD says: The bodies you have thrown there are the meat and this city is the pot, but I will drive you out of it. ⁸You fear the sword, and the sword is what I will bring against you, declares the Sovereign LORD. ⁹I will drive you out of the city and hand you over to foreigners and inflict punishment on you. ¹⁰You will fall by the sword, and I will execute judgment on you at the borders of Israel. Then you will know that I am the LORD. ¹¹This city will not be a pot for you, nor will you be the meat in it; I will execute judgment on you at the borders of Israel. ¹²And you will know that I am the LORD, for you have not followed my decrees or kept my laws but have conformed to the standards of the nations around you."

¹³Now as I was prophesying, Pelatiah son of Benaiah died. Then I fell face-down and cried out in a loud voice, "Ah, Sovereign LORD! Will you completely destroy the remnant of Israel?"

JUDGMENT OF JERUSALEM (11:1-13). **11:1-3** Ezekiel returned in a vision to the east gate of the temple near where he saw twenty-five men, apparently the same leaders he saw in 8:16. Only two were named, Jaazaniah, the son of Azzur (a different Jaazaniah from 8:11), and Pelatiah, son of Benaiah (v. 1). There is nothing known of these men other than that they were leaders in Jerusalem. This meant they were state officials responsible for some facet of governing the populace. Recent archaeological discoveries in the excavations of the city of David have yielded over two hundred and fifty bullae (clay seals used on official documents) from the period just prior to the fall of Jerusalem. They were preserved because they were burned when the building in which they were housed was destroyed, probably in the destruction of 586 B.C. Both the names Jaazaniah and Pelatiah appeared in this archive of seals of royal officials. In addition to these, the name Jeremiah and the seal of Jeremiah's scribe, Baruch, the son of Neriah, were found.[52]

Ezekiel was told these men were "plotting evil" and giving "wicked advice" in Jerusalem (v. 2). As leaders they were responsible for the moral, social, and spiritual direction of the people. God gave Ezekiel two illustrations of their bad counsel. First, "Will it not soon be time to build houses?" (v. 3). As translated in the NIV the phrase suggests that the cri-

---

[52] Avigad, *Hebrew Bullae;* see his "Conclusions" for date (p. 130) and for reference to Baruch (pp. 129-30). Seals of the officials named are Jaazaniah (p. 102) and Pelatiah (pp. 67, 72, 79-80, 90). There seems to have been more than one Pelatiah, one of the sons of Hoshea, and Pelatiah, son of Heleq (pp. 94-96). Benaiah, the name of Pelatiah's father, appeared on one seal (p. 45). The name "Jeremiah" also was found, but this probably was not the prophet (p. 64). See also T. Schneider, "Six Biblical Signatures," *BAR* XVII, 4 (1991): 26-33.

sis would soon pass and life would return to normal. It is also possible that this was a denial of the crisis and should be translated, "The time (of destruction) is not near; let us build houses." Another possibility is that it is a reference to house-building in the exile. Thus the phrase would mean, "The time is not near to build houses (in exile)." Still another interpretation is that it may have been a declaration of defiance against Babylon. The meaning would be, "It is not time to build houses (but time to prepare for battle)." Of the possible interpretations this last one seems to fit the context best.[53]

The second phrase, "This city is a cooking pot, and we are the meat" (v. 3), is equally enigmatic. At face value it seems to be a reference to the judgment of Judah, but the context suggests the opposite. Most interpreters agree that the cooking pot, a clay vessel for cooking food, was used to protect the choice meats from the fire while being prepared.[54] The city, with its walls and fortifications, was the protection of the people from the "fire" of Babylon's armies. This interpretation fits the statement in v. 11 that the "city will not be a pot for you, nor will you be the meat in it." If true, this meant they were relying on the inviolability and military fortifications of Jerusalem for their security and protection. This was a condemnation of the misplaced trust because Judah should have relied on God. We are to trust God and not our own ability or understanding (11:1-3; cf. Prov 3:5-7). He will direct our lives and give us the keys for knowing and doing his will (Rom 12:1-8).[55]

**11:4-13** The Lord's response and command to Ezekiel was literally, "Therefore, prophesy, prophesy against them, O Son of man." The verb form (related to *nābîʾ*, "prophet") was used twice for emphasis and to stress the urgency of the assignment.

God knew what the leaders were thinking and saying (v. 5). The "saying" in vv. 3 and 5 may have been internal, defined by the phrase following in v. 5 translated, "What is going through your mind."[56] The clause

---

[53] Compare Zimmerli, *Ezekiel 1*, 258; Fisch, *Ezekiel*, 57; Taylor, *Ezekiel*, 109.

[54] See Eichrodt, *Ezekiel*, 136; Fisch, *Ezekiel*, 57; Feinberg, *Ezekiel*, 65; Cooke, *Ezekiel*, 122.

[55] While recognizing that any interpretation here is conjecture, D. Stuart (*Ezekiel*, 101) suggests that the two sayings mean that "the people could go ahead and build, that is, make long-term plans (cf. Jer 32:6-15) because they belonged in Jerusalem like meat in a cooking pot whereas the exiles were like the entrails, hooves, etc. of an animal—discarded as unfit to go into the pot for cooking."

[56] The verb אָמַר can mean "say in the heart" (BDB, 56). The word for "mind" is רוּחַ. The word וּמַעֲלוֹת is a hapax, whose meaning is clear from the verb עלה ("go/come up"; cf. 20:32; 38:10). See D. Block, "The Prophet of the Spirit: The Use of *rwḥ* in Ezekiel," *JETS* 32 (1989): 45.

that contains that phrase, interpreted by the NIV as contrastive, "but I know," may rather be parenthetical or explanatory. As Brownlee translates the sentence, "Thus you think, O Israel, for the thoughts of your mind I know!" (see also KJV, NKJV, NRSV, NASB, REB, NJB).[57] The Lord knows our thoughts, whether good or bad, conscious or unconscious, even if we can no longer remember them (cf. Ps 139:1-6; Dan 2:30; Acts 1:24).

In defying God's judgment they had already been responsible for the death of many people.[58] In the coming judgment only the slain would be the meat that would remain in the pot, that is, Jerusalem (v. 7). As for the leaders, the city would not be their protection but the site of their execution. God would use the sword of Babylon (v. 8) as his chastening instrument. He would drive his people from Jerusalem and turn them over to their captors for punishment (v. 9).

Judgment would fall on the borders of the land (vv. 10-11), a possible allusion to the massacre at Riblah in Hamath (2 Kgs 25:18-24).[59] The city would not be a pot of protection for them (v. 11) but would be an object of God's wrath. Because of these punishments the people would know Yahweh is God (v. 12) and that it was foolish for God's people to pattern their values and behavior after the nations (cf. 1 Sam 8:5; Rom 12:2).

When Ezekiel prophesied, Pelatiah, the son of Benaiah, one of the leaders, died (v. 13). The prophet's reaction was compassionate, and he offered a prayer of intercession for those receiving judgment. There was no explanation why Pelatiah's death was such an ominous sign. He doubtless was a figure of importance in the city of Jerusalem. The meaning of the name "Pelatiah" is "Yahweh rescues." Perhaps Ezekiel felt that Pelatiah's sudden death signaled a decision by God that there would be no remnant, hence his cry, "Will you completely destroy the remnant of Israel?" (v. 13).[60]

**[14]The word of the LORD came to me: [15]"Son of man, your brothers—your brothers who are your blood relatives and the whole house of Israel—are those of whom the people of Jerusalem have said, 'They are far away from**

---

[57] W. H. Brownlee, *Ezekiel 1–19* (Waco: Word, 1986), 154; also Greenberg, *Ezekiel 1–20*, 185.

[58] Stuart (*Ezekiel,* 101) understands both vv. 6 and 7 as predictive of future slaying connected with God's judgment.

[59] Fisch, *Ezekiel,* 59. Riblah in the land of Hamath was on the frontier of the Northern Kingdom (Jer 52:24-26).

[60] R. M. Hals, *Ezekiel,* FOTL (Grand Rapids: Eerdmans, 1989), 67; see 6:12 and note on Diblah as Riblah.

the Lord; this land was given to us as our possession.'

16"Therefore say: 'This is what the Sovereign LORD says: Although I sent them far away among the nations and scattered them among the countries, yet for a little while I have been a sanctuary for them in the countries where they have gone.'

17"Therefore say: 'This is what the Sovereign LORD says: I will gather you from the nations and bring you back from the countries where you have been scattered, and I will give you back the land of Israel again.'

18"They will return to it and remove all its vile images and detestable idols. 19I will give them an undivided heart and put a new spirit in them; I will remove from them their heart of stone and give them a heart of flesh. 20Then they will follow my decrees and be careful to keep my laws. They will be my people, and I will be their God. 21But as for those whose hearts are devoted to their vile images and detestable idols, I will bring down on their own heads what they have done, declares the Sovereign LORD."

GLIMMER OF HOPE (11:14-21). **11:14-16** In 597 B.C., when Ezekiel and others were taken to Babylon, not everyone was taken captive. Those left in Jerusalem after 597 B.C. concluded that it was the exiles who were under judgment and thus the land belonged to those who remained (vv. 14-15). They invoked the rite to redeem property granted under Levitical law. The law provided for such redemption of property within family and tribal groups in association with the Jubilee Year (Lev 25:25-35).

But God did not totally abandon the exiles in Babylon. He was a "sanctuary" to them (v. 16). God wanted these people, who suddenly were without the temple as a place of worship, to learn to worship him in spirit and truth.[61] Also, God promised that even though Israel would be taken captive, a remnant would return and once again possess the land.

**11:17-21** In a message anticipating those of chaps. 34–36, especially 36:24-28, the Lord promised through Ezekiel a physical return to the land of those Jews scattered in the exile and dispersion (v. 17). However, the promise involved more than a mere physical presence in the land. There would also be sweeping spiritual reforms and a general spiritual revival. The returnees would remove all the "vile images" and "detestable idols," both phrases translating Hebrew words meaning "something abominable/

---

[61] Zimmerli, *Ezekiel 1*, 262; May, "Ezekiel," 122. The Targums interpret this as a "little sanctuary," taking it to be an allusion to the synagogue; the AV also has "little sanctuary," but the NIV correctly reflects the Heb. text. The idea that worship of God was the sanctuary suggests the same lesson Jesus imparted in his encounter with the Samaritan woman in John 4:1-42. She raised the dispute over which was the true sanctuary, Jerusalem or Samaria. By his response Jesus showed her that worship of God was not tied to a sanctuary. God is a Spirit and must be worshiped in spirit and truth (John 4:24).

detestable" (v. 18; cf. 5:11 and 7:20, where the same terms are used).[62] Such deep and widespread revival would be driven by Yahweh's gift of a new heart and a new spirit. The heart was considered the center of human reason and volition, what leads someone to reject one path and choose another (cf. Exod 14:5; 1 Sam 14:7; 27:1; 2 Sam 7:3).[63] The new heart would be "undivided" (lit. "one heart," v. 19; cf. 36:26; Jer 32:39). Israel had attempted to follow both the Lord and idols (cf. 1 Kgs 11:4; 15:3,14; 2 Kgs 20:3), an ill-considered, aimless course that leads nowhere but to destruction (cf. Hos 4:11, where "understanding" is lit. "heart," and Hos 7:11, where "senseless" is "without heart").[64] Henceforth they would follow only the Lord in singlehearted devotion, loving and serving him with *all* their heart, obeying him completely and unconditionally (Deut 6:4-5; 10:12; 1 Kgs 8:61; Ps 86:11; Jer 3:10; Joel 2:12).[65]

The "new spirit" the Lord promises also seems to refer to a renovation of Israel's mental processes, which had become perverse ("mind" in v. 5 translates *rûah*). The parallel with "heart" would support this interpretation, as would the parallel in Ps 51:10[Heb. 12] between a "pure heart" and a "steadfast spirit."[66] D. Block notes, however, that in 36:26-27 the new spirit is associated with God's Spirit, which he promises to put in Israel; thus there may be an intentional ambiguity in the use of the term.[67]

---

[62] The first word is שִׁקּוּץ, which is always associated with idolatry (e.g., Jer 16:18; Dan 9:27; 12:11; Hos 9:10; 2 Chr 15:8). The related verb שָׁקַץ ("detest, contaminate") is used in Lev 11:11,13,43; 20:25 of unclean animals and those who eat them. See *TWOT*, 955. The second word is תּוֹעֵבָה (rendered "abomination" in KJV), related to the verb תָּעַב ("loathe/exclude"; *hiphil*, "commit abominations"). Some of the practices labeled "abominations" are homosexuality, idolatry, human sacrifice, eating or sacrificing unclean animals, occult worship, dishonesty, and prostitution (see Lev 18:22-30; 20:13; Deut 7:25; 12:31; 14:3-8; 17:1; 18:9-14; 25:13-16; 1 Kgs 14:24; Prov 6:16-19). It is often used as here as a synonym for "idol" (e.g., Deut 7:26; Isa 44:19; 2 Kgs 23:13).

[63] H. W. Wolff says that "the Israelite finds it difficult to distinguish linguistically between 'perceiving' and 'choosing,' between 'hearing' and 'obeying'" (*Anthropology of the Old Testament* [Philadelphia: Fortress, 1974], 51).

[64] Ibid., 46-55.

[65] Perhaps this promise of singlehearted devotion suggests the ultimate integration of will and conscience so that such struggles as Paul described in Rom 7:7-25 will be a thing of the past (cf. 1 Sam 24:6; Ps 51:10). It could be argued as well that Israel's heart had been divided in that they pretended to serve Yahweh while really following idols. Block ("Prophet of the Spirit," 46) notes that Ps 12:3[Eng., 2] describes flattery as speaking בְּלֵב וָלֵב ("with heart and heart"). See also 1 Chr 12:34[Eng., 33].

[66] M. Tate (*Psalms 51–100*, WBC [Dallas: Word, 1990], 22) says, "The spirit of a person has much the same meaning as heart, and indeed seems to be a synonym in v. 12." Note also Van Groningen (*Messianic Revelation*, 750): "The spirit in this context refers to a person's spiriual life, mindset, desires, and impulses."

[67] Block, "Prophet of the Spirit," 45-46.

The change from a "heart of stone" to a "heart of flesh" (v. 19) is also promised in 36:26. A hard heart is stubborn and unresponsive to God (Exod 4:21, etc.). In 2 Chr 34:27 the Lord blessed King Josiah because unlike his predecessors, his "heart was 'soft' ["responsive"] and [he] humbled [himself] before God." After his encounter with David, Nabal's heart is said to have "failed him, and he became like a stone." Ten days later he died (1 Sam 25:37-38). He seems to have been stricken with paralysis, perhaps due to a stroke. H. W. Wolff applies the sense to Ezek 11:19-20; 36:26-27: "The heart of stone is the dead heart . . . which is unreceptive and makes all the limbs incapable of action. The heart of flesh is the living heart, full of insight, which is at the same time ready for new action. The new *rūaḥ* brings to the perception and will of the heart the new vital power to hold on steadfastly in willing obedience."[68]

Ezekiel saw a new day when God's covenant people would again be in the land, devoted only to the Lord and enjoying fellowship with him (v. 20; cf. 14:11 and note there). After the exile when many Jews returned to a restored province of Judah in fulfillment of prophecy (Ezra 1:1), they were careful to avoid idolatry (Ezra 4:1-3; 6:19-21; Neh 8–10). Nevertheless, their obedience was not complete (Ezra 9:1-2,10-15; 10:15,44; Neh 5:1-9; 13:7-29), nor was their experience of promised blessings (Ezra 9:8-9; Neh 9:32-37).[69] Thus the radical spiritual transformation of the people and the associated physical blessings promised in this and other prophecies of the new covenant (Jer 31:31-34; Ezek 34:20-31; 36:24-38; 37:15-28) await fulfillment in a future messianic age.[70] Such promises, however, would be only for those who would receive the new heart and spirit by faith (18:31). Those who refused would be judged and eliminated (11:21). The remnant would be made up of those who repented and returned to the standard of the single heart (cf. 34:17-22). Single-hearted devotion is what God expects from us. Whenever we fail to give him our single-hearted commitment, we invite the chastening of God.[71]

---

[68] Wolff, *Anthropology of the Old Testament,* 29, 40-41, 54. Van Groningen (*Messianic Revelation,* 750) explains, "Persons with a heart of stone are spiritually dead, following their own lusts and passions."

[69] See J. G. McConville, "Ezra-Nehemiah and the Fulfillment of Prophecy," *VT* 36 (1986): 205-24.

[70] G. Van Groningen, *Messianic Revelation in the Old Testament* (Grand Rapids: Baker, 1990), 751. The question of whether 11:14-21 is a messianic prophecy is considered by Van Gronigen, who concluded that it is not messianic in the narrow sense of identifying a royal person. Nevertheless, it does present some of the plans and purposes that will ultimately be achieved in the messianic age to come.

[71] This single-minded devotion to God was the seedbed of the NT standard of one heart (mind) totally dedicated to God (Matt 4:10; 6:24-34; Eph 6:5; Col 3:22).

**22**Then the cherubim, with the wheels beside them, spread their wings, and the glory of the God of Israel was above them. **23**The glory of the LORD went up from within the city and stopped above the mountain east of it. **24**The Spirit lifted me up and brought me to the exiles in Babylonia in the vision given by the Spirit of God.

Then the vision I had seen went up from me, **25**and I told the exiles everything the LORD had shown me.

DEPARTURE OF GOD'S GLORY (11:22-25). **11:22-25** When the details of this vision were completed, the prophet witnessed the departure of the glory of God from the sanctuary and the city to the mountains east of Jerusalem, which is the Mount of Olives (vv. 22-23). Later he would witness the return of the glory from the same direction (43:1-4). According to rabbinic tradition, the glory of God tarried on the Mount of Olives for three and a half years awaiting some sign of repentance and when there was none, ultimately departed.[72]

The departure of the glory of God from the Mount of Olives was the final step in the judgment process. The removal of his blessing signaled the end of his longsuffering with a disobedient and rebellious people. God had exhausted every means of soliciting repentance from the people. Therefore he removed the glory that was the sign of his presence so that judgment might run its full course. The absence of the glory signaled the last stage in the process of reprobation of the self-willed people of the nation.

Romans 1, especially vv. 18-32, presents a similar overview of those who have chosen their own idols and set their self-will against the will of God and the word of God. In rejecting his word and his will, they have rejected him; so he departed, leaving them to their own devices, a process described in Rom 1:24ff. as reprobation (i.e., "God gave them over"). The end result is ever the same as it was for the nation of Ezekiel's day. The wages of sin is judgment and death (Rom 1:32; 3:23; 6:23).

Ezekiel returned to Babylon by the Spirit after the departure of the glory of God (v. 24; cf. "the Spirit of the LORD" in 37:1). This chapter concludes the visions of the pollution of the temple that began in 8:1. The prophet's return in a vision to Babylon as he had departed (8:3) confirmed

---

[72] Fisch, *Ezekiel*, 62; see also Greenberg, *Ezekiel 1–20*, 191. Rabbinic sources trace steps of the movement of the glory (1) from one cherub on the ark to the other (Ezek 9:3 uses the singular cherub), (2) to the threshold of the temple (10:4), (3) back to the cherubim (10:18), (4) to the east gate (10:19), (5) to the court of the temple (10:4), (6) to the altar (Amos 9:1), (7) to the roof of the temple (Prov 21:9), (8) to the temple wall (Amos 7:7), (9) to the city (Mic 6:9), and (10) then to the Mount of Olives (11:23) for three and a half years (Greenberg, *Ezekiel 1–20*, 201).

that visit to Jerusalem was visionary rather than physical.[73] Upon his return from Jerusalem, Ezekiel told the exiles in Babylon everything the Lord had shown him (11:25).[74]

---

[73] Wevers, *Ezekiel,* 98. The word מַרְאָה ("vision") was a technical term for a visionary experience as in 8:3 and 43:3.

[74] Note the repetition in vv. 22-25 of references to the exiles, the Spirit, and the glory found in reverse order in 8:1-4, thus signifying the end of a section.

3. Prophecies of Judgments to Befall Judah and Jerusalem
    (12:1–19:14)
    (1) Prophecy of Jerusalem in Captivity (12:1-20)
    (2) Prophecy of the False Proverb (12:21-28)
    (3) Prophecy Condemning False Prophets and
        Prophetesses (13:1-23)
    (4) Prophecy of Judgment for Consulting Idols (14:1-11)
    (5) Prophecy of the Fourfold Judgment of Jerusalem
        (14:12-23)
    (6) Prophecy of Jerusalem: The Useless Vine (15:1-8)
    (7) Prophecy of Jerusalem: The Orphan Who Became a
        Harlot (16:1-63)
    (8) Prophecy (Parable) of the Eagles and the Vine (17:1-24)
    (9) Prophecy of Individual Responsibility (18:1-32)
    (10) Prophecy Lamenting Jerusalem's Leaders (19:1-14)

## 3. Prophecies of Judgments to Befall Judah and Jerusalem (12:1–19:14)

The prophecies of judgment in 12:1–19:14 are the third cycle of prophecies in 4:1–24:27. These messages focus on specific reasons for the fall of Judah that go beyond the obstinacy and pagan worship already condemned in 8:1–11:25. Ten separate prophecies are in this section, each of which begins with the introductory formula, "The word of the LORD came to me" (12:1,17,21; 13:1; 14:1,12; 15:1; 16:1; 17:1; 18:1; 19:1).

Seven reasons for the fall of Jerusalem are set forth in this section. These are listed in summary at the end of 19:1-14 and form a thematic outline of this section. God's purpose was to set forth the reasons for the judgment of Judah and fall of Jerusalem over against the people's charge that they were being judged for the sins of their forefathers (cf. 18:1-4). Ezekiel also gave eight additional reasons for the exile of the people to Babylon in his longest message of the book in 16:15-34.

### (1) Prophecy of Jerusalem in Captivity (12:1-20)

There are four parts to this message. First, the rebellious nature of the people is declared (12:1-2). Second, there is the drama of the packed luggage (12:3-7). Third, there is the explanation of the prophet's actions (12:8-16). Fourth, there is the drama of the nervous eater (12:17-20).

**¹The word of the LORD came to me: ²"Son of man, you are living among a rebellious people. They have eyes to see but do not see and ears to hear but do not hear, for they are a rebellious people.**

A REBELLIOUS PEOPLE (12:1-2).    **12:1-2**    Sinfulness blinded the people of Jerusalem; therefore consistently they refused to heed Ezekiel's warnings about impending judgment. God told Ezekiel about their obstinacy in his call vision in 2:3-8. The people rejected all the signs of the impending destruction of Judah and Jerusalem. The fall of the Northern Kingdom in 722 B.C. was a lesson in the consequences of national sin that Judah would not learn.

Equally representative of their blindness was the way Jeremiah's message had been largely ignored and at one point clearly rejected by Jehoiakim (Jer 36:1-32) and the priests (Jer 20:1-6). The rise of Babylon and the establishment of Judah as a vassal state under Jehoiakim in 605 B.C. and subsequently under Jehoiachin and Zedekiah in 597 B.C. failed to bring about any sign that the leaders or people were ready to listen to God's prophets. Instead they chose to remain rebellious and hardhearted as God had predicted.[1] Sin blinds the heart and mind. Like Samson, who could not see that his chosen path was leading to the loss of his ministry, the sinner does not see the ultimate consequences of sin that produces death and destruction (Judg 13–16; cf. Ezek 12:1-2; Isa 6:9-13; Rom 6:23).

**³"Therefore, son of man, pack your belongings for exile and in the daytime, as they watch, set out and go from where you are to another place. Perhaps they will understand, though they are a rebellious house. ⁴During the daytime, while they watch, bring out your belongings packed for exile. Then in the evening, while they are watching, go out like those who go into exile. ⁵While they watch, dig through the wall and take your belongings out through it. ⁶Put them on your shoulder as they are watching and carry them out at dusk. Cover your face so that you cannot see the land, for I have made you a sign to the house of Israel."**

**⁷So I did as I was commanded. During the day I brought out my things packed for exile. Then in the evening I dug through the wall with my hands. I**

---

[1] S. Fisch, *Ezekiel* (London: Soncino, 1950), 63; J. W. Wevers, *Ezekiel,* NCB (Grand Rapids: Eerdmans, 1969), 100. "Eyes to see" and "ears to hear" signified the rejection of Ezekiel's messages as expressed both in dramatic signs and in words.

took my belongings out at dusk, carrying them on my shoulders while they watched.

THE PACKED LUGGAGE (12:3-7).   **12:3-7**   In a manner not unlike the symbolic actions and dramatizations of chaps. 4–7, Ezekiel was given another role in God's series of instructive dramas. God told him to prepare baggage like one about to go into exile (vv. 3-4). An exile's baggage probably included only the barest essentials—a skin for water, a mat for sleeping, and a bowl for food.[2] Then in the evening of the same day, he was to depart, suggesting that the "night" of the exile would be a time of spiritual darkness for the nation. While the people watched his drama, Ezekiel dug through a wall (v. 5),[3] the wall of his house. This suggested the unsettled conditions during the siege of Jerusalem and may have been an allusion to the attempt by Zedekiah to flee the invading armies of Babylon by slipping from the city through the breaches in the wall (2 Kgs 25:4-7).[4]

[8]In the morning the word of the Lord came to me: [9]"Son of man, did not that rebellious house of Israel ask you, 'What are you doing?'

[10]"Say to them, 'This is what the Sovereign LORD says: This oracle concerns the prince in Jerusalem and the whole house of Israel who are there.' [11]Say to them, 'I am a sign to you.'

"As I have done, so it will be done to them. They will go into exile as captives.

[12]"The prince among them will put his things on his shoulder at dusk and leave, and a hole will be dug in the wall for him to go through. He will cover his face so that he cannot see the land. [13]I will spread my net for him, and he will be caught in my snare; I will bring him to Babylonia, the land of the Chaldeans, but he will not see it, and there he will die. [14]I will scatter to the winds all those around him—his staff and all his troops—and I will pursue them with drawn sword.

[15]"They will know that I am the LORD, when I disperse them among the nations and scatter them through the countries. [16]But I will spare a few of them from the sword, famine and plague, so that in the nations where they go they may acknowledge all their detestable practices. Then they will know that I am the LORD."

THE PROPHET'S ACTIONS EXPLAINED (12:8-16).   **12:8-16**   The prophet's response to the people when they asked, "What are you doing?"

---

[2] M. Greenberg, *Ezekiel 1–20*, AB (Garden City: Doubleday, 1986), 209.

[3] The word קִיר means "the wall of a house" and is used here rather than חוֹמָה, which refers to a city wall. Some houses were built against the city wall, so the house wall could also be the city wall (see Fisch, *Ezekiel*, 64.)

[4] Greenberg, *Ezekiel 1–20*, 210; Fisch, *Ezekiel*, 64.

(v. 8) was to explain that his actions were a "sign" of the soon-coming captivity and exile. This drama was about the "prince" and the whole house of Israel (vv. 10-11). Placing the bags on his shoulder and covering his face was Ezekiel's symbolic prophecy of the blinding of Zedekiah by Nebuchadnezzar and his exile in Babylon (v. 12).

Zedekiah was called "the prince."[5] Ezekiel carefully avoided the Hebrew word *melek,* which meant "king," because he considered Jehoiachin the legitimate king, who was in exile. Zedekiah had been appointed by Nebuchadnezzar, not God or the people (2 Kgs 25:17-20).

The "net" (v. 13) referred to a snare used to hunt fowl (see 2 Kgs 25:4-7).[6] Zedekiah was taken captive and transported to Babylon but did not see the land because he was blinded after witnessing the execution of his sons (2 Kgs 25:7; Jer 39:4; 52:7). Some survivors fled to other countries (v. 15). Only a small group of survivors remained in Jerusalem. Others were dispersed among foreign nations as witnesses that the nation was in exile because of their iniquity and not because of God's lack of care or inability to defend them (v. 16).[7]

**[17]The word of the LORD came to me: [18]"Son of man, tremble as you eat your food, and shudder in fear as you drink your water. [19]Say to the people of the land: 'This is what the Sovereign LORD says about those living in Jerusalem and in the land of Israel: They will eat their food in anxiety and drink their water in despair, for their land will be stripped of everything in it because of the violence of all who live there. [20]The inhabited towns will be laid waste and the land will be desolate. Then you will know that I am the LORD.'"**

THE DRAMA OF THE NERVOUS EATER (12:17-20).  **12:17-20**  Ezekiel performed a second dramatic action. He trembled while eating (vv. 17-19) as a sign of fear and anxiety over the exile. The people would be forced to eat meager rations in fear not knowing if there would be another meal.[8] The result would be that they would know Yahweh was the one true God.

---

[5] The term "prince" is the word נָשִׂיא, which also may be translated "leader." It is related to the verb נָשָׂא, "to lift up," and may mean literally "uplifted one" or "exalted one." See Greenberg, *Ezekiel 1–20,* 213, and R. H. Alexander, "Ezekiel," EBC 6 (Grand Rapids: Zondervan, 1986), 797.

[6] Greenberg, *Ezekiel 1–20,* 214; Fisch, *Ezekiel,* 66. The fowler or bird hunter spread nets on the ground to capture his prey as in Hos 7:12.

[7] Alexander, "Ezekiel," 797. This would be a natural interpretation of Israel's misfortune due to the common view in the ancient Near East of each nation having a patron deity.

[8] Fisch, *Ezekiel,* 66 (cf. 2 Kgs 6:24-29).

Unfortunately they learned this by receiving his judgment (v. 20).[9]

Brownlee has argued that Ezekiel was presenting a reversal of Joshua's seven stages in the conquest of Canaan by presenting seven stages in the loss of the land. Joshua's stages included invading the land (Josh 3–4), laying siege to Jericho (Josh 6:1-14), the celebration at Gilgal (Josh 5:10-12), the panic of the Canaanites (Josh 5:1), the destruction of the Canaanites (Josh 8–11), the rejoicing of Israel (Josh 10:22-27), and Israel's possessing the land (Josh 11:23; 1 Kgs 8:56). Contrast this with Ezekiel's inclusion of a settled people fleeing (Ezek 12:1-14,19b-20), Israel under siege in Jerusalem (4:1-3), Israel starved in Jerusalem (4:9-16; 5:10), Israel panicked (4:16; 7:26-27; 12:17-19a), Israel destroyed and expelled from the land (5:1-12), Israel's enemies rejoicing (6:11-12), and decadence ending with the loss of the land (7:1-9).[10]

The moral depravity and decadence of Israel had led to the fall of the capital of the Northern Kingdom, Samaria, in 722 B.C. That example of the consequences of sin did not deter Judah. Those under sin's power often mistakenly conclude that though sin destroys others, they will not be affected (12:3-20; see 2 Sam 12:10-12, where the consequences of David's sin were foretold).

### (2) Prophecy of the False Proverb (12:21-28)

[21]The word of the LORD came to me: [22]"Son of man, what is this proverb you have in the land of Israel: 'The days go by and every vision comes to nothing'? [23]Say to them, 'This is what the Sovereign LORD says: I am going to put an end to this proverb, and they will no longer quote it in Israel.' Say to them, 'The days are near when every vision will be fulfilled. [24]For there will be no more false visions or flattering divinations among the people of Israel. [25]But I the LORD will speak what I will, and it shall be fulfilled without delay. For in your days, you rebellious house, I will fulfill whatever I say, declares the Sovereign LORD.'"

[26]The word of the LORD came to me: [27]"Son of man, the house of Israel is saying, 'The vision he sees is for many years from now, and he prophesies about the distant future.'

[28]"Therefore say to them, 'This is what the Sovereign LORD says: None of my words will be delayed any longer; whatever I say will be fulfilled, declares the Sovereign LORD.'"

---

[9] W. H. Brownlee (*Ezekiel 1–19*, WBC [Waco: Word, 1986], 177-80) has noted the relationship of 12:17-20 to Ezekiel's statement in 4:16 regarding the eating of "rationed food in anxiety" and drinking "rationed water in despair." He wants to relocate vv. 17-20, however, and place them with 4:16-17 but offers no sufficient reason for doing so.

[10] Ibid., 181. The lack of lexical echoes of Joshua in Ezekiel, however, and Brownlee's need to rearrange events makes this correlation purely conjectural.

There are two parts to this message, each introduced by "the word of the LORD came to me." In each part God responds to a saying of the people.

**12:21-25** The disdain of the people for Ezekiel's ministry and probably Jeremiah's may be seen in the popular proverb "The days go by and every vision comes to nothing" (v. 22).[11] The obvious meaning of this proverb was that the people did not take seriously the messages of God's prophets.[12] The people were appealing to the prophetic test of truth in Deut 18:20-22, which stated that if a prophet's words did not come to pass, he was a false prophet. Jeremiah and Ezekiel were considered prophets of doom, so the people rejected their messages and held to a false hope of restoration.[13]

The divine response was to give Ezekiel a counter-proverb, literally, "The days are near, and the fulfillment [matter/content/word] of every vision" (v. 23). "Every vision" referred to those, like Ezekiel's and Jeremiah's, that legitimately warned of imminent judgment and exile. False visions and "flattering divinations" would cease (v. 24).[14] Divination is the attempt to communicate with the supernatural by observing natural

---

[11] The root מָשָׁל is especially significant in Ezekiel, which accounts for about a third of its occurrences in the OT. It is applied to different literary forms from a pithy saying, as here (also 16:44; 18:2), to a narrative in the style of a parable, allegory, or fable (see 17:2; 24:3). Because of its apparent relationship to the verb מָשַׁל ("to be like"), the basic meaning of מָשָׁל is often said to be "simile" (see W. McKane, *Proverbs* [Philadelphia: Westminster, 1970], 22-33; G. Landes, "Jonah: A *Mašal*?" in *Israelite Wisdom* [Missoula, Mont.: Scholars Press, 1978], 140). But T. Polk explains that sometimes a מָשָׁל is intended only to encourage the reader to draw a comparison ("Paradigms, Parables, and *Měšālîm*: On Reading the *Māšāl* in Scripture," *CBQ* 45 [1983]: 567). See also C. Fontaine, *Traditional Sayings in the Old Testament* (Sheffield: Almond, 1982).

[12] See similar sentiments regarding Jeremiah's message in Jer 5:12-14; 17:15; 26:17-24.

[13] Alexander ("Ezekiel," 795) lists eight rationalizations the people used for rejecting the messages of the "prophets of doom" and holding to false hope and security. (1) If judgment came, it would not be in their lifetime (12:1-28). (2) Why believe Ezekiel and Jeremiah rather than the other prophets who predicted a quick end to the exile (13:1–14:23)? (3) Judgment should be for the leaders, not the people (14:1-11). (4) Any righteous person could intercede, and judgment could be averted (14:12-23). (5) God would not judge his chosen people so severely (15:1–16:63). (6) Judgment for their ancestors' sins would be unfair (17:1-24). (7) If judgment were inevitable, as the "prophets of doom" said, repentance would be useless (18:1-32). (8) Zedekiah their king would find a way to defeat Babylon (19:1-14).

[14] The word "false" in v. 24 translates שָׁוְא, which also means "empty," "unproductive," "deceitful" (cf. 13:6-9,23; 21:29; 22:28; Deut 5:20; Job 15:31; Ps 119:37; Isa 59:4; Lam 2:14). All of these meanings describe the false prophets' message. The term מִקְסַם ("divination") occurs only here and in 13:7, but the verb קָסַם ("practice divination," Deut 18:10,14) and the noun קֶסֶם ("divination," Num 23:23; 1 Sam 15:23) occur several times. (cf. 8:16; 21:21; Gen 44:5,15; Lev 19:26; Deut 18:11; 1 Sam 15:23; 28:8; 2 Kgs 21:6; Isa 48:13; Jer 10:2; Zech 10:2). See I. Mendelssohn, "Divination," in IDB (Nashville: Abingdon, 1962), 856-58; J. S. Wright, "Divination," NBD, 320-21.

phenomena (e.g., stars, entrails of sacrificial animals, clouds, births), manipulating certain objects (arrows, oil and water, lots, etc.), or consulting mediums. T. Polk argues that a *mašal* ("proverb/saying/parable") presents its hearers with a paradigm and calls upon them to make application and self-judgment. Here "those who hear the new saying are to see themselves not only under the judgment of having wrongly judged the prophet's authenticity; they must also take seriously what he had said, which means seeing themselves under the judgment announced in vv. 19-20."[15]

**12:26-28** Another saying was that even if the vision were true, it was for some distant future time. The people conceded that Ezekiel's message might be true, but it was irrelevant to their situation. These verses demonstrate that there are many ways to despise God's word, whether by outright denial or by diverting its message to other times and applications. Again God's response was simple and direct. As someone has said, God does not necessarily pay at the end of every week; nevertheless, he pays.

### (3) Prophecy Condemning False Prophets and Prophetesses (13:1-23)

There are four parts to the message against false prophets and prophetesses. First is God's denunciation of the false prophets (13:1-7), then his judgment against them declared in two stages (13:8-12,13-16). Next is the condemnation of false prophetesses (13:17-19), followed by God's declaration of judgment (13:20-23).

**[1]The word of the LORD came to me: [2]"Son of man, prophesy against the prophets of Israel who are now prophesying. Say to those who prophesy out of their own imagination: 'Hear the word of the LORD! [3]This is what the Sovereign LORD says: Woe to the foolish prophets who follow their own spirit and have seen nothing! [4]Your prophets, O Israel, are like jackals among ruins. [5]You have not gone up to the breaks in the wall to repair it for the house of Israel so that it will stand firm in the battle on the day of the LORD. [6]Their visions are false and their divinations a lie. They say, "The LORD declares," when the LORD has not sent them; yet they expect their words to be fulfilled. [7]Have you not seen false visions and uttered lying divinations when you say, "The LORD declares," though I have not spoken?**

DENUNCIATION OF FALSE PROPHETS (13:1-8). **13:1-3** Ezekiel,

---

[15] T. Polk, "Paradigms, Parables, and *Měšālîm*," 574. Basing his analysis upon speech act theory, he explains that "when used in and as *religious* discourse, the *māšāl* wants to do something to, with, or for its hearers/readers" (p. 567). It "requires the participation of the readers in a special way, by requesting their assent and a decision about their life-relation to the subject" (p. 573).

prophet "in the midst" of the exiles, was painfully aware of competitive voices and alternative messages from others who also claimed to be prophets of God. His contemporary, Jeremiah, labored under the same tension. It is no surprise, therefore, that Jeremiah's book contained a denunciation of false prophets in words similar to those of Ezekiel (see Jer 14:14; 23:9-40). Jeremiah contrasted the ministry of these false prophets with the ministry of the ideal prophet (Jer 23:1-8) in a messianic prophecy.

This prophetic message from Ezekiel opened with an exhortation to prophesy or preach against these false prophets (Ezek 13:1-2), who did not speak God's word but spoke out of their own minds, giving false information (cf. Num 16:28; 1 Kgs 12:33). D. Block suggests there may be sarcasm in the redundant "prophets of Israel who are now prophesying."[16] They were nothing but words. He called such individuals fools, those who are spiritually and morally insensitive and may even be guilty of blasphemy and atheism (see Job 2:10; 30:8; Pss 14:1; 74:18; Prov 17:7; 30:32; 1 Sam 25:25; 2 Sam 13:13; Isa 32:5-6).[17] By contrast a true prophet was one who spoke only God's will and was led by God's Spirit (cf. 2 Pet 1:21; 1 Cor 2:13).[18]

**13:4-7**    Had these false prophets been true to God as Ezekiel and Jeremiah were, they would have warned the people of judgment to come. But instead of helping repair the "breaks in the wall" (v. 5) by strengthening the moral and spiritual lives of the people, they contributed to the decay. The false prophets were the "jackals" or scavengers, and the people were their prey.[19] Instead of receiving a sure word from God, they had imagined false visions and declared lies obtained by human invention (v. 6). They sought to foretell the future by the use of human devices, not divine insight (Deut 18:14). What they said were delusions from their own minds when God had, in fact, not spoken through them (v. 7).[20]

---

[16] D. Block ("The Prophet of the Spirit: The Use of *rwḥ* in the Book of Ezekiel," *JETS* 32 [1989]: 42. He includes a helpful summary of the characteristics of these false prophets (pp. 42-43). He also argues that one of the uses of רוּחַ (v. 3) is as a synonym for לֵב, "mind" (pp. 43-46). It could also refer to the divine Spirit as an "agency of prophetic inspiration (2:2; 3:24; and especially 11:5)," which is also implied in v. 3.

[17] See Fisch, *Ezekiel,* 69.

[18] Greenberg (*Ezekiel 1–20,* 235) regards Num 16:28 as an antecedent to these verses. See also 1 Kgs 12:33 and Jer 23:16.

[19] Wevers, *Ezekiel,* 106; Greenberg, *Ezekiel 1–20,* 236. The sight of jackals scavenging in ruins was a familiar one after the fall of Jerusalem (Lam 5:18; Neh 3:35).

[20] Wevers, *Ezekiel,* 106; G. A. Cooke, *The Book of Ezekiel,* ICC (Edinburgh: T & T Clark, 1986), 139; Fisch, *Ezekiel,* 70. On divination, see comments at 12:24.

[8]"'Therefore this is what the Sovereign LORD says: Because of your false words and lying visions, I am against you, declares the Sovereign LORD. [9]My hand will be against the prophets who see false visions and utter lying divinations. They will not belong to the council of my people or be listed in the records of the house of Israel, nor will they enter the land of Israel. Then you will know that I am the Sovereign LORD.

[10]"'Because they lead my people astray, saying, "Peace," when there is no peace, and because, when a flimsy wall is built, they cover it with whitewash, [11]therefore tell those who cover it with whitewash that it is going to fall. Rain will come in torrents, and I will send hailstones hurtling down, and violent winds will burst forth. [12]When the wall collapses, will people not ask you, "Where is the whitewash you covered it with?"

[13]"'Therefore this is what the Sovereign LORD says: In my wrath I will unleash a violent wind, and in my anger hailstones and torrents of rain will fall with destructive fury. [14]I will tear down the wall you have covered with whitewash and will level it to the ground so that its foundation will be laid bare. When it falls, you will be destroyed in it; and you will know that I am the Lord. [15]So I will spend my wrath against the wall and against those who covered it with whitewash. I will say to you, "The wall is gone and so are those who whitewashed it, [16]those prophets of Israel who prophesied to Jerusalem and saw visions of peace for her when there was no peace, declares the Sovereign LORD.'"

GOD'S JUDGMENT DECLARED (13:8-16).    **13:8-16**   Because of their deliberate deception of the leaders and people, Ezekiel announced that these false prophets would be cut off and no record of their personal ministries would remain (v. 9). The phrase "counsel of my people" probably refers to places of leadership and may be compared to the counsel of the elders (Ps 107:32; cf. Ps 111:1).[21] The Jew familiar with the exodus account could not help but recall Exod 7:5— "And the Egyptians will know that I am the LORD when I stretch out my hand against Egypt and bring the Israelites out of it." The revelation of God's character should have come through judgment on Israel's enemies, but the wickedness of God's people made it necessary for him to reveal himself in judgment upon them also.[22] The truth of the threat to remove the false prophets was confirmed. The names of at least forty people referred to as "prophet" or "prophetess" who were legitimate representatives of God have been preserved in the Old Testament. But not one false prophet from this period was named,

---

[21] The similar phrase "counsel of the LORD" in the parallel context of Jer 23:18 may suggest that it is also connected with receiving instructions from God (cf. Ps 25:14).

[22] The phrase "I am against you" is used of Israel elsewhere in Ezekiel only in 21:3 (but see Jer 21:13; 50:31; 51:25). Elsewhere it is used of foreign nations (Ezek 26:3; 28:22; 29:3; 29:10; 35:3; 38:3; 39:1; cf. Nah 2:13; 3:5).

though we have accounts of their evil misdeeds (see, e.g., 1 Kgs 22:1-53).

These fraudulent spokesmen gave false hope of a peace that was not to be (Ezek 13:10). Their words were like an unstable wall. The "wall" they built would not protect the people but was something that would collapse at the slightest touch, though they had dressed it handsomely.[23] When the stormy weather came, the wall would collapse (cf. Jesus' lesson of the two foundations in Matt 7:24-29).

The analogy of the wall was extended to refer to Jerusalem in Ezek 13:14. God declared his intention to bring down the wall (i.e., the city of Jerusalem). The people, their leaders, and the false prophets would be judged (vv. 15-16).

**[17]"Now, son of man, set your face against the daughters of your people who prophesy out of their own imagination. Prophesy against them [18]and say, 'This is what the Sovereign LORD says: Woe to the women who sew magic charms on all their wrists and make veils of various lengths for their heads in order to ensnare people. Will you ensnare the lives of my people but preserve your own? [19]You have profaned me among my people for a few handfuls of barley and scraps of bread. By lying to my people, who listen to lies, you have killed those who should not have died and have spared those who should not live.**

**[20]"'Therefore this is what the Sovereign LORD says: I am against your magic charms with which you ensnare people like birds and I will tear them from your arms; I will set free the people that you ensnare like birds. [21]I will tear off your veils and save my people from your hands, and they will no longer fall prey to your power. Then you will know that I am the LORD. [22]Because you disheartened the righteous with your lies, when I had brought them no grief, and because you encouraged the wicked not to turn from their evil ways and so save their lives, [23]therefore you will no longer see false visions or practice divination. I will save my people from your hands. And then you will know that I am the LORD.'"**

CONDEMNATION AND JUDGMENT (13:17-23). **13:17-23** In addition to the false prophets, false prophetesses were singled out for a special word of condemnation (vv. 17-19). This passage is one of only four Old Testament prophetic passages specifically critical of women (cf. Isa 3:16–4:1; 32:9-13; Amos 4:1-3). Only four female prophets, all true prophets of God, are mentioned by name in the Old Testament: Deborah (Judg 4:4–5:31), Huldah (2 Kgs 22:14), Miriam (Exod 15:20), and Noadiah (Neh

---

[23] תָּפֵל ("whitewash," v. 10) refers to plaster that dresses but does not strengthen a wall. It suggests a wall that may appear to be good but is in fact useless. The word חַיִץ refers to a "flimsy wall" of stacked stones that are not cemented together and are very weak unless fortified (see Fisch, *Ezekiel,* 71).

6:14). By contrast the false prophetesses of Ezekiel's day suffered the same condemnation as their male counterparts. God preserved neither their names nor their specific ministries (cf. Ezek 13:9).

The activities attributed to these women suggest that they were more like witches or sorcerers than prophets.[24] Perhaps they were like the witch of Endor mentioned in 1 Sam 28:7. As Greenberg notes, the terms translated "magic charms" and "veils" are of uncertain meaning, and the practices are unknown. Nevertheless, it is clear that some type of magic was involved that was intended to "ensnare people" (vv. 18,20) in some sense.[25] By their forbidden activities in Israel they profaned God for a "few handfuls of barley and scraps of bread" (v. 19), which was the price of their services.[26] Perhaps in addition to promises of peace their lies consisted of predicting death for some and life for others regardless of guilt or innocence. Thus they "disheartened the righteous" and "encouraged the wicked," enticing both to trust in them and their magic rather than in God and the words of his prophets. But God warned these false prophetesses that he was going to take away their clients (v. 21), an obvious reference to the captivity. He said, "You will no longer practice divination" (v. 23), meaning his judgment on Judah would put them out of business.

A review of the characteristics of false prophets and prophetesses as presented by Ezekiel helps to show how these men and women led a whole nation astray. This passage stands out in the Old Testament as one clear description of the characteristics of these false prophets and prophetesses and of the jealousy and compassion God feels for his people when they are being led astray (note the repeated "my people" throughout chaps. 13–14). This is a message that needs to be reviewed in every generation because everyone is vulnerable to the leadership of those who claim to have a word from God but who in fact have none.

These false representatives of God exhibited at least ten negative characteristics. First, they spoke out of their own will, not God's will (vv. 1-3,17). Second, they made the people a prey instead of performing a ministry for them (v. 4). They scavenged among ruined lives for personal gain and self-gratification. Third, they had no crisis ministry (v. 5). They could not strengthen the breaks in the walls (i.e., people or nations) or fortify broken lives. Fourth, they claimed their revelations were divine to deceive

---

[24] Taylor, *Ezekiel*, 123; Cooke, *Ezekiel*, 144-45. The use of magic was rife in the time of Jeremiah and Ezekiel. Magic was especially practiced by the women of Jerusalem (Jer 7:18; 44:17,19) and penetrated all parts of life in Babylon.

[25] Greenberg, *Ezekiel 1–20*, 239; see also Fisch, *Ezekiel*, 73; Wevers, *Ezekiel*, 109.

[26] Greenberg prefers to translate "with handfuls of barley and bread crumbs" and understands it probably as offerings to God accompanying their divination (*Ezekiel 1–20*, 244).

their followers (vv. 6-7) and easily deceived others because they were deceived themselves. Fifth, they failed to stand against sin (vv. 6-9) and declared an empty message without truth. Sixth, they preached a message of peace, prosperity, and safety in the face of imminent judgment (vv. 10-12) because they failed to relate the consequences of sin. Seventh, their ministry provoked the wrath of God and invited his judgment (vv. 13-16). Eighth, they often used false methods and occult practices to legitimize their work and control their victims (vv. 17-21). Ninth, they encouraged iniquity by word and personal example (vv. 22-23). Tenth, they set up the worst idols, their own self-will (14:1-7).

Through their methods, messages, and ministries these men and women led the nation to believe that those in Babylon would soon be returned and Israel restored. They condemned Ezekiel and Jeremiah as troublemakers. Instead of impending judgment they preached peace, prosperity, freedom, and a do-as-you-please (really a do-as-*we*-please) philosophy that kept the people under their control.[27] They appealed to what the people wanted to hear as a means of maintaining control. All this sounds uncomfortably familiar when applied to many self-styled "prophets" today. In days of moral crisis there are always those who seek personal profit by establishing counterfeit ministries, who preach man-made systems instead of divine truth, proclaim peace instead of repentance, use materialistic methods, and set up idols in human hearts (14:1-11).

### (4) Prophecy of Judgment for Consulting Idols (14:1-11)

**¹Some of the elders of Israel came to me and sat down in front of me. ²Then the word of the LORD came to me: ³"Son of man, these men have set up idols in their hearts and put wicked stumbling blocks before their faces. Should I let them inquire of me at all? ⁴Therefore speak to them and tell them, 'This is what the Sovereign LORD says: When any Israelite sets up idols in his heart and puts a wicked stumbling block before his face and then goes to a prophet, I the Lord will answer him myself in keeping with his great idolatry. ⁵I will do this to recapture the hearts of the people of Israel, who**

---

[27] Compare with Jer 23:9-40, where he says that the false prophets (1) set no righteous example (vv. 9-11), (2) teach false doctrines (vv. 13,27), (3) align themselves with evildoers (v. 14), (4) preach out of their own hearts (will) (vv. 16,23-30), (5) present false hope (v. 17), (6) lack God's counsel (vv. 18-22), and (7) ridicule the true messengers of God (vv. 31-40). Also note vv. 5-8, where Jeremiah presents the perfect prophet, who is (1) a righteous Branch of David, (2) a King whose reign will prosper, (3) who will execute justice and righteous judgment, (4) in whose days Judah will be saved, (5) and who will be called the Lord Our Righteousness. Jesus gave a further test of a true prophet in Matt 7:15-20— "By their fruits" they will be known.

have all deserted me for their idols.'

⁶"Therefore say to the house of Israel, 'This is what the Sovereign LORD says: Repent! Turn from your idols and renounce all your detestable practices!

⁷"'When any Israelite or any alien living in Israel separates himself from me and sets up idols in his heart and puts a wicked stumbling block before his face and then goes to a prophet to inquire of me, I the LORD will answer him myself. ⁸I will set my face against that man and make him an example and a byword. I will cut him off from my people. Then you will know that I am the LORD.

⁹"'And if the prophet is enticed to utter a prophecy, I the LORD have enticed that prophet, and I will stretch out my hand against him and destroy him from among my people Israel. ¹⁰They will bear their guilt—the prophet will be as guilty as the one who consults him. ¹¹Then the people of Israel will no longer stray from me, nor will they defile themselves anymore with all their sins. They will be my people, and I will be their God, declares the Sovereign Lord.'"

Two prophecies are presented in chap. 14. The first in vv. 1-11 forms a conclusion to the message against the false prophets and prophetesses in 13:1-23. This prophecy warned that those who patronized false prophets would share in the same judgment that would befall them. Ezekiel pointed out that those who frequented these prophets were responsible for their apparent success. If they had not traded on the lies of these false representatives of God, there would have been no market for their services. Their practices would have long since ceased.

There are two parts to this message. First, the elders seek a word from the prophet (14:1-5). Second is the announcement of judgment against Israel (14:6-11).

**14:1-5** A group of elders or leaders of Israel came to Ezekiel for instruction (v. 1). These leaders already had demonstrated a halfhearted piety. They prayed for deliverance from Babylon but were not ready to give God his rightful place in their hearts.[28] They had adopted Babylonian values, goals, and standards but still considered themselves worshipers of Yahweh. So God asked, "Should I let them inquire of me at all?" (v. 3).

These leaders served the worst idols, the idols of their minds (v. 4). Their thoughts were under pagan control, so they were open to all forms of apostate practices. The same word used here for idols (*gillûlîm*) is also in 6:4-6,9,13, where they are characterized as "dung pellets."[29] Such sin

---

[28] W. Zimmerli, *Ezekiel 1*, Her (Philadelphia: Fortress, 1979), 309. Cf. Jer 38:14-28.

[29] See note on 6:4. This is Ezekiel's favorite word for idols and is so used thirty-nine times in the book.

was grounds for excluding a person from the community of worship because it was a spiritual "stumbling block" (v. 4).[30]

"Any Israelite" who worshiped such self-made idols was liable for judgment (v. 4). The same judgment formula also was used in Leviticus to affirm liability for judgment (e.g., Lev 17:3,10,13; 22:14).[31] Verse 5 begins literally, "In order to seize/capture the house of Israel in/by their heart." An alternative to the NIV interpretation is that of Greenberg: even though Israel's sin was presently only in their heart, that is, "idolmindedness," God was able to catch them "at their thoughts" (cf. Num 5:13).[32] Both ideas are in the passage, and either fits the context (cf. v. 11). In the midst of such an idolatrous culture, a battle for the minds of Israel was being fought.

**14:6-11** A double imperative of the decisive Hebrew verb *šub,* "turn/return," was used to give added force to the call to forsake their idolatry and self-willed choices.[33] The verse literally reads "turn and cause to turn." The language of personal liability used in v. 4 continues in v. 7. "Any Israelite," or "any alien," was admonished to turn back to God. Reference to the "alien" may mean those in Jerusalem who were taken to Babylon at the time of the Babylonian invasion or perhaps those in Babylon who became worshipers of Yahweh.[34]

Those who inquired of false prophets and followed their advice would be punished personally by God. Their judgment would become an example to everyone, "archetypes of a bad fate," resulting from "a bad life" (cf. Isa 14:16).[35]

The false prophets were not exempt from judgment about to befall the land. God warned them also of impending judgment (v. 9). This verse clearly states that the deception of these false prophets was allowed by

---

[30] Zimmerli, *Ezekiel 1,* 305-6. The exclusion from the community meant exclusion from worship and hence the "life" of the individual.

[31] Greenberg, *Ezekiel 1–20,* 248.

[32] Ibid., 249, 253-55.

[33] The first imperative is שׁוּבוּ, a *qal,* and the second is וְהָשִׁיבוּ, *hiphil,* which is usually transitive. BDB (999) explains its meaning here as "show a turning away from your idols." Greenberg (*Ezekiel 1–20,* 249) suggests it may be a longer, more emphatic variation of *qal.* See also Ezek 18:30,32; 21:35[30, Eng.], where שׁוּב also is used. The identical verbal expression is found in 18:30.

[34] Taylor, *Ezekiel,* 126-27; Fisch, *Ezekiel,* 77; Cooke, *Ezekiel,* 151. The use of the term גּוּר shows that the warning applied to native Israelites as well as temporary residents; see also Alexander, "Ezekiel," 806.

[35] T. Polk, "Paradigms, Parables, and *Měšālîm,* 577. The words are אוֹת and מָשָׁל, "a sign" (or, as Polk prefers, "symbol" [p. 578]) and "a proverb." See also Zimmerli, *Ezekiel 1,* 308.

and even encouraged by God as a part of the judgment process.[36] A similar judgment was mentioned, for example (1 Kgs 22:23), against the false prophets who misinformed Ahab. In so doing they were contributing factors of God's judgment on the king and kingdom. So the people and prophets of the exile equally bore the guilt and were equally liable for the judgment of God (cf. 20:25-26; Deut 4:27-28; 13:1-3; Rom 1:18-32).[37] But this was to be punishment with a purpose (Ezek 14:11). It was to purge idolatry from the lives and minds of the people and to renew their covenant relationship and fidelity to the Lord.[38]

## (5) Prophecy of the Fourfold Judgment of Jerusalem (14:12-23)

[12]**The word of the** LORD **came to me:** [13]**"Son of man, if a country sins against me by being unfaithful and I stretch out my hand against it to cut off its food supply and send famine upon it and kill its men and their animals,** [14]**even if these three men—Noah, Daniel and Job—were in it, they could save only themselves by their righteousness, declares the Sovereign** LORD.

[15]**"Or if I send wild beasts through that country and they leave it childless and it becomes desolate so that no one can pass through it because of the beasts,** [16]**as surely as I live, declares the Sovereign** LORD, **even if these three men were in it, they could not save their own sons or daughters. They alone would be saved, but the land would be desolate.**

[17]**"Or if I bring a sword against that country and say, 'Let the sword pass throughout the land,' and I kill its men and their animals,** [18]**as surely as I live, declares the Sovereign** LORD, **even if these three men were in it, they could not save their own sons or daughters. They alone would be saved.**

[19]**"Or if I send a plague into that land and pour out my wrath upon it through bloodshed, killing its men and their animals,** [20]**as surely as I live, declares the Sovereign** LORD, **even if Noah, Daniel and Job were in it, they could save neither son nor daughter. They would save only themselves by their righteousness.**

[21]**"For this is what the Sovereign** LORD **says: How much worse will it be**

---

[36] Cooke, *Ezekiel,* 151-52; Fisch, *Ezekiel,* 77. The Scriptures sometimes overlook secondary causes and attribute everything to God. W. Eichrodt (*Theology of the Old Testament* [Philadelphia: Westminster, 1967], 2:179) explains that passages on divine providence like this one portray "the power of evil to grow and spread, whereby it becomes ripe for judgment."

[37] Greenberg, *Ezekiel 1–20,* 251; cf. also Jer 14:15-16; 27:15-22.

[38] Greenberg (ibid., 254) points out that the covenantal expression "they will be my people, and I will be their God" is derived from the terminology of marriage and adoption (he cites Y. Muffs, "Studies in Biblical Law, IV: The Antiquity of P," mimeographed [lectures held at the Jewish Theological Seminary of America, New York, 1965]; cf. Exod 6:7; Lev 26:12; Jer 7:23; 11:4; 30:21; 32:38; Ezek 11:20; 36:28; 37:23). See also Ezek 16:8 and comments there.

**when I send against Jerusalem my four dreadful judgments—sword and famine and wild beasts and plague—to kill its men and their animals! [22]Yet there will be some survivors—sons and daughters who will be brought out of it. They will come to you, and when you see their conduct and their actions, you will be consoled regarding the disaster I have brought upon Jerusalem— every disaster I have brought upon it. [23]You will be consoled when you see their conduct and their actions, for you will know that I have done nothing in it without cause, declares the Sovereign LORD."**

The second prophecy of this chapter continues the same judgment theme by explaining the fourfold judgment to befall Jerusalem and the irrevocable nature of that judgment. The fourfold judgment of Jerusalem was introduced in Ezek 5:1-17 and is again reviewed here: famine (14:12-14), wild beasts (14:15-16), the sword (14:17-18), and pestilence (14:19-21). The chapter concludes with an assurance that such devastation was just and necessary (14:22-23). These four devastations were among the most feared threats to life in the ancient Near East.[39] They also were part of divine judgment associated with the end time in Rev 6:1-8.

**14:12-14**   The language of v. 13 seems incongruous. "If a country sins" implies that the situation would apply to any nation on earth, whereas the act of "being unfaithful" is not elsewhere applied to non-Israelites.[40] Unfaithfulness is a violation of trust, an act of treachery, which presumes a prior relationship. It usually refers to religious sins (e.g., 2 Chr 36:14).[41] It probably is sufficient simply to note that the hypothetical situation has both a general character (note that Noah, Daniel, and Job are all associated with non-Israelite contexts) and a specific application to Israel. The point of the passage is that Israel was under a divine judgment that was irreversible in its very nature.[42]

Furthermore, God's judgment was fourfold (cf. Lev 26:14-39; Deut 28:15-68; 32:15-27). The choice of words suggests that the nation as a whole would be punished for breaking its covenant commitment to God, which was the cornerstone of its life (Exod 19:1-8). The first plague mentioned was famine. Ezekiel portrayed a severe famine that resulted in the

---

[39] Taylor (*Ezekiel,* 130) compares with 5:17.

[40] See Greenberg, *Ezekiel 1–20,* 257.

[41] For examples of sins of unfaithfulness, see Job 31:3-40 (note v. 28); Lev 6:1-3. For a discussion of מעל ("transgress/act unfaithfully") see *TWOT,* 519-20.

[42] The only other place in Scripture where אֶרֶץ is part of a כִּי clause but occurs before כִּי is in Ezek 33:2, suggesting perhaps an intentional connection between the two passages. Zimmerli (*Ezekiel 1,* 315) compares this passage with its references to "any country" to 33:1-20, which introduced the "watchman" passage as the background for the restoration passages in chaps. 34–37.

loss of life for humans and animals.

The famine would be so serious that its effect would not be averted though righteous men of the quality of Noah, Job, and Daniel were found in the midst (Ezek 14:14). There is universal agreement that Noah and Job were characters from Old Testament history. Events of their lives revealed them to be outstanding examples of righteousness (Gen 6:9,22; Job 1:1–2:10). Noah was the only righteous man of his day, but he could not avert the judgment of the flood upon the rest of humanity. Job was righteous but could not avert the test of faith that cost him his family and possessions. There is some question among interpreters regarding the identity of Daniel, mentioned here and in Ezek 28:3. It is not clear whether Daniel the prophet was intended or a hero from second millennium B.C. Ugaritic literature named Danel. If the Canaanite Danel were intended, then Ezekiel chose as an example one who was not a Yahwist. The spelling of the name in Ezekiel has the same consonants as Danel (*dn'l*), but this is not conclusive proof.[43]

Ample evidence exists to sustain the conclusion that Daniel, the prophet and writer of the book that bears his name, was the one Ezekiel mentioned as a third and contemporary example of righteousness. First, Daniel the prophet, exiled in 605 B.C. (Dan 1:1), would have had time to establish his reputation as a wise and righteous man by the time Ezekiel ministered, as especially by the time the book was written. Second, the use of a pagan as an example of God's righteousness is unknown elsewhere in Scripture (cf. Deut 18:14-22). Third, as Dressler argues, the text where he is found (The Story of Aqht) "does not portray Dnil as either king, or wise, or righteous."[44] By contrast Daniel the prophet was well known for his righteousness, wisdom, and understanding (Dan 1:17-21; 2:14,48; 5:12). Fourth, if Danel were the intended example, Ezekiel was using an idol worshiper as an example of righteousness in a context that

---

[43] Daniel of the biblical book is דָּנִיֵּאל, while in Ezek 14:14 and 28:3 it is דָּנִאֵל. Scholars are divided on the identification of Daniel. Alexander ("Ezekiel," 808) and H. H. P. Dressler ("The Identification of the Ugaritic Dnil with the Daniel of Ezekiel," *VT* 29 [1979]: 152-61) favor an identification with Daniel the prophet. Though the spelling is slightly different, the name would be vocalized as Daniel in West Semitic dialect (Alexander, "Ezekiel," 808). The difference involves a vowel letter/*mater* (Dressler, "Identification of the Ugaritic Dnil," 156). Most others, such as Taylor (*Ezekiel,* 129, 196), Wevers (*Ezekiel,* 115), J. Day ("The Daniel of Ugarit and Ezekiel and the Hero of the Book of Daniel," *VT* 30 [1980]: 174-84), Brownlee (*Ezekiel 1–19,* 207), Greenberg (*Ezekiel 1–20,* 257), and Zimmerli (*Ezekiel 1,* 314-15) at least tentatively favor identification with Danel. Zimmerli sees the reference to Danel as a move to include the whole world, not simply the covenant people Israel. If so, it adds to the general nature of the hypothetical situation.

[44] Dressler, "Identification of the Ugaritic Dnil," 154.

condemns idolatry.[45] Daniel the prophet, on the other hand, stood firm against idolatry even when it was difficult to do so (Dan 2:8-20). Fifth, it is unlikely that Ezekiel would have chosen two examples from Scripture and one from Canaanite religion. On the other hand, it seems reasonable that he would choose a pre-Israelite (Noah), a non-Israelite (Job), and an Israelite in a foreign context (Daniel) as examples of righteousness in the midst of unrighteousness. This passage makes the most sense if Ezekiel referred to Daniel the prophet. The presence of godly people in society will not alone deter deserved judgment (Ezek 14:14,20). People must respond personally to God by confession, repentance, and faith.

**14:15-16** The second judgment mentioned was the visitation of wild beasts. This judgment pointed to the utter desolation of the land. Wild beasts would leave the country childless so that it was robbed of further hope of renewal. This is similar to the warning of Lev 26:22, which mentioned "wild animals" that would "rob you of your children" (cf. Deut 32:24).

Neither sons nor daughters would be delivered (Ezek 14:16). Noah's sons were saved with him, but Job's children were lost (Job 1:18-19). The Job pattern would be Judah and Jerusalem's pattern. Children would be victims of the judgment that would befall the land. This is a perennial consequence of war and conquest. Children often suffer the most.

**14:17-18** The third judgment was the "sword" that obviously represented warfare (v. 17).[46] Though righteous men such as Noah, Job, or Daniel were found in the land, their cumulative righteousness could not prevent the inevitability of judgment to come. The certainty of their peril was assured by God's personal oath, "as surely as I live," accompanying each of the last three devastations (vv. 16,18,20). This oath formula is found sixteen times in Ezekiel and only six times elsewhere. It is a variation of the formula "as the LORD lives" (forty-one times in the OT) and "as God lives" (2 Sam 2:27; Job 27:2), which involves invoking God to watch over the oath to see that it is kept (cf. 1 Sam 20:23). It is connected to the concept of Yahweh as "the Living God," which means that he "acts effectually."[47] Unlike the pagan gods, who were thought to die and rise or to sleep, the Lord is always watching and working on behalf of his people and his word (Ps 121:3-5; Josh 3:10; 1 Sam 17:26; Jer 1:12; 10:3-16; Dan

---

[45] Ibid., 158-59.

[46] חֶרֶב, "sword," occurs at least eighty times in Ezekiel. See comments/notes at 5:7-12.

[47] *TDOT,* 338-40. B. Ramm (*The God Who Makes a Difference* [Waco: Word, 1972], 46) explains the significance of the expression as referring to the God who "makes a difference," who "acts in our world and in our history."

6:20-26). There is nothing more certain than "as surely as I live."

**14:19-21**   The fourth judgment was plague or disease, especially epidemics. These were considered acts of divine judgment (the first use of *deber,* "plague," is in Exod 5:3; see also 9:3,15). The use here probably is to be associated with the effects of a siege (cf. Lev 26:25). God plagued the Philistines (1 Sam 5:7) and the Assyrians (Isa 37:36), who were enemies of his people. This time the warning of the judgment by plague was aimed at Judah and Jerusalem. Therefore God promised a bloody death in which no son or daughter would be spared. Ezekiel's message closely resembled the message of Amos 9:1-10, which warned that God's judgments are inescapable (see also Amos 5:18-19).

This mention of the deterrent power of the righteous is an obvious allusion to Gen 18:22-33. There Abraham sought to intercede on behalf of Sodom, and God agreed to spare the cities if ten righteous were found. Yet Yahweh would not spare Jerusalem though the three outstanding examples of righteousness and integrity in the face of wickedness were found in it (v. 20).

The plague was used as an illustration of coming judgment as had been done in the prophecy of 5:1-17. Ezekiel 14:21 clinches the argument with a return from the hypothetical to the real—how much worse it will be for Israel. What a tragedy when the heathen invite God's punishment. What an unthinkable tragedy when God's own people, who should know better, incur greater judgment.[48]

**14:22-23**   Ezekiel, like Jeremiah (Jer 44:27ff.) and Amos (Amos 9:8, 11-15), spoke of total annihilation but also predicted the survival of a small remnant (Ezek 14:22). The appearance of the remnant would be a cause for consolation (cf. 11:14-20 in response to 11:13). The comfort would not come "in the midst" of judgment but "out of" (v. 22) or "by" it. Encountering the wickedness of those who escaped the destruction of Jerusalem in 586 B.C. would enable the exiles to see that judgment had been deserved and necessary to produce a righteous remnant (v. 23). The older captives would take comfort in this fact since it would teach them that by loyalty to him they could escape a similar fate.[49] Comfort would come only after judgment had been fully exercised.

*(6) Prophecy of Jerusalem: The Useless Vine (15:1-8)*

**¹The word of the LORD came to me: ²"Son of man, how is the wood of a**

---

[48] See Greenberg's (*Ezekiel 1–20,* 260) note on the use of כִּי.

[49] Fisch, *Ezekiel,* 80-81.

vine better than that of a branch on any of the trees in the forest? [3]Is wood ever taken from it to make anything useful? Do they make pegs from it to hang things on? [4]And after it is thrown on the fire as fuel and the fire burns both ends and chars the middle, is it then useful for anything? [5]If it was not useful for anything when it was whole, how much less can it be made into something useful when the fire has burned it and it is charred?

[6]"Therefore this is what the Sovereign LORD says: As I have given the wood of the vine among the trees of the forest as fuel for the fire, so will I treat the people living in Jerusalem. [7]I will set my face against them. Although they have come out of the fire, the fire will yet consume them. And when I set my face against them, you will know that I am the LORD. [8]I will make the land desolate because they have been unfaithful, declares the Sovereign LORD."

Like Isaiah's parable of the vine (Isa 5), Ezekiel's brief prophecy of the useless vine may be divided into two parts. Verses 1-5 present the parable and vv. 6-8 the interpretation and application of the parable.[50]

**15:1-5**   The representation of Israel as a vine is not unique to Ezekiel. There was a well-established pattern among Old Testament prophets of using the vine to represent Israel. Hosea made the comparison (see Hos 10:1). Other passages that identified Israel as the vine of the Lord were Gen 49:22; Deut 32:32; Ps 80:8-16; Isa 5:1-7; Jer 2:21; cf. John 15. Ezekiel's use of this parable was an answer to those who thought that the vine, that is, Israel, was sacred and indestructible. The only purpose of a grapevine is to produce grapes. Otherwise it is useless except as fuel to burn. Israel was punished because it had abandoned the purpose that gave it value, the bearing of fruit.[51]

The wood of a vine was useless as a source of lumber. It was not good for making furniture or even for use as a peg for a tent or a wall hanging (v. 3).[52] Hence the question posed in v. 2, "How is the wood of the vine

---

[50] L. Boadt argues that chaps. 15–19 form a unity. They all "employ highly developed metaphors, allegories, or case studies before a much shorter announcement of judgment." Such a pattern "contrasts with the earlier oracles of chapters 5–7, 12–14, which generally have shorter introductory accusations and include more extensive announcements of judgment" ("Rhetorical Strategies in Ezekiel's Oracles of Judgment," in *Ezekiel and His Book,* ed. J. Lust (Leuven: University Press, 1986), 194-95)

[51] D. M. G. Stalker, *Ezekiel* (London: SCM, 1968), 135; Taylor, *Ezekiel,* 131. The use of the vine traditions goes back at least to Gen 49:22. Ezekiel ignored the fruitbearing properties that were lacking in Israel and focused instead on the quality of wood for which the vine was notoriously useless.

[52] Some translations have "vine tree" for "wood of the vine" in v. 2; the word עֵץ may mean "tree" or the "wood" of a tree and is used in both senses in this passage. The word "peg" in v. 3 is יָתֵד and is used either of a tent peg, a wall peg, or a reliable person, as in Isa 22:23-25 (see Zimmerli, *Ezekiel 1,* 317, and Taylor, *Ezekiel,* 132).

better than that of a branch or any other of the trees of the forest?" The implied answer was that any other wood was better.[53]

Vines usually were pruned twice annually in late winter and again in summer. Branches that bore no fruit were cut off and bundled for firewood. Fruit-producing branches were pruned to make them more fruitful.[54] If a whole unfruitful branch were of no value, a part of that branch would be less than worthless. The partial branch presented in v. 5 has been pruned and partially burned, which also depreciated its limited usefulness. This was an obvious reference to Jerusalem, which twice was invaded by Nebuchadnezzar in 605 B.C. and again in 597 B.C. In that sense it had already been "charred" (v. 5). These words also anticipated the final destruction that came in 586 B.C. when the city was burned and looted (2 Kgs 25:8-21).

**15:6-8** Ezekiel stated the interpretation of the parable in unmistakable language. Jerusalem was the vine that God had consigned to the "fire" of judgment, a reference to the coming Babylonian destruction. While Jerusalem was only charred in the earlier invasions, the coming judgment was to be decisive. The city and its people would be severely punished for their unfaithfulness and treachery (v. 8).

Without God no individual or nation will ever realize their true potential or purpose. Like an unproductive vine, they have no purpose beyond fruitbearing. When they bear no fruit, they are replaced (15:1-8; Isa 5:1-30; Luke 13:6-17).

### (7) Prophecy of Jerusalem: The Orphan Who Became a Harlot (16:1-63)

This chapter is the longest single prophetic message in the Book of Ezekiel, sixty-three verses, beginning with the revelation formula in 16:1. It follows logically after the declaration of uselessness and consequent judgment in chap. 15, since it graphically portrays the cause for Yahweh's anger. The vine had not just failed to produce good fruit; it had produced vile, disgusting fruit. This prophetic oracle is a parable about a despised orphan who became the wife of the king, then gave away all his gifts to become a harlot. A figurative biography of Israel, it is a parable about

---

[53] The word "branch" is זְמוֹרָה and is from the root זָמַר, which means "to prune." Greenberg (*Ezekiel 1–20*, 265) probably is correct in understanding it as a branch of the vine rather than another tree (as NIV). The second half of v. 2 (lit., "the branch which was among the trees of the forest"), then, is in poetic apposition to "the wood of a vine." See also Alexander, "Ezekiel," 809.

[54] Greenberg, *Ezekiel 1–20*, 267-68.

grace and ingratitude, of God's love spurned and his riches squandered. As such, it is reminiscent of the story of Hosea and Gomer (Hos 1–3). The chapter has six divisions: the orphan who became a queen (16:1-14); the queen who became a harlot (16:15-34); the harlot who became a convict (16:35-43); the convict who became a proverb (16:44-52); the convict and her companions who repented (16:53-58); and the convict who was saved, cleansed, and restored (16:59-63).

[1]**The word of the LORD came to me:** [2]**"Son of man, confront Jerusalem with her detestable practices** [3]**and say, 'This is what the Sovereign LORD says to Jerusalem: Your ancestry and birth were in the land of the Canaanites; your father was an Amorite and your mother a Hittite.** [4]**On the day you were born your cord was not cut, nor were you washed with water to make you clean, nor were you rubbed with salt or wrapped in cloths.** [5]**No one looked on you with pity or had compassion enough to do any of these things for you. Rather, you were thrown out into the open field, for on the day you were born you were despised.**

[6]**"'Then I passed by and saw you kicking about in your blood, and as you lay there in your blood I said to you, "Live!"** [7]**I made you grow like a plant of the field. You grew up and developed and became the most beautiful of jewels. Your breasts were formed and your hair grew, you who were naked and bare.**

[8]**"'Later I passed by, and when I looked at you and saw that you were old enough for love, I spread the corner of my garment over you and covered your nakedness. I gave you my solemn oath and entered into a covenant with you, declares the Sovereign LORD, and you became mine.**

[9]**"'I bathed you with water and washed the blood from you and put ointments on you.** [10]**I clothed you with an embroidered dress and put leather sandals on you. I dressed you in fine linen and covered you with costly garments.** [11]**I adorned you with jewelry: I put bracelets on your arms and a necklace around your neck,** [12]**and I put a ring on your nose, earrings on your ears and a beautiful crown on your head.** [13]**So you were adorned with gold and silver; your clothes were of fine linen and costly fabric and embroidered cloth. Your food was fine flour, honey and olive oil. You became very beautiful and rose to be a queen.** [14]**And your fame spread among the nations on account of your beauty, because the splendor I had given you made your beauty perfect, declares the Sovereign LORD.**

THE ORPHAN WHO BECAME QUEEN (16:1-14).   **16:1-14**   God commanded Ezekiel again to confront Jerusalem with its "detestable practices" (v. 2).[55] This message was so forceful and explicit that it was

---

[55] The term תּוֹעֵבָה ("something abominable/detestable") occurs over forty times in Ezekiel, especially in chaps. 5–8. See Deut 32:16; 1 Kgs 14:22-24.

excluded from use as a public reading in later synagogue practice. The denunciation of the apostasy of Israel was considered an unhealthy topic for devotional reading in general worship.[56]

The birth of the nation as God's covenant people is portrayed in parable form and compared to the untimely birth of an unwanted female child (v. 4). God had chosen Israel from among its Canaanite neighbors, principally the Amorites and Hittites, to be specially related to and used by him (v. 3).[57] When David captured Jerusalem from the Jebusites, he made it the capital and crown jewel of the Hebrew nation. The Jebusites retained control of Jerusalem until its conquest by David (2 Sam 5:6-9).[58]

The nativity of Israel was traced to Egypt when the Hebrews were delivered and "born" as a nation at Mount Sinai (Exod 19:1-8). Ezekiel described normal birth practices such as rubbing the newborn with salt, water, and oil, then wrapping the baby in cloth strips for seven days and repeating the process for forty days. This was supposed to enhance the child's character and promote general health and well-being for newborn children.[59] But Israel's nativity was deprived of these rites. Instead, Israel was portrayed as a female abandoned at birth with no one to care for or have pity on her helplessness. This practice of exposure of sickly, deformed, and unwanted children was common in the ancient Near East, especially for unwanted female babies.[60] When she was unlovely and no one else wanted her (Israel), God had compassion on her as she lay struggling in her own blood, and he rescued her and decreed her life by the word of his power.[61]

God then cared for the nation and caused it to increase and flourish like sprouts in a field, language reminiscent of the growth of the nation in Egypt as described in Exod 1:7,12. So she (Israel) prospered until she

---

[56] Fisch, *Ezekiel*, 83.

[57] Greenberg, *Ezekiel 1–20*, 274. The term "Canaanites" can also be used synonymously with or as a subset of "Amorites." Furthermore, it can refer to different groups, the former occupying regions near the Mediterranean and the latter in the hills and east of Palestine. See R. de Vaux, *The Early History of Israel* (Philadelphia: Westminster, 1978), 132-39.

[58] B. Mayer, "Jerusalem in the Biblical Period," in *Jerusalem Revealed* (New Haven: Yale University Press, 1976), 4; see also Greenberg, *Ezekiel 1–20*, 274; Eichrodt, *Ezekiel*, 204.

[59] Fisch, *Ezekiel*, 84; Greenberg, *Ezekiel 1–20*, 274.

[60] Zimmerli, *Ezekiel 1*, 338; Fisch, *Ezekiel*, 84-85; Greenberg, *Ezekiel 1–20*, 275; Wevers, *Ezekiel*, 121. Baby girls often were abandoned because of poverty and fear of disgrace because of the low estate afforded women in the ancient Near East. This was especially true of malformed and weak children.

[61] See Exod 33:19; 34:6; Deut 8:3; Neh 9:16-25; Isa 55:11; Luke 7:14; John 6:68; Rom 5:8; Phil 2:16; Heb 4:12.

reached the maturity of womanhood. As a beautiful young woman of marriageable age, she became the wife of Yahweh.[62] "Spreading the corner" of a garment over a young woman was the ritual for claiming a bride. Unlike a marriage arranged by the parents, the arrangement in which the woman had no part, God made a "covenant" with her in which he pledged to care for her with words that are reminiscent of Sinai (Exod 19:1-8).[63]

The language of the marriage ritual continues through the passage. Ezekiel reported how God cleansed her (v. 9), clothed her luxuriously with the garments of a princess (v. 10), gave her bridal jewelry, the best food usually reserved for royalty, and crowned her as his queen. As a result she became renowned for her beauty (vv. 10-14).[64] Israel was the orphan who became a queen. All the figures used in the description were reminders of the providential care God gave Israel from the time of Abraham to nationhood and onward.

The love and compassion of God offers hope to those ruined by sin. He offers new hope and new life (see Eph 1:1-6, according to which God chose us, predestined us, adopted us, and accepted us because he loved us). God transforms the lives of those who respond to his love. They become new creatures (2 Cor 5:17), enfranchised as the people of God (Eph 2:11-22).

**[15]"'But you trusted in your beauty and used your fame to become a prostitute. You lavished your favors on anyone who passed by and your beauty became his. [16]You took some of your garments to make gaudy high places, where you carried on your prostitution. Such things should not happen, nor should they ever occur. [17]You also took the fine jewelry I gave you, the jewelry made of my gold and silver, and you made for yourself male idols and engaged in prostitution with them. [18]And you took your embroidered clothes to put on them, and you offered my oil and incense before them. [19]Also the food I provided for you—the fine flour, olive oil and honey I gave you to eat—you offered as fragrant incense before them. That is what happened, declares the Sovereign LORD.**

**[20]"'And you took your sons and daughters whom you bore to me and sac-**

---

[62] Taylor, *Ezekiel,* 135; Greenberg, *Ezekiel 1–20,* 276; Fisch, *Ezekiel,* 85; Deut 8:1-20 was a message from Moses in which he warned of the consequences of forgetting God was their source and provider.

[63] Greenberg, *Ezekiel 1–20,* 277; Fisch, *Ezekiel,* 86. This was another way to express the double obligation clause, "You shall be my people, and I shall be your God." These words constituted a covenant in which Israel became God's as a wife becomes a husband's and a husband a wife's in a marriage.

[64] Wevers, *Ezekiel,* 122; Greenberg, *Ezekiel 1-20,* 279; Fisch, *Ezekiel,* 87. Israel's fame became worldwide during David's reign (1 Chr 14:17).

rificed them as food to the idols. Was your prostitution not enough? [21]You slaughtered my children and sacrificed them to the idols. [22]In all your detestable practices and your prostitution you did not remember the days of your youth, when you were naked and bare, kicking about in your blood.

[23]"'Woe! Woe to you, declares the Sovereign LORD. In addition to all your other wickedness, [24]you built a mound for yourself and made a lofty shrine in every public square. [25]At the head of every street you built your lofty shrines and degraded your beauty, offering your body with increasing promiscuity to anyone who passed by. [26]You engaged in prostitution with the Egyptians, your lustful neighbors, and provoked me to anger with your increasing promiscuity. [27]So I stretched out my hand against you and reduced your territory; I gave you over to the greed of your enemies, the daughters of the Philistines, who were shocked by your lewd conduct. [28]You engaged in prostitution with the Assyrians too, because you were insatiable; and even after that, you still were not satisfied. [29]Then you increased your promiscuity to include Babylonia, a land of merchants, but even with this you were not satisfied.

[30]"'How weak-willed you are, declares the Sovereign LORD, when you do all these things, acting like a brazen prostitute! [31]When you built your mounds at the head of every street and made your lofty shrines in every public square, you were unlike a prostitute, because you scorned payment.

[32]"'You adulterous wife! You prefer strangers to your own husband! [33]Every prostitute receives a fee, but you give gifts to all your lovers, bribing them to come to you from everywhere for your illicit favors. [34]So in your prostitution you are the opposite of others; no one runs after you for your favors. You are the very opposite, for you give payment and none is given to you.

THE QUEEN WHO BECAME A HARLOT (16:15-34). **16:15-34** This Cinderella story turned tragic because Israel's repayment for God's love and care was betrayal. The girl once left for dead, who was nurtured to maturity and who became the bride of her benefactor, also became unfaithful. The reasons for the fall of the nation are presented poignantly in this section. Ezekiel enumerated at least eight reasons for the exile: pride (v. 15a), spiritual prostitution (vv. 15b-19), materialistic idolatry (vv. 16-19), human sacrifices (vv. 20-21), forgetting God (v. 22), propagating her prostitution (vv. 23-25), trusting relations with pagan nations (vv. 26-29), and a weak will that cast off all moral restraints (vv. 30-34).

The language of this whole passage is most explicit. Pride and self-sufficiency were the foundation for all its harlotry (v. 15). Israel ignored the warnings given in the early days of its national life. Deuteronomy 6:10-12 was a clear warning against the danger of becoming self-sufficient and forgetting God. Deuteronomy 8:1-20 was an additional warning that the nation must not forget its heritage. It was to bear in mind continually that God found it, nurtured it in the wilderness, made it his own, and gave it a land of promise and blessing. Israel ignored these clear warnings and became what Ezekiel portrayed as an "adulterous wife" who preferred strangers to her husband (Ezek 16:32).[65]

Israel exchanged Yahweh worship for worship of pagan gods at pagan shrines called "high places" (v. 16; cf. 2 Kgs 21:3). It was wickedly ironic that the people used God's gifts to build shrines and make idols of gods that were nonexistent. They took fine jewelry and constructed male idols and engaged in ritual sex as part of the fertility cult (v. 17).[66] They put fine clothing on their idols, offered the finest food before them, and burned incense to them (vv. 18-19).

Yet all these things had been gifts of God and were not theirs to use indiscriminately. The proliferation of personal pronouns in this passage tells the story of the sin of ingratitude for God's marvelous provision. They wantonly misused these provisions. God said these were things "*I* gave you" (v. 17), "*my* gold and silver," "food *I* provided for you" (v. 19), "fine flour, olive oil and honey *I* gave you to eat," "sons and daughters which you bore to *me*" (v. 20); "you slaughtered *my* children" (v. 21). These were undeniable evidences of their greed, selfishness, and self-will that are true of any materialistic society. Such conduct produced injustice, violence, immorality, decadence, and blindness to the sanctity of human life.

Children also were sacrificed to pagan gods such as Molech, a practice strictly forbidden in the law (see Lev 18:21; 20:1-5; Deut 12:30-32). This practice was a tragic fact of history before the fall of Israel and Judah. Ahaz practiced child sacrifice (2 Kgs 16:3; 2 Chr 28:3), as did Manasseh (2 Kgs 21:6). When Josiah tried to eradicate child sacrifice, it had become a widespread general practice (2 Kgs 23:10).[67] These practices mark a climax of the surrender of the fundamental convictions of the ancient faith of Yahweh in favor of Canaanite heathenism.[68]

The basic cause behind all the evil excesses presented in v. 22 was neglect of the covenant. They "did not remember the days of their youth." They forgot God in the sense that he made no difference in their daily lives. They were practical atheists, professing to worship Yahweh along with other gods but failing to believe and obey his word.[69]

God's response was to cry, "Woe, Woe" to the nation (v. 23), an ex-

---

[65] Wevers, *Ezekiel*, 123. "Strangers" refers to alliances with various nations and paying bribes to them in order to secure Judah's political future.

[66] Greenberg, *Ezekiel 1–20*, 280 (cf. Isa 57:8).

[67] See Stalker, *Ezekiel*, 143; Eichrodt, *Ezekiel*, 207; and Alexander, "Ezekiel," 813.

[68] See Eichrodt, *Ezekiel*, 207.

[69] P. C. Craigie, *Ezekiel* (Philadelphia: Westminster, 1983), 112.

pression of lament and horror that was uttered at the arrival of disaster.[70] God was horrified that they would not listen to his prophets but multiplied altars for sinning. They placed hope for present and future security on alliances with idolatrous neighbors who further prostituted the nation. Ezekiel mentioned specifically Egypt (v. 26) and Assyria (v. 28), who captured some of Judah's territory in Sennacherib's invasion in 701 B.C., and Babylon (v. 29).[71] The people's conduct was so depraved that even the Philistines, noted for their debauchery, were "shocked" by their lewd conduct (v. 27).

Israel had failed to remember their history of grace received from God. Their annual festivals and daily worship were designed to remind them of this grace, but they became deaf to the message (v. 22). Failing to remember their history, they became proud of who they were and of what they had (v. 15). The result was that they cast off all moral restraint and gave themselves to permissiveness and perversions (v. 30). So Israel was an "adulterous wife" who preferred strangers to her own husband (v. 32). Furthermore, while most harlots exacted a price for their services, Israel the harlot bribed her clients and paid them to commit adultery with her (vv. 33-34), thus voluntarily enslaving herself to them (cf. 1 Cor 7:22-23). With this record of the sordid deeds of the queen who became a harlot, the message turns to the theme of judgment.

[35]"'Therefore, you prostitute, hear the word of the LORD! [36]This is what the Sovereign LORD says: Because you poured out your wealth and exposed your nakedness in your promiscuity with your lovers, and because of all your detestable idols, and because you gave them your children's blood, [37]therefore I am going to gather all your lovers, with whom you found pleasure, those you loved as well as those you hated. I will gather them against you from all around and will strip you in front of them, and they will see all your nakedness. [38]I will sentence you to the punishment of women who commit adultery and who shed blood; I will bring upon you the blood vengeance of my wrath and jealous anger. [39]Then I will hand you over to your lovers, and they will tear down your mounds and destroy your lofty shrines. They will strip you of your clothes and take your fine jewelry and leave you naked and bare. [40]They will bring a mob against you, who will stone you and hack you to pieces with their swords. [41]They will burn down your houses and inflict

---

[70] See Prov 23:29; 1 Sam 4:8; Isa 3:9.

[71] "Canaanites" appears in some translations for NIV "merchants" in v. 29. The word כְּנַעַן literally means "merchants" and is here descriptive of Israel's relationship with Babylon (see Hos 12:8[Eng., 7]; Zeph 1:11; also see Alexander, "Ezekiel," 814). For their dependence on these nations and God's attitude toward it, see 20:6-8; 2 Kgs 16:7-9; 17:4; Isa 30:1-5; 31:1-3.

punishment on you in the sight of many women. I will put a stop to your prostitution, and you will no longer pay your lovers. [42]Then my wrath against you will subside and my jealous anger will turn away from you; I will be calm and no longer angry.

[43]"'Because you did not remember the days of your youth but enraged me with all these things, I will surely bring down on your head what you have done, declares the Sovereign LORD. Did you not add lewdness to all your other detestable practices?

THE HARLOT WHO BECAME A CONVICT (16:35-43). **16:35-43** The queen who became a harlot was tried, convicted, and sentenced as a criminal. Her lovers were to be the agents of her destruction. Judah paid the penalty for the spiritual adultery of its idolatry and the murder of its children in sacrifice to false gods. The judgment of a harlot prescribed in the law included tearing off the clothes, public humiliation in nakedness, public trial, public stoning till death, dismemberment of the body, and burning of the house (cf. vv. 37-41; Lev 20:10-12; Deut 22:22).

Israel's lovers were all the nations with which there was an alliance and from which there was a syncretistic appropriation of pagan religious ideals and practices.[72] Through judgment Israel the harlot was to return to the same despised condition of shame, helplessness, and exile she was in before God found and rescued her ("naked and bare" in v. 39, also in vv. 7,22).[73] The nation would be an example of the justice and judgment of God. The phrase "in the sight of many women" (v. 41) was a reminder that women were made to watch the judgment of an adulteress so her judgment might be an example and deterrent. God would not rest until he had so punished unfaithful Israel (v. 42).[74] The idea of v. 43 is repeated from v. 22 as a reminder that all these calamities came because they failed to remember their history and their covenant with Yahweh. Judah was unfaithful and ungrateful for all God had done for the nation.[75]

---

[72] Fisch, *Ezekiel,* 93, and cf. Hos 2:9.

[73] The word for "nakedness" in v. 37 is עֶרְוָה, also used in Gen 9:22; 42:9,12 ("unprotected"); Deut 23:15[Eng., 14] ("indecent"). A different word, עָרוֹם "naked," is used in Gen 2:25; 1 Sam 19:24. In v. 39 "naked" is עֵירֹם (23:29; Gen 3:7,10; Deut 28:48), and "bare" is עֶרְיָה (also in vv. 7,22; 22:10 ["bed"]; 23:29; Mic 1:11). The literal result of God's judgment would be loss and exile. The verb גלה means both "uncover/expose" and "go into exile," since exile involves the loss of protection. At least part of the judgment of nakedness involved exile. See 16:36-37,57; 23:10,18; 39:23; D. Stuart, *Ezekiel* (Dallas: Word, 1989), 141,143.

[74] Greenberg, *Ezekiel 1–20,* 288.

[75] Ezekiel portrays God as relentless in his determination to punish Israel for idolatry and its compromise of faith. See Eichrodt, *Ezekiel,* 212; Fisch, *Ezekiel,* 95.

[44]"'Everyone who quotes proverbs will quote this proverb about you: "Like mother, like daughter." [45]You are a true daughter of your mother, who despised her husband and her children; and you are a true sister of your sisters, who despised their husbands and their children. Your mother was a Hittite and your father an Amorite. [46]Your older sister was Samaria, who lived to the north of you with her daughters; and your younger sister, who lived to the south of you with her daughters, was Sodom. [47]You not only walked in their ways and copied their detestable practices, but in all your ways you soon became more depraved than they. [48]As surely as I live, declares the Sovereign LORD, your sister Sodom and her daughters never did what you and your daughters have done.

[49]"'Now this was the sin of your sister Sodom: She and her daughters were arrogant, overfed and unconcerned; they did not help the poor and needy. [50]They were haughty and did detestable things before me. Therefore I did away with them as you have seen. [51]Samaria did not commit half the sins you did. You have done more detestable things than they, and have made your sisters seem righteous by all these things you have done. [52]Bear your disgrace, for you have furnished some justification for your sisters. Because your sins were more vile than theirs, they appear more righteous than you. So then, be ashamed and bear your disgrace, for you have made your sisters appear righteous.

THE CONVICT WHO BECAME A PROVERB (16:44-52) **16:44-52** The next stage in the judgment of the orphan who became a queen, a harlot, and finally a convicted criminal was the revelation that her story would become a "proverb" (cf. 14:8).[76] The proverb was, "Like mother, like daughter." The point was that if Jerusalem wanted a shocking look at her disgraceful character and her dismal future, she could look at her cultural ancestors the Hittites and Amorites, who had transmitted their heritage of wickedness to Sodom, Samaria, and Jerusalem.[77] In depravity and idolatry Israel had followed the bad example of the Canaanites and thus would be judged like them.[78]

"Samaria" (v. 46) refers to the Northern Kingdom, which was not "older" in a chronological sense but was larger and was the first to mature for judgment. The term "daughter" (vv. 46,49) could be used to refer to small villages dependent on the larger cities such as Samaria, Sodom, and Jerusalem.[79] These cities influenced the villages in the vicinity. Jerusalem, in this sense, had become the "daughter" of Samaria. Together they became

---

[76] Concerning מָשָׁל see comments on 12:21-25.
[77] Polk, "Paradigms, Parables, and Mĕšālîm, 575.
[78] See Greenberg, *Ezekiel 1–20,* 288; cf. also Hos 5:1-4; 2 Kgs 17:19; Fisch, *Ezekiel,* 95.
[79] See Cooke, *Ezekiel,* 177.

harlots and in so doing influenced others to become harlots as well (v. 45).

The abominations of Judah quickly followed the fall of Samaria (vv. 46-47). Soon moral depravity and idolatry exceeded that of fellow Israel and even of Sodom (Gen 18:20). Judah's security and prosperity produced pride and self-sufficiency that in turn resulted in disregard for moral righteousness (vv. 49-50).[80] Thus because Samaria and Sodom did not escape judgment, neither would Judah (v. 51). So reprehensible were the sins of Judah that Sodom and Samaria appeared more righteous by comparison. This was a cutting indictment filled with irony since the name Sodom was not even spoken by Jews of Judah out of contempt for its evil example.[81] Judah's actions therefore served as a mitigating influence on the severe punishment and hope of restoration for her sisters in sin, Sodom and Samaria (v. 52).[82] Had God not severely punished Judah, Sodom and Samaria could have received comfort (v. 54) by pointing to Judah, justifying themselves and accusing God of violating his righteousness.

Even the people of God receive judgment for sin. Judah was judged as an adulteress, lost its possessions, became a proverb for spiritual harlotry, and was destroyed (vv. 36-58).

**[53]"'However, I will restore the fortunes of Sodom and her daughters and of Samaria and her daughters, and your fortunes along with them, [54]so that you may bear your disgrace and be ashamed of all you have done in giving them comfort. [55]And your sisters, Sodom with her daughters and Samaria with her daughters, will return to what they were before; and you and your daughters will return to what you were before. [56]You would not even mention your sister Sodom in the day of your pride, [57]before your wickedness was uncovered. Even so, you are now scorned by the daughters of Edom and all her neighbors and the daughters of the Philistines—all those around you who despise you. [58]You will bear the consequences of your lewdness and your detestable practices, declares the LORD.**

**[59]"'This is what the Sovereign LORD says: I will deal with you as you deserve, because you have despised my oath by breaking the covenant. [60]Yet I will remember the covenant I made with you in the days of your youth, and I will establish an everlasting covenant with you. [61]Then you will remember your ways and be ashamed when you receive your sisters, both those who are older than you and those who are younger. I will give them to you as daughters, but not on the basis of my covenant with you. [62]So I will establish my covenant with you, and you will know that I am the LORD. [63]Then, when I make atonement for you for all you have done, you will remember and be**

---

[80] Fisch, *Ezekiel,* 96-97, and cf. Jer 3:11.

[81] Ibid., 98; cf. Ezek 16:56.

[82] Alexander, "Ezekiel," 817; Wevers, *Ezekiel,* 131; cf. Jer 3:6-11.

**ashamed and never again open your mouth because of your humiliation, declares the Sovereign LORD.'"**

THE CONVICT AND HER COMPANIONS (16:53-63).   This message about the orphan who became first a queen, then a harlot, and finally an object of judgment does not end with solemn words of judgment but with assurance of restoration.[83] The hope of forgiveness and restoration was not new. Moses and the other prophets who spoke of judgment for both Israel and Judah also had envisioned a future restoration.[84] Ezekiel saw hope for restoration of the harlot but only after judgment had been fulfilled.

**16:53-58**   Because Judah had exceeded the sins of Sodom and Samaria, any hope of restoration also must include them, since God is just (v. 53). Ezekiel envisioned not only their restoration but also that it would take precedence over that of Judah (note "your fortunes along with them," lit. "in their midst" in v. 53).[85] This was an astonishing development, especially since Sodom and Samaria were bywords for evil and object lessons of God's wrath against evil (cf. Isa 1:9-23; 3:9; 13:19; Jer 49:18; 50:40; Amos 4:11). The irony of this was that Judah had become a byword (vv. 56-57) to its pagan neighbors such as Edom and Philistia for destruction and judgment (v. 58).

The fact that Sodom was destroyed rather than exiled (Gen 19:24-25) makes it clear that Ezekiel was not predicting a literal return for them. We perhaps also should not expect from this promise a literal rebuilding of Sodom and Samaria. D. Stuart may be correct that the point is that "God will one day bless other cities as well, forgiving many people their sins, and that He will eventually establish an existence where righteousness prevails and rebellion against Him is no more."[86] Sodom, then, may rep-

---

[83] The phrase "restore the fortunes" (שְׁבִית/שְׁבוּת שׁוּב) is translated "bring again/turn the captivity" in KJV, understanding שְׁבִית/שְׁבוּת as from the root שׁבה ("take captive"). Most today, however, understand it as a cognate accusative from שׁוּב; thus the meaning is "bring about a restoration" (note its use in Job 42:10; see KB[3], 1289-90; J. M. Bracke, "šûb šebût: A Reappraisal," *ZAW* 97 [1985]: 233-44; M. Dahood, *Psalms III* [Garden City: Doubleday, 1970], 217-18; W. Holladay, *The Root šûbh in the Old Testament* [Leiden: Brill, 1958], 110-14). G. Van Groningen explains that the expression involves "restoration to either spiritual, physical, social, economic, or political well-being or a combination of these" (*Messianic Revelation in the Old Testament* [Grand Rapids: Baker, 1990], 752).

[84] Zimmerli (*Ezekiel 1*, 351) notes that the idea of restoring fortunes is not unique to Ezekiel. See Deut 30:3; Pss 14:7; 53:7[6]; 85:2[1]; 126:4; Jer 29:14; 30:3,18; 31:23; 32:44; 33:7,11,26; 48:47; Hos 6:11[7:1]; Joel 4:1[3:1]; Amos 9:14; Zeph 2:7; 3:20; cf. Ezek 29:14; 39:25. There is even found elsewhere the idea of restoring the fortunes of the nations (Jer 48:47; 49:6,39).

[85] Greenberg, *Ezekiel 1–20*, 289-90. The same order of salvation is found in Rom 11.

[86] Stuart, *Ezekiel*, 143.

resent the Gentile peoples whose widespread repentance is predicted else-where.[87] "In His mercy He has even loved the 'citizens of Sodom,' as it were. And they are we!"[88]

**16:59**    This message of judgment for breaking God's moral laws was presented as a story of marital unfaithfulness. Judah, the wife, was un-faithful to Yahweh, the husband. Judah broke her marriage covenant (v. 59), which probably was a reference to the covenant at Sinai (Exod 19:1-8). According to Hebrew law, when adultery was discovered a husband could not ignore it. He was compelled by law to take action against his wife for her promiscuity. Likewise, God was obligated to punish Judah for breaking the covenant (v. 59).[89]

**16:60-61**    In spite of the inevitability of judgment, God declared he indeed would restore Judah with its sisters, Sodom and Samaria. The as-surance in v. 60 contrasts with v. 59 by the use of an emphatic "I"—Judah had forgotten Yahweh's covenant, but "I myself will remember it."[90] God pledged to remember the former broken covenant and to make a new, ev-erlasting, and therefore unbreakable covenant (cf. Exod 2:24; Lev 26:42-45).[91] This new covenant would not only be permanent but it would be the basis for Judah's sense of conviction and sorrow for sin (cf. 20:43; 36:31; Zech 12:10-14). The word "receive" in v. 61 refers to the endow-ment of the new creation as an inheritance from God.[92]

The new covenant promised here and elsewhere (17:22-24; 34:23-29; 37:26; Jer 31:31-34) would have a new covenant Mediator who would be the Messiah.[93] Therefore the restoration Ezekiel presented was not based on the renewal of a broken covenant but on a new and everlasting cove-nant. Both Jeremiah and Ezekiel foresaw a new covenant for Israel, which would be everlasting and therefore permanent.[94]

---

[87] See Gen 12:2-3; Ps 86:9; Isa 19:23-25; 60:1-22; 66:18; Jer 12:14-16; Mic 4:1-4; Zech 8:20-23; Rev 15:4; cf. Rom 11:11; Gal 3:14.

[88] Stuart, *Ezekiel*, 144.

[89] Fisch, *Ezekiel*, 98-99; Greenberg, *Ezekiel 1–20*, 290-91; Zimmerli, *Ezekiel 1*, 353.

[90] Note the same construction translated "I myself" in 17:22.

[91] On various views of the "everlasting covenant," see M. Woudstra, "The Everlasting Covenant in Ezekiel 16:59-63," *CTJ* 6 (1971): 22-48.

[92] The same word, לָקְחָה, is used in Num 34:14-28; Josh 13:8; 18:7 regarding the inher-itance of the tribes of Israel (Greenberg, *Ezekiel 1–20*, 292).

[93] Fisch, *Ezekiel*, 99; cf. 34:23-25; 37:26; Jer 31:30. For the relation of the new cove-nant motif to the messianic hope, see J. Jocz, *The Covenant: A Theology of Human Destiny* (Grand Rapids: Eerdmans, 1968), 240; E. Jacob, *Theology of the Old Testament* (New York: Harper & Row, 1958), 216 and note 1.

[94] To explore the concept of covenant renewal and covenant renewal formulary in the OT, see K. Baltzer, *The Covenant Formulary* (Philadelphia: Fortress, 1971). See especially p. 62, where he notes the new covenant of Jer 31 was an eternal covenant that never needed to be renewed. See also P. P. Enns, *Ezekiel* (Grand Rapids: Zondervan, 1986), 85.

**16:62**   Verse 62 uses the same emphatic construction (literally) "I myself" as v. 60. Though Israel despised and broke the covenant, God himself would establish it and restore his relationship with them. The NIV has reversed the order of clauses in v. 63. It could be rendered more literally, "In order that you may remember and be ashamed and not open your mouth again because of your humiliation, when I make atonement for all you did." God's establishing his covenant with his rebellious people will be based on his all-important work of atonement, not overlooking but covering their sin by his marvelous grace.[95] Israel's departure from God had come because they had failed to remember who they were in relationship to him (15:22). But as a result of his atoning work, they would remember and return in humility and gratitude. The grace of God always is available to those who repent. God will remove the guilt of sin and will heal, forgive, and save people and nations (16:59-63; cf. 2 Chr 7:14).

### (8)  Prophecy (Parable) of the Eagles and the Vine (17:1-24)

[1]The word of the LORD came to me: [2]"Son of man, set forth an allegory and tell the house of Israel a parable. [3]Say to them, 'This is what the Sovereign LORD says: A great eagle with powerful wings, long feathers and full plumage of varied colors came to Lebanon. Taking hold of the top of a cedar, [4]he broke off its topmost shoot and carried it away to a land of merchants, where he planted it in a city of traders.

[5]"'He took some of the seed of your land and put it in fertile soil. He planted it like a willow by abundant water, [6]and it sprouted and became a low, spreading vine. Its branches turned toward him, but its roots remained under it. So it became a vine and produced branches and put out leafy boughs.

[7]"'But there was another great eagle with powerful wings and full plumage. The vine now sent out its roots toward him from the plot where it was planted and stretched out its branches to him for water. [8]It had been planted in good soil by abundant water so that it would produce branches, bear fruit and become a splendid vine.'

[9]"Say to them, 'This is what the Sovereign LORD says: Will it thrive? Will it not be uprooted and stripped of its fruit so that it withers? All its new growth will wither. It will not take a strong arm or many people to pull it up by the roots. [10]Even if it is transplanted, will it thrive? Will it not wither com-

---

[95] The verb כָּפַר is used here in the sense that Judah's sin would be covered/atoned for and the former sentence of judgment reversed (Deut 21:8; Isa 22:14). See Greenberg (*Ezekiel 1–20*, 298-99) on the uniqueness of this chapter and its relationship to Hosea. See also Van Groningen, *Messianic Revelation,* 754-55, where he identifies the covenant renewal and atonement of vv. 59-63 as that which will be finalized by the Messiah. The atonement for the covenant people is the topic of Isa 52:13–53:12.

pletely when the east wind strikes it—wither away in the plot where it grew?'"

[11]Then the word of the LORD came to me: [12]"Say to this rebellious house, 'Do you not know what these things mean?' Say to them: 'The king of Babylon went to Jerusalem and carried off her king and her nobles, bringing them back with him to Babylon. [13]Then he took a member of the royal family and made a treaty with him, putting him under oath. He also carried away the leading men of the land, [14]so that the kingdom would be brought low, unable to rise again, surviving only by keeping his treaty. [15]But the king rebelled against him by sending his envoys to Egypt to get horses and a large army. Will he succeed? Will he who does such things escape? Will he break the treaty and yet escape?

[16]"'As surely as I live, declares the Sovereign LORD, he shall die in Babylon, in the land of the king who put him on the throne, whose oath he despised and whose treaty he broke. [17]Pharaoh with his mighty army and great horde will be of no help to him in war, when ramps are built and siege works erected to destroy many lives. [18]He despised the oath by breaking the covenant. Because he had given his hand in pledge and yet did all these things, he shall not escape.

[19]"'Therefore this is what the Sovereign LORD says: As surely as I live, I will bring down on his head my oath that he despised and my covenant that he broke. [20]I will spread my net for him, and he will be caught in my snare. I will bring him to Babylon and execute judgment upon him there because he was unfaithful to me. [21]All his fleeing troops will fall by the sword, and the survivors will be scattered to the winds. Then you will know that I the LORD have spoken.

[22]"'This is what the Sovereign LORD says: I myself will take a shoot from the very top of a cedar and plant it; I will break off a tender sprig from its topmost shoots and plant it on a high and lofty mountain. [23]On the mountain heights of Israel I will plant it; it will produce branches and bear fruit and become a splendid cedar. Birds of every kind will nest in it; they will find shelter in the shade of its branches. [24]All the trees of the field will know that I the LORD bring down the tall tree and make the low tree grow tall. I dry up the green tree and make the dry tree flourish.

"'I the LORD have spoken, and I will do it.'"

This prophetic parable of 17:1-24 returns to the basic imagery of 15:1-8, where the vine was identified as Judah (15:6). Here Israel is represented by a cedar from Lebanon as well as a vine. This message may have been delivered shortly before the third invasion of Nebuchadnezzar in 586 B.C. It is an undated prophecy in contrast to the many dated prophecies in Ezekiel (see Introduction, "Dated Prophecies in Ezekiel"). There are six parts to the prophecy. First is an introduction (17:1-4) depicting the great eagle, Nebuchadnezzar, who crops the top of the tree. Second, new seed is planted that grows into a vine (17:5-6). Third, a second great eagle, Pharaoh Hophra, appears; and the vine extends its roots to him (17:7-8). Fourth, the vine is denounced and withers because of its treachery (17:9-10). Fifth is the interpretation of the prophetic parable (17:11-21). Sixth is a promise that God will restore the vine/tree one day as the messianic kingdom (17:22-24).

**17:1-4** This message is in the form of an "allegory" (*ḥîdâ*), better rendered "riddle," which usually designates an enigmatic saying designed "to disguise an idea so that the hearers might be confused or challenged to search for its meaning" (cf. Judg 14:12-18; 1 Kgs 10:1).[96] Here it identifies the chapter as "having a riddling quality, as if it entailed a mystery to be discerned."[97] The chapter is also called a *māšāl,* translated here "parable" but elsewhere also rendered "proverb" (12:22-23; 16:44; 18:2-3) or "byword" (14:8).[98] This chapter contains the longest *māšāl* in the Old Testament. It presents a prophetic parable about Judah's treachery during its last days and God's consequent judgment.

The story concerned a great eagle who took the top "shoot" of a cedar and carried it to a land of merchants, already identified as Babylon in 16:29. Cedars were plentiful in Lebanon in ancient times, and it was not uncommon for them to be transported to Mesopotamia, where timber was scarce.[99] The mention of Lebanon, therefore, may not be significant otherwise, as suggested by the interpretation in vv. 11-21. The top of the tree, the most prominent part, represented Judah's king and other leaders, who were taken to Babylon when Ezekiel was exiled in 597 B.C.

**17:5-10** In v. 5 the image changes. The remaining state of Judah, no longer a mighty cedar after its fall to Babylon, became a lowly vine in the land of Palestine. Nevertheless, it flourished, being amply cared for and protected as long as it subjected itself to Nebuchadnezzar, the eagle (cf. vv. 13-14). But a second eagle appeared, looking powerful and impressive, and the vine stretched its roots and branches toward him (vv. 7-8).

---

[96] C. H. Bullock, *An Introduction to the Old Testament Poetic Books* (Chicago: Moody, 1979), 22.

[97] Polk, "Paradigms, Parables, and *Měšālîm,*" 578.

[98] For מָשָׁל see comments at 12:21-25. Greenberg (*Ezekiel 1–20,* 309, 321-23) understands the form as riddle and fable. See also Wevers (*Ezekiel,* 104) and Alexander ("Ezekiel," 6:820-21).

[99] Stuart, *Ezekiel,* 148. Boadt ("Rhetorical Strategies," 193-94) notes the connection made between Lebanon and Jerusalem in Jer 22:6,23; 1 Kgs 7:2. More significant, he thinks, are similarities to Ezek 31, where Assyria is traced to a "cedar in Lebanon" (v. 3), alluding to "the myth of a cosmic world tree." Boadt suggests that in Ezek 17 Zedekiah is being compared to the Egyptian pharaoh of chap. 31, who also was guilty of "divine *hubris.*"

This represented Zedekiah's rebellious appeal to Egypt for help against Babylon (cf. v. 15). But Ezekiel warned that such rebellion, which apparently had begun at the time of the message, would be disastrous (vv. 9-10; cf. vv. 16-17). Though the soil and water favored growth and productivity, the vine would wither away (vv. 9-10). Even if transplanted, its survival was doubtful.

**17:11-21**    Verses 11-21 leave little doubt about the meaning of the parable or the identity of its symbols. The first great eagle was Nebuchadnezzar, and the cedar tree top was Jehoiachin and the "nobles" of Judah. The seed planted in the fertile soil of Canaan was Zedekiah, Jehoiachin's uncle, who was placed on the throne by Nebuchadnezzar.[100] He made a secret treaty with Pharaoh Hophra of Egypt to overthrow the rule of Nebuchadnezzar. Would the plot succeed? The answer was a resounding no! Ezekiel warned that Zedekiah would be taken captive and die in Babylon. Zedekiah brought further disgrace on God by breaking the oath of allegiance to Nebuchadnezzar that he had taken invoking the divine name, Yahweh, to confirm his pledge (cf. 2 Chr 36:13).[101] After judgment became inevitable, God's will for Judah was submission to their foreign conquerors as a sign of their submission to him (Jer 38:17-23). As king, Zedekiah had pledged to lead God's people in obedience to the divine covenant (cf. 16:59).[102] Therefore despising his oath and breaking his covenant with Nebuchadnezzar also amounted to an act of treachery and rebellion against God.[103]

Zedekiah was just as unfaithful to Nebuchadnezzar as he had been to God. Therefore God allowed him to be taken captive to Babylon. All Zedekiah's troops fled and were killed by the invading army of Babylon (vv. 19-21). The accuracy of this description of the destruction of Jerusalem confirmed the truth of this prediction.

**17:22-24**    The closing verses elaborate on the theme of messianic hope found in 16:60-63. Whereas the "great eagle" would transplant Israel and their king to the "city of traders" in the "land of merchants" (vv. 3-4), the Sovereign Lord himself ("I myself," emphatically) promised in v. 22 to provide a new Davidic king and transplant Israel again to a place of protection

---

[100] Fisch, *Ezekiel,* 104. The text has מִזֶּרַע הַמְּלוּכָה, which is literally "from the seed of kingship." Mattaniah, who took the throne name Zedekiah (2 Kgs 24:17), was another son of Josiah, which made him "royal seed" also.

[101] Wevers, *Ezekiel,* 107.

[102] Greenberg, *Ezekiel 1–20,* 322-23.

[103] The Hebrew word translated "treaty" in v. 16 (בְּרִית) is the same as that translated "covenant" in vv. 18-19.

and prominence on "the mountain heights of Israel."[104] "Take" is the same verb (*lāqaḥ*) as in v. 3. But there its object is "the top of a cedar," whereas v. 22 reads (literally), "I will take from the high top of a cedar," with no expressed object.[105] The addition of the adjective "high," together with the more narrow "from," suggests an individual more prominent than Jehoiachin and the leaders of v. 3. Yet the reappearance of the symbolic "cedar" calls attention to the fact that the new planting (community/nation) would be an extension of the old.[106] The verb *nātan,* translated "plant" in v. 22, usually means "give." It can also mean "place" and so can be translated "plant" here; but if so, it is out of logical order and is sometimes excised as a textual error.[107] In its more general sense of "give," however, it is reminiscent of Isa 9:6, another messianic prophecy.

The verb translated "break off" (*qāṭap*) is the same as in v. 4, where its object is (literally) "the top of its shoots." Again v. 22 uses the same words (except that "shoot" translates different forms of the root *ynq*[108]) but adds the preposition "from" and an additional modifier, "tender," yielding (literally) "from the top of its tender shoots" (again leaving the verb without an explicit object). The suggestion again is of a special shoot that will provide a fresh new beginning. The words translated "shoot" in vv. 4 and 22 are both derivatives of a verb meaning "to suck" (Job 3:12; Song 8:1; Isa 60:16). Another derivative (*yônēq*) is used of the messianic figure in Isa 53:2, where it is translated "tender shoot," an unpromising "sucker" usually pruned to prevent it from draining strength from the main plant.[109] The synonyms *ḥōṭer,* "shoot," and *nēṣer,* "branch," in Isa 11:1 and *ṣemaḥ,* "branch," in Isa 4:2; Jer 23:5; 33:15; Zech 3:8; and 6:12

---

[104] Van Groningen (*Messianic Revelation,* 755-60) dates the prophecy ca. 590 B.C. and believes it follows a literal chronology of the last days of Judah. He considers vv. 22-24 messianic both in the broad general sense of an envisioned restoration and also in the more narrow sense of a future royal figure, the Messiah, who will be preeminent over all kings and nations.

[105] The word "top" is צַמֶּרֶת, found only in 17:3,22; 31:3,10,14.

[106] Van Groningen, *Messianic Revelation,* 757. He explains further, "The overall emphasis of the two phrases, *I will take* and *I will set,* is on Yahweh's firm intention to undo what Babylon's king has done to the house of David by exceeding him, going to the highest twig, and placing it himself where it will grow and function as it should."

[107] Greenberg, *Ezekiel 1–20,* 216. An alternative would be to interpret God's words in v. 22 as a couplet consisting of two synonymous lines.

[108] Verse 4 uses יְנִיקָה (a hapax), and v. 22 uses יוֹנֶקֶת, a *qal* participle "sucker," occurring six times in the OT. See *TDOT* 6:106-8; *TWOT,* 383-84.

[109] The word is found eleven times in the OT. It is also a participial form and elsewhere refers to an infant (e.g., Num 11:12; Deut 32:25; 1 Sam 15:3; 22:19; Jer 44:7).

are also used figuratively of the Messiah.[110]

Planted on the highest mountain in Israel, his people will flourish beyond anything they experienced in the past (cp. v. 23 and v. 8) and will furnish shelter to "birds of every kind" (v. 23).[111] Furthermore, "all the trees of the field," that is, all nations, will acknowledge what Yahweh has done in humbling the proud and in exalting and restoring languishing Israel and the Davidic line in the Messiah (v. 24).[112]

The concluding statement of the chapter affirms the certainty of the Lord's promised restoration. Although some have understood it to have been fulfilled in the restoration of Judah under Zerubbabel, Ezra, and Nehemiah, the language goes beyond such limited scope (cf. Ezra 9:8-9)[113] to a time yet future when Israel will have its perfect King, the Messiah, reigning on the earth in righteousness.

### (9) Prophecy of Individual Responsibility (18:1-32)

**[1]The word of the LORD came to me: [2]"What do you people mean by quoting this proverb about the land of Israel:**

**"'The fathers eat sour grapes,**
**and the children's teeth are set on edge'?**

**[3]"As surely as I live, declares the Sovereign LORD, you will no longer quote this proverb in Israel. [4]For every living soul belongs to me, the father as well as the son—both alike belong to me. The soul who sins is the one who will die.**

**[5]"Suppose there is a righteous man**
**who does what is just and right.**

**[6]He does not eat at the mountain shrines**
**or look to the idols of the house of Israel.**
**He does not defile his neighbor's wife**
**or lie with a woman during her period.**

**[7]He does not oppress anyone,**
**but returns what he took in pledge for a loan.**
**He does not commit robbery**

---

[110] See E. J. Young, *The Book of Isaiah* (Grand Rapids: Eerdmans, 1965), 1:173-78, 378-80; F. B. Huey, Jr., *Jeremiah, Lamentations,* NAC (Nashville, Broadman, 1993), 211-12; J. G. Baldwin, "*Şemah* as a Technical Term in the Prophets," *VT* 14 (1964): 93-97.

[111] According to Van Groningen, "It will be above all other trees, above all vegetation, above the entire animal and insect world, and above all of mankind" (*Messianic Revelation,* 758).

[112] Zimmerli, *Ezekiel 1,* 367-68. This messianic promise is found again in 34:23-31 and 37:24-28.

[113] Cf. M. Breneman, *Ezra, Nehemiah, Esther,* NAC (Nashville: Broadman, 1993), 152-53.

but gives his food to the hungry
  and provides clothing for the naked.
[8]He does not lend at usury
  or take excessive interest.
He withholds his hand from doing wrong
  and judges fairly between man and man.
[9]He follows my decrees
  and faithfully keeps my laws.
That man is righteous;
  he will surely live,
    declares the Sovereign LORD.

[10]"Suppose he has a violent son, who sheds blood or does any of these other things [11](though the father has done none of them):

"He eats at the mountain shrines.
He defiles his neighbor's wife.
[12]He oppresses the poor and needy.
He commits robbery.
He does not return what he took in pledge.
He looks to the idols.
He does detestable things.
[13]He lends at usury and takes excessive interest.

Will such a man live? He will not! Because he has done all these detestable things, he will surely be put to death and his blood will be on his own head.

[14]"But suppose this son has a son who sees all the sins his father commits, and though he sees them, he does not do such things:

[15]"He does not eat at the mountain shrines
  or look to the idols of the house of Israel.
He does not defile his neighbor's wife.
[16]He does not oppress anyone
  or require a pledge for a loan.
He does not commit robbery
  but gives his food to the hungry
  and provides clothing for the naked.
[17]He withholds his hand from sin
  and takes no usury or excessive interest.
He keeps my laws and follows my decrees.

He will not die for his father's sin; he will surely live. [18]But his father will die for his own sin, because he practiced extortion, robbed his brother and did what was wrong among his people.

[19]"Yet you ask, 'Why does the son not share the guilt of his father?' Since the son has done what is just and right and has been careful to keep all my decrees, he will surely live. [20]The soul who sins is the one who will die. The son will not share the guilt of the father, nor will the father share the guilt of the son. The righteousness of the righteous man will be credited to him, and

the wickedness of the wicked will be charged against him.

[21]"But if a wicked man turns away from all the sins he has committed and keeps all my decrees and does what is just and right, he will surely live; he will not die. [22]None of the offenses he has committed will be remembered against him. Because of the righteous things he has done, he will live. [23]Do I take any pleasure in the death of the wicked? declares the Sovereign LORD. Rather, am I not pleased when they turn from their ways and live?

[24]"But if a righteous man turns from his righteousness and commits sin and does the same detestable things the wicked man does, will he live? None of the righteous things he has done will be remembered. Because of the unfaithfulness he is guilty of and because of the sins he has committed, he will die.

[25]"Yet you say, 'The way of the LORD is not just.' Hear, O house of Israel: Is my way unjust? Is it not your ways that are unjust? [26]If a righteous man turns from his righteousness and commits sin, he will die for it; because of the sin he has committed he will die. [27]But if a wicked man turns away from the wickedness he has committed and does what is just and right, he will save his life. [28]Because he considers all the offenses he has committed and turns away from them, he will surely live; he will not die. [29]Yet the house of Israel says, 'The way of the LORD is not just.' Are my ways unjust, O house of Israel? Is it not your ways that are unjust?

[30]"Therefore, O house of Israel, I will judge you, each one according to his ways, declares the Sovereign LORD. Repent! Turn away from all your offenses; then sin will not be your downfall. [31]Rid yourselves of all the offenses you have committed, and get a new heart and a new spirit. Why will you die, O house of Israel? [32]For I take no pleasure in the death of anyone, declares the Sovereign LORD. Repent and live!

God planned a new kingdom that would rise out of the decadence, ashes, and life-and-death struggle of the fall of Judah and Jerusalem. This struggle is portrayed on a personal level by the message of individual responsibility in 18:1-32. The invitation of the message is to choose life rather than judgment and death.[114] Portions of this chapter are often mistakenly used to present a case for impermanent salvation. Verses like 18:26 sometimes are taken out of context to claim that salvation once attained can be lost. For this reason it is very important to understand that neither spiritual salvation nor permanent versus perishable salvation were issues under discussion in chap. 18. The theme of the chapter is judgment deserved, and the central issue is who will receive judgment from God. Ezekiel presented the basis for deliverance from certain judgment versus visitation of certain judgment.

---

[114] Ibid., 387.

Judgment is a theme sometimes mistakenly applied only to those not saved. Ezekiel rightly declared that the prospect of divine punishment is a reality for everyone. The Bible clearly teaches that those lost are judged because of sin and a lack of a Savior-Redeemer (e.g., John 3:18; Rev 20:11-15). But the Bible also teaches that the saved will be judged according to their stewardship of life (see Rom 14:10-12; 1 Cor 3:11-15; 2 Cor 5:10).

Ezekiel eloquently made the case that everyone was equally accountable before God for the stewardship of life and the opportunity to avoid God's anger. Judgment was coming, and the people were accountable directly to God. The unrepentant were responsible for hearing the word of God and turning from sin by repentance. The repentant were responsible for warning others and doing the work God assigned. Even the prophet was responsible to warn and exhort both the unrepentant and repentant (see 3:18-21). This message on individual responsibility, then, was part of Ezekiel's assignment as "watchman" for the house of Israel (3:16-21). As a watchman the prophet was to warn, exhort, and thus protect the people by heralding God's word (Isa 21:6). If those warned refused to listen, the prophet had fulfilled his responsibility to God, and those who had sinned would be liable.

Chapter 18 develops the same theme with the same conclusion and results. There are two main emphases and thus two divisions in 18:1-32. First, individuals were not guilty for sins committed by others or by their families (18:1-20).[115] The thesis is stated in vv. 1-4, then illustrated with three examples. Verse 20 summarizes the first division and previews the second.[116] The point of the second division (18:21-32) is that individuals were not bound by former sins, their own or others, but could alter the sit-

---

[115] The argument has often been made or assumed since the nineteenth century that the concept of individual responsibility developed during the exile. More recently this view has been refuted both on the grounds that the concept was present in the earliest biblical literature and that the point of the exilic prophets was primarily that the current generation was guilty and therefore was suffering for their own sins. See especially P. Joyce, "Individual Responsibility in Ezekiel 18?" in *Studia Biblica 1978*, ed. E. A. Livingstone (Sheffield: JSOT, 1979), 185-96; idem, *Divine Initiative and Human Response in Ezekiel* (Sheffield: JSOT, 1989); idem, "Ezekiel and Individual Responsibility," in *Ezekiel and His Book*, ed. J. Lust (Leuven: University Press, 1986), 317-21; G. H. Matties, *Ezekiel 18 and the Rhetoric of Moral Discourse* (Atlanta: Scholars Press, 1990), 113-58; T. C. Vriezen, *An Outline of Old Testament Theology* (Oxford: Basil Blackwell, 1970), 386-87.

[116] See the helpful discussion of the structure of chap. 18 in Matties, *Ezekiel 18*, 34-43. Matties notes its complexity resulting from a lack of clear internal boundary markers (p. 34). Nevertheless, he demonstrates its unity by noting the presence of "lexical, grammatical, and rhetorical" devices (p. 35). He calls v. 20 a "hinge" between the two main sections (p. 43).

uation through repentance and faith. The proposition is stated in vv. 21-24. Then there is a response to charges of divine injustice in vv. 25-29. The chapter concludes with a call to repentance in vv. 30-32.[117]

**18:1-4** As if to answer the query of those who were trying to fix responsibility for the success of Babylon against Judah, Ezekiel discussed the proverb used by the people to disavow personal responsibility. It no doubt was a popular one among the Jews in Ezekiel's day. Jeremiah also mentioned this proverb in Jer 31:29. Like Jeremiah, Ezekiel concluded that it was not valid (18:3). The fathers, meaning their predecessors, had been guilty of gross sins deserving judgment. As a result, the people had concluded that they were having to suffer for the sins of their ancestors, an injustice brought upon their nation by God (18:25). The practice of transferring responsibility and blame to someone else apparently is a characteristic of sinful human nature. Their situation, they claimed, was not their fault, and there was nothing they could do about it. They were innocent victims of an unfair God.

Taylor makes two important observations that help to show why the proverb was so popular. First, the idea of continuing effects of ancestral sins is found in the Ten Commandments: "I the LORD your God am a jealous God, visiting the iniquity of the fathers upon the children to the third and the fourth generation of those who hate me" (Exod 20:5).[118] Second, it had been the basis of much of Ezekiel's own teaching, namely, that the sufferings of the exile could be traced back to the persistent rebellion, idolatry, and unfaithfulness to the covenant of previous generations of Israelites (e.g., 16:1-59). The exile was, in effect, the due consequence of these accumulating acts of disobedience. Furthermore, there was the element of apparent injustice in the way in which God's judgment fell indiscriminately upon both the bad and the good.[119] The people had seized upon these ideas, however, to remove themselves from blame or accountability and to throw the spotlight back onto God.

God's response through Ezekiel was that although sin had continuing effects, he never *punished* the righteous for the sins of the guilty.[120] In place of the invalid proverb, he declared a new thesis, "The soul that sins is the one who will die" (vv. 4,20). The word "soul" here carries the

---

[117] See Greenberg, *Ezekiel 1–20,* 334-36.

[118] The phrase "those who hate me" refers to the children, not the fathers.

[119] See Taylor, *Ezekiel,* 147.

[120] Stuart, *Ezekiel,* 153. The argument of H. W. Robinson that in Israel prior to Ezekiel and Jeremiah individuals and groups were thought to share guilt because the idea of individual personality was unknown has been shown to be false. See especially J. W. Rogerson, "The Hebrew Conception of Corporate Personality: A Re-Examination," *JTS* 21 (1970): 1-16.

meaning "life" or "person" and should not be confused with the concept of a "soul" as the spiritual and eternal part of a person.[121] Such a concept was foreign to the Hebrew mind-set, which regarded every person as a "life" or "soul." So the meaning of this declaration was, "The person who sins will be judged because of that sin" (cf. Rom 6:23).[122] All people are personally responsible to God for their own sin.

Ezekiel was not contradicting the biblical concept of corporate solidarity that was an essential part of Hebrew thought; nor was he introducing a new doctrine.[123] G. H. Matties argues that whereas H. W. Robinson felt that Ezek 18:4 was "untrue to the facts of life,"[124] Ezek 18 combines corporate and individual dimensions of personality in a way that is not contradictory. Ezekiel's goal was to reconstruct Israel as the holy people of God. Such a community would have to be created on the basis of individual choice. So it is through the commitment of the individual that the social and religious orders are to be saved.[125]

The story of Achan in Josh 7:1-26 is a classic example of corporate responsibility. Achan sinned, but his whole family suffered for his sin. Such a passage is difficult to understand unless we see the biblical distinction between guilt and consequences. In Achan's case he was the guilty party (7:21), but his family, who may have shared guilt by remaining silent about his misdeed, shared at least the consequences of his guilt, which was death by stoning. This was the point made in Exod 20:5 and 34:6-7. Individually each person is responsible for his or her own guilt of sin. But we must always be aware that the consequences of sin will affect others who may be innocent of the guilt for that particular sin. This is true even when the sin is forgiven. God promised to remove the guilt of sin, but

---

[121] The word נֶפֶשׁ refers to the whole person, not to a segmented part. In the OT view humans were neither a dichotomy (two parts, soul and body) nor a trichotomy (three parts, body, mind, and spirit) but a unity. See H. W. Wolff, *Anthropology of the Old Testament* (Philadelphia: Fortress, 1974), 18-25. This is also consistent with NT theology that envisions the redemption of the whole person, a concept confirmed by the resurrection and glorification of the physical body (1 Cor 15:1-58).

[122] Zimmerli (*Ezekiel 1,* 378-79) sees the ideal of life and death connected with the covenant of Noah (Gen 9:1-7).

[123] Taylor, *Ezekiel,* 148. The term "corporate solidarity" is used in W. C. Kaiser, *Toward Old Testament Ethics* (Grand Rapids: Zondervan, 1983), 67-72. He argues that sometimes a group was treated as a unit, sometimes an individual represented a group, and sometimes there was "oscillation" between a representative and the group represented. An individual can "implicate" a group.

[124] H. W. Robinson, *The Christian Doctrine of Man* (Edinburgh: T & T Clark, 1911), 34.

[125] Matties, *Ezekiel 18,* 118-24, 157-58. See also 130-46 for a comparison of other texts in Ezekiel that reflect the concepts of individual and corporate responsibility (e.g., chaps. 7; 9; 14; 16–17; 20; 33).

most often the consequences remain. David is a good example. Though he was forgiven of his sins of adultery and murder, he still suffered the consequences (2 Sam 12:11-20).

**18:5-20** Having stated his thesis, Ezekiel presented three examples: (1) the righteous person who does "right" (vv. 5-9), (2) the wicked son of a righteous father (vv. 10-13), and (3) the righteous son of a wicked father (vv. 14-20).

As part of the first example, Ezekiel presents a code of ethics for a righteous person (repeated in different form in vv. 10-13 and 14-17). Five principles characterize the life of this kind of person.[126] The first is the general principle that they do "what is just and right" (v. 5).[127] Second, the righteous person worships Yahweh alone as the one true God (v. 6a). Pagan practices and false gods are rejected.[128] Third, the righteous person carefully guards and maintains marital fidelity and moral purity (v. 6b). Fourth, the righteous person is a good neighbor (vv. 7-8). Others are treated with kindness, generosity, and justice. This person does not steal, nor does he wrong or take advantage of anyone, especially the needy, but rather gives food and clothing to the poor. He also promotes ethical behavior in others. The last principle summarizes the others: the righteous person respects and observes divine and human law (v. 9). If this principle is kept, all others will result.

In the second example (vv. 10-13) the righteous man's son was the antithesis of his father. He indulged in all those unjust and evil things from which his father abstained.[129] Should the wicked son go unpunished because he has a righteous father? The answer is an unqualified no (v. 13).

Example three is the case of the righteous man's grandson, the son of the wicked man. He had compared his grandfather's life and the life-style of his father (v. 14) and chose to follow the example of his godly grandfa-

---

[126] Greenberg (*Ezekiel 1–20*, 342) notes that the list begins and ends with general statements (vv. 5,9), between which there are twelve particulars (vv. 6-8). All but two are acts the righteous person avoids.

[127] The words צַדִּיק and מִשְׁפָּט indicate equitable dealings with all parties, human and divine. Ezekiel 18 has affinities with both the so-called priestly and deuteronomic traditions. Ezekiel describes sin as transgression of sacral orders which he equates with moral transgression. He thus saw the fall of Israel as failure in the holy ordinances (Matties, *Ezekiel 18*, 12; see also his "Legal Lists," 88-91, where he compares correspondences of the laws in chap. 18 as presented by various other scholars).

[128] Wevers (*Ezekiel*, 109-10) notes the combination of elements from the Decalogue dealing with levitical laws that deal with sexual mores.

[129] Notice the list in vv. 10b-13a parallels the list of vv. 6-9. See Greenberg's chart (*Ezekiel 1–20*, 342-43) comparing vv. 5-9,10-13, and 14-17. He also makes a helpful observation regarding the similarity to the crimes of Jerusalem presented in 22:6-12.

ther (cp. vv. 15-17 with vv. 6-9). So the conclusion of the matter was, Should a godly, righteous son assume the guilt of a wicked, ungodly father? The answer again was a resounding no (v. 17).

The question at issue in the three examples was restated and summarized in v. 19. Why did the son of vv. 14-20 not share the guilt of his father as presented in vv. 10-13? Because he had done what is just and righteous. So the person who practices the principles of righteousness will live and avert the judgment of God.[130] This section concludes with a restatement of the original thesis (v. 4). Persons who sin will die bearing the guilt of their own sin (v. 20). As Zimmerli states, "Righteousness and ungodliness, according to the formulation of the concluding sentence of the first speech in vv. 2-20, are not only causes but powers, which carry life and death within themselves."[131]

Greenberg makes the observation that Ezekiel's theological principle (vv. 4,20) is a literary inversion of and, therefore, an intentional reference to the law of individual responsibility in Deut 24:16 ("Fathers shall not be put to death for their children, nor children put to death for their fathers; each is to die for his own sin"):[132]

| Deut 24:16 | Ezek 18:20 |
|---|---|
| 1. not fathers for children | 3. the soul sinning dies |
| 2. children not for fathers | 2. son not with the father |
| 3. each dies for his sin | 1. father not with the son |

**18:21-24** A generation is not predetermined for judgment or for blessing by the previous one. Even within a generation, or within an individual life, the past does not necessarily determine the present or the future.[133] Ezekiel here set forth his proposition that God honors true repentance and genuine faith. The person who truly repents is able to put the guilt of sin in the past (v. 22). God erases it from one's record (cf. Ps 51:1,9).[134] God will forgive and receive anyone who turns to him from sin in repentance and faith, regardless of past sins (v. 21; Rom 5:6-11; Eph 2:1-8; Col 1:20-22; 2 Pet 3:9).[135] Verse 21 gives an excellent defini-

---

[130] See Zimmerli, *Ezekiel 1*, 385.

[131] Ibid.

[132] The chart is adapted from Greenberg, *Ezekiel 1–20*, 333.

[133] See Stuart, *Ezekiel*, 160-62.

[134] Fisch, *Ezekiel*, 112.

[135] שׁוּב is the most prominent word for repentance and literally means "to turn," or "to change direction." The word can be used in a physical sense connoting a change of physical movement but also is used in a spiritual sense to describe a new spiritual direction (BDB, 996-1000). See comments on 14:6-11 and 16:53. Also see the discussion of repentance in R. L. Smith, *Old Testament Theology: Its History, Method, and Message* (Nashville: Broadman & Holman, 1993), 304-6; Huey, *Jeremiah, Lamentations*, 70-79.

tion of true repentance based on faith. It involves two stages: first, a turning away from sin and second, a determination of loyal obedience to God.

God is not vindictive and takes no pleasure in bringing judgment on the wicked (v. 23). Matties notes that vv. 21-24 is a chiasm with God's rhetorical question at the place of prominence in the center. The idea is repeated as a statement in v. 32 as grounds for the call to repent.[136] God is righteous yet loving, just yet merciful. Judgment is to God a necessity; but what delights him is the repentance of the wicked because it allows him to forgive and restore.

God responds to faith and repentance (18:21-23). When the wicked repent, he forgives. When the God-fearing repent, he forgives. True repentance involves confession, sorrow for sin, desire for cleansing, and restoration (see Ps 51:1-12).

**18:25-29** This paragraph begins and ends with God's response to charges of injustice. Apparently the charges were based on the claim that Judah was innocent of wrongdoing but was paying for the sins of past generations. They believed they were caught in an unfair process of retribution that meted out punishment indiscriminately. There was nothing, then, the people could do about it. The phrase "is not just" translates the negation of the uncommon verb *tākan,* meaning "to measure/examine" (cf. 1 Sam 2:3; 2 Kgs 12:11[Heb., 12]; Job 28:25; Prov 16:2; 21:2; 24:12; Isa 40:12-13). The related noun *tōken* is used in Ezek 45:11 (elsewhere only Exod 5:18) meaning "measure/amount." The people's claim in 18:25,29, then, seems to be that God does not measure or examine his actions but acts arbitrarily. His response is to turn the charge on his accusers. It is they, he says, who do not measure their actions but act according to their own pleasure and will. God acts according to a clear principle: the wicked are punished, and the righteous are rewarded. Because God is just, his righteousness demands judgment for those who disobey his law. Since God clearly warns all people of this divine principle, the death of the wicked is not capricious or arbitrary but the choice and responsibility of each individual. Therefore when the righteous person abandons righteousness, judgment will be dispensed (v. 24).

Judgment that must be executed on a true believer is called chastening (see Heb 12:1-29). Believers are warned of God's chastening. Aside from its corrective purpose, chastening is an evidence of true faith (Heb 12:8). If a person sins and is not chastened, that person is illegitimate and not a genuine believer (Heb 12:8). If salvation could be lost, as some argue, "chastening" as a category of divine punishment has no meaning. A be-

---

[136] Matties, *Ezekiel 18*, 38. The repetition confirms the unity of vv. 21-32.

liever who sinned would be lost and simply once again would be in need of being saved. Consequently, Ezekiel was not discussing the issue of being lost or saved but how all people, lost and saved alike, can avert the judgment of God for sin.

As often is the case, when the guilty person is exposed there is a tendency to blame God (v. 29) or others. Ezekiel eloquently made the point that there is no basis on which the guilty may fix blame on others but rather they must accept their own personal accountability to God (v. 29). God's dealings are always just and equitable; he gives ample, clear warning of the consequences of sin.

**18:30-32** Having firmly and eloquently made his case, Ezekiel stated his final proposition. God desired to deliver, but he would bring judgment if necessary. Verses 30-32 also contain a final call to Judah to cease their faithlessness, turn to God, and be delivered. Such a radical course correction would involve a change of heart, meaning a change of thinking and volition (see discussion at 11:17-21). Individuals who would change their thinking and commit themselves wholeheartedly in faith to the Lord would be saved. In 11:19 God had already promised a day when all in Israel would experience such a transformation, and he repeats that promise in 36:25-27. The command here may be understood as based on that promise.[137] As A. H. Strong explained:

> Since the relation between the divine and the human activity is not one of chronological succession, man is never to wait for God's working. If he is ever regenerated, it must be in and through a movement of his own will, in which he turns to God as unconstrainedly and with as little consciousness of God's operation upon him, as if no such operation of God were involved in the change. And in preaching, we are to press upon men the claims of God and their duty of immediate submission to Christ, with the certainty that they who do so submit will subsequently recognize this new and holy activity of their own wills as due to a working within them of divine power.[138]

The message closes with the sad interrogative refrain, "Why will you die, O house of Israel?" (v. 31). God takes no pleasure in judgment, so "Repent and live!" (cf. v. 23).

### (10) Prophecy Lamenting Jerusalem's Leaders (19:1-14)

[1]"Take up a lament concerning the princes of Israel [2]and say:
"'What a lioness was your mother

---

[137] Wolff, *Anthropology of the Old Testament,* 54.
[138] A. H. Strong, *Systematic Theology* (Philadelphia: Judson, 1907), 830.

among the lions!
She lay down among the young lions
  and reared her cubs.
³She brought up one of her cubs,
  and he became a strong lion.
He learned to tear the prey
  and he devoured men.
⁴The nations heard about him,
  and he was trapped in their pit.
They led him with hooks
  to the land of Egypt.

⁵"'When she saw her hope unfulfilled,
  her expectation gone,
she took another of her cubs
  and made him a strong lion.
⁶He prowled among the lions,
  for he was now a strong lion.
He learned to tear the prey
  and he devoured men.
⁷He broke down
their strongholds
  and devastated their towns.
The land and all who were in it
  were terrified by his roaring.
⁸Then the nations came against him,
  those from regions round about.
They spread their net for him,
  and he was trapped in their pit.
⁹With hooks they pulled him into a cage
  and brought him to the king of Babylon.
They put him in prison,
  so his roar was heard no longer
  on the mountains of Israel.

¹⁰"'Your mother was like a vine in your vineyard
  planted by the water;
it was fruitful and full of branches
  because of abundant water.
¹¹Its branches were strong,
  fit for a ruler's scepter.
It towered high
  above the thick foliage,
conspicuous for its height
  and for its many branches.

<sup>12</sup>**But it was uprooted in fury**
   **and thrown to the ground.**
**The east wind made it shrivel,**
   **it was stripped of its fruit;**
**its strong branches withered**
   **and fire consumed them.**
<sup>13</sup>**Now it is planted in the desert,**
   **in a dry and thirsty land.**
<sup>14</sup>**Fire spread from one of its main**
**branches**
   **and consumed its fruit.**
**No strong branch is left on it**
   **fit for a ruler's scepter.'**
**This is a lament and is to be used as a lament."**

Chapter 19 comprises two funeral laments, one for the king (vv. 1-9) and one for the people of Judah (vv. 10-14). In that the scroll Ezekiel ate (2:10) contained "words of lament and mourning and woe," this chapter may be intended as a conclusion not only to chaps. 12–19 but also the entire first part of the book.[139] These two poems are dirges, which are set in the poetic meter specifically used for funerary poems.[140] Both poems are allegorical. The first poem presents a lioness, representing the Davidic line in the tribe of Judah. One lion cub, representing King Jehoahaz, grew up under the direction of the lioness but was captured and brought to Egypt (vv. 3-4). Jehoahaz, succeeding his father Josiah in 609 B.C., reigned only three months and then was taken to Egypt (2 Kgs 23:31-34).

He was replaced by Jehoiakim, who reigned as a vassal to Nebuchadnezzar. Jehoiakim is not referred to in the laments, since he was not exiled. He was deposed, however, for rebellion in 598/597 and replaced by his son Jehoiachin, represented by the second cub in the lament (vv. 5-9). Like Jehoahaz, he reigned only three months until he was taken captive, but his captivity was in Babylon (2 Kgs 24:8-17).

The second poem focuses on the reign of Zedekiah. He was Jehoiachin's uncle, a brother of Jehoahaz and son of Josiah. Given the throne by Nebuchadnezzar, his reign of treachery ended in a rebellion against Babylon that resulted in the destruction of Jerusalem in 586 B.C. It is little wonder that Judah earned a reputation as a rebellious kingdom (2 Kgs

---

[139] Boadt, "Rhetorical Strategies," 195.

[140] "Lament" (v. 1) is a translation of קִינָה, from which is named the lament meter, the dominant pattern of the laments in Lamentations as well as poems written commemorating the death of political leaders (see Amos 5:1-3; Isa 14:4-21; 2 Sam 1:17-27; 3:33-34). See Wevers, *Ezekiel,* 146-47.

24:20; 2 Chr 36:13; Neh 2:19).[141]

The funeral dirge is an appropriate form for chap. 19 since it is about the last days of Judah, the death of the kings, the death of Jerusalem, and the death of the nation. This poem has three parts: (1) a lament for the loss of a leader (19:1-4), (2) a lament for the loss of another leader (19:5-9), and (3) a lament for the fall of Judah (19:10-14).

**19:1-4**    Ezekiel called the last kings of Judah by the term "prince" rather than "king" because he did not recognize their legitimate right to reign.[142] The first poem uses hunting terminology, beginning in v. 4 with the mention of a "pit" and "hooks." Other terms are employed in vv. 8-9, such as "net" and "cage."[143]

The lion was a figure commonly associated with Judah and especially the line of David (Gen 49:9; Num 23:24; 1 Kgs 10:19-20; Mic 5:8; Rev 5:5). The lioness reared her cubs, one of which became a strong lion (v. 3), Jehoahaz, whose father Josiah was killed by Pharaoh Neco at Megiddo (2 Kgs 23:28-30).

Parallels of the description "they led him with hooks" (cf. v. 9) may be found in an Assyrian inscription from King Assurbanipal that says of a conquered king, "I pierced his cheeks, . . . put the ring to his jaw, placed a dog collar around his neck, and made him guard the east gate of Nineveh."[144] An Assyrian relief also shows King Esarhaddon holding a rope tied to rings in the lips of two captives.[145]

**19:5-9**    After the loss of one cub the lioness took a second and trained him as another "strong lion," a characterization emphasizing strength and prowess. This lion became a feared warrior who devoured men, destroyed strongholds, and devastated towns so that everyone was terrified of him.[146]

Some have identified the second cub as Zedekiah, who reigned as the last king of Judah from 597 to 586 B.C., since he and Jehoahaz had the same mother (2 Kgs 23:31; 24:18). But he is the subject of the second

---

[141] See the discussion of Jehoahaz, Jehoiakim, Jehoiachin, and Zedekiah in E. H. Merrill, *Kingdom of Priests* (Grand Rapids: Baker, 1987), 446-53.

[142] See Alexander, "Ezekiel," 831.It must be noted, however, that David is called a prince and is appointed by God to be king.

[143] Fisch, *Ezekiel,* 116; Zimmerli, *Ezekiel 1,* 395. See also Greenberg, *Ezekiel 1–20,* 351, who suggests reference to shackles used to transport prisoners. He also acknowledges these as hunting terms.

[144] *ANET,* 300.

[145] *ANEP,* no. 447. Both illustrations are mentioned in Greenberg, *Ezekiel 1–20,* 351.

[146] See Alexander ("Ezekiel," 831) for an extensive note on the translation of וַיֵּדַע ("he knew") in v. 7. The NIV has followed K. Elliger (BHS) in reading וַיָּרַע from רעע II ("to break") and אַרְמְנוֹתֵיהֶם ("their strongholds") for the MT אַלְמְנוֹתָיו ("their widows").

poem in Ezek 19:10-14. Most agree that the cub was not Jehoiakim, who reigned from 605 to 598/597 B.C. and was the immediate successor to Jehoahaz. The king was most likely Jehoiachin, who was captured and taken prisoner to Babylon (vv. 8-9).[147] Like the first cub, he is said to have been trapped in a pit and led away with hooks, but the second was put in a "cage." This may refer to neckstocks[148] or to an animal cage used by Assyrians to display and humiliate captured rulers.[149]

**19:10-14**   In this second lament concerning the "princes of Israel" (v. 1), they are no longer compared to lion cubs and their "mother," the Davidic line, a lioness; now they are branches on their "mother" a vine. The vine metaphor was used by Ezekiel previously in 15:1-8 and 17:5-10 (cf. Isa 24:7; Jer 2:21; 6:9) with reference to the decline and fall of Judah.

The fruitfulness and strength of the vine were signs of God's favor rather than evidence of the assurances of Babylon's help as in 17:5,8.[150] God had "planted" Israel "in a home of their own" and given them "rest" (2 Sam 7:10-11). In his charter for the Davidic dynasty he had promised that his strength would sustain them and his faithful love would cause their exaltation (Ps 89:19-29).[151] But if they forsook his law and violated his decrees, he would "punish their sin with the rod, their iniquity with flogging," although the Davidic line would not be destroyed (Ps 89:30-37). Ezekiel described in his figure of the vine the outworking of this Davidic covenant. The Lord in anger had uprooted the vine, stripped it of fruit, caused it to wither, and consumed it with fire (v. 12; cf. Ps 89:38-45). This clearly refers to the capture and death of Zedekiah and the destruction of Jerusalem in the siege of 586 B.C. But the vine was not destroyed. Rather, it was transplanted to the desert, where it languished, with no fruit and no strong branch left on the vine (vv. 13-14).[152] Thus the exile in Babylon is depicted, the Israelite monarchy apparently a thing of the past. The first poem (vv. 1-9) laments the end of two kings of Judah; the second poem (vv. 10-14) laments the end of kingship itself.[153]

This message concludes the prophecies of judgments to befall Judah

---

[147] On the succession of kings and their identity in the allegory see Fisch, *Ezekiel,* 117; Zimmerli, *Ezekiel 2,* 395; Wevers, *Ezekiel,* 148; Eichrodt, *Ezekiel,* 252-56.

[148] See Greenberg, *Ezekiel 1–20,* 352; Zimmerli, *Ezekiel 1,* 395-96.

[149] Fisch, *Ezekiel,* 118.

[150] Zimmerli, *Ezekiel 1,* 397. This is a reference to the grace assured to the Davidic line.

[151] Cf. W. J. Dumbrell, *Covenant and Creation* (Grand Rapids: Baker, 1984), 145.

[152] Wevers, *Ezekiel,* 150; Fisch, *Ezekiel,* 119; this refers to Zedekiah's revolt against Babylon (2 Kgs 24:20b).

[153] Stuart, *Ezekiel,* 170. He interprets the "fire" in v. 14 as Zedekiah, "whose leadership as a rebellious and godless king ruined Judah at the end of its history."

and Jerusalem that began in 12:1 (and perhaps also the entire first part of the book). As noted in the introduction to chap. 12, Ezekiel set forth in these messages seven reasons for the fall of Judah that may be used to summarize the theme and point of this section that began in chap. 12. They show that God was justified in bringing severe judgment on Judah. These failures will disintegrate the life of any nation or individual. They may be summarized as follows:

1. Judah failed to submit to God's chastening and rebelled in the face of captivity (12:1-20).

2. Judah rejected divine revelation. True prophets were ignored while false prophets and the idolatry they approved were accepted (13:1–14:23).

3. Judah failed to fulfill the purpose of fruitfulness for which God had created it (15:1-8).

4. Judah had a long history of unfaithfulness to God (16:1-63).

5. Judah depended on political alliances for security rather than looking to God to sustain the nation (17:1-24).

6. Judah was responsible to God for sin though there was reluctance to accept it (18:1-32).

7. Judah already was spiritually dead, so its political life also was allowed to die (19:1-14).

4. Prophecies concerning Judah (20:1–24:27)
   (1) Enumeration of the Rebellions of Judah (20:1-49)
   (2) Prophecy of the "Sword" of the Lord (21:1-27)
   (3) Prophecy of Judgment on the Ammonites (21:28-32)
   (4) Enumerations of Further Sins of Jerusalem (22:1-31)
   (5) Parable of the Two Sisters (23:1-49)
   (6) Parable of the Boiling Pot (24:1-14)
   (7) Parable at the Death of Ezekiel's Wife (24:15-27)

## 4. Prophecies concerning Judah (20:1–24:27)

This section of prophecies is the final collection of messages of judgment concerning the fall of Judah and Jerusalem. While thematically it is related to the previous section (12:1–19:14), Ezekiel focused more on the idea of God's motives behind judgment in chaps 20–24. For example, he addressed the matter of Yahweh's concern for his name and reputation. The name of Yahweh was considered synonymous with his character. So the character and reputation of Yahweh were set forth and contrasted with the sins and immorality of Judah's leaders and people.[1]

Chapter 20 is a historical review of the sins of Judah. Similar to 12:1–19:14 (esp. chap. 16), chap. 20 presents a catalog of the iniquities of the nation. It is one of the most forcefully structured units of the entire book. It also is like the overview of the waywardness of Israel and Judah as presented in chap. 23.[2]

The chapter may be seen in two areas of focus. The first, 20:1-29, is a dated prophecy that focuses on God's dealings with Israel and the nation's rebelliousness. The second, 20:30-49, focuses on the future and gives an affirmation of respect for Yahweh's name and concern over the defilement of his name by Israel that made judgment necessary.

---

[1] J. B. Taylor, *Ezekiel*, TOTC (Downers Grove: InterVarsity, 1969), 155-56.
[2] R. M. Hals, *Ezekiel*, FOTL (Grand Rapids: Eerdmans, 1989), 135. The structure of this passage reveals a prophetic message in which old tradition and new reinterpretation are present.

## *(1)  Enumeration of the Rebellions of Judah (20:1-49)*

There are eight divisions to this message: (1) the prophet speaks to the elders (20:1-4); (2) lessons from the exodus (20:5-9); (3) lessons from the wilderness days (20:10-14); (4) lessons for the forty years of wandering (20:15-22); (5) past rebellions committed in the land (20:23-29); (6) present rebellions and the coming exile (20:30-39); (7) the purification after the exile (20:40-44); (8) the call for judgment to begin (20:45-49).

**¹In the seventh year, in the fifth month on the tenth day, some of the elders of Israel came to inquire of the LORD, and they sat down in front of me.**
**²Then the word of the LORD came to me: ³"Son of man, speak to the elders of Israel and say to them, 'This is what the Sovereign LORD says: Have you come to inquire of me? As surely as I live, I will not let you inquire of me, declares the Sovereign LORD.'**
**⁴"Will you judge them? Will you judge them, son of man? Then confront them with the detestable practices of their fathers**

SPEECH TO THE ELDERS (20:1-4).　**20:1-4**　This is the fourth dated prophecy in the Book of Ezekiel.[3] It was August 591 B.C. A contingent of elders gained an audience with the prophet (v. 1). This scene is similar to the elders' approach recorded in 14:1-11.[4] God said, "I will not let you inquire of me," meaning he would not give Ezekiel any information for them. Instead God promised to give him the words they needed to hear (vv. 2-3). The double statement, "Will you judge them? Will you judge them?" (v. 4) had the force of a command. Thus it meant, "Be their advocate and confront them with their iniquities."[5] In essence, as an introduction to what followed, God instructed Ezekiel to tell these elders to listen to the record of the past sins of Israel, which the prophet was going to rehearse for them. God's judgment is never capricious. He always brings judgment in response to disobedience and unfaithfulness; thus it is always deserved judgment. This leaves no logical or legal basis on which to question his motives. The second of past sins serves to establish the basis for God's action.

**⁵and say to them: 'This is what the Sovereign LORD says: On the day I chose Israel, I swore with uplifted hand to the descendants of the house of Ja-**

---

[3] See "Dated Prophecies in Ezekiel" chart in the Introduction.
[4] Hals (*Ezekiel,* 138) believes this to be a clear parallel with 14:1-11.
[5] See W. Zimmerli, *Ezekiel 1,* Her (Philadelphia: Fortress, 1979), 406; Taylor, *Ezekiel,* 156-57.

cob and revealed myself to them in Egypt. With uplifted hand I said to them, "I am the LORD your God." ⁶On that day I swore to them that I would bring them out of Egypt into a land I had searched out for them, a land flowing with milk and honey, the most beautiful of all lands. ⁷And I said to them, "Each of you, get rid of the vile images you have set your eyes on, and do not defile yourselves with the idols of Egypt. I am the LORD your God."

⁸"'But they rebelled against me and would not listen to me; they did not get rid of the vile images they had set their eyes on, nor did they forsake the idols of Egypt. So I said I would pour out my wrath on them and spend my anger against them in Egypt. ⁹But for the sake of my name I did what would keep it from being profaned in the eyes of the nations they lived among and in whose sight I had revealed myself to the Israelites by bringing them out of Egypt.

LESSONS FROM THE EXODUS (20:5-9). **20:5-9** God appeared to the Hebrews in the time of Moses while in captivity in Egypt and promised them a land of milk and honey (Exod 6:8). He brought them out of bondage and chose Israel to be his special people (Exod 19:1-8; Deut 7:6-9). "I chose Israel" is covenant language and is a reminder of the relationship between God and Israel at the time he led them from bondage in Egypt and chose them to be his people by the covenant made at Sinai (Exod 19:1-8).[6] The phrase "I swore with uplifted hand" (v. 5) suggests that God took a solemn oath to fulfill the promises of the covenant.[7] Based on their covenant relationship with him, God commanded them to stop all vile, foreign religious practices (v. 7; Josh 24:14). He had delivered them to bring them into the land "flowing with milk and honey" (Deut 6:3), and they should be faithful to him.

Instead of obeying, the people rebelled and refused to listen (*šĕmaʾ*[8]) to God's request. Ezekiel probably had in mind the rebellion of the people while still in Egypt (e.g., Exod 5:20-23) or in the early days of wilderness wandering (e.g., Exod 14:11-12; 15:24; 16:3; 17:2). This was either an unrecorded event or a possible reference to the golden calf incident of Exod 32:1-35.[9] This sin occurred shortly after their departure from Egypt and was an example of how quickly they abandoned faithfulness to Yahweh and appealed to Egypt's gods for deliverance.[10]

---

[6] Cf. Deut 7:6-7; 14:52; 18:5; Jer 33:24.

[7] See S. Fisch, *Ezekiel* (London: Soncino, 1950), 121.

[8] "Listen" also can be translated "obey" and is from the root שׁמע (cf. Deut 6:4).

[9] M. Greenberg (*Ezekiel 1–20,* AB [Garden City: Doubleday, 1986], 365) believes that the reference is to Exod 32 and Num 14.

[10] Greenberg (*Ezekiel 1–20,* 365-66) notes that the Midrash presents the Hebrews as unwilling to totally separate themselves from the gods of Egypt and unwilling to be redeemed on Yahweh's terms.

Whatever incident Ezekiel had in mind, he stated that God spared the people because of his name, Yahweh, which embodied his character (Ezek 20:9).[11] This statement strongly suggests that God referred to the golden calf incident of Exod 32. Moses appealed to God with this line of argument (Exod 32:11-14) to spare the people. God had expressed his desire to annihilate them for their "stiff-necked" rebellion and start a new nation with Moses (Exod 32:7-10). Moses appealed to God to spare the people and based his petition on concern for the character and reputation of God (Exod 32:11-14).[12]

Though people are sinful and rebellious, God seeks to redeem them and faithfully fulfills his promises of life and blessing for them. Such an example is the story of the exodus from Egypt and the subsequent rebellion in the wilderness. This is a reminder of the truth concerning all people (Rom 5:6-8).

**[10]Therefore I led them out of Egypt and brought them into the desert. [11]I gave them my decrees and made known to them my laws, for the man who obeys them will live by them. [12]Also I gave them my Sabbaths as a sign between us, so they would know that I the LORD made them holy.**

**[13]"'Yet the people of Israel rebelled against me in the desert. They did not follow my decrees but rejected my laws—although the man who obeys them will live by them—and they utterly desecrated my Sabbaths. So I said I would pour out my wrath on them and destroy them in the desert. [14]But for the sake of my name I did what would keep it from being profaned in the eyes of the nations in whose sight I had brought them out.**

LESSONS FROM THE WILDERNESS DAYS (20:10-14). **20:10-14** Continuing to follow the story line of the exodus from Egypt, Ezekiel turns to the wilderness experience as a second example of Israel's rebellion. God freed them from Egypt and gave them laws, decrees, and rules for living (e.g., Exod 20–24). Two words were employed for "law," and some distinction of the two is necessary. The term "decrees" means "laws that were general axioms or principles." The word here translated "law" means "rules that were associated with an incurred penalty if broken."[13]

---

[11] Taylor, *Ezekiel*, 157. The name of God represents his total personality and is parallel to his glory. It therefore refers to his reputation in the human family.

[12] See Zimmerli, *Ezekiel 1*, 409.

[13] R. H. Alexander ("Ezekiel, EBC 6 [Grand Rapids: Zondervan, 1986], 836) makes this observation regarding the use of מִשְׁפָּט and חֹק, although the terms are generally synonymous. Following A. Alt, the concept of apodictic versus casuistic law has been made by W. Eichrodt in *Theology of the Old Testament*, vol. I (Philadelphia: Westminster, 1961), 71, 94. Cf. Exod 20; Deut 5.

In addition to providing his "law," God also provided the Sabbath. The mention of the Sabbath (Ezek 20:12) goes beyond reference to a day of rest observed weekly. It also was considered a perpetual sign of God's presence with the Hebrews and his pledge to keep his covenant with them. The observance of the Sabbath was "a constantly recurring acknowledgment of God as Creator of the universe. It would be an open denial of God for an Israelite to desecrate the Sabbath."[14] But the people rebelled against the "decrees" and laws and desecrated the Sabbath anyway. This is another example of people who professed to believe in and serve Yahweh but whose daily practice proceeded as if God did not exist. God gave them laws, decrees, and the Sabbath so that they would "know" him. The word "know," *yāda²*, is also the word translated "revealed" in vv. 5,9 (cf. v. 20). It speaks specifically of knowledge by personal experience. Despite the Hebrews' not "knowing" God, Moses appealed to God not to abandon or annihilate them. The basis of his appeal was the name, which represents the character and reputation of God (vv. 13-14; see Num 14:13-19). Again, for his name's sake, God spared Israel.

**15Also with uplifted hand I swore to them in the desert that I would not bring them into the land I had given them—a land flowing with milk and honey, most beautiful of all lands— 16because they rejected my laws and did not follow my decrees and desecrated my Sabbaths. For their hearts were devoted to their idols. 17Yet I looked on them with pity and did not destroy them or put an end to them in the desert. 18I said to their children in the desert, "Do not follow the statutes of your fathers or keep their laws or defile yourselves with their idols. 19I am the LORD your God; follow my decrees and be careful to keep my laws. 20Keep my Sabbaths holy, that they may be a sign between us. Then you will know that I am the LORD your God."**

**21"'But the children rebelled against me: They did not follow my decrees, they were not careful to keep my laws—although the man who obeys them will live by them—and they desecrated my Sabbaths. So I said I would pour out my wrath on them and spend my anger against them in the desert. 22But I withheld my hand, and for the sake of my name I did what would keep it from being profaned in the eyes of the nations in whose sight I had brought them out.**

LESSONS FROM YEARS OF WANDERING (20:15-22). **20:15-22** In spite of their history of rebellion, God gave them the land of promise, but once again they rebelled and would not enter (Num 13:26–14:12). So he left them to wander in the wilderness for forty years until all that genera-

---

[14] J. H. Hertz, *The Pentateuch and Haftorahs* (London: Soncino, 1967), 356.

tion had died (Num 14:26-39). Only those twenty years old and under were allowed to enter the land (Ezek 20:15-16; cf. Num 14:29-30). Though God took care of their needs and exhorted them not to follow idols, the people again rebelled against the law and desecrated the Sabbath. This reference to rebellion even after the judgment of the wilderness wandering was reminiscent of the Hebrew's choice to follow Baal worship prior to their entry into the land of promise at Jericho (see Num 22:1–25:18; 31:16). God withheld judgment again as he "drew back his hand" (v. 22) and spared the nation.[15]

**[23]Also with uplifted hand I swore to them in the desert that I would disperse them among the nations and scatter them through the countries, [24]because they had not obeyed my laws but had rejected my decrees and desecrated my Sabbaths, and their eyes [lusted] after their fathers' idols. [25]I also gave them over to statutes that were not good and laws they could not live by; [26]I let them become defiled through their gifts—the sacrifice of every firstborn—that I might fill them with horror so they would know that I am the LORD.'**

**[27]"Therefore, son of man, speak to the people of Israel and say to them, 'This is what the Sovereign LORD says: In this also your fathers blasphemed me by forsaking me: [28]When I brought them into the land I had sworn to give them and they saw any high hill or any leafy tree, there they offered their sacrifices, made offerings that provoked me to anger, presented their fragrant incense and poured out their drink offerings. [29]Then I said to them: What is this high place you go to?'" (It is called Bamah to this day.)**

PAST REBELLIONS (20:23-29). **20:23-29** Further, God promised to disperse them among the nations if they continued to rebel. This was an obvious reference to the exile in Babylon, which was current history for Ezekiel and his people. The concept of the exile was not a new one. Moses gave a prophetic warning that the exile would come because of disobedience (see Lev 26:14-46; Deut 28; 32). God gave his law, but the people rejected it, desecrated the Sabbath, and "lusted" after idols (v. 24). They took the land of promise and filled it with pagan altars and made offerings to idols. They offered their children in sacrifice to these pagan gods and rejected the law (vv. 25-26). They burned incense, offered gifts, and blasphemed God at these "high places." The word *bamoth,* "high places," is a reference to those altars built on the mountains (see 16:16).[16]

---

[15] Greenberg, *Ezekiel 1–20,* 368. For "drew back my hand" see Lam 2:8 and Ps 74:11.

[16] Alexander ("Ezekiel," 837) believes that בָּמָה refers to Gibeon, which was a worship center because of that city's role in Israel's early history in Canaan (see 1 Sam 9; 1 Kgs 3:4; 11:7; 1 Chr 16:39; 21:9; 2 Chr 1:3,13).

Verse 24 contains the fifth reference in this chapter to the Sabbath, four of which specifically meant the desecration of this holy day (vv. 13,16,20,21,24). Ezekiel's constant reference to the Sabbath seems to have a wider significance than the censure for failing to observe the weekly holy seventh day commanded in Exod 20:8-11. It also may include reference to the Sabbatical Year and Jubilee Year observances of Lev 25:1-34. It is extremely important to recognize that Lev 26 follows chap. 25 with a prophetic warning against idolatry and its consequences and includes a list of the blessings of obedience. Ezekiel issued the same warning.[17]

Israel and Judah perhaps owed God at least seventy sabbatical years by the time the Babylonian exile occurred, according to Jer 25:11-12 and 29:10. But that Jeremiah was referring to seventy sabbatical years is conjecture. The writer of 2 Chronicles specifically states that the seventy years of Jeremiah's prophecy were Sabbath years that God was collecting because of Israel and Judah's disobedience (2 Chr 36:21).

God used Babylon as an instrument of chastening to discipline Judah (cf. Isa 45:1). The Babylonian Empire lasted seventy years as a world power. Babylon's reign over Judah began in 609 B.C. with the death of Josiah. Four years later Nebuchadnezzar forced Jehoiakim to become a vassal. Babylon ended its role as a world power in 539 B.C. when the kingdom was defeated by the Medo-Persians. The people of Judah were captives from 605 B.C. until the first return and the foundation of the second temple was laid in 535 B.C. During those seventy years the land lay at rest to "enjoy her sabbaths" (2 Chr 36:21). Ezekiel's continual reference to the Sabbath in this passage seems to suggest an awareness of this connection between the breaking of the Sabbath, disregard for the Sabbatical Year, and the exile.

God therefore "gave them over" to the practice of idolatry and the abandonment of his laws (v. 25; cf. Rom 1:26-32). He let them become defiled (Ezek 20:26) to prepare them for judgment so that they might realize Yahweh alone was God. "Therefore" of v. 27 introduces a new word for the people. Their sins of the past continued so Ezekiel centered on the

---

[17] The largest portion of Lev 26 presents five cycles of discipline that God would apply to the nation if the people were disobedient and deliberately practiced idolatry. These cycles of discipline were (1) loss of courage (vv. 14-17); (2) loss of power and strength (vv. 18-20); (3) loss of domestic and public tranquility (vv. 21-22); (4) loss of national peace and prosperity (vv. 23-26); and (5) loss of freedom (vv. 27-46). One consequence of the loss of freedom was the predicted exile in a foreign land (26:30-33). One stated reason for that exile is given in vv. 34-35. It was to let the land "rest and enjoy her sabbaths." The implication was that among the sins of Israel was a failure to observe the Sabbath Years and Jubilee Years besides repeated violation of the weekly Sabbath.

primary sin of the people, which was idolatry. The rhetorical question "What is this place you go to?" indicts the people without allowing a response. The people must have thought they could worship other gods without God knowing. But God knows the actions and hearts of his people. So the people took the land God gave them and filled it with pagan altars and "high places" (vv. 27-29).

**³⁰"Therefore say to the house of Israel: 'This is what the Sovereign LORD says: Will you defile yourselves the way your fathers did and lust after their vile images? ³¹When you offer your gifts—the sacrifice of your sons in the fire—you continue to defile yourselves with all your idols to this day. Am I to let you inquire of me, O house of Israel? As surely as I live, declares the Sovereign LORD, I will not let you inquire of me.**

**³²"'You say, "We want to be like the nations, like the peoples of the world, who serve wood and stone." But what you have in mind will never happen. ³³As surely as I live, declares the Sovereign LORD, I will rule over you with a mighty hand and an outstretched arm and with outpoured wrath. ³⁴I will bring you from the nations and gather you from the countries where you have been scattered—with a mighty hand and an outstretched arm and with outpoured wrath. ³⁵I will bring you into the desert of the nations and there, face to face, I will execute judgment upon you. ³⁶As I judged your fathers in the desert of the land of Egypt, so I will judge you, declares the Sovereign LORD. ³⁷I will take note of you as you pass under my rod, and I will bring you into the bond of the covenant. ³⁸I will purge you of those who revolt and rebel against me. Although I will bring them out of the land where they are living, yet they will not enter the land of Israel. Then you will know that I am the LORD.**

**³⁹"'As for you, O house of Israel, this is what the Sovereign LORD says: Go and serve your idols, every one of you! But afterward you will surely listen to me and no longer profane my holy name with your gifts and idols.**

PRESENT REBELLIONS (20:30-39).   **20:30-39**   Having focused on Israel's past rebellions, the message in the remainder of chap. 20 turned to the future. The elders came to the prophet for a word from God. God said that because of their idolatry, child sacrifice, and continuance of sins of their fathers, he would not answer them (vv. 30-31). The people who came to Ezekiel were as guilty as their ancestors, a point made at length in Ezek 18. Therefore they were to be judged by the wrath of God and would go into exile (v. 33). Finally, God promised to gather a remnant of them from the nations (vv. 34-36) for a new wilderness experience.

The exodus story continued to be a model for the message as Ezekiel spoke of the wilderness days as a time of purification in vv. 37-39. There is a double analogy in v. 37. Reference to those who "pass under my rod" was first an allusion to the tithe (Lev 27:32). Every tenth animal that passed under a "rod" held over the sheep was separated and declared to be holy. The purification of the exile, likewise, would separate the righteous and the wicked.[18] The "rod" also was an instrument of discipline, correction, and punishment.[19] This was another way of communicating the purpose of the exile, which was to "purge" and purify those who rebelled against God (v. 38). The second part of the analogy is the "bond of the covenant." The Hebrew for "bond" rarely occurs and means "to be in obligation to the covenant."[20]

"Go and serve your idols every one of you" is a remarkable command (v. 39). Like v. 25, this is a parallel to Rom 1:24,26,28, which refers to those who consistently rejected God. Paul stated that "God gave them over to a depraved mind, to do what ought not to be done" (v. 28). At some point God gives in to those who consistently reject him and allows them to become wholly devoted to the destructive power of sin. Israel and Judah had repeatedly rejected God in favor of worshiping Baal, Molech, and other idols. Ezekiel's message was a declaration of the inevitability of judgment that results from such a disposition toward idols. God was therefore saying, "Go and serve your idols" because judgment is irrevocable.

Those who consistently reject God and his Word favor self-willed idolatry and immorality and are finally given over by him to reprobation (20:30-39), a process described in detail in Rom 1:24-28.

---

**[40]For on my holy mountain, the high mountain of Israel, declares the Sovereign LORD, there in the land the entire house of Israel will serve me, and there I will accept them. There I will require your offerings and your choice gifts, along with all your holy sacrifices. [41]I will accept you as fragrant incense when I bring you out from the nations and gather you from the countries where you have been scattered, and I will show myself holy among you in the sight of the nations. [42]Then you will know that I am the LORD, when I bring you into the land of Israel, the land I had sworn with uplifted hand to give to your fathers. [43]There you will remember your conduct and all the ac-**

---

[18] Fisch, *Ezekiel,* 129. This practice from Lev 27:32 meant that the tithe or tenth was holy because it belonged to God.

[19] The שֵׁבֶט was a short club used for remedial or corrective punishment for animals and slaves alike. The term also is used in association with discipline (Prov 10:13; 13:24; 22:15; 23:13-14; 26:3; 29:15; cf. Ps 23:4). God used Assyria and Babylon as "rods" with which he chastened Israel and Judah (see *TWOT,* 897).

[20] בְּמָסֹרֶת הַבְּרִית. See Greenberg, *Ezekiel 1-20,* 362, 372-73. The problem is whether מָסֹרֶת is from אסר, "to bind," or from מסר, "to count or deliver up." Regardless, one who passes under the שֵׁבֶט is judged to be with or against God in covenant relationship.

tions by which you have defiled yourselves, and you will loathe yourselves for all the evil you have done. [44]You will know that I am the LORD, when I deal with you for my name's sake and not according to your evil ways and your corrupt practices, O house of Israel, declares the Sovereign LORD.'"

PURIFICATION AFTER THE EXILE (20:40-44).   **20:40-44**   In the future, after the exile purified the nation, the Hebrews would return to the land and to the "holy mountain" (v. 40). This is a reference to Zion, Jerusalem, and the temple as used elsewhere (e.g., Isa 27:13; 56:7; 66:20; Joel 2:1; 4:17; Zeph 3:11; Zech 8:3).[21] This future restoration presented by Ezekiel encompassed four things. First, Yahweh, would be sanctified or *show* himself holy among his people in such a way the non-Israelite nations would recognize God's hand on them (v. 41).[22] Second, Israel and Judah would again know Yahweh as God when he fulfills this promise and restores them to the land (v. 42). The emphasis here is on "knowing" or experiencing God and therefore a reaffirmation that Yahweh is the only true God. Third, once back in the land the people would repent, turn to God, and express deep remorse for their sinfulness (v. 43). Fourth, then they would see that God has dealt with them in a way that is consistent with his name and character (v. 44).

These verses are very much like those of Zech 12:10-14; 13:1-9; 14:1-20. Both Ezekiel and Zechariah prophesied a future restoration based on repentance. Out of this experience God again would be glorified through his people. This is a subject to which Ezekiel would return in chaps. 36 and 37. The observation of 20:43 is repeated in the restoration passage in 36:31. God's motive for judgment in this life is always redemptive (20:40-44). He never judges vindictively but always with the desire to bring the rebellious to repentance, faith, and purity of life so that he may bless them and they may be a blessing to others.

[45]The word of the LORD came to me: [46]"Son of man, set your face toward the south; preach against the south and prophesy against the forest of the southland. [47]Say to the southern forest: 'Hear the word of the LORD. This is what the Sovereign LORD says: I am about to set fire to you, and it will consume all your trees, both green and dry. The blazing flame will not be quenched, and every face from south to north will be scorched by it. [48]Everyone will see that I the LORD have kindled it; it will not be quenched.'"

---

[21] Greenberg, *Ezekiel 1–20,* 374; Fisch, *Ezekiel,* 130. The temple mount is intended here rather than the mountainous regions of Israel.

[22] Taylor, *Ezekiel,* 160. Presentation of choice offerings in the temple was a means of showing all other nations God's holiness.

[49]Then I said, "Ah, Sovereign LORD! They are saying of me, 'Isn't he just telling parables?'"

THE CALL FOR JUDGMENT (20:45-49).   **20:45-49 (Heb. 21:1-5)**   In order for the restoration to begin, judgment must be dispensed. The process of purging the land will begin with the refining fires of judgment on Judah and Jerusalem. As a sign of the coming purge, Ezekiel was told to turn toward the south and deliver the brief message of judgment.[23] Use of the words for "south" and "forests of the southland" are references that point to Judah and Jerusalem (vv. 45-46).[24] God promised a fire would consume all trees, green and dry, of the south (v. 47). Ezekiel portrayed, in this parable form, the invasion of Judah by the Babylonian armies and the destruction of Jerusalem that was inevitable. The destruction will be of a scope and severity that everyone would recognize it as an act of divine retribution (vv. 48-49).[25]

This section closes with the prophet's complaint that he was not being taken seriously because he spoke in parables rather than plain, direct words. The message that follows in 21:1-27 therefore was presented in clear terminology in which all the subjective elements of the message were identified.[26]

Judgment of sin is a prerequisite to blessing. The wrath of God's judgment precedes the restoration of his blessings and the fulfillment of his promises. This pattern was true for Ezekiel's day, and it is also the pattern of the end time when God will purge the earth (Rev 17–18) in preparation for the rule of the Messiah (Rev 19–20).

### (2) Prophecy of the "Sword" of the Lord (21:1-27)

Ezekiel's vision message of the sword of the Lord may be divided into three sections. (1) The sword of the Lord is drawn against Judah and Jerusalem and will not return to the sheath until judgment is complete (21:1-7).

---

[23] The Hebrew text includes 20:45-49 as part of chap. 21 (21:1-5). Verse 46 uses three different words for "south." (1) תֵּימָ֫נָה means "right" as opposed to "left." Directions were determined by facing east with west to the rear, north to the left, and south to the right. (2) דָּרוֹם is a word that was used to designate south in a geographical sense. (3) נֶ֫גֶב is the word that refers to the southern portion of the land of Israel as a geographical entity (see Alexander, "Ezekiel," 841 note).

[24] See Zimmerli, *Ezekiel 1,* 423; Fisch, *Ezekiel,* 132. The use of "south" here may simply be the antithesis to the woe from the north, which was to come against Judah.

[25] See Fisch, *Ezekiel,* 132-33. The major public buildings of Jerusalem were destroyed. The defensive walls of the city were reduced to rubble, and all temple valuables were carried to Babylon. See E. H. Merrill, *Kingdom of Priests* (Grand Rapids: Baker, 1987), 453.

[26] Zimmerli, *Ezekiel 1,* 424.

He could then speak of judgment to come (21:6-7). (2) The destruction of the sword is presented in four phrases (21:8-17). (3) Nebuchadnezzar consults methods of divination and chooses to attack Jerusalem (21:18-27).

**¹The word of the LORD came to me: ²"Son of man, set your face against Jerusalem and preach against the sanctuary. Prophesy against the land of Israel ³and say to her: 'This is what the LORD says: I am against you. I will draw my sword from its scabbard and cut off from you both the righteous and the wicked. ⁴Because I am going to cut off the righteous and the wicked, my sword will be unsheathed against everyone from south to north. ⁵Then all people will know that I the LORD have drawn my sword from its scabbard; it will not return again.'**

**⁶"Therefore groan, son of man! Groan before them with broken heart and bitter grief. ⁷And when they ask you, 'Why are you groaning?' you shall say, 'Because of the news that is coming. Every heart will melt and every hand go limp; every spirit will become faint and every knee become as weak as water.' It is coming! It will surely take place, declares the Sovereign LORD."**

SWORD OF THE LORD DRAWN (21:1-7). **21:1-7 [Heb. 21:6-12]** The phrase "Son of man, set your face against" occurs nine times in the Bible, all in Ezekiel.[27] Each time the phrase is in the context of judgment. Here Ezekiel is commanded to prophesy judgment against Jerusalem. There is a New Testament parallel to this text. In Luke 9:51 the Son of Man, Jesus, "set his face to go to Jerusalem." Jesus pronounced judgment against Jerusalem similar to Ezekiel (Luke 19:41; 21:20-24).[28]

This collection of "sword" theme oracles is a continuation of the messages of judgment against Judah and Jerusalem. All three figures mentioned in v. 2, "Jerusalem," the "sanctuary," and the "land," were included to show that judgment will be complete and indiscriminate.[29] God called the sword, which actually was the Babylonian armies who conquered Judah, "my sword" (vv. 3-5). This was another clear indication that God was using Babylon as his instrument or "sword" of chastisement for Judah.[30]

Some interpreters note the apparent contradiction between vv. 2 and 4 regarding indiscriminate judgment of the righteous and wicked and the theme of Ezek 18:1-20, which stated that each person would be responsi-

---

[27] Ezek 6:2 (see comment there); 13:17; 20:46; 21:2; 25:2; 28:21; 29:2; 35:2; 38:2.

[28] C. A. Evans, *Luke*, NIBC (Peabody, Mass.: Hendrickson, 1990), 161, 164.

[29] Wevers, *Ezekiel*, 163. This is 21:6 in the Heb. text.

[30] The entire message of the brief Book of Habakkuk is devoted to this theme and its resulting difficulties for the Hebrew mind. They could not understand how or why God would use the Babylonians as an instrument of chastening. The Book of Habakkuk was written sometime between 605 and 597 B.C. (See J. M. P. Smith, W. H. Ward, J. A. Bewer, *Micah, Zephaniah, Nahum, Habakkuk, Obadiah, Joel,* ICC [London: T & T Clark, 1911], 4; and Taylor, *Ezekiel,* 1.)

ble only for his or her own sins.[31] There is no contradiction between Ezek 18 and this chapter. It must be remembered that Ezek 18 focuses on responsibility for judgment, that is, each person only bears personal guilt. The Bible does have a concept of corporate responsibility when it comes to the effect of individual sins. Exodus 34:6-7 states this principle, and the case of Achan in Josh 7:1-26 illustrates the principle (see discussion of Ezek 18:1-4). The wicked were guilty, but many people, including some righteous, would suffer because of the sins of the wicked.

Because of the judgment described, all people, or literally "all flesh" (v. 5), will know that these judgments were of divine origin. God would begin this judgment and not assuage it until he had completed his work.[32] So the prophet was told to "groan" and give signs of despair (v. 6). When asked for the reason behind his depression, he was to respond with warnings of impending judgment (v. 7).

The language of v. 7, "It is coming! It will surely take place," heightens the sense of apprehension concerning the coming judgment. Amos employed the same device in the "three"-for-"four" judgments that he announced at the beginning of his book (see Amos 1:1–2:16). The Hebrew text of Amos literally says, "For the three transgressions of," after which each country is named. Then he said, "I will not turn 'it' away." The use of "it" by Amos and by Ezekiel was deliberately ambiguous to heighten the fear element of these messages.[33] Imagine the reaction should someone run into a crowded room with a look of terror, shout, "It is coming!" and then bolt out the door. Such was the intended effect of these "sword" messages. Consistent rebellion leads to inevitable judgment. God will reveal himself in either blessing or judgment. He will bless the faithful and obedient and bring judgment upon the faithless and disobedient (cf. Deut 11:26-32; 28:1–29:29).

**[8]The word of the LORD came to me: [9]"Son of man, prophesy and say, 'This is what the LORD says:**

**"'A sword, a sword,**
**sharpened and polished—**
**[10]sharpened for the slaughter,**
**polished to flash like lightning!**
**"'Shall we rejoice in the scepter of my son [Judah]? The sword despises every such stick.**

---

[31] See, e.g., Zimmerli, *Ezekiel 1,* 424, and Fisch, *Ezekiel,* 133.

[32] Wevers *(Ezekiel,* 163) relates v. 5 to 20:48. The sword is the unquenchable fire that will not be returned to its sheath until judgment is complete.

[33] A. Cohen, *The Twelve Prophets* (London: Soncino, 1969), 84; A. Bentzen, "The Ritual Background of Amos i:2-ii:16" *OTS* 8 (1950): 85-99.

[11]" 'The sword is appointed to be polished,
  to be grasped with the hand;
  it is sharpened and polished,
    made ready for the hand of the slayer.
[12]Cry out and wail, son of man,
    for it is against my people;
  it is against all the princes of Israel.
  They are thrown to the sword
    along with my people.
  Therefore beat your breast.
[13]" 'Testing will surely come. And what if the scepter [of Judah], which
the sword despises, does not continue? declares the Sovereign LORD.'
[14]"So then, son of man, prophesy
    and strike your hands together.
  Let the sword strike twice,
    even three times.
  It is a sword for slaughter—
    a sword for great slaughter,
    closing in on them from every side.
[15]So that hearts may melt
    and the fallen be many,
  I have stationed the sword for slaughter
    at all their gates.
  Oh! It is made to flash like lightning,
    it is grasped for slaughter.
[16]O sword, slash to the right,
    then to the left,
    wherever your blade is turned.
[17]I too will strike my hands together,
    and my wrath will subside.
  I the LORD have spoken."

DESTRUCTION OF THE SWORD (21:8-17; Heb. 21:13-23).   This section
is a predominantly poetic one with some prose statements interspersed. It
may be an adaptation of some well-known song that the people would
have recognized.[34] Ezekiel's sword song pictured judgment unfolding in
four phases: (1) the sword is sharpened and readied for slaughter (vv. 8-
11); (2) Ezekiel must cry and smite his chest as a symbol of the carnage
(vv. 12); (3) the sword struck twice, then three times to emphasize the extent of judgment (vv. 13-15); and (4) the sword was instructed to do its
work (vv. 16-17).

---

[34] Cf. the Song of Lamech in Gen 4:23-24 (Taylor, *Ezekiel,* 162; Zimmerli, *Ezekiel 1,*
432-33) and the Song of the Sword (see S. R. Driver, *The Book of Genesis,* WC [London:
Methuen, 1906], 70).

**21:8-11** The sight of a highly polished weapon would strike fear in the hearts of potential victims. This one was especially terrifying, "sharpened and polished," ready for the hand of Nebuchadnezzar to wield against Judah. The interpretation of v. 10b is uncertain. It literally reads, "Or we shall rejoice; the scepter/rod of my son [*or* the scepter, my son] despises every stick." Some take the scepter to refer to a rod of discipline. So the NRSV translates: "How can we make merry? You have despised the rod, and all discipline." The REB ventures further in rendering, "(Look, the rod is brandished, my son, to defy all wooden idols!)." Zimmerli concludes that the line "in spite of all the effort expended on it, so far eludes any satisfactory interpretation."[35] It apparently has suffered in transmission.

**21:12** Ezekiel was to act out the horror of this impending judgment by crying, wailing, and beating his chest, which were signs of grief (v. 12). This death lament was for Judah and was comparable to that of Amos, who lamented the death of the virgin Israel (see Amos 5:1-3).[36]

**21:13-14** The warnings of Ezekiel and other prophets were a test to see whether the people would listen. It was clear the people had despised the evidences and warnings of impending judgment (v. 13). Therefore Ezekiel was commanded to "prophesy" and "to strike" his hands together, probably as a sign of anger, and let the sword strike three times (v. 14). The mention of three strikes of the sword may refer to the three attacks of Nebuchadnezzar against Jerusalem. The first attack was in 605 B.C. during the reign of Jehoiakim, the second in 597 B.C. during the reign of Jehoiachin, and the third from 588 B.C. to 586 B.C. during the reign of Zedekiah.[37]

**21:15-17** Ezekiel told of great slaughter with many fallen and many fearful (v. 15). The sword of slaughter was stationed at the gates to intercept those who might flee. The sword would slash until its work was done (v. 16). So God struck his hands together to indicate his determination to dispense judgment until his fury was spent (v. 17).

God's judgment will be swift, severe, indiscriminate, and final upon those who refuse to heed his warnings. To reject God is to choose sin and guarantee punishment (Jer 18:1-12; Rom 3:23; 6:23; Rev 20:11-15). Ezekiel had formerly spoken of the six men who went forth with the

---

[35] Zimmerli, *Ezekiel 1*, 426-27. See L. C. Allen, "The Rejected Scepter in Ezek 21:15b, 18a," *VT* 39 (1989): 67-71. He understands both verses as glosses.

[36] Eichrodt, *Ezekiel*, 295. Eichrodt does not believe there is a connection with the Song of Lamech in Gen 4:23-24 or that the message has been moved by a redactor. Placed where it is, it adds to the intensification of the pending message of judgment.

[37] Fisch, *Ezekiel*, 136. The third disaster will be twice as destructive as the first two, hence the striking of hands in dismay in v. 19.

sword to carry out indiscriminate judgment (cf. Ezek 9:1-11, esp. v. 6).

**[18]The word of the LORD came to me: [19]"Son of man, mark out two roads for the sword of the king of Babylon to take, both starting from the same country. Make a signpost where the road branches off to the city. [20]Mark out one road for the sword to come against Rabbah of the Ammonites and another against Judah and fortified Jerusalem. [21]For the king of Babylon will stop at the fork in the road, at the junction of the two roads, to seek an omen: He will cast lots with arrows, he will consult his idols, he will examine the liver. [22]Into his right hand will come the lot for Jerusalem, where he is to set up battering rams, to give the command to slaughter, to sound the battle cry, to set battering rams against the gates, to build a ramp and to erect siege works. [23]It will seem like a false omen to those who have sworn allegiance to him, but he will remind them of their guilt and take them captive.**

**[24]"Therefore this is what the Sovereign LORD says: 'Because you people have brought to mind your guilt by your open rebellion, revealing your sins in all that you do—because you have done this, you will be taken captive.**

**[25]"'O profane and wicked prince of Israel, whose day has come, whose time of punishment has reached its climax, [26]this is what the Sovereign LORD says: Take off the turban, remove the crown. It will not be as it was: The lowly will be exalted and the exalted will be brought low. [27]A ruin! A ruin! I will make it a ruin! It will not be restored until he comes to whom it rightfully belongs; to him I will give it.'**

NEBUCHADNEZZAR'S DECISION (21:18-27; Heb. 21:23-32). **21:18-23** The "sword" of the Lord's chastening was the sword of Nebuchadnezzar. Ezekiel made a drawing of the road by which Nebuchadnezzar approached Judah. The king had two choices. He could attack Rabbah, a city of the Ammonites, or Jerusalem. Faced with the decision of which one to attack, the king of Babylon sought the help of imitative magic, common in ancient Near Eastern prophecy. Three forms of soothsaying are mentioned in v. 21. *Belomancy* was the shaking of arrows, letting them fall and interpreting the pattern. Consulting the *teraphim* or idols was a second method of divination. The third was *hepatoscopy*, or the examination of the liver of an animal to determine the future.[38] By divination Nebuchadnezzar chose to attack Jerusalem instead of Rabbah. The inhabitants of Jerusalem refused to take this warning seriously; as a result they would be taken captive.

**21:24-27** "Therefore" introduces the fundamental reason for Judah's exile: "open rebellion" against God. The "profane and wicked prince of Israel" is a reference to Zedekiah (v. 25); he would lose his crown, and the

---

[38] See Taylor, *Ezekiel,* 163-64; cf. note on Ezek 12:24.

kingdom of Judah would end (v. 26). The crown would be held in reserve until "he comes to whom it rightfully belongs" (v. 27). This messianic prophecy echoes the words of Gen 49:10, which depicts the Messiah as a future King (see also Ps 2:6; Jer 23:5-6; Ezek 37:24; Zech 6:12-15). Zedekiah would be dethroned and humiliated (vv. 25-27), and his kingdom, including Jerusalem, would be a ruin (v. 27).[39]

Those who reject God may turn to other forms of worship and religious commitment in an attempt to find deliverance. All means apart from God are futile, empty, and hopeless.

### (3) Prophecy of Judgment on the Ammonites (21:28-32)

[28]"And you, son of man, prophesy and say, 'This is what the Sovereign LORD says about the Ammonites and their insults:
"'A sword, a sword,
   drawn for the slaughter,
   polished to consume
   and to flash like lightning!
[29]Despite false visions concerning you
   and lying divinations about you,
   it will be laid on the necks
   of the wicked who are to be slain,
   whose day has come,
   whose time of punishment has reached its climax.
[30]Return the sword to its scabbard.
   In the place where you were created,
   in the land of your ancestry,
   I will judge you.
[31]I will pour out my wrath upon you
   and breathe out my fiery anger against you;
   I will hand you over to brutal men,
   men skilled in destruction.
[32]You will be fuel for the fire,
   your blood will be shed in your land,
   you will be remembered no more;
   for I the LORD have spoken.'"

**21:28-29** God turns Ezekiel's attention to the Ammonites with the command to prophesy the punishment of the Ammonites with the "sword" of judgment (v. 28). The image of the "sword, drawn for slaughter" is viv-

---

[39] G. Van Groningen, *Messianic Revelation in the Old Testament* (Grand Rapids: Baker, 1990), 760-69.

idly described. It will strike with the speed of "lightning," and its sole purpose is to "consume" the Ammonites who had aided the Babylonian conquest of Jerusalem.[40] The Ammonites were descendants of Lot. Ben-Ammi, the father of the Ammonites, was the son of Lot born to him by one of his daughters, who fled Sodom with Lot and his wife. When Lot's wife was lost in judgment for her disobedience, the daughters employed immoral methods to try to preserve the family name (Gen 19:30-38). They made Lot drunk and had sexual relations with him, each conceiving a child by their father. The children born of this immoral union were named Moab and Ben-Ammi. Both groups who descended from this immoral encounter, the Moabites and Ammonites, became bitter enemies of God's people. They were known for idolatry (1 Kgs 11:7,33), condemned for cruelty (Amos 1:13), condemned for pride (Zeph 2:9-10), and were enemies of God's people (Deut 23:3-4; Judg 3:13; 1 Sam 11:1-3; 2 Sam 10:1-4; 2 Kgs 24:2; Neh 4:3,7-8).

**21:30-32**    The Ammonites would be judged in their homeland (v. 30). Verses 31-32 are similar to vv. 8-17. Though the Ammonites participated in the judgment of Jerusalem, they too would be the object of God's wrath. God vowed to pour out his wrath in judgment and destroy them (vv. 31-32). Their fate was worse than Judah's since they would be remembered no more.[41] This anticipates the message of judgment Ezekiel later delivered against Ammon in 25:1-7. Judgment is for the wicked and ungodly, (21:18-32; cf. 1 Pet 4:17-18), but the people of God are not exempt (21:1-17).

### (4)  Enumeration of Further Sins of Jerusalem (22:1-31)

There are four divisions to this chapter. First, God declares that he knows their sins (22:1-5). Second, specific sins are listed (22:6-12). Third, God promises judgment for these sins (22:13-22). Fourth, the total disintegration of society is portrayed (22:23-31).

**[1]The word of the LORD came to me: [2]"Son of man, will you judge her? Will you judge this city of bloodshed? Then confront her with all her detestable practices [3]and say: 'This is what the Sovereign LORD says: O city that brings on herself doom by shedding blood in her midst and defiles herself by making idols, [4]you have become guilty because of the blood you have shed**

---

[40] Fisch, *Ezekiel,* 141. The Ammonites were hostile toward Judah at the time (cf. 2 Kgs 24:2).

[41] Taylor, *Ezekiel,* 165. In the Semitic mind nothing was more horrible than the thought of no restoration, no future generations, no memorial but only oblivion.

and have become defiled by the idols you have made. You have brought your days to a close, and the end of your years has come. Therefore I will make you an object of scorn to the nations and a laughingstock to all the countries. ⁵Those who are near and those who are far away will mock you, O infamous city, full of turmoil.

GOD'S DECLARATION (22:1-5). **22:1-5** This new indictment against Jerusalem was different from the historical review presented in 20:1-49. Chapter 22 presents a list of specific crimes of which Jerusalem and Judah were guilty. This catalog of crimes falls into two categories: social injustices and spiritual apostasies. The sins enumerated parallel those mentioned in the holiness code of Lev 17–26. These Levitical laws were practical applications of the standards of holiness embodied in the Ten Commandments.[42]

Both moral and cultic sins were reviewed to show the hostility that existed for the law.[43] The first two sins mentioned included bloodshed and idolatry. These two were linked to remind the people of the close relationship between violence and idolatry. Those who worshiped false gods in Israel and Judah also had participated in human sacrifice (2 Kgs 17:17-18). Disregard for the law of God led to a dramatic increase in crimes of violence so that Jerusalem was called the "city of bloodshed" (vv. 2-3).

Because of its wicked, violent reputation, nations near and far made Jerusalem an object of scorn. The phrase "O infamous city full of turmoil" (v. 5) is specific in the Hebrew text and can be translated "O defiled of the Name, abounding in tumult." This literal translation shows the ungodly, violent reputation of Jerusalem. They defiled "the Name," meaning the person and character of God, especially his holiness. "Name" regularly was used with the definite article ("The Name") as a substitute for the personal name of God, Yahweh, which represented his holy nature and character.[44]

Those who receive more light, such as Judah and Jerusalem, also would be held to a greater accountability for their knowledge and failure to follow it or share it. God knows about specific sins and will hold all

---

[42] Ibid., 167. Compare this with 18:15-17 and see Taylor's discussion of this list of sins as compared with the Ten Commandments and the holiness code of Lev 17–26.

[43] Eichrodt, *Ezekiel,* 309.

[44] Most commentators, e.g., Zimmerli, Allen, Wevers, understand הַשֵּׁם to refer to either the people of Jerusalem or to the city itself. However, in Gen 6:4; Lev 24:11; and Deut 28:58, הַשֵּׁם (used only five times in the Heb. text) can be understood to be used as a substitute for the divine name יהוה (although Gen 6:4 is a difficult text to interpret). The fifth use of הַשֵּׁם is as a personal name in 1 Chr 11:34. Use of the divine name became minimal in the Jewish tradition out of reverence and respect for the holiness of the name of God (cf. Amos 6:9-10).

people responsible for repentance and faith (22:1-5).

**[6]"'See how each of the princes of Israel who are in you uses his power to shed blood. [7]In you they have treated father and mother with contempt; in you they have oppressed the alien and mistreated the fatherless and the widow. [8]You have despised my holy things and desecrated my Sabbaths. [9]In you are slanderous men bent on shedding blood; in you are those who eat at the mountain shrines and commit lewd acts. [10]In you are those who dishonor their fathers' bed; in you are those who violate women during their period, when they are ceremonially unclean. [11]In you one man commits a detestable offense with his neighbor's wife, another shamefully defiles his daughter-in-law, and another violates his sister, his own father's daughter. [12]In you men accept bribes to shed blood; you take usury and excessive interest and make unjust gain from your neighbors by extortion. And you have forgotten me, declares the Sovereign LORD.**

SINS LISTED (22:6-12).   **22:6-12**   The list of crimes continues in vv. 6-12 with bloodshed or violence and idolatry or disregard for God's law. A most helpful comparison, made by Greenberg, contrasts the sins listed in 18:5-17, which focus on individual responsibility, and the sins of 22:6-12, which recount Jerusalem's crimes. Chapter 18 contains three contrasting lists in vv. 5-17, which name at least twelve sins that the righteous avoid but which the wicked embrace. The righteous do what is just and right and avoid all the sins listed in vv. 5-9. The second list in vv. 10-13 includes seven of the twelve that the wicked person does. The third list in vv. 14-17 notes ten of the items that the righteous person avoids. Ezekiel 22:6-12 includes all the sins of chap. 18 and adds three additional sins for a total of fifteen.[45]

The lists of 18:5-9,10-13,14-17 contrast the social and moral sins in light of accepted standards based on the laws of the Old Testament, especially the Decalogue.[46] Chapter 22 reads like a bill of indictment for the many specific sins that made judgment inevitable. The priestly dimension of Ezekiel's understanding of the law was revealed in his use of legal terms and his special concern for shedding of blood (vv. 2-4).[47]

---

[45] Greenberg, *Ezekiel 1-20*, 342-43. His excellent analysis maintains that the lists of 18:5-17 and 22:6-12 are Ezekiel's work. He notes that the resemblance between the two cannot be missed. The differences between the two lists are in terms of purpose. The list of 18:5-17 intends to present the ideal person, while chap. 22 is a bill of indictment (hence the addition of desecration and sexual offenses).

[46] See Greenberg's list of sins based on Ezek 22 (*Ezekiel 1-20*, 343; and Taylor, *Ezekiel*, 167). Ezekiel lists at least fifteen specific sins of which Judah had been guilty.

[47] Hals, *Ezekiel*, 157-58. The language for making known abominable deeds is presented in priestly terms; cf. 16:2 and 20:4.

Having laid the foundation for his discussion of specific sins by identifying the first three sins of bloodshed, idolatry, and the violation of God's law, Ezekiel continued his listing of specific crimes. The fourth sin he mentioned was the perversion of power (v. 6). The princes had used their power to shed blood. This charge is reminiscent of Amos's call for justice "in the gate" (Amos 5:10,15), where he indicted the leaders of his day for misuse of their power. These leaders, like those to whom Ezekiel spoke, had forgotten that their power to rule came from God.[48]

The fifth sin Ezekiel identified was the loss of discipline in the home and lack of parental respect (v. 7). This concern was at the heart of the Ten Commandments (Exod 20:12; Deut 5:16; Lev 19:3). The sixth and seventh sins were the lack of hospitality shown to foreigners and oppression of the orphans and widows (v. 7). These two were placed together because both suggest a lack of concern for those who are in need (Exod 22:20; 23:9,12; Deut 14:29; 16:11,14; 24:19-21; 26:12-19).

Another pair of sins were presented in v. 8. The eighth and ninth sins were the profaning of holy things (sanctuary, sacrifices, temple vessels) and the desecration of the Sabbath (see discussion of 20:12). Violation of the Sabbath specifically was mentioned in the prophetic warning about the exile in Lev 26:34-35 and in 2 Chr 36:21 (see 20:24).

Verse 9 lists a triad of sins. The tenth sin mentioned was slanderous men who gave false witness to shed blood (Lev 19:16). The eleventh sin was worshiping or "eating" communal meals at pagan shrines, and the twelfth was reference to the "lewd" immoral acts also associated with the pagan worship of a degenerate society. Verses 10-11 list additional examples of immoral behavior that illustrate the "lewdness" of the people. They disregarded laws concerning sexual purity and committed incest (Lev 18:19). Additional sexual sins in v. 11 include adultery with a neighbor's wife and with a daughter-in-law and incest with a sister (Lev 18:20; Ezek 22:10,12,17), each of which suggests the total breakdown of respect for the laws concerning moral purity.

The final triad of sins is listed in v. 12. The thirteenth sin named was accepting bribes to promote injustice (Exod 23:8; Deut 10:17; 16:19; 27:25; Isa 1:23; Amos 5:12; Mic 3:11). The fourteenth sin named was the exacting of exorbitant interest rates because of greed (see 18:8). Finally, the fifteenth sin mentioned summarizes all previous sins and offers the motive behind them. The people had forgotten God.[49] Although to forget

---

[48] Zimmerli, *Ezekiel 1,* 457. Ezekiel sets aside Judah's claim to honor by setting forth its humiliation not only in its deserved conquest but also in the reputation it had made for itself in social injustice, violence, immorality, and ungodliness.

God precedes all sin, here it is listed last. The reason is that it is the summation of all that is wrong, that is, the proverbial last nail in the coffin.

Ezekiel joined Jeremiah and Hosea in condemning the lack of concern for God's will on an individual basis (e.g., Jer 3:6-25; 7:9; 17:1-6; Hos 4:1-6; 11:7). This individual immorality had left the collective morality of the nation bankrupt and under sentence of judgment. The sins mentioned were not intended to be an exhaustive list but represent the kinds of offenses that made divine judgment a necessity.[50]

The Bible is very specific about the nature and identity of sin. Such sins are the works of the flesh, such as those presented in Gal 5:19-21, where they are contrasted with the fruit (sing. in Greek) of the Spirit.

[13]"'I will surely strike my hands together at the unjust gain you have made and at the blood you have shed in your midst. [14]Will your courage endure or your hands be strong in the day I deal with you? I the LORD have spoken, and I will do it. [15]I will disperse you among the nations and scatter you through the countries; and I will put an end to your uncleanness. [16]When you have been defiled in the eyes of the nations, you will know that I am the LORD.'"

[17]Then the word of the LORD came to me: [18]"Son of man, the house of Israel has become dross to me; all of them are the copper, tin, iron and lead left inside a furnace. They are but the dross of silver. [19]Therefore this is what the Sovereign LORD says: 'Because you have all become dross, I will gather you into Jerusalem. [20]As men gather silver, copper, iron, lead and tin into a furnace to melt it with a fiery blast, so will I gather you in my anger and my wrath and put you inside the city and melt you. [21]I will gather you and I will blow on you with my fiery wrath, and you will be melted inside her. [22]As silver is melted in a furnace, so you will be melted inside her, and you will know that I the Lord have poured out my wrath upon you.'"

PROMISE OF JUDGMENT (22:13-22).    **22:13-22**    In vv. 1-12 the pronoun "you" occurs twenty-one times, indicating that Judah was guilty of all charges, crimes, and sin. The pronoun "I" occurs eleven times, indicating that God, who is the speaker, would bring about the judgment on Judah. In response to the sins enumerated in vv. 1-12, God promised he

---

[49] The word שָׁכַח does not refer to a lack of mental recall. It was not that they could not remember God but that they had wandered away from him and the standards of his word. They had forgotten God in the sense that they ceased to care about God's holy standards (BDB, 1013).

[50] Zimmerli's observation (*Ezekiel 1,* 459) on this point is significant. He says it becomes clear that within the full listing of laws that have been broken, it is ultimately only one thing: the turning away from the Lord, who gives to everything in life its order (cf. Hos 4:2; Jer 7:9).

would do five things. God's first four responses are listed in vv. 13-16, and the final one is in vv. 17-22. First, God said he would "strike" his hands (v. 13) as a sign of extreme displeasure. This emotional response was especially appropriate considering the violence and injustices that had been described in vv. 1-12.[51] Second, God posed a rhetorical question that presupposed a negative response. The question related to their will and endurance. The word "courage" (v. 14) literally means "will."[52] So the question was, "Will you have the will, resolve, and strength to stand against the enemy?" The implied answer was, "No, you will not!"[53] Third, God warned that he would scatter them among the nations and "put an end to [their] uncleanness" (v. 15). This was a paradoxical statement because the foreign nations were considered unclean. The fourth response was that the scattered people would know that Yahweh is God by the acts of judgment present in their midst, such as extortion, violence, bloodshed, injustice, immorality, incest, and the multiplication of false religions.[54]

The fifth and final response was presented in the symbol of the smelting furnace (vv. 17-18). Judgment will be like a smelting furnace that burns away the dross and impurities, leaving the purified precious metal. This was a common figure used for purification in Scripture (see, e.g., Isa 1:22,25; 48:10; Jer 9:7; Zech 13:9; Mal 3:2-3).[55] The smelting process was used to purify all kinds of metals (Ezek 22:18). In this analogy Jerusalem was the smelting furnace (v. 19), and Judah was the object to be refined (v. 20). The wrath of God supplied the heat (v. 21), and because of this judgment Judah would know God judged the nation (v. 22).

God promised to purge the land of sin and unrepentant sinners (21:13-22). The figure of the smelter's fire was used by Ezekiel to represent the final purge God planned for Judah, which he also plans for the end time when he will purge his creation of sin (2 Pet 3:9-14; Rev 20:15).

**23Again the word of the LORD came to me: 24"Son of man, say to the land, 'You are a land that has had no rain or showers in the day of wrath.' 25There is a conspiracy of her princes within her like a roaring lion tearing its prey; they devour people, take treasures and precious things and make many wid-**

---

[51] Wevers, *Ezekiel,* 174; Zimmerli, *Ezekiel 1,* 459; Fisch, *Ezekiel,* 145.

[52] The word לֵב is used consistently to refer to the "will" or seat of volitional choice (see discussion of 16:30 note).

[53] Fisch, *Ezekiel,* 145. The implied answer is negative. There will be no strength to stand against the enemy.

[54] Taylor, *Ezekiel,* 168. There is a terrifying description of any nation whose end is near. Political commentators take note.

[55] Wevers, *Ezekiel,* 174-75. See his extended note on the use of the smelting figure.

ows within her. [26]Her priests do violence to my law and profane my holy things; they do not distinguish between the holy and the common; they teach that there is no difference between the unclean and the clean; and they shut their eyes to the keeping of my Sabbaths, so that I am profaned among them. [27]Her officials within her are like wolves tearing their prey; they shed blood and kill people to make unjust gain. [28]Her prophets whitewash these deeds for them by false visions and lying divinations. They say, 'This is what the Sovereign LORD says'—when the LORD has not spoken. [29]The people of the land practice extortion and commit robbery; they oppress the poor and needy and mistreat the alien, denying them justice.

[30]"I looked for a man among them who would build up the wall and stand before me in the gap on behalf of the land so I would not have to destroy it, but I found none. [31]So I will pour out my wrath on them and consume them with my fiery anger, bringing down on their own heads all they have done, declares the Sovereign LORD."

SOCIETY'S DISINTEGRATION (22:23-31). This passage depicts the tragic and total disintegration of every area of leadership that should have given moral and spiritual guidance to Judah. Their failure in these areas made judgment inevitable. No one escaped arraignment for responsibility of the moral and spiritual delinquency of the nation. Ezekiel indicted five specific groups that encompassed all segments of society and spelled out the reasons for the disintegration of leadership in Judah.

**22:25** *Princes.* These were the nobility or ruling class of Judah.[56] These members of the royal house were responsible for insuring law and order but had instead promoted murder, robbery, greed, and lawlessness. They only were interested in personal gain and lacked concern for the consequences that befell the nation or individuals.

**22:26** *Priests.* These men were responsible for instruction in the law (cf. Hos 4:6) and guarding the holiness and purity of the temple. They were to make a clear demarkation between holy and profane, the clean and unclean (Lev 10:10; 11:47; 20:25; Jer 5:30-31). Instead the priests violated the laws of God, distorted the line between holy and profane, and closed their eyes to desecration of the Sabbath.[57]

---

[56] The Hebrew text here has נְבִיאֶ֫יהָ ("her prophets") rather than נְשִׂיאֶ֫יהָ ("her princes" read by the LXX and followed by the NIV). "Princes" is used because of the nature of the sin of the ones being described as taking treasures and precious things, which princes had the power to do. The prophets "whitewashed" the situation (v. 28) with "false visions and lying divinations." The differing characteristics and the mention of both priests (v. 26) and "officials" (v. 27) between princes and prophets suggest that we follow both the LXX and the NIV. See Wevers, *Ezekiel*, 176; Zimmerli, *Ezekiel 1*, 468.

[57] Wevers, *Ezekiel*, 176-77; Zimmerli, *Ezekiel 1*, 468. G. W. Harrison ("Covenant Unfaithfulness in Malachi 2:1-16," *CTR* 2, 1, [1987]: 63-72) discusses how Malachi shows the failure of the priests to have been covenant unfaithfulness.

**22:27** *Government Officials.* "Officials" is used in this context by Ezekiel to refer to those appointed as government officials rather than nobility. These officials were compared to wolves attacking and tearing their prey. They were supposed to serve the people but instead had made them their victims.

**22:28** *False Prophets.* These spokesmen were to serve as the moral and spiritual conscience of the nation. Instead of preaching against sin, they gave false prophecies and lying divinations; they whitewashed sin in general. In the face of the impending destruction of Jerusalem and fall of Judah, they continued to preach peace[58] and safety. Ezekiel's indictment was consistent with his earlier exposé of false prophets and prophetesses in 13:4-23.

**22:29** *People of the Land.* What kind of people would such leadership produce? It should be no surprise that the people were extortioners, robbers, oppressors, the inhospitable, and subverters of justice. Their society was a showcase of violence, greed, graft, indifference to suffering, and general neglect of God's word. There was no discipline in the homes (22:7). Moral and sexual perversions and indiscretions were commonplace (22:9-11). Crime and general lack of moral restraint was the order of the day (22:12).

One hardly could read such a list of crimes that so thoroughly pervaded society of Ezekiel's day without seeing the parallel to the Western world at the close of the twentieth century. The latter years of this century have been marked by decadence, moral and spiritual decay, loss of integrity, violence, and injustices that mirror what Ezekiel must have witnessed.[59] Such a crisis calls for renewed spiritual and moral leadership that is the by-product of genuine spiritual renewal. S. Briscoe notes that Judah lacked the clear-sighted, highly motivated leadership and call of loving obedience. Like Judah, the countries of the Western world are wallowing in a morass of their own making. Some groups are concerned about injustice, violence, pornography, and crime; but their best efforts seem devoted to fighting it and banning it. While this is commendable, it should be done along with denouncing it as primarily anti-God and then working for a spiritual revival that will counter it.[60]

---

[58] Cf. Jer 23:16-22 and see F. B. Huey, Jr., *Jeremiah, Lamentations*, NAC (Nashville: Broadman, 1993), 215-17, with regard to the "prophets of peace." See also J. Sisson, "Jeremiah and the Jerusalem Conception of Peace," *JBL* 105,3 (1986): 429-42.

[59] See T. W. Engstrom with R. C. Larson, *Integrity* (Waco: Word, 1987); see especially pp. 26-27; and C. Colson, *Against the Night* (Ann Arbor: Servant Publications, 1989), 35-69.

[60] See Briscoe, *All Things Weird and Wonderful,* 112.

**22:30-31** Whenever such moral and spiritual crises have gripped nations, God has sought for a solitary individual who would be willing to be used (v. 30). He found such a person in Noah, in Moses, in Deborah, in Daniel, and in Ezekiel.

God was looking for someone to take the lead and stand in the breaches of the wall so he would not destroy the land. This proposal was similar to that found in Gen 18:22-33, where God promised to spare Sodom and Gomorrah if but ten righteous persons were found there. The situation in Judah was even more serious. God was looking for just one person willing to stem the tide of immorality and "stand before [him] in the gap." The analogy of a breach or hole in the wall was chosen because of its obvious overtones about the impending fall of Jerusalem.[61] But there was no one who would respond to the plaintiff plea of God. Therefore God would pour out his wrath and consume them in his fiery anger (v. 31).

God's plan for reaching ungodly people and nations is still the same. He uses godly men and women to stand in the breaches in morality and spirituality and make the difference by calling the nation and individuals to repentance, faith, righteousness, and commitment to God in Christ.

Those who have places of leadership also are doubly responsible. They are responsible for their own lives, but they also are responsible for those whom God places under their charge. When those who lead distort or misrepresent the truth of God, they not only deceive themselves but others also (22:23-31; cf. Heb 13:17; 1 Pet 5:1-5).

### (5) Parable of the Two Sisters (23:1-49)

The relationship between chaps. 16 and 23 should not be overlooked. Chapter 16 is the message of the orphan who became a harlot. The theme of chap. 16 centers on the seduction of Judah by Canaanite worship. Chapter 23 addresses the political alliances with ungodly nations that spelled doom for both Israel (Samaria), the Northern Kingdom, and Judah (Jerusalem), the Southern Kingdom. Chapter 16 focuses on Judah alone while chap. 23 focuses on both Judah and Samaria (Israel).[62]

In this parable Oholibah, Judah, observed the degradation and ultimate

---

[61] Fisch, *Ezekiel,* 149. The word פֶּרֶץ refers to a breach in the wall that usually was the result of a battering ram used for entering a city under siege. Ezekiel's call was for someone willing to גָּדַר־גָּדֵר ("erecting, to erect" or "indeed erect") a wall. This form especially was used of a wall protecting a vineyard. (For Israel as Yahweh's vineyard, see Isa 5:1-30.) Ezekiel 13:5 used the same terminology regarding the failure of the prophets (see Zimmerli, *Ezekiel 1,* 469).

[62] See Cooke, *Ezekiel,* 247-48; Wevers, *Ezekiel,* 178; Hals, *Ezekiel,* 168; and Cody, *Ezekiel,* 113.

downfall of its sister Oholah, Samaria, which fell to Assyria in 722 B.C. Tragically, Judah did not learn from the things it saw in the demise of its sister. Judah too became a harlot worse than her sibling.[63] This parable declared that Judah also was marked for a fall that came in 586 B.C.

Chapter 23 may be divided into four sections: (1) vv. 1-10 introduce the two sisters and describe the harlotry of Oholah (Samaria); (2) vv. 11-21 describe the harlotry of Oholibah (Judah); (3) vv. 22-35 presents four oracles of judgment concerning Oholibah; (4) vv. 36-49 review the record of the two sisters and predicted judgment.[64]

[1]The word of the LORD came to me: [2]"Son of man, there were two women, daughters of the same mother. [3]They became prostitutes in Egypt, engaging in prostitution from their youth. In that land their breasts were fondled and their virgin bosoms caressed. [4]The older was named Oholah, and her sister was Oholibah. They were mine and gave birth to sons and daughters. Oholah is Samaria, and Oholibah is Jerusalem.

[5]"Oholah engaged in prostitution while she was still mine; and she lusted after her lovers, the Assyrians—warriors [6]clothed in blue, governors and commanders, all of them handsome young men, and mounted horsemen. [7]She gave herself as a prostitute to all the elite of the Assyrians and defiled herself with all the idols of everyone she lusted after. [8]She did not give up the prostitution she began in Egypt, when during her youth men slept with her, caressed her virgin bosom and poured out their lust upon her.

[9]"Therefore I handed her over to her lovers, the Assyrians, for whom she lusted. [10]They stripped her naked, took away her sons and daughters and killed her with the sword. She became a byword among women, and punishment was inflicted on her.

THE TWO SISTERS (23:1-10). **23:1-4** This parable is about two daughters who are introduced in vv. 1-4. Several facts are presented about the two sisters in these opening remarks. First, they had the same mother (v. 2). This meant their rearing and opportunities were similar if not identical while in Egypt. Second, these sisters became prostitutes while in Egypt (v. 3). This was a reference to the roots of their idolatry that could be traced to their common experience in Egyptian bondage (v. 3). Third, their prostitution began in their youth (v. 3). Fourth, they had names that identified their character (v. 4). Fifth, they belonged to their father.

The "mother" of these daughters is a reference to the common origin of Jerusalem/Judah and Samaria/Northern Israel. Fisch suggests that this re-

---

[63] Enns, *Ezekiel,* 108.

[64] See Taylor, *Ezekiel,* 171. The sisters represent cities, Samaria and Jerusalem, their inhabitants, and their common sins.

fers to the common origin in the United Kingdom under Saul, David, and Solomon, 1051–931 B.C.,[65] and roots that went all the way to the common origin Abraham (Gen 12:1). The mention of Egypt makes specific reference to the bondage common to both Israel and Judah prior to the Exodus. They did not learn their prostitution at home but from foreigners in Egypt (Ezek 23:3). Egypt has overtones of early examples of idolatry and spiritual "prostitution." When the Israelites came out of Egypt, they rebelled against God and Moses (Exod 6:9; 16:2-3; 17:3) and finally made a golden calf that they worshiped as a substitute for Yahweh (Exod 32:1-35). From the days of her youth, Israel was guilty of unfaithfulness. God did not discard Israel but was faithful to his promises made to Abraham (Deut 7:6-11).

These two daughters represented the period of the divided kingdoms. The Northern Kingdom after 931 B.C. was Israel, and the capital was at Samaria. This kingdom-daughter was named Oholah, which means "her tent" (v. 4). This is a probable reference to a place of worship such as the pagan shrines so prevalent in the north.[66] The other kingdom-daughter was Jerusalem, who was called Oholibah, meaning "my tent is in her" (v. 4). This name is a reminder that God had selected Jerusalem as the place for his "tent" (2 Sam 6:17; Ps 48:1-14) or place of worship.[67]

Oholah was called the "older" sister probably because the Northern Kingdom was the first to set up official shrines; they endorsed pagan worship under Jeroboam I (1 Kgs 12:25-33). Also the Northern Kingdom was the first to establish political alliances with foreign nations, particularly the Assyrians (Hos 8:9).[68]

**23:5-10**    Oholah's record of prostitution with Assyria is summarized by describing how she lusted for the handsome young Assyrian warriors (vv. 5-6).[69] Israel's political prostitution was of particular concern to Ho-

---

[65] Fisch, *Ezekiel,* 149; cf. Ezek 16:46; Jer 3:7.

[66] Alexander, "Ezekiel," 851. He notes that the existence of heathen tent-shrines in the Northern Kingdom has been confirmed by recent excavations. The omission of the *mappiq* in the final Hebrew letter ה in both girls' names has been questioned about whether it should be translated third feminine singular. The omission is not uncommon and occurs elsewhere in the OT in the use of proper names.

[67] The word אֹהֶל means "tent" and may refer to a dwelling (Gen 4:20) or sometimes was translated "tabernacle" in reference to God's dwelling (Exod 26:36; 27:21). Esau's wife was אָהֳלִיבָמָה (Oholibamah, Exod 36:2) or "tent of the high place."

[68] Howie, *Ezekiel, Daniel,* 54-55; Alexander, "Ezekiel," 851.

[69] The Assyrians are described as קְרוֹבִים, which is translated "warriors," probably from the root קָרַב (sometimes meaning "war," e.g., 1 Kgs 20:29). See Alexander, "Ezekiel," 852-53 note; Taylor, *Ezekiel,* 172 note. The Assyrians wore beautiful uniforms that were very attractive; see Fisch, *Ezekiel,* 152.

sea, and the same idea of harlotry was the basis of his message (Hos 5:13; 7:11; 8:9; 12:1). The Black Obelisk of Shalmaneser III shows Jehu prostrating himself before the Assyrian king. This record has been dated ca. 840 B.C. near the beginning of Jehu's reign.[70]

The political alliance and fixation on Assyria also spilled over into the realm of worship. Assyrian forms of idolatry were adopted into Hebrew worship as modified forms of the idolatries learned in Egypt (vv. 7-8).[71] Judgment came with the deliverance of Samaria into the hands of her lovers, the Assyrians (v. 9). The capture of sons and daughters and the slaying of Oholah with the sword referred to the exile that came with the fall of Samaria in 722 B.C. at the hands of Shalmaneser V (2 Kgs 18:9).[72] The Assyrians "stripped her naked . . . took away sons and daughters," and "she became a byword" for punishment (v. 10). Parts of the land literally were denuded as the Assyrians cut all the lumber and carried away many natural resources.

[11]"Her sister Oholibah saw this, yet in her lust and prostitution she was more depraved than her sister. [12]She too lusted after the Assyrians—governors and commanders, warriors in full dress, mounted horsemen, all handsome young men. [13]I saw that she too defiled herself; both of them went the same way.

[14]"But she carried her prostitution still further. She saw men portrayed on a wall, figures of Chaldeans portrayed in red, [15]with belts around their waists and flowing turbans on their heads; all of them looked like Babylonian chariot officers, natives of Chaldea. [16]As soon as she saw them, she lusted after them and sent messengers to them in Chaldea. [17]Then the Babylonians came to her, to the bed of love, and in their lust they defiled her. After she had been defiled by them, she turned away from them in disgust. [18]When she carried on her prostitution openly and exposed her nakedness, I turned away from her in disgust, just as I had turned away from her sister. [19]Yet she became more and more promiscuous as she recalled the days of her youth, when she was a prostitute in Egypt. [20]There she lusted after her lovers, whose genitals were like those of donkeys and whose emission was like that of horses. [21]So you longed for the lewdness of your youth, when in Egypt your bosom was caressed and your young breasts fondled.

---

[70] See Thomas, *DOTT,* 48-49 and plate 3; Taylor, *Ezekiel,* 172.

[71] Fisch, *Ezekiel,* 152. This suggests that Israel was never really able to distance itself from the negative influences of Egyptian idolatry.

[72] Wevers, *Ezekiel,* 181. The exile of the Northern Kingdom occurred in the sixth year of Hezekiah's reign over Judah and the ninth year of Hoshea's reign over Israel.

OHOLIBAH (23:11-21).   **23:11-21**   The younger sister, Oholibah
(Judah), witnessed the perversions of the older sister Oholah (Samaria),
as well as her destruction but did not profit from the knowledge of tragic
consequences. Instead she indulged in the same life-style and became
more depraved than her sister (v. 11). She lusted after the same kind of
political alliances that proved to be the downfall of Samaria (vv. 12-13).
Just as Oholah had been attracted to the Assyrians, Oholibah was attracted
to the Babylonians.

Oholibah saw figures of the men of Babylon portrayed on a wall (v.
14). The Assyrians and Babylonians were noted for decorating walls with
carved bas-reliefs, some ten to twelve feet high, depicting the glories and
conquests of the empire.[73] Many such reliefs were painted red (vermilion,
AV), which may be the meaning of Jeremiah's statement that the buildings were decorated with red by Jehoiakim (Jer 22:14).[74]

The sight of the Babylonians, with their warrior's belts and turbans, at
once aroused a desire to be allied with them (Ezek 23:15-16). Messengers
were sent, the alliance was consummated, and Judah's defilement was
complete.[75] But the alliance was no sooner complete than she was repulsed by the Babylonians. Judah turned away in disgust.

God likewise was repulsed by Judah's actions, and he turned away from
her in disgust (v. 18). The language employed shows God's strong displeasure with Judah and Jerusalem. The phrase "she turned away" from her
lovers (Babylon) in v. 17 is parallel to God's statement that "I turned
away" (v. 18) from her just as "I turned away" (v. 18) from her sister.

She (Judah) also played the harlot and became more and more promiscuous. Judah's conduct was reminiscent of those days in the youth of the
nation when the people worshiped the golden calf in the wilderness (cf.
Rom 1:18-32; esp. v. 24). This incident produced lewd, sensual worship
and unrestrained idolatry (Exod 32:1-10).

Also Judah's political prostitution was presented in explicit sexual terminology. This idolatry produced the same revulsion by God that
prompted him to annihilate their forefathers in the wilderness for the
worship of the gods of Egypt (v. 21; Exod 32:11-18). Judah lusted for her
lovers whose "genitals were like those of donkeys, and whose emission
was like that of horses" (v. 20). These proverbial phrases were intended
to show divine contempt for those attracted by the military power por-

---

[73] See Cooke, *Ezekiel,* 251; Wevers, *Ezekiel,* 181.

[74] See Zimmerli, *Ezekiel 1,* 486-87.

[75] Fisch, *Ezekiel,* 153. Jerusalem "lusted" (v. 12) in the sense that the sight of the Babylonian soldiers aroused a desire to be allied with them.

trayed by reference to sexual potency.[76]

The trite but true principle that "The one thing we learn from history is that we fail to learn from history" is true for individuals as well as nations. All the examples of the sins of the past that are recorded in the Word of God shout the warnings of sin's ultimate consequences, but, amazingly, people still reject God and choose a life of sin and rebellion (23:11-21; cf. Gal 6:7-10).

**22"Therefore, Oholibah, this is what the Sovereign LORD says: I will stir up your lovers against you, those you turned away from in disgust, and I will bring them against you from every side— 23the Babylonians and all the Chaldeans, the men of Pekod and Shoa and Koa, and all the Assyrians with them, handsome young men, all of them governors and commanders, chariot officers and men of high rank, all mounted on horses. 24They will come against you with weapons, chariots and wagons and with a throng of people; they will take up positions against you on every side with large and small shields and with helmets. I will turn you over to them for punishment, and they will punish you according to their standards. 25I will direct my jealous anger against you, and they will deal with you in fury. They will cut off your noses and your ears, and those of you who are left will fall by the sword. They will take away your sons and daughters, and those of you who are left will be consumed by fire. 26They will also strip you of your clothes and take your fine jewelry. 27So I will put a stop to the lewdness and prostitution you began in Egypt. You will not look on these things with longing or remember Egypt anymore.**

**28"For this is what the Sovereign LORD says: I am about to hand you over to those you hate, to those you turned away from in disgust. 29They will deal with you in hatred and take away everything you have worked for. They will leave you naked and bare, and the shame of your prostitution will be exposed. Your lewdness and promiscuity 30have brought this upon you, because you lusted after the nations and defiled yourself with their idols. 31You have gone the way of your sister; so I will put her cup into your hand. 32"This is what the Sovereign LORD says:**

**"You will drink your sister's cup,
    a cup large and deep;
  it will bring scorn and derision,
    for it holds so much.
33You will be filled with drunkenness and sorrow,**

---

[76] Reference to the wild donkey and the horse is an epithet for sexual potency since the sexual heat of these animals was well known; see Keil, *Biblical Commentary on the Prophecies of Ezekiel,* vol. I, 327-28.

the cup of ruin and desolation,
  the cup of your sister Samaria.
³⁴You will drink it and drain it dry;
  you will dash it to pieces
  and tear your breasts.

I have spoken, declares the Sovereign LORD.

³⁵"Therefore this is what the Sovereign LORD says: Since you have forgotten me and thrust me behind your back, you must bear the consequences of your lewdness and prostitution."

ORACLES OF JUDGMENT (23:22-35). This passage contains four messages of judgment to come upon Oholibah (Judah, especially Jerusalem). First, her lovers would become the instruments of judgment against her. The Babylonians, with other conquered vassals, would attack Jerusalem (vv. 22-27). They would mutilate her, strip her, and take her away. Second, she would be despised by those who were formerly her lovers (vv. 28-31). Disloyalty to God leads to idolatry and ultimately is expressed in contempt for all involved. Third, she would suffer the same fall as her sister Oholah. Jerusalem would be destroyed and her citizens taken captive because of the wrath (cup) of God (vv. 32-34).[77] Fourth, she would bear her sin, abandoned of any source of help (v. 35). Because Jerusalem forgot God, she was left alone. Greater punishment for sin does not exist than to be isolated in a time of judgment and despair.[78]

**23:22-27** In the first message God pledged he would "stir" against her the lovers with which Oholibah had committed prostitution. The Babylonians clearly were used by God as a chastening instrument against Judah and Jerusalem. They came against Jerusalem from all sides, with the men of Pekod, Shoa, Koa, and Assyria, all groups in the eastern part of the Babylonian Empire.[79]

God's intention to use military action as a means of judgment was reinforced by the military terms "governors," "commanders," "chariot officers," "men of high rank," "all [men] mounted on horses," "chariots," "weapons," "wagons," "shields," and "helmets" (vv. 23-24). The cutting

---

[77] See the same idea in Jer 25:15-31; 49:12; Lam 4:21; Hab 2:16; Obad 16; Isa 51:17,22 and Ps 75:8.

[78] Ellison, *Ezekiel: The Man and His Message,* 94.

[79] פְּקוֹד also was mentioned with Babylon in Jer 50:21 and שׁוֹעַ in Isa 22:5 (translated as "crying" in NIV). See I. W. Slotki, *Isaiah* (London: Soncino, 1972), 100, and Alexander, "Ezekiel," 856.

"off your noses and ears" (v. 25) is an accurate description of the barbaric
practices of mutilating enemies and prisoners of war. This was widely accepted military strategy in the ancient Near East. The Assyrians and Babylonians especially were known for their cruelty.[80] God promised that by
the method of chastening he would end the "lewdness" and "prostitution"
of Oholibah's (Judah's) idolatry and foreign political alliances (v. 27).

Nations who rely on political agreements and military might alone to
sustain their security will ultimately incur the judgment of God for failure
to allow him to have first place in their commitments (vv. 1-15). Judgment often comes by the very nations in which trust was placed as a false
sense of security. Israel trusted Egypt and Babylon, both of which God
used as chastening instruments (vv. 16-31).

The second message condemned idolatry and its influence on foreign
involvement that began when the people left Egypt (Exod 32). It continued in the wilderness even to the end of the forty years of wandering. The
Moabites introduced Baal worship in the Balaam/Balak incident of Num
22–25 (see especially Num 31:16). Following the Babylonian exile, idolatry was never again a problem.[81] So God reaffirmed his commitment to
the exile as a means of chastening (see Ezek 23:28-30). He said, "I will
put her cup into your hand" (v. 31). This "cup" was a reference to the fall
of Samaria and the captivity of the Northern Kingdom. Judah would receive the same "cup."

The third message was a reminder that the "cup" he had given to her
sister Oholah (Samaria) contained the wrath of God's judgment that also
would be given to Judah (vv. 32-34). The first strophe of these verses describes the size of the cup and the consequences of drinking its contents
(e.g., scorn, derision) because it holds much (v. 32). The second strophe
describes the drunkenness and sorrow that are the consequences of the
ruin and desolation that resulted from drinking the cup (v. 33). The final
strophe describes the anguish of the finality of judgment (v. 34).[82] The
"cup" of God's wrath is a common feature in the Old Testament prophet
who proclaimed God's judgment on Israel and Judah (Isa 51:7,22; Jer
25:15-17,28; Hab 2:16; Zech 12:2). The motif of the cup places Ezekiel in
"a long prophetic chain that was to culminate in Jesus, who absorbed in
his own person the horror of God's judgment accepting it from his hand

---

[80] See Zimmerli, *Ezekiel 1,* 488-89; Wevers, *Ezekiel,* 184, cf. 2 Kgs 25:7.

[81] Fisch, *Ezekiel,* 155; cf. Ezek 22:15.

[82] Zimmerli, *Ezekiel 1,* 490-91. The images and motifs are characters of those used by
Ezekiel and may be compared with the song of the sword in 21:23-32.

without a shudder (Mark 14:36)."[83]

The final of the four messages states that the chief purpose for Jerusalem's judgment was that Judah had forgotten God. He had been discarded like an object deliberately flung behind one's back as worthless (Ezek 23:35). Therefore Judah had to bear the consequences of her sins.[84] God judged Jerusalem, the city of God, for its sins. This should be a sober warning that no one will escape God's chastening or judgment against sin.

[36]The LORD said to me: "Son of man, will you judge Oholah and Oholibah? Then confront them with their detestable practices, [37]for they have committed adultery and blood is on their hands. They committed adultery with their idols; they even sacrificed their children, whom they bore to me, as food for them. [38]They have also done this to me: At that same time they defiled my sanctuary and desecrated my Sabbaths. [39]On the very day they sacrificed their children to their idols, they entered my sanctuary and desecrated it. That is what they did in my house.

[40]"They even sent messengers for men who came from far away, and when they arrived you bathed yourself for them, painted your eyes and put on your jewelry. [41]You sat on an elegant couch, with a table spread before it on which you had placed the incense and oil that belonged to me.

[42]"The noise of a carefree crowd was around her; Sabeans were brought from the desert along with men from the rabble, and they put bracelets on the arms of the woman and her sister and beautiful crowns on their heads. [43]Then I said about the one worn out by adultery, 'Now let them use her as a prostitute, for that is all she is.' [44]And they slept with her. As men sleep with a prostitute, so they slept with those lewd women, Oholah and Oholibah. [45]But righteous men will sentence them to the punishment of women who commit adultery and shed blood, because they are adulterous and blood is on their hands.

[46]"This is what the Sovereign LORD says: Bring a mob against them and give them over to terror and plunder. [47]The mob will stone them and cut them down with their swords; they will kill their sons and daughters and burn down their houses.

[48]"So I will put an end to lewdness in the land, that all women may take warning and not imitate you. [49]You will suffer the penalty for your lewdness and bear the consequences of your sins of idolatry. Then you will know that I am the Sovereign LORD."

---

[83] Allen, *Ezekiel 20–48,* 52. See also C. A. Blaising, "Gethsemane: A Prayer of Faith," *JETS* 22,4 (1979): 333-43.

[84] Alexander, "Ezekiel," 855; Fisch, *Ezekiel,* 157. Fisch calls v. 35 the most significant verse of the judgment messages in that it contains the cause of the judgment: the people forgot God, meaning they no longer regarded him or his Word in their daily lives.

RECORD REVIEWED AND JUDGMENT PREDICTED (23:36-49). **23:36-49** The chapter concludes with additional statements about the sins and judgment of the two harlot sisters Oholah and Oholibah. These statements form the conclusion of the words of judgment for sin that was the central theme of the prophet in chaps. 20–23. The last two parables, the boiling pot (24:1-14) and the death of Ezekiel's wife (24:15-27), have the theme of Jerusalem's destruction. The verdict was reached in 23:36-49, and the sentence was executed in 24:1-27.

Seven "detestable practices" were reviewed (23:36-44) prior to the verdict (vv. 45-49). These practices or "abominations" restate all former charges presented in chaps. 20–23. These "detestable things" relate to spiritual infidelity, moral impurity, and political indiscretion. The list includes desecration of the Sabbath (v. 38), desecration of the temple (v. 39), forbidden foreign alliances (vv. 40-41), adultery (vv. 42-44), innocent bloodshed (v. 45), child sacrifice (vv. 46-47), and idolatry (vv. 48-49).[85]

Though alliances with foreign, ungodly nations were strictly forbidden (Deut 17:14-20), Judah pursued them aggressively. She prepared herself as a harlot advertising her trade (vv. 40-41).[86] She attracted the drunken rabble of the desert who wore her out with adulteries and used her as a prostitute to gratify their own lusts.

The two sisters, Samaria and Judah, were sentenced by "righteous" men (v. 45). This probably meant that heathen paramours were more righteous, by comparison, than the two sisters.[87] So a mob ("an assembly," Heb.) will be brought against the two sisters in judgment (vv. 46-47). They will stone them, use the sword against them, kill their children and burn their houses. So these two sisters will be an example to all people of the consequences of unfaithfulness (vv. 48-49). While most parables and messages concerning sin in the Old Testament seek to produce repentance, that is not so here. The message closed with a note of finality. "Then," when judgment has been dispensed, "you will know that I am the Sovereign LORD."[88] The arrival of judgment will confirm the truth of God's warnings and the ministry and message of Ezekiel. This concluded

---

[85] תּוֹעֲבוֹתֵיהֶן ("their detestable practices"), translated "abominations" in NKJV, refers to acts of a physical, ritual, or ethical nature (cf. Lev 18:22-30; 20:13; Deut 7:25; 12:31; 14:3-8; 18:9-14; 1 Kgs 14:23; Prov 6:16-19).

[86] Alexander, "Ezekiel," 857; Fisch, *Ezekiel,* 158; Enns, *Ezekiel,* 111. The use of cosmetics to enhance the appearance in order to entice lovers was a common practice (2 Kgs 9:30; Jer 4:30).

[87] Fisch, *Ezekiel,* 159. The Targum takes this as a reference to Babylonian and Assyrian judges who were, by comparison to the sisters, righteous.

[88] Hals, *Ezekiel,* 170.

the prophecies of Ezekiel, which addressed the sins of Judah and the reasons for impending judgment.

God demands holiness and a standard of righteousness that will reveal his love and his character to all people (23:36-49). He demands that the standards of holiness that are found in the demands of the law (Exod 20:1-17). They are to be lived out in the daily lives of his people (cf. Matt 5–7).

### (6) Parable of the Boiling Pot (24:1-14)

¹In the ninth year, in the tenth month on the tenth day, the word of the LORD came to me: ²"Son of man, record this date, this very date, because the king of Babylon has laid siege to Jerusalem this very day. ³Tell this rebellious house a parable and say to them: 'This is what the Sovereign LORD says:

"'Put on the cooking pot; put it on
  and pour water into it.
⁴Put into it the pieces of meat,
  all the choice pieces—the leg and the shoulder.
 Fill it with the best of these bones;
⁵take the pick of the flock.
 Pile wood beneath it for the bones;
  bring it to a boil
  and cook the bones in it.
⁶"'For this is what the Sovereign LORD says:
 "'Woe to the city of bloodshed,
  to the pot now encrusted,
  whose deposit will not go away!
 Empty it piece by piece
  without casting lots for them.

⁷"'For the blood she shed is in her midst:
  She poured it on the bare rock;
 she did not pour it on the ground,
  where the dust would cover it.
⁸To stir up wrath and take revenge
  I put her blood on the bare rock,
  so that it would not be covered.
⁹"'Therefore this is what the Sovereign LORD says:
 "'Woe to the city of bloodshed!
  I, too, will pile the wood high.
¹⁰So heap on the wood
  and kindle the fire.
 Cook the meat well,
  mixing in the spices;

and let the bones be charred.
**11**Then set the empty pot on the coals
 till it becomes hot and its copper glows
so its impurities may be melted
 and its deposit burned away.
**12**It has frustrated all efforts;
 its heavy deposit has not been removed,
 not even by fire.

**13**" 'Now your impurity is lewdness. Because I tried to cleanse you but you would not be cleansed from your impurity, you will not be clean again until my wrath against you has subsided.

**14**" 'I the LORD have spoken. The time has come for me to act. I will not hold back; I will not have pity, nor will I relent. You will be judged according to your conduct and your actions, declares the Sovereign LORD.' "

The date of this prophecy is significant. It was written on the day when Nebuchadnezzar's siege of Jerusalem began in January 588 B.C. At that point judgment was no longer a future prospect but a present reality. The date became an appointed fast day and was observed as early as the time of Zechariah (Zech 8:19).[89] The prophecy consisted of three poems, each introduced with, "This is what the Sovereign LORD says" (vv. 3,6,9).

The first is the song of the cooking pot in vv. 3-5. The second and third are interpretive speeches in poetic form in vv. 6-8 and vv. 9-12. This message has three divisions: (1) the assignment of the message to the messenger (24:1-5), (2) the announcement of woe (24:6-8), and (3) the announcement of judgment (24:9-14).[90]

**24:1-5**   The prophet was told to make a record of the date (Jan. 15, 588[91]) because on that date the king of Babylon began the siege of Jerusalem. Ezekiel was instructed to tell the people a parable that began in poetic form in the last part of vv. 3-5. In the parable a cooking pot was placed on a fire. This "cooking pot song" is like the "sword song" of 21:8-17 and the "cup song" of 23:32-34.[92]

A cooking pot was placed on the fire, and choice pieces of meat were

---

[89] Fisch, *Ezekiel,* 160; see Jer 52:4-34 and 2 Kgs 25:1-30.

[90] For an analysis of the structure and form of Ezek 24:1-14 as a disputation speech, see D. I. Block, "Ezekiel's Boiling Cauldron: A Form-Critical Solution to Ezekiel XXIV: 1-14," *VT* XLI (1991): 12-37.

[91] See Zimmerli, *Ezekiel 1,* 498; Taylor, *Ezekiel,* 177; and "Dated Prophecies in Ezekiel" chart in the Introduction.

[92] Alexander, "Ezekiel," 860. This song is followed by two poetic verdict speeches that expand and interpret the song.

placed in it for cooking (vv. 3-4).[93] Such pots usually were made of clay, but this one was made of copper (v. 11). The meat was placed in the pot and the pot heated to a boil (vv. 3-5). The cooking pot represented Jerusalem, and the meat represented the inhabitants.[94] "Bring it to a boil" (v. 5) is an emphatic statement in the Hebrew text, which literally means "cause its boilings to boil." This statement was an allusion to the ferocity of the Babylonian attack against Jerusalem.[95]

**24:6-8** The second poem is an interpretive song expressed as a cry of woe for the city of Jerusalem.[96] "Woe" (v. 6) was pronounced on Jerusalem because it was a city known for bloodshed and violence that previously was described in 22:1-16. This pot was encrusted with residue and could not be cleansed. The terminology describes an unclean, filthy cooking pot that could not be cleaned and was therefore unusable (v. 6; cf. vv. 12-13). Jerusalem's bloody crimes were in its midst, and no attempt was made to cover them (v. 7). The lack of concern for covering the blood of people slain was further evidence of the cruelty and heartlessness of the people since the law required that the blood of a sacrifice be covered (Lev 17:13).[97]

God noted Jerusalem's callous disregard for the sanctity of human life and vowed to preserve the bloodstains as a witness to the city's guilt (v. 8).[98] So in spite of the destruction brought by the early stages of the exile, the guilt of the city remained. Jerusalem had not even tried to cover the murder and violence in its midst. There was such total disregard for the law of God that human life was of little value. Their unabashed transgressions of the law deliberately provoked the righteous indignation of a holy God.[99]

**24:9-14** The third song contains another interpretive song of woe like the one in vv. 6-8. Again the theme was God's response to the bloodshed of Jerusalem (v. 9). God declared he would pile the wood high so the fire of judgment would be hot. The contents of the pot were cooked, then

---

[93] Taylor, *Ezekiel,* 178 note; this סִיר ("pot") was a wide-mouthed cauldron made of copper instead of clay and used for cooking. See also Zimmerli, *Ezekiel 1,* 499.

[94] Cooke, *Ezekiel,* 266. Prophets sometimes received inspiration from ordinary events like cooking (see e.g., Amos 7:15; Jer 1:11,13; 18:1-23).

[95] Fisch, *Ezekiel,* 162. Boiling bones is an allusion to the barbarism of the Babylonians.

[96] Use of the word אוֹי suggests a situation of extreme distress especially associated with judgment. In Ezekiel it is used only in Ezek 16:23; 24:6,9 (see comment on 16:23) but was a favorite term of Jeremiah (Jer 4:13,31; 6:4; 10:19; 13:27; 15:10; 45:3; 48:46).

[97] Fisch, *Ezekiel,* 162-63. Human blood was given less concern than animal blood, which had to be covered with dust.

[98] Wevers, *Ezekiel,* 191. The exposed blood was left so that the "wrath" of Yahweh would be stirred.

[99] Eichrodt, *Ezekiel,* 339. By failure to seek God's forgiveness, they served intent upon arousing his wrath.

charred (v. 10), poured on the fire, and finally burned away like the impurities in the smelting process (v. 11). The act of pouring the contents on the fire and burning the leftovers is a demonstration to state there is no hope for Jerusalem; rather, destruction is certain to come.[100] This refining process began with the first deportation in 605 B.C. It continued with the second siege of Jerusalem in 597 B.C. and again at the fall of Jerusalem in 586 B.C. This message was a prelude to the prophecy of 36:22-32, which predicted a final cleansing in the end time after Israel has returned to the land (vv. 11-12).[101]

All God's efforts to bring moral restoration through the ministry of the prophets had proven fruitless (v. 13). Therefore God announced that the time to act had come. He would not restrain judgment (v. 14); he would have no pity, nor would he relent.[102]

God especially condemned Judah for callous disregard for the sanctity of human life (24:1-14). This indifference to human life was evident in the proliferation of crimes of violence and the lack of compassion for the innocent victims of those crimes. The severe judgment sent by God upon Judah should be ample warning to those today who share the same callous disregard for the value of human life, both the born and the unborn.

### (7) Parable at the Death of Ezekiel's Wife (24:15-27)

**[15]The word of the LORD came to me: [16]"Son of man, with one blow I am about to take away from you the delight of your eyes. Yet do not lament or weep or shed any tears. [17]Groan quietly; do not mourn for the dead. Keep your turban fastened and your sandals on your feet; do not cover the lower part of your face or eat the customary food [of mourners]."**

**[18]So I spoke to the people in the morning, and in the evening my wife died. The next morning I did as I had been commanded.**

**[19]Then the people asked me, "Won't you tell us what these things have to do with us?"**

**[20]So I said to them, "The word of the LORD came to me: [21]Say to the house of Israel, 'This is what the Sovereign LORD says: I am about to desecrate my sanctuary—the stronghold in which you take pride, the delight of your eyes, the object of your affection. The sons and daughters you left behind will fall by the sword. [22]And you will do as I have done. You will not cover the lower part of your face or eat the customary food [of mourners]. [23]You will keep your turbans on your heads and your sandals on your feet. You will not**

---

[100] Block, "Ezekiel's Boiling Cauldron," 37.

[101] Alexander, "Ezekiel," 861.

[102] Fisch, *Ezekiel,* 164; the use of פָּרַע, meaning "to let loose" or "to refrain," suggests unrestrained judgment.

mourn or weep but will waste away because of your sins and groan among yourselves. <sup>24</sup>Ezekiel will be a sign to you; you will do just as he has done. When this happens, you will know that I am the Sovereign LORD.'

<sup>25</sup>"And you, son of man, on the day I take away their stronghold, their joy and glory, the delight of their eyes, their heart's desire, and their sons and daughters as well— <sup>26</sup>on that day a fugitive will come to tell you the news. <sup>27</sup>At that time your mouth will be opened; you will speak with him and will no longer be silent. So you will be a sign to them, and they will know that I am the LORD."

The last word of judgment against Judah and Jerusalem was without a doubt the most painful for Ezekiel. The parable on the occasion of the death of Ezekiel's wife raises the question of how we are tonderstand the love of God as it related to the prophet and especially to Ezekiel's wife. Did God commit an unprovoked act of cruelty in taking the life of Ezekiel's wife, who was call "the delight" of his eyes (v. 16), just to illusstrate a point? Any attempt to answer this question involves a struggle with the meaning, purpose, and existence of suffering in the world.

Suffering is a reality in the life of men and wome of faith. God does not promise to remove suffering from human experienc, but he does promise to sustain the faithful in the midst of suffering (Ps 23:4). Suffering may serv e a godly purpose in our lives. It may be a means to test our faith (1 Pet 1:7; 4:12-13), to strengthen our faith (Matt 15:28; Acts 6:5; Rom 4:19-20), to discipline and educate (Heb 12:7), to humble (Deut 8:2-3; 1 Cor 12:1-9), to purify (Mal 3:3; 1 Pet 1:7), to enable us to help other sufferers (2 Cor 1:3-7), and to demonstrate the suffering of God's grace (2 Cor 12:9; Phil 1:23).

God informed Ezekiel of the imminent death of his wife and used the occasion to prepare his people for judgment. The passage does not say that God put her to death as an object lesson. God would not arbitrarily take the life of Ezekiel's wife to clarify his word to an unrepentant people.[103] But he would speak in the misdst of the inevitable suffering of life to show them that he knows, he cares, and he will use the usffering as a basis for a hope of new life. The new nation, purified and restored, could not begin to take shape until the old had gone. This was an important aspect of Jesus' message. We live by death, and we gain by losing (Matt 9:16-17; 16:25; cf. Rom 6:6; 2 Cor 5:17; Heb 8:13). This is the message of the cross, which was "foolishness to those who are perishing" (1 Cor

---

[103] Hals (*Ezekiel,* 176) sees in this event a miror of the NT message that God would go so far as to allow an innocent person to die to demonstrate the intensity of his love and his judgment and concludes that such a concept is only at home in that context.

1:18), a "stumbling block to the Jews" (1 Cor 1:23), but the power of God and wisdom of God to all who believe (1 Cor 1:24).

**24:15-17**   God revealed to the prophet that his wife would die suddenly and unexpectedly (v. 15). The closeness of their relationship was heightened by the reference to her as the "delight" of his eyes (v. 16). She would be taken with "one blow." This usually described sudden death in battle (1 Sam 4:17; 2 Sam 17:9; 18:7) or from plague or disease (Num 14:37; 17:13-15; 25:8-9). Here it probably meant that she contracted some disease that was sudden and fatal.[104]

God told Ezekiel that when his wife died, he was to forego all visible signs of mourning.[105] Funerary rites usually included tearing one's clothing (2 Sam 3:31), removing one's shoes and turban (2 Sam 15:30), and shaving the head and putting dust and ashes on the head (1 Sam 4:12). The mourner's face was covered, and other mourners, some friends and some professional mourners, joined in wailing for the dead. The family sat or rolled in dust as a sign of their grief. Sometimes mourning also was accompanied by fasting. The family would eat only mourner's bread that was supplied by friends or neighbors.[106] Ezekiel was to adopt none of these usual responses but was told to "groan quietly" or literally "sigh in silence" (v. 17) for the death of his wife.

**24:18-24**   In the morning Ezekiel gave this unusual message to the people, and the same day in the evening his wife died. The following morning Ezekiel did as God had requested (v. 18). The circumstances may mean that Ezekiel's wife already was ill at the time God revealed the impending death of his mate.

Ezekiel's unorthodox conduct in light of his grief inevitably drew questions. The people asked, "What do these things have to do with us?" (v. 19). The question is ironic. With it, the people unknowingly spoke of their own deaths. The fall of Jerusalem resulted in the desecration and destruction of the temple. Jerusalem suddenly "died," as had Ezekiel's wife, and with it the temple and worship. The temple was characterized as the "delight" of their eyes (vv. 20-21), the same words used to describe the prophet's wife in v. 16.[107]

Besides the loss of the temple, they lost another "delight," namely, their sons and daughters (v. 21). Like Ezekiel, those in Jerusalem would

---

[104] Enns, *Ezekiel,* 114. The use of the term מַגֵּפָה refers to both slaughter and plague.

[105] Jeremiah, another prophet who witnessed the siege and fall of Jerusalem, is likewise instructed not to mourn (Jer 16:5-13).

[106] Alexander, "Ezekiel," 862; Enns, *Ezekiel,* 114. See both, who give brief discussions of mourning practices in the time of Ezekiel.

[107] Zimmerli, *Ezekiel 1,* 508, cf. vv. 16,21.

be unable to mourn because they would immediately be taken away as captives to Babylon. For the captives to lament could be perceived as seditious. Therefore they would, like the prophet, be forced to "groan quietly" (v. 17).[108] When this happened, it was to be a confirmation of the truth of God's word and the integrity of Ezekiel (v. 24).

**24:25-27**    All former restrictions on Ezekiel (3:25-27) would be removed with the fall of Jerusalem (vv. 26-27). From that point, when the prophet's message changed from primarily judgment to restoration and hope, he would be free to move among the people and to relate his messages.[109] This was a significant word placed after the messages of judgment against Judah and Jerusalem because it anticipated the messages of hope and restoration that begin in chap. 33. This prophecy of a fugitive from fallen Jerusalem and the end of Ezekiel's silence is fulfilled in 33:21-22 in anticipation of the additional messages of restoration in 33:30–39:29.

God is not the author of personal tragedy, but he does often use such experiences as unique opportunities and special windows through which people will come to "know" that he is the Lord. Such a knowledge of God tells of his grace, mercy, love, and blessing but also his wrath, resolve, and determination to deal with sin that brought death into the world (24:15-27; cf. Rom 8:28-29).

---

[108] Hals, *Ezekiel,* 176; Fisch, *Ezekiel,* 166. Cf. Prov 5:11-12. D. Stuart (*Ezekiel,* 243) suggests as another possibility that "mourning is not appropriate in cases of capital punishment," which the destruction of Jerusalem, in effect, would be. He also notes (p. 244) a parallel with Jesus' statement, "Let the dead bury their own dead."

[109] Alexander, "Ezekiel," 863. The removal of the prophet's silence would be another confirmation of Ezekiel's prophetic gifts and calling.

## III. PROPHETIC MESSAGES CONCERNING FOREIGN NATIONS (25:1–32:32)

1. Prophecy against Ammon (25:1-7)
2. Prophecy against Moab (25:8-11)
3. Prophecy against Edom (25:12-14)
4. Prophecy against Philistia (25:15-17)
5. Prophecy against Tyre (26:1–28:19)
   (1) Tyre's Sin Identified (26:1-6)
   (2) Details of the Immediate Destruction of Tyre (26:7-14)
   (3) Effect of Judgment on Tyre's Neighbors (26:15-18)
   (4) Tyre's Descent into the Pit (26:19-21)
   (5) Lament over the Loss of Tyre (27:1-36)
   (6) Prophecy against the King of Tyre (28:1-10)
   (7) Final Lament for the King of Tyre (28:11-19)
6. Prophecy against Sidon (28:20-26)
7. Prophecy against Egypt (29:1–32:32)
   (1) Egypt's Sin Exposed and Judged (29:1-16)
   (2) Egypt to Suffer the Fate of Tyre (29:17-21)
   (3) Egypt and Allies Devastated (30:1-19)
   (4) Egypt Helpless in the Day of Yahweh (30:20-26)
   (5) Fall of Pharaoh, the "Cedar" of Egypt (31:1-18)
   (6) Lament for the Fall of Pharaoh (32:1-16)
   (7) Pharaoh Condemned to the Pit (32:17-32)

## III. PROPHETIC MESSAGES CONCERNING FOREIGN NATIONS (25:1–32:32)

Ezekiel's collection of prophetic messages against foreign nations is not unlike those in Isa 13:1–23:18; Jer 46:1–51:64; and Amos 1:3–2:3.[1] These messages separate the oracles denouncing the sins of Judah in

---

[1] On the differences between the oracles against the nations in Amos and the major prophets, see J. B. Geyer, "Mythology and Culture against the Nations," *VT* XXXVI (1986): 129-45.

chaps. 1–24 from the oracles of future restoration in chaps. 33–48.[2] As such, they form an ideal transition suggesting that all nations will answer for acts of ungodliness like those for which Israel and Judah were condemned.[3] Ezekiel, then, is structured in three basic movements: words of judgment for Judah and Israel (chaps. 1–24), judgment against the nations (chaps. 25–32), and words of hope and restoration (33–48).[4] This section emphasizes the fact that God had not overlooked the guilt of foreign nations and that they also would be judged for their sins.

There are seven messages in this series, the first four of which are in chap. 25.[5] These were the prophecies against Ammon (25:1-7), Moab (25:8-11), Edom (25:12-14), and Philistia (25:15-17). Ezekiel brought separate messages against Tyre (26:1–28:19) and Sidon (28:20-29), which were sister city-states. The final series of messages were directed against Egypt (29:1–32:32).[6] A comparison of Ezekiel's messages with those of other Old Testament prophets shows him to be in the mainstream of prophetic consciousness. He was aware that the foreign nations also must be judged for their personal sins and for their cruelty and inhumanity to Israel. He spoke against all the foreign nations mentioned by other prophets except Damascus and Babylon.

This collection of messages against foreign nations served two important purposes. First, they were a reminder that all those who oppose God and his people will be judged. All the nations named had either taken part

---

[2] The oracles do not, however, represent a later writer or tradition but rather the "genius" of the prophet Ezekiel, who placed the oracles where they are to join the words of judgment against Israel (chaps. 1–24) and the words of hope for Israel (chaps. 33–48). See L. Boadt, "Rhetorical Strategies in Ezekiel's Oracles of Judgment," in *Ezekiel and His Book*, ed. J. Lust (Leuven: Leuven University Press, 1986), 182-200.

[3] G. A. Cooke, *The Book of Ezekiel*, ICC (Edinburgh: T & T Clark, 1986), 281; A. B. Davidson, *The Book of the Prophet Ezekiel* (Cambridge: University of Chicago Press, 1892), 178.

[4] R. W. Klein, *Ezekiel: The Prophet and His Message* (Columbia: University of South Carolina Press, 1988), 139. Klein also points out that Isaiah (and the LXX of Jeremiah) is also so structured: words of judgment (chaps. 1–12), words of judgment against the nations (chaps. 13–23), and words of hope (chaps. 24–39 [24–66]).

[5] Ezekiel presents seven messages against foreign nations in 25:1–32:32. The extended use of messages against foreign nations may also be found in Isaiah and Jeremiah, both of which also have seven messages. Such messages are deeply rooted in the prophetic tradition from the time of Amos. The six messages of Amos were brief and included prophecies against Damascus (1:3-5), Gaza (1:6-8), Tyre (1:9-10), Edom (1:11-12), Ammon (1:13-15), and Moab (2:1-3). Cf. also the prophecies of Zephaniah.

[6] W. Zimmerli, *Ezekiel 2* (Philadelphia: Fortress, 1983), 3. Such messages were understood in the ancient Near East as a means of placing a curse on one's enemies. God had revealed to his true prophets that he would fulfill the judgments of these messages.

in the destruction of Jerusalem or rejoiced over it. According to Jer 27:3, five of the nations Ezekiel prophesied against were involved in a conspiracy against Judah. Jeremiah viewed this as outright rebellion against the Lord.[7] Second, these nations were filled with ungodly pride and idolatries. As a result of these judgments announced by Ezekiel, these nations also would know that Yahweh is God.[8]

The notable omission in Ezekiel's list of prophecies of judgment was any reference to Babylon. This is somewhat of a surprise since so much detail was given to Babylon's destruction by Jeremiah, Ezekiel's contemporary. Zimmerli suggests that perhaps the book was put in its final form at a time before the fall of Babylon was so apparent, hence no mention of it by Ezekiel. Later when the doom of Babylon was certain, prophetic writers spoke more freely.[9] Such an explanation fails to account for the lengthy message by Jeremiah, who was highly regarded by the Babylonians (Jer 50:1–51:63) and whose ministry began prior to that of Ezekiel but continued at least until the fall of Jerusalem in 587/586 B.C.

Another explanation is that God used the Babylonians as an instrument of chastening to punish Judah and Jerusalem. Ezekiel was therefore reluctant to include them in the list of nations mentioned for judgment.[10] Such reasoning also fails to account for inclusion of messages of judgment against Babylon by other major prophets including Jeremiah and Isaiah.

Jeremiah's longest prophecy of judgment in his messages against the nations was against Babylon. This is rather remarkable because Jeremiah encouraged submission to the Babylonians. He believed they were God's instrument of judgment (Jer 37:1-10; 39:11-14; 40:1-12). When Jerusalem was attacked, Jeremiah was treated as a friend of Babylon in spite of his lengthy and vivid account of its destruction.

Since Ezekiel was in Babylon instead of in Jerusalem, it may have been more difficult for him to write openly about the fall of his captors. If he did so, one would not be surprised if he did it in cryptic, symbolic language. The one judgment message remaining after his prophecies against foreign nations is the judgment of Gog and Magog (38:1–39:29). In our discussion of the Gog-Magog judgment, we will explore the possibility that this message was a cryptic judgment prophecy against Babylon and thus would have been Ezekiel's missing message.

Each of the seven messages contain at least three parts. First there was

---

[7] Klein, *Ezekiel*, 130.

[8] Davidson, *Ezekiel*, 179.

[9] Zimmerli, *Ezekiel 2*, 4.

[10] Cooke, *Ezekiel*, 281.

## MESSAGES AGAINST FOREIGN NATIONS

|  | ISAIAH | JEREMIAH | EZEKIEL | AMOS |
|---|---|---|---|---|
| AMMON | None | 49:1-6 Ammon destroyed and later restored | 25:1-7 Ammon destroyed and taken captive | 1:13-15 Ammon destroyed and taken captive |
| MOAB | 15:1–16:14 Moab ruined and destroyed | 48:1-47 Moab destroyed until last days | 25:8-11 Moab conquered and forgotten | 2:1-3 Moab destroyed by fire |
| EDOM | 21:11-12; 34:5-17 Edom will be a place of silence | 49:7-22 Edom destroyed and desolate | 25:12-14 Edom's stronghold a desolation | 1:11-12 Edom devoured by fire |
| PHILISTIA | 14:29-32 Philistia will be destroyed | 47:1-7 Philistia will be destroyed and silenced | 25:15-17 Philistia cut off as seafarers | 1:6-8 Philistia will perish |
| TYRE AND SIDON | 23:1-18 Tyre & Sidon destroyed but rebuilt after seventy years | None | 26:1–28:26 Tyre & Sidon destroyed as an example of ungodliness | 1:9-10 Tyre devoured with fire |
| EGYPT | 19:1-25 Egypt will fall and fade as a world power | 46:1-26 Egypt will be conquered by Nebuchadnezzar | 29:1–32:32 Egypt will fall and fade as a world power | None |
| DAMASCUS | 17:1-14 Damascus will be destroyed except for small remnant | 49:23-27 Damascus will be destroyed | None | 1:3-5 Damascus will be destroyed and broken |
| BABYLON | 13:1–14:23 Babylon destroyed like Sodom and Gomorrah | 50:1–51:64 Babylon will be destroyed, devastated, obliterated | 38:1–39:29(?) See discussion of this passage at 38:1 | None |

the identity of the recipient by the statement of the name, Ammonites, Moab, Edom, and so on. Second, the crimes for which each nation was judged were listed. Third, the judgment to befall each nation was described. Finally, there is a phrase, "know I am the LORD," that occurs nineteen times in chaps. 25–32: 25:5,7,11,14,17; 26:6; 28:22,23,24,26; 29:6,9,16,21; 30:8,19,25,26; 32:15. As in the rest of the book, this phrase signifies the importance of "knowing that the LORD is the one and only God. An intimate relationship with him is lacking in the case of Judah and the nations. According to Ezekiel, not knowing God is to reject God; such rejection must be punished.[11]

## 1. Prophecy against Ammon (25:1-7)

**[1]The word of the LORD came to me: [2]"Son of man, set your face against the Ammonites and prophesy against them. [3]Say to them, 'Hear the word of the Sovereign LORD. This is what the Sovereign LORD says: Because you said "Aha!" over my sanctuary when it was desecrated and over the land of Israel when it was laid waste and over the people of Judah when they went into exile, [4]therefore I am going to give you to the people of the East as a possession. They will set up their camps and pitch their tents among you; they will eat your fruit and drink your milk. [5]I will turn Rabbah into a pasture for camels and Ammon into a resting place for sheep. Then you will know that I am the LORD. [6]For this is what the Sovereign LORD says: Because you have clapped your hands and stamped your feet, rejoicing with all the malice of your heart against the land of Israel, [7]therefore I will stretch out my hand against you and give you as plunder to the nations. I will cut you off from the nations and exterminate you from the countries. I will destroy you, and you will know that I am the LORD.'"**

**25:1-2** The "Ammonites" (v. 2) is a one-word translation for the literal phrase "children of Ammon," which appears in the Hebrew text. The Hebrew phrase suggests both their name and their identity. The children of Ammon were the descendants of Lot, who was both their father and grandfather. The Ammonites were descended from Ben-Ammi, born to the younger daughter of Lot after they fled from Sodom and Gomorrah (Gen 19:38). Ezekiel had already given one message of judgment against Ammon prior to this one (21:28-32 [Heb. 21:33-37]).[12]

The Ammonites were known for their excesses in idolatries (1 Kgs 11:7,33), cruelty (Amos 1:13), pride (Zeph 2:9-10), and opposition to God's people (Deut 23:3-4; Judg 3:13; 1 Sam 11:1-3; 2 Sam 10:1-14; 2

---

[11] See W. Zimmerli, *I Am Yahweh* (Atlanta: John Knox, 1982), 29-98.

[12] See discussion of 21:28-32.

Kgs 24:2; Neh 4:3,7-8). They were among the bitterest enemies of Israel and Judah, a somber testimony to the ungodliness that Lot and his daughters brought with them when they left Sodom. The daughters thought there was no one to carry the family name. They did not look to God for a solution but instead made their father drunk, then had sexual relations with him and became pregnant by him (Gen 19:30-36). Their descendants became enemies of all that was good and godly (v. 2).[13]

**25:3**  Next, Ezekiel reviewed their crimes. They said, "Aha!" over God's sanctuary, an expression of malicious delight over the destruction of the temple and the fall of Jerusalem. They were pleased that Judah was ravaged and the people were carried captive to Babylon (v. 3).[14] Earlier the prophet had condemned them for their open hostility and prophecies of doom against Judah (21:28-29; Heb 21:33-34).

These hostilities were not new. From the earliest days of Israel's history the relations with Ammon were unfriendly. In the days of the judges they harassed the tribes on the east of the Jordan and finally were crushed by Jephthah (Judg 10–11). Saul had defeated the Ammonites in the early days of the monarchy (1 Sam 11). Amos condemned them for their savagery in warfare (Amos 1:13-15) and predicted their ultimate destruction.[15]

**25:4-6**  Ezekiel prophesied four coming judgments upon the Ammonites. First, they too would be taken captive. They would not escape unscathed the invasion of Nebuchadnezzar. Their land would be occupied by the desert tribes of Arabs who lived to the east of the Ammonites (v. 4). Second, their capital, Rabbah, would be destroyed. It would no longer be a great city but would become a habitation and pasture for camels (v. 5). The former capital, Ammon, would be desolate and overgrown after visitation of God's judgment (see 21:25). The reason for this judgment is restated. Ammon gloated and rejoiced over the fall of Jerusalem (v. 6).

**25:7**  Third, Ammon would be plundered by the nations around them. They would become a spoil of war. Fourth, the country would disappear from the family of nations. Jeremiah predicted a return of the Ammonites (Jer 49:6), suggesting that perhaps his prophecy referred to an earlier occasion. The truth of Ezekiel's prophecy is a matter of historical record. Ammon, as a nation, no longer existed after its destruction by Nebuchadnezzar and plunder by Bedouins from the east (v. 7).[16] The fate of Am-

---

[13] Zimmerli, *Ezekiel 2*, 12-13. See also "Ammon," *ABD* (New York: Doubleday, 1992), 1:194-196

[14] See, e.g., S. Fisch, *Ezekiel* (London: Soncino, 1950), 168.

[15] Davidson, *Ezekiel*, 180.

[16] Ibid.

mon confirmed the truth of the messages of judgment announced by his prophets.

## 2. Prophecy against Moab (25:8-11)

**[8]"This is what the Sovereign LORD says: 'Because Moab and Seir said, "Look, the house of Judah has become like all the other nations," [9]therefore I will expose the flank of Moab, beginning at its frontier towns—Beth Jeshimoth, Baal Meon and Kiriathaim—the glory of that land. [10]I will give Moab along with the Ammonites to the people of the East as a possession, so that the Ammonites will not be remembered among the nations; [11]and I will inflict punishment on Moab. Then they will know that I am the LORD.'"**

**25:8** The Moabites[17] descended from the older daughter of Lot in the same illicit union that produced Ammon (Gen 19:37) and thus also were related to the Hebrews. The Moabites inhabited the land to the east of the Dead Sea. When the Hebrews first approached the land after forty years in the wilderness, it was the Moabites who introduced them to Baal worship (see Num 21:1–25:5; 31:16).

Ezekiel listed Moab's crime as mocking Judah for being like all the other nations (v. 8). The purpose of their taunts was to contradict Judah's claim that they were God's chosen people. The Moabites joined the Ammonites in assisting the Babylonians in 605 B.C, when Jerusalem was attacked by Nebuchadnezzar.[18]

**25:9-11** Ezekiel prophesied that God would expose the flank or border of Moab to invading forces. Towns on the usually well-guarded frontier especially were vulnerable. If the Moabites could not protect their border, the whole country would be at risk (v. 9). The people of Moab were to suffer a similar fate as the Ammonites. They would be overtaken by the desert people to their east and would not be remembered in the family of nations (vv. 10-11). This prediction also was historically accurate. The Moabites like the Ammonites ceased to exist in the family of nations.[19]

The judgment of God on Ammon and Moab is a commentary on the tragic consequences of wrong choices (vv. 1-11). Lot never dreamed that when he chose to live in Sodom that the choice would affect his descendants forever. His children born to him in an immoral union with his

---

[17] See J. M. Miller, "Moab," *ABD* 4:882-93, and A. Dearman, ed., *Studies in the Mesha Inscription and Moab* (Atlanta: Scholars Press, 1989).

[18] Zimmerli, *Ezekiel 2,* 15. Moabite troops fought with Babylonian soldiers (2 Kgs 29:2; Jer 27:3).

[19] J. W. Wevers, *Ezekiel,* NCB (Grand Rapids: Eerdmans, 1969), 197.

daughters became bitter enemies of God's people and Abraham's descendants (Gen 19:1-18). After such punishment, all will "know that I am the LORD" (Ezek 25:11). Both the Ammonites (v. 7) and the Moabites will finally realize that there is no god but the God of Judah.

### 3. Prophecy against Edom (25:12-14)

[12]"This is what the Sovereign LORD says: 'Because Edom took revenge on the house of Judah and became very guilty by doing so, [13]therefore this is what the Sovereign LORD says: I will stretch out my hand against Edom and kill its men and their animals. I will lay it waste, and from Teman to Dedan they will fall by the sword. [14]I will take vengeance on Edom by the hand of my people Israel, and they will deal with Edom in accordance with my anger and my wrath; they will know my vengeance, declares the Sovereign LORD.'"

**25:12-14** Located just south of Moab, Edom[20] also was associated with the area around Mount Seir mentioned in v. 8. Edom and Moab were closely allied because they were neighbors and because of ancestral ties. The Edomites were descendants of Esau (Gen 25:25), who was characterized as red and hairy. The word "Edom" means "red."

There was a natural enmity between Edomites, Esau's descendants, and Israelites, Jacob's descendants (v. 12). That enmity was perpetuated in successive generations by memory of the deception of Jacob that had cost Esau his birthright (Gen 25:29-34) and blessing (27:1-40). The Edomites would never forgive or forget what they had lost by Jacob's treachery (Gen 27:41-46). Like the Moabites and Ammonites, they were a warring (Gen 27:40), idolatrous (2 Chr 25:14,20), proud (Isa 49:16-17), cruel (Amos 1:11-12), and vengeful (Ezek 25:12-14) people.

Esau despised his birthright and thus held the promises of God in contempt (25:12-14; cf. Gen 25:29-34; Heb 12:16-17). It is no surprise that his descendants, the Edomites, also were bitter enemies of God and his people. Edom had consistently taken sides with the enemies of Israel and often aided them (2 Chr 20:10). They had called for the destruction of Jerusalem (Ps 137:7), and Amos said they bought Hebrew slaves from the men of Tyre (Amos 1:9-10; 11–12).

Ezekiel prophesied that the whole country would be laid waste (v. 13). Teman was the extreme northern district of Edom while Dedan was in the south; thus the mention of these two cities was a way of referring to the whole nation. Both Isaiah (34:5-17) and Jeremiah (49:7-22) have lengthy denunciations of Edom that describe the consequences of judgment as

---

[20] J. R. Bartlett and B. MacDonald, "Edom," *ABD,* 287-301.

rendering it a desolate, empty place. The entire Book of Obadiah predicts the doom of Edom for conspiracy against the Hebrews, who were their kinsmen. So Ezekiel predicted that the Hebrews would be the "hand" by which God's anger and wrath would be administered to Edom. The prophecy was fulfilled when Edom finally was defeated by the Maccabees and incorporated into the Jewish state (vv. 13-14).[21]

### 4. Prophecy against Philistia (25:15-17)

[15]"This is what the Sovereign LORD says: 'Because the Philistines acted in vengeance and took revenge with malice in their hearts, and with ancient hostility sought to destroy Judah, [16]therefore this is what the Sovereign LORD says: I am about to stretch out my hand against the Philistines, and I will cut off the Kerethites and destroy those remaining along the coast. [17]I will carry out great vengeance on them and punish them in my wrath. Then they will know that I am the LORD, when I take vengeance on them.'"

**25:15-17** Ezekiel's fourth prophecy was against the Philistines, a seafaring people who came to the coast of Israel from the area around the Aegean Sea. They formed a confederation of five city-states, Gath, Gaza, Ekron, Ashdod, and Askelon.[22] From the time of the judges they were adversaries of the Hebrews. A strong Jewish state was always a threat to their control over the region. So they opposed Israel in the early years of its statehood under the monarchs. The Philistines were a threat even before the monarchy when the judges Shamgar (Judg 3:31), Jephthah (Judg 10:7), and Samson (Judg 13–16) faced them as a constant danger to the security of Israel.

Threats and continued opposition from Philistia gave impetus to the desire for a king in Israel. Early defeats and the capture of the ark of the covenant by the Philistines (1 Sam 4–5) led the Hebrews to call for a king who could be a military leader (1 Sam 8:4-22). Saul was chosen king in the context of this political-military tension (1 Sam 9:1-10). But it was David who finally subdued Philistia during his reign (2 Sam 5:17-25). Hostilities continued to erupt between the two nations until the Philistines were confronted by Hezekiah (2 Kgs 18:8), Jehoram (2 Chr 21:16-17), and Ahaz (2 Chr 28:18), after which they were no longer a threat.

Ezekiel's indictment against the Philistines summarized all those years of hatred and opposition. He said, "They took revenge with malice in

---

[21] See Fisch, *Ezekiel,* 171.

[22] Zimmerli, *Ezekiel 2,* 18; see also T. Dothan and M. Dothan, *People of the Sea: The Search for the Philistines* (New York: Macmillan, 1992), 13-28.

their hearts" (v. 15). A literal translation of the Hebrew text of this passage is most emphatic. "Because the Philistines acted with vengeance and have committed vengeful vengeance [meaning a great vengeance] with malice in some to destroy with hatred forever" (Heb.).[23]

So God promised to act for Israel and execute a "great vengeance" against Philistia (v. 17). That vengeance included cutting off the Kerethites (v. 16),[24] one of two fierce fighting forces once employed by David (2 Sam 8:18) as his personal army. The other group also employed by David was called Pelethites. So God promised to cut off the best of the fighting forces of the Philistines and to destroy the remnant of the sea coast that was their homeland.[25]

Because of the hatred of the Philistines toward Israel, Ezekiel prophesied God's vengeance on them. Those who oppose God and his people never gain by their opposition. The prophecies against foreign nations show both God's concern for the redemption of all people and his determination to judge sin wherever and whenever the standards of his word are violated (25:1–32:32).

## 5. Prophecy against Tyre (26:1–28:19)

While Tyre also was condemned by Isaiah (23:1-18), Zechariah (9:3-4), and Amos (1:9-10), none had as much to say against Tyre as did Ezekiel, who devoted three chapters to its judgment. This may have been due to his belief that God was using Nebuchadnezzar to punish all the enemies of Israel, of which Tyre and Egypt were the most formidable.[26] These chapters alternate between judgment speech (26:1-21; 28:1-10) and funeral dirge (27:1-36; 28:11-19).[27] The first judgment speech may be further divided into four sections, resulting in an analysis of the prophecy against Tyre in seven sections:[28] (1) Tyre's sin identified (26:1-6); (2) details of the immediate destruction of Tyre (26:7-14); (3) the effects of judgment on Tyre's neighbors (26:15-18); (4) Tyre's descent into the pit (26:19-21); (5) lament over the loss of Tyre (27:1-36); (6) prophecy against the king of Tyre (28:1-10); (7) final lament for the king of Tyre (28:11-19).

---

[23] The MT reads בִּנְקָמָה וַיִּנָּקְמוּ נָקָם. The emphatic nature of this text states the depth of hatred and vengeance that the Philistines manifested toward the Hebrews.

[24] Exacting vengeance is one of God's rights (Rom 12:19); cf. Zimmerli, *Ezekiel 2,* 19.

[25] Fisch, *Ezekiel,* 172.

[26] See Wevers, *Ezekiel,* 199; H. J. van Dijk, "Ezekiel's Prophecy on Tyre," *BibOr,* 20 (Rome: Pontifical Biblical Institute, 1968), 1-47.

[27] Alexander, "Ezekiel," 882.

[28] D. R. Edwards, "Tyre," *ABD,* 686-92.

John the apostle employed parts of these messages in a significant way in his prophecy of the kingdom of the Antichrist in Rev 17–18. Also his vision of the destruction of end-time Babylon used several figures from Ezekiel's prophecy of Tyre (cp. Rev 18:9,13,18-19,22 and Ezek 26:16; 27:13,30; 26:13).

## *(1) Tyre's Sin Identified (26:1-6)*

**[1]In the eleventh year, on the first day of the month, the word of the LORD came to me: [2]"Son of man, because Tyre has said of Jerusalem, 'Aha! The gate to the nations is broken, and its doors have swung open to me; now that she lies in ruins I will prosper,' [3]therefore this is what the Sovereign LORD says: I am against you, O Tyre, and I will bring many nations against you, like the sea casting up its waves. [4]They will destroy the walls of Tyre and pull down her towers; I will scrape away her rubble and make her a bare rock. [5]Out in the sea she will become a place to spread fishnets, for I have spoken, declares the Sovereign LORD. She will become plunder for the nations, [6]and her settlements on the mainland will be ravaged by the sword. Then they will know that I am the LORD.**

Tyre was a principal city of Phoenicia. The name "Tyre" means "rock" and referred to the main fortress that was located on a rock outcropping one-half mile offshore.[29] The city was built in two parts, one on shore and the other on the offshore island. It was mentioned as a chief city of the Phoenicians by Joshua (19:29). The Egyptians and Assyrians sought to maintain control of Tyre because of its strategic importance as a port city and a military outpost.[30]

Nebuchadnezzar continued attempts first begun by the Assyrians to conquer the city. They subdued Tyre in 722 B.C. after a five-year siege, but the offshore island was never conquered. Nebuchadnezzar besieged the city for an additional thirteen years (587–572 B.C.) but was unsuccessful in his campaign to conquer the rock fortress offshore.[31] Alexander the Great was the first one actually to conquer the city. He did so by constructing a causeway from the shore and then using his fleet to attack from the sea as well.[32] Until that time Tyre ranked as a great commercial center whose wealth knew no bounds.

---

[29] See A. Cohen, *The Twelve Prophets* (New York: Soncino, 1969), 304.

[30] See Zimmerli, *Ezekiel 2*, 22-23, for a brief history of Tyre.

[31] See Zimmerli, *Ezekiel 2*, 23; Wevers, *Ezekiel*, 199; Taylor, *Ezekiel*, 190; and S. Smith, "The Ship Tyre," *PEQ* LXXXV (1953): 97-110.

[32] Zimmerli, *Ezekiel 2*, 24. The alluvial deposits on the causeway Alexander built created a permanent link to the mainland.

The ability to withstand some of the greatest armies and commanders in history gave the inhabitants a pride and arrogance that made them insensitive to human suffering. This lack of concern is illustrated by the malicious joy of the people of Tyre at the destruction of Jerusalem (v. 2). Ezekiel used the same language employed in describing Ammon's delight over Jerusalem's fall in 25:3.[33]

**26:1** Verse 1 contains the sixth dated prophecy in the book (see table "Dated Prophecies in Ezekiel," p. 54). The date as stated by Ezekiel omitted the specific month of the eleventh year which began April 23, 587 B.C. The message probably dated from the eleventh month, which would have been February 13, 586 B.C. or the twelfth month, March 15, 586 B.C. The solution to the date problem is compounded further because Jerusalem was not destroyed until the twelfth year of the captivity (see 33:21).

**26:2** Judgment of Tyre was due, in part, to the attitude of the people of the city toward news of the destruction of Jerusalem. They said: "Aha! The gate of the nations is broken, and its doors have swung open to me; now that she lies in ruins I will prosper." This phrase represents the animosity the people of Tyre had toward Israel.

**26:3-6** God promised to bring six judgments upon Tyre (vv. 3-6). First come words usually associated with military engagements. Many nations would "come against" the city (v. 3). The proliferation of the military opponents of Tyre was pictured as unrelenting waves pounding the city.[34] Second, Ezekiel stated evidence of divine opposition to Tyre (v. 3). The emphasis of the text literally states, "Behold [I am] coming against you," which calls attention to the events of judgment as having been divinely orchestrated. Third, the walls of Tyre would be destroyed (v. 4). In spite of all those who fought against Tyre, it was not until its conquest by Alexander the Great that this prophecy was fulfilled. Nevertheless, the prediction did come true.

Fourth, God promised that the island fortress would become a pile of rubble that would be scraped away. There would be no trace of the once-invincible city. Only a bare rock where fishermen would dry their nets would mark the spot (v. 4).[35] Fifth, Tyre, known for its commercial and political power, would be an object of plunder for all the nations (v. 5). Sixth, the city on the mainland also would be destroyed and the area rav-

---

[33] Fisch, *Ezekiel*, 172-73.

[34] Wevers, *Ezekiel*, 201.

[35] Fisch, *Ezekiel*, 173.

aged by the sword (v. 6).[36]

Nations who distinguish themselves as special centers of evil and ungodliness receive special attention as objects of God's judgment. Such nations in history also received special attention in the Word of God. Tyre, Egypt, and Babylon all share this dubious distinction. Egypt was used as a byword for the slavery of sin, immorality, and idolatry. Babylon is a byword for godless government, and Tyre is a byword for pride and self-sufficiency (26:1-6).

### (2) Details of the Immediate Destruction of Tyre (26:7-14)

[7]"For this is what the Sovereign LORD says: From the north I am going to bring against Tyre Nebuchadnezzar king of Babylon, king of kings, with horses and chariots, with horsemen and a great army. [8]He will ravage your settlements on the mainland with the sword; he will set up siege works against you, build a ramp up to your walls and raise his shields against you. [9]He will direct the blows of his battering rams against your walls and demolish your towers with his weapons. [10]His horses will be so many that they will cover you with dust. Your walls will tremble at the noise of the war horses, wagons and chariots when he enters your gates as men enter a city whose walls have been broken through. [11]The hoofs of his horses will trample all your streets; he will kill your people with the sword, and your strong pillars will fall to the ground. [12]They will plunder your wealth and loot your merchandise; they will break down your walls and demolish your fine houses and throw your stones, timber and rubble into the sea. [13]I will put an end to your noisy songs, and the music of your harps will be heard no more. [14]I will make you a bare rock, and you will become a place to spread fishnets. You will never be rebuilt, for I the LORD have spoken, declares the Sovereign LORD.

**26:7-14** This passage specifically focuses on Nebuchadnezzar's attack against Tyre. It has already been noted that Nebuchadnezzar launched a campaign against Tyre that lasted for thirteen years from 586 to 573 B.C.[37] He was named in v. 7 as the perpetrator of this attack, and

---

[36] Zimmerli, *Ezekiel 2*, 35. The term "daughter" does not mean a female child but here refers to related villages or settlements often referred to as daughters (e.g., Josh 15:45). The KJV renders v. 6, "Her daughters which are in the field shall be slain." The word "daughters" often was used to describe surrounding rural settlements and smaller villages that were called "daughters" of larger towns. "Settlements on the mainland" is an excellent rendering.

[37] The Hebrew text has five variant spellings of Nebuchadnezzar that are all correct. The most common is נְבוּכַדְנֶאצַּר, used fifty-eight times mostly in Daniel and 2 Chronicles. נְבוּכַדְרֶאצַּר occurs thirty-three times, was used by Jeremiah and Ezekiel and may represent an Aramaic form (see A. Even-Shoshan, *A New Concordance of the Bible* (Jerusalem: Kiryat-Sefer, 1989), 732. Other forms are נְבוּכַדְנֶצַּר, נְבֻכַדְנֶצַּר, and נְבֻכַדְרֶצַּר; see G. Lisowsky, *Konkordanz Zum Hebraischen Alten Testament* (Stuttgart: Deutsche Bibelgesellschaft, 1981), 1644. "Nebuchadnezzar" means "may Nabu protect my crown," or "may Nabu protect my labor." See Alexander, "Ezekiel," 871 note, and Fisch, *Ezekiel*, 174.

use of pronouns "he" and "his" abound (nine times in the NIV of vv. 8-12). The last two verses refer to something Nebuchadnezzar was not able to accomplish but which did happen later under Alexander. Note the person changed to "I" in vv. 13 and 14, speaking of what God would do by that future destruction by the hands of Alexander. What God began with Nebuchadnezzar (v. 7), he continued until the time of Alexander and the complete fulfillment of all that Ezekiel predicted.

Nebuchadnezzar was called King of Babylon and the "king of kings" (v. 7) who would come with his great army, chariots, and horsemen to battle against Tyre. The title "king of kings" referred to the many vassal kings Nebuchadnezzar brought to fight with him. These vassals included Jehoiakim, Jehoiachin, Zedekiah, and the king of Tyre.[38] With his armies he ravaged the mainland settlement of Tyre and thus isolated the island fortress (vv. 8-10). Reference to the fall of the "strong pillars" (v. 11) may be to two famous pillars in the temple of Melkart mentioned by Herodotus or to the fall of the general strength and leadership of the city.[39] In either case the city was marked for a violent fall and plunder (v. 12).

### (3) Effect of Judgment on Tyre's Neighbors (26:15-18)

[15]"This is what the Sovereign LORD says to Tyre: Will not the coastlands tremble at the sound of your fall, when the wounded groan and the slaughter takes place in you? [16]Then all the princes of the coast will step down from their thrones and lay aside their robes and take off their embroidered garments. Clothed with terror, they will sit on the ground, trembling every moment, appalled at you. [17]Then they will take up a lament concerning you and say to you:

"'How you are destroyed, O city of renown,
    peopled by men of the sea!
You were a power on the seas,
    you and your citizens;
you put your terror
    on all who lived there.
[18]Now the coastlands tremble
    on the day of your fall;
the islands in the sea
    are terrified at your collapse.'

**26:15-18** The "coastlands" (v. 15) refers to the neighboring states that were vassals of Tyre and therefore depended on the city for their own

---

[38] Zimmerli, *Ezekiel 2*, 36; Fisch, *Ezekiel*, 174; cf. Dan 2:37; Ezra 7:12.
[39] See Wevers, *Ezekiel*, 202, and Herodotus, *Histories II*, 44.

security. The lament, or funeral song, of v. 18 was preceded by a brief prophetic message that described the shock and fright of these neighboring villages on learning of the fall of Tyre (v. 16). The people's conduct depicted the usual response of a person to the death of a close friend or loved one. Normally clothing was torn and mourners sat on the ground and sang funeral dirges. These leaders removed their royal garments because of their costliness and adopted other signs of remorse (v. 16).

The lament of vv. 17-18 was set in a special poetic meter known as a funeral dirge. This poetic form was used by Ezekiel in 19:1,14 to describe a funeral lament over the loss of the leaders of Jerusalem.[40] The song here depicted the fear and uncertainty shared by those who were dependent on Tyre's welfare. God takes a personal interest in the destruction of those who had become special emissaries of the adversary. Those who oppose God must answer to him personally (Num 32:23; Rom 14:10-12).

### (4) Tyre's Descent into the Pit (26:19-21)

[19]"This is what the Sovereign LORD says: When I make you a desolate city, like cities no longer inhabited, and when I bring the ocean depths over you and its vast waters cover you, [20]then I will bring you down with those who go down to the pit, to the people of long ago. I will make you dwell in the earth below, as in ancient ruins, with those who go down to the pit, and you will not return or take your place in the land of the living. [21]I will bring you to a horrible end and you will be no more. You will be sought, but you will never again be found, declares the Sovereign LORD."

**26:19-21** Having mentioned the funeral, Ezekiel followed with the interment of the "body" of Tyre into the "pit." God promised Tyre would be a desolate, uninhabited place. The depths of the ocean would cover the spot where the city once stood (v. 19). Tyre would be brought "down to the pit" like people of old and like ancient ruins. The city would never return to the land of the living, meaning it would never be rebuilt (v. 20). This was usual language for describing a burial, and "pit" is a synonym used to describe the "grave" and a favorite term employed by Ezekiel.[41]

---

[40] See introductory remarks to 19:1-14 and note. The קִינָה or funeral dirge was a feature of funerary customs of the ancient Near East. The rhythm of the קִינָה dirge was three beats followed by two beats and often was used by professional mourners employed to mourn the dead. See Alexander, "Ezekiel," 831, 872. The קִינָה is mentioned in Ezekiel 19:1,14; 26:17; 27:2,32; 28:12; 32:2,16.

[41] Ezekiel used בּוֹר as a synonym for שְׁאוֹל and clearly intended for it to refer to the grave (31:16; 32:18,23-25,29-30). בּוֹר ("pit or cistern") is commonly used for שְׁאוֹל ("the grave" or "the place of the dead" or "the underworld"); see *TWOT* I:88, 892-93.

The last two verses of this chapter use a new series of images to convey the concept of judgment. Tyre's trip to the "pit" will not be one that will lead to peace and rest but to a "horrible end" (v. 21). While the existence of Tyre produced fear of reprisal in all opponents (v. 17), the absence of Tyre would produce the fear of dismay and uncertainty (v. 21). Tyre would disappear from the family of nations forever.[42]

### (5) *Lament over the Loss of Tyre (27:1-36)*

A second funeral dirge was offered for the destruction of Tyre (see 26:15-18 note). This funeral song was in two parts (vv. 3b-9 and vv. 25-36) with a prose introduction in vv. 1-3a and a prose interlude in vv. 10-24.[43] The message has three sections: First is the presentation of the city of Tyre (27:1-9). Second, the city was a source of world commerce (27:10-24). Third, the city would be destroyed (27:25-36).

**[1]The word of the LORD came to me: [2]"Son of man, take up a lament concerning Tyre. [3]Say to Tyre, situated at the gateway to the sea, merchant of peoples on many coasts, 'This is what the Sovereign LORD says:**
**"'You say, O Tyre,**
**"I am perfect in beauty."**
**[4]Your domain was on the high seas;**
**your builders brought your beauty to perfection.**
**[5]They made all your timbers**
**of pine trees from Senir;**
**they took a cedar from Lebanon**
**to make a mast for you.**
**[6]Of oaks from Bashan**
**they made your oars;**
**of cypress wood from the coasts of Cyprus**
**they made your deck, inlaid with ivory.**
**[7]Fine embroidered linen from Egypt was your sail**
**and served as your banner;**
**your awnings were of blue and purple**
**from the coasts of Elishah.**
**[8]Men of Sidon and Arvad were your oarsmen;**
**your skilled men, O Tyre, were aboard as your seamen.**
**[9]Veteran craftsmen of Gebal were on board**
**as shipwrights to caulk your seams.**

---

[42] Zimmerli, *Ezekiel 2*, 39. The addition of לְעוֹלָם, meaning "forever," underscores the finality of judgment.

[43] See Wevers, *Ezekiel,* 204-5.

**All the ships of the sea and their sailors
came alongside to trade for your wares.**

PRESENTATION OF THE CITY (27:1-9). **27:1-9** Tyre was situated in a strategic location for trade and military purposes. The city was well known for its pride, conceit, and the belief that it was impregnable. God warned that such pride was the prelude to destruction (Prov 6:17; 8:13; 16:18). The people of Tyre thought their city to be a model of perfection with all its wealth, commerce, and trade with other nations. But God marked the city for destruction because of its moral and spiritual bankruptcy (vv. 1-3).[44]

The "gateway to the sea" is actually a plural, "gateways," and referred to the two entrances to the harbor, one known as the Sidonian entrance and the other as the Egyptian entrance (v. 3). Ironically the phrase "perfect in beauty" also was the same one used in Lamentations to describe the pride of Jerusalem that led to its fall (Lam 2:15).[45]

The lament compared Tyre to a magnificent merchant ship. The builders perfected the beauty of the ship in the midst of the seas (v. 4). Pine trees from Senir, also called Mount Hermon, were used for the ship's timber, and a mast was made from Lebanon's cedars (v. 5).[46] The ship's oars were made of oak from Bashan, and the deck of cypress was from Cyprus.[47] The deck also was inlaid with ivory (v. 6), adding to its beauty and worth. Woven linen from Egypt was used for the sail that also served as a flag or banner. The deck awning was blue and purple (regal colors) from Elishah (v. 7). Elishah is mentioned in Gen 10:4 as a son of Javan, who founded the maritime nations.[48]

The ship's oarsmen were men of Sidon and Arvad, a city near Sidon renown for its seamen. The pilots were skilled men of Tyre (v. 8). Skilled craftsmen from Gebal, which was Byblos, were on the ships, and shipwrights were on board for repairing cracks in the seams. Ships came alongside the magnificent vessel to trade and sell cargo (v. 9).[49]

---

[44] Alexander, "Ezekiel," 874. Tyre would be lamented as the wreck of a magnificent ship; see also E. M. Good, "Ezekiel's Ship: Some Extended Metaphors in the Old Testament," *Semitics* 1 (1970): 79-103.

[45] Fisch, *Ezekiel,* 178-79.

[46] בְּרוֹשׁ, translated "pine," may refer to a "cypress" or "fir" tree. שְׂנִיר is associated with Mount Hermon, which was called Senir by the Ammonites and Sirion by the Phoenicians. See Zimmerli, *Ezekiel 2,* 57, and Alexander, "Ezekiel," 875.

[47] כִּתִּים refers to the city of Kittim, the capital of Cyprus. See Zimmerli, *Ezekiel 2,* 57.

[48] אֱלִישָׁה has been associated with several sites including Italy, Sicily, Greece, Carthage, Peloponnese, the Canary Islands, or Cyprus.

[49] Wevers, *Ezekiel,* 207.

¹⁰"'Men of Persia, Lydia and Put served as soldiers in your army.
They hung their shields and helmets on your walls,
    bringing you splendor.
¹¹Men of Arvad and Helech manned your walls on every side;
men of Gammad were in your towers.
They hung their shields around your walls;
    they brought your beauty to perfection.
¹²"'Tarshish did business with you because of your great wealth of goods;
they exchanged silver, iron, tin and lead for your merchandise.
¹³"'Greece, Tubal and Meshech traded with you; they exchanged slaves
and articles of bronze for your wares.
¹⁴"'Men of Beth Togarmah exchanged work horses, war horses and mules
for your merchandise.
¹⁵"'The men of Rhodes traded with you, and many coastlands were your
customers; they paid you with ivory tusks and ebony.
¹⁶"'Aram did business with you because of your many products; they exchanged turquoise, purple fabric, embroidered work, fine linen, coral and ru-
bies for your merchandise.
¹⁷"'Judah and Israel traded with you; they exchanged wheat from Minnith and confections, honey, oil and balm for your wares.
¹⁸"'Damascus, because of your many products and great wealth of goods,
did business with you in wine from Helbon and wool from Zahar.
¹⁹"'Danites and Greeks from Uzal bought your merchandise; they exchanged wrought iron, cassia and calamus for your wares.
²⁰"'Dedan traded in saddle blankets with you.
²¹"'Arabia and all the princes of Kedar were your customers; they did
business with you in lambs, rams and goats.
²²"'The merchants of Sheba and Raamah traded with you; for your merchandise they exchanged the finest of all kinds of spices and precious stones,
and gold.
²³"'Haran, Canneh and Eden and merchants of Sheba, Asshur and Kilmad traded with you. ²⁴In your marketplace they traded with you beautiful
garments, blue fabric, embroidered work and multicolored rugs with cords
twisted and tightly knotted.

SIGNIFICANCE OF THE CITY (27:10-24).    **27:10-24**   Mercenaries were
hired to assist the defense of Tyre. These men were from Persia, Lud (Lydia), and Put (Lybia). Local mercenaries also came from Arvad (v. 8),
Helech, and Gammad (vv. 10-11). They "hung their shields" and "helmets" on the walls as a sign that they were on the job and would assist in
the protection of the city.

The scope of the commerce of Tyre was extensive. Twenty nations are
mentioned as having direct trade relations with Tyre. Another three nations had indirect trade. Minnith (v. 17) in Ammon sold wheat to Judah

and Israel to use in trade with Tyre. Helbon, a wine center northwest of Damascus, and Zahar, a desert area also northwest of Damascus, traded wine and wool with Damascus for use in trade with Tyre (v. 18). Thirty-seven different products are named as the trade merchandise of Tyre including metals, horses, ivory and ebony, fabric, coral, precious stones, foodstuffs, wool, saddle blankets, cattle, garments, and rugs.

Many nations with which Tyre conducted commerce still exist today by the same name used in the text. Among these are Greece, Rhodes, Israel, Damascus, Syria, and Arabia. Others have changed their names or no longer exist. Examples of these are Tubal and Meshech (Gen 10:2), regions of eastern Asia Minor; Togarmah, which became Armenia; Aram, which became Syria; Minnith, which became Ammon; Helbon and Zahar, located northwest of Damascus; Dedan, northwest of Edom; Kedar, part of Arabia, with Sheba and Raamah; Haran, Cannah, and Eden, located in Mesopotamia, with Asshur and Kilmad.[50]

Those who place their dependence on the power and wealth of God's opponents will suffer irreparable loss. God alone is a resource who never fails (26:19–27:36). People and nations who reject him not only can but will ultimately fail.

> [25]" 'The ships of Tarshish serve
>    as carriers for your wares.
> You are filled with heavy cargo
>    in the heart of the sea.
> [26]Your oarsmen take you out to the high seas.
> But the east wind will break you to pieces
>    in the heart of the sea.
> [27]Your wealth, merchandise and wares,
>    your mariners, seamen and shipwrights,
>    your merchants and all your soldiers,
>    and everyone else on board
>    will sink into the heart of the sea
>    on the day of your shipwreck.
> [28]The shorelands will quake
>    when your seamen cry out.
> [29]All who handle the oars
>    will abandon their ships;
>    the mariners and all the seamen
>    will stand on the shore.
> [30]They will raise their voice

---

[50] See Wevers, *Ezekiel,* 198, 208-10; Zimmerli, *Ezekiel 2,* 59-60, 65-69; Fisch, *Ezekiel,* 181-85; Alexander, "Ezekiel," 876-77.

and cry bitterly over you;
they will sprinkle dust on their heads
    and roll in ashes.
[31]They will shave their heads because of you
    and will put on sackcloth.
They will weep over you with anguish of soul
    and with bitter mourning.
[32]As they wail and mourn over you,
    they will take up a lament concerning you:
"Who was ever silenced like Tyre,
    surrounded by the sea?"
[33]When your merchandise went out on the seas,
    you satisfied many nations;
with your great wealth and your wares
    you enriched the kings of the earth.
[34]Now you are shattered by the sea
    in the depths of the waters;
your wares and all your company
    have gone down with you.
[35]All who live in the coastlands
    are appalled at you;
their kings shudder with horror
    and their faces are distorted with fear.
[36]The merchants among the nations hiss at you;
    you have come to a horrible end
    and will be no more.'"

DESTRUCTION OF THE CITY (27:25-36).   **27:25-36**   The perfect ship[51] described in vv. 3-9, laden with merchandise for many nations described in vv. 10-24, was headed for tragic shipwreck. Ships from Tarshish, a Phoenician port also called Tartessus located in southern Spain, had a fleet of large ships that brought goods to trade for the many products available at Tyre.[52] Tyre is pictured as a ship that traded with the large ships of Tarshish and was overloaded with "heavy cargo" (v. 25). The sea became no match for the oarsmen, and the east wind broke the ship in pieces. The cargo, Tyre's wealth and merchandise, with all on board—mariners, seamen, shipwrights, merchants, soldiers, and all passengers—were lost. Such storms with a strong east wind are still known today.[53]

---

[51] Some take the ship to be metaphor for all of Tyre; cf. Newsome, "A Maker of Metaphors;" Boadt, "Rhetorical Strategies," (he calls it an allegory); Allen, *Ezekiel 20-48*; Good, "Ezekiel's Ship."

[52] Fisch, *Ezekiel*, 181, 185.

[53] See Wevers, *Ezekiel,* 211, and cf. Ps 48:7.

All other seamen and mariners would stand on shore and mourn. They would be overtaken with grief at the sinking of Tyre, for if mighty Tyre could fall to Babylon, then all could fall (vv. 28-29).[54] These men of the sea exhibited all the outward signs of mourning for Tyre, including bitter wailing, sprinkling dust and ashes on their heads, shaving their heads, wearing sackcloth, weeping, and singing a funeral dirge (vv. 30-32).[55]

The closing lines of the funeral lament review the splendor of Tyre. Who was like Tyre? No other city or nation could compare with the wealth, power, commerce, and beauty of Tyre. Many nations were satisfied with the commerce and many kings made rich (vv. 32-33). But Ezekiel envisioned that the splendor of Tyre was gone and everyone was astonished at the fall of the great city (v. 35). The nations hissed, a sign of amazement and dismay, at the end of Tyre, which "will be no more" (v. 36).[56] When the storm of judgment comes, those who do not rest safely in God will be removed. Those who build their lives on the solid foundation of his word will stand (Isa 40:8; Matt 7:24-28).

### (6) Prophecy against the King of Tyre (28:1-10)

There are two divisions to this section. First is the indictment of the ruler of Tyre for his arrogance and greed (28:1-5). Second is the announcement of his punishment (28:6-10).

**[1]The word of the LORD came to me: [2]"Son of man, say to the ruler of Tyre, 'This is what the Sovereign LORD says:**

> **"'In the pride of your heart
>   you say, "I am a god;
> I sit on the throne of a god
>   in the heart of the seas."
> But you are a man and not a god,
>   though you think you are as wise as a god.
> [3]Are you wiser than Daniel?
>   Is no secret hidden from you?
> [4]By your wisdom and understanding
>   you have gained wealth for yourself
> and amassed gold and silver
>   in your treasuries.
> [5]By your great skill in trading**

---

[54] Zimmerli, *Ezekiel 2,* 61.

[55] See R. de Vaux, *Ancient Israel* (London: Darton, Longman, and Todd, 1968), 59-61, for a discussion of funerary practices, rites of mourning, and lamentations.

[56] Alexander, "Ezekiel," 878-79.

> **you have increased your wealth,**
> **and because of your wealth**
> **your heart has grown proud.**

INDICTMENT OF THE KING   (28:1-5).   **28:1**   Rulers are responsible for the character of their kingdom. In the case of Tyre the arrogance of the nation was a reflection of the personal pride of the ruler. Although he was not mentioned by name, the king of Tyre during this period was Ethbaal II (585–573 B.C.).[57] He is called "ruler" (the word sometimes translated "prince"), a word used in older texts to refer to a charismatic leader (1 Sam 9:16; 10:1) or a dynastic king (1 Kgs 1:35).[58]

**28:2**   Tyre's ruler was guilty of the same sins of pride and self-aggrandizement as the people (see 27:1-9; Prov 6:17–8:13; 16:18). The king's pride was "of your heart," self-willed. The word "heart" refers to the mind or will. It was the pride of self-will that prompted the king's conclusion, "I am a god" (v. 2).[59] The last part of the verse gives a small portrait of this process. "You think you are as wise as a god" is literally, "You have given your heart [will] as the heart [will] of a god." The decision to recognize himself as a god was determined by his own intellect and self-will. [60]

The king's conclusion about his status was immediately and strongly controverted, "But you are a man and not a god." He never was nor could he be anything but "man."

**28:3**   Two rhetorical questions follow, both of which presuppose a negative answer. The king was not wiser than Daniel, nor did he possess all knowledge (v. 3). The identity of Daniel has been discussed previously under 14:12-14. Those who prefer the mythical Ugaritic Dan'el in the earlier passage do so here as well. There is enough justification, however, to warrant the identification with Daniel, the contemporary of Ezekiel in Babylon.[61] It is significant that the character of the Daniel of the Bible is antithetical to the pride and arrogant self-sufficiency of the king of Tyre (v. 3).[62]

**28:4-5**   The king of Tyre did possess wisdom, but it was wisdom related to making money (cf. Luke 16:8-9). He was doubtless a skilled trad-

---

[57] See Cooke, *Ezekiel,* 313.

[58] Zimmerli, *Ezekiel 2,* 76. נָגִיד means "chief overseer" or "prince."

[59] See 11:17-21 note and 18:30-32.

[60] See Fisch, *Ezekiel,* 189. The word אֵל and the longer אֱלֹהִים are both used in the verse. Both words can refer either to a false god or the true God, Yahweh, according to the context. See Zimmerli, *Ezekiel 2,* 77-78.

[61] Although spelled דָּנִאֵל in the text, the *qere* is דָּנִיאֵל.

[62] Taylor, *Ezekiel,* 196.

er, merchant, and businessman. But because of his material success he had grown proud and self-sufficient (vv. 4-5). God warned Israel in the wilderness about such arrogant self-sufficiency: "You may say to yourself, 'My power and the strength of my hands have produced this wealth for me.' But remember the LORD your God, for it is he who gives you the ability to produce wealth" (Deut 8:17-18). That warning was also appropriate to Tyre. L. C. Allen points out that the threefold use of *ḥîl*, "wealth," in vv. 4-5 is balanced by a threefold use of the root *ḥll* in the announcement of punishment in vv. 7-9. It is translated "pierce" in v. 7 and "slay" in v. 9. The literal translation of "die a violent death" (v. 8) is "die the death of the slain" (*ḥll*). Although wealth is not inherently evil, it contains in it the seeds of destruction if one fails to acknowledge it as a gift of God.[63]

> [6]"'Therefore this is what the Sovereign LORD says:
> "'Because you think you are wise,
>   as wise as a god,
> [7]I am going to bring foreigners against you,
>   the most ruthless of nations;
> they will draw their swords against your beauty and wisdom
>   and pierce your shining splendor.
> [8]They will bring you down to the pit,
>   and you will die a violent death
>   in the heart of the seas.
> [9]Will you then say, "I am a god,"
>   in the presence of those who kill you?
> You will be but a man, not a god,
>   in the hands of those who slay you.
> [10]You will die the death of the uncircumcised
>   at the hands of foreigners.
> I have spoken, declares the Sovereign LORD.'"

PUNISHMENT OF THE KING (28:6-10). **28:6-8** The last line from v. 2 also begins v. 6. "Because you think you are wise, as wise as a god" also here is literally, "Because you have given your heart [will] as the heart [will] of a god." Because of the ruler's arrogance, judgment would come upon the kingdom as well as its king. God said, "I am going to bring foreigners against you" (v. 7). The "foreigners" who would come against Tyre refers to Nebuchadnezzar and his army (26:7).[64] God promised that

---

[63] L. C. Allen, *Ezekiel 21–48,* WBC (Dallas: Word, 1990), 92, 96.

[64] Wevers, *Ezekiel,* 214-15. The word עַל ("against") regularly is used to describe the military engagement of two or more armies in combat; BDB, 757-58.

these soldiers, noted for ruthlessness, would destroy the city and bring its ruler down to the "pit" (v. 8).[65]

**28:9-10**   Another question follows in v. 9. When the king of Tyre had come to "ruin," the absurdity of his divine claims would be clear even to him. In fact, the king would die like the "uncircumcised" (v. 10), a statement of contempt used for someone whose corpse was treated with disrespect and left unburied.[66] Ungodly nations are led by ungodly rulers. These self-styled, wise-in-their-own-eyes leaders promise much but can provide nothing of eternal value.

### (7)  Final Lament for the King of Tyre (28:11-19)

Numerous interpretations have been proposed for this passage, differing in the way the figurative language is construed and the source for the imagery.[67] Some see the figures as simply metaphorical, describing the king of Tyre with various images, stated in bold and exaggerated terms. Others identify the form as allegory, in which another real or simply familiar character (i.e., Satan or a pagan god) is directly addressed, making the connection to the king of Tyre more indirect or inferred. For the imagery some suppose a source in ancient Near Eastern ideology and myth, especially that which was known to be associated with Tyre.[68] Others find the source in either a loose rendering of the Genesis creation account of the fall of humankind[69] or in supposing alternative accounts of the fall known through tradition.[70] A variant of this approach, favored by several

---

[65] The word for "pit" here is שַׁחַת, from the verb meaning "to ruin/corrupt." It is used either of a pit for trapping animals (Ezek 19:4,8) or of a grave or the place of the dead (as here). The word translated "pit" in 26:20 is בּוֹר, used of a cistern (Exod 21:33) or of a grave or place of the dead (Ezek 31:14,16; 32:18-30). See Zimmerli, *Ezekiel 2,* 79.

[66] See Wevers, *Ezekiel,* 215; Fisch, *Ezekiel,* 190.

[67] Compare the discussions in Wevers, *Ezekiel,* 215; Taylor, *Ezekiel,* 196-97; and Zimmerli, *Ezekiel 2,* 90-91.

[68] See Cooke, *Ezekiel,* 315; A. J. Williams, "The Mythological Background of Ezekiel 28:12-19?" *BTB* 6 (1976): 49-61.

[69] Taylor (*Ezekiel,* 197) understands the dirge as a metaphorical description of Tyre's sin and destruction, drawing on the Genesis account of Adam's fall supplemented by Ezekiel's imaginative use of "a wide variety of symbolical background." Craigie's view (*Ezekiel,* 208) is that the fall was reenacted in Ezekiel's message, as it is by all when they first choose to sin; but in 28:11-19 the figure clearly returned to the king of Tyre.

[70] Allen (*Ezekiel 20–48,* 94) mentions the two possibilities without choosing one. He does not reject the possibility, however, that Ezekiel was also drawing on various creation myths. Craigie (*Ezekiel,* 207) believes that Ezekiel has "taken the ancient stories of primeval paradise, both the biblical story of Eden (v. 13) and Canaanite traditions concerning a holy mountain (v. 14), and adapted the themes to his immediate purpose."

of the church fathers, is to understand for the background of the lament an account of the fall of Satan not given in Scripture but alluded to elsewhere, especially in Isa 14:12-17. Ezekiel would have been relying on his listeners/readers' familiarity with such an account, and they would have understood the comparison between the fall of Satan and the fall of the king of Tyre. The difficulty of the text makes it unwise to insist upon a particular interpretation,[71] but the latter traditional view appears to the present writer to account best for the language and logic of the passage.

**[11]The word of the LORD came to me: [12]"Son of man, take up a lament concerning the king of Tyre and say to him: 'This is what the Sovereign LORD says:**

    **"'You were the model of perfection,**
      **full of wisdom and perfect in beauty.**
**[13]You were in Eden,**
      **the garden of God;**
    **every precious stone adorned you:**
      **ruby, topaz and emerald,**
      **chrysolite, onyx and jasper,**
      **sapphire, turquoise and beryl.**
    **Your settings and mountings were made of gold;**
      **on the day you were created they were prepared.**
**[14]You were anointed as a guardian cherub,**
      **for so I ordained you.**
    **You were on the holy mount of God;**
      **you walked among the fiery stones.**
**[15]You were blameless in your ways**
      **from the day you were created**
      **till wickedness was found in you.**
**[16]Through your widespread trade**
      **you were filled with violence,**
      **and you sinned.**
    **So I drove you in disgrace from the mount of God,**
      **and I expelled you, O guardian cherub,**
      **from among the fiery stones.**
**[17]Your heart became proud**
      **on account of your beauty,**
    **and you corrupted your wisdom**
      **because of your splendor.**
    **So I threw you to the earth;**
      **I made a spectacle of you before kings.**

---

[71] See discussion in Ellison, *Ezekiel,* 110-11.

**[18]**By your many sins and dishonest trade
    you have desecrated your sanctuaries.
So I made a fire come out from you,
    and it consumed you,
and I reduced you to ashes on the ground
    in the sight of all who were watching.
**[19]**All the nations who knew you
    are appalled at you;
you have come to a horrible end
    and will be no more.'"

**28:11-15**  The context of chaps. 26–28 and the stated subject, "concerning the king of Tyre," make it clear that the primary message here regards the literal king of Tyre.[72] The word "king" (*melek*) is used elsewhere in Ezekiel primarily of the kings of Babylon (e.g., 17:12; 19:9; 21:19; 24:2; 26:7; 29:18; 30:10; 32:11) and Egypt (29:2; 30:21; 31:2; 32:2).[73] The fact that the "ruler" (*nāgîd*) of Tyre in 28:1 is here called "king" suggests to some that there is something different about the one addressed in the lament. One suggestion is that it is the patron god of Tyre in view here, whose name, Melkart, means "king of the city." This view is difficult, as Zimmerli argues, since "king" elsewhere in Ezekiel describes an earthly ruler.[74] In a parallel verse in 32:2 it refers to the Egyptian pharaoh—"Son of man, take up a lament concerning Pharaoh king of Egypt." Zimmerli's alternative explanation, however, that the different terms betray the separate origins of the two oracles is at least as unlikely.

The statement "you were in Eden, the garden of God" (v. 13; cf. 31:8-9) must mean that the king of Tyre is being compared to someone who was in the garden of Eden. The verses describe someone in an exalted position who was favored by God[75] but who became corrupt and lost that position. This could describe the first man, Adam.[76] Yet even granting the figurative nature of language, it seems that something more than a human

---

[72] Fisch, *Ezekiel*, 191-93.

[73] Otherwise it is used once of Jehoiachin (1:2) and twice of the future messianic King (37:22,24). Its use in 7:27 is problematic, perhaps referring to Jehoiachin or to the kings of Israel generally.

[74] Zimmerli, *Ezekiel 2*, 90.

[75] The verb translated "created" in vv. 13,15 is בָּרָא, which stresses that he was a special creation of God (cf. *TWOT*, 127). Special divine involvement is also stressed by the use of נָתַן, "to give," in v. 14 ("ordained"), v. 17 ("made"), and v. 18 ("reduced").

[76] Craigie, *Ezekiel*, 207; Taylor, *Ezekiel*, 196. This is surely true of "blameless" in v. 15. תָּמִים also sometimes is translated "perfect." The word does not necessarily mean sinless perfection but "wholeness" or "blameless" regarding moral character. See Alexander, "Ezekiel," 886.

creature is in view. Perhaps Adam was a "model of perfection," "full of wisdom," and "perfect in beauty" (v. 12), but Scripture never describes him as such.[77] Nor does it speak of him as adorned with "every precious stone" (v. 13). The difficulty, however, is that no one else is described in such terms either. Some suggest that adornment with precious stones is an allusion to the Jewish high priest (Exod 28:17-20),[78] but such a confusion of images would hardly communicate a coherent message.

Especially significant is that the one addressed was "anointed" (v. 14) and "ordained" as "a guardian cherub" by the God who was speaking through Ezekiel (v. 14) and that he previously dwelt not on the earth (v. 17)[79] but "on the holy mount of God" and "walked among the fiery stones" (v. 14).[80] Such descriptions make it unlikely that a strictly human creature is in view.

Furthermore, the cause for his loss of favor and exalted position do not match the biblical account of the fall of humanity. The woman was driven by a desire to gain wisdom and become like God (Gen 3:5-6). But this character's sin is said to have arisen from pride on account of his "beauty" (v. 17) and "splendor." Consequently, he "corrupted" his divine gifts and became full of "wickedness" and "violence" (vv. 15-17).

Some of the difficulties of identification may result from a shift of focus back and forth between the king of Tyre and the figurative character. The comparison has surely been temporarily abandoned when "widespread trade" is said to be the expression, cause, or occasion for his wickedness and violence (v. 16). This apparently was something true of Tyre but not of anyone in Eden. However, this shift of focus does not explain all the divergencies unless the figurative character was a supernatural one. Nor does Scripture ascribe this specific kind of wickedness or the resulting judgment to humankind generally after the fall. The flood is said to have been God's judgment on the "wickedness" of a "corrupt" world "full of violence" (Gen 6:5,11-13), and the people in the "plain of Shinar" exhibited great pride in desiring to "make a name" for themselves by build-

---

[77] Note Tyre describes itself as "perfect in beauty" in 27:3, and its ruler claims great wisdom in 28:3-5.

[78] E.g., Taylor, *Ezekiel*, 196. He prefers the text of the LXX, which has twelve stones listed rather than the nine of the MT.

[79] It is also possible to understand the clause "I threw you to the earth" as "I threw you to the ground," i.e., in humiliation. The sense also can be either literal or figurative. If two individuals are being addressed as one, the literal king of Tyre and also Satan, there is intentional ambiguity here.

[80] The hapax legomenon אַבְנֵי־אֵשׁ ("stones of fire") appears here and v. 16. This may refer to the jewels mentioned in v. 13 (Fisch, *Ezekiel,* 192) but otherwise remains enigmatic.

ing "a tower that reaches to the heavens" (Gen 11:1-4). But in neither case was the judgment described as being driven "in disgrace from the mount of God," "expelled . . . from among the fiery stones,"[81] or thrown "to the earth" (Ezek 28:16-17), although Adam and his wife were "banished" and driven from "the Garden of Eden" (Gen 3:24).

The suggestion that the passage has borrowed from some creation account other than Gen 1–3 is purely conjectural and highly speculative. Borrowing is not the best answer to the question of the interpretation of Ezek 28. To suggest that it is purely an imaginary story about creation that also involved the king of Tyre, composed from the mind of Ezekiel, stretches our own imagination.

Who, then, was the person whose character was like the king of Tyre that fulfilled the elements of vv. 12-17? The serpent was known for his craftiness (Gen 3:1), his deceit, and his anti-God attitude (3:4), leading humanity to sin (3:6-7).[82] Elsewhere he is presented as a deceiver (Rev 12:9; 20:2), an instigator of evil (John 13:2,27), one who seeks worship as a god (Luke 4:6-8; 2 Thess 2:3-4), and one who seeks to get others to renounce God (Job 2:4-5). He appears as an angel of God (2 Cor 11:14) and as the father of lies and violence (John 8:44), distorts Scripture (Matt 4:6), opposes believers (2 Cor 2:11), and finally is judged (Matt 25:41; Rev 19:20-21; 20:13-15). Therefore the conclusion that the figure behind the poetic symbol is the serpent (also known as the adversary, the devil, Satan; Rev 12:9) is a logical one.

Ezekiel began with a funeral lament for the city of Tyre (27:1-36), calling attention to its materialism, pride, and self-sufficiency. He then moved to a discussion of the king of Tyre presenting his arrogance and self-will (28:1-19). Overlaid in these prophetic messages are many elements that extend beyond the characteristics of the city or the king. This is not an unusual prophetic phenomenon. Ezekiel presented the king of Tyre as an evil tyrant who was animated and motivated by a more sinister, unseen tyrant, Satan. The picture presented by the prophet goes beyond what we know about the adversary in other passages. It tells us of his wisdom, beauty, appearance of perfection, appointment as a guardian and his expulsion from the presence of God.

Of the twenty elements associated with the king of Tyre in 28:11-19

---

[81] The word "expelled" is a translation of אָבַד (lit. "to destroy"). The name is used to describe a place of judgment and destruction in Rev 9:11, where it appears as "Abaddon," meaning "place of destruction." It is synonymous in that verse with the "abyss."

[82] Identification of elements in this vision that may be applied to characteristics of Satan has been made by Enns, *Ezekiel,* 131-32; Feinberg, *The Prophecy of Ezekiel,* 162-63; and W. A. Criswell, *Expository Sermons on the Book of Ezekiel* (Grand Rapids: Zondervan), 149.

most also are found in Isaiah's indictment of another tyrannical ruler, the king of Babylon (14:12-17). These passages sometimes are compared and related to Satan as the figure behind the elements.[83] Of the twenty elements, fourteen also are found in Isaiah.

The sinister character of the mastermind behind God's enemies is not always recognized. The real motivating force behind the king of Tyre was the adversary, the satan, who opposed God and his people from the beginning (28:6-19).

| EZEKIEL 28:1-19 | ISAIAH 14:12-17 |
| --- | --- |
| 1. Was motivated by pride (v. 2) | verse 13 |
| 2. Claimed to be God (v. 2) | verse 14 |
| 3. Claimed to sit on God's throne (v. 3) | verse 13 |
| 4. Claimed divine wisdom (v. 2) | verse 13, "like" God |
| 5. Claimed superior human wisdom (v. 3) | verse 16 |
| 6. Proud of wealth and power (vv. 4-5) | verse 16 |
| 7. Condemned to violent judgment (vv. 6-10) | verse 19 |
| 8. Claimed to be model of perfection (v. 12) | verse 13 |
| 9. Known for his beauty (v. 12) | verse 12 |
| 10. Was in Eden (v. 13) | |
| 11. Was a guardian cherub (v. 14) | |
| 12. Was on holy mount of God (v. 14) | |
| 13. Considered himself blameless (v. 15) | |
| 14. Chose the way of evil (v. 15) | |
| 15. Was expelled from his position (v. 16) | verse 12 |
| 16. Was corrupted by pride (v. 17) | verse 13 |

---

[83] Enns, *Ezekiel,* 131; Criswell, *Expository Sermons,* 149; both Enns and Criswell note the parallel nature of Isa 14:12-17 and Ezek 28:11-19.

| Ezekiel 28:1-19 | Isaiah 14:12-17 |
|---|---|
| 17. Was thrown down to earth (vv. 17-18) | |
| 18. Desecrated many sanctuaries (v. 18) | |
| 19. Suffered fiery judgment (v. 18) | verse 15 |
| 20. Nations appalled who knew him (v. 19) | verses 16-17 |

### 6. Prophecy against Sidon (28:20-26)

[20]The word of the LORD came to me: [21]"Son of man, set your face against Sidon; prophesy against her [22]and say: 'This is what the Sovereign LORD says:

" 'I am against you, O Sidon,
and I will gain glory within you.
They will know that I am the Lord,
when I inflict punishment on her
and show myself holy within her.
[23]I will send a plague upon her
and make blood flow in her streets.
The slain will fall within her,
with the sword against her on every side.
Then they will know that I am the LORD.
[24]" 'No longer will the people of Israel have malicious neighbors who are painful briers and sharp thorns. Then they will know that I am the Sovereign LORD.
[25]" 'This is what the Sovereign LORD says: When I gather the people of Israel from the nations where they have been scattered, I will show myself holy among them in the sight of the nations. Then they will live in their own land, which I gave to my servant Jacob. [26]They will live there in safety and will build houses and plant vineyards; they will live in safety when I inflict punishment on all their neighbors who maligned them. Then they will know that I am the LORD.

**28:20-24** Sidon was a sister Phoenician city to Tyre, and they often are mentioned together (Jer 27:3; 47:4; Joel 4:4). Sidon was located about twenty-three miles north of Tyre and was much more exposed to military assault.[84] One of the most infamous Sidonians was the woman who married Ahab, king of Israel. Ahab sought to strengthen his reign over the

---

[84] Zimmerli, *Ezekiel 2*, 97; Enns, *Ezekiel*, 132.

Northern Kingdom and took Jezebel, daughter of Ethbaal, king of Sidon, for his wife (1 Kgs 16:31-34). This move proved unwise because Jezebel reinstituted Baal worship in Israel and hastened the fall of the Northern Kingdom by contributing to its moral and spiritual decay.

God promised to execute judgment against Sidon by means of "plague," "blood," and "sword" (vv. 22-23), a three-pronged judgment used earlier by Ezekiel (6:11-12; 14:21). Because of God's judgment, the fall of Sidon would be acknowledged as more than a chance event. It would be viewed as a fulfillment of God's promise of judgment (v. 23).

While v. 24 applied to Sidon and Tyre, it also applied to the larger context of the judgment messages. The summary statement applied to all the nations beyond Israel-Judah that have been considered thus far.[85]

**28:25-26** These two verses add to the summary statement of v. 24. They plant the seed of hope of restoration for Israel that germinates, grows, and blossoms in 33:1–39:29. These verses anticipate the day when Israel will be regathered and restored (v. 25). The nation will dwell in safety and again enjoy divine protection (v. 26).[86] "Build houses" and "plant vineyards" are operations that only were undertaken in a time of security. Those fellow travelers who either endorsed or condoned the rule of the ungodly also would be judged (28:20-26).

## 7. Prophecy against Egypt (29:1–32:32)

Seven messages of judgment to befall Egypt conclude the series of judgments against the nations.[87] Much more attention is given to Egypt than any other of the nations against which Ezekiel spoke. Much of the long-standing hostility Israel had toward Egypt can be traced to the time of the Egyptian bondage. Even beyond that time Israel was always caught between Egypt and other powers in Mesopotamia that were struggling for world domination. Although much more extensive, Ezekiel's messages against Egypt follow the same plan as those of Jeremiah (Jer 46:1-26).[88]

---

[85] Zimmerli, *Ezekiel 2*, 99; Fisch, *Ezekiel*, 194. Judgment on all the nations who have opposed Israel will provide the needed security to insure the success of their reestablishment in the land of promise.

[86] Enns, *Ezekiel*, 132-33. This anticipates the extended discussion of the restoration in chaps. 36–37. It is an allusion to the millennial kingdom of the Messiah when Israel is regathered and will dwell in security and prosperity.

[87] For a detailed analysis see L. Boadt, *Ezekiel's Oracles Against Egypt: A Literary and Philological Study of Ezekiel 29-32. Biblica et Orientalia* 37 (Rome: Biblical Institute Press, 1980).

[88] See Zimmerli (*Ezekiel 2*, 102-5) for a comprehensive overview of the political nuances of Egypt's relationship to Israel and other nations.

Six of the seven messages are dated prophecies.[89] The seven messages are: (1) Egypt's sins exposed and judged (29:1-16; Jan. 587 B.C.); (2) Egypt would suffer same fate of Tyre (29:17-21; Apr. 571 B.C.); (3) Egypt and allies devastated (30:1-19; undated, 587 B.C.?); (4) Egypt helpless in the Day of Yahweh (30:20-26; Apr. 587 B.C.); (5) fall of Pharaoh, the "cedar" of Egypt (31:1-18; June 587 B.C.); (6) lament for the fall of Pharaoh (32:1-16; Mar. 585 B.C.); (7) Pharaoh condemned to the pit (32:17-32; Mar. 585 B.C.). These messages are in chronological order with the exception of 29:17-21. Chronological sequence has been a matter of discussion regarding these messages.[90] Ezekiel generally followed chronological sequence, but setting forth a complete dated history of opposition to Egypt was not his major purpose.

### (1) Egypt's Sins Exposed and Judged (29:1-16)

**[1]In the tenth year, in the tenth month on the twelfth day, the word of the LORD came to me: [2]"Son of man, set your face against Pharaoh king of Egypt and prophesy against him and against all Egypt. [3]Speak to him and say: 'This is what the Sovereign LORD says:**

**"'I am against you, Pharaoh king of Egypt,**
**you great monster lying among your streams.**
**You say, "The Nile is mine;**
**I made it for myself."**
**[4]But I will put hooks in your jaws**
**and make the fish of your streams stick to your scales.**
**I will pull you out from among your streams,**
**with all the fish sticking to your scales.**
**[5]I will leave you in the desert,**
**you and all the fish of your streams.**
**You will fall on the open field**
**and not be gathered or picked up.**
**I will give you as food**
**to the beasts of the earth and the birds of the air.**
**[6]Then all who live in Egypt will know that I am the LORD.**

**"'You have been a staff of reed for the house of Israel. [7]When they grasped you with their hands, you splintered and you tore open their shoulders; when they leaned on you, you broke and their backs were wrenched.**

**[8]"'Therefore this is what the Sovereign LORD says: I will bring a sword against you and kill your men and their animals. [9]Egypt will become a deso-**

---

[89] See "Dated Prophecies in Ezekiel" in Introduction. See also Alexander, "Ezekiel," 888-89.

[90] Wevers, *Ezekiel,* 221, and Alexander, "Ezekiel," 888-89.

late wasteland. Then they will know that I am the LORD.

"'Because you said, "The Nile is mine; I made it," [10]therefore I am against you and against your streams, and I will make the land of Egypt a ruin and a desolate waste from Migdol to Aswan, as far as the border of Cush. [11]No foot of man or animal will pass through it; no one will live there for forty years. [12]I will make the land of Egypt desolate among devastated lands, and her cities will lie desolate forty years among ruined cities. And I will disperse the Egyptians among the nations and scatter them through the countries.

[13]"'Yet this is what the Sovereign LORD says: At the end of forty years I will gather the Egyptians from the nations where they were scattered. [14]I will bring them back from captivity and return them to Upper Egypt, the land of their ancestry. There they will be a lowly kingdom. [15]It will be the lowliest of kingdoms and will never again exalt itself above the other nations. I will make it so weak that it will never again rule over the nations. [16]Egypt will no longer be a source of confidence for the people of Israel but will be a reminder of their sin in turning to her for help. Then they will know that I am the Sovereign LORD.'"

This message has two parts: the introduction of the monster, Pharaoh (29:1-6a), and the judgment that would befall Egypt (29:6b-16).

**29:1-6a**  This prophecy has been dated January 7, 587 B.C., about seven months before the fall of Jerusalem.[91] This message against Pharaoh was directed at Pharaoh Hophra (588–569 B.C.), whose grandfather, Pharaoh Neco killed Josiah at Megiddo in 609 B.C. (vv. 1-2).[92] Pharaoh was compared to a "monster" lying among the streams, who claimed the Nile as his domain.[93] The "monster" was doubtless a crocodile. The "hooks" in the jaws to render the "monster" helpless described the standard method for capture and destruction of a crocodile (v. 4).[94]

The "monster" of the stream will be left in the desert, which would mean certain death for a crocodile as well as the fish that were his food (v. 5). There was no burial, but the beast would become food for the scavengers of land and air (v. 5). When the destruction of Egypt becomes a reality, everyone will know God did it (v. 6a).

**29:6b-16**  Ezekiel portrayed Egypt as a crumpled reed used as a staff for support, which splintered when weight was applied. The same figure

---

[91] See Zimmerli, *Ezekiel 2*, 110; Fisch, *Ezekiel*, 195.

[92] See Wevers, *Ezekiel*, 221, who gives a brief history of the Saite Dynasty of Egypt 663–525 B.C. of which Neco was the second ruler and Hophra his grandson.

[93] תַּנִּים is translated "crocodile," "jackal," "monster," "serpent," "dragon" and obviously refers to a feared creature. The "monster" of the streams in Egypt was the "crocodile," as some translate it. See Alexander, "Ezekiel," 892; Fisch, *Ezekiel*, 190; Zimmerli, *Ezekiel 2*, 110; BDB, 1072.

[94] See Enns, *Ezekiel*, 133; Fisch, *Ezekiel*, 196.

was used in 2 Kgs 18:21 and also applied to Egypt. When the reed broke, the shoulders of those nations, including Israel, who leaned on it were dislocated.[95] As a result those who tried to lean on the splintered reed, Egypt, were forced to stand on their own or perish (vv. 6-7).

So Egypt was judged by the sword and desolation for two reasons. First, pride; Egypt said the Nile was theirs (v. 9). Such self-sufficient pride was punished by God in Tyre (28:2) and was punished in Egypt as well. Pharaoh Hophra was known for his arrogance and inflated self-image. He felt no one could defeat him.[96] Second, Egypt had seduced Israel. Pharaoh Hophra had pledged to help them confront Nebuchadnezzar, but when the battle came, he abandoned them like the brittle staff (v. 7). Therefore God promised to ruin the streams (v. 9) and make the land uninhabitable for forty years (v. 11; related to forty years of wandering after the Exodus?). The people of Egypt would be dispersed forty years like the Hebrews in the wilderness (v. 12).

After forty years the nation was to be restored. The restoration was to be a limited one, and the weakened nation was to be a "lowly kingdom" (vv. 13-14). Never again would Egypt be a world power. Never again would Egypt be exalted over nations. Never again would it be a source of confidence for Israel, but it only would be a reminder of their sin in turning to Egypt instead of God for help (vv. 15-16; see Isa 30:1–31:9).

Spiritual pride always produces a self-sufficient attitude of rebellion against God and opposition to his people and his work (2 Chr 26:16). Those nations who have championed idolatry and immorality and used their influence to subvert the work of God will be especially marked for judgment.

### *(2) Egypt to Suffer the Fate of Tyre (29:17-21)*

[17]In the twenty-seventh year, in the first month on the first day, the word of the LORD came to me: [18]"Son of man, Nebuchadnezzar king of Babylon drove his army in a hard campaign against Tyre; every head was rubbed bare and every shoulder made raw. Yet he and his army got no reward from the campaign he led against Tyre. [19]Therefore this is what the Sovereign LORD says: I am going to give Egypt to Nebuchadnezzar king of Babylon, and he will carry off its wealth. He will loot and plunder the land as pay for his

---

[95] Wevers, *Ezekiel,* 224; Fisch, *Ezekiel,* 197. Both suggest that this refers to a dislocated shoulder, meaning that those who attempted to rely on Egypt were not strengthened but crippled.

[96] Alexander, "Ezekiel," 891. Hophra felt so secure he believed no one, not even the gods of Egypt, could dislodge him from his position as king.

army. <sup>20</sup>I have given him Egypt as a reward for his efforts because he and his army did it for me, declares the Sovereign LORD.

<sup>21</sup>"On that day I will make a horn grow for the house of Israel, and I will open your mouth among them. Then they will know that I am the LORD."

**29:17-21**    Ezekiel's second message against Egypt was given on New Year's Day, April 26, 571 B.C.[97] Nebuchadnezzar campaigned against Tyre for thirteen years and came away without a final victory.[98] God, in this message, promised to deliver Egypt to him as a consolation. The loot and plunder that his armies would take was much-needed pay for his men, who came away from Tyre unrewarded (vv. 17-19). Nebuchadnezzar's military campaign against Tyre therefore was divinely motivated. What he did was done for "me," God said (v. 20). So God promised that Egypt would be given to Nebuchadnezzar as repayment to his men for their thirteen years of opposition to Tyre.[99]

This brief message concludes with a one-verse statement of messianic hope. Ezekiel foresaw that when the subjugation of Egypt was accomplished, God would "make a horn grow" for Israel. A "horn" meant any kind of animal horn (ram, cow, deer) and sometimes was mentioned as a symbol of strength or power (1 Sam 2:1; 1 Kgs 22:11; Ps 92:10; Jer 48:25). As used here it meant the rise of a leader of unusual strength and power. That "horn" would "grow" for Israel. The word "grow" is a specific messianic term. It means a "sprout" or "shoot" of new growth as when a tree sprouts and grows from a seed. Isaiah, Jeremiah, and Zechariah use this word in key messianic passages to speak of the coming of the Messiah.[100] The character of the Messiah is revealed throughout the prophets. (1) He is "The Lord Our Righteousness" (Jer 23:5-6). The Messiah was called a "righteous branch" (ṣemaḥ). Zedekiah was the last king of Judah. His name literally means "Yahweh Is Righteous," a paradox because he was an unrighteous ruler. (2) He is the "beautiful and glorious branch" (ṣemaḥ, Isa 4:2-6). In his day there will be restoration and cleansing of the impurity of Zion. (3) He is the "branch" (neṣer), the root and stem of Jesse (Isa 11:1-5) and will reinstate the line of David. (4) He is the "servant branch" (ṣemaḥ, Zech 3:8-10). He will come as servant of both God and humankind (see Isa 42:1-3; 49:1-7; 50:4-11; 52:13–53:12). His hu-

---

<sup>97</sup> Taylor, *Ezekiel*, 36.

<sup>98</sup> See chapter note at 26:7-14.

<sup>99</sup> Taylor, *Ezekiel*, 201 (cf. Jer 43:8-13; 46:1-25). The thirteen-year siege of Tyre ended with the fortress still unconquered. This meant the armies of Nebuchadnezzar were left with no booty for pay. Egypt is presented as a consolation.

<sup>100</sup> צֶמַח is a "branch" or "sprig" and was used to describe the hope of Messiah (Jer 23:5; Isa 4:2; Zech 3:8).

mility will be the key to his greatness (Matt 20:26-27). (5) He is the man called the "branch" (*ṣemaḥ*, Zech 6:12-13). The God-man, who is a perfect high priest, will rebuild the temple and be a perfect mediator between God and humanity (1 Tim 2:5).

This fivefold picture of the "Righteous Branch" was fulfilled in the person of Christ, who is (1) our Righteousness (Rom 3:22; 10:3-4; 1 Cor 1:30; Phil 3:9; 2 Pet 1:1); (2) our Redeemer, Restorer, Protector, Defender (Eph 2:17; 6:10-12; Col 1:14; 4:4-5); (3) our Wisdom, Understanding, Strength (Luke 2:52; 1 Cor 1:24; Rev 5:12); (4) our Servant (Matt 12:18; 20:26-27; Phil 2:27); (5) our Priest/King[Mediator] (1 Tim 2:5; Heb 7:25-28; 10:10-12).

Egypt's subjugation by Nebuchadnezzar was portrayed by Ezekiel as a forerunner of the advent of the Messiah. When the prophecy became a reality, God promised the prophet, "I will open your mouth among them" (Ezek 29:21). Although Ezekiel once was restrained from speaking (3:26), God promised a time when he would speak freely. This promise, when realized, gave boldness and authenticity to Ezekiel's message.[101]

The long-standing enemies of God will one day be removed so that he can set up his perfect kingdom of righteousness (29:17-21), ruled by his ideal king, the Messiah (29:21; Pss 2:1-12; 8:1-9).

### (3) Egypt and Allies Devastated (30:1-19)

[1]The word of the LORD came to me: [2]"Son of man, prophesy and say: 'This is what the Sovereign LORD says:

"'Wail and say,
  "Alas for that day!"
[3]For the day is near,
  the day of the LORD is near—
a day of clouds,
  a time of doom for the nations.
[4]A sword will come against Egypt,
  and anguish will come upon Cush.
When the slain fall in Egypt,
  her wealth will be carried away
  and her foundations torn down.
[5]Cush and Put, Lydia and all Arabia, Libya and the people of the covenant land will fall by the sword along with Egypt.
[6]"'This is what the LORD says:

---

[101] Wevers, *Ezekiel*, 227; Enns, *Ezekiel*, 136. With the conquest of Egypt, Israel would receive new boldness.

"'The allies of Egypt will fall
   and her proud strength will fail.
From Migdol to Aswan
   they will fall by the sword within her,
      declares the Sovereign LORD.
⁷"'They will be desolate
   among desolate lands,
and their cities will lie
   among ruined cities.
⁸Then they will know that I am the LORD,
   when I set fire to Egypt
   and all her helpers are crushed.
⁹"'On that day messengers will go out from me in ships to frighten Cush
out of her complacency. Anguish will take hold of them on the day of Egypt's
doom, for it is sure to come.

¹⁰"'This is what the Sovereign LORD says:
   "'I will put an end to the hordes of Egypt
   by the hand of Nebuchadnezzar king of Babylon.
¹¹He and his army—the most ruthless of nations—
   will be brought in to destroy the land.
They will draw their swords against Egypt
   and fill the land with the slain.
¹²I will dry up the streams of the Nile
   and sell the land to evil men;
by the hand of foreigners
   I will lay waste the land and everything in it.
I the LORD have spoken.

¹³"'This is what the Sovereign LORD says:
   "'I will destroy the idols
   and put an end to the images in Memphis.
No longer will there be a prince in Egypt,
   and I will spread fear throughout the land.
¹⁴I will lay waste Upper Egypt,
   set fire to Zoan
   and inflict punishment on Thebes.
¹⁵I will pour out my wrath on Pelusium,
   the stronghold of Egypt,
   and cut off the hordes of Thebes.
¹⁶I will set fire to Egypt;
   Pelusium will writhe in agony.
Thebes will be taken by storm;
   Memphis will be in constant distress.
¹⁷The young men of Heliopolis and Bubastis

> will fall by the sword,
>   and the cities themselves will go into captivity.
> [18]Dark will be the day at Tahpanhes
>   when I break the yoke of Egypt;
>   there her proud strength will come to an end.
> She will be covered with clouds,
>   and her villages will go into captivity.
> [19]So I will inflict punishment on Egypt,
>   and they will know that I am the LORD.'"

No date was included for this third prophecy that presented specific details about the fall of Egypt. This message has four parts, each introduced with, "This is what the Sovereign LORD says" (vv. 2,6,10,13); and each concluded with a final word, "declares the Sovereign LORD" (v. 6), "they will know that I am the LORD" (vv. 8,19), and "I the LORD have spoken" (v. 12).[102]

**30:1-9**    This was not a funeral lament such as the lament for Tyre in 27:1-36. It began with a cry of distress at the nearness of the Day of the Lord (v. 2).[103] That "day" is sometimes used in a general sense to mean a day of judgment. Sometimes it is used to refer to God's judgment on the nations at the end of human history. Sometimes it refers to a day of blessing and deliverance for Israel (v. 3).[104] It is used in 30:3 in the first sense of a general approaching day of judgment called the "time of doom for the nations" (v. 3). Ezekiel's prophecies are similar in impact to "the prophet Joel, who faced with a spiritually apathetic audience, stabbed it awake with the theme of the day of the Lord (Joel 1:15–2:11)."[105] Ezekiel utilized the same theme as Joel in announcing judgment on the former ally of Judah.

Judgment for Egypt and its allies was symbolized by the sword (v. 4). The "sword" would bring judgment on Egypt, Cush or Ethiopia, Put or northern Africa in the vicinity of Lydia, Arabia, and Libya (vv. 4-5). Even the "people of the covenant land" (a possible reference to those who had fled to Egypt in the wake of Nebuchadnezzar's invasion) would fall by the

---

[102] Wevers, *Ezekiel,* 227. The absence of a date in this passage led some to conclude that vv. 1-19 are not Ezekiel's words. The absence of a date, however, is not compelling evidence.

[103] הֵילִילוּ is a *hiphil* imperative of יָלַל ("to howl") and is a cry of distress. The anguish of the approach of the Day of the Lord is heightened by the addition of הָהּ, meaning "Woe!" or "Alas!"

[104] See Ezek 7:7. Enns, *Ezekiel,* 136; "the day of the LORD" is a phrase with eschatological overtones (cf. Isa 13:1-22; 19:1-25; Joel 1:15; 2:1-11; 3:14-16; Amos 5:18; Obad 15; Zeph 1:7-18).

[105] Allen, *Ezekiel 20–48,* 116.

sword (vv. 4-5).[106] All Egypt would fall from Migdol to Aswan, the northern and southern extremities (meaning all the land). All Egypt's allies would fail and fall by the sword (v. 6).[107] Then they would know that Yahweh is God when Egypt is afire and its allies are crushed (vv. 7-8). Messengers who tell of the plight of Egypt would bring fear of doom on the allies (v. 9).

**30:10-19** Nebuchadnezzar would wield the "sword" of destruction.[108] He and his army were described as the most ruthless national armies (28:7; 31:12; 32:12). They would fill Egypt with slain, which was the same fate described for Tyre in 28:7, fulfilling the prediction of 29:17-21 (vv. 10-11).

Nebuchadnezzar would dry the "streams of the Nile." Destruction of the canal system of irrigation would hasten the desolation of Egypt.[109] This canal system was the only way to irrigate the limited but fertile, arable land. The land would fall to evil men who would exploit it and its people (v. 12).

God would destroy the idols of Egypt (v. 13).[110] This was a remarkable claim considering the scope of Egyptian religion. Elements of Egyptian religion are so complex and contradictory from one period to another that sweeping generalities would be difficult. Religion in Egypt developed out of a system of local village gods and lesser spirits whose purposes included both help and hindrance of humanity. These traditions were preserved as some of these villages grew to become cities. Ptah was the god of Memphis; Atum, god of Heliopolis; Montu, god of Thebes. In the villages gods were associated with every area of daily life. There were gods to assist childbearing, household duties, harvest of crops; there were river gods and others. The gods at one point numbered more than twelve hundred.[111]

Eight cities that were prominent centers of religious, political, and military might in Egypt were marked for judgment. They represent the pun-

---

[106] Alexander, "Ezekiel," 895. Even Judeans who fled to Egypt at the death of Gedeliah (2 Kgs 25:23-26) would be affected when Egypt is judged.

[107] Fisch, *Ezekiel*, 198. See his note on 27:10.

[108] See 26:7-14 note on the name "Nebuchadnezzar."

[109] Fisch, *Ezekiel*, 204. Egypt depended on the Nile and the irrigation canal system that it fed to support its agricultural productivity (cf. Isa 19:5-9).

[110] גִּלּוּלִים is Ezekiel's favorite word for idols (8:10; 14:4[see note],7; 16:36; 18:6,12,15; 20:7-8,24,39; 22:4).

[111] E. A. W. Budge, *The Gods of the Egyptians*, vol. I (New York: Dover, 1969), ix-x; *Religion in Ancient Egypt: Gods, Myths, and Personal Practice*, B. E. Shafer, ed. (Ithaca: Cornell University Press, 1991), 7-87.

ishment inflicted on Egypt. Their fall represented the passing of Egypt as a military, religious, and political power in the world and represented the fulfillment of 29:14. These cities were (1) Memphis (vv. 13,16), which was the capital of Lower Egypt (north) and center of worship of Ptah and Apis; (2) Pathros (v. 14), which was a fortified area in Upper Egypt (south); (3) Zoan (v. 14), the Hyksos's capital of Egypt under their occupation; (4) Thebes (vv. 15-16), the most important city in Egypt, capital of Upper Egypt, center for Amun worship, adjacent to Luxor, and across the Nile from the Valley of the Kings; (5) Pelusium (vv. 15-16), an old fortress in the northeastern Nile delta; (6) Heliopolis (v. 17), also called Aven and On, the center of sun worship and located in Lower Egypt (Jer 43:13); (7) Bubastis (v. 17), capital during the twenty-second and twenty-third dynasties; it was located forty miles northeast of Cairo; (8) Tahpanhes (v. 18), one of the main fortresses of ancient Egypt (Jer 2:16).[112]

### (4) Egypt Helpless in the Day of Yahweh (30:20-26)

**[20]In the eleventh year, in the first month on the seventh day, the word of the LORD came to me: [21]"Son of man, I have broken the arm of Pharaoh king of Egypt. It has not been bound up for healing or put in a splint so as to become strong enough to hold a sword. [22]Therefore this is what the Sovereign LORD says: I am against Pharaoh king of Egypt. I will break both his arms, the good arm as well as the broken one, and make the sword fall from his hand. [23]I will disperse the Egyptians among the nations and scatter them through the countries. [24]I will strengthen the arms of the king of Babylon and put my sword in his hand, but I will break the arms of Pharaoh, and he will groan before him like a mortally wounded man. [25]I will strengthen the arms of the king of Babylon, but the arms of Pharaoh will fall limp. Then they will know that I am the LORD, when I put my sword into the hand of the king of Babylon and he brandishes it against Egypt. [26]I will disperse the Egyptians among the nations and scatter them through the countries. Then they will know that I am the LORD."**

**30:20-26** Ezekiel's fourth message has been dated April 29, 587 B.C.[113] When Nebuchadnezzar attacked Jerusalem in 588 B.C., Pharaoh Hophra initially came to Zedekiah's assistance. Hophra's armies were defeated and returned to Egypt. When Jerusalem fell, Hophra, whose strength was broken, was defeated by Ahmose in a civil war. Nebuchadnezzar invaded and easily conquered Egypt, which subsequently was nev-

---

[112] For the identity of these cities compare Wevers, *Ezekiel*, 231; Fisch, *Ezekiel*, 199, 205; Alexander, "Ezekiel," 895; and Zimmerli, *Ezekiel 2*, 131-35.

[113] See Taylor, *Ezekiel*, 36 and Zimmerli, *Ezekiel 2*, 137.

er a prominent world power.[114] Like the Hebrews, the Egyptians would be dispersed as exiles among the nations (vv. 23,26).

This message bears sober testimony in graphic detail to the events associated with the fall of Egypt. Ezekiel said that Pharaoh's arms would be broken (vv. 21-22,24) and that his arms would fall limp (v. 25). This passage presents Pharaoh as helpless and unable to hold a weapon and therefore unable to defend against invading armies (v. 21).[115] Additional references to the defeat of Egypt may be found in Isaiah (30:1-14), Jeremiah (37:5ff.; 46:1-26), and the writer of Kings (2 Kgs 24:7). The repetition of the ideas in the last four verses was for emphasis (Ezek 30:23-25). Egypt's devastation and its loss of standing in the family of nations is a constant testimony to the truth of God's word (30:1-19). The great civilization would exist only in ruins and in historical records (30:20-26).

## (5) Fall of Pharaoh, the "Cedar" of Egypt (31:1-18)

This message has two parts. First, the fall of Egypt is like the fall of Assyria (31:1-9). Second, the reasons for the fall of Assyria and Egypt are given (31:10-18). The prophetic rhetoric lulls the reader into a state of indifference before the door of hope slams with a resounding "therefore" (v. 10). Judgment, not hope, is the message for Egypt.

**[1]In the eleventh year, in the third month on the first day, the word of the LORD came to me: [2]"Son of man, say to Pharaoh king of Egypt and to his hordes:**

**" 'Who can be compared with you in majesty?**
**[3]Consider Assyria, once a cedar in Lebanon,**
**with beautiful branches overshadowing the forest;**
**it towered on high,**
**its top above the thick foliage.**
**[4]The waters nourished it,**
**deep springs made it grow tall;**
**their streams flowed**
**all around its base**
**and sent their channels**
**to all the trees of the field.**
**[5]So it towered higher**

---

[114] Zimmerli, *Ezekiel 2*, 138; Alexander, "Ezekiel," 897-98; Enns, *Ezekiel*, 138; Cooke, *Ezekiel*, 334-35. The fall of Egypt was a prelude to the complete destruction God would bring on both Egypt and Babylon.

[115] Alexander, "Ezekiel," 898. Nebuchadnezzar would ultimately break both arms of Hophra so that they could not hold weapons, thereby rendering him and Egypt defenseless.

   than all the trees of the field;
  its boughs increased
   and its branches grew long,
   spreading because of abundant waters.
⁶All the birds of the air
   nested in its boughs,
  all the beasts of the field
   gave birth under its branches;
  all the great nations
   lived in its shade.
⁷It was majestic in beauty,
   with its spreading boughs,
  for its roots went down
   to abundant waters.
⁸The cedars in the garden of God
   could not rival it,
  nor could the pine trees
   equal its boughs,
  nor could the plane trees
   compare with its branches—
  no tree in the garden of God
   could match its beauty.
⁹I made it beautiful
   with abundant branches,
  the envy of all the trees of Eden
   in the garden of God.

THE FALL OF EGYPT AND THE FALL OF ASSYRIA (31:1-9). **31:1-9** This message has been dated June 21, 587 B.C. to the time of the final siege before the fall of Jerusalem.[116] Ezekiel prophesied against the king of Egypt. The Song of the Cedar in 17:1-24 was about the king of Assyria and recounted the pride and the fall of that nation (Prov 16:18). Depicting rulers as "trees" was a common literary device in the ancient Near East.[117] Similar use of "trees" for people in biblical passages may be seen as early as the Jotham story in Judg 9:7-21. Jotham compared his brother to other "trees" in a story that exposed Abimelech's weaknesses as a ruler. Daniel also used this device to characterize Nebuchadnezzar (Dan 4:10-37).

The poem of 31:1-9 has similarities to Isa 14:1-8, a portion of the prophecy against the king of Babylon, as well as to Daniel's poem about

---

[116] Zimmerli, *Ezekiel 2,* 148; the city was under siege at least three times from Jan. 15, 588 B.C. (24:1). The siege of June 21, 587 B.C. probably was the second, and the final stage of destruction came in early 586 B.C.

[117] See Hals, *Ezekiel,* 220; cf. Judg 9:7-21 and Dan 4:1-18.

Nebuchadnezzar (Dan 4:1-37).[118] This poem begins with recounting the fall of the king of Assyria, who is compared to a cedar of Lebanon. The cedars of Lebanon were known for their height and durability.[119] These trees grew taller than all other trees (vv. 3,5), a symbolic reference to Assyria's former position of world dominance. All the birds nested in the cedar (v. 6), a reference to the small nations that became dependant on Assyria. This "tree" was a model of beauty and majesty for all to see (v. 7). None of the cedars in the garden of God could rival it (v. 8). "Garden of God" is a reference to Eden (v. 9) but also represents the whole world order as initially created by God.[120] Assyria was the greatest nation in world history up to the point of its rise as a dominant world power. The point of the image of the tree in vv. 3-9 is to present the matchless splendor and power of Egypt.[121]

**10"'Therefore this is what the Sovereign LORD says: Because it towered on high, lifting its top above the thick foliage, and because it was proud of its height, 11I handed it over to the ruler of the nations, for him to deal with according to its wickedness. I cast it aside, 12and the most ruthless of foreign nations cut it down and left it. Its boughs fell on the mountains and in all the valleys; its branches lay broken in all the ravines of the land. All the nations of the earth came out from under its shade and left it. 13All the birds of the air settled on the fallen tree, and all the beasts of the field were among its branches. 14Therefore no other trees by the waters are ever to tower proudly on high, lifting their tops above the thick foliage. No other trees so well-watered are ever to reach such a height; they are all destined for death, for the earth below, among mortal men, with those who go down to the pit.**

**15"'This is what the Sovereign LORD says: On the day it was brought down to the grave I covered the deep springs with mourning for it; I held back its streams, and its abundant waters were restrained. Because of it I clothed Lebanon with gloom, and all the trees of the field withered away. 16I made the nations tremble at the sound of its fall when I brought it down to the grave with those who go down to the pit. Then all the trees of Eden, the choicest and best of Lebanon, all the trees that were well-watered, were consoled in the earth below. 17Those who lived in its shade, its allies among the nations, had also gone down to the grave with it, joining those killed by the sword.**

---

[118] Cooke (*Ezekiel,* 338) compares Isa 14:4-20; Ezek 31–32 with Dan 4 and concludes that Isaiah is the superior poetic form and most likely should be given priority.

[119] Alexander, "Ezekiel," 899; Zimmerli, *Ezekiel 2,* 149. The cedars of Lebanon were the tallest trees known in the ancient Near East.

[120] See Fisch, *Ezekiel,* 209.

[121] Alexander, "Ezekiel," 899.

<sup>18</sup>"'Which of the trees of Eden can be compared with you in splendor and majesty? Yet you, too, will be brought down with the trees of Eden to the earth below; you will lie among the uncircumcised, with those killed by the sword.

"'This is Pharaoh and all his hordes, declares the Sovereign LORD.'"

REASONS FOR THE FALL OF ASSYRIA AND EGYPT (31:10-18). **31:10-18** Precisely because of Assyria's pride and perversion of powers, God determined to bring judgment on it (vv. 10-11), the most ruthless nation in history. So God raised the most "ruthless," literally "brutal" (v. 12), nations against it, and it fell. All nations abandoned Assyria and left it to fall (vv. 12-13). No other trees would ever reach such height, but God would consign them all to the "pit" (v. 14).[122]

On the day Assyria went into the grave, God assisted its burial.[123] Nations trembled and mourned at the sound of its fall and descent into Sheol.[124] The allies went down with the "cedar," and all the nations were consoled (vv. 16-17).

All that was said to this point has laid the foundation for the conclusion in v. 18. If Assyria, with its splendor, power, and majesty, could not escape the judgment of God, neither would Egypt. The same fate that befell Assyria would befall Pharaoh, who would be Egypt's fallen "cedar" (v. 18).[125] The story of the cedar revisits several familiar themes that occurred in the prophecies against foreign nations. First, God hates pride because it leads people and nations to ruin (Ezek 27:3; 28:1-2; Prov 16:18). Second, the mighty fall as do the weak (cf. 27:27-36). When the mighty fall, it is also a loss for the weak and dependant. Third, the fall of the tree was a reminder of the mortality of human beings and individual accountability to God (cf. 3:16-21; 18:1-32).[126]

The pride and perversion of Egypt were its downfall. This example warns that the same characteristics will bring the downfall of any individual or nation. For Judah the message was equally devastating. If they had any hope that Egypt would save them from the hands of the Babylonians, Ezekiel had just pronounced that their "deliverer," that is, Pharaoh, would fall. Not only would Egypt be judged, but also Israel's last (false) hope had failed.[127]

---

[122] See 28:6-10 note on בּוֹר; see BDB, 92.

[123] Ibid., and Wevers, *Ezekiel*, 238.

[124] Fisch, *Ezekiel*, 212; see 32:17-26 and note on בּוֹר and שְׁאוֹל and cp. with 26:19-21.

[125] Enns, *Ezekiel*, 140.

[126] Craigie, *Ezekiel*, 225-26.

[127] See Allen, *Ezekiel 20–48*, 127.

## (6) *Lament for the Fall of Pharaoh (32:1-16)*

[1]In the twelfth year, in the twelfth month on the first day, the word of the
LORD came to me: [2]"Son of man, take up a lament concerning Pharaoh king
of Egypt and say to him:

"'You are like a lion among the nations;
  you are like a monster in the seas
 thrashing about in your streams,
  churning the water with your feet
  and muddying the streams.
[3]"'This is what the Sovereign LORD says:

"'With a great throng of people
  I will cast my net over you,
  and they will haul you up in my net.
[4]I will throw you on the land
  and hurl you on the open field.
 I will let all the birds of the air settle on you
  and all the beasts of the earth gorge themselves on you.
[5]I will spread your flesh on the mountains
  and fill the valleys with your remains.
[6]I will drench the land with your flowing blood
  all the way to the mountains,
  and the ravines will be filled with your flesh.
[7]When I snuff you out, I will cover the heavens
  and darken their stars;
 I will cover the sun with a cloud,
  and the moon will not give its light.
[8]All the shining lights in the heavens
  I will darken over you;
  I will bring darkness over your land,
   declares the Sovereign LORD.
[9]I will trouble the hearts of many peoples
  when I bring about your destruction among the nations,
  among lands you have not known.
[10]I will cause many peoples to be appalled at you,
  and their kings will shudder with horror because of you
  when I brandish my sword before them.
 On the day of your downfall
  each of them will tremble
  every moment for his life.
[11]"'For this is what the Sovereign LORD says:

"'The sword of the king of Babylon
  will come against you.
[12]I will cause your hordes to fall
  by the swords of mighty men—

the most ruthless of all nations.
They will shatter the pride of Egypt,
  and all her hordes will be overthrown.
[13]I will destroy all her cattle
  from beside abundant waters
no longer to be stirred by the foot of man
  or muddied by the hoofs of cattle.
[14]Then I will let her waters settle
  and make her streams flow like oil,
    declares the Sovereign LORD.
[15]When I make Egypt desolate
  and strip the land of everything in it,
when I strike down all who live there,
  then they will know that I am the LORD.'
[16]"This is the lament they will chant for her. The daughters of the nations
will chant it; for Egypt and all her hordes they will chant it, declares the Sovereign LORD."

The sixth message in the series of prophecies against Egypt characterizes Pharaoh as a sea monster and uses language similar to the earlier
message in chap. 29. This is another funeral dirge that has six parts: (1) an
introduction (vv. 1-2), (2) the description of the judgment of the sea monster (vv. 3-8), (3) the reaction of the nations (vv. 9-10), (4) the identity of
the "sword" of judgment (vv. 11-14), (5) a proof saying (v. 15), and (6) a
conclusion (v. 16).[128]

**32:1-8**   The message has been dated March 3, 585 B.C.[129] The lament
was a device Ezekiel employed several times through these prophetic
messages against the nations.[130] Egypt is compared to a lion among the
nations. This was a view Egypt had of itself. But the lion was really a sea
monster or crocodile, the same designation used in 29:3 to describe Pharaoh Hophra (vv. 1-2).[131]

Ezekiel announced the judgment of Pharaoh beginning with v. 3. God
said, "I will cast my net over you." This was not the snare of the fowler
but the dragnet of the seaman.[132] When caught in the net, the crocodile
would be dragged on dry land and left for the birds of prey (cf. 29:5) and
the beasts of the field (v. 4). The message meant that the people of Egypt

---

[128] See Wevers, *Ezekiel,* 239-40.

[129] See Zimmerli, *Ezekiel 2,* 158.

[130] Ezekiel used the קִינָה ("funeral dirge") more than any other OT writer (19:1,14;
27:2,32; 28:12; 32:2,16).

[131] See 29:1-6a note; Fisch, *Ezekiel,* 213.

[132] Zimmerli, *Ezekiel 2,* 159. Ezekiel used the term חֵרֶם ("dragnet" of the fisherman)
rather than מְצוֹדָה, which was the net of the hunter of fowl.

would meet a violent end in a foreign land. Their flesh and blood would fill the mountains and the valleys (vv. 5-6).

Pharaoh's judgment also would be part of the eschatological Day of the Lord. He would be snuffed out or extinguished like a shining star (vv. 7-8). On that Day of the Lord, Egypt, like all other nations, will be judged by God (Joel 2:10,31; 3:14; Isa 13:10; 34:4; Matt 24:29; Rev 6:12; 8:12).[133]

**32:9-16**   Egypt's destruction would bring distress among the nations who saw it. God would brandish his "sword," which was Babylon, and the nations would tremble (vv. 9-10).[134] So that there be no doubt that Babylon was the "sword" of the Lord, Ezekiel specifically made the identity clear in v. 11. The ruthless mighty men of Babylon would shatter the pride of Egypt (v. 12; cf. 30:6,18). The cattle also would be destroyed, and the water (v. 13) probably of the Nile would no longer be available.[135] With neither human nor animal to disturb the water, it would flow smoothly like oil (v. 14). Because of God's judgment on Egypt, they would know he is the true God. Then everyone would chant this funeral dirge (v. 16).

### (7) Pharaoh Condemned to the Pit (32:17-32)

[17]In the twelfth year, on the fifteenth day of the month, the word of the LORD came to me: [18]"Son of man, wail for the hordes of Egypt and consign to the earth below both her and the daughters of mighty nations, with those who go down to the pit. [19]Say to them, 'Are you more favored than others? Go down and be laid among the uncircumcised.' [20]They will fall among those killed by the sword. The sword is drawn; let her be dragged off with all her hordes. [21]From within the grave the mighty leaders will say of Egypt and her allies, 'They have come down and they lie with the uncircumcised, with those killed by the sword.'

[22]"Assyria is there with her whole army; she is surrounded by the graves of all her slain, all who have fallen by the sword. [23]Their graves are in the depths of the pit and her army lies around her grave. All who had spread terror in the land of the living are slain, fallen by the sword.

[24]"Elam is there, with all her hordes around her grave. All of them are slain, fallen by the sword. All who had spread terror in the land of the living went down uncircumcised to the earth below. They bear their shame with those who go down to the pit. [25]A bed is made for her among the slain, with all her hordes around her grave. All of them are uncircumcised, killed by the sword. Because their terror had spread in the land of the living, they bear

---

[133] Zimmerli, *Ezekiel 2,* 60, and Enns, *Ezekiel,* 141.

[134] Fisch, *Ezekiel,* 215.

[135] Ibid., 216. Fisch refers to the destruction of the canals for irrigation; cf. 31:12 note.

their shame with those who go down to the pit; they are laid among the slain. ²⁶"Meshech and Tubal are there, with all their hordes around their graves. All of them are uncircumcised, killed by the sword because they spread their terror in the land of the living. ²⁷Do they not lie with the other uncircumcised warriors who have fallen, who went down to the grave with their weapons of war, whose swords were placed under their heads? The punishment for their sins rested on their bones, though the terror of these warriors had stalked through the land of the living.

²⁸"You too, O Pharaoh, will be broken and will lie among the uncircumcised, with those killed by the sword.

²⁹"Edom is there, her kings and all her princes; despite their power, they are laid with those killed by the sword. They lie with the uncircumcised, with those who go down to the pit.

³⁰"All the princes of the north and all the Sidonians are there; they went down with the slain in disgrace despite the terror caused by their power. They lie uncircumcised with those killed by the sword and bear their shame with those who go down to the pit.

³¹"Pharaoh—he and all his army—will see them and he will be consoled for all his hordes that were killed by the sword, declares the Sovereign LORD. ³²Although I had him spread terror in the land of the living, Pharaoh and all his hordes will be laid among the uncircumcised, with those killed by the sword, declares the Sovereign LORD."

**32:17-25**   Ezekiel's final message against Egypt has been dated April 1, 585 B.C. (v. 17).[136] The message is a review of the demise of the past political powers with the conclusion that Egypt would join them (v. 18). This was not technically a funeral dirge but a wailing song. The poetic meter is different from the lament, but it is classified as a song of mourning as well.[137] The mourners were to bewail the descent of Egypt into the "pit," which represents the grave (v. 18).[138] Egypt would go into the grave and join the "uncircumcised" nations that represent all others who have suffered the judgment of God.[139] These nations would recognize Egypt's arrival as a fulfillment of God's judgment against those who "killed by the sword" (vv. 19-21).

Already in the "pit" to receive Egypt was Assyria, who had been over-

---

[136] See Zimmerli, *Ezekiel 2*, 171.

[137] Wevers (*Ezekiel*, 244) calls this the only example of a mourning song in the OT. Zimmerli (*Ezekiel 2*, 170) notes the use of a two plus two meter, which makes this a wailing song, not the three plus two meter of the funeral dirge קִינָה. He does not believe the distinction between the two types to be great.

[138] בּוֹר is again used as a synonym for שְׁאוֹל (see vv. 23-25,29-30). See also 26:19-21, note and Alexander, "Ezekiel," 903; Zimmerli, *Ezekiel 2*, 172.

[139] See Fisch, *Ezekiel*, 190.

thrown by the Babylonians (vv. 22-23), and Elam, located east of Babylon. Elam had its capital at Susa and was destroyed by Ashurbanipal ca. 650 B.C. Jeremiah still recognized Elam as a power to be destroyed, but for all practical purposes the nation was already dead (vv. 24-25).[140]

**32:26-32**   Another two groups, Meshech and Tubal, also were in the "pit." These two groups were older nations in Asia Minor (see 27:13) known for their terror and ruthlessness (v. 26). These mighty warriors who had "fallen" are an allusion to the mighty men of old described in Gen 6:4 as Nephilim.[141] Like these people and nations, Pharaoh also would descend into the "pit" as a result of divine judgment (v. 28).

Edom also was in the "pit" (v. 29). The appearance of Edom confirmed the earlier message of judgment in 25:12-14. With Edom were the "princes of the north" and Sidonians (v. 30). This is a reference to the Phoenician coastal towns of which Tyre and Sidon were the chief cities.[142] All the nations in the pit were those who had killed by the "sword," a reference to their cruelty (vv. 22-23,25-26,28-30). Pharaoh joined them because he, too, had "killed by the sword" (vv. 30-31). God therefore consigned him to the "pit" to dwell with the "uncircumcised" who killed ruthlessly and indiscriminately (v. 32).[143]

The oracles against the nations in Ezek 25–32 were originally delivered to the people of Judah. Although the words written seem to be solely for those particular nations, they are foremost for the people of Judah in Jerusalem and Babylon and serve at least three purposes. First, the oracles in Ezek 25–32 reveal God's judgment against the nations that either mocked or aided in Jerusalem's fall. Second, as with both the king of Tyre and the Pharaoh of Egypt, God would throw them down from their self-elevated positions of power—there is no room for such arrogance and pride in God's creation. Third, the oracles are essentially a dismantling of the gods of the nations, which is in turn a dismantling of the gods Judah had begun to rely wrongly upon, and the proclamation that Yahweh is the one and only true God for all nations. As mentioned in the introduction to this section, the phrase "know I am the LORD" occurs nineteen times. The primary purpose of these oracles is that everyone should come to "know the LORD."

---

[140] Wevers, *Ezekiel*, 247.

[141] "Nephilim" is a transliteration of נְפִלִים in Gen 6:4. גִּבּוֹרִים נֹפְלִים, "mighty men, Nephilim" were ancient warriors of renown who had fallen into the sinful life-style that made necessary the flood judgment; see Zimmerli, *Ezekiel 2*, 176.

[142] See Enns, *Ezekiel*, 145.

[143] See Fisch, *Ezekiel,* 190.

IV. PROPHECIES AND VISIONS OF THE RESTORATION
(33:1–48:35)
1. Prophetic Messages concerning the Restoration of Israel
(33:1–39:29)
(1) The Watchman and the Fall of Jerusalem (33:1-33)
(2) False Shepherds and the True Shepherd (34:1-31)
(3) Edom's Desolation and Israel's Repossession (35:1–36:15)
(4) Future Restoration of Fruitfulness in Israel (36:16-38)
(5) Restoration of National Life for Israel (37:1-28)
(6) God's Defense of Restored Israel (38:1–39:29)

## IV. PROPHECIES AND VISIONS OF THE RESTORATION (33:1–48:35)

Chapter 33 is a turning point in the Book of Ezekiel. After his initial commissioning in chaps. 1–3, Ezekiel delivered messages of judgment against Judah in chaps. 4–24, concluding with an announcement that the siege of Jerusalem had begun. Chapters 25–32 form a transition to the oracles of restoration that follow in chaps. 33–48 by announcing God's judgment against Israel's enemies. After echoing from chaps. 1–24 the themes of Ezekiel's role as watchman of Judah and of Judah's responsibility and opportunity to heed and repent and thus find life (33:1-20), the announcement was made that Jerusalem had fallen (v. 21). Yet the people of Israel were still unrepentant (vv. 22-33). Against the background of Israel's refusal to heed the watchman's warning and of the clear vindication of his message of judgment in the fall of Jerusalem, Ezekiel's ministry and messages turned to a theme of hope and restoration. Only two dated prophecies are in chaps. 33–48 (33:21; 40:1), both of which were written after the fall of Jerusalem.[1]

Israel and especially Judah had been victimized by the messages of false prophets (13:1–14:23), who had predicted an imminent return to peace and glory that never came. Out of the despair of the exile, Ezekiel had the opportunity to introduce the truth about the coming Messiah, who

---

[1] See R. M. Hals, *Ezekiel*, FOTL (Grand Rapids: Eerdmans, 1989), 230. See the chart "Dated Prophecies in Ezekiel," p. 54.

would be a servant-shepherd and set up a glorious new kingdom.[2]

Chapters 33–39 comprise words of restoration and hope, and chaps. 40–48 present details of the restored community. False shepherds are condemned in chap. 34, and the true Shepherd is presented as the purveyor of the coming restored kingdom.

Edom receives special mention in a judgment message in chap. 35, which is an expanded sequel to the brief message against Edom in the prophecies against the nations (25:12-14). The appearance of this message in the restoration section reflects the continued animosity of these kinsmen of the Hebrews who had helped Nebuchadnezzar in his destruction of Jerusalem. Also, the Edomites occupied the southern borders of Israel after the fall of the nation, settling the entire Negev. Any hope of reclaiming all the land had to include a plan for the expulsion of the Edomites.[3]

The return to "Edom" is its representative value for the enemies of Israel—its demise is necessary for the security Israel will enjoy and the blessings promised. Malachi 1:1-5 makes this clear, and Amos 9:11-15 shows how eventually "Edom" (humankind) will come into the sacrifice orbit of Israel's future kingdom.

Chapter 36 introduces an account of the cleansing and restoration of Israel, which climaxes in its resurrection from the dead in chap. 37. The section climaxes with an apocalyptic judgment message upon the enemies of Israel, Gog and Magog, who oppose the resurrection and restoration of the Hebrew nation.

## 1. Prophetic Messages concerning the Restoration of Israel (33:1–39:29)

These messages outline God's program of restoration for his people. The God who had been faithful in judgment would also be faithful in redemption.

### (1) The Watchman and the Fall of Jerusalem (33:1-33)

Chapter 33 can be divided into three sections: (1) warning to heed the watchman (vv. 1-9), (2) exhortation to turn from evil (vv. 10-20), (3) and Jerusalem's fall and Israel's failure to heed (vv. 21-33). This message also summarized the principles of the new kingdom: (1) God desired that all

---

[2] P. P. Enns, *Ezekiel* (Grand Rapids: Zondervan, 1986), 149.
[3] J. W. Wevers, *Ezekiel,* NCB (Grand Rapids: Eerdmans, 1969), 264-65.

people should live (v. 11); (2) the new kingdom would be populated by those who enter by choice as individuals (v. 12); (3) the conditions for entering the kingdom were repentance and faith (vv. 14-16); (4) individuals are free to chose repentance or continue their evil lives (vv. 17-20).[4]

**[1]The word of the LORD came to me: [2]"Son of man, speak to your countrymen and say to them: 'When I bring the sword against a land, and the people of the land choose one of their men and make him their watchman, [3]and he sees the sword coming against the land and blows the trumpet to warn the people, [4]then if anyone hears the trumpet but does not take warning and the sword comes and takes his life, his blood will be on his own head. [5]Since he heard the sound of the trumpet but did not take warning, his blood will be on his own head. If he had taken warning, he would have saved himself. [6]But if the watchman sees the sword coming and does not blow the trumpet to warn the people and the sword comes and takes the life of one of them, that man will be taken away because of his sin, but I will hold the watchman accountable for his blood.'**

**[7]"Son of man, I have made you a watchman for the house of Israel; so hear the word I speak and give them warning from me. [8]When I say to the wicked, 'O wicked man, you will surely die,' and you do not speak out to dissuade him from his ways, that wicked man will die for his sin, and I will hold you accountable for his blood. [9]But if you do warn the wicked man to turn from his ways and he does not do so, he will die for his sin, but you will have saved yourself.**

WARNING TO HEED THE WATCHMAN (33:1-9).   **33:1-9**   This message parallels 3:16-21, where Ezekiel first was appointed watchman over Israel (3:17; 33:7).[5] It rehearses the principle of the watchman in vv. 1-6 and identifies Ezekiel as Israel's watchman in vv. 7-9. The purpose of returning to this theme was to show that Ezekiel had been faithful to his assignment and to place the responsibility upon Israel to heed his warning. The purpose of the message in the structure of the book is to reintroduce the theme of the prophet calling God's people to repentance in the context of the watchman's warning coming true (v. 21). The death of those who hear the watchman's alarm but refuse to listen is their own fault. A watchman was guiltless if the alarm was sounded but no one responded, but he was guilty of the blood of those who perished if an attack came and the

[4] A. B. Davidson, *The Book of the Prophet Ezekiel* (Cambridge: Cambridge University Press, 1892), 239. Ezekiel is the medium through whom the principles of the kingdom and its implementation are enunciated.

[5] See note on Ezek 3:16-21. Zimmerli (*Ezekiel 2,* 185) sees this as an "oracle of appointment," a divine message of ordination.

people were not warned (vv. 5-6).[6]

Cities were constructed with towers on the walls where watchmen kept their vigil (Isa 21:5). The "trumpet" (v. 3) was a *shofar,* or ram's horn, that was used to sound the warning of an approaching enemy. This horn was used for both military and religious purposes (Josh 6:4; 2 Sam 2:28; Ps 81:3; Joel 8:15; Amos 3:6; Hos 5:8; Jer 4:19).[7] Ezekiel was a divinely called servant whose "trumpet" was his messages for Judah and Jerusalem (chaps. 1–24), sounding the alarm to warn of impending judgment.

Ezekiel's "alarming" messages were divinely imparted (v. 7)[8] and specifically directed to the people of Judah. As a watchman Ezekiel did not use his own powers of observation but was the channel of divine warning. God explained that when the prophet delivered the messages he fulfilled his responsibility as a watchman whether or not the people heard or responded (v. 9; cf. 2:7; 3:4-11).

Warning others of the consequences of judgment inherent in sin is never a popular assignment. Believers have a duty to be "watchmen" who warn those who are in the world and are without God of the destructive nature of sin and its final irrevocable result—death and hell (33:1-33). Our responsibility is to warn and proclaim as persuasively as possible, but how the message is received is beyond our control.

[10]"Son of man, say to the house of Israel, 'This is what you are saying: "Our offenses and sins weigh us down, and we are wasting away because of them. How then can we live?"' [11]Say to them, 'As surely as I live, declares the Sovereign LORD, I take no pleasure in the death of the wicked, but rather that they turn from their ways and live. Turn! Turn from your evil ways! Why will you die, O house of Israel?'

[12]"Therefore, son of man, say to your countrymen, 'The righteousness of the righteous man will not save him when he disobeys, and the wickedness of the wicked man will not cause him to fall when he turns from it. The righteous man, if he sins, will not be allowed to live because of his former righteousness.' [13]If I tell the righteous man that he will surely live, but then he trusts in his righteousness and does evil, none of the righteous things he has done will be remembered; he will die for the evil he has done. [14]And if I say to the wicked man, 'You will surely die,' but he then turns away from his sin and does what is just and right— [15]if he gives back what he took in pledge for a loan, returns what he has stolen, follows the decrees that give life, and does no evil, he will surely live; he will not die. [16]None of the sins he has committed

---

[6] W. Zimmerli, *Ezekiel 2,* Her (Philadelphia: Fortress, 1983), 184-85.

[7] J. B. Taylor, *Ezekiel,* TOTC (Downers Grove: InterVarsity, 1969), 214.

[8] Cf. Wevers, *Ezekiel,* 251.

will be remembered against him. He has done what is just and right; he will
surely live.

[17]"Yet your countrymen say, 'The way of the Lord is not just.' But it is
their way that is not just. [18]If a righteous man turns from his righteousness
and does evil, he will die for it. [19]And if a wicked man turns away from his
wickedness and does what is just and right, he will live by doing so. [20]Yet, O
house of Israel, you say, 'The way of the Lord is not just.' But I will judge
each of you according to his own ways."

EXHORTATION TO TURN FROM EVIL (33:10-20). **33:10-11**  Verse 10
begins with an emphatic, "You, Son of Man, say to the house of Israel."
These verses bear a close resemblance to 18:21-32, focusing on the responsibility of those who hear the messages of the watchman. Their structure is the reverse of vv. 1-9. There the principle of the watchman is
followed by an exhortation. Here an exhortation is followed by the principle of individual responsibility. The people said: "Our offenses and sins
weigh us down, and we are wasting away because of them. How can we
live?" (v. 10). God's answer was that individuals have the opportunity to
repent and are commanded to do so. "Turn! Turn from your evil ways!"
(v. 11). This was a call to repent so they could be healed and restored.[9]
God took no pleasure in the death of the wicked, so he was always careful
to warn of judgment and to call for repentance (cf. 18:23,32).

**33:12-16**  As in Ezekiel's earlier message of individual responsibility
in chap. 18, he included some examples to illustrate this theme. People
who do wicked things are responsible for their actions, but the wicked
who repent will be forgiven. The statement at the end of v. 16 affirms
God's openness to all who repent. They will be accepted because by re-
penting they (even the wicked) have "done what is just and right" and
"will surely live" (v. 16).[10]

**33:17-20**  As in 18:25-29, the prophet discussed the charge that God
was not just in his dealings with Judah (vv. 17-20). He reaffirmed the
justice of God and noted that he judges all on their "own ways" or mer-
its (v. 20). No attempt should be made to understand this passage without also consulting Ezekiel's earlier message in 18:1-32. God is a
champion of justice. Justice demands that he eradicate sin and reestablish universal righteousness (33:10-20). Those who repent and turn to
him by faith will be spared (John 3:16-18).

---

[9] The imperative is from שׁוּב ("to turn"), the OT word for repentance. The word presents
the idea of the change in direction in one's life that results from true repentance; see 14:6-
11; 18:21-24 note and Criswell, *Expository Sermons,* 172-73.

[10] See introduction to 18:1-32 and discussion at 18:5-24; see also Taylor, *Ezekiel,* 215.

²¹In the twelfth year of our exile, in the tenth month on the fifth day, a man who had escaped from Jerusalem came to me and said, "The city has fallen!" ²²Now the evening before the man arrived, the hand of the LORD was upon me, and he opened my mouth before the man came to me in the morning. So my mouth was opened and I was no longer silent.

²³Then the word of the LORD came to me: ²⁴"Son of man, the people living in those ruins in the land of Israel are saying, 'Abraham was only one man, yet he possessed the land. But we are many; surely the land has been given to us as our possession.' ²⁵Therefore say to them, 'This is what the Sovereign Lord says: Since you eat meat with the blood still in it and look to your idols and shed blood, should you then possess the land? ²⁶You rely on your sword, you do detestable things, and each of you defiles his neighbor's wife. Should you then possess the land?'

²⁷"Say this to them: 'This is what the Sovereign LORD says: As surely as I live, those who are left in the ruins will fall by the sword, those out in the country I will give to the wild animals to be devoured, and those in strongholds and caves will die of a plague. ²⁸I will make the land a desolate waste, and her proud strength will come to an end, and the mountains of Israel will become desolate so that no one will cross them. ²⁹Then they will know that I am the Lord, when I have made the land a desolate waste because of all the detestable things they have done.'

³⁰"As for you, son of man, your countrymen are talking together about you by the walls and at the doors of the houses, saying to each other, 'Come and hear the message that has come from the LORD.' ³¹My people come to you, as they usually do, and sit before you to listen to your words, but they do not put them into practice. With their mouths they express devotion, but their hearts are greedy for unjust gain. ³²Indeed, to them you are nothing more than one who sings love songs with a beautiful voice and plays an instrument well, for they hear your words but do not put them into practice.

³³"When all this comes true—and it surely will—then they will know that a prophet has been among them."

JERUSALEM'S FALL AND ISRAEL'S FAILURE TO HEED (33:21-33). **33:21-22** On January 8, 585 B.C., an eyewitness arrived with the news of Jerusalem's fall (vv. 21-22). The date was eighteen months after the destruction of the city. There was no explanation why it would have taken so long for word to reach Babylon. The time lag seems unrealistic since actual travel time from Jerusalem to Babylon would have been about four or five months.[11] One suggestion is that the "twelfth" year

---

[11] The descriptions of Ezra's journey to Jerusalem ca. 458 B.C. give the time of the trip as approximately five months (Ezra 7:6-9). D. Stuart (*Ezekiel*, 315) suggests that "a refugee who had waited in hiding, then dodged Babylonian troops, taking the back roads and relying on his wits," would have taken longer.

should read "eleventh." There is only one consonant difference in the Hebrew words for eleven and twelve, and it may have been a minor copyist's
error. The original reading may have been "eleventh" year, in which case
the elapsed travel time would have been about six months, which was
normal.[12]

A second suggestion is that Ezekiel reckoned by the Babylonian calendar, which began the year in the spring, whereas Jeremiah (Jer 39:2; 52:6-
7,12) and Kings (2 Kgs 25:1) followed the Hebrew calendar, which began
the year in the fall. Adjusting the difference would result in a time lapse
of a more realistic five or six months. This second explanation is the more
probable.[13]

**33:23-29** At last the prophet was vindicated as his messages of doom
proved true. He might have expected the repentance of those left in Judah
and obedient hearts among his fellow exiles. If so, the Lord warned him,
he would be disappointed. Those left among the ruins responded with un-
deserved pride (vv. 23-26). "Abraham was only one man. . . . But we are
many" (v. 24) reflects the arrogance that kept the people from true repentance even in the face of total destruction. God reminded them that they
still sacrificed to idols, ate meat with the blood (Lev 19:26), and committed acts of violence and sexual immorality (cf. Acts 15:29), actions detri-
mental to the restoration, rather than submitting to the standards of God's
word (vv. 25-26).[14]

These refugees among the ruins thought they had escaped judgment
because they were left in the land. But God promised that they too would
be visited by the sword, wild beasts, and plague, familiar instruments of
judgment (vv. 27-28).[15] The land would be devastated, and no one would
cross it again. Everyone would know from this judgment that the Lord is
God (v. 29). If people do not seek to "know" God through repentance and
faith, they will ultimately "know" him in judgment (v. 29; Rev 6:13-17).

**33:30-33** Although the response of Ezekiel's fellow exiles was more

---

[12] Compare עַשְׁתֵּי שְׁתֵּי עֶשְׂרֵה ("twelfth") with עַשְׁתֵּי עֶשְׂרֵה. There is some manuscript support for this change, e.g., the LXX (Lucian Recension) and the Syriac. See Taylor, *Ezekiel,*
216; Zimmerli, *Ezekiel 2,* 191-92. This would mean Ezekiel delivered the prophecies of
chaps. 33–39 before those of chap. 32.

[13] Wevers, *Ezekiel,* 179; Cooke, *Ezekiel,* 366; Fisch, *Ezekiel,* 225. Another explanation,
favored by many, is that Jerusalem fell in the summer of 586 rather than 587. See Alexander,
"Ezekiel," 741, 910; A. Malamat, "The Last Kings of Judah and the Fall of Jerusalem," *IEJ*
18 (1968): 137-56.

[14] Fisch, *Ezekiel,* 226; Zimmerli, *Ezekiel 2,* 199. The levitical laws prohibit idolatry and
bloodshed for which the Canaanites were expelled from the land (see Lev 18:24).

[15] See discussion of 5:1-2; 6:11; 7:15; 14:12; Zimmerli, *Ezekiel 2,* 199.

encouraging, making him a celebrity, the Lord informed him that his popularity among the people was superficial. They listened to him out of curiosity but had no intention of changing their way of life. They found his words entertaining, but they neglected to put the principles into practice (vv. 30-32).[16]

God was not through, however, making himself known to his people. There was much yet to be revealed in word and in deed. Since Jerusalem had already fallen, "when all this comes true" may refer to the further prophecies Ezekiel was about to proclaim (v. 33). God's closing words to Ezekiel in chap. 33 are similar to those given him in his call in 2:5. Whether or not the people would hear and respond, Ezekiel was to continue proclaiming God's word. By his faithful ministry they would know that a "prophet had been among them." Faithfulness to God by believers often means that the unbelieving world will not take them seriously (v. 32). But faithfulness will one day be vindicated by God (v. 33; cf. Gal 6:9).

### (2) False Shepherds and the True Shepherd (34:1-31)

Chapter 34 is a sequel to chap. 22. Both passages present the sins of the nation and the failure of its leaders. Instead of the figures of dross (22:17-22) and the lion (22:25) or wolf (22:27) and its prey, here Ezekiel employed the metaphor of a flock and its selfish and corrupt shepherds. Similarities also can be found with the indictment of the false prophets and prophetesses in 13:1–14:11. One problem of restoration was determining what should be done about the corrupt leaders who led the nation to ruin. Chapter 34 addresses this question. Kings and leaders often were called "shepherds" in the ancient Near East (see Isa 44:28; Jer 2:8; 10:21; 23:1-6; 25:34-38; Mic 5:4-5; Zech 11:4-17).[17] These "shepherds" were more than military-political leaders. They bore a primary responsibility for the moral and spiritual direction of the nation.

The dynamic link between these leaders and the future hope of restoration is reflected in these messages. The false shepherds' failure on the one hand was presented in contrast to the hope of the coming ideal Shepherd, the Lord. Chapters 34 and 36 abound in references to restoration hope under the leadership of this ideal future King. Because of God's determination to redeem Israel and Judah, the people will return to the land (34:13-

---

[16] Taylor, *Ezekiel*, 218. Religious meetings were popular. People attended, listened, and said good things; but their actions revealed their true priorities (cf. Acts 8:18-28).

[17] See Taylor, *Ezekiel*, 219; Hals, *Ezekiel*, 250-54; W. H. Brownlee, "Ezekiel's Poetic Indictment of the Shepherds," *HTR* 51 (1958): 191-203.

16; 36:1-12,24,35; 37:11-14,21); in the land they will be cleansed and converted (36:25-27), reunified as one nation (37:11,15-23), ruled by the Messiah (34:11-16,23-24; 37:24-28), victorious over enemies (34:27; 36:7,12; 38:17-23; 39:1-6), and will achieve lasting peace and security.[18]

Chapter 34 comprises figurative messages to the leaders of Israel as shepherds (vv. 1-16) and to the people as sheep (vv. 17-24), followed by a literal message to the people (vv. 25-31). The figurative message to the shepherds consists of condemnation and the announcement of their removal (vv. 1-10), then the Lord's announcement that as owner of the flock he would take over as shepherd (vv. 11-16). In the figurative message to the flock, God announced his determination to judge and to deliver (vv. 17-24). The final message to the people is a promise to provide them with a "covenant of peace" (vv. 25-31).

[1]The word of the LORD came to me: [2]"Son of man, prophesy against the shepherds of Israel; prophesy and say to them: 'This is what the Sovereign LORD says: Woe to the shepherds of Israel who only take care of themselves! Should not shepherds take care of the flock? [3]You eat the curds, clothe yourselves with the wool and slaughter the choice animals, but you do not take care of the flock. [4]You have not strengthened the weak or healed the sick or bound up the injured. You have not brought back the strays or searched for the lost. You have ruled them harshly and brutally. [5]So they were scattered because there was no shepherd, and when they were scattered they became food for all the wild animals. [6]My sheep wandered over all the mountains and on every high hill. They were scattered over the whole earth, and no one searched or looked for them.

[7]"'Therefore, you shepherds, hear the word of the LORD: [8]As surely as I live, declares the Sovereign LORD, because my flock lacks a shepherd and so has been plundered and has become food for all the wild animals, and because my shepherds did not search for my flock but cared for themselves rather than for my flock, [9]therefore, O shepherds, hear the word of the LORD: [10]This is what the Sovereign LORD says: I am against the shepherds and will hold them accountable for my flock. I will remove them from tending the flock so that the shepherds can no longer feed themselves. I will rescue my flock from their mouths, and it will no longer be food for them.

CONDEMNATION OF CORRUPT SHEPHERDS (34:1-10). **34:1-6** Ezekiel was commanded to prophesy against the "shepherds" of Israel (v. 1). Any examination of the history of the Northern Kingdom beginning with Jeroboam I (1 Kgs 12:25-33) will reveal the apostasy of the leadership that

---

[18] See Enns, *Ezekiel*, 152.

proved to be Israel's ruin. Jeroboam immediately introduced idolatry by erecting two golden calves at Dan and Bethel. From this spiritual low point Israel descended even further into the depths of sin and immorality until the nation was destroyed in 722 B.C. (2 Kgs 17:5-7). Ezekiel already emphasized that Judah did not learn from the judgment that befell her harlotrous sister Israel (23:1-49). After Josiah the last kings of Judah were all corrupt. They led the nation to spiritual and political ruin. A prophetic preview of the monarchy's effects on the life of the nation found in 1 Sam 8:11-18 was a sobering prediction of these events.[19]

The indictment against these shepherds is in vv. 1-6. First, they did not seek to meet the needs of the people but only used the people for their own selfish ends (vv. 2-3). Second, they did not take special care of those in need, the helpless members of society. Rather, they met weakness and injury with callous cruelty (v. 4). For lack of positive moral or spiritual leadership the people wandered from the Lord and became a prey to idolatry and immorality (vv. 5-6).

**34:7-10** For their irresponsible and selfish lack of leadership the Lord counted them guilty of violating his trust and announced their removal. The Lord himself would come to the aid of his flock and rescue them out of the mouths of their corrupt leaders (cf. Matt 20:25-28).

**11**"'For this is what the Sovereign LORD says: I myself will search for my sheep and look after them. **12**As a shepherd looks after his scattered flock when he is with them, so will I look after my sheep. I will rescue them from all the places where they were scattered on a day of clouds and darkness. **13**I will bring them out from the nations and gather them from the countries, and I will bring them into their own land. I will pasture them on the mountains of Israel, in the ravines and in all the settlements in the land. **14**I will tend them in a good pasture, and the mountain heights of Israel will be their grazing land. There they will lie down in good grazing land, and there they will feed in a rich pasture on the mountains of Israel. **15**I myself will tend my sheep and have them lie down, declares the Sovereign LORD. **16**I will search for the lost and bring back the strays. I will bind up the injured and strengthen the weak, but the sleek and the strong I will destroy. I will shepherd the flock with justice.

ANNOUNCEMENT OF THE LORD AS SHEPHERD (34:11-16). **34:11-16** Ezekiel contrasted the exploitation of the corrupt shepherds with the diligent care he himself would exercise on behalf of his flock. The role of Yahweh as a shepherd was a familiar one in the Old Testament. The title

---

[19] See Introduction, "Historical Background."

"shepherd" was one of the oldest designations used for God and appeared in Gen 49:24. Perhaps the best known example of his shepherd image was that presented by David in Ps 23.[20] David provided insight not only into God's role as "Shepherd" but also into the responsibility of kings to be rightly related to God. The king was to be the undershepherd and God the true King and Shepherd. Psalm 23 was David's personal commitment to this principle. "The LORD is my shepherd" (Ps 23:1) was a personal declaration that he, David the king, had a King/Shepherd, who was Yahweh.

Ezekiel 34:11-16 abounds in first person promises. God repeatedly promised, "I will" go after them, and "I will" meet the needs of my people. While there is some overlap and repetition, there are twenty-five such promises in this and the following paragraphs of the chapter. These promises include elements of judgment as well as deliverance. Yahweh promised to hold the shepherds accountable for the sheep, remove them from tending the flock, rescue his flock from their mouths, search for and look after his sheep, look after and gather them, rescue them from clouds and darkness, and gather them from among the nations. He would bring them to their own land, place them on the mountains of Israel, tend the flock in good pasture so that they could lie down in safety, search out the lost and the strayed of the flock, bind up the injured, and destroy the strong who oppose the flock. In addition he would shepherd the flock with justice, judge between one sheep and another, judge between the fat and the lean sheep, save the flock, place over them one shepherd, be their God, make a covenant of peace with them, bless them, send showers in season, and provide for them (vv. 10-29).

No longer would any human figure mediate between God and his people. Only God and his Messiah (v. 23) would be the "Shepherd" of his people. This message of hope is a glaring contrast with the picture in 34:1-15 with its message of the neglect and exploitation of human kings.[21] The proliferation of "I wills" in 34:10-29 suggests Yahweh's determination personally to be involved in the lives and destinies of his people.

---

**17**"'As for you, my flock, this is what the Sovereign LORD says: I will judge between one sheep and another, and between rams and goats. **18**Is it not enough for you to feed on the good pasture? Must you also trample the rest of your pasture with your feet? Is it not enough for you to drink clear water? Must you also muddy the rest with your feet? **19**Must my flock feed on what you have trampled and drink what you have muddied with your feet?

---

[20] P. C. Craigie, *Ezekiel* (Philadelphia: Westminster, 1983), 243.

[21] Zimmerli, *Ezekiel 2*, 216; cf. also Jer 23:1-6.

<sup>20</sup>"'Therefore this is what the Sovereign LORD says to them: See, I myself will judge between the fat sheep and the lean sheep. <sup>21</sup>Because you shove with flank and shoulder, butting all the weak sheep with your horns until you have driven them away, <sup>22</sup>I will save my flock, and they will no longer be plundered. I will judge between one sheep and another. <sup>23</sup>I will place over them one shepherd, my servant David, and he will tend them; he will tend them and be their shepherd. <sup>24</sup>I the LORD will be their God, and my servant David will be prince among them. I the LORD have spoken.

DETERMINATION TO JUDGE AND DELIVER (34:17-24). **34:17-22** Here the Lord ceased addressing the corrupt shepherds and began speaking to his flock. Not only would he rescue and tend, but the coming divine Shepherd also would be a righteous judge. Former "shepherds" allowed and even participated in the oppression of the weak of the flock (vv. 17-19). The Lord would oppose those who were "greedy for unjust gain" (33:31) and who took advantage of the weak. Like a shepherd who must judge between sheep to be bred or sold or butchered, the Lord will judge between people who need his care and those who deserve his judgment. Yahweh has promised to be a righteous judge who would "save" his flock and distinguish between those who were truly his and those who were not (v. 22; cf. Rom 2:28-29; 9:6-8).<sup>22</sup>

**34:23-24** These verses are transitional to the final section on the covenant of peace (vv. 25-31). They are clearly unified by the repetition of "my servant David" in both verses and by the parallelism between the last clause of v. 23 and the first clause of v. 24 (literally): "And he will be to them for a shepherd / and I Yahweh will be to them for a God." Nevertheless, v. 23 continues the figure of shepherd/flock, whereas v. 24 abandons it for the literal "prince/people" in anticipation of the literal message in vv. 25-31 (which reverts to the figure in v. 31).

The coming Shepherd will be known as "my servant David" (v. 23; see 37:22-26 for a parallel passage). He was one from the line of David who was a fulfillment of the promise made in the Davidic covenant in 2 Sam 7:16. He will establish an everlasting throne of David. The use of "my servant David" represents the hope of a future resurrection of the golden age of Israel. David was characterized as a man after God's own heart (1 Sam 13:14).<sup>23</sup> Unlike the corrupt former Davidic rulers who only served themselves, this new king will be a servant of the Lord (cf. Matt 4:10;

---

<sup>22</sup> The use of the term מוֹשִׁיעַ from יָשַׁע ("to save" or "to deliver") suggests God's intention to deliver the weak and oppressed; see Zimmerli, *Ezekiel 2*, 218.

<sup>23</sup> See Wevers, *Ezekiel*, 262; Taylor, *Ezekiel*, 223; J. L. McKenzie, "Royal Messianism," *CBQ* XIX, 1 (1957): 25-52.

6:24; 12:18; 20:28; Luke 1:69; Acts 3:13,26; 4:25-30). He will also be God's personal representative, who will reconfirm the Davidic covenant of 2 Sam 7:12-16. He will tend the Lord's flock, be Yahweh's shepherd (Ezek 34:23) and a prince among them (34:24).

**[25]"'I will make a covenant of peace with them and rid the land of wild beasts so that they may live in the desert and sleep in the forests in safety. [26]I will bless them and the places surrounding my hill. I will send down showers in season; there will be showers of blessing. [27]The trees of the field will yield their fruit and the ground will yield its crops; the people will be secure in their land. They will know that I am the LORD, when I break the bars of their yoke and rescue them from the hands of those who enslaved them. [28]They will no longer be plundered by the nations, nor will wild animals devour them. They will live in safety, and no one will make them afraid. [29]I will provide for them a land renowned for its crops, and they will no longer be victims of famine in the land or bear the scorn of the nations. [30]Then they will know that I, the Lord their God, am with them and that they, the house of Israel, are my people, declares the Sovereign LORD. [31]You my sheep, the sheep of my pasture, are people, and I am your God, declares the Sovereign LORD.'"**

PROMISE OF A COVENANT OF PEACE (34:25-31). **34:25-31** Ezekiel concluded this series of messages with the Lord's promise of a "covenant of peace" with his people (v. 25), referring to what Jeremiah called the "new covenant" (Jer 31:31). The designation here indicates that this new covenant relationship will provide his people with peace (cf. Num 25:12; Josh 9:15; 10:1; Pss 29:11; 85:8; Isa 54:10). It was peace and rest which humanity lost through sin (Gen 3:15; 4:8) and which the Mosaic covenant promised as a result of obedience (Lev 26:6). But in spite of Israel's disobedience, the prophets envisioned a coming restoration of peace and all the other characteristics of life before the fall (Isa 9:6-7; 52:7 53:5; 66:12; Jer 30:10; 33:6,9; Hag 2:9). This will come to pass in the Messianic Age with the restoration of the ideals of life as it was lived in Eden (see "Restoration of Edenic Ideals," p. 349).

This covenant is the same as the one promised in Ezek 16:60 (see discussion of 16:53-63), which will establish an unbreakable bond between God and his people. By it he will assure their well-being and personally act as covenant mediator (v. 25).[24]

"I will bless them" (v. 26) begins a list of the benefits of the "covenant

---

[24] Zimmerli, *Ezekiel 2*, 220. The covenant of peace was to be permanent (cf. 34:25; 37:26; Isa 54:10).

of peace." There will be showers at the right season (v. 27a) that produce bountiful crops. The people will dwell in security and freedom (v. 27b-28). There will be no famine or threats from enemies (v. 29). The people will know that God, their Shepherd, is with them and that Israel his flock is his people (v. 30).

This covenant anticipates events and promises never realized in the first return of Israel from captivity. When the people came back to the land after 535 B.C., they were under the control of every world-dominating power including Medo-Persia, Greece, and finally Rome until A.D. 70 when the nation was destroyed by Rome.

There are only two possible conclusions concerning the meaning of the "covenant of peace" and the promises of Ezek 34:23-31. Either the restoration Ezekiel envisioned was only an unrealistic hope and therefore never came to pass or the prophecy concerned some future return beyond the scope of the return in 535 B.C. under Zerubbabel and later returns under Ezra and Nehemiah. Even the author of Ezra-Nehemiah recognized that the restoration community was not the final fulfillment of Old Testament promises of redemption (see comments on 11:17-21). Yet God's promises themselves and the incomplete fulfillments that God's people have experienced gave the people of Ezekiel's and later times renewed strength and courage to face daily trials, knowing that God is faithful and will bring it to pass (Pss 31:24; 37:9; 42:11; Isa 40:31; Lam 3:19-40; 2 Cor 3:12; Col 1:5; 1 Thess 1:3; 4:13; 5:8; Heb 6:19; 1 John 3:3).

The four remaining messages in chaps. 35–39 expanded the promises of the covenant of peace in 34:11-16. The message against Edom (35:1-15) expanded the promise of security and victory over plundering in 34:27-28. The cleansing and restoration of the land in 36:1–37:14 was an expansion of the promise to return to the Israelites' own land in 34:13,26. The message of the resurrection of the nation and the reunification under one shepherd in 37:1-28 was an expansion of the "one shepherd" promise of 34:20-24. The defeat of Israel's enemies in 38:1–39:29 was an expansion of the promise of peace and security in 34:25-31.[25]

The central figure of chap. 34 is God's ideal Shepherd-King, who was the antithesis of the corrupt leadership that resulted in the exile. Eight character traits about this promised future King may be gleaned from 34:11-31. These characteristics were fulfilled in the life and ministry of Jesus as recorded in the Gospels. But their significance was not exhausted by analogies with his first earthly ministry. They also characterize his future earthly and heavenly ministries.

---

[25] Alexander, "Ezekiel," 914.

First, he has a special relationship with Yahweh. In vv. 11-16 the shepherd is God (34:16), but in vv. 23 and 24 the shepherd is "my servant David." The use of the personal pronouns "I" more than thirty times and "my" more than fifteen times suggests that this shepherd would be God in a personal form. The same phenomenon may be found in the good Shepherd passage in John's Gospel in which Jesus said, "I and the Father are one" (John 10:30; cf. 1 Tim 2:5).

Second, he will feed his sheep (34:13,26-27,29). Like the shepherd of Ps 23:1, his sheep will not "want." Jesus is the Bread of life (John 6:31-35) and the Water of life (John 4), satisfying the needs of his "sheep."

Third, he will gather his sheep together (34:12-13). No longer were they to be a scattered flock. In the New Testament the church was unified through Christ (Matt 12:30; Eph 4:3-7). Ezekiel envisioned the day when the Messiah would gather all his sheep in a wonderful union (see Matt 13:30-31).

Fourth, he will reestablish his people peacefully in their land (34:14-15). This echoes Ps 23, which tells of the shepherd's care for his flock. Under his rule the flock has no want (23:1), no worry (23:2), no weakness (23:3), no wickedness (23:4), no death (23:4), no fear (23:4), no defeat (23:5), no deficit (23:5), no judgment (23:6), and no end (23:6), all qualities that promote peace and security (see John 1:1-42; 14:27).

Fifth, he will rule with justice and compassion (Ezek 34:16). Jesus began his public ministry by claiming the role of the servant of the Lord: "The Spirit of the LORD is upon me, because the LORD has anointed me to preach good news to the poor. He has sent me to bind up the brokenhearted, to proclaim freedom for the captives and release from the darkness for the prisoners" (Isa 61:1-2; cp. Luke 4:16-21). Justice and compassion also will characterize his reign in the latter days (Rev 20:4).

Sixth, he will personally judge his people (34:17,20,22). Unlike the ruthless kings of Israel and Judah, he will judge with equity and righteousness. Jesus was presented as a righteous judge of his people who rendered to each a just reward (Rom 14:10-12; 2 Cor 5:10-11; 1 Cor 3:11-15).

Seventh, he will be the only true shepherd (34:23). There will be no rivals to his ministry. Jesus was and is *the* way, *the* truth, and *the* life (John 10:9,11-12,14; 14:6; Acts 4:12).

Eighth, he will mediate a covenant of peace (Ezek 34:25). When people enter a covenant of peace with the Shepherd, they also make peace with God (John 10:27-28). This covenant of peace is an everlasting covenant (Ezek 16:60; Isa 54:10; John 10:29).

Perhaps this is another one of those passages that Ellison had in mind when he said that the prophets often spoke more than they knew.[26] We can see much more in this passage than Ezekiel was privileged to see. He only saw the promises as a future hope of redemption to be realized. On the other hand, we can see them both in their historical setting and in their fulfillment in Christ. Ezekiel 34:1-31 is closely related to both Ps 23:1-6 and the Good Shepherd passage of John 10:1-42. A comparative study of the three passages reveals similar characteristics of God's ideal Shepherd. The hope of the Messiah soared with God's promise of "one shepherd" (v. 23) who would regather the people and reinstate the line of David to bring people to a personal knowledge of God.

### (3) Edom's Desolation and Israel's Repossession (35:1–36:15)

A second prophecy against Edom seems somewhat unnecessary if not a bit out of place in the midst of these messages of restoration and hope. The easy way to handle the passage is to use scissors-and-paste exegesis and move the passage to a thematically more appropriate section. Such passages often are viewed as having been moved by an editor for some reason or regarded as material added by some later editor.[27] Zimmerli rejects both ideas. He observes that 35:1 begins with the single message formula, "The word of the LORD came to me," which occurs again in 36:16, announcing the next prophetic message. Zimmerli regards chaps. 35 and 36 as a unit in which the "mountain" of 35:2 was contrasted with the "mountains" of 36:1-15. In this unit the message of 35:1-15 is an integral part. The judgment of Edom in 35:1-15 was the basis for the salvation of the "mountains" of Judah in 36:1-15. He calls chap. 35 a "motivated declaration of judgment," which in chap. 36 resulted in a "motivated declaration of salvation."[28]

L. Allen has noted that there are many connecting links between 35:1-15 and 36:1-15. These form strong contrasts and comparisons between Edom and Israel, making the judgment of Edom "a foil for Israel's salvation in 36:1-15."[29] For the desolation Edom brought upon Israel, God would bring desolation upon Edom and fruitfulness to Israel. The first

---

[26] See H. L. Ellison, *The Old Testament Prophets* (Grand Rapids: Zondervan, 1971), 15.

[27] Taylor (*Ezekiel*, 224) notes that redaction is the often-used solution to what some see as the misplaced message against Edom. To see it as an editor's mistake is the easy way out, but it will not solve the problem because chap. 35 is closely related to chap. 36, in which case the idea of redaction is unnecessary.

[28] Zimmerli, *Ezekiel 2*, 232-34. See his discussion of the concepts of "motivated declaration of salvation" and "motivated declaration of judgment."

[29] L. C. Allen, *Ezekiel 20–48*, WBC (Dallas: Word, 1990), 170-71.

message (35:1-15) begins with instructions to the "son of man" to set his face "against Mount Seir" (*ʿal har śēʿîr*). In the second message the "son of man" is told to prophesy "to the mountains of Israel" (*ʾel hārê yiśrāʾēl* in 36:1; note the expression "mountains of Israel" also in 35:12). The first message declares that Edom's "mountains," "hills," "valleys," and "ravines" (35:8) would become "a desolate waste" (*šĕmāmâ ûmĕšammâ*, 35:3; cf. vv. 4,7,9,14-15) because of their "hostility" (*ʾêbat* in v. 5, related to *hāʾôyēb*, "enemy" in 36:2) and their rejoicing (35:15; the same word translated "glee" in 36:5) at the desolation of Israel (35:12—"laid waste" is *šāmēmû*; and v. 15). In the second message the Lord says to "the mountains and hills, to the ravines and valleys" (vv. 4,6) of Israel that although their enemy "ravaged" (*šammôt*) them (v. 3) so that they became "desolate" (*haššōmĕmôt*, v. 4), he was going to make Israel fruitful and full of "men and animals" (36:8-11).[30] "You and all of Edom" in 35:15 is literally "and all Edom, all of it." Parallel to that expression of the extent of Edom's desolation is the expression in 36:10 of blessing upon "even the whole house of Israel," which is literally "all the house of Israel, all of it."

Ezekiel quotes Israel's "enemy" in 36:2 boasting, "The ancient heights have become our *possession*" (cf. 36:3,5). Also in 35:10 Edom is quoted, "These two nations and countries will be ours and we will take possession of them." But in 36:12 the Lord announces that the mountains of Israel will again be the *possession* of his people Israel. Israel's towns had become deserted ruins (36:4), but the Lord declared that he would turn Edom's "towns into ruins" (35:4), while Israel's "towns will be inhabited and the ruins rebuilt" (36:10). In 35:11 the Lord swears ("as surely as I live") that he will treat Edom with the same "anger," "jealousy," and "hatred" they gave to Israel; and that promise is repeated ("I swear with uplifted hand") in 36:5-7 ("zeal" in 36:5 is the same word translated "jealousy" in 35:11 and "jealous" in 36:6). Because of Edom's speaking against Israel and their God (35:13; cf. 35:10,12; 36:2-3), the Lord spoke against Edom and the nations (36:5), and declared, "I am against you" (*hinnî ʾēleykā* in 35:3), while to Israel he declared, "I am concerned for you" (*hinnî ʾălekem* in 36:9).

A further link may be found by comparing 35:1–36:15 to the prophecy of judgment against the mountains of Israel in chap. 6 (see the comments

---

[30] The word אֱדֹם occurs once in each of the vv. 10-14 and is surely a wordplay on the name "Edom." This is unfortunately obscured in translation, especially since אֱדֹם is translated "men" in vv. 11,13-14 but "people" in vv. 11-12. In v. 12 the first "people" is אֱדֹם while the second is עַם.

at 36:1-7). As Ezekiel was told, "Set your face against the mountains of Israel" in 6:2 and to prophesy destruction and desolation, so here Ezekiel was to set his face against Mount Seir (Edom), which was an instrument of that judgment. As God determined for the mountains of Israel, "I will stretch out my hand against them and make the land a desolate waste" (6:14), so he determined for Edom, "I will stretch out my hand against you and make you a desolate waste (35:3). As the people of Israel were to "fall slain among" (6:7) the "mountains and hills, . . . ravines and valleys" (6:3), so the Lord declared to Edom, "I will fill your mountains with the slain; those killed by the sword will fall on your hills and in your valleys and in all your ravines" (35:8). All these connections highlight the eye-for-an-eye nature of the judgment declared against Edom and the nations who scorned Israel (cf. 35:6,11,14-15; 36:6-7; cf. Jer 30:12-17).

[1]**The word of the LORD came to me:** [2]**"Son of man, set your face against Mount Seir; prophesy against it** [3]**and say: 'This is what the Sovereign LORD says: I am against you, Mount Seir, and I will stretch out my hand against you and make you a desolate waste.** [4]**I will turn your towns into ruins and you will be desolate. Then you will know that I am the LORD.**

[5]**"'Because you harbored an ancient hostility and delivered the Israelites over to the sword at the time of their calamity, the time their punishment reached its climax,** [6]**therefore as surely as I live, declares the Sovereign LORD, I will give you over to bloodshed and it will pursue you. Since you did not hate bloodshed, bloodshed will pursue you.** [7]**I will make Mount Seir a desolate waste and cut off from it all who come and go.** [8]**I will fill your mountains with the slain; those killed by the sword will fall on your hills and in your valleys and in all your ravines.** [9]**I will make you desolate forever; your towns will not be inhabited. Then you will know that I am the LORD.**

[10]**"'Because you have said, "These two nations and countries will be ours and we will take possession of them," even though I the LORD was there,** [11]**therefore as surely as I live, declares the Sovereign LORD, I will treat you in accordance with the anger and jealousy you showed in your hatred of them and I will make myself known among them when I judge you.** [12]**Then you will know that I the LORD have heard all the contemptible things you have said against the mountains of Israel. You said, "They have been laid waste and have been given over to us to devour."** [13]**You boasted against me and spoke against me without restraint, and I heard it.** [14]**This is what the Sovereign LORD says: While the whole earth rejoices, I will make you desolate.** [15]**Because you rejoiced when the inheritance of the house of Israel became desolate, that is how I will treat you. You will be desolate, O Mount Seir, you and all of Edom. Then they will know that I am the LORD.'"**

DESOLATION OF EDOM (35:1-15). Two factors suggest the appropriateness and validity of this message of judgment.[31] First, the malicious joy of the Edomites over the fall of Jerusalem marked them for a double portion of judgment. It also was fitting that the message of judgment to befall Edom be given twice to suggest certainty. Second, Edom had taken territorial possession of portions of Judah especially in the south.[32] If there was to be a future restoration of the land to the Israelites, one obvious question would have been, What about the territory taken over by the Edomites? This sequel to the brief prophecy of 25:12-14 addressed these issues. The message against Edom has two parts, the declaration of judgment against Edom and the reasons for the judgment of Edom.

*Declaration of Judgment (35:1-4).* **35:1-4** The Edomites were descendants of Esau (Gen 25:25). Genesis 27; 32 reveals the enmity that existed between Jacob and Esau. That animosity was perpetuated among their progeny in spite of their personal reconciliation (Gen 33:1-20). The Edomites inhabited the region southeast of the Dead Sea and south of Moab around Mount Seir.[33] Esau's descendants were known as a cruel (Amos 1:11-12), vengeful (Ezek 25:12-14), warring (Gen 27:40), idolatrous (2 Chr 25:14,20), and proud people (Isa 49:16-17).

God was "against" them (Ezek 35:3) because they consistently took sides with the enemies of his people and even helped them in attacks against Israel (2 Chr 20:10). Therefore God promised that Edom would one day be desolate (see Isa 34:5-17; Jer 49:7-22; Obadiah) because of their implacable thirst for revenge against the Hebrews.[34]

*Reasons for Judgment (35:5-15).* **35:5-15** Ezekiel enumerated at least five specific reasons for the judgment of Edom.[35] First, Edom was to be judged for its "ancient" enmity against the Hebrews, still harbored after hundreds of years following the deception of Esau by Jacob (v. 5).

Second, the Edomites had encouraged Israel's enemies to execute the Jews by the sword. They missed no opportunities to endorse and even to participate in attacks against Israel (v. 5; Obad 10-14). Third, their desire to possess the land of Israel was fueled by their feelings that the land still belonged to them because Jacob had obtained it by deception (v. 10; Gen 27:1-40).[36] Because of these feelings God said they would be victims of

---

[31] The expression "Set your face against" first occurs in the judgment speech to the mountains of Israel in 6:2. See comments there.

[32] Davidson, *Ezekiel,* 253.

[33] See Fisch, *Ezekiel,* 235; Zimmerli, *Ezekiel 2,* 234. Cf. Gen 36:8-10; Deut 1:2; 2:1.

[34] Zimmerli, *Ezekiel 2,* 234.

[35] Cf. Alexander, "Ezekiel," 916-17.

[36] Wevers (*Ezekiel,* 265) treats the history of the ancestral enmity between the descendants of Esau and Jacob from Gen 25:27-34; 27:41-45 forward.

bloodshed since they perpetrated bloodshed and violence against Israel (v. 6). So Edom was to be destroyed (v. 7), and the land, filled with the slain, would remain a perpetual desolation (v. 8). The cities of Edom would vanish, never to return (v. 9). The accuracy of this prophecy is confirmed by the absence of Edom from the family of nations and the desolation of the region they formerly inhabited.[37]

Fourth, the Edomites blasphemed the mountains of Israel by saying, "They have been laid waste and have been given over to us to devour" (v. 12). Their words were blasphemous because they disregarded Yahweh's desire for the allotment of the land to Israel. Fifth, they had spoken against God "without restraint" (v. 13). This spirit of defiance was the subject of Malachi's message and insight into the bitterness of the descendants of Esau (Mal 1:1-5). They exhibited an attitude of defiance that ignored God's will for themselves as well as for the Israelites.[38]

God promised judgment for Edom and announced that since the Edomites rejoiced over Israel's calamity the whole world would rejoice over its destruction (v. 14).[39] Gloating over Israel and trying to confiscate the territory caused the destruction, desolation, and loss of their land and national identity (v. 15).[40]

[1]"Son of man, prophesy to the mountains of Israel and say, 'O mountains of Israel, hear the word of the LORD. [2]This is what the Sovereign LORD says: The enemy said of you, "Aha! The ancient heights have become our possession."' [3]Therefore prophesy and say, 'This is what the Sovereign LORD says: Because they ravaged and hounded you from every side so that you became the possession of the rest of the nations and the object of people's malicious talk and slander, [4]therefore, O mountains of Israel, hear the word of the Sovereign LORD: This is what the Sovereign LORD says to the mountains and hills, to the ravines and valleys, to the desolate ruins and the deserted towns that have been plundered and ridiculed by the rest of the nations around you— [5]this is what the Sovereign LORD says: In my burning zeal I have spoken against the rest of the nations, and against all Edom, for with glee and with malice in their hearts they made my land their own possession so that they might plunder its pastureland.' [6]Therefore prophesy concerning the land of Israel and say to the mountains and hills, to the ravines and valleys: 'This is what the Sovereign LORD says: I speak in my jealous wrath be-

---

[37] See R. Alexander, *Ezekiel* (Chicago: Moody, 1976), 110.

[38] Fisch, *Ezekiel*, 237.

[39] Wevers, *Ezekiel*, 267.

[40] Fisch, *Ezekiel*, 237. Attempts to separate Israel from the land God gave them resulted in permanent loss for the Edomites of their own land.

cause you have suffered the scorn of the nations. [7]Therefore this is what the Sovereign LORD says: I swear with uplifted hand that the nations around you will also suffer scorn.

[8]"'But you, O mountains of Israel, will produce branches and fruit for my people Israel, for they will soon come home. [9]I am concerned for you and will look on you with favor; you will be plowed and sown, [10]and I will multiply the number of people upon you, even the whole house of Israel. The towns will be inhabited and the ruins rebuilt. [11]I will increase the number of men and animals upon you, and they will be fruitful and become numerous. I will settle people on you as in the past and will make you prosper more than before. Then you will know that I am the LORD. [12]I will cause people, my people Israel, to walk upon you. They will possess you, and you will be their inheritance; you will never again deprive them of their children.

[13]"'This is what the Sovereign LORD says: Because people say to you, "You devour men and deprive your nation of its children," [14]therefore you will no longer devour men or make your nation childless, declares the Sovereign LORD. [15]No longer will I make you hear the taunts of the nations, and no longer will you suffer the scorn of the peoples or cause your nation to fall, declares the Sovereign LORD.'"

REPOSSESSION OF THE MOUNTAINS OF ISRAEL (36:1-15). **36:1-7** Ezekiel 36:1-15 presents three accusations against Edom and the nations (vv. 1-7; note the repeated "because" or "for" and "therefore") and four promises of restoration for Israel (vv. 8-15; note "but you" in v. 8 and the recurring "I will").[41] As a message to the "mountains of Israel," it is the restoration counterpart to the judgment message of 6:1-14. As here (v. 4), the message in chap. 6 also is addressed to the "mountains and hills, to the ravines and valleys" (6:3,6). It is a message of judgment because of Israel's idolatry at the "high places" (bāmôt in 6:3; cf. 20:29), the same word translated "heights" in 36:2.[42] At these sites of pagan worship the people multiplied sins through idolatrous Baal worship.[43] These pagan altars to Baal, Asherah, Molech, and others covered wooded areas of the mountains. For the idolatry at these high places, the Lord had announced that he would destroy the pagan shrines (6:3-4,6) and would "bring the sword" (6:3) to slay the people (6:4,7,11-13) "because of all the wicked and detestable practices of the house of Israel" (6:11). The Lord would express his wrath by "sword, famine, and plague" (6:11-12) and "make

---

[41] Alexander, *Ezekiel,* 111-12.

[42] בָּמוֹת was used regularly to refer to the groves and pagan shrines on the mountains. Although it can have a less technical sense, the use of the term in 36:2 does allow the hearer to remember the misuse of those mountain shrines (see Ellison, *Ezekiel,* 126).

[43] Wevers, *Ezekiel,* 267-68.

the land a desolate waste from the desert to Diblah—wherever they live" (6:14). Through Edom and the "rest of the nations" (36:3-5) the Lord had fulfilled his word. They had wielded the sword (35:5) and made desolate "the inheritance of the house of Israel" (35:15; cf. 36:4).

Nevertheless, the Lord would not leave them unpunished for their "malicious talk and slander" (36:3), their "scorn" (36:6,15; cf. 36:4; 35:12-13), or for the "glee" (or "rejoicing") and "malice in their hearts" (36:5; cf. "hostility," "bloodshed," "anger," "jealousy," and "hatred" in 35:5-6,11) with which they acted. Most important, he would not allow them to retain possession of his land but would return it to his people, "the whole house of Israel" (36:10; cf. 35:15).[44]

The three accusations brought against the enemies of Israel in vv. 1-7 expand the ideas of 35:1-15. First, the nations and Edom had taken possession of the mountains of Israel (36:2-3,5). Second, the nations and Edom plundered Judah and left the land desolate (36:3-4). Third, the nations and Edom ridiculed and scorned Judah (36:3-4,6,15). Edom is mentioned specifically only in v. 5, but the accusations are comparable to those of 35:1-15. The "nations" meant the Gentile nations, of which the most recent and cruel was Babylon. Clearly Edom is especially significant in 35:1–36:15 as "the epitome of nations that sought to overrun and acquire Israel's land for themselves."[45]

**36:8-12** Within these verses are four promises to Israel regarding the land. First, the land will again be fruitful (vv. 8-9; cf. 6:8-10). Second, all the house of Israel will return and multiply in the land (vv. 10-11). Third, their return to the land will be permanent (vv. 12-14).[46] Fourth, God's people will again be ridiculed and scorned (v. 15).

The enemies of the land had said, "Aha, the ancient high places have become our possession" (v. 2). These "heights" were the "high places" for pagan worship especially of Baal and Asherah. As ancient cultic sites they were thought to have special power and thus were considered a prized possession.

Ownership of the land was by divine commission. Every family was entrusted with a portion of land protected by the law of the Jubilee Year (Lev 25:8-24), when all property was restored to the original owner or surviving family. Thus the land was viewed as a divine stewardship. It was this reason, for example, that Naboth refused to sell his portion of land to Ahab (1 Kgs 21:3; Lev 25:23). In this way divine ownership of the land was ac-

---

[44] Craigie, *Ezekiel,* 252-53.
[45] Alexander, "Ezekiel," 916.
[46] Alexander, *Ezekiel,* 111-12.

knowledged. When an enemy claimed possession of the land, they claimed ownership of what was not theirs to take. It was God's land.[47]

Edom and the nations including Babylon took the land by force in spite of God's grant of the territory to Israel. The land became an object of contempt and malicious talk (vv. 3-4). Six terms in succession were used in v. 4 to depict every feature of the land to describe the total destruction of the "mountains," "hills," "ravines," "valleys," "desolate ruins," and "deserted towns." So the nations, especially Babylon and Edom, had attacked the land with malice and declared it to be their own (v. 5; cf. 6:3).[48]

The use of "my land" in 36:5 called attention to the fact that the land was God's. "My people" affirmed the unique relationship that Israel had with Yahweh (v. 12).[49] Ezekiel spoke to the land and relayed a divine oath. God promised to scorn the enemies of his land and his people (vv. 6-7). While the land of Edom will be desolate forever, Israel will again be productive (v. 8; cf. 17:23).[50]

Ezekiel said the people would "soon" return (v. 8). "Soon" was used in a relative sense given from the prophet's perspective.[51] After the return they will multiply and prosper in the land (vv. 10-11,13) and will never again be separated from it (v. 12). This promise obviously applied to some time after the initial return from Babylon under Zerubbabel, Ezra, and Nehemiah, since the Jews were dispossessed in A.D. 70. The permanent return to the land, which Ezekiel saw, as well as other aspects of these promises, seem to have an eschatological element in their fulfillment that will be identified in further discussion of this section (vv. 24-38).

**36:13-15**   When the spies described the land after their reconnaissance, they said that it was a land that "devours those living in it" (Num 13:32). God promised that in the restoration the land would no longer "devour" its inhabitants (Ezek 36:14). No longer will people taunt Israel in it; no longer will they scorn them nor cause them to fall (v. 15). God assured them that these things would "never" happen again.[52]

---

[47] Ibid., 124-25.

[48] Fisch (*Ezekiel*, 239) notes that this is a reversal of the prophecy of 6.3.

[49] Alexander ("Ezekiel," 919) notes that the use of אַרְצִי ("my land," v. 5) and עַמִּי ("my people," v. 12) was to emphasize the land and the people as God's unique possession (36:20; Gen 12:1-7; 15:7; Exod 19:5-6; Lev 25:23; Deut 32:43; Ps 78:54; Jer 2:7). God's actions in 35:1–36:15 were based on his covenant with Israel.

[50] Wevers, *Ezekiel*, 270; Zimmerli, *Ezekiel 2*, 238; and D. E. Gowan (*Eschatology in the Old Testament* [Philadelphia: Fortress, 1986], 101-3) discuss the theme of the transformation of nature as a characteristic of the restoration.

[51] Fisch, *Ezekiel*, 240.

[52] לֹא occurs five times in vv. 14 and 15 with עוֹד.

The destruction of Edom as a judgment for their opposition to God, his work, and his people is a sobering testimony to the fate of those who aggressively oppose him. Edom missed no opportunity to attack God's people. Consequently they would suffer annihilation, and their land would be desolate (34:1-15; cf. Isa 34:5-17; Jer 49:7-22; Obadiah).

God promised that the restoration would reverse the physical consequences of judgment for Israel. The land would again be fruitful and productive (36:8-15; cf. Amos 9:11-15).

### (4)  Future Restoration of Fruitfulness in Israel (36:16-38)

The revelation formula in 36:16 (cf. 35:1) announces a new message. Having settled in 35:1–36:16 the issue of who owned the land of Israel, Ezekiel presents in this message an extensive treatment of the basis and nature of the restoration.

This message may be divided into three parts: reasons for the coming restoration (36:16-23), seven elements of the coming restoration (36:24-32), and a summary of the benefits of the restoration (36:33-38).

The first section explains that the land had been defiled by the Hebrews' disobedience to the Mosaic covenant (vv. 16-18). These acts of disobedience centered in two areas: (1) bloodshed and violence (vv. 16-17) and (2) idolatry (v. 18). Their abominations were so offensive that God compared them to the bloody discharge of a woman during her menstrual cycle that rendered her ceremonially impure (v. 17; cf. Lev 12:2-5; 15:9-10; Isa 64:6).[53]

**16Again the word of the LORD came to me: 17"Son of man, when the people of Israel were living in their own land, they defiled it by their conduct and their actions. Their conduct was like a woman's monthly uncleanness in my sight. 18So I poured out my wrath on them because they had shed blood in the land and because they had defiled it with their idols. 19I dispersed them among the nations, and they were scattered through the countries; I judged them according to their conduct and their actions. 20And wherever they went among the nations they profaned my holy name, for it was said of them, 'These are the LORD'S people, and yet they had to leave his land.' 21I had concern for my holy name, which the house of Israel profaned among the nations where they had gone.**

**22"Therefore say to the house of Israel, 'This is what the Sovereign LORD says: It is not for your sake, O house of Israel, that I am going to do these**

---

[53] Alexander, "Ezekiel," 920. See his discussion of Israel's defilement of the land, which rendered both them and the land unclean.

things, but for the sake of my holy name, which you have profaned among the nations where you have gone. <sup>23</sup>I will show the holiness of my great name, which has been profaned among the nations, the name you have profaned among them. Then the nations will know that I am the LORD, declares the Sovereign LORD, when I show myself holy through you before their eyes.

REASONS FOR THE RESTORATION (36:16-23).    **36:16-23**    God judged the Hebrews by dispersing them, a reference to the Assyro-Babylonian exile. But they were a reproach and profanation of God's holy name because they made it appear that he had not been able to keep them safe (Ezek 36:19-20). Therefore God intended to restore them not because the people deserved restoration (vv. 21-22,32) but for the sake of his holy name, that is, his reputation (note "my holy name" in vv. 20-22 and "I will show the holiness of my great name" in v. 23).

The Lord's name also was an issue at times other than during the exile. Not only did the Hebrews' idolatry defile the land, but it also profaned God's name (20:39). The revelation of God's name or character was a major aspect of God's dealing with Israel from the beginning (cf. Exod 5:2; 9:16; Lev 18:21; 20:3; 22:31-33), and it would continue to be God's concern (Ezek 39:7-8,25; 43:7-9). Moses effectively used the appeal to God's name and character to stay the judgment of annihilation upon Israel after the incident of the golden calf in Exod 32:11-18. He gave the same appeal when the people chose not to enter the land of promise in Num 14:13-19.

The restoration of Israel would serve as a signal to the nations, including Babylon and Edom, that Yahweh was still in control and still regarded Israel as his people. God promised to reestablish his reputation, or "name," among them.

<sup>24</sup>"'For I will take you out of the nations; I will gather you from all the countries and bring you back into your own land. <sup>25</sup>I will sprinkle clean water on you, and you will be clean; I will cleanse you from all your impurities and from all your idols. <sup>26</sup>I will give you a new heart and put a new spirit in you; I will remove from you your heart of stone and give you a heart of flesh. <sup>27</sup>And I will put my Spirit in you and move you to follow my decrees and be careful to keep my laws. <sup>28</sup>You will live in the land I gave your forefathers; you will be my people, and I will be your God. <sup>29</sup>I will save you from all your uncleanness. I will call for the grain and make it plentiful and will not bring famine upon you. <sup>30</sup>I will increase the fruit of the trees and the crops of the field, so that you will no longer suffer disgrace among the nations because of famine. <sup>31</sup>Then you will remember your evil ways and wicked deeds, and you will loathe yourselves for your sins and detestable practices. <sup>32</sup>I want you to know that I am not doing this for your sake, declares the Sovereign LORD. Be

**ashamed and disgraced for your conduct, O house of Israel!**

ELEMENTS OF THE RESTORATION (36:24-32). **36:24-32** Seven additional elements of restoration are present in these verses that expand ideas first presented in 11:14-21 (see the discussion there).[54] First, God promised to return his people to their land (v. 24; cf 11:16-17; 20:34; 34:13; 37:21). The use of "nations" and "countries" echoes v. 19 in reverse, which recalled their dispersion. But the breadth of the reference, especially with the addition of "all," suggests an eschatological setting. The return to the land in 535 B.C. after the exile in Babylon involved a return from one nation, Babylon, allowed by another nation, the Medo-Persians. Technically three nations were involved in the return of the exiles, Assyria, Babylon, Egypt, and Medo-Persia. Israel, the Northern Kingdom, went captive to Assyria in 722 B.C. Babylon took captives from Judah in 605, 597, and 587 B.C. Babylon was overthrown by the Medo-Persians in 539 B.C., after which the Hebrews began to return to the land under Zerubbabel, Ezra, and Nehemiah.

The reference in Ezekiel to a gathering from "all countries" seems to imply a wider scope for the return that looked beyond the first return from the Assyro-Babylonian captivity. This prophecy reflected the hope of a regathering after the A.D. 70 dispersion among all nations of the world (cf. 11:16-17; Isa 11:12; Jer 16:15).

Second, God will cleanse them from their impurities and especially their idolatry, which had defiled the land (v. 25; cf. vv. 17-18). Ezekiel used his favorite word, *gillûlîm*, for "idols" (vv. 18,25; see comments on 6:3-7). Cleansing and forgiveness were symbolized by sprinkling with clean water to wash away their impurities (cf. Ps 51:7). While the reference was to ceremonial cleansing that was necessary to reestablish worship (Num 19:13,20), it is important to remember that ceremonial cleansing was an external rite, but it was a ritual that also called for internal repentance.

Third, God promised to regenerate the people spiritually by giving them a "new heart" and a "new spirit" (v. 26). No longer would they be characterized by perverse thinking and unresponsiveness to God (see comments at 11:17-21). The change of will from "stone" to "flesh" would be made possible by the new covenant presented in Jer 31:31-34. This new internalized covenant would lead the people to turn to the new shepherd, the Messiah, and exchange their rebelliousness for a new heart, sensitive to the will of God. The enabling power to do this would be provided

---

[54] Davidson, *Ezekiel,* 260-61.

by a "new spirit" within them. God called this new spirit "my Spirit" (v. 27), meaning Yahweh's Holy Spirit (11:19-20; 18:31; 37:14; 39:29; Joel 2:28-29), who would empower them to obey the law of God.

The temptation to find the fulfillment of the "new heart" and "new spirit" of 36:25-27 exclusively in Christian conversion in this age should be resisted. New Testament conversion is only a preview of the massive spiritual revival God has in store for all of true Israel and Gentiles who believe. The New Testament concept of redemption came out of the theology of the Old Testament. The similarities exist because what God wants to do for Israel is what he wants to do for everyone. The point of Israel's election to nationhood in Exod 19:1-8 was that they be mediators of the message of God's salvation by fulfilling their missionary role as a "kingdom of priests." When Israel did not fulfill its role, God used the New Testament church as a means of presenting the message of redemption. So the church will be used ultimately to reach Israel as well (Rom 10:1; 11:25-33).

Fourth, the Spirit of God will "move" them to follow ("walk in") his laws (v. 27).[55] Inability to keep the law was a primary concern presented by the apostle Paul. He lamented his struggle and failure to keep the law in his own strength (Rom 7:13-25) and followed that lament with the solution in Rom 8:1-39. The solution to his dilemma was living in the power of the Holy Spirit (cf. Gal 5:16-26).

Fifth, the people will live permanently in the land that God gave their forefathers (v. 28). The word "live" is from the root $y\bar{a}s\check{a}b$, which means "to dwell" as a permanent resident and is antithetical to $g\hat{u}r$, "sojourner," or "a temporary resident or resident alien." The covenant relationship of the Hebrews will be reaffirmed (cf. 11:20; 14:11).

Sixth, God promised a new level of productivity (Amos 9:11-15). God instructed the grain to produce and the trees and crops to yield bountifully (vv. 29-30; cf. v. 8; Hos 2:21-22; Amos 9:13-15). No longer would famine disgrace God's people or drive them from the land (see comments on 5:12; also cf. Gen 12:10; 26:1; 42:5; 43:1; 47:4; Ruth 1:1; 2 Sam 21:1).

Seventh, the people will remember their former practices, immorality and idolatry, and will "loathe" themselves (v. 31). This terminology was used in 6:9 to describe Israel's repentance in exile. Here and in 20:43 it describes their feeling of revulsion after the return when they would recall their former life-style.[56]

Verse 32 concludes the entire section with another reminder that none

---

[55] "Move" translates an unusual use of עָשָׂה, "to do, make." BDB (795) gives the sense here (also Eccl 3:14) as "bring about." Allen (*Ezekiel 20–48,* 175) translates "ensure."

[56] Allen, *Ezekiel 20–48,* 179.

of these restoration promises was provided because the Hebrews deserved them. Ezekiel reaffirmed the primary motive expressed in vv. 20-23, which was to demonstrate God's greatness and holiness.

**[33]" 'This is what the Sovereign LORD says: On the day I cleanse you from all your sins, I will resettle your towns, and the ruins will be rebuilt. [34]The desolate land will be cultivated instead of lying desolate in the sight of all who pass through it. [35]They will say, "This land that was laid waste has become like the garden of Eden; the cities that were lying in ruins, desolate and destroyed, are now fortified and inhabited." [36]Then the nations around you that remain will know that I the LORD have rebuilt what was destroyed and have replanted what was desolate. I the LORD have spoken, and I will do it.'**

**[37]"This is what the Sovereign LORD says: Once again I will yield to the plea of the house of Israel and do this for them: I will make their people as numerous as sheep, [38]as numerous as the flocks for offerings at Jerusalem during her appointed feasts. So will the ruined cities be filled with flocks of people. Then they will know that I am the LORD."**

BENEFITS OF THE RESTORATION (36:33-38).     **36:33-38**   This is a final review of the benefits of the restoration that God will provide. Those benefits include cleansing from sin, resettlement, rebuilding, replanting, and productivity of the land (vv. 33-34). Mention of the "garden of Eden" in v. 35 suggests that Ezekiel saw a future fulfillment of his prophecy that went beyond the return from Babylon under Zerubbabel, Ezra, and Nehemiah. While many aspects of the fulfillment of these prophetic promises were immediate and limited, there was also to be a distant, complete fulfillment in a messianic age.[57] The ideal qualities of life, work, rest, peace, companionship, knowledge by revelation, dominion, productivity, and security characterized human existence before the fall. All were either lost or greatly diminished after sin entered the world. Ezekiel's use of the garden of Eden revealed a hope for the restoration and development of the characteristics of life in Eden.

God is faithful. When he promised he would bless the descendants of Abraham (Gen 12:1-3), the promise was unconditional, confirmed by the marvelous restoration that God promised in Ezek 36:1-38.

The love, grace, mercy, and salvation that God offers is never deserved by human recipients. He gives these gifts because of his holy and righteous character (36:22-23,32), which is embodied in his name (Exod 3:14-15; 34:6-7 [the OT version of John 3:16]; John 8:58).

---

[57] Alexander, "Ezekiel," 923. See also 28:13 and "Restoration of Edenic Ideals," p. 349.

## (5) Restoration of National Life for Israel (37:1-28)

One of the most amazing and well-known prophecies in the Old Testament is found in chap. 37. Few other passages have suffered more from the extremes of interpreters who see either too much or too little in both meaning and application of the figures, symbols, and types. This passage employs an apocalyptic form, the use of which was on the rise in the seventh and sixth centuries B.C.[58] This literature presented its message in symbols and visions whose meanings were not immediately apparent. Some apocalyptic sections of Ezekiel, like Ezek 37:11-14, Daniel, and Revelation, were accompanied by interpretation passages that explained the symbols.[59]

Before looking at the first vision of the valley of dry bones, two questions need to be addressed. First, does this passage convey Old Testament ideas concerning the bodily resurrection of the dead? Second, what, if anything, does this passage reveal about the relationship of Israel and the church of the New Testament?

Regarding the resurrection of the dead, there is nothing in the Old Testament that can compare to New Testament passages like 1 Cor 15:1-58. Most interpreters agree that teaching a doctrine of the resurrection of the dead was not the main point of Ezek 37. Zimmerli denies any thought in the passage of the resurrection of individuals.[60] Wevers also denies any hint of the resurrection in vv. 1-14 but does acknowledge the belief that Yahweh was the author of life, and the possibility of the resurrection is left open.[61] Cooke simply said that the passage referred to the "present state of the living, not to the future state of the dead." But then he admitted that vv. 1-14 must have contributed to the development of the resurrection ideas in the Old Testament, especially in its most highly developed expression in Dan 12:2-3.[62]

Hals similarly noted that only a national resurrection was in view but admitted he found curious the imagery of vv. 1-14 portrayed on the wall of a synagogue in Dura-Europos as an illustration of the promise of resurrection from the grave.[63]

Several interpreters deny the possibility that Ezekiel would have been

---

[58] Alexander, "Ezekiel," 924. See his discussion of vv. 1-2, which includes a brief overview of apocalyptic literature in the ancient Near East.

[59] Ibid., 744-45.

[60] See Zimmerli, *Ezekiel 2*, 264-66.

[61] Wevers, *Ezekiel*, 278.

[62] Cooke, *Ezekiel*, 397.

[63] Hals, *Ezekiel*, 270-71.

aware of a developed concept of the resurrection of the human body as we already have noted. Death in most of the Old Testament was viewed as an impossible situation from which there was no return. All who died went to the grave called *sheol* from which no one returned. Hals was therefore surprised by the imagery of vv. 1-14, which obviously rose above this view of death.[64]

Ezekiel's primary purpose was not to teach a doctrine of the resurrection. The main purpose of the vision was the restoration of Israel. Yet the images of dead bones that were scattered, bleached dry by the sun, but revived and lived again as a "vast army" was startling and unexpected. Recent work by D. I. Block has shed additional light on understanding this passage.[65] While acknowledging that the concept of life after death was prevalent in non-Hebrew cultures and that Ezekiel reflects a knowledge of afterlife images used outside Israel (without affirming their truth), Block believes there was sufficient basis in Hebrew teachings for the concepts found in Ezekiel's vision of the Valley of Dry Bones. First, the idea of bodily resurrection could have developed as a natural corollary to Hebrew views of anthropology. Human beings were considered living souls (*nepeš ḥayyâ*). As such, a human being was a unity rather than a dichotomy or trichotomy (Gen 2:7). At death the physical body and the life-giving breath are separated (Job 34:14-15; Ps 104:29; Eccl 18–21; 12:7). Any hope of victory over death would require a reunion of the physical body and the life-giving breath. This is what Ezekiel saw in 37:1-14.

Second, resurrection of human beings was not a totally new idea. Both Elijah and Elisha had been involved in the resurrection of individuals who had died (1 Kgs 17:17-24; 2 Kgs 4:18-37; 13:20-21). While none of these compare to what Ezekiel saw in his vision, they do represent two earlier prophets as being the instruments of the breath of life.

Third, at least two psalms present the idea of *sheol* as a place where death reigns. Deliverance from *sheol* is presented as being brought back from death to life (Pss 16:9-11; 49:14-15).

Fourth, Ezekiel was not the first one to portray the idea of restoration

---

[64] Ibid., 271.

[65] D. I. Block, "Beyond the Grave: Ezekiel's Vision of Death and Afterlife," *BBR* 2 (1992): 112-41. Block gives attention to the language and concepts of death and the afterlife in Ezek 26:19-21; 31:14-18; 32:17-32 in the prophecies against the nations and 37:1-14, the national resurrection of Israel. The concepts that emerge in Ezekiel's view of the afterlife in the oracles against the nations describe the netherworld as an extension of the grave in which the dead exist as "living corpses." Nevertheless, while Ezek 37:1-14 may contain a metaphor used primarily for its rhetorical effect, the underlying doctrinal truths, however basic, should not be discounted too quickly, as previously has been the situation in OT studies (pp. 134-36).

as a national resurrection. Both Hos 6:1-3 and Isa 26:19 hint at the idea of a national resurrection at least a century and a half before Ezekiel.[66]

Fifth, in addition to Block's observations, one might also add Job 14:7-10, where Job observes that even the trees are resuscitated after they have been cut down. He contemplates the apparent incongruity of the fact that human life seems to end without hope of a revival. From this low point Job rises to a leap of faith in 19:25-27 in which he declares a hope that in some future time he will have a redeemer who will resurrect him so that his innocence can be vindicated.[67] Such a dim hope was a hope nonetheless, and it was a part of that seedbed of nourishment that rises to a higher revelation in Ezekiel.

There was then present for Ezekiel to believe that the power of God could bring new life to a hopeless situation such as a nation gone into exile. Only Yahweh could replace the hopelessness of the death of the nation with new life and a new nation. While clearly the prophet had a national resurrection for Israel in mind, it also is but a small step from what he saw concerning Israel to the realization that the same God who could resurrect a dead nation also had the power to conquer humanity's great enemy, death. It is no coincidence that the one Old Testament passage that bridged that narrow gap appeared in the writings of Ezekiel's contemporary, Daniel.[68] The hope of a bodily resurrection in the Old Testament was dim but nevertheless a hope. The development of that hope can be traced from longing for it as in Job 14:7-10 and 19:25-27 to visualizing it as in Ezek 37:1-14 to belief in it as a real possibility in Dan 12:2-3.

The second question concerning Ezek 47:1-14 is how its message relates to the church. It is certainly true that the church belongs to God and in that sense is the people of God. It is also true that the New Testament applied some Old Testament figures to the church (e.g., 1 Pet 2:9; Gal 3:6-18; 1 Cor 10:1-13). But vv. 1-14 are not presented as a preview of the birth of the New Testament church. Many early Christians also were Jewish, but they never applied the name Israel to the church. On the contrary, the New Testament teaches that though salvation came to the Gentiles (Rom 11:11-24), God also intended to restore Israel (Rom 11:1-10,25-36).

---

[66] Block, "Beyond the Grave," 140. Block notes the similarity of the language and images used in Hos 6:2, where Hosea uses חָיָה (*piel* "to make alive) and קוּם (*hiphil* "to raise up") and those of Ezek 37:10, where he uses חָיָה ("to live) and עָמַד ("to stand"). See also A. R. Johnson, *The Vitality of the Individual in the Thought of Ancient Israel* (Cardiff: University of Wales, 1964), 19; H. W. Wolff, *Anthropology of the Old Testament* (Philadelphia: Fortress, 1974), 22; O. Kaiser, *Isaiah 13–39*, OTL (Philadelphia: Westminster, 1974), 213.

[67] See R. L. Alden, *Job*, NAC (Nashville: Broadman & Holman, 1993), 166-69, 205-9.

[68] See Criswell, *Expository Sermons on the Book of Ezekiel*, 191-211.

Some of the restoration promises of Ezek 36:24-32, especially the "new heart" and "new spirit" (vv. 24-28), are features of the church age as well.[69] The new covenant of Jer 31:31-34 has much in common with the gospel of the New Testament. But the Old Testament promises of a new everlasting covenant are all addressed to a remnant within ethnic Israel, not to the church. The New Testament inclusion of Gentiles in the blessings of the new covenant is not clearly envisioned in the Old Testament and does not warrant the equation of Israel with the church.

While Ezekiel is not quoted in the New Testament, the Jeremiah passage lies behind Mark 14:24 and is quoted in Heb 8:8-12 and 10:16ff. There it is given as a description rather than fulfillment with no suggestion that the promise has been exhausted in the church's claim to it. To regard such passages otherwise is to *spiritualize* them to mean something other than it possibly could have meant to its original hearers.

Ezekiel clearly envisioned the transformed land of Israel in chap. 36 and the national resurrection of Israel in chap. 37. We must take care not to banish the Israel of the old covenant from the picture in favor of the church. Thus the promises of Israel are not promises to be collected exclusively by the church. When Jesus established the church and turned to the Gentiles (Matt 21:33-46; 1 Pet 2:4-8; Luke 2:32; 13:6-10), it was with the same missionary purpose he had for Israel. His plan was to include all people in the presentation of salvation. That missionary purpose was set forth in Exod 19:1-8. The arrival of the church age did not circumvent Israel but was God's plan to share his salvific love with all people (Rev 22:17). It also assured that Israel would someday be included in the fulfillment of this promise (Rom 10:1-21; 11:25-33).

Ezekiel 37 easily may be divided into two sections by the introductory phrases "the hand of the LORD was upon me" in v. 1 and "the word of the LORD came to me" in v. 15. The vision of the valley of dry bones (37:1-10) followed by its interpretation (vv. 11-14) is the first message. The second complementary message concerned a symbolic action, binding two sticks together (vv. 15-17) with an interpretation in vv. 18-28.

---

[1]**The hand of the LORD was upon me, and he brought me out by the Spirit of the LORD and set me in the middle of a valley; it was full of bones.** [2]**He led me back and forth among them, and I saw a great many bones on the floor of the valley, bones that were very dry.** [3]**He asked me, "Son of man, can these bones live?"**

**I said, "O Sovereign LORD, you alone know."**

---

[69] See the seven elements of restoration in the discussion of 36:24-32.

[4]Then he said to me, "Prophesy to these bones and say to them, 'Dry bones, hear the word of the LORD! [5]This is what the Sovereign LORD says to these bones: I will make breath enter you, and you will come to life. [6]I will attach tendons to you and make flesh come upon you and cover you with skin; I will put breath in you, and you will come to life. Then you will know that I am the LORD.'"

[7]So I prophesied as I was commanded. And as I was prophesying, there was a noise, a rattling sound, and the bones came together, bone to bone. [8]I looked, and tendons and flesh appeared on them and skin covered them, but there was no breath in them.

[9]Then he said to me, "Prophesy to the breath; prophesy, son of man, and say to it, 'This is what the Sovereign LORD says: Come from the four winds, O breath, and breathe into these slain, that they may live.'" [10]So I prophesied as he commanded me, and breath entered them; they came to life and stood up on their feet—a vast army.

[11]Then he said to me: "Son of man, these bones are the whole house of Israel. They say, 'Our bones are dried up and our hope is gone; we are cut off.' [12]Therefore prophesy and say to them: 'This is what the Sovereign LORD says: O my people, I am going to open your graves and bring you up from them; I will bring you back to the land of Israel. [13]Then you, my people, will know that I am the LORD, when I open your graves and bring you up from them. [14]I will put my Spirit in you and you will live, and I will settle you in your own land. Then you will know that I the LORD have spoken, and I have done it, declares the LORD.'"

RESTORATION OF LIFE FOR ISRAEL (37:1-14). **37:1-10**    "The hand of the LORD was upon me" is Ezekiel's usual expression for a visionary experience (v. 1; cf. 1:3; 8:1). He was taken in a vision to a valley filled with human bones that were dried, bleached, and scattered. The location of the valley was not given, but the one mentioned in 3:22 has been suggested.[70] These bones may have been remnants of people slain during the conquest (v. 1).[71] The prophet walked "back and forth" (lit. "around") in the valley taking care not to touch any of the bones. As a priest he would have taken such precautions since touching a dead body, including these bones, was forbidden (Lev 21:11).[72] The bones were characterized as "very dry," indicating that they had been there for some time (Ezek 37:2).

Any suggestion that there could ever again be life in the bones would appear preposterous. Yet as Ezekiel surveyed the scene in the valley of

---

[70] See Fisch, *Ezekiel*, 246.

[71] Davidson, *Ezekiel*, 267.

[72] Fisch (*Ezekiel*, 246-47) notes that the question of ritual impurity of touching a dead body may be a moot point since this was a vision and not a real experience, which means that Ezekiel did not really touch anyone.

bones, he heard a question, "Son of man, can these bones live?" (v. 3). The prophet's answer was restrained and filled with his awareness of human helplessness in the face of death (cf. 24:15-27, the death of his wife) but also respect for the mystery of God's power.[73] He knew that if the bones could live it was a matter only God knew and that the giving of life was a deed only God could perform (v. 3). Thus when God told him to preach to the dead, dry bones, he obeyed despite its apparent absurdity (cf. John 11:43). The message he was to deliver was a simple one, "Dry bones, hear the word of the LORD!" (Ezek 37:4). That word consisted of a promise to give breath, life, tendons, flesh, and skin to these bones so they would know that he is Yahweh (vv. 5-6).

Ezekiel's obedience produced immediate results. Even before he had finished (cf. Acts 10:44), he heard the "noise" of the fulfillment of God's promise (Ezek 37:7). The bones came together and were clothed with flesh but they still were not alive (v. 8). So God again commanded the prophet to preach to the *rûaḥ* ("breath," "wind," or "spirit") to fill these corpses (v. 9). The same word, *rûaḥ,* may be translated by any one of these three words according to the context. "Winds" in the expression "from the four winds" is also the plural of *rûaḥ*.[74] The imperative "breathe" is the verb *nāpaḥ,* "to breathe/blow," reflecting its use in the creation context of Gen 2:7 (cf. its use in Ezck 22:20-21). It clearly was God's Spirit who was to give breath to these corpses, and Ezekiel was given the extraordinary task of summoning him. So he preached to the "breath," life entered these corpses, and they stood as a vast, living, reconstituted army (vv. 9-10).

**37:11-14**   God interpreted the vision for Ezekiel. It was God's response to the people's expression of hopelessness, "Our bones are dried up and our hope is gone; we are cut off" (v. 11). These "bones" were "the whole house of Israel" (3:7; 5:4; 12:10; 20:40; 36:10; 37:16; 39:25; 45:6), meaning both the Northern and Southern Kingdoms (v. 11). The question "Can these bones live?" was designed to show him the impotence of Israel during the exile.[75] God made marvelous promises to the nation in chaps. 33–36, but the real issue was, "Can these bones live?" Can a dead and impotent nation in exile and under the control of a godless nation be resurrected and become a living, thriving kingdom once again?

Sin had brought about the death of the nation of Israel (cf. Rom 6:23).

---

[73] Zimmerli, *Ezekiel 2,* 260. Ezekiel, like Job (14:14), did not know of a general eschatological resurrection but did not deny the possibility of Yahweh's power to awaken the dead.

[74] Fisch, *Ezekiel,* 248; Davidson, *Ezekiel,* 268.

[75] See Hals, *Ezekiel,* 271.

Sin's destructive power is most apparent on a personal level, where it destroys human lives (37:1-3; cf. Eph 2:1-22; 1 Pet 1:3-12). Only God can produce life for those who are physically and/or spiritually dead (37:3). Nothing but a miracle will resurrect the dead (John 11:25; 1 Cor 15:1-58).

The Sovereign Lord, however, said, "I am going to open your graves and bring you up from them," signifying all their places of exile (the "nations" and "all the countries" of 36:24). Stress was given in this promise to the revival of the nation as a manifestation of divine, not human, power (vv. 12-14).[76]

What a marvelous message of encouragement this was, both to Ezekiel and to the people in exile. If the prophet remained faithful to his call and proclaimed the word of God, the ultimate consequence would be a life-transforming experience that would result in a national resurrection. There is no finer illustration of the life-changing power of the preached word than what the prophet saw in his vision. It has the power to transform those who are dead in trespasses and sins (Eph 2:1-22) and make them new, living creatures in Christ (2 Cor 5:17). God has always used the "foolishness of what was preached to save those who believe" (1 Cor 1:21).

The enabling power of the Holy Spirit also is portrayed in this passage. The Spirit empowered the dead, dry bones and gave them life and animation. This was Paul's testimony. He was unable to live the life of a believer (Rom 7:13-25), faithful to the commands of God, without the enabling power of God's Spirit (Rom 8:1-17).

**[15]The word of the LORD came to me: [16]"Son of man, take a stick of wood and write on it, 'Belonging to Judah and the Israelites associated with him.' Then take another stick of wood, and write on it, 'Ephraim's stick, belonging to Joseph and all the house of Israel associated with him.' [17]Join them together into one stick so that they will become one in your hand.**

**[18]"When your countrymen ask you, 'Won't you tell us what you mean by this?' [19]say to them, 'This is what the Sovereign LORD says: I am going to take the stick of Joseph—which is in Ephraim's hand—and of the Israelite tribes associated with him, and join it to Judah's stick, making them a single stick of wood, and they will become one in my hand.' [20]Hold before their eyes the sticks you have written on [21]and say to them, 'This is what the Sovereign LORD says: I will take the Israelites out of the nations where they have gone. I will gather them from all around and bring them back into their own land. [22]I will make them one nation in the land, on the mountains of Israel. There will be one king over all of them and they will never again be two nations or be divided into two kingdoms. [23]They will no longer defile themselves with**

---

[76] See Fisch, *Ezekiel,* 249.

their idols and vile images or with any of their offenses, for I will save them from all their sinful backsliding, and I will cleanse them. They will be my people, and I will be their God.

[24]"'My servant David will be king over them, and they will all have one shepherd. They will follow my laws and be careful to keep my decrees. [25]They will live in the land I gave to my servant Jacob, the land where your fathers lived. They and their children and their children's children will live there forever, and David my servant will be their prince forever. [26]I will make a covenant of peace with them; it will be an everlasting covenant. I will establish them and increase their numbers, and I will put my sanctuary among them forever. [27]My dwelling place will be with them; I will be their God, and they will be my people. [28]Then the nations will know that I the LORD make Israel holy, when my sanctuary is among them forever.'"

REUNIFICATION OF ISRAEL (37:15-28). **37:15-23** These verses present a new vision that is a sequel to the vision of 37:1-14 and an extension of Ezekiel's message of national resurrection. Ezekiel was commanded to perform a symbolic action as he had done in several of his other messages (e.g., 4:1-16; 24:15-24). He took two sticks and identified them with inscriptions as representing the two former kingdoms of Judah and Israel.[77] Each inscription mentioned Israel, indicating that the two kingdoms were always recognized as an ethnic/theological unity. Ezekiel made one stick of the two by holding them together (vv. 15-17). Through this symbolic act he portrayed the reunification of the revived nation. Ezekiel avoided the use the name "Israel" for the Northern Kingdom, instead using the name "Joseph" or "Ephraim" (vv. 16,19). The Northern Kingdom had consisted largely of Ephraim and Manasseh. Jeroboam I was an Ephraimite (1 Kgs 12:25). Ephraim became a popular designation for the tribes of the northern secessionist kingdom under his leadership (Hos 4:16-17).

The public performance of this symbolic act prompted the question, "Won't you tell us what you mean?" (v. 18). Ezekiel explained that God was going to join (lit. "give") Joseph to Judah (v. 19), perhaps since David, the new king (v. 24), was of the tribe of Judah (cf. Gen 49:10). Thus God was going to restore and reunite the nation under one king (vv. 18-22). Furthermore, the nation would never again be divided (v. 22), and never again would the people serve idols (v. 23).[78]

---

[77] The inscriptions each begin with לְ, which may be a *lamed* of specification to be left untranslated rather than of possession as NIV's "belonging."

[78] לוֹא, "not," is used three times in vv. 22-23 with עוֹד ("again"), and עוֹד is used by itself a fourth time (at the end of v. 22), thus making a major point of the permanence of the new nation.

**37:24-28**   As Ezekiel previously had informed them in 34:23-24 (see comments there), the restored nation would have "my servant David" as their king. Thus they would be united under "one shepherd." Also as he already had told them (36:27), in this new relationship with God they would be led by God's Spirit to obey his laws (v. 24). They would live in the very land first given to them under the "covenant of peace" (v. 26; cf. 34:25). Two new elements were added in this restatement of the promise. First, the people would be restored to the land forever (v. 26; cf. 16:60). The word ʿolām ("forever/everlasting") is used five times in vv. 25-28. Second, a sanctuary would again be constructed among them that would remain forever. Mention of this house of worship here is a prelude to the temple vision of 40:1–44:31. The reestablished kingdom will have an everlasting king who will be "my servant David," an everlasting "covenant of peace," an everlasting "sanctuary," and an everlasting blessing (vv. 24-28).[79]

It is clear from our vantage point that all of these promises were not fulfilled after the first return from Babylon.[80] Prophecy often had an immediate, limited fulfillment but also a long-range, more complete fulfillment. If this was the case, it meant that Ezekiel was describing details, many of which would be fulfilled in a future permanent return beyond the immediate purview of the return from Babylon. This explains why so many symbols, figures, and verses from Ezekiel were incorporated into John's view of the last days in Revelation. The truth is that both were describing the same events.

There were thirteen promises made to Israel in 37:15-28 that illustrated God's determination to revive, revitalize, restore, and reestablish the nation of Israel.[81] First, God will personally find Israel and gather the people from among the nations (v. 21a). Second, God will bring them again into their land that will be restored to them (v. 21b). Third, God will make one nation of the two that had been in the land (v. 22a). Fourth, God will set one king over the nation (v. 22b,24a). Fifth, God will insure the unity of the restored kingdom that will never again be divided (v. 22c). Sixth, God will insure that the people will never again serve idols (v. 23a). Seventh, God will save them, cleanse them, and establish an intimate person-

---

[79] This restoration will be accomplished by the covenant of peace (cf. 16:60; 34:25) and the resulting construction of the new temple in the middle of the land (48:8; 10:21).

[80] Craigie, *Ezekiel*, 263-64. The passage anticipates the future work of God with Israel in bringing about a complete restoration of the nation.

[81] Van Groningen (*Messianic Revelation*, 779-83) argues rightly that the king in 37:24-28 is the coming Messiah who will effectively carry out the work of the Good Shepherd of 34:23-31.

al relationship with them (v. 23b). Eighth, God will enable them to walk in obedience to his law (v. 24b). Ninth, God will establish them in their land forever (v. 25). Tenth, God will establish his new covenant of peace with them (v. 26a; cf. 34:25; Jer 31:31-34). Eleventh, God will multiply them in the land, and they will enjoy prosperity with peace (v. 26b). Twelfth, God will establish his sanctuary among them and personally dwell there forever (vv. 26c,27). Thirteenth, God will make Israel a testimony to the nations of his saving grace (v. 28).

God has not finished with Israel. He plans a permanent reunification and restoration of his people in his land (37:15-24). The realization of this promise was tied to the development of the messianic hope (37:25-28; cf. Rom 11:25-36).

### (6) God's Defense of Restored Israel (38:1–39:29)

This closing section of the prophecies of restoration addresses a final but crucial question. If Israel was to be restored permanently to the land, what about future enemies? What about the opposition of the premier enemy of God's people in every age, the adversary, Satan? If God's people are to enjoy permanent residence, permanent blessing, and permanent peace in the restoration, what will be done about the struggle between good and evil, God and Satan? These final chapters of the restoration section speak to these questions.

Ezekiel 38:1–39:29 was composed as a series of seven oracles against Gog, the enemy of Israel (note the formula "This is what the Sovereign LORD says" beginning each oracle). These seven messages are: (1) Yahweh will bring Gog and his allies against Israel (38:1-9; cf. Rev 16:13-14; 20:7-8). (2) Gog's evil thoughts and intentions will lead him to invade Israel (38:10-13). (3) Gog will advance against Israel from the north (38:14-16). (4) God will display his awesome judgment against Gog (38:17-23). (5) It will take seven years to plunder and seven months to bury Gog's fallen army (39:1-16). (6) The birds of the air and beasts of the field will be invited to a great feast at which Gog is the meal (39:17-24). (7) Through this deliverance God will conclude the salvation and restoration of Israel as foreseen in 33:1–37:28 (39:25-29).

The eschatological themes and symbolic language of Ezek 38–39 suggests categorizing them as biblical apocalyptic.[82] While lacking such elements as visions and angelic interpreters, they do contain other

---

[82] P. L. Redditt ("Apocalyptic Literature," *MDB*, 38) notes that Ezek 38–39 and Isa 24–27; 34–35; 56–66; Joel; and Zech 1–6; 9–14 were all OT antecedents of NT apocalyptic.

characteristics: (1) a setting in the end times; (2) a conflict between God and the forces of evil, represented by Gog's army; (3) a cataclysmic display of divine power; (4) the replacement of this present age of violence and wickedness with a new age of peace, righteousness, and divine presence; and (5) encouragement to patient faith for God's oppressed people.[83]

In the following comments on these chapters, several principles of interpretation are followed. (1) The message is interpreted as literally as the context and language allow. (2) Since the biblical canon is considered ultimately the product of divine revelation, these chapters are assumed to harmonize rather than conflict with apparently parallel passages encountered elsewhere in Scripture. (3) The present shape of the Book of Ezekiel is believed to have come from a single divinely guided individual. (4) Context is understood to constrain meaning and so is taken as a reliable guide. (5) Divine revelation is believed to have unfolded gradually or progressively so that later prophecies illuminate, elaborate, or expand earlier ones. The present writer believes that these principles lead to an interpretation of the following chapters in accordance with a dispensation premillennial framework.

Other millennial views are believed inadequate when applied to apocalyptic passages such as Ezek 38–39 and 40–48. The premillennial approach is more consistent with the biblical facts, answers more questions, and solves more problems than any of the other approaches. It views history as headed for a literal grand climax that will conclude with a literal battle between Christ and Satan. Jesus will be victorious and establish an earthly kingdom of peace for a thousand years in preparation for the eternal state. This is the general approach that has been adopted in the discussion and interpretation of eschatological passages in Ezekiel and elsewhere.

Most of Old Testament prophecy called for repentance and reformation of human society as the solution to the problem of evil in the world. Thus it focused on the establishment of social, economic, and political justice. The key ideas were "repent" and "return" to the divine standards of God's Word. On the other hand, Ezek 38 and 39 describe one of the most significant apocalyptic confrontations in eschatological prophecy. Like apocalyptic prophecies encountered in Daniel and Zechariah, most of Ezekiel focuses more on revolution than reformation. It is written from the perspective of inevitable and even present judgment. Thus it looks ahead to a grand climax in history. At the end of time God will confront the forces of

---

[83] See "Apocalyptic Literature" in the Introduction.

evil and defeat them. Then he will set up a new golden age of peace and prosperity. The present age and present world will ultimately be dissolved by fire and replaced by a new heaven and a new earth. The Book of Ezekiel combines elements of both traditional prophecy that sought reform and repentance and apocalyptic prophecy that looked for a revolutionary divine intervention in history. Chapters 38 and 39 are a prophetic-apocalyptic view of the cataclysmic initiation of the age of peace to come.[84] Like the messages of judgment against the nations in chaps. 25–32, this speech identifies the recipients, then lists their crimes, then pronounces judgment. This fact lends some additional support to the idea that this may be a symbolic speech against eschatological Babylon, an issue that will be considered in discussion of 38:1-3.

Several questions immediately come to the forefront in consideration of Ezekiel 38 and 39. Who was Gog? What battle was described? When did this battle take place? Where did this battle take place? Why did this battle take place? The discussion of chaps. 38–39 will address these questions.

**¹The word of the LORD came to me: ²"Son of man, set your face against Gog, of the land of Magog, the chief prince of Meshech and Tubal; prophesy against him ³and say: 'This is what the Sovereign LORD says: I am against you, O Gog, chief prince of Meshech and Tubal. ⁴I will turn you around, put hooks in your jaws and bring you out with your whole army—your horses, your horsemen fully armed, and a great horde with large and small shields, all of them brandishing their swords. ⁵Persia, Cush and Put will be with them, all with shields and helmets, ⁶also Gomer with all its troops, and Beth Togarmah from the far north with all its troops—the many nations with you.**

**⁷"'Get ready; be prepared, you and all the hordes gathered about you, and take command of them. ⁸After many days you will be called to arms. In future years you will invade a land that has recovered from war, whose people were gathered from many nations to the mountains of Israel, which had long been desolate. They had been brought out from the nations, and now all of them live in safety. ⁹You and all your troops and the many nations with you will go up, advancing like a storm; you will be like a cloud covering the land.**

GOG'S CALL TO ARMS (38:1-9). *The Identity of Gog (38:1-3).* **38:1-3** The meaning of the name "Gog" is uncertain.[85] The name appears

---

[84] Russell, *Jewish Apocalyptic,* 104-17, and Gowan, *Eschatology,* 49. Gowan asserts that Ezekiel 38–39 is clearly to be viewed as end time, i.e., eschatological in nature.

[85] Alexander ("Ezekiel," 929) gives options for the meaning of Gog, whom he regards as a person.

only here and in 1 Chr 5:4 in the Old Testament, where it identifies one of the sons of Reuben. In the New Testament it appears only once in Rev 20:8. The associated place name, Magog, appears in the table of nations in Gen 10:2 with Gomer, Madai, Javan, Tubal, Meshech, and Tiras, all sons of Japheth. It also is found in Rev 20:8.

Many suggestions have been offered for the identity of Gog. Some of these include: (1) Gugu or Gyges, a ruthless ruler of Lydia; (2) Gagu, a ruler of the land of Sakhi, an area north of Assyria; (3) an unidentified ruler whose name is from a Sumerian loan word *gug,* which means "darkness"; (4) an official title for a ruler comparable to pharaoh or king; (5) a general term for any enemy of God's people.[86]

Gog is called the "chief prince" of Meshech and Tubal.[87] Meshech and Tubal were provinces of Asia Minor in an area associated with the Scythians. The geographical area would today include parts of Iran, Turkey, and southern provinces of Russia.[88] These were the locations of Gog's allies but still furnish no conclusive evidence of Gog's identity. Allen favors the first possibility above, that Gog refers to a former great ruler of Lydia. Meshech and Tobal as well were former powers in Asia Minor. These symbols of former greatness are thus used "to define a future threat, as we might speak fearfully of a new Hitler."[89]

One interesting interpretation identifies Gog as a cryptogram for Babel or Babylon.[90] This identification bears some consideration, especially since Babylon was omitted from the nations mentioned in the messages of judgment of 25:1–32:32. It is strange that Ezekiel would omit the one nation that had to be judged to secure the release of the Hebrew captives. Jeremiah's prophecy against Babylon, for example, devoted more attention to its destruction than any other foreign nation condemned in his prophecies against the nations. He was convinced that God would use Babylon to chasten Judah and encouraged submission and cooperation (Jer 37:1-10; 39:11-14; 40:1-12). Yet he devoted two lengthy chapters totalling 110 verses (50:1–51:64) to a description of the total, massive destruction of Babylon. This prophecy of the fall of Babylon was not

---

[86] For a discussion of possible identifications see Alexander, "Ezekiel," 929, who gives six; Zimmerli, *Ezekiel 2,* 301-2; Cooke, *Ezekiel,* 408-10; Wevers, *Ezekiel,* 284; S. H. Hooke, "Gog and Magog," *ExpTim* 26 [1914]: 317; W. F. Albright, "Gog and Magog," *JBL* 43 [1924]: 378-85.

[87] A possible alternate but highly unlikely translation is "prince of Rosh, Meshech, and Tubal." The NIV translation best fits the grammar and syntax.

[88] Ibid., and Wevers, *Ezekiel,* 284; Fisch, *Ezekiel,* 253.

[89] Allen, *Ezekiel 20–48,* 204-5.

[90] Zimmerli (*Ezekiel 2,* 301) and Wevers (*Ezekiel,* 284) raise this possibility.

fulfilled when it fell to the Medo-Persians in 539 B.C. (Dan 5:1ff.). Why then did Ezekiel omit any hint of the destruction of Babylon in his messages against foreign nations in 25:1–32:32? The answer may lie here in chaps. 38 and 39. These chapters may be a cryptic catalog of the details of the fall of Babylon (see "Messages against the Nations" chart, p. 244).

Using Gog as a symbol of Babylon would fit the apocalyptic nature of these chapters. If such is the case, Babylon itself is being used to represent the nations of the world aligned against God's people in the end times (cf. Rev 14:8; 16:19; 17:1-18; 18:2-24). Ezekiel was concerned not about the destruction of sixth century B.C. Babylon but of the Babylon of the last days, whose destruction would be necessary to facilitate the messianic restoration of Israel that he envisioned in 33:1–37:28. The establishment of the messianic kingdom is the theme of this entire section on restoration. In order for that restoration to take place, Babylon would have to be overthrown. This means Ezekiel 38–39 would be an appropriate prelude to visions of the messianic kingdom. It is no coincidence, therefore, that this is exactly what follows in chaps. 40–48.

If this identification is correct, Gog was a symbol of the forces of Antichrist foreseen by Ezekiel.[91] If the word Gog is from the Sumerian *gug* (meaning "darkness"), that would be additional support for treating him as a symbol of "the prince of this world" (John 12:31; 14:30), an appropriate designation that fits the character of the ruler of end-time Babylon.[92]

Babylon's control of Israel began in 605 B.C. when Nebuchadnezzar laid siege to Jerusalem and forced Jehoiakim to submit as his vassal. Babylon was overthrown exactly seventy years later in one night at the hands of the Medo-Persians (see Dan 5; Isa 41:2; 44:28; 45:1-7). But this would not be the end of Babylon. The kingdom that began under Nimrod (Gen 10:8-10) as a byword for godless government would resurface in the last days under the direction of the wicked prince Gog, and it would be defeated. His defeat would be incontrovertible evidence that the Messiah's reign of peace and security for his people had begun.

One additional clue to this cryptographic identity of Gog as "Mystery Babylon" (Rev 17:5) lies with the role of Nebuchadnezzar in Babylon's rise to power. His father, Nabopolassar, engineered the overthrow of Assyria to establish Babylon as the dominant world power of that time. He did so by forming an alliance with the Median king Cyaxares.[93] With the

---

[91] Ibid., 125.

[92] See Alexander, "Ezekiel," 929, and Albright, "Gog and Magog," 378-85.

[93] See Merrill, *Kingdom of Priests,* 449-50, for a discussion of the historical developments associated with the rise of Nebuchadnezzar.

help of the Medes and Scythians he captured Nineveh in 612 B.C. The alliance that made this great military feat possible was sealed by the marriage of Nabopolassar's son, crown prince Nebuchadnezzar, to Amytis, the daughter of Cyaxares. This gave Nebuchadnezzar a direct link to the very provinces identified as allies of Gog: Meshech, Tubal, Gomer, and Togarmah (38:6).

Ezekiel was most concerned about the final form of the Babylonian Empire, "Mystery Babylon," which he called "Gog." Using subtle cryptic clues, he identified Gog as the future Babylon that would appear in the last days to oppose God and his people. The anti-God kingdom Ezekiel saw is similar to the picture in Rev 16:13-14 of "Mystery Babylon" gathering all nations against God and his people.

One should be cautious, however, about making certain identification of exactly which nation in modern or future history will fill this role. In the twentieth century Germany, Russia, Iran, and Iraq have all been nominated to fill this role; but none of these is certain. The nation that both Ezekiel and John saw will be whatever nation or other group Satan chooses as a means to oppose God at that crucial time. Rabbinic writers identify Gog and Magog as the final enemy who will attack Israel in the messianic age.[94]

God declared, "I am against you, O Gog, chief prince of Meshech and Tubal" (Ezek 38:3; cf. Jer 51:25; Ezek 26:3; 28:22; 29:3; 35:3; 39:1; Nah 2:13; 3:5). The timeless truth of Rom 8:31, "If God is for us, who can be against us?" appears in antithetical form here. If God is against us, who can be for us? The obvious point of v. 3 was that God held no hope for the success of Gog.

John's version of this battle, found in Rev 17–19, suggests that the conflict will be halted for a thousand years of peace under the rule of Messiah (Rev 20:1-3). After the thousand years the battle again resumes with Satan (symbolized by Gog) inciting the nations to revolt against God (Rev 20:7-8). It is significant that the apostle John drew on Ezekiel's language to describe the hostile forces that will oppose Christ's rule. This is strong evidence that John understood that he was describing the same event.

*The Announcement of the Invasion* (38:4-9). **38:4-9** These verses present answers for two additional questions. When will these events happen? What was the main point of 38:1–39:29? Ezekiel was not the first prophet to envision a future apocalyptic battle against the people of God. Several other Old Testament prophets as well as John in Revelation used

---

[94] See Fisch, *Ezekiel*, 253.

apocalyptic language and style to describe future battles.[95]

Some of these prophecies referred to battle in the immediate purview of the prophet, such as the destruction of Jerusalem or Babylon (e.g., Isa 13:1-22; Jer 4:5-6:30; Zeph 1:1-13). Some seem to blend immediate and long-range eschatological fulfillment. Jeremiah 50 and 51 are good examples. These two chapters predict the destruction of Babylon, but their description extends considerably beyond the magnitude of destruction by Medo-Persia in 535 B.C. One may conclude that the reference is to some later time. Other predictions of end-time warfare are purely eschatological and are concerned only with end-time events such as Zech 14:1-21 and Rev 18:1-24. Ezekiel 38–39 was concerned with immediate events as well as end-time events.[96]

In the progression of Ezekiel's prophetic messages the reader is surprised at first by this announcement of a coming battle. One of the occurring themes of the previous chapters is that following the Lord's restoration and reformation of Israel they will "no longer" be victims of the nations or any other calamities but will live securely in their land "forever" (cf. 34:25-29; 36:12-15,30; 37:25-28). When one realizes that the land the Lord will bring Gog's army against is Israel's (vv. 8-9), there is considerable confusion. The solution must be that a major purpose for the invasion will be to demonstrate just how secure Israel will be in their land.

Gog's army would be well equipped, having a mounted calvary, shields, swords, and many soldiers who were called a "great horde" (v. 4). The army would be allied with Persia (Iran), Cush (Ethiopia), Put (Lybia), Gomer (Armenia), and Togarmah (also Armenia).[97] These nations would be called to battle "after many days" and "in future years" against Israel (v. 8). Use of phrases such as "the Day of the LORD," "in that day," "in the latter days," "in future years" were all typical of eschatological passages. These prophetic idioms, "after many days" and "in future years," were

---

[95] Scripture has at least fourteen such apocalyptic passages: (1) Isa 13:1-22; Babylon destroyed by Medo-Persia; (2) Isa 29:1-8; Jerusalem attacked by enemies; (3) Isa 66:1-24; Jerusalem restored after a great battle; (4) Jer 4:5-6:30; Jerusalem to be destroyed; (5) Jer 50:1-51:64; Babylon to be destroyed by many nations; (6) Joel 1:6-12; 2:1-32; Israel's enemies invade and are destroyed; (7) Amos 5:18-20; Samaria to be destroyed; (8) Zeph 1:1-13; Jerusalem to be destroyed; (9) Zech 12:1-9; Jerusalem to be destroyed; (10) Zech 14:1-21; Jerusalem delivered when attacked; (11) Mal 4:1-6; future judgment, the Day of the Lord; (12) Rev 18:1-24; mystery Babylon destroyed; (13) Rev 19:17-21; battle at the return of Messiah; (14) Rev 20:7-8; battle at the end of the millennium.

[96] Cooke, *Ezekiel,* 408.

[97] See 27:10-24.

used nowhere else in Ezekiel and clearly mark this passage as an eschatological reference to end-time events. The future is suggested again in the
expression in v. 16, "in days to come," which is more literally "in the latter days."[98]

Ezekiel envisioned a future time when Israel will have recovered, regathered in the land, and will be dwelling in security (v. 8; cf. 36:33-36).
The armies of Gog would advance like a "storm" and a "cloud" covering
the land (v. 9). Gog at that time would come against the "mountains" of
Israel (cf. 36:1).[99]

There are at least seven views of the time when the invasion of Gog will
take place.[100] One view regards this passage as entirely symbolic. Another
considers that the battle will occur before the tribulation either just prior
to or at the time of the rapture of the church.[101] A third view is that the
battle will occur in the middle of the tribulation and is associated with Rev
14:14-20 and Dan 11:40-41. Fourth, the battle will occur at the end of the
tribulation and is equated with the battle of Rev 19:11-21. Fifth, the battle
will occur during a transitional period that is between the end of the tribulation and the beginning of the millennium to destroy the weapons of
Babylon and cleanse the land prior to the advent of the millennium. Sixth,
the battle will occur at the end of the millennium and should be equated
with Rev 20:7-8. A final view combines the fourth and sixth views and
considers that the battle will occur at the end of the tribulation (Rev 19:17-
21). It will be held in pause for one thousand years, after which it will re-
sume and be concluded as the battle of Rev 20:7-8.

---

[98] Cooke (*Ezekiel,* 407) notes that Jeremiah also used the same expressions (e.g., Jer
4:6,13,24-26; 5:15; 6:1,22; 10:22). The exact expression מִיָּמִים רַבִּים ("after many days")
is found elsewhere only in Josh 23:1. Daniel 8:26 uses לְיָמִים רַבִּים ("the distant future").
The exact expression בְּאַחֲרִית הַשָּׁנִים, "in future years," is found only here. "In days to
come" is בְּאַחֲרִית הַיָּמִים. BDB (31) explains this as "a prophetic phrase denoting the final
period of the history so far as the speaker's perspective reaches; the sense thus varies with
the context, but it often equals the ideal or messianic future." Cf. Deut 4:30; Hos 3:5; Isa 2:2;
Jer 23:20; 30:24; 48:47; 49:39; Dan 2:28; 10:14.

[99] Zimmerli, *Ezekiel 2,* 307. Use of the phrase "mountains of Israel" was intended to
indicate all of the restored nation.

[100] See Enns, *Ezekiel,* 166-69.

[101] The Bible presents a pattern of events associated with the end of time including an
increase of apostasy (1 Tim 4:1,3; 2 Tim 3:1-5), resurrection of the righteous dead and rapture of the righteous living (1 Cor 15:20-24,35-50; 1 Thess 4:13-18), seven years of tribulation on earth (Rev 6:1–16:21), the salvation of Israel in the tribulation (Rev 7:1-8), the battle
of Armageddon (Rev 19:11-16), the establishment of an earthly millennial kingdom with
Christ as the King (Rev 20:1-6) followed by a final confrontation with evil (Rev 20:7-8), the
final judgment with the unregenerate consigned to the lake of fire (Rev 20:11-15), creation
of the new heavens and new earth (Rev 21:1-27), advent of the eternal state (Rev 22:1-21).

None of these suggestions is problem free. The first suggestion fails on the premise that a purely symbolic battle would hardly be described in such detail. The second suggestion does not correlate with the scheme of end-time events in which Israel already would have begun to enjoy its "covenant of peace" (Dan 9:27). The third suggestion does not fit since there is no battle mentioned at midtribulation. It also would be difficult to classify the midtribulation as a time of security (38:14). The fourth suggestion fails to explain the battle of Rev 20:7-8 and what its relation would be to the other apocalyptic battles as well as the use of the name Gog. The fifth suggestion is unacceptable because there is no biblical evidence to suggest that a battle occurs in the transition period mentioned in Dan 12:11-12.[102]

The sixth suggestion places the battle at the end of the millennium. This seems to have fewer problems than the previous ones. Not all the elements of Ezek 38–39 fit neatly into Rev 20:7-8. The information in fifty-two verses would hardly fit into two verses. But Revelation does have the important feature of exact name identity with Gog and Magog. The seventh view has the advantages of both four and six and is strongly suggested by John's use of Ezek 39:4ff. in Rev 19:17-18.[103]

This battle probably takes place at the end of the tribulation, bringing it to a conclusion and ushering in the thousand-year reign of peace. The battle starts again, however, at the end of the thousand years. Revelation 20:2-3 refers to the binding of Satan in the abyss for the thousand years "to keep him from deceiving the nations any more until the thousand years were ended. After that, he must be set free for a short time." Revelation 20:7-8 adds that "when the thousand years are over, Satan will be released from his prison and will go out to deceive the nations in the four corners of the earth—Gog and Magog—to gather them to battle." This seems clearly to suggest a second stage of the Gog-Magog battle that be-

---

[102] An extra month appears in the chronology of the last half of the tribulation (1,290 days instead of the usual 1,260 days). In Dan 12:12 another forty-five days were added for a total of 1,335 days in the last half of the tribulation. These are sometimes called the transition days between the end of the tribulation and the beginning of the millennium. Placing the battle of Ezek 38–39 in Dan 12:11-12 is conjecture and places a great weight of evidence on the chronology of days in Daniel, which no one really understands. For a discussion of various interpretations of Dan 12:11-12, see E. J. Young, *The Prophecy of Daniel* (Grand Rapids: Eerdmans, 1970), 261-64; L. Wood, A *Commentary on Daniel* (Grand Rapids: Zondervan, 1973), 327-29; F. M. Wood, *The Dilemma of Daniel* (Nashville: Broadman, 1985), 213-15.

[103] Enns (*Ezekiel,* 166-69) discusses the weakness of each of five views. Alexander ("Ezekiel," 937-40), after a lengthy excursus, takes the position that the battles of Rev 19:11-21 and 20:7-8 are the same battle.

gan in Rev 19 at the coming of Messiah and conclusion of the tribulation. The purpose would be the final defeat of Satan before the beginning of the eternal state.

[10]"'This is what the Sovereign LORD says: On that day thoughts will come into your mind and you will devise an evil scheme. [11]You will say, "I will invade a land of unwalled villages; I will attack a peaceful and unsuspecting people—all of them living without walls and without gates and bars. [12]I will plunder and loot and turn my hand against the resettled ruins and the people gathered from the nations, rich in livestock and goods, living at the center of the land." [13]Sheba and Dedan and the merchants of Tarshish and all her villages will say to you, "Have you come to plunder? Have you gathered your hordes to loot, to carry off silver and gold, to take away livestock and goods and to seize much plunder?" '

GOG'S EVIL SCHEME (38:10-13). **38:10-13** These verses disclose the plan of the invasion. Verses 10-11 give further insight into the occasion for the battle. Verses 4,16 show that the battle will take place according to the plan and purpose of God. According to Rev 20:7-8, Gog was satanically inspired and hated both God and his people. Verse 10 explains only the human experience, that "thoughts will come into your mind." This is one of several cases in Scripture where several causes that seem to conflict are given for an event that is contrary to the revealed will of God. Pharaoh's refusal to allow Israel to leave Egypt (cp. Exod 7:3 and 8:15) and the crucifixion of Jesus (cp. Matt 26:20-25; John 6:70-71; 10:18; 13:2; 14:27; and Acts 2:23) are two preeminent examples. The viewpoint of Scripture is that neither human wickedness nor the powers of darkness can thwart God's purpose. God's sovereign power and infinite wisdom enable him to use even the schemes of the devil and of wicked individuals to achieve his ends. These chapters promise a day when God's people will no longer need walled villages to be secure. And in order to demonstrate the greatness of his power and of his faithfulness and the powerlessness of evil to thwart his plans to bless his redeemed people, God will lure Gog to his doom.

Gog will notice that Israel is a land of unwalled and therefore unprotected villages (cf. Zech 2:4,8; Esth 9:19), and he will think that the people are easy prey for a swift, formidable attack.[104] God will allow this attack in order to bring swift and decisive judgment against Gog (v. 16) so that he may once and for all correct the damage his people have done to

---

[104] Fisch, *Ezekiel,* 255; Zimmerli (*Ezekiel 2,* 310) notes the use of פְּרָזוֹת ("undefended"), which means "unwalled or unprotected."

his name and may proclaim the greatness of his holy character to all the world.

Gog will seek to loot and plunder those who have resettled Israel in the "center of the land" (v. 12). The word "center" is *tabur,* which means "navel." It is similar to the name for Mount Tabor, located in north central Israel just north of the valley of Jezreel. The same area was associated with the battle of Armageddon based on Rev 16:16.[105] The commodities of end-time Babylon would be of interest to Sheba, Dedan, and Tarshish, who are viewed as trading partners and always interested in plundered goods (vv. 12-13; cf. 27:12,15,22).[106]

[14]"Therefore, son of man, prophesy and say to Gog: 'This is what the Sovereign LORD says: In that day, when my people Israel are living in safety, will you not take notice of it? [15]You will come from your place in the far north, you and many nations with you, all of them riding on horses, a great horde, a mighty army. [16]You will advance against my people Israel like a cloud that covers the land. In days to come, O Gog, I will bring you against my land, so that the nations may know me when I show myself holy through you before their eyes.

GOG'S ADVANCE (38:14-16).    **38:14-16**    Although Gog's intention would be the elimination of Israel for the sake of greed, God would use this desire as an opportunity to confront evil. Gog was not a mindless pawn of Yahweh but one who imagined personal glory in defeating God. But the judgment of Gog was an act God turned to his glory.[107] Divine purpose overrides human motive. The same lesson was given in Habakkuk's message about the Babylonian invasion (Hab 1:5-11).

[17]"'This is what the Sovereign LORD says: Are you not the one I spoke of in former days by my servants the prophets of Israel? At that time they prophesied for years that I would bring you against them. [18]This is what will happen in that day: When Gog attacks the land of Israel, my hot anger will be aroused, declares the Sovereign LORD. [19]In my zeal and fiery wrath I declare that at that time there shall be a great earthquake in the land of Israel. [20]The fish of the sea, the birds of the air, the beasts of the field, every creature that moves along the ground, and all the people on the face of the earth will

---

[105] Zimmerli (*Ezekiel 2,* 311) notes the similarity between טַבּוּר ("navel") and תָּבוֹר ("Tabor"). Jerusalem also was called the "navel" of the earth (D. W. Thomas, "Mount Tabor: The Meaning of the Name," *VT* 1 [1951]: 230). But Jerusalem is not the location since 39:5,11 suggests that this battle takes place in an open valley.

[106] Fisch, *Ezekiel,* 256. Merchants were interested in the purchase of booty taken in battle.

[107] Cooke, *Ezekiel,* 414; Taylor, *Ezekiel,* 246; God's purpose overrules human motives.

tremble at my presence. The mountains will be overturned, the cliffs will crumble and every wall will fall to the ground. <sup>21</sup>I will summon a sword against Gog on all my mountains, declares the Sovereign LORD. Every man's sword will be against his brother. <sup>22</sup>I will execute judgment upon him with plague and bloodshed; I will pour down torrents of rain, hailstones and burning sulfur on him and on his troops and on the many nations with him. <sup>23</sup>And so I will show my greatness and my holiness, and I will make myself known in the sight of many nations. Then they will know that I am the LORD.'

GOD'S WRATH AGAINST GOG (38:17-23).  **38:17-23**  These verses reveal the purpose and outcome of the invasion. Interpreters of v. 17 have offered many suggestions for the identification of the prophecy or prophecies from "former days." Such prophecies as Isa 14:24-25; 26:20-21; Jer 4:5; 6:26; 30:18-24; Joel 3:9-21; Zeph 1:14-18; 3:8 are possibilities.[108] The Gog-Magog message is very similar to Zech 12:3-9; 14:1-8, but these do not come from "former days" (the dating of Joel is controverted). D. I. Block has made a cogent argument that none of these prophecies would fit Ezek 38:17.[109] Nor does he find acceptable a reference to general prophecies of "the final destruction of the enemies of God's people."[110] Equally unconvincing are the attempts of Zimmerli and Fishbane to see Ezekiel's prophecy as a reinterpretation and reapplication of earlier prophecies, especially Jeremiah's "foe from the north."[111] Block's most significant argument is that the question in v. 17 should be translated, "Are you he of whom the prophets spoke?" This is the clear reading of the Hebrew text as it stands. It is frequently emended to a statement, "You are he," but this is unnecessary. The translation "are you not" assumes an introductory particle (*hălō*), which is not in the text. Block notes the striking similarity between Ezek 38:17 and 2 Sam 7:5, "Are you the one to build me a house to dwell in?" This expects a negative reply, confirmed by the parallel in 1 Chr 17:4, where it is a statement, "You are not the one." The point of the Lord's question in Ezek 38:17, then, may be that Gog is not a divinely commissioned agent of judgment like Jeremiah's "foe from the north" (though Gog may have thought so) but strictly an enemy of God and his people to

---

[108] Wevers, *Ezekiel*, 289; Taylor, *Ezekiel*, 246; Fisch, *Ezekiel*, 257; Alexander, "Ezekiel," 933.

[109] See D. I. Block, "Gog in Prophetic Tradition: A New Look at Ezekiel 38:17," *VT* 42 (1992): 166-72.

[110] Alexander, "Ezekiel," 933.

[111] Zimmerli, *Ezekiel 2*, 303; M. Fishbane, *Biblical Interpretation in Ancient Israel* (Oxford: Oxford University Press, 1985), 477. See also Allen (*Ezekiel 20–48*, 206), who sees Ezek 38–39 as a "typological" fulfillment of earlier prophecies.

be dealt with in "zeal and fiery wrath" (v. 19).

When God allows Gog to come against Israel, several events will take place. First, the hot, fiery anger of God will be released (v. 18).[112] Second, there will be an earthquake of major force (vv. 19-20). An earthquake sometimes was a sign of a theophany,[113] but the "day of the LORD" was also a theophany.[114] Third, the sword will be summoned against Gog. The attack is a picture of confusion and demoralization in which the army of Gog attacks itself (v. 21).[115] Fourth, other signs of divine judgment follow, including rain, hailstones, blood, and burning sulfur that will descend on Gog and the many nations who fight with him (v. 22). These are obvious signs of a supernatural divine judgment.[116] This demonstration of divine power will result in two things. One is the deliverance of Israel from the invading forces of Gog. Another is the universal recognition of the sovereignty of Yahweh.[117]

Chapter 39 is a continuation and expansion of details concerning the destruction of Gog. The details given in 39:1-29 are more vivid and numerous, and they reiterate the same purposes presented in chap. 38. In Block's analysis the two chapters of the Gog prophecy comprise two parallel panels, each consisting of four units and having a conclusion. Panel A in chap. 38 he titles "The Disposal of Gog." The first panel concludes in 38:23 and the second panel in 39:21-24. The final message in 39:25-29 is the conclusion to the whole oracle.[118] Although not without problems, this analysis directs attention to the five "acknowledgment" passages ("that . . . may know") that reveal God's purposes. Each panel has two acknowledgment passages, the second being its conclusion (38:16,23; 39:6-8,21-24); the whole prophecy ends in a final acknowledgment passage (39:25-29).

[1]**"Son of man, prophesy against Gog and say: 'This is what the Sovereign LORD says: I am against you, O Gog, chief prince of Meshech and Tubal. [2]I will turn you around and drag you along. I will bring you from the far north and send you against the mountains of Israel. [3]Then I will strike your bow from your left hand and make your arrows drop from your right hand. [4]On**

---

[112] Fisch, *Ezekiel,* 257. This denotes divine anger; see Deut 32:22 and Ps 18:9.

[113] Cooke, *Ezekiel,* 414; cf. 1 Kgs 19:11; Ps 18:16.

[114] Zimmerli, *Ezekiel 2,* 313. The idea of a cosmic earthquake was a significant one associated with the end of time in later apocalyptic (see Joel 2:10; 3:3ff.; 4:15).

[115] Taylor, *Ezekiel,* 247; see also Judg 7:22; 1 Sam 14:20; Hag 2:22; Zeph 14:13.

[116] Alexander, "Ezekiel," 934.

[117] Fisch, *Ezekiel,* 258.

[118] Block, "Gog in Prophetic Tradition," 157.

the mountains of Israel you will fall, you and all your troops and the nations with you. I will give you as food to all kinds of carrion birds and to the wild animals. [5]You will fall in the open field, for I have spoken, declares the Sovereign Lord. [6]I will send fire on Magog and on those who live in safety in the coastlands, and they will know that I am the LORD.

[7]"'I will make known my holy name among my people Israel. I will no longer let my holy name be profaned, and the nations will know that I the LORD am the Holy One in Israel. [8]It is coming! It will surely take place, declares the Sovereign LORD. This is the day I have spoken of.

[9]"'Then those who live in the towns of Israel will go out and use the weapons for fuel and burn them up—the small and large shields, the bows and arrows, the war clubs and spears. For seven years they will use them for fuel. [10]They will not need to gather wood from the fields or cut it from the forests, because they will use the weapons for fuel. And they will plunder those who plundered them and loot those who looted them, declares the Sovereign LORD.

[11]"'On that day I will give Gog a burial place in Israel, in the valley of those who travel east toward the Sea. It will block the way of travelers, because Gog and all his hordes will be buried there. So it will be called the Valley of Hamon Gog.

[12]"'For seven months the house of Israel will be burying them in order to cleanse the land. [13]All the people of the land will bury them, and the day I am glorified will be a memorable day for them, declares the Sovereign LORD.

[14]"'Men will be regularly employed to cleanse the land. Some will go throughout the land and, in addition to them, others will bury those that remain on the ground. At the end of the seven months they will begin their search. [15]As they go through the land and one of them sees a human bone, he will set up a marker beside it until the gravediggers have buried it in the Valley of Hamon Gog. [16](Also a town called Hamonah will be there.) And so they will cleanse the land.'

THE MAGNITUDE OF GOG'S DEFEAT (39:1-16). **39:1-8** These verses restate the divine initiative in the invasion and elaborate upon the fall of Gog and God's purposes. The parallel nature of the two chapters is suggested by the repetition in vv. 1-2 from 38:2-4. The identity of Gog, chief prince of Meshech and Tubal, has been discussed (vv. 1-2; see 38:1-3). Gog came from the mountains of the "far north," a designation associated with Meshech and Tubal. God promised that the weapons of Gog would be taken from him (v. 3); he would lose his power and fall on the "mountains of Israel" (v. 4). The AV makes reference to a "sixth part" of the armies of Gog in v. 2. This was based on a mistranslation of the verb rendered here "drag you along" (שֵׁשֵׁאתִיךָ).[119] God will "drag" the army of Gog to

---

[119] שֵׁשֵׁאתִיךָ is a hapax legomenon, which means "to lead" or perhaps "to drive."

a stunning and miraculous defeat.

The defeat will be so awesome that bodies of the soldiers will become food for the birds of prey and the wild animals of the land. Verses 4-9 are similar to Rev 19:17-18, obviously references to the same event. Alexander reached the same conclusion in a lengthy excursus that explains the "birds of prey" passage as unique to Ezek 39 and Rev 19. He correctly concluded that Rev 19 was at least a partial fulfillment of Ezek 39:4.[120] The idea of the "birds of prey" in 39:4 is discussed more fully in 39:17-20.

Another clue for fixing the location of this battle is given in v. 5. Gog will fall along with his army in the "open field" (v. 6). As noted in the discussion of 38:12, this event may take place near Mount Tabor in north central Israel where the valley of Jezreel is situated.[121] This valley, which also was called the plain of Esdraelon, would certainly qualify for a large open area suitable for a battlefield. Gog will be destroyed, and destruction will come even on his homeland and the surrounding "coastlands" so that they too will know that Yahweh is God. Wevers takes the "coastlands" as a reference to the western end of the Jezreel Valley, which will witness the awesome fiery destruction portrayed in v. 6, but Allen is more likely correct that Gog's neighbors in western Asia Minor are in view.[122]

Recognition of the holiness of God's name and character (v. 7) is an echo of 36:20-23 that mentioned Israel's profaning the name of Yahweh (see also 20:39; 39:25; 43:7ff.). Through this act of miraculous judgment on Gog and deliverance of Israel, Yahweh will vindicate his name, and everyone will know he is the Holy One in Israel (v. 7).[123] The certainty of these events was confirmed by the declaration, "It is coming!" (v. 8).[124]

**39:9-16**    These verses describe the disposal of Gog's army and offer two illustrations of the magnitude of Gog's defeat. First, Gog's weapons will supply Israel with fuel for seven years (vv. 9-10). Gog came to plunder Israel (38:12) but instead will become Israel's (v. 10).

Second, the debacle will be such that a valley in Israel will be required as a graveyard for the slain soldiers of the army of Gog. The valley is not identified other than that it was a route for those traveling "east toward the sea" (v. 11). Most interpreters identify the "sea" as the Dead Sea since it is the one sea that lies to the east of Israel.[125]

---

[120] See Alexander, "Ezekiel," 937-40; cf. Ezek 29:5.

[121] See 38:10-16 note; cf. 39:11.

[122] Wevers, *Ezekiel,* 291-92; Allen, *Ezekiel 20–48,* 207.

[123] Zimmerli, *Ezekiel 2,* 315. This is the antithesis of profaning God's name in 36:20-23.

[124] Ibid., Fisch, *Ezekiel,* 260; see notes of 21:1-7.

[125] See Fisch, *Ezekiel,* 261; Cooke, *Ezekiel,* 419; Taylor, *Ezekiel,* 247; Wevers, *Ezekiel,* 292, as examples of those who identify the sea to the east as the Dead Sea.

Wevers notes that the use of the word "travelers" (ʿōbĕrîm) is similar to the name of the mountains of northern Moab ("Abarim") with a large valley on the east side of the Dead Sea. He identified this valley in the central area east of the Dead Sea as the valley of 39:11. He admits that this territory is outside the land of Israel. It was not part of postexilic Israel but was part of the Davidic empire.[126] Yet the geographical location of this valley to the east of the Dead Sea creates the same problem as with Jezreel. It would be impossible to travel east toward the sea (39:11) that lies due west of this valley. Second, the size of this valley would accommodate neither the battle nor the burial mentioned in 39:11-16.

The Jezreel Valley near Mount Tabor mentioned in discussion of vv. 5-6 runs east/west, but the Mediterranean or Great Sea is at the western end, not the eastern end. East of the Jezreel Valley was the Jordan River and the Sea of Galilee, which usually was called Lake Gennesaret and probably was not the "sea" of v. 11.

A simpler solution lies in translating "east *of* the Sea." This translation would allow for the travelers' movement east from the sea, which would be to their rear. Then the sea could indeed be the Mediterranean and the valley the Jezreel Valley.[127]

The Jezreel Valley is the only major east/west valley in Israel.[128] It has at least three names including the valley of Jezreel, plain of Esdraelon and valley of Megiddo. This valley was identified by the apostle John in Rev 16:13-16 as the location of the battle of "Armageddon." The valley is a natural battlefield and could even serve as a large graveyard such as mentioned in v. 11. This site also has the proximity with Mount Tabor mentioned in 38:11 as the "navel of the earth."

At the time of the burial the valley will be renamed the valley of "Hamon Gog," meaning "hordes of Gog." A city located in the valley will be named Hamonah, Hebrew for "multitude," a reference to the scope of the destruction (v. 16).[129]

The devastation of this battle will be so great that burial of the dead will proceed for seven months. All the dead will be buried to cleanse the land. An unburied corpse was considered unclean (Deut 21:23), and burial was done as soon as possible after death.[130] Though everyone participated in the burial of Gog's army (v. 13), a full-time burial corps was em-

---

[126] See Wevers, *Ezekiel,* 292, for a description of the valley. Allen (*Ezekiel 20–48,* 201) thinks the text originally had "Abarim."

[127] See BDB, 870.

[128] See Alexander, "Ezekiel," 936.

[129] See Zimmerli, *Ezekiel 2,* 317.

[130] Fisch, *Ezekiel,* 261.

ployed (v. 14). Anyone who found a bone, skeleton, or any human remains placed a marker on it for the burial corps to find and bury in the valley of Hamon-Gog.[131]

<sup></sup>

**17"Son of man, this is what the Sovereign LORD says: Call out to every kind of bird and all the wild animals: 'Assemble and come together from all around to the sacrifice I am preparing for you, the great sacrifice on the mountains of Israel. There you will eat flesh and drink blood. 18You will eat the flesh of mighty men and drink the blood of the princes of the earth as if they were rams and lambs, goats and bulls—all of them fattened animals from Bashan. 19At the sacrifice I am preparing for you, you will eat fat till you are glutted and drink blood till you are drunk. 20At my table you will eat your fill of horses and riders, mighty men and soldiers of every kind,' declares the Sovereign LORD.**

**21"I will display my glory among the nations, and all the nations will see the punishment I inflict and the hand I lay upon them. 22From that day forward the house of Israel will know that I am the LORD their God. 23And the nations will know that the people of Israel went into exile for their sin, because they were unfaithful to me. So I hid my face from them and handed them over to their enemies, and they all fell by the sword. 24I dealt with them according to their uncleanness and their offenses, and I hid my face from them.**

THE FEAST OF GOG AND THE GLORY OF THE LORD (39:17-24).   **39:17-24**   Verses 17-20 develop the "birds of prey" theme from v. 4.[132] God speaks through Ezekiel to the birds and animals, inviting them to a sacrificial meal at which Gog will be the only item on the menu (vv. 17-19). These birds and animals are invited to feast on the dead corpses of the army of Gog. Bodies will lie in the open as the burial corps proceeds with their work for seven months (cf. v. 12). Little imagination is needed to realize the gruesome fact that the birds of prey and wild animals will feed on carrion. Reference to setting a marker by a bone (v. 15) suggests that often by the time burial took place there was not much remaining to bury in the valley called "Hamon Gog."

The army of Gog will be eaten as if it were consumed by the altar fires like a sacrificial animal.[133] God said he was preparing his sacrifice, and the birds and animals at his table will eat their fill (vv. 17-20). The idea of

---

[131] Zimmerli, *Ezekiel 2,* 318; Wevers, *Ezekiel,* 293. The language used suggests that the people were professionals in the art of burial.

[132] Alexander ("Ezekiel," 937-40) discusses the relationship of Ezek 38–39 to Rev 19:17-21 and 20:7-10 and concludes that both predict the ultimate defeat for all those who oppose Israel.

[133] See Fisch, *Ezekiel,* 262-63.

the Lord's sacrifice as a divine judgment also may be found in Isa 34:6-17; Jer 46:10; Zeph 1:7-18; and Rev 19:17-21.[134]

Gog's army will be a glorious sight when it appears with horses and "horsemen fully armed," a "great horde with large and small shields, all of them brandishing their swords" (38:4). An alliance of many nations, it will come against Israel like a storm cloud, and God's people will be helpless before them (38:9). A compassionate observer would wince at the prospect of such an imminent slaughter of "a peaceful and unsuspecting people" (38:11). But just as disaster is about to strike God's people, they will see a massive and spectacular display of the power and wrath of God against their enemies. They will stand by and watch in amazement as the great army of Gog is annihilated by earthquake, flood, hail, fire, and their own swords (38:19–39:6).

The amount of plunder will be awesome and the stench of bodies overpowering as the birds of prey devour the flesh of what was perhaps the greatest army ever assembled (39:9-20). All the nations of the world will see and learn as all the pretense of human glory is extinguished before the pure and ineffable glory of the Holy God of Israel. No longer will the accusation be heard that Israel's God had abandoned them in unfaithfulness or proved unable to defend them against the nations and their gods. It will be clear to all that it was Israel's sin and unfaithfulness that led to their exile, that their troubles had been recompense for their uncleanness and their offenses.

**²⁵"Therefore this is what the Sovereign LORD says: I will now bring Jacob back from captivity and will have compassion on all the people of Israel, and I will be zealous for my holy name. ²⁶They will forget their shame and all the unfaithfulness they showed toward me when they lived in safety in their land with no one to make them afraid. ²⁷When I have brought them back from the nations and have gathered them from the countries of their enemies, I will show myself holy through them in the sight of many nations. ²⁸Then they will know that I am the LORD their God, for though I sent them into exile among the nations, I will gather them to their own land, not leaving any behind. ²⁹I will no longer hide my face from them, for I will pour out my Spirit on the house of Israel, declares the Sovereign LORD."**

THE EPITAPH OF GOG'S DEFEAT (39:25-29). **39:25-29** In these verses the focus shifts back from the eschatological future to the situation of the exiles in Babylon. This passage provides a conclusion to the Gog-

---

[134] Taylor, *Ezekiel,* 248.

Magog passage but also the six restoration messages of 33:1–39:29.[135] In this summary Ezekiel listed seven purposes that God would achieve by ending the exile.[136] First, God would initiate a new era in relationship with Israel, hence the use of "now."[137] Second, God had demonstrated the discipline of love by chastening his people (Prov 3:11-12; Heb 12:5-8). He would show the compassion of love by restoring them to their former place. Third, God would be zealous for his holy name's sake. He would reverse the profaning of his name that was reported in 36:20-23 and promote the sanctification of his name among the heathen (36:23).

Fourth, Israel would forget their shame and unfaithfulness (v. 26) in that their time of disgrace would be past (36:30-31). Fifth, God would demonstrate his holiness through regathering Israel from the countries of their enemies and reestablishing them in their land (v. 27). Sixth, Israel would know that Yahweh is their God, for he would leave none in exile but return everyone to the land (v. 28). Seventh, God would pour out his spirit on the house of Israel as he promised (36:27; Joel 2:29), a promise that was associated with the messianic age (v. 29).[138]

These verses are very similar to the concluding verses of the preceding section (39:21-24). They both declare what the Lord was going to do and how Israel and the nations would respond, and they both refer to the exile and the Lord hiding his face. Both passages mention the nations seeing what the Lord does, but the Lord's actions in vv. 21-24 involve only judgment on the army of Gog, while in vv. 25-29 they include all aspects of the restoration of Israel.[139] Both passages stress the resultant revelation of the knowledge of God for both Israel and the nations. For Israel, receiving the Spirit (v. 29) will be "a sign and seal of the covenant," repre-

---

[135] Cooke (*Ezekiel,* 421-22) concludes the Gog oracles with 39:16; Wevers (*Ezekiel,* 285) and Zimmerli (*Ezekiel 2,* 289-90) conclude it with 39:20; Eichrodt (*Ezekiel,* 521) concludes it with 39:24 and considers vv. 25-29 as the link between chaps. 37 and 40. Block rejects attempts to trace the history of the composition of the passage and focuses on its function. He considers vv. 21-29 as the conclusion of the Gog oracle and also of the preceding chapters of restoration. See D. I. Block, "Gog and the Pouring out of the Spirit: Reflections on Ezekiel 39:21-29," *VT* 37 (1987): 257-70.

[136] Alexander, "Ezekiel," 942. The six messages stressed the covenant promises that reflect God's will for Israel at the end of the exile.

[137] Fisch, *Ezekiel,* 264; Taylor, *Ezekiel,* 249. "Now" refers to the time when the decree of God's punishment of Israel has been fulfilled so that the new era will be inaugurated for the blessing and benefit of the people.

[138] Fisch (*Ezekiel,* 265) understands that the restoration of the prophetic phenomenon in the coming new age for Israel will indicate the return of the Spirit's power and result in permanent redemption.

[139] See Block, "Gog and the Pouring out of the Spirit," 264.

senting "the divine mark of ownership" (cf. Isa 32:15; 44:1-5; Joel 3:1; Zech 12:10), the "guarantee of new life, peace, and prosperity." It will be "the definitive act whereby he [Yahweh] claimed and sealed the newly gathered nation of Israel as his own."[140]

Yet those who think that Pentecost is the final fulfillment of this prophecy and that the church has replaced Israel in the plan of God must reckon with the stress of these chapters on the need for an eschatological vindication of God's name in his dealings with Israel. These prophecies call for Israel's literal return to the land in peace and prosperity, followed by the threat of massive invasion and a spectacular annihilation of Israel's enemies. Only then will the revelation of the uniqueness and glory of God be complete and will the purpose of Israel as a light to the nations be fulfilled.[141] As R. L. Saucy has written, "It is not that God *simply chooses* to reveal to all people his grace and power in the reestablishment and blessing of his people." More than that, "God's reputation is at stake." Thus just as his holiness required him to judge Israel for rebellion, so also it requires him to regather and restore it. So "the restoration of Israel is not only a display of God's love and power in behalf of his people, but also *'an event necessary to the preservation of the honor of the true God.'*"[142]

This great section of hope and restoration beginning in 33:1 presents three significant themes that are crystallized in chaps. 38–39. First, God will triumph in the end of things. Whenever individuals set themselves against God, they always fail. God will judge those who oppose him and chasten those who love him but stray. He may grant the brief illusion of success, but ultimately judgment will come. In the end God will be the victor who will establish his name, his glory, and his people at the end of human history. "If God is for us, who can be against us?" (Rom 8:31). If God is against us, who can be for us? (38:3).

Second, God offers salvation to individuals. For those who will approach him in humility, repentance, and faith, he will provide a "new heart" and a "new spirit" (36:26-27). This offer is an ever-present possibility, which he offers to the human predicament of sin. The shadow of calvary was cast in two directions. It stretched from Christ back to cre-

---

[140] Ibid., 268-69.

[141] See R. L. Saucy, *The Case for Progressive Revelation* (Grand Rapids: Zondervan, 1993), 297-323. He notes that Israel's election was particularly to be a witness to the nations of the uniqueness of Yahweh (p. 301-2). He also notes regarding these prophecies of acknowledgment in Ezek 39:21-29: "We cannot say that history thus far reveals *the nations* as truly recognizing God's hand in the suffering of Israel. That awakening is still future" (p. 313).

[142] Ibid., 315, quoting G. F. Oehler.

ation to embrace all those who were saved by faith, looking forward to the salvation he provided. It stretched from Christ to the end of creation, providing salvation to all people in all ages of human history. Salvation will be available as long as people are lost and human history continues. That salvation includes security insured by divine power that results in victory over all that opposes God and his people (39:26).

Third, even the evil of those who oppose him will ultimately bring glory to God. Whenever the judgment of God comes upon ungodliness and unrighteousness, his holiness and righteousness are established (39:7). One day every knee will bow and every tongue confess the glory of Yahweh and Jesus Christ his son (Phil 2:9-11). Long ago Habakkuk wrestled with the question of why God would use the wicked Babylonians as an instrument of judgment on Israel. He discovered that even the wicked will bring glory to God either by receiving the life-transforming gift of a new heart and new spirit or by receiving judgment to establish his holiness, righteousness, and name (Hab 1:1–2:20).

## Table 5: Restoration of Edenic Ideals

The ideal characteristics of life in Eden were forfeited because of sin. The OT prophets developed the theme of restoration of these ideals and the hope of a coming ideal community. Ezekiel developed every aspect of this restoration hope of a new Eden (Ezek 36:35).

| Ideals of Eden | Loss Due to Sin | Restoration |
|---|---|---|
| Life<br>Gen 2:7-9 | Death<br>Gen 3:19; 4:8 | NEW LIFE (everlasting)<br>Ezek 36:25-27; 37:1-14; 47:1-2,5-10; Rev 22:1-2,14 |
| Work<br>Gen 2:15 | Toil, Labor<br>Gen 3:17-19 | WORK (rewards for labor): Jer 31:15-17; Ezek 36:8-11,33-36; 1 Cor 3:11-15; 15:58 |
| Rest<br>Gen 2:3 | No Rest<br>Gen 3:19a | REST (cessation of human efforts)<br>Jer 6:16; Ezek 34:27-28; Matt 11:28; Heb 4:8-11; Rev 14:13 |
| Peace (harmony)<br>Gen 2:8-20 | Enmity<br>Gen 3:15; 4:8 | PEACE (new harmony)<br>Isa 9:6; 11:6-8; Ezek 34:25; 37:26; Jer 31:31-34; Mic 4:1-3; Eph 2:14 Rev 22–23 |
| Companionship Gen 2:18,21-25 | Discord<br>Gen 3:12,16<br>(polygamy 4:19) | COMPANIONSHIP<br>Isa 11:11-12; Ezek 34:13,16,23-24,30; 36:28; 37:15-28; Rev 22:3 |
| Knowledge<br>Gen 2:9,17<br>(by revelation and discernment) | Knowledge<br>Gen 3:7 (by experience)<br>Amos 8:11-12; Hos 4:6 | KNOWLEDGE (by revelation and experience)<br>Jer 31:31-34; Ezek 34:30; 36:26-27; Col 1:9; 1 Tim 2:3-4; 2 Tim 3:16-17 |
| Dominion<br>(stewardship Gen 1:26-28; 2:19-20 | Domination<br>Gen 3:6;<br>4:17; 6:5 | DOMINION (stewardship renewal)<br>Ezek 34:29; 36:28-38; Zech 9:10; Rev 22:3-5 |
| Productivity | Unproductivity<br>Gen 3:17-18 | PRODUCTIVITY<br>Joel 2:23-24; Ezek 29:21; 34:26-31; 36:8-12,30-32,37-38; 47:12; Amos 9:11-15; Rev 22:2-3 |
| Security (garden = sheltered, protected area Gen 2:8 | Fear | SECURITY (eternal)<br>Ezek 34:28; 37:27-28; Mic 4:4; 1 John 4:18; Rev 7:14-17; 21:3,8; 22:3-4 |

2. Visions concerning the Restored Community (40:1–48:35)
    (1)  Vision of a Restored Temple (40:1–42:20)
    (2)  Return of Yahweh to His Sanctuary (43:1-12)
    (3)  Vision of Restored Worship (43:13–46:24)
    (4)  Vision of the River Flowing from the Throne (47:1-12)
    (5)  Vision of the New Boundaries (47:13–48:35)

## 2. Visions concerning the Restored Community (40:1–48:35)

Ezekiel 40–48 was written later than all the prophecies of the book except 29:17-21.[1] The visions recorded in this section continue the theme of the hope of restoration that began in chap. 33. Chapters 33–37 present the promise of hope; the triumph of hope follows in chaps. 38–39, and finally Ezekiel presents the realization of hope in chaps. 40–48. The focus on a new temple and reinstituted offerings is foreshadowed in 20:40 as well as 37:24-28.[2] Following the destruction of Gog and Magog in chaps. 38–39, the prophet foresaw the establishment of a glorious new kingdom. These messages came thirteen years after the six vision messages of restoration in 33:1–39:29.[3]

Several approaches have been taken to chaps. 40–48. One approach is to view these chapters strictly historically as Ezekiel's hopes and dreams for the restored community when Israel returned to their homeland.[4] If this is true, then his hope was never realized. Nothing that took place after the return from Babylon matched the details of these predictions. No temple built after the return resembled the structure that the prophet envisioned in 40:1–42:20. There has never been a reinstatement of the

---

[1] See Introduction, "Dated Prophecies in Ezekiel," p. 54.

[2] Cf. M. Greenberg, "The Design and Themes of Ezekiel's Program of Restoration," *Int* 38 (1984): 181-82. He takes chaps. 40–48 as "a proleptic corroboration" of the book's earlier promises. This and other factors lead him to the conclusion that this final section "is the product of a single mind (and hand) and that, as carrying forward ideas and values found in the preceding prophecies, it may reasonably be attributed to their author, the priest-prophet Ezekiel" (p. 181).

[3] R. H. Alexander, "Ezekiel," EBC 6 (Grand Rapids: Zondervan, 1986), 952; Greenburg, "Ezekiel's Program of Restoration," 181-208; S. Talmon and M. Fishbane, "The Structures of Biblical Books: Studies in the Book of Ezekiel," *ASTI* 10 (1975-76): 138-54.

[4] See J. B. Taylor, *Ezekiel,* TOTC (Downers Grove: InterVarsity, 1969), 251-53.

priesthood or sacrifices, or tribal allotments as suggested in 43:13–46:24, or geographical changes as in 47:1–48:35. There has been no literal fulfillment down to the present that compares to what Ezekiel saw.[5] Furthermore, such a historical view does not fit the eschatological context of the previous chapters.

Second, some regard the visions of Ezek 40–48 as symbolically portraying the present age following the salvific work of Christ. In this view the symbols represent the church and for that reason were used by John in Revelation.[6] The weakness of this approach is that it fails to account for the detailed descriptions of people, places, and events in the restored community. A spiritualized interpretation of chaps. 40–48 ignores the warning of Ezekiel's angel-guide that he should carefully record the minute details of the physical structures in his vision (40:4). If these structures are only symbols of greater spiritual realities and nothing more, then such details would be irrelevant. This symbolic approach also fails if the church is not the new Israel.[7]

Somewhat similar to the spiritualized approach is that of S. Tuell, who believes chaps. 40–48 are neither prophetic, apocalyptic, nor a practical hope for the future. He believes the section represents a symbolic declaration that worship was the center of life in the shuffle of world events. The temple, at the heart of Ezekiel's vision, was a symbol that worship was at the heart of world culture.[8]

A third view is that these chapters describe symbolically an eschatological kingdom. These symbols were idealized pictures of spiritual truths that present the character of the coming kingdom but make no attempt to define its form. The view suffers from the same weakness of the previous one. The detail with which the restored community was described exceeds the use of apocalyptic merely as a literary device.[9] Also no distinction is made between Israel and the church.

Fourth, the passage is apocalyptic and therefore filled with highly sym-

---

[5] Alexander, "Ezekiel," 943. See his excellent discussion of approaches to the interpretation of chaps. 40–48.

[6] Taylor (*Ezekiel,* 252) calls this the "symbolic Christian" approach.

[7] Alexander, "Ezekiel," 943. See discussion of the church and Israel in the introduction to 37:1-28. See also P. D. Hanson, *Old Testament Apocalyptic* (Nashville: Abingdon, 1987), 59. He notes that "properly used the historical-critical method is an indispensable tool in the effort to interpret the apocalyptic writings for contemporary individuals and communities of faith" (p. 59).

[8] S. Tuell, *The Law of the Temple in Ezekiel 40–48* (Atlanta: Scholars Press, 1992), 175-78.

[9] Hanson, *Old Testament Apocalyptic,* 945-46.

bolic imagery, but it is also prophetic in the sense that it describes literal future events. The prophetic-apocalyptic view of the passage regards the chapters as an essentially literal description of a real future kingdom. This restored kingdom is not the church but Israel. But while describing literal features of a restored kingdom, Ezekiel also conveys spiritual truth. The very objects he describes, such as a literal temple, priesthood, and sacrifices also function as symbols of the character of the kingdom and its King. For example, the eight steps that lead to the inner court of the sanctuary (40:31,34,37) will be eight literal steps, but they are also a symbol of the Messiah, who is "the way" of access to fellowship with God (John 14:6).[10]

Chapters 40–48 present details of the millennial temple, priesthood, sacrifices, and tribal divisions to be set up on earth during the millennium as forerunners of the eternal state. Obvious questions arise about this approach, such as: Why a temple? Why reinstate animal sacrifices? Why the return to the requirements of the Mosaic law? Answers to these issues will be presented in the discussion that follows. Others perhaps would conclude that the detailed discussion of the temple complex is somewhat tedious. If the prophet was discussing a literal structure, it is easier to understand his extreme attention to detail. If one takes this seriously as a literal future temple, then the attention to detail is no surprise.

Chapters 40–48 may be divided into five sections concerning (1) the presentation of the temple (40:1–42:20); (2) the return of the glory of God (43:1-12); (3) the priesthood and sacrifices (43:13–46:24); (4) the river of life (47:1-12); and (5) the land and the city (47:13–48:35).[11]

### (1) Vision of a Restored Temple (40:1–42:20))

A sanctuary for worship was associated with Israel from the foundation of its existence (cf. Exod 33:7-11). The tabernacle, constructed in the wilderness as the visible sign of the Mosaic covenant (Exod 26:1; 36:8–38:20), was the forerunner of the permanent sanctuary, the temple, both in precedent and design.[12] M. Haran lists thirteen "Israelite temples from

---

[10] See discussion of 34:23-31 and the eight characteristics of the ideal Shepherd.

[11] Tuell (*Law of the Temple*, 20) proposes a seven-part division of chaps. 40–48. (1) Introduction (40:1-4); (2) Survey of the Temple Complex (40:5–42:20); (3) Return of the Divine Glory (43:1-9); (4) The Law of the Temple (43:10–46:24); (5) The Course of the River of Life (47:1-12); (6) Survey of Territorial Allotments and Borders (47:13–48:29); (7) Conclusion (48:30-35).

[12] See R. E. Clements, *God and Temple* (Philadelphia: Fortress, 1965), 40-43. See also "Temple" in the standard Bible dictionaries.

the Old Testament period which are attested explicitly or indirectly." These worship centers were at Shiloh, Dan, Bethel, Gilgal, Mizpah, Hebron, Bethlehem, Nob, the house of Micah (Judg 17–18), Ophrah, Gibeah, Arad, and Jerusalem.[13]

Beginning with Solomon's temple there are seven sanctuaries of Israel in Scripture:[14]

1. *Solomon's Temple*. Details Solomon's construction are reported in 1 Kgs 6–8. It was destroyed by Nebuchadnezzar in 587/586 B.C. (Jer 32:28-44).

2. *Zerubabbel's Temple*. When the Hebrews returned from Babylon in 535 B.C., one of the first priorities was to lay the foundation for a new temple. The structure was dedicated in 516 B.C. (Ezra 3:1-8; 4:1-14). Zerubbabel, a descendant of David (1 Chr 3:19), was in charge of this reconstruction.

3. *Herod's Temple*. The existing structure desecrated by Antiochus Epiphanes in 169 B.C. was refurbished and enlarged by Herod the Great. The work began in 19 B.C. and continued until the fall of Jerusalem in A.D. 70.

4. *The Present Temple*. The present temple of the Lord is the life of a believer (1 Cor 6:10-20; 2 Cor 6:16-18). The human heart will be the sacred sanctuary of God's presence until the Messiah, Jesus Christ, returns and builds the millennial temple foreseen by Ezekiel in 40–48.

5. *The Temple of Revelation 11*. The temple of Rev 11:1-2 appears some time after the rapture (Rev 4:1). The Antichrist will set up world headquarters in this temple at Jerusalem (Dan 11:45).

6. *Ezekiel's Millennial Temple*. Ezekiel 40–48 refers to the temple to be built in Jerusalem during the millennium for Israel's use in worship commemorating the new covenant with Messiah.

7. *The Eternal Temple*. John records the end of the first heaven and the first earth (Rev 21:1-3) and declares that God himself will dwell with his people and will be the temple of the new Jerusalem (Rev 21:22).

H. Parunak has noted a chiastic structure to chaps. 40–42, centering around the description of the inner court. After the introduction to the vision in 40:1-4, Ezekiel's angelic tour guide begins his tour outside the temple (40:5-16). Then they move into the outer court (40:17-27) and fi-

---

[13] See M. Haran, *Temples and Temple Service in Ancient Israel* (Winona Lake, Ind.: Eisenbrauns, 1985), 26-39.

[14] See H. P. Lee, "Temple of Jerusalem," *HBD*, 1325-33; Haran, *Temples and Temple Service in Ancient Israel*, 26-39. Andre' Parrot, *The Temple of Jerusalem* (London: SCM, 1957); G. E. Wright, "Solomon's Temple Resurrected," *BA* (1941): 4:18-31; P. L. Garber, "Reconstructing Solomon's Temple," *BA* (1951): 14:2-24; "Temple," *IBD* 3:1522; "Temples," *IDB* 4:498; "Temple of Jerusalem," *HBD*, 1325-31.

nally into the inner court and the focus of the tour (40:28–41:26). Ezekiel
and his guide then move back through the outer court (42:1-14) and out of
the temple (42:15-20).[15]

**[1]In the twenty-fifth year of our exile, at the beginning of the year, on the
tenth of the month, in the fourteenth year after the fall of the city—on that
very day the hand of the LORD was upon me and he took me there. [2]In visions
of God he took me to the land of Israel and set me on a very high mountain,
on whose south side were some buildings that looked like a city. [3]He took me
there, and I saw a man whose appearance was like bronze; he was standing in
the gateway with a linen cord and a measuring rod in his hand. [4]The man
said to me, "Son of man, look with your eyes and hear with your ears and pay
attention to everything I am going to show you, for that is why you have been
brought here. Tell the house of Israel everything you see."**

INTRODUCTION (40:1-4).  **40:1-4**   This is the final dated prophecy in
the book but not the last in chronological sequence. The vision of 29:17-
21 is the final chronological vision (see "Dated Prophecies in Ezekiel" in
the Introduction). Ezekiel received this message more than twelve years
after his initial messages of restoration hope in 33:21-33. The date for this
prophecy is April 19, 573 B.C.[16] It is not clear why this new year began
on the tenth day of the month since the new year usually began on the first
day of month. It is possible that Ezekiel was referring to a Jubilee Year,
which according to Lev 25:9 began on the tenth day of the seventh month.
If this is true, the date for the message would be October 22, 573 B.C.[17]

Zimmerli notes the dominance of the number twenty-five and its multi-
ples in this passage (v. 1). He believes that by using this number Ezekiel
was calling to the attention of the captives in Babylon that they were half-
way to the next Jubilee Year still another twenty-five years away.

Isaiah 61:1-4 used the Jubilee Year as a symbol of the dawn of the messianic age. He portrayed the Jubilee Year as a time of release from captivity.[18] Isaiah's prophecy has long been viewed by premillennialists as an
announcement of the millennium.[19] Ezekiel's use of terms similar to the
Jubilee Year lends support to the conclusion that he prophesied the advent
of the millennial kingdom and the millennial temple. Of the elements in

---

[15] Parunak, "Literary Architecture," 71.

[16] See Introduction, "Dated Prophecies in Ezekiel."

[17] W. Zimmerli, *Ezekiel 2,* Her (Philadelphia: Fortress, 1983), 345-46. This places the
date eighteen months prior to the chronologically final message in 29:17-21.

[18] Ibid., 346; Fisch, *Ezekiel,* 266.

[19] C. C. Ryrie, *The Basis of the Premillennial Faith* (Neptune, N.J.: Loizeaux, 1953), 86.

this vision, four features regularly appear in introductory sections of apocalyptic literature.[20] First, apocalyptic visions often were dated. Second, the recipients of visions were identified in apocalyptic writings. Ezekiel clearly was identified as the recipient by using his characteristic phrase "the hand of the Lord was on me" (Ezek 40:1). Third, apocalyptic writers often mentioned the location of the recipient of a vision at the time the revelation was received. Ezekiel suggested that he was taken to the land of Israel as he had been in an earlier vision (see 8:1-18). Fourth, any additional circumstances of importance related to the intended message were also included in apocalyptic writings. Such a detail was the appearance of the "man" who looked like bronze and had a linen cord and a measuring rod in his hands (v. 3). Both implements were used for measuring distances. As the vision unfolds, clearly this "man" was not a human being but a heavenly messenger.[21] He instructed the prophet to pay careful attention and observe all he was about to see. By including such details, Ezekiel was underscoring the importance of his message, which was consistent with his commission to report all that he had seen (v. 4).

The wording of this introduction also encourages the reader to compare this vision with those of chaps. 1–3 and chaps. 8–11.[22] First, the phrase *mar$^{ɔ}$ôt $^{ɔ}$ĕlōhîm,* "visions of God," only occurs in 1:1; 8:3; and 40:2. Second, the date formula is found in conjunction with the hand of the Lord upon the prophet only in 1:1–3; 8:1; and 40:1. And third, only in 3:12,14; 8:3; 11:1,24; 43:5 is the Spirit said to "lift up" (*nāśa$^{ɔ}$*) the prophet. Parunak has also observed that whereas we are informed of the prophet's visionary translation to and from Babylon in the vision of chaps. 8-11 (8:3; 11:24), we are only told of his translation back to Babylon in the first vision (3:14-15) and only of his translation to Israel in the last (40:2). Parunak comments that "it poignantly summarizes the career of Ezekiel. Though he was a priest among the captives when he was called, he ministered among them in an entirely new sense when, as a prophet, he returned from his ordination. It was as though he came among them for the first time. And at the end of the book, having traced not only Israel's sin and punishment, but also her future restoration, his task is finished. He has come home to the land of Israel, in prophecy if not yet in fact, and home he will stay."[23]

The restoration of the temple would be a significant step in the reestab-

---

[20] Alexander, "Ezekiel," 953-54.
[21] See Alexander, "Ezekiel," 953. See "Weights and Measures," *IDB* 4:828.
[22] Parunak, "Literary Architecture," 61-62.
[23] Ibid., 61.

lishment of Israel's national and spiritual identity (cf. 37:26-27). The departure of the glory of God that he had reported in chaps. 10–11 along with the final destruction of Jerusalem were difficult theological problems that superseded the physical, political, social, and economic circumstances. The vision of the restored temple was a statement of affirmation about the future of the nation. The magnitude and magnificence of the temple and its complex indicated that Ezekiel clearly foresaw the restored community as supplanting that of David and Solomon. The temple of the last days would be a source of blessing and a lamp of truth to the whole world.[24] The restored temple represents God's desire to be in the midst of his people and suggests his accessibility to them and desire to bless them (see, e.g., 48:35; Rev 21:3-4; 22:1-4).

**[5]I saw a wall completely surrounding the temple area. The length of the measuring rod in the man's hand was six long cubits, each of which was a cubit and a handbreadth. He measured the wall; it was one measuring rod thick and one rod high.**
**[6]Then he went to the gate facing east. He climbed its steps and measured the threshold of the gate; it was one rod deep. [7]The alcoves for the guards were one rod long and one rod wide, and the projecting walls between the alcoves were five cubits thick. And the threshold of the gate next to the portico facing the temple was one rod deep.**
**[8]Then he measured the portico of the gateway; [9]it was eight cubits deep and its jambs were two cubits thick. The portico of the gateway faced the temple.**
**[10]Inside the east gate were three alcoves on each side; the three had the same measurements, and the faces of the projecting walls on each side had the same measurements. [11]Then he measured the width of the entrance to the gateway; it was ten cubits and its length was thirteen cubits. [12]In front of each alcove was a wall one cubit high, and the alcoves were six cubits square. [13]Then he measured the gateway from the top of the rear wall of one alcove to the top of the opposite one; the distance was twenty-five cubits from one parapet opening to the opposite one. [14]He measured along the faces of the projecting walls all around the inside of the gateway—sixty cubits. The measurement was up to the portico facing the courtyard. [15]The distance from the entrance of the gateway to the far end of its portico was fifty cubits. [16]The alcoves and the projecting walls inside the gateway were surmounted by narrow parapet openings all around, as was the portico; the openings all around faced inward. The faces of the projecting walls were decorated with palm trees.**

---

[24] See E. H. Merrill ("A Theology of Ezekiel and Daniel," in *A Biblical Theology of the Old Testament* [Chicago: Moody, 1991], 382) for his discussion of the importance of Ezekiel's emphasis on the temple as God's dwelling place among his people.

THE SURROUNDING WALL AND EAST GATE (40:5-16). **40:5-16** Ezekiel first saw the wall that surrounded the temple area. There are numerous measurements given in the description of the temple complex (chaps. 40–42), all of which are calculated in cubits (40:5). Use of cubit measurement is problematic because the standard for these calculations was determined by parts of the human body that vary from person to person. A regular cubit was measured from the tip of a man's elbow to the tip of the middle finger, approximately eighteen inches. Ezekiel's cubit was a longer cubit known as a royal cubit that added a "handbreadth." This was the width of a man's hand at the base of the fingers, approximately three inches. A royal cubit is estimated to be twenty-one inches. The measuring rod that Ezekiel saw in this vision was six cubits or about 10.5 feet.[25]

The wall that Ezekiel saw around the temple complex (v. 5; cf. 42:17) was one rod thick (10.5 ft.) and one rod high (10.5 ft.). The gates in this wall are described in detail beginning with the east gate (vv. 6-19), the north gate (vv. 20-23), and south gate (vv. 24-27), each having the same design. The design features of each of the three gates are illustrated by their floor plan. Each gate had seven steps that led to an outer porch (v. 8). The porch was eight cubits deep with door jambs two cubits thick (v. 9). Inside each gate were six side chambers of equal size (v. 10). They were one rod or six cubits square (vv. 7,12). Each side chamber also had a wall one cubit high in front of it (v. 12).

The inside dimensions from one side chamber wall to the opposite wall was twenty-five cubits (v. 13). As one continued past the six side chambers, there was an inner porch that was the exit chamber that opened into the outer courtyard. The distance around the walls of the inner porch was sixty cubits (v. 14). The entire gate structure was fifty cubits long (v. 15) and twenty-five cubits wide (v. 13) plus the steps leading up to the outer porch.[26] Such intricate details are somewhat extraneous if the purpose of the vision is only to relate truths of a spiritual restoration. The attention to detail seems rather to suggest a literal structure that also has great spiritual significance.

These gates resembled gate complexes of walled cities that have been excavated and dated to the Solomonic period. City gates of this period featured side chambers that were guard rooms and council chambers for

---

[25] See Zimmerli, *Ezekiel 2*, 349; Alexander, "Ezekiel," 955-56; Fisch, *Ezekiel*, 267. Both Alexander and Fisch discuss the various estimates of the length of the royal cubit.

[26] No unanimity exists on the features of the gates. For descriptions and diagrams see also Taylor, *Ezekiel*, 255, and Alexander, "Ezekiel," 957.

the city elders.[27] The gates represent access while the walls represent security for those within and limited access or even exclusion to those without. The presentation of the temple anticipates the return of God's glory, which departed as an act of judgment reported in chaps. 10–11. God was returning to a place of proximity and accessibility to his people.

### Gates of the Temple

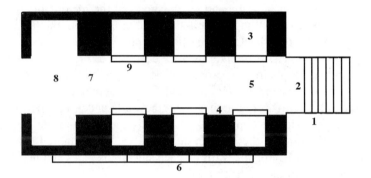

1. Seven steps (vv. 6,22,26)       5. Threshold (outer, vv. 6,11)
2. Porch (outer, v. 8)             6. Chamber windows (v. 16)
3. Guard chambers (vv. 7,10,12)    7. Threshold (inner, v. 7)
4. Chamber walls (v. 7)            8. Porch (inner, vv. 6,11)
                    9. Chamber door walls (v. 12)

The gates are a foreshadowing of the accessibility God gave to all people through Jesus, who presents himself as the door by which one can enter to God and be saved (see John 10:9-21). The choice of three gates for this temple rather than four or more may suggest a deeper significance of the means of access God provides for humans to approach him, since God manifests himself in three ways to the human family as Father, Son, and Holy Spirit.

**[17]Then he brought me into the outer court. There I saw some rooms and a pavement that had been constructed all around the court; there were thirty rooms along the pavement. [18]It abutted the sides of the gateways and was as**

---

[27] Zimmerli (*Ezekiel 2*, 353) compares the gate of Ezekiel's temple to the city gates of Hazor, Gezer, and Megiddo. See also Alexander, "Ezekiel," 956; H. G. May, "The Book of Ezekiel: Introduction and Exegesis," in *IB* 6 (Nashville: Abingdon, 1956), 285-86.

wide as they were long; this was the lower pavement. ¹⁹Then he measured the distance from the inside of the lower gateway to the outside of the inner court; it was a hundred cubits on the east side as well as on the north.

THE OUTER COURT (40:17-27). **40:17-19** The three gates of the temple led to a large outer courtyard that surrounded the temple sanctuary on three sides: north, east, and south. The sanctuary was separated from the outer courtyard by a wall in which there were three additional gates leading to an inner courtyard (vv. 28-37). These gates were opposite and identical with those in the outer court.

The combination of walls and gates conveyed the idea of limited access. God was again making himself available to Israel, but the limits that were part of the tabernacle and earlier temples also were preserved in Ezekiel's temple. These limitations were designed to protect God's holiness. The contrast of God's approachableness on the one hand and his holiness on the other hand is a familiar Old Testament theme.[28]

In the outer court were rooms around the walls under a portico on the three sides opposite the temple (v. 17). The distance from inside the outer eastern gate to outside the inner eastern gate was one hundred cubits. A pavement was laid along the walls on each side of the gates and in front of the thirty rooms of the portico (v. 18).

²⁰Then he measured the length and width of the gate facing north, leading into the outer court. ²¹Its alcoves—three on each side—its projecting walls and its portico had the same measurements as those of the first gateway. It was fifty cubits long and twenty-five cubits wide. ²²Its openings, its portico and its palm tree decorations had the same measurements as those of the gate facing east. Seven steps led up to it, with its portico opposite them. ²³There was a gate to the inner court facing the north gate, just as there was on the east. He measured from one gate to the opposite one; it was a hundred cubits.

**40:20-23** The north gate was identical in size and design to the east gate (cf. vv. 5-16). It has been suggested that the seven steps mentioned in v. 22 were only associated with the north gate since it may have been slightly higher in elevation.[29] But the gates were identical in every detail, so the mention of seven steps likely applied to all three gates.[30] Seven

---

[28] See the discussion of God's inapproachable majesty versus his immanence and approachableness in W. Eichrodt, *Theology of the Old Testament I* (Philadelphia: Westminster, 1961), 111, 205, 211, 214, 384.

[29] Fisch (*Ezekiel*, 270-72) believes the gate was on a higher level; see his discussion of v. 18 (pp. 270-71) and the discussion of vv. 19-23 (pp. 271-72).

[30] Zimmerli, *Ezekiel 2*, 354.

steps also are mentioned in v. 26 as a feature of the south gate. The identical physical structure and appearance of these gates suggests their equality in form and function. This idea also is consistent with concepts related to the Trinity, which considers God as three coequal manifestations of the one divine being (see John 10:22-30).

**²⁴Then he led me to the south side and I saw a gate facing south. He measured its jambs and its portico, and they had the same measurements as the others. ²⁵The gateway and its portico had narrow openings all around, like the openings of the others. It was fifty cubits long and twenty-five cubits wide. ²⁶Seven steps led up to it, with its portico opposite them; it had palm tree decorations on the faces of the projecting walls on each side. ²⁷The inner court also had a gate facing south, and he measured from this gate to the outer gate on the south side; it was a hundred cubits.**

**40:24-27** The south gate is the third of these identical gate structures that gave access to the outer courtyard of the temple area as described in vv. 5-16. Like the other two gates, the posts had ornamental tops shaped like palm trees (vv. 16,26).[31] Reference to the inner court was another reminder that its three gates were opposite the three gates of the outer courtyard. This outer court was known as the "court of the women" in Talmudic literature.[32]

THE INNER COURT (40:28–41:26). From 40:28 to 41:26 the prophet describes what he saw while in the inner court (48:28). It is here that Ezekiel would receive the visions of chaps. 43–46. He describes features east of the sanctuary first (40:28-47), then he describes the rest of the inner court including the sanctuary itself (40:48–41:26).

**²⁸Then he brought me into the inner court through the south gate, and he measured the south gate; it had the same measurements as the others. ²⁹Its alcoves, its projecting walls and its portico had the same measurements as the others. The gateway and its portico had openings all around. It was fifty cubits long and twenty-five cubits wide. ³⁰(The porticoes of the gateways around the inner court were twenty-five cubits wide and five cubits deep.) ³¹Its portico faced the outer court; palm trees decorated its jambs, and eight steps led up to it.**

---

[31] Palm trees carved in the woodwork of the sanctuary were symbols of peace (40:16,22,26,31; 41:18-20,25-26) and long life. Isaiah revealed that the Messiah would be known as the Prince of peace (Isa 9:6). The people unknowingly acclaimed him to be the King of peace when he entered Jerusalem on the Sunday before his crucifixion (John 12:13; Ps 92:12; see Garber, "Reconstructing Solomon's Temple," *BA* XIV [1951]: 11).

[32] Fisch, *Ezekiel,* 271; see his discussion of 40:17.

³²Then he brought me to the inner court on the east side, and he measured the gateway; it had the same measurements as the others. ³³Its alcoves, its projecting walls and its portico had the same measurements as the others. The gateway and its portico had openings all around. It was fifty cubits long and twenty-five cubits wide. ³⁴Its portico faced the outer court; palm trees decorated the jambs on either side, and eight steps led up to it.

³⁵Then he brought me to the north gate and measured it. It had the same measurements as the others, ³⁶as did its alcoves, its projecting walls and its portico, and it had openings all around. It was fifty cubits long and twenty-five cubits wide. ³⁷Its portico faced the outer court; palm trees decorated the jambs on either side, and eight steps led up to it.

*The Gates of the Inner Court (40:28-37).*   **40:28-37**   The measurements and features of the gates of the inner court were identical with those of the gates of the outer courtyard in vv. 5-16 in every detail but one. Each gate leading to the inner courtyard had eight steps instead of seven (vv. 31,34,37). The use of the number eight was considered in rabbinic literature to have messianic overtones. The eight steps typologically pictured the Messiah as a means of access to the inner court and sanctuary, therefore the presence of Yahweh.[33]

³⁸A room with a doorway was by the portico in each of the inner gateways, where the burnt offerings were washed. ³⁹In the portico of the gateway were two tables on each side, on which the burnt offerings, sin offerings and guilt offerings were slaughtered. ⁴⁰By the outside wall of the portico of the gateway, near the steps at the entrance to the north gateway were two tables, and on the other side of the steps were two tables. ⁴¹So there were four tables on one side of the gateway and four on the other—eight tables in all—on which the sacrifices were slaughtered. ⁴²There were also four tables of dressed stone for the burnt offerings, each a cubit and a half long, a cubit and a half wide and a cubit high. On them were placed the utensils for slaughtering the burnt offerings and the other sacrifices. ⁴³And double-pronged hooks, each a handbreadth long, were attached to the wall all around. The tables were for the flesh of the offerings.

*The Sacrifice Preparation Rooms (40:38-43)*   **40:38-43**   Exact location of the washing rooms where sacrifices were cleansed by each gate is uncertain (v. 38). Perhaps they were outside and next to the entrance or perhaps even part of the inner porch (see Fig. 1). Also in this porch on the

---

[33] Bullinger, *Number in Scripture* (Grand Rapids: Kregel, 1967), 196-234; R. D. Johnston, *Numbers in the Bible* (Grand Rapids: Kregel, 1990), 75-76; G. B. Caird, *The Revelation of St. John the Divine* (New York: Harper & Row, 1966), 174-76; A. Deismann, *Light from the Ancient East* (Grand Rapids: Baker, 1965), 278 note; see 34:23-31.

north side were four tables for the sacrifice of animals (v. 39). Four additional tables were located outside, two on either side of the steps. While this information was given for the north gate only, it is possible that the other two gates also had eight of these tables for sacrifice associated with it. The use of sets of eight tables for sacrifice also may have messianic overtones (vv. 40-41). These slaughter tables were made of dressed stone and were one and a half cubits square and one cubit high (v. 42). On these tables were implements used in the preparation of animals for sacrifice on the altar.

Ebla in northern Syria is known for the large quantity (over twenty thousand) of clay tablets excavated in the library storage area. Not as well known are two of the finest examples of dressed stone slaughter tables of almost the same size and design as those described by Ezekiel. These tables had channels around the edge for collection of the blood and a smaller side table attached to hold the implements. They were made of black basalt and found in the sanctuary. These tables are excellent examples of the slaughter tables Ezekiel saw by the north gate (v. 42).[34] On the walls near these tables were hooks used for hanging the slaughtered animals to be skinned and prepared for sacrifice by the priests (v. 43).[35] This temple, like its predecessor, will be a place for celebrating sacrifices and worship.

**[44]Outside the inner gate, within the inner court, were two rooms, one at the side of the north gate and facing south, and another at the side of the south gate and facing north. [45]He said to me, "The room facing south is for the priests who have charge of the temple, [46]and the room facing north is for the priests who have charge of the altar. These are the sons of Zadok, who are the only Levites who may draw near to the LORD to minister before him."**

**[47]Then he measured the court: It was square—a hundred cubits long and a hundred cubits wide. And the altar was in front of the temple.**

*The Priests' Quarters (40:44-47).* **40:44-47** Beside the northern gate of the inner court were two rooms. Beside the eastern gate was one room. The rooms of the northern gate had openings that faced south. The room by the eastern gate opened to the north. The NIV translates "south" gate in v. 44 instead of "east" as in the Hebrew text. This translation is based on the logic that the south gate would be open toward the north, but

---

[34] See these photographs in the details of the sanctuary B2, room L.2113 located in the unnumbered section between 160 and 161 of P. Matthiae, *Ebla: An Empire Rediscovered* (New York: Doubleday, 1981).

[35] Fisch, *Ezekiel,* 276.

the Hebrew text "east gate" is likely the correct reading.[36] The purpose of the rooms by the north gate facing south is not clear. They may have been for use by the priests preparing for duty in the sanctuary or by singers (v. 45).[37] The room facing north by the east gate was for the priests who administered the altar of sacrifice (v. 46).

The only priests who could minister at the altar were the descendants of Zadok, a priest who remained loyal to David during the insurrection of Absalom (2 Sam 15:24-29), and whose descendants remained loyal to Yahweh through the course of Israel's growing idolatry (Ezek 44:15).[38] Zadok also anointed Solomon as David's successor (1 Kgs 1:32-35) and refused to join Abiathar in support of Adonijah's vain attempt to supplant Solomon (1 Kgs 1:5-26). Solomon appointed as high priest Zadok, a descendant of Aaron through Eleazar, instead of Abiathar, a descendant through Ithamar (1 Sam 2:31-33; 1 Kgs 2:26-27,35; 1 Chr 6:3-8; 24:3). The reward for faithfulness to David continued to Zadok's descendants, who also remained faithful during the exile. Some have suggested that Zadok was a Jebusite priest of Yahweh in Jerusalem when David conquered the city.[39] But the designation "Levites" in v. 46 rules out this possibility. Presentation of the Zadokite priesthood because of its loyalty to David anticipates the New Testament concept of the priesthood of believers who are to be loyal to the new David, the Messiah, and his kingdom (see 1 Pet 2:9-10).

After describing these details, Ezekiel's guide measured the inner court. It was one hundred cubits wide and one hundred cubits long, a perfect square, conveying the idea of symmetry and order. In this courtyard the altar of sacrifice sat in front of the temple sanctuary (v. 47).

**[48]He brought me to the portico of the temple and measured the jambs of the portico; they were five cubits wide on either side. The width of the entrance was fourteen cubits and its projecting walls were three cubits wide on either side. [49]The portico was twenty cubits wide, and twelve cubits from front to back. It was reached by a flight of stairs, and there were pillars on each side of the jambs.**

---

[36] Ibid., 276-77. He identifies the gate as the east gate whose entrance faced north.

[37] Alexander, "Ezekiel," 960. Singing was a priestly function in OT worship (see, e.g., 1 Chr 16:4-6; 23:5; 2 Chr 29:26-29).

[38] Tuell (*Law of the Temple,* 102) concludes that the Persians installed the Zadokite priests in the rebuilt temple in Jerusalem as a political move. They no doubt were certain that by returning these men to power they would insure their loyalty to Persia.

[39] Cooke, *Ezekiel,* 439; H. H. Rowley, "Zadok and Nehushtan," *JBL* LVIII (1939): 113-41. But see F. M. Cross, *Canaanite Myth and Hebrew Epic* (Cambridge: Harvard University Press, 1973), 208-15.

*The Temple Portico (40:48-49).*   **40:48-49**   Ezekiel was led to the temple sanctuary that was accessed by a flight of stairs (v. 49; see Fig. 3). He entered the doors that had door jambs five cubits wide and an opening fourteen cubits wide (v. 48). Through the doorway was an outer porch twenty cubits wide and twelve cubits deep with a pillar on either side of the entrance (v. 49). Pillars such as these were a feature of the temple that Solomon constructed (see 1 Kgs 7:16-20). The pillars of Solomon's temple were made of brass. Their purpose may have been to represent the pillar of cloud and of fire from the wilderness days (Exod 13:17-22). These pillars were signs of God's presence and preservation of his people.[40]

**[1]Then the man brought me to the outer sanctuary and measured the jambs; the width of the jambs was six cubits on each side. [2]The entrance was ten cubits wide, and the projecting walls on each side of it were five cubits wide. He also measured the outer sanctuary; it was forty cubits long and twenty cubits wide.**

**[3]Then he went into the inner sanctuary and measured the jambs of the entrance; each was two cubits wide. The entrance was six cubits wide, and the projecting walls on each side of it were seven cubits wide. [4]And he measured the length of the inner sanctuary; it was twenty cubits, and its width was twenty cubits across the end of the outer sanctuary. He said to me, "This is the Most Holy Place."**

**[5]Then he measured the wall of the temple; it was six cubits thick, and each side room around the temple was four cubits wide. [6]The side rooms were on three levels, one above another, thirty on each level. There were ledges all around the wall of the temple to serve as supports for the side rooms, so that the supports were not inserted into the wall of the temple. [7]The side rooms all around the temple were wider at each successive level. The structure surrounding the temple was built in ascending stages, so that the rooms widened as one went upward. A stairway went up from the lowest floor to the top floor through the middle floor.**

**[8]I saw that the temple had a raised base all around it, forming the foundation of the side rooms. It was the length of the rod, six long cubits. [9]The outer wall of the side rooms was five cubits thick. The open area between the side rooms of the temple [10]and the [priests'] rooms was twenty cubits wide all around the temple. [11]There were entrances to the side rooms from the open area, one on the north and another on the south; and the base adjoining the open area was five cubits wide all around.**

---

[40] Zimmerli, *Ezekiel 2,* 356-57; G. E. Wright, "Solomon's Temple Reconstructed," *BA* IV:2 (1941): 18-31; P. L. Garber, "Reconstructing Solomon's Temple," *BA* XIV:1 (1951): 2-24; and C. G. Howie, "The East Gate of Ezekiel's Temple Enclosure and the Solomonic Gateway of Megiddo," *BASOR* 117 (1950): 13-19.

¹²**The building facing the temple courtyard on the west side was seventy cubits wide. The wall of the building was five cubits thick all around, and its length was ninety cubits.**

*The Temple Sanctuary (41:1-12).*  **41:1-12**  The temple sanctuary had three divisions: (1) a porch, (2) an outer sanctuary known as the holy place, and (3) an inner sanctuary known as the most holy place or holy of holies. Ezekiel's guide took him into the outer sanctuary. As he entered, he measured the door jambs that were six cubits on each side, and the entrance was ten cubits wide. The outer sanctuary was twenty cubits wide and forty cubits long (vv. 1-2).

Then he was taken into the inner sanctuary that had door jambs two cubits wide, and the entrance was six cubits wide. The walks on either side of the entrance were seven cubits wide. The inner sanctuary was twenty by twenty cubits, and the guide with Ezekiel said, "This is the Most Holy Place" (v. 4). The guide speaks little in these chapters (cf. 40:4,45; 41:22; 42:13; 43:18; 46:20,24; 47:8) and always regarding key elements of the restoration—priests, offerings, holy of holies, altar, and river.

The temple sanctuary had three levels. The inner wall of the temple was six cubits thick. Between the inner wall and the outer wall were side rooms on three levels with thirty side chambers on each level (vv. 5-6). These side rooms had supports that made them independent of the wall of the temple. The rooms on the lowest level were the smallest. The second and third stories were successively wider than the level below it so that the largest rooms were on the top level. These side chambers could only be accessed by two side entrances, one on the north and one on the south side of the temple and only through a doorway on the middle level (v. 7). The purpose of these rooms is unclear. They may have been storage areas or rooms for the temple treasure. Nebuchadnezzar took treasure from the temple when he destroyed Jerusalem according to Dan 1:2. Belshazzar later used this treasure in the final night of his reign of debauchery (Dan 5:3). The chambers may have been used for private worship.

The use of three levels and the placement of these divisions may be additional symbols of the triune nature of the God who would reside here. If the side rooms on each of the three levels were areas for individual worship, they were used only by the priests. They could only be entered through the middle level. Just so the Messiah, the second Person of the Godhead, is the one through which we gain access to all three (John 14:6).

The whole superstructure of the temple was built on a raised platform base (v. 8).[41] The outer wall of the side rooms and the temple superstruc-

---

[41] Wevers, *Ezekiel,* 306.

ture was five cubits thick. An open space about twenty cubits wide separated the side rooms from the priests' rooms on either side of the temple
(v. 10). The two entrances to the side chambers already have been mentioned in vv. 5-7.

The base extended away from the building for five cubits on every side
(v. 11). Behind the temple was another building seventy by ninety cubits
with a wall five cubits thick (v. 12). The exact function of this building is
unknown (see Figs. 2 and 3),[42] although it has been associated with the
*parbār* ("court") of 1 Chr 26:18, which probably was an open area. This
open area may have been in front of the building, or it may refer to the
open area of the large room inside the building, whose purpose is unclear.[43]

[13]**Then he measured the temple; it was a hundred cubits long, and the
temple courtyard and the building with its walls were also a hundred cubits
long.** [14]**The width of the temple courtyard on the east, including the front of
the temple, was a hundred cubits.**

[15]**Then he measured the length of the building facing the courtyard at the
rear of the temple, including its galleries on each side; it was a hundred cubits.**

**The outer sanctuary, the inner sanctuary and the portico facing the court,**
[16]**as well as the thresholds and the narrow windows and galleries around the
three of them—everything beyond and including the threshold was covered
with wood. The floor, the wall up to the windows, and the windows were covered.** [17]**In the space above the outside of the entrance to the inner sanctuary
and on the walls at regular intervals all around the inner and outer sanctuary**
[18]**were carved cherubim and palm trees. Palm trees alternated with cherubim. Each cherub had two faces:** [19]**the face of a man toward the palm tree on
one side and the face of a lion toward the palm tree on the other. They were
carved all around the whole temple.** [20]**From the floor to the area above the
entrance, cherubim and palm trees were carved on the wall of the outer sanctuary.**

[21]**The outer sanctuary had a rectangular doorframe, and the one at the
front of the Most Holy Place was similar.** [22]**There was a wooden altar three
cubits high and two cubits square; its corners, its base and its sides were of
wood. The man said to me, "This is the table that is before the LORD."** [23]**Both
the outer sanctuary and the Most Holy Place had double doors.** [24]**Each door
had two leaves—two hinged leaves for each door.** [25]**And on the doors of the
outer sanctuary were carved cherubim and palm trees like those carved on
the walls, and there was a wooden overhang on the front of the portico.** [26]**On
the sidewalls of the portico were narrow windows with palm trees carved on**

---

[42] See Alexander, "Ezekiel," 964.
[43] Cooke, *Ezekiel*, 449.

**each side. The side rooms of the temple also had overhangs.**

*Auxiliary Buildings (41:13-26).*   **41:13-26**   The length and width of the inner courtyard in front of the temple was one hundred cubits. The temple sanctuary sat on the west central side of the court and was also one hundred cubits long (vv. 13-14).

The building behind the sanctuary was one hundred cubits on its outside measurement (v. 15a). This measurement at first seems to contradict v. 12, which said it was seventy by ninety cubits. There are two possible explanations. The dimensions of v. 12 may have been the measurement of the building interior that would make it ninety cubits plus the walls that were five cubits thick on each end, making the total one hundred cubits.[44] Another possibility lies in the qualification stated in v. 15, "including its galleries on each side." Apparently there were galleries or porches on either side of the building that were five cubits wide, making the total one hundred cubits. The second explanation seems the correct one.

All the interior walls of the sanctuary were decorated with wood. Wood covered the floors, the walls up to the windows, and the windows (vv. 15b-16). Carved on the walls of the outer and inner chambers of the sanctuary were cherubim and palm trees.[45] These cherubim were like the ones the prophet had seen in his visions in 1:5-25 and 10:9-17. Cherubim appear several places in Scripture and are always guardians of the holiness of God. They were there specifically to remind the priests not to enter the holy of holies. Cherubim appeared in the garden of Eden to protect the presence of God and prevent any person from approaching him after human sin entered the world (Gen 3:22-24).[46] Cherubim were placed on the veil of the tabernacle to guard the presence of God in the holy of holies (Exod 26:31). Inside the holy of holies two cherubim sat atop the ark of the covenant, again as guardians of the presence of God (Exod 25:18-22; see also discussion of 1:5-25; 10:1-2,9-17).

The meaning of the palm tree and its use in the sanctuary is associated with the covenant of peace expressed in 34:25 and 37:26.[47] Elsewhere in Scripture the palm tree symbolized righteousness (Ps 92:12) and longevity (vv. 18-20). Cherubim and palm trees were also featured in the Solomonic temple (see 1 Kgs 6:29,32,35-36).

---

[44] See Alexander, "Ezekiel," 964; Zimmerli, *Ezekiel 2*, 379-80, for descriptions of these features of the sanctuary.

[45] See the discussion of 40:24-27 and the note on the use of palm trees.

[46] Cooke, *Ezekiel*, 451. Also see Garber, "Reconstructing Solomon's Temple," *BA* XIV:1 (1951): 12-16.

[47] See 40:24-27 note.

According to the statement in the Hebrew text, the doors to the sanctuary had square corners (v. 21).[48] Within the outer sanctuary was an altar like the altar of incense in the tabernacle and Solomonic temple. It was three cubits high and two cubits square (v. 22).[49] Zimmerli suggests since it is called the "table that is before the LORD" it was not an altar of incense but the table for the bread of the presence of the Lord first used in the tabernacle of Exod 25:23-30 and mentioned in 1 Kgs 7:48.[50]

Both the inner and outer sanctuaries had double doors that hung on hinges and covered the entrances (vv. 23-24). Cherubim were carved on the doors to the outer sanctuary. The "wooden overhang" described in v. 25 consisted of beams that supported the wall of the superstructure.[51] The porch of the sanctuary had narrow windows with palm trees on either side (v. 26).

Both the inner and outer courts of the temple area had three doors, and the sanctuary had three inner divisions, each having a doorway (see 40:5–42:20). The temple sanctuary of Ezekiel's vision was a house of worship and a statement of God's desire to dwell among his people. The divisions and separations placed in the temple plan and in the sanctuary itself were designed to preserve the idea of God's holiness and separation from sin yet his availability to sinful humanity (see discussion of 40:17-19 and note). The Messiah was the Word who became flesh and "tabernacled" among humans.[52]

The messianic ideas that were in the tabernacle, temple of Solomon, and here in Ezekiel's temple were recognized by the New Testament writer of Hebrews (see, e.g., Heb 8:3-5). These sanctuaries were a pattern of the coming of Messiah, who would dwell or "tabernacle" among humans. The perfect symmetry of the temple seen in these types were symbols of the perfect Law and Word of God and the fulfillment of his plan of redemption (see Heb 9:23-24; 10:1-4).[53]

**[1]Then the man led me northward into the outer court and brought me to the rooms opposite the temple courtyard and opposite the outer wall on the**

---

[40] See Fisch, *Ezekiel,* 285, for his discussion of v. 21.

[49] Alexander, "Ezekiel," 964. This is the only piece of sanctuary furniture mentioned.

[50] Zimmerli, *Ezekiel 2,* 389. See his discussion of vv. 21-22b. According to Greenberg ("Program of Restoration," 191), it could be either.

[51] Fisch, *Ezekiel,* 286, and Garber, "Reconstructing Solomon's Temple," *BA* XIV:1 (1951): 10-12.

[52] The word ἐσκήνωσεν in John 1:14 is translated "made his dwelling among us," which does not reflect the connection between the tabernacle and our Lord that the writer may have intended. See *TDNT* VII:368-83.

[53] See B. Childs, *Exodus,* OTL (Philadelphia: Westminster, 1974), 546-47.

north side. [2]The building whose door faced north was a hundred cubits long and fifty cubits wide. [3]Both in the section twenty cubits from the inner court and in the section opposite the pavement of the outer court, gallery faced gallery at the three levels. [4]In front of the rooms was an inner passageway ten cubits wide and a hundred cubits long. Their doors were on the north. [5]Now the upper rooms were narrower, for the galleries took more space from them than from the rooms on the lower and middle floors of the building. [6]The rooms on the third floor had no pillars, as the courts had; so they were smaller in floor space than those on the lower and middle floors. [7]There was an outer wall parallel to the rooms and the outer court; it extended in front of the rooms for fifty cubits. [8]While the row of rooms on the side next to the outer court was fifty cubits long, the row on the side nearest the sanctuary was a hundred cubits long. [9]The lower rooms had an entrance on the east side as one enters them from the outer court.

[10]On the south side along the length of the wall of the outer court, adjoining the temple courtyard and opposite the outer wall, were rooms [11]with a passageway in front of them. These were like the rooms on the north; they had the same length and width, with similar exits and dimensions. Similar to the doorways on the north [12]were the doorways of the rooms on the south. There was a doorway at the beginning of the passageway that was parallel to the corresponding wall extending eastward, by which one enters the rooms.

[13]Then he said to me, "The north and south rooms facing the temple courtyard are the priests' rooms, where the priests who approach the LORD will eat the most holy offerings. There they will put the most holy offerings— the grain offerings, the sin offerings and the guilt offerings—for the place is holy. [14]Once the priests enter the holy precincts, they are not to go into the outer court until they leave behind the garments in which they minister, for these are holy. They are to put on other clothes before they go near the places that are for the people."

THE OUTER COURT (42:1-14). **42:1-12** Ezekiel was led out of the temple sanctuary into the inner court and around the building to the north side (see Fig. 2). He stood before the building described as one hundred cubits long and fifty cubits wide (vv. 1-2; see Fig. 2, nos. 12-13). This building had three levels and several galleries with a ten-cubit-wide passageway in front of the structure (vv. 3-4). There were rooms in the building along fifty cubits of its length. The uppermost rooms were the smallest but had the largest galleries. The middle and lower stories had larger rooms, but the gallery on the second level was narrower than the third level. The lower floor had no gallery (v. 5). The rooms of the upper level had no pillars for support, so they had to be made smaller than the lower floors (v. 6).

Extending beyond the rooms was a wall that was attached to the corner of the building and advanced fifty cubits toward the east so that the length of the building and the wall combined was one hundred cubits. Across the ten-cubit-wide passageway on the side toward the sanctuary was another building that was one hundred cubits long and fifty cubits wide. This had no wall attached but had a row of rooms one hundred cubits long (v. 8). The entrance to the lower rooms was on the east side facing the outer court (v. 9). On the south side of the temple was an exact duplicate of the buildings on the north. Their size and orientation were exactly the same with entrances that faced east toward the outer court (vv. 10-12).[54]

**42:13-14** Use of these buildings and rooms was reserved for the priests when they ate communal offering meals. The buildings and rooms were used for both dining and storage of offerings until they were needed (vv. 13-14). According to the Mosaic system, the priests received a portion of some offerings that were eaten. From the whole burnt offering they received only the skin of the animal (Lev 7:8). A memorial portion of grain offerings was burned on the altar of burnt offering and the remainder given to the priests (Lev 2:3,10; 6:16-18; 7:14-15). The priests received the brisket and right thigh from the peace offering (Lev 7:30-34). The fat of the sin offering and trespass offering was burned on the altar of burnt offering and the remainder eaten by the priests (Lev 6:26; 7:6-7). These regulations for the priests were observed in the tabernacle and temple. The offerings were types of the perfect sacrifice, Jesus Christ the Messiah (Heb 10:1-39; see discussion of 41:13-26).

[15]**When he had finished measuring what was inside the temple area, he led me out by the east gate and measured the area all around:** [16]**He measured the east side with the measuring rod; it was five hundred cubits.** [17]**He measured the north side; it was five hundred cubits by the measuring rod.** [18]**He measured the south side; it was five hundred cubits by the measuring rod.** [19]**Then he turned to the west side and measured; it was five hundred cubits by the measuring rod.** [20]**So he measured the area on all four sides. It had a wall around it, five hundred cubits long and five hundred cubits wide, to separate the holy from the common.**

MEASURING THE SURROUNDING WALL (42:15-20)  **42:15-20** After touring the inner and outer courts, Ezekiel was taken out the east gate to the outer perimeter of the sanctuary, where the angel-guide measured the outer wall of the entire complex. It was a perfect square five hundred cubits on each side (vv. 15-19). The NIV margin note states that the Hebrew text has "rods" instead of "cubits" as the unit of the measurement. Some

---

[54] Zimmerli follows others in labeling these buildings as "temple sacristies" that were restricted buildings reserved for the use of the priests only; see *Ezekiel 2*, 398-401.

rabbinic interpreters calculate one rod to be six cubits based on the statement in 40:5, which said that the walled area was measured by a rod that was six cubits in length (see discussion of 40:5-16).

If the unit of measurement was a six-cubit rod, then the complex would have been three thousand cubits on each side instead of five hundred. A temple complex this size would be problematic since it would be larger than the topography of Jerusalem.[55] The misunderstanding lies in the assumption that the rod of 40:5 is the unit of measure in 42:15ff. for the temple area. The measuring rod of 40:5 was indeed six cubits long, but it was to be used for measuring cubits in the same way feet are sometimes measured with a yardstick. The size of the complex was five hundred cubits measured with the measuring rod that was six cubits long and therefore measured six cubits at a time.[56] The five-hundred-cubit measurement is consistent with the size of the land allotted for the sanctuary described in 45:1-2.

One cannot but be impressed by the detail and careful plan that unfolded in Ezekiel's description of the temple. He was shown by his angel-guide the future temple that would exceed all former temples in size and beauty. He saw a temple that had perfect symmetry and was symbolic of the holiness of God. The graduated levels and divisions that led to the holy of holies provided a line of demarcation and separation between the common and the holy (42:20). This was a temple that was clearly designed for worship and sacrifice to Yahweh, who had promised to restore his people Israel to their land.

After discussing Moses and the Israelites in the wilderness, the apostle Paul wrote, "Now these things occurred as our examples [Greek *tupos*], to keep us from setting our hearts on evil things as they did" (1 Cor 10:6). He also wrote, "These things happened to them as our examples were written down as warnings for us whom the fulfillment of the ages has come" (1 Cor 10:11).

The word translated "example" is the one from which we get the English word "type."[57] It means an "image" or an "impression" like those struck on the face of metal coins. The image is a representation of a real person or object. In the Old Testament "types" were in the form of images painted with words. Descriptions of the temple, priesthood, and worship

---

[55] Fisch, *Ezekiel*, 291-92. See his discussion of the two traditional rabbinic interpretations. Also see Taylor, *Ezekiel*, 263-64.

[56] Zimmerli (*Ezekiel 2*, 404) proposes this solution and concludes that the cubit was still the basic unit of measurement intended.

[57] BAGD, 837; *TDNT* VII:246-59; see "Typology," *HBD*, 1377-78; "Number Systems and Number Symbolism," *HBD*, 1029-31.

regulations such as those envisioned by Ezekiel were all prophetic "types" of the life and work of Christ. The following represents a summary of some of the more obvious typological associations in chaps 40-42.

First, the sanctuary was the third division of the temple complex and the most holy place in the temple area. Like the tabernacle and temples before it, this structure will be a reminder of God's desire to dwell among his people. It was for this reason that the Messiah came and the "Word became flesh and lived ["tabernacled"] for a while among us" (John 1:14).[58]

Second is the use of the number eight.[59] There were eight steps leading up to the inner court of the priests in the temple area (40:31,34,37). Why not seven or five or fifteen? Eight seems to have symbolized the Messiah. Eight steps showed that Messiah was the way to the inner sanctuary of God (John 14:6). There were eight slaughter tables for preparing sacrifices. These tables were a foreshadowing of the perfect Lamb of sacrifice that God sent for all people in the Messiah, Jesus Christ (John 1:29). The sacrifices of Ezekiel's temple were done on the eighth day (43:27), the day of new beginning. These were dim but discernible allusions to the Messiah, who would be the "way" and the "sacrifice" (Heb 10:1-18; esp. v. 10).

Third were the three levels. The three temple sanctuary levels and the placement of these divisions are dim types of the triune nature of God the Father, Son, and Holy Spirit. There were side rooms on each of the three levels, which presumably were areas for individual worship. These side chambers could only be entered through the middle level (41:7). Just so the Messiah, the second Person of the Godhead, is the one through which we gain access to all three (John 14:6).

Fourth are the doors. Both the inner and outer courts of the temple area had three doors, and the sanctuary had three inner divisions, each having a doorway (see 40:5–42:20). Jesus used the figure of a door as a self-characterization (John 10:9).

Fifth were the palm trees. The use of palm trees carved in the woodwork of the sanctuary symbolized peace (40:16,22,26,31; 41:18-20,25-26) and long life.[60] Isaiah revealed that the Messiah would be known as the Prince of peace (Isa 9:6). The people unknowingly acclaimed him to

---

[58] See discussion of 41:13-26 (esp. v. 26) and n. 48 and the use of ἐσκήνωσεν in John 1:14, which may refer to the tabernacle, a portable worship center with the same floor plan and pattern as the temple.

[59] Caird, *Revelation,* 174-75; Deissman, *Light from the Ancient East,* 278 note; see also 40:28-37 note and 34:23-31 note.

[60] Garber, "Reconstructing Solomon's Temple," *BA* XIV (1951): 11.

be the King of peace when he entered Jerusalem on the Sunday before his crucifixion (John 12:13; Ps 92:12).

Sixth was the altar of sacrifice (41:47), a reminder of the sacrificial work of Messiah (Isa 53:7-10; Heb 10:1-18; John 1:29; see 43:13-27).[61]

Seventh, was the year of release. The language of Ezek 40:1-4 makes a subtle but clear allusion to the year of release or Jubilee Year (Lev 25:8-17). Isaiah made it clear that the Messiah would come and initiate a glorious and eternal year of release (Isa 61:1-4). When Jesus began his first earthly ministry, he did so by announcing the advent of the year of release and by reading Isa 61:1-2, therefore claiming to be the Messiah (Luke 4:18-19).[62] These seven examples are representative and serve to illustrate both subtle and overt messianic ideas in the temple of Ezekiel's vision.

### (2) Return of Yahweh to His Sanctuary (43:1-12)

Like several other visions in Ezekiel, this vision (43:1-5) is followed by an interpretation (43:6-12). As the glory of God filled the tabernacle after its construction at the beginning of Israel's history (Exod 40:34-38), and as it filled the temple following its construction by Solomon (1 Kgs 8:10-11), so Ezekiel was assured in a vision that once again God's glory will reside with Israel. As the exiles despaired at the departure of God's glory in Ezekiel's vision, a departure confirmed by the destruction of the temple, so Israel had once before despaired when the Philistines took the ark and Eli and his sons all died. Eli's daughter-in-law named her son Ichabod, which meant "no glory" (1 Sam 4:19-22). But as the ark and the glory were restored when the Davidic covenant was revealed to David (2 Sam 6–7) and confirmed in the building of the temple (2 Sam 7:12-13; 1 Kgs 8:10-11), so will the glory of the Lord be restored to the new temple in the messianic age when the Davidic covenant is completely fulfilled.

God's glory was manifested as a bright light that signified his presence. The glory of God appeared to Moses and the elders on Mount Sinai (Exod 24:9-17). It has been called the *shekinah* glory, although this term is not used in the Bible. The word *shekinah* comes from the Hebrew verb *šākan*, which means "to rest" or "to abide." This verb was used in Exod 24:16 when the glory of Yahweh "settled" (*šākan*) on Mount Sinai. Moses spent a lengthy time in God's presence; his face glowed with the reflection of God's glory when he came down from the mountain (Exod 34:29-30). When the temple of Solomon was dedicated (1 Kgs 8:11), the sanctuary

---

[61] "Altar," *HBD*, 37-40.

[62] J. D. Pentecost, *Things to Come* (Grand Rapids: Zondervan, 1970), 452, 489-90.

was filled with the glory of God's presence. The shepherds of Bethlehem also experienced the glory of God at the announcement of the birth of Jesus (Luke 2:8-10).

In the first vision when he received his call to the ministry, Ezekiel saw the glory of God emerge from the storm that came from the north (1:4-28). In a later vision he had seen the glory of God depart from the sanctuary (10:4,18-19) and move to the east gate of the temple area and pause. Then the glory moved from the east gate to the Mount of Olives (11:22-25). From there at some unspecified later time the glory of God disappeared. According to rabbinical sources, the glory of God tarried for three and a half years atop the Mount of Olives. The midrash traced ten stages of the withdrawal of God's glory from the temple and city.[63]

Most agree chaps. 40–48 have three major divisions. That the second division begins at 43:1 is suggested by the relationship between the three "visions of God" passages in 1:1; 8:3; and 40:2 (see comments at 40:1-4). As Parunak has observed, some of the elements from 8:1-4 introducing the second vision are repeated in 40:1-4, and other elements are repeated in 43:1-5. "It is as though the author, at the start of 40, begins to give a vision on the plan of 8–11." Then "he pauses to describe the new temple, before resuming his prologue and the oracular temple tour in chap. 43."[64] The similarity of 44:5-6 to 40:4, however, causes some to begin the second division at 44:1. It probably is best to treat chap. 43 independently, as having connections both to chaps. 40–42 and to chaps. 44–46.[65]

**¹Then the man brought me to the gate facing east, ²and I saw the glory of the God of Israel coming from the east. His voice was like the roar of rushing waters, and the land was radiant with his glory. ³The vision I saw was like the vision I had seen when he came to destroy the city and like the visions I had seen by the Kebar River, and I fell facedown. ⁴The glory of the LORD entered the temple through the gate facing east. ⁵Then the Spirit lifted me up and brought me into the inner court, and the glory of the LORD filled the temple.**

VISION OF GOD'S GLORY (43:1-5). **43:1-5** Ezekiel's guide brought him toward the east side of the city where the Mount of Olives lies just across the Kidron Valley from the temple mount. As Ezekiel looked to-

---

[63] See Greenberg, *Ezekiel 1–20,* 191, 201; Fisch, *Ezekiel,* 62.

[64] Parunak, "Literary Architecture," 70-71.

[65] Greenberg ("Program of Restoration," 189) ends the first division with 43:12 and considers 43:13-27 as transitional to the second division while "formally attached to what precedes." J. G. McConville ("Priests and Levites in Ezekiel," *TynBul* 34 [1983]: 18-22) argues that chap. 43 is introductory to chaps. 44–46.

ward the east, where the glory of the Lord had departed in the vision of chaps. 8–11, he saw God's glory return, accompanied by the sound of "rushing waters" (cf. 1:24). What he saw also reminded him of his first vision of the glory of God that he had seen by the Kebar River (1:4-28). But it was apparent to Ezekiel that the Lord's coming here was not a summons to ministry or a sign of judgment. It was a sign of his covenant love bringing blessings to his people that would never be taken away. The verb translated "was radiant" is found often suggesting the Lord's favor, as in the priestly blessing in Num 6:25— "The LORD *make* his face *shine* upon you and be gracious to you" (cf. Ezra 9:8; Job 33:30; Pss 19:8; 31:16; 67:1; Isa 60:1).

Ezekiel's response was the same as in his first encounter with God's glory. He fell on his face (v. 3; cf. 1:28). But the Spirit lifted him up and brought him into the inner court (v. 5). As Ezekiel watched, God's glory entered the east gate by which it had departed, continued into the inner court, and then entered the sanctuary (v. 5).[66]

**⁶While the man was standing beside me, I heard someone speaking to me from inside the temple. ⁷He said: "Son of man, this is the place of my throne and the place for the soles of my feet. This is where I will live among the Israelites forever. The house of Israel will never again defile my holy name—neither they nor their kings—by their prostitution and the lifeless idols of their kings at their high places. ⁸When they placed their threshold next to my threshold and their doorposts beside my doorposts, with only a wall between me and them, they defiled my holy name by their detestable practices. So I destroyed them in my anger. ⁹Now let them put away from me their prostitution and the lifeless idols of their kings, and I will live among them forever.**

**¹⁰"Son of man, describe the temple to the people of Israel, that they may be ashamed of their sins. Let them consider the plan, ¹¹and if they are ashamed of all they have done, make known to them the design of the temple—its arrangement, its exits and entrances—its whole design and all its regulations and laws. Write these down before them so that they may be faithful to its design and follow all its regulations.**

**¹²"This is the law of the temple: All the surrounding area on top of the mountain will be most holy. Such is the law of the temple.**

INTERPRETATION OF THE VISION (43:6-12). **43:6-12** God personally interpreted this vision for Ezekiel, thus adding even more importance to

---

[66] The word רָאָה ("to see") occurs seven times in this verse. The rabbis counted plural uses as two and calculated that the root was used nine times. Moses was allowed to see the glory of God. All other prophets must receive a ninefold obscuration of his glory, hence the use of the word "to see" for vision nine different times (see Fisch, *Ezekiel,* 293).

what Ezekiel saw (v. 6). The vision contained the fulfillment of promises that had deep theological significance for the people to whom Ezekiel ministered. God wanted to be sure Ezekiel understood the significance of what he had seen, so he gave him a personal interpretation. God said, "This is the place of my throne. . . . This is where I will live among the Israelites forever" (v. 7). God promised that his return would be a permanent return (vv. 7,9). Further, he promised that restored Israel would "never again" defile God's name or turn to idolatry.[67] The exile indeed was a cure of idolatry and Baal worship. After the Babylonian captivity Israel never again turned to idols.

The reference to idolatry and "detestable practices" (v. 8) was reminiscent of the scene in 8:1-18, where the prophet witnessed pagan cultic practices being performed inside the temple. God told Ezekiel to "describe the temple to the people of Israel, that they may be ashamed of their sins" (v. 10). The presence of the restored temple with Yahweh in residence was to serve as a reminder of his holiness and their sinfulness. It was to be a visible call to repentance and faith by both its presence and its rituals, laws, and feasts (vv. 10-11).

Verses 6-12 not only contain a vision of the fulfillment of the promise of restoration found in chaps. 33–37 but also present an outline of the theological significance of the temple. Ezekiel's future temple, like Solomon's temple, was to be the center of worship for Israel. Its religious significance was presented by Ezekiel in five important theological statements in vv. 7-12, which form a conclusion to the section (40:1–43:12) and present a summary of the theology of the temple.[68]

First, the temple was the throne house of God (43:7). The ark enshrined in the most holy place of the temple of Solomon was considered to be the throne of God. When the ark of the covenant was placed there, God was understood to be taking possession of his house of worship and affirming his desire to dwell among his people. A cloud filled Solomon's temple as a sign of God's presence and approval (1 Kgs 8:10). This cloud was accompanied by the glory of God (1 Kgs 8:11). The divine name represented the person of God to the Semitic mind. Therefore the name of God was enshrined in the temple (1 Kgs 8:17). Though the Hebrews understood that God was too great to be contained in an earthly temple (1 Kgs 8:27), they

---

[67] See Alexander, "Ezekiel," 969.

[68] See de Vaux, *Ancient Israel,* 322-30, and Clements, *God and Temple,* 104-7, who discuss the theological significance of the temple and its fixtures and provide the source of these summary statements. See also Morgenstern, "The Book of the Covenant," *HUCA* V (1928): 72-81; J. F. Drinkard, Jr., "Altar," *HBD,* 37-40.

also knew that in some unique and mystical way God was enthroned in the temple that Solomon built and dedicated to God's glory. As a part of the restoration God promised he would again be the Shepherd of Israel and that he would dwell with them in a unique way (Ezek 34:30). The temple of Ezekiel's vision made that promise a reality by looking to a future day when God would personally dwell again with his people (Rev 7:15-17; 21:3-4).

Second, the temple was a sign of God's election of Israel (43:7). Yahweh had chosen Israel as the people through whom his redemptive purpose would be realized for all humanity (Deut 7:6-11; Ezek 34:30). He chose Jerusalem and Zion (Pss 68:17; 132:13) as the place where his temple was built and where worship was centralized. Because the temple was spared in the invasion of Sennacherib in 701 B.C. (2 Kgs 18:1–19:37) its deliverance was viewed as a sign of God's special unfailing protection.[69] This deliverance created the belief that Jerusalem and the temple were inviolable and would always be afforded such protection. This was one reason that Ezekiel's preaching ministry was so unpopular. He predicted the fall of Jerusalem and the destruction of the temple, which the people had always thought to be impossible. The vision of God's return to the temple was a reconfirming sign of God's determination to keep his promise of the election of Israel and selection of Jerusalem, where his name would be enshrined forever.

Third, the temple was a visible sign of the holiness of God (43:7c). Yahweh's name repeatedly had been profaned by Israel's "detestable practices" (43:8; cf. 5:11; 44:6-7,13). They had profaned the temple by allowing pagan worship to infiltrate its courts as noted by Ezekiel in chaps. 8–9 and by their negligence (cf. 22:26).[70] The temple was the center of society. A corrupt temple was the sad witness of a corrupt nation (36:23). Ezekiel saw the millennial temple where God's holiness and name would again be established. He also envisioned a new holiness among the people, suggesting a new order based on the holiness and righteousness of Yahweh, who would reign forever as the monarch of this coming kingdom (43:8-9). McConville suggests that 43:12 ("All the surrounding area on top of the mountain will be most holy") together with Zech 14:20-21 be understood to describe "the beginning of a reclaiming of the whole creation as holy to God."[71]

Fourth, the temple was a visible witness of God's redemptive love.

---

[69] de Vaux, *Ancient Israel,* 327-28.
[70] McConville, "Priests and Levites in Ezekiel," 19.
[71] Ibid., 15.

God promised he would gather Israel from among the nations and return them to their land. After they returned to the land, he promised to cleanse them, give them a new heart, a new spirit, and save them from their uncleanness (36:21-29). The reconstructed temple was to be a confirmation of this promise and a witness to its fulfillment (43:10-12). The permanent presence of God would bring a vivid awareness of sins forgiven and uncleanness removed. The design of the temple with its graduated sections approaching the holy of holies pointed to the holy God in residence. The perfect law that he endorsed will call his future people Israel to serve him again in humility, faith, and repentance (43:10-11). This was, is, and will be the law of the temple (43:12). God's determination to restore Israel, cleanse them, and permanently dwell with them was an affirmation of his redemptive love for them and for all humanity.

Fifth, the temple was a physical sign of the new covenant (43:11-12). All the significant covenants of the Old Testament had a visible sign of their confirmation and perpetuity. Adam's covenant was sealed by the sign of the seed of the woman (Gen 3:15). Noah's covenant was sealed by the rainbow (Gen 9:11-13). Circumcision was the seal and sign of the Abrahamic covenant (Gen 17:1-14). The Mosaic covenant was sealed by the observance of the Sabbath and by the tabernacle and its laws (Exod 24:1-18; 25:8-10.). David's covenant promise of a permanent dynasty for his descendants was sealed by the temple that his son built for God's glory (2 Sam 7:13-14). Ezekiel and others envisioned a covenant of peace, whose spiritual sign would be the outpouring of the Spirit (36:26-28). The temple, the vision of which unfolded in chaps. 40–42, would be the physical confirmation of the covenant of peace and of the future restoration (Ps 48:1-14, esp. v. 8). The millennial temple will stand as a witness to the immutability of God's covenant of peace with Israel and with all humanity (43:11-12).

### (3) Vision of Restored Worship (43:13–46:24))

Reinstatement of the laws of the sacrificial system appeared to be a retrogression from the New Testament ideals in force before the beginning of the millennium. It seems to return to the more primitive typological pictures of redemption that the Mosaic system represented. Yet it should be no surprise that Ezekiel would have been shown sacrifices as a vital part of worship in the temple. He was a priest and therefore vitally concerned with worship. If Ezekiel's future temple is taken to be a literal institution, then there must be some understanding of exactly why there would be a return to the sacrificial system when Jesus had already fulfilled those types (Matt 5:17-18).

It must be remembered that chaps. 40–48 only present the Hebrew perspective of worship in the millennium.[72] In the previous discussion of vv. 1-12 five theological purposes for the temple were presented. These purposes define worship in the millennial temple from the Hebrew viewpoint. Still the question remains, How can the New Testament ideals in force today be set aside at some future time for a return to the Mosaic system?

When the descendants of Abraham were constituted as a nation at Mount Sinai, God appointed them to be a "kingdom of priests and a holy nation" (Exod 19:1-6). This role as a kingdom of priests included a missionary purpose that would involve all humanity. They were not simply to be a kingdom *with* priests to minister to themselves. They were to be priestly mediators of God's covenant promises to all people. But from the time of their constitution as a nation to the present, Israel has never fulfilled that missionary mandate. Israel as a nation has never given witness to the truth that the Messiah was Jesus Christ. Zechariah 4:1-14 presented a prophecy of the fulfillment of Isa 60:1-3 in which the nation of Israel witnessed to the world concerning the Messiah, God's true Light, Jesus Christ. Zechariah, Isaiah, and Jeremiah (31:31-34) foretold a day when Israel would be a kingdom of priests mediating a new covenant of the saving grace of Yahweh through the Messiah.

Ezekiel also had foreseen the promise of a new covenant in his earlier prophecies (34:24-25; 36:22-31; 37:26-28). In these temple visions he also saw a future day when Israel will witness to the Messiah's salvation during the time of the tribulation. John the apostle received a similar message in Rev 7:1ff. that presented the conversion of 144,000 Jews who will go forth as witnesses of the Messiah. As a result of their work, a great unnumbered host will be saved (Rev 7:9-10). In Rev 12 Israel is portrayed as a sun-clad woman and is said to have the testimony of the Messiah, Jesus Christ (Rev 12:17). John's message seems to suggest that Israel's testimony of Jesus as Messiah will be acquired during the time of the tribulation. From that time Israel will begin to fulfill their assignment to be a kingdom of priests and a holy nation and to witness of Jesus as Messiah.

In addition to this future prospect of Israel's missionary zeal is another aspect of the covenant the nation was given that has never been fulfilled. Israel has never used the sacrificial system with the proper perspective,

---

[72] See Alexander, "Ezekiel," 946-52, for an in-depth discussion of issues related to harmonizing the apparent contradiction of returning to temple worship and the sacrificial system.

that is, with the person of the Messiah, the Suffering Servant (Isa 52:13–53:12), in view as the supreme sacrifice for sin. Israel rejected Jesus because they could not accept the idea of a nonpolitical, humble, self-sacrificing savior for their Messiah. The millennial kingdom will afford an opportunity for Israel to realize and practice its missionary purpose in the plan of God and practice the symbols of their covenant for the first time, in retrospect, to commemorate the redemptive work of Jesus as Messiah.

A return to the system of sacrifices has no place in the present church age. Why then would Israel in the millennium, after the church age, return to the sacrificial system of the time of Moses? The new covenant was sealed not with the blood of bulls and goats as was the old (Heb 10:1-8) but with the precious blood of Jesus (Matt 26:28). To commemorate his new covenant and this redemptive work, he established two ordinances, baptism and the Lord's Supper (Rom 6:1-23; Matt 26:26-30; 1 Cor 11:17-34). These ordinances celebrate and commemorate, in retrospect, the redemptive work of Jesus. In like manner Israel will worship God with sacrifices of fellowship as a commemoration and confirmation, in retrospect, of the redemptive work of Jesus as their Messiah as well.

Both the church ordinances and the ordinances of the sacrificial system share a common purpose. They were commissioned to be instructive and commemorative. These systems of worship were intended to employ rituals to communicate spiritual truths. Both the covenant of law and the covenant of grace have similar goals: to lead worshipers to cast themselves on the mercy and grace of a loving, forgiving God (cf. Exod 34:6-7; Ps 51:1-13; Eph 2:11-16).

Since the church will be taken out of the world, or raptured, prior to the tribulation (Rev 4:1), the tribulation will be the era of conversion for Israel (Rev 7:1ff.), and the millennium will afford them the opportunity to reinstate their covenant to celebrate and commemorate the redemptive work of Jesus the Messiah. The existence of the millennial temple and the reinstatement of the sacrificial system is not only understandable but predictable. Ezekiel's vision of a restored sacrificial system was really not so amazing after all. The millennium will afford Israel the opportunity for the first time in its history to use the symbols of their covenant with Jesus as Messiah in view. It will be their first time to be a kingdom of priests and a holy nation showing forth to the world the redemptive work of Yahweh in the person of Jesus Christ the Messiah (Isa 53:7; 61:1-3; Zech 4:1; John 1:29; Acts 8:32-35; 1 Pet 1:19; Rev 7:13-14; 5:9; 13:8; 15:3).

DEDICATION OF THE ALTAR AND RESTORATION OF SACRIFICES (43:13-27). There are two parts to this vision. First is the description of the altar

(43:13-17). Second are the regulations for use of the altar (43:18-27).

[13]"These are the measurements of the altar in long cubits, that cubit being a cubit and a handbreadth: Its gutter is a cubit deep and a cubit wide, with a rim of one span around the edge. And this is the height of the altar: [14]From the gutter on the ground up to the lower ledge it is two cubits high and a cubit wide, and from the smaller ledge up to the larger ledge it is four cubits high and a cubit wide. [15]The altar hearth is four cubits high, and four horns project upward from the hearth. [16]The altar hearth is square, twelve cubits long and twelve cubits wide. [17]The upper ledge also is square, fourteen cubits long and fourteen cubits wide, with a rim of half a cubit and a gutter of a cubit all around. The steps of the altar face east."

*Description of the Altar (43:13-17).* **43:13-17** The first element of temple worship that Ezekiel described was the altar of burnt offering. The measurements of the altar were based on the longer royal cubit, approximately twenty-one inches (see 40:5). The altar was built in four stages consisting of a base plus three stages. Each stage was two cubits smaller than the one below. Around the base was a one-cubit gutter with a rim on the outer edge one cubit high (v. 13). The perimeter of the base was eighteen cubits. The lowest stage was two cubits high and sixteen cubits on each side (v. 14) and the second four cubits high and fourteen cubits on each side (v. 15); the third stage that was the hearth was four cubits high and twelve cubits on each side. On the four corners of the fourth stage hearth were horns or projections. The upper ledge on the edge of the second stage also had a rim one-half cubit high and a gutter one cubit wide (v. 17). There were steps on the east side of the altar for access to the hearth.[73] The altar was a visible sign of the consequences of sin that encouraged people to confess and repent of deliberate sins (43:18-19; see discussion of 45:13-17).

[18]Then he said to me, "Son of man, this is what the Sovereign LORD says: These will be the regulations for sacrificing burnt offerings and sprinkling blood upon the altar when it is built: [19]You are to give a young bull as a sin offering to the priests, who are Levites, of the family of Zadok, who come near to minister before me, declares the Sovereign LORD. [20]You are to take some of its blood and put it on the four horns of the altar and on the four corners of the upper ledge and all around the rim, and so purify the altar and make atonement for it. [21]You are to take the bull for the sin offering and burn it in the designated part of the temple area outside the sanctuary.

---

[73] Taylor, *Ezekiel,* 267; Alexander, "Ezekiel," 972; H. G. May, "Ezekiel," *IB* VII (Nashville: Abingdon, 1956), 272.

²²"On the second day you are to offer a male goat without defect for a sin offering, and the altar is to be purified as it was purified with the bull. ²³When you have finished purifying it, you are to offer a young bull and a ram from the flock, both without defect. ²⁴You are to offer them before the LORD, and the priests are to sprinkle salt on them and sacrifice them as a burnt offering to the LORD.

²⁵"For seven days you are to provide a male goat daily for a sin offering; you are also to provide a young bull and a ram from the flock, both without defect. ²⁶For seven days they are to make atonement for the altar and cleanse it; thus they will dedicate it. ²⁷At the end of these days, from the eighth day on, the priests are to present your burnt offerings and fellowship offerings on the altar. Then I will accept you, declares the Sovereign LORD."

*Regulations for Use of the Altar (43:18-27).*  **43:18-27**  The Lord continued to speak to Ezekiel and gave him regulations for sacrificing on the altar. Two purposes for the altar were specified: (1) it was to be used for offering whole burnt offerings, and (2) it was to be used for "sprinkling blood" (v. 18).[74] Burnt offerings included all the five offerings in Lev 1–7.[75] "Sprinkling blood" is literally "throwing blood" (Heb. text) and was associated with priestly ordination (Exod 29:16,20), burnt offerings (Lev 1:5,11; 9:12), and peace offerings (Lev 3:2,8; 9:18).[76]

Jewish interpreters believe the command for the prophet to give the "bull" to the priests (v. 19) was a prophetic sign that Ezekiel will be one of the priests to officiate in the messianic temple.[77] But the best interpretation is that of Zimmerli, who views this section as similar to the charge given to Moses to see that worship procedures were carried out correctly (Exod 25:1ff.). Ezekiel was only officiating as an administrator in the vision that should not necessarily be taken as a prophetic promise that he will be a priest in the millennial temple.[78]

The altar was a symbol of the consequences of sin. The wages of sin produced the death of the sacrificial animal (Rom 6:23). The altar also presented the grace and love of God, who provided a means to atone for unintentional sins (43:19). Blood was sprinkled on the horns of the altar (v. 20). These projections on the four corners of the hearth were consid-

---

[74] Taylor, *Ezekiel,* 268; see his discussion of v. 18.

[75] The word עוֹלָה was the specific name for the whole burnt offering of Lev 1:3-17; 6:8-13. The four remaining offerings had only a portion of the sacrifice that was burned on the altar.

[76] Wevers, *Ezekiel,* 315. This practice goes back to Exod 24:6, where blood was a symbol of the covenant.

[77] Fisch (*Ezekiel,* 299) holds the position that Ezekiel thought he would be the high priest in the restored temple.

[78] Zimmerli, *Ezekiel 2,* 432-33.

ered the most holy and sacred part of the altar (Exod 29:12) and a place of mercy and refuge (1 Kgs 1:50; 2:28).[79] Excellent examples of altars have come to light in recent archaeological excavations. A small horned altar was found at Megiddo that may have been an incense altar. The most magnificent example of a horned sacrificial altar was found in the fifth season at Beersheba. This was the first time that the remnant of a horned sacrificial altar was discovered. This large dressed stone altar was approximately one and a half meters high and one and a half meters on each side. On each corner of the hearth were horns that were part of the cornerstones of the top. The author was a participant in the excavations in the Negev at Beer Sheba where the altar was discovered. It is on display at the museum of Beer Sheba, which houses the artifacts from the seven years of excavation at the site.[80]

The horns of the altar that Ezekiel saw were sprinkled with blood to purify the altar and make atonement for it (v. 20).[81] Also a bull was offered as a sin offering and burned outside the inner court but inside the temple complex (v. 21).[82] On the second day of the dedication of the altar a male goat was offered outside the inner court and the altar purified as in v. 20. Then a bull and a ram were offered as a whole burnt offering mixed with salt (vv. 23-24). The use of salt with an offering has specific overtones and association with the idea of covenant (Num 18:19; 2 Chr 13:5).[83] Salt was used as part of sacrificial communal meals and was a sign of purification and preservation. This procedure was repeated for seven days, meaning until seven days had ended rather than for an additional seven days.[84] The seven days for these ceremonies were for the atonement, cleansing, and dedication of the altar (v. 26).

The theological significance of the altar and sacrifices is an important

---

[79] Taylor, *Ezekiel*, 268. See his brief statement regarding the sanctity of the horns of the altar.

[80] *Excavations in the Negev Beer Sheba and Tel Masos,* bulletins of the 1973, 1974, 1975, and 1976 seasons, Tel Aviv University; J. Murphy-O'Conner, *The Holy Land* (Oxford: University Press, 1980), 138.

[81] Use of the words הֶחֱטֵא ("to purify") and כִּפֶּר ("to expiate" or "to cover") also are used in Exod 29:36 in the rites of consecration of the altar. These terms with טָהֵר ("to cleanse," v. 26) suggest the rites were designed to transfer the altar from secular to sacred. The rite of cleansing removes all possible contamination of being associated with the sinful secular world.

[82] See Fisch, *Ezekiel*, 300. Although the exact spot is not given, the sin offering was burnt inside the wall of the temple mount but outside the inner court.

[83] Zimmerli, *Ezekiel 2*, 434. בְּרִית מֶלַח refers to the use of salt with sacrifices to seal a covenant, a practice that came from the use of salt at sacral meals.

[84] Fisch, *Ezekiel*, 300.

concept in Ezekiel.[85] McConville considers this section on the altar to be
the central section ("midpoint") or peak of chaps. 40–48. He observes an
"inward movement" in the chapters to this point and the beginning from
here of an "outward movement" as regulations are given for the temple
(44:5), then measurements of the land belonging to the temple (chap. 45).
He also observes a "change of idiom" in 43:13-27 so that rather than describing what Ezekiel saw it describes the altar and its regulations as the
very words of God.[86]

At least seven theological concepts are associated with the altar and
the sacrifices. First, the altar sometimes was regarded as the "table" of
Yahweh (Ezek 44:16; Mal 1:7,12). It was where the sacrifice was transformed by fire into smoke that rose to heaven and to God. Because it was
burned, it became an irrevocable gift.

Second, since the temple was regarded as the "house" of God, a house
normally had a hearth, which was a repository of fire. The altar was considered to be the "hearth" of God (Ezek 43:15-16). The fire of God was on
the altar, and priests were admonished to keep the fire pure (see Lev 10:1-
7). Fire is a symbol in Scripture for God's presence (Exod 19:18), power
(Exod 9:24), wrath (2 Kgs 1:9-12), approval (Lev 9:24), guidance (Exod
13:21-22), protection (Zech 2:5), purity (Isa 6:5-7), deliverance (2 Kgs
2:11), God's word (Jer 5:14), the Messiah (Mal 3:2), the Holy Spirit (Acts
2:3), judgment (Matt 25:41), the return of Christ (2 Thess 1:8), and the
end of the present age (2 Pet 3:10-12).

Third, the altar was a sign of God's presence among his people (43:27).
It was commemorative of a theophany (Gen 12:7; 26:24-25). Such manifestations of God were often accompanied by fire (Exod 19:18; Judg
13:16-22).

Fourth, the altar was associated with the idea of holiness, purity, and
mercy, especially the horns of the altar (43:15,20; 1 Kgs 1:50-51; 2:28).
The sprinkling of blood on the horns of the altar was a rite of purification
(43:18-21).

Fifth, the altar was an instrument of mediation (40:47; 43:19). Offerings were translated from the physical world by burning and given to
God as they rose to heaven in smoke. By keeping the commandments,
the offerings, sacrifices, and feast days, the covenant promises were

---

[85] Vaux (*Ancient Israel,* 413-16; 451-54) discusses the theological significance of the altar and of sacrifices providing the basis for this summary. Many today agree with de Vaux
that the altar was the "hearth" of God's house. G. von Rad (*Old Testament Theology,* I [New
York: Harper & Row, 1962], 44-45) asserts that the altar gave legitimacy to Jerusalem as the
central place of worship.

[86] McConville, "Priests and Levites in Ezekiel," 20-22.

maintained (Lev 1:1–7:38).

Sixth, sacrifices were considered a gift to God (Ps 50:1-2; Ezek 43:27). A domesticated animal that was needed for food and work was given to God. The sacrifice was burned for two reasons: (1) burning made the gift irrevocable, and (2) it translated it to the invisible world where God lived. Thus the sacrifice was a means of communication with God and was considered a form of prayer (Ps 141:2).

Seventh, sacrifice was for expiation of sins committed unknowingly and unintentionally (43:25-27; Lev 4:2,13,22,27; 5:3-4,15,18; Num 15:22-31).

When the altar had been properly dedicated and the seven days fulfilled, God said, "Then I will accept you." From the eighth day onward the altar was used for the sacrifice of burnt offerings (v. 27). The beginning of the service of the altar of sacrifice from the eighth day has significant messianic overtones. The eighth day and the use of eight as a messianic number is an important part of the new temple of Ezekiel's vision. The use of the number eight and especially the eighth day in Scripture is significant (Ezek 43:27).

First, every seventh year was considered a Sabbatical Year. During the Sabbatical Year all land was to lie untilled. The pattern of six days of work followed by a Sabbath of rest was fixed in the years just as in the weeks (Lev 23:3). This principle probably had some agricultural value, but it also was to help the Hebrews guard against covetousness. A year without tilling the ground or harvesting any crops required careful planning and storing in preparation for the Sabbatical Year. But the Sabbath Year was followed by the eighth year that was to be a year of new beginning. It was to be a time for plowing the ground, sowing seeds, and harvesting crops once again. Jesus the Messiah is the person of the eighth day and eighth year of new beginnings. He is our Sabbath rest who satisfied both the Sabbath Day and Sabbath Year of rest (Matt 11:28-29; Heb 4:1-13). He will lead his people to a final time of eternal rest (Rev 14:13).

Second, priests were chosen and prepared for a seven-day period (Lev 8:1). The eighth day was the day for consecration and beginning their priestly duties (Lev 9:1-2). Nazirites were people who made a special personal consecration to the Lord similar to the priests. They were cleansed and consecrated on the eighth day (Num 6:10). Every believer in the New Testament era is a priest who ministers on the eighth day. Ezekiel saw a time of worship when the priesthood of the Old Testament would be reestablished for Israel. The worship in the temple over which they will officiate will take place on the eighth day (43:27). This perhaps suggests that the millennial calendar will appropriate eight-day weeks including worship on both the Sabbath and the Lord's Day.

Third, the sign of the covenant of Abraham, circumcision, to be received by all male Jews was to be administered on the eighth day after birth (Gen 17:12; Lev 12:3; Rom 2:28-29). The signs of the new covenant such as baptism, worship, and faith in Christ are part of the new eighth day of worship called the Lord's Day, made possible by the Messiah and envisioned by Ezekiel (43:27).

Fourth, those who were healed of sickness were to present themselves to the priest to be examined and pronounced clean. This ritual of purification took place on the eighth day following the healing. Lepers were pronounced clean in such eighth-day ceremonies (Lev 14:10,23); cleansing of running sores was done on the eighth day (Lev 15:14,29).

Fifth, the eighth day was a day of holy convocation and gathering. A holy convocation was called on the eighth day of the Feast of Tabernacles, and an offering was made unto the Lord (Lev 23:36,39; Num 29:35). When the law was reinstated after the Babylonian exile, it was done by Ezra and Nehemiah in a holy convocation on the eighth day (Neh 8:18). The Sabbath of the Old Testament was not a day of gathering for worship but a day of rest from work. The eighth day convocations beautifully anticipated the observance of the Lord's Day as a day of worship.

Sixth, animals to be used for sacrifice had to be at least eight days old (Lev 22:26-27). The grace of God could be sought through obedience to the sacrificial system from the eighth day and beyond. The eighth day was the beginning point of grace and mercy anticipating the messianic work of Jesus in providing salvation by grace (Eph 2:8-9) by being our perfect sacrifice (Heb 10:1-18; esp. v. 10).

DUTIES OF THE PRINCE AND THE PRIESTS (44:1-31). This chapter has three divisions: (1) the vision of the prince and the gate (44:1-3), (2) the return to the sanctuary (44:4-14), and (3) the Zadokite priesthood (44:15-31).

**¹Then the man brought me back to the outer gate of the sanctuary, the one facing east, and it was shut. ²The LORD said to me, "This gate is to remain shut. It must not be opened; no one may enter through it. It is to remain shut because the LORD, the God of Israel, has entered through it. ³The prince himself is the only one who may sit inside the gateway to eat in the presence of the LORD. He is to enter by way of the portico of the gateway and go out the same way."**

*Vision of the Prince and the Gate (44:1-3).*  **44:1-3**  Again Ezekiel's angel-guide brought him back to the eastern gate of the inner court of the sanctuary. When they arrived, the gate was shut. The prophet heard the voice of the Lord declare that the gate is to remain shut.

This enigmatic passage immediately raises several questions. Why was the gate shut? When was the gate shut? Who is the prince of the gate? The answer to the first question is suggested in the text. Yahweh returned to the temple through the east gate just as he had departed through the east gate (10:1-22; 11:22-25). When God returned, he promised never again to depart the city or temple (37:28; cf. 14:11; 34:30-31; 37:24-28). Closing the east gate was a way of providing an affirming sign of his intention to remain in permanent residence.[87]

The time of the gate's closure is more difficult to decide. Ezekiel was not told when the gate was closed. There is no evidence to suggest that the eastern gate of either Zerubbabel's temple or Herod's temple was permanently closed. The eastern gate that overlooks the Kidron Valley today is closed as it has been since the Crusades, nearly a thousand years ago. Crusaders walled up the gate because they believed that Jesus entered the temple mount by this gate on Palm Sunday and that it should be closed until he returns to reenter the temple mount.[88] Zechariah 14:4-5 presents the Messiah coming to the valley on the eastern side of the temple in preparation for his entry into the temple area. This has been regarded as biblical evidence that the gate should remain closed until Jesus returns.

Today the eastern gate, also called the Golden Gate, is a significant holy site for three major world religions, Judaism, Christianity, and Islam. Jews believe that when the Messiah comes he will open the east gate and enter the temple mount first and then enter the city of Jerusalem.[89] Moslems believe that the gate is the site of final judgment and call it the gate of heaven and hell. They believe the final judgment of humanity will take place before the eastern gate and the redeemed are those who will be allowed to enter the temple mount; all others will be outcasts.[90]

---

[87] Zimmerli, *Ezekiel 2*, 441; Fisch, *Ezekiel,* 302; May, "Ezekiel," 307.

[88] S. Gafni and A. van der Heyden, *The Glory of Jerusalem* (Cambridge: University Press, 1982), 18-19; L. C. Berrett, *Discovering the World of the Bible* (Nashville: Nelson, 1979), 224.

[89] Berrett, *Discovering the World of the Bible,* 224. In the summer of 1980 the author met with Professor Yigael Yadin, excavator of Masada, Hazor, and the Judean Caves, who was then Deputy Prime Minister of Israel. On the wall of his office was a picture of himself with other key military leaders entering St. Stephen's Gate just to the north of the Golden Gate when the Israelis took Jerusalem in the 1967 war. He told me: "We talked at the time about opening the Golden Gate and entering the temple mount and the city. Someone there reminded us that the Messiah was to be the one to open that gate, so we decided to enter the city through St. Stephen's Gate instead."

[90] Gafni and van der Heyden, *Glory of Jerusalem,* 18; Berrett, *Discovering the World of the Bible,* 224.

The gate was open in Jesus' day, and perhaps he did use it on Palm Sunday and at other times. Within thirty to forty years after Jesus' death, this gate along with the temple and the city of Jerusalem was destroyed. The gate that is there today is a seventh century A.D. structure, perhaps modified by the Crusaders and partially destroyed by the Ottoman Turks, who rebuilt the gate in the early sixteenth century. The Turkish governor of Jerusalem closed and walled up the gate in A.D. 1530. Since then it has remained closed. For the last thousand years there has been no gate of access to the temple on the eastern side. Any future opening and closing of this gate awaits the events of the end time and millennium.[91] Perhaps only then will we understand the full significance of the eastern gate.

Equally intriguing is the "prince" who may sit inside the gate to "eat in the presence of the LORD," probably meaning to eat a communal meal. Not even the prince used the entrance of the gate. When he entered it, he entered by the porch (v. 3).

Because of the messianic associations with the eastern gate, some have identified the "prince" as the Messiah, since 37:25 says, "David my servant will be their prince forever." In spite of this reference, two important details suggest that the "prince" of 44:3 is not the Messiah.[92] First, the prince is not a priest but has priests who minister for him. The Messiah is portrayed in Old Testament prophecy as the coming Priest-King (Zech 6:13). The offices of priest and king are always kept separate because the Messiah is to be the only one in whom these two offices are combined (2 Chr 26:16-21). Second, the prince is required to offer a sin offering for himself (Ezek 45:22) every day for seven days during feasts (45:23). By contrast, the Messiah was the sinless sacrifice for all people and a perfect High Priest (Heb 9:22-28).

If the prince is not the Messiah, then who is he? Some have identified the prince as David resurrected and serving in the temple during the millennium. More likely the prince is a special representative of the Messiah who will serve as an administrator of the temple, temple area, and sacred district. Such a conclusion is suggested by Levenson, who sees the prince as an apolitical messianic leader or a David-like administrator.[93]

---

[91] A gate that possibly dates to NT times or to the first temple has been found underneath the Golden Gate of the wall today, but excavation at this time is not possible. See J. Fleming, "The Undiscovered Gate Beneath Jerusalem's Golden Gate," *BAR* 9.1 (1983): 24-27.

[92] Alexander, "Ezekiel," 974; see his discussion of v. 3.

[93] J. D. Levenson, *Theology of the Program of Restoration of Ezekiel 40–48* (Atlanta: Scholars Press, 1986), 61, 67. Levenson agrees with Noth that the term נָשִׂיא has an amphictyonic origin. It looks to an earlier stage of Hebrew history prior to the monarchy to suggest that the prince would be an apolitical leader (pp. 75-77) who would be the administrator of the kingdom of Ezekiel's new order (pp. 111-13).

The word *nāsîʾ*, "prince" (v. 3), usually was associated with royalty but prior to the monarchy was a general term that meant a "leader."[94] The use of this term to describe the officer of the eastern gate seems consistent with the view that he is to be an administrative representative of the Messiah. The physical posture of sitting "in the gate" is also a familiar term of leadership in a municipality. Lot was "sitting in the gateway" of Sodom when the angel messengers came to warn him of the destruction of the city (Gen 19:1-29). This was an indication that he was a city official.

Gates were more than entrances to cities in the ancient Near East. Archaeological excavations have revealed that these ancient gates were actually buildings with rooms on either side of the entrance. In these rooms the elders of the city sat to rule in civil and judicial matters. The city gates functioned as a town council, chamber of commerce, city court, and welcome wagon all in one.[95] Amos decried the lack of justice in the gate and indicted the city fathers because they were corrupt and could be bribed into perverting justice. Thus the rich were able to secure whatever injustice they could buy, and the poor were disadvantaged (Amos 5:10,12,15; Prov 22:22).

The prince of Ezekiel's temple is a godly representative of the messianic King. He will sit in the gate, commune with God, and serve as a guarantor of mercy, justice, and righteousness. He will be the perfect spiritual-administrative leader of the new kingdom. The eternal security of believers in the millennium and beyond is guaranteed by God's determination to dwell permanently among his people (44:1-3; cf. John 10:28; Heb 7:24; Jude 4).

**⁴Then the man brought me by way of the north gate to the front of the temple. I looked and saw the glory of the Lord filling the temple of the LORD, and I fell facedown.**

**⁵The LORD said to me, "Son of man, look carefully, listen closely and give attention to everything I tell you concerning all the regulations regarding the temple of the LORD. Give attention to the entrance of the temple and all the**

---

[94] Alexander, "Ezekiel," 974. נָשִׂיא normally was associated with royalty, but earlier usage would seem to suggest that it also was used for any important leader. Tuell (*The Law of the Temple*, 117-20) believes that the term נָשִׂיא was given messianic associations because of what he calls the "messianic hysteria" surrounding the appointment of Zerubbabel as the governor of the restored Jerusalem. Sheshbazzar, Zerubbabel, and Nehemiah are all identified as נָשִׂיא, "governor" (see Ezra 5:14; Hag 1:1,14). In the restored temple of Ezekiel's vision, the נָשִׂיא has an important role in the temple as a patron of the liturgy.

[95] Such an administrative gate complex was found at Beer Sheba. It had two side chambers on either side of the entrance to the city.

exits of the sanctuary. <sup>6</sup>Say to the rebellious house of Israel, 'This is what the Sovereign LORD says: Enough of your detestable practices, O house of Israel! <sup>7</sup>In addition to all your other detestable practices, you brought foreigners un-circumcised in heart and flesh into my sanctuary, desecrating my temple while you offered me food, fat and blood, and you broke my covenant. <sup>8</sup>In-stead of carrying out your duty in regard to my holy things, you put others in charge of my sanctuary. <sup>9</sup>This is what the Sovereign LORD says: No foreigner uncircumcised in heart and flesh is to enter my sanctuary, not even the for-eigners who live among the Israelites.

<sup>10</sup>"'The Levites who went far from me when Israel went astray and who wandered from me after their idols must bear the consequences of their sin. <sup>11</sup>They may serve in my sanctuary, having charge of the gates of the temple and serving in it; they may slaughter the burnt offerings and sacrifices for the people and stand before the people and serve them. <sup>12</sup>But because they served them in the presence of their idols and made the house of Israel fall into sin, therefore I have sworn with uplifted hand that they must bear the consequences of their sin, declares the Sovereign LORD. <sup>13</sup>They are not to come near to serve me as priests or come near any of my holy things or my most holy offerings; they must bear the shame of their detestable practices. <sup>14</sup>Yet I will put them in charge of the duties of the temple and all the work that is to be done in it.

*Return to the Sanctuary (44:4-14).*    **44:4-14**   Since the east gate was shut, Ezekiel's guide brought him into the temple court through the north gate. As he stood in front of the temple, the glory of God filled the sanctu-ary (v. 4). Wevers' conclusion that most of 44:1-5 is a late addition, partly because of the repetition of what Ezekiel reported in 43:3-5, is unwarrant-ed.[96] Zimmerli states that the prophet was led for a second time into the inner court, and the glory filled the temple. He does not believe that this necessarily means that there were two separate fillings but correctly con-cludes that the glory was there all the time.[97] Ezekiel's reaction was pre-dictable. He fell on his face at the sight of the glory of God out of fear and reverence (v. 4; cf. 1:28; 43:1-5). The return of the glory was the sign of the restoration of God's presence that Ezekiel saw withdraw from the temple in chaps. 10 and 11. Regarding its repetition in 44:4, McConville explains, "The new reference to the glory of God simply makes clear that it is the return of God to the temple that serves as a basis for the regula-

---

[96] Wevers, *Ezekiel*, 219.

[97] See Zimmerli, *Ezekiel 2*, 444. He unnecessarily concludes, however, that the passage is secondary. To him the only original sections of chaps. 40–48 are those where Ezekiel is an observer (pp. 547-53). All the regulations are secondary. See the response to this view and the related view of Eichrodt (*Ezekiel*, 555-56) in McConville, "Priests and Levites in Ezekiel," 10-22.

tions to follow."[98]

Again the prophet was instructed to pay close attention to what he saw and heard (v. 5; cf. 40:4).[99] These regulations regarding the priesthood are commonly used by proponents of the documentary source theory of the Pentateuch to prove that the so-called "priestly document" (much of Genesis through Numbers) was compiled after Ezekiel.[100] Ezekiel 44:6-16 is frequently said to mean that the distinction between priests and Levites taught in Num 3–4 actually originated in Ezekiel. According to Wellhausen, Ezekiel was awarding the disenfranchised priests of the high places, whom Ezekiel calls "Levites," an inferior status in the Jerusalem temple, replacing the heathen temple slaves. The reason was that they had served as (legitimate) priests of the high places (v. 10) before King Josiah abolished the high places. The priests who had served in Jerusalem, however, called "sons of Zadok," Ezekiel rewarded with preeminence in the new temple system. Deuteronomy had tried (in the seventh century B.C.) to make the non-Jerusalem priests equal with those in Jerusalem but had failed (2 Kgs 23:9).[101]

This reconstruction of history is afflicted with unfounded assumptions and unlikely interpretations, as many have noted.[102] Nothing in the verses of Ezekiel that mention the distinction in temple personnel demand that Ezekiel was creating that distinction (40:45-46; 43:19; 44:10-16; 45:4-5; 46:20-24; 48:11-13).

The practices being condemned in vv. 7-8—bringing foreigners into the sanctuary (cf. Neh 13:4-9), giving unauthorized individuals charge over holy things, and desecrating the temple with unholy foreign worship

---

[98] McConville, "Priests and Levites in Ezekiel," 18.

[99] On the structural significance of the similarity of 44:5-6 to 40:4 see the discussion of structure in the introduction to chap. 43.

[100] See, e.g., E. Sellin and G. Fohrer, *Introduction to the Old Testament* (Nashville: Abingdon, 1968), 185; H. J. Flanders, et al., *People of the Covenant* (New York: Oxford University Press, 1988), 78,188. Several scholars now argue for an early date of P. See Y. Kaufmann, The *Religion of Israel* (New York: Schocken, 1960), 174-211; A. Hurvitz, "The Evidence of Language in Dating the Priestly Code," *RB* 81 (1974): 25-46; J. Misgrom, *Leviticus 1–16*, AB (New York: Doubleday, 1991), 3-13.

[101] J. Wellhausen, *Prolegomena to the History of Ancient Israel* (Gloucester, Mass.: Peter Smith, 1983), 123-24. See also Wevers, *Ezekiel*, 220-21. Regarding the date, of P. Wellhausen states (p. 124): "That the prophet should know nothing about a priestly law with whose tendencies he is in thorough sympathy admits of only one explanation,—that it did not then exist. His own ordinances are only to be understood as preparatory steps towards its own exactment."

[102] See the analysis in McConville, "Priests and Levites in Ezekiel," 3-31. See also M. Haran, "The Law Codes of Ezekiel XL-XLVIII and Its Relation to the Priestly School," *HUCA* 50 (1979): 45-71; R. Abba, "Priests and Levites in Ezekiel," *VT* 28, 1978, 138-49.

(44:7-8) cannot be identified historically with certainty. Rabbinic tradition says the "detestable practices" consisted of the employment of priests who were unqualified to minister before the Lord because of their evil deeds. It also may refer to the unauthorized use of prisoners of war to perform menial tasks in the temple.[103] Perhaps these sins were committed during Ezekiel's exile in Babylon. They are not directly attributed to the Levites, however, whose sin is said to have been idolatry and encouraging Israel in idolatry (vv. 10,12). There is nothing to suggest that their guilt involved serving as priests at the high places.

Because of their idolatry the Levites were confirmed in their subordinate status they are given in Numbers. Furthermore, for their faithfulness the priesthood is entrusted to the Zadokites, who are enjoined to protect the holiness of the temple (44:15). In spite of their sin the Levites were allowed to have a part in the temple service but only as ministers in charge of the temple, in contrast to the priests who would be in charge of the altar (v. 10; cf. 40:45-46). The Levites' responsibilities would be similar to those given in the wilderness. There they were to serve at the tabernacle (Num 16:8-11), guard the tabernacle from defilement (Num 1:53; 3:10), and redeem the firstborn (Num 3:12-13,40-43; 8:14-19). Ezekiel mentions all but the last. They were to guard the temple gates and slaughter the animals of sacrifice brought by the people, but they could not minister as priests or "come near," meaning they could not go into the inner court (vv. 11-12).[104]

The principles for service to the Lord are based on high moral and spiritual standards. The Levites compromised their convictions and became immoral and idolatrous (Mal 1:6-14; 3:1-4). Those who serve God in leadership roles must present an unblemished example (1 Tim 3:1-13). A holy God demands no less. The unbeliever will never take seriously the message of an unholy messenger (Ezek 44:4-14).

God has a place of service for everyone. Though the Levites were disqualified from leadership roles, they still had a significant part in the service of the temple. Past moral failure does not exclude one from worship or service in the house of God. It may, however, preempt one from serving in leadership roles where a moral failure would present a compromised testimony (44:11-14).

---

[103] Fisch, *Ezekiel*, 303; May, "Ezekiel," 308-9. Prisoners sometimes were used for menial tasks in temple service (Josh 9:27). Excavations of the second temple in A.D. 1870 uncovered an inscription in Greek (now in the museum at Istanbul) that warned Gentiles against entering the prohibited areas of the temple under penalty of death.

[104] Taylor, *Ezekiel*, 271. See his discussion of vv. 10-14, where the Levites would be allowed to serve.

<sup>15</sup>" 'But the priests, who are Levites and descendants of Zadok and who faithfully carried out the duties of my sanctuary when the Israelites went astray from me, are to come near to minister before me; they are to stand before me to offer sacrifices of fat and blood, declares the Sovereign LORD. <sup>16</sup>They alone are to enter my sanctuary; they alone are to come near my table to minister before me and perform my service.

<sup>17</sup>" 'When they enter the gates of the inner court, they are to wear linen clothes; they must not wear any woolen garment while ministering at the gates of the inner court or inside the temple. <sup>18</sup>They are to wear linen turbans on their heads and linen undergarments around their waists. They must not wear anything that makes them perspire. <sup>19</sup>When they go out into the outer court where the people are, they are to take off the clothes they have been ministering in and are to leave them in the sacred rooms, and put on other clothes, so that they do not consecrate the people by means of their garments.

<sup>20</sup>" 'They must not shave their heads or let their hair grow long, but they are to keep the hair of their heads trimmed. <sup>21</sup>No priest is to drink wine when he enters the inner court. <sup>22</sup>They must not marry widows or divorced women; they may marry only virgins of Israelite descent or widows of priests. <sup>23</sup>They are to teach my people the difference between the holy and the common and show them how to distinguish between the unclean and the clean.

<sup>24</sup>" 'In any dispute, the priests are to serve as judges and decide it according to my ordinances. They are to keep my laws and my decrees for all my appointed feasts, and they are to keep my Sabbaths holy.

<sup>25</sup>" 'A priest must not defile himself by going near a dead person; however, if the dead person was his father or mother, son or daughter, brother or unmarried sister, then he may defile himself. <sup>26</sup>After he is cleansed, he must wait seven days. <sup>27</sup>On the day he goes into the inner court of the sanctuary to minister in the sanctuary, he is to offer a sin offering for himself, declares the Sovereign LORD.

<sup>28</sup>" 'I am to be the only inheritance the priests have. You are to give them no possession in Israel; I will be their possession. <sup>29</sup>They will eat the grain offerings, the sin offerings and the guilt offerings; and everything in Israel devoted to the LORD will belong to them. <sup>30</sup>The best of all the firstfruits and of all your special gifts will belong to the priests. You are to give them the first portion of your ground meal so that a blessing may rest on your household. <sup>31</sup>The priests must not eat anything, bird or animal, found dead or torn by wild animals.

*The Zadokite Priesthood (44:15-31).* **44:15-31** The line of Zadok is to be the only legitimate line of priests allowed to minister in the inner court and in the sanctuary before the Lord (v. 15). This priority of the line of Zadok has previously been discussed (see 40:46; 43:19). They were rewarded for their faithfulness to David and his descendants (v. 16) and for standing against idolatry.

Several regulations for the Zadokite priests are described in vv. 17-21. First, their clothing would be only linen when they administered their office (v. 17). Linen was a symbol of purity in contrast to wool, which was an animal by-product and therefore unclean.[105] The priests were to wear linen turbans and linen undergarments. They were to avoid any weight of cloth of any kind that would cause excessive perspiration (v. 18). The sacred vestments were only to be worn in the administration of their duties as priests before the Lord. Upon entering or leaving the inner sanctuary they were to change clothes (v. 19). Second, their hair must neither be too long nor totally shaved (v. 20). Third, they could drink no wine in the inner court (v. 21). Fourth, they could marry but only a virgin or the widow of another priest (v. 22).

Verse 23 breaks into the flow of regulations to interject the reason for these regulations: "They are to teach my people the difference between the holy and the common and show them how to distinguish between the unclean and the clean," teaching by example as well as precept. The priests were to provide the kind of unblemished example that would encourage Israel to worship God and attract unbelieving nations to serve him.

Fifth, the priests will serve as judges in civil disputes. They were to see that all the laws of God were observed, especially the feasts days and the Sabbath (v. 24). Sixth, the priests will refrain from touching the dead. Any priest who violated this law must remain unclean for seven days. When he returned to duty, he had to offer a sin offering for himself (v. 27). Seventh, God was the only legitimate possession of the priests. All food, clothing, and needs will come from temple service (vv. 28-29). They received the firstfruits of the harvest and the best of each household (v. 30). Eighth, the priests will eat nothing that died a natural death or that had been killed by a wild animal (v. 31).

These regulations are very similar to the laws of the Nazirites in Num 6:1-21, which were laws of special consecration. The priests of the tabernacle and first temple also had similar regulations (see Lev 21:1-9). These rules were to insure that the priests were examples of holiness, faithfulness, and had unblemished characters.[106]

Those who are called to leadership roles must make whatever personal sacrifices necessary to maintain their moral purity. Both the character and conduct of those in leadership roles should demonstrate an obedience of and conformity to the physical, moral, and spiritual principles of the Word of God (44:15-31).

---

[105] Wevers, *Ezekiel,* 321.

[106] Taylor, *Ezekiel,* 272; see his discussion of vv. 20-27.

DIVISION OF THE LAND FOR THE PRIESTS, LEVITES, AND PRINCE (45:1-8). Two sections discuss the allotment of land in the future kingdom, 45:1-8 and 47:13–48:35. Ezekiel 45:1-8 gives the details of the apportionment of the central sacred district of the land that is to be assigned to the priests, Levites, and the prince. The sacred district that Ezekiel saw had a central area twenty-five thousand by twenty thousand cubits flanked on either side by areas for the prince (see also 48:8-20).

[1]"'When you allot the land as an inheritance, you are to present to the LORD a portion of the land as a sacred district, 25,000 cubits long and 20,000 cubits wide; the entire area will be holy. [2]Of this, a section 500 cubits square is to be for the sanctuary, with 50 cubits around it for open land. [3]In the sacred district, measure off a section 25,000 cubits long and 10,000 cubits wide. In it will be the sanctuary, the Most Holy Place. [4]It will be the sacred portion of the land for the priests, who minister in the sanctuary and who draw near to minister before the LORD. It will be a place for their houses as well as a holy place for the sanctuary. [5]An area 25,000 cubits long and 10,000 cubits wide will belong to the Levites, who serve in the temple, as their possession for towns to live in.

[6]"'You are to give the city as its property an area 5,000 cubits wide and 25,000 cubits long, adjoining the sacred portion; it will belong to the whole house of Israel.

[7]"'The prince will have the land bordering each side of the area formed by the sacred district and the property of the city. It will extend westward from the west side and eastward from the east side, running lengthwise from the western to the eastern border parallel to one of the tribal portions. [8]This land will be his possession in Israel. And my princes will no longer oppress my people but will allow the house of Israel to possess the land according to their tribes.

**45:1-8** Within the central sacred district a portion five hundred cubits square was set aside for the sanctuary bordered by a fifty-cubit-wide open perimeter (vv. 1-2). There has been some confusion about the unit of measurement used to determine distances in these allotments. The Hebrew text used the term "rods" instead of cubits. These rods were previously described as six cubits long (see 40:5-16). The NIV translated the measurement into cubits, and that is the unit used in this discussion (see 42:15-20).

In the middle of the sacred district was a section twenty-five thousand cubits by ten thousand cubits with the sanctuary located in the center. This land was allotted to the Zadokite priests. They will live in this section and minister in the sanctuary (Ezek 45:3-4). Just to the north of this section was the land assigned to the Levites. This section was twenty-five thousand by ten thousand cubits (v. 5).[107]

A third section twenty-five thousand by five thousand cubits will be allotted for the new city (new Jerusalem, v. 6). On either side of the central district allotted to the Zadokite priests, Levites, and city is the land allotment of the prince (v. 7). He received two sections of land on either side of the central district that are also twenty-five thousand cubits from north to south but extend from the sacred central district to the borders of the land to the east and west (v. 8). This land will belong to the prince who will oversee the allotments of the land for all the tribes (see 47:13–48:35). The land of the priests will be a sacred district belonging to the Lord. Those who commit themselves to God's service are his and are to live by what his people provide for his work (45:1-8; 1 Cor 9:14).

REGULATIONS FOR OFFERINGS AND FEAST DAYS (45:9–46:24). Seven sets of regulations were given to the prince and the priests. These regulations are presented in the seven divisions of this section. First is a demand for just standards (45:9-12). Second are offerings for the prince (45:13-17). Third are regulations for the feasts (45:18-25). Fourth are regulations for the Sabbath (46:1-8). Fifth are general regulations for worship (46:9-15). Sixth are regulations concerning the prince and his property (46:16-18). Seventh are regulations for cooking (46:19-24).

**[9]"'This is what the Sovereign LORD says: You have gone far enough, O princes of Israel! Give up your violence and oppression and do what is just and right. Stop dispossessing my people, declares the Sovereign LORD. [10]You are to use accurate scales, an accurate ephah and an accurate bath. [11]The ephah and the bath are to be the same size, the bath containing a tenth of a homer and the ephah a tenth of a homer; the homer is to be the standard measure for both. [12]The shekel is to consist of twenty gerahs. Twenty shekels plus twenty-five shekels plus fifteen shekels equal one mina.**

*The Demand for Just Standards (45:9-12).* **45:9-12** This section is a rebuke of the priests for their dishonesty in the use of scales, weights, and measures used to weigh offerings brought to the temple. Abuse of these tools of the marketplace was a source of frequent mention in the Old Testament (Lev 19:35; Deut 25:13-16; Prov 11:1; Amos 8:5; Mic 6:10-12).[108] Amos preached against insincere worship and dishonest practices (Amos 8:1-6). He painted a sordid picture of people who were impatient

---

[107] See map "Millennial Tribal Allotments," p. 428. Ibid., 273-74; Alexander, "Ezekiel," 979,81.

[108] Taylor, *Ezekiel,* 274; Angelo Segrè, "A Documentary Analysis of Ancient Palestine Units of Measure," *JBL* 64 (1945): 357-75; "Weights and Measures," *IDB* 4:828.

because of the arrival of the Sabbath that interrupted their dishonest and deceitful business practices perpetrated on the populace.[109] The people of Amos's day loved dishonest gain more than they loved God. They were selfish and covetous.[110] Their lack of morality in the market reflected their loose attitude toward all standards of righteousness. These dishonest merchants tampered with the scales, placed false bottoms in the measure used in the sale of grain, mixed chaff with the salable wheat, and shaved metal off the coins used in exchange (Amos 8:5-6).[111] Concern for honesty applied to the temple precincts as well as the marketplace. In the temple animals were bought and money was exchanged by those who came to worship.

Ezekiel already had soundly rebuked the community leaders for their injustices (22:1-31). That he also here rebuked the priests was another reminder of how seriously God views honesty and probity in dealings between individuals. It was a sad testimony to the lack of honesty among the spiritual leaders of Ezekiel's day and a warning for spiritual leaders in every age (cf. 22:1-22). Such dealings reveal the sincerity or lack of it that is necessary for acceptable worship. Jesus mentioned it in the Sermon on the Mount as a basis for our acceptance before God (Matt 5:23-24).

The "princes" (v. 9), perhaps a reference to leaders in general or perhaps to the prince and his family, will be responsible for setting and enforcing a system of standard weights and measures to insure honesty in trade and exchange not only in the temple but for all commercial enterprises as well.[112] God admonished the princes to avoid violence and oppression and to enforce justice. Also the priests will be responsible for receiving money, gifts for offerings such as grain and oil, and were also involved in exchange. Standard weights and measures were necessary for acceptable offerings.[113] This law set a standard to enforce justice that the prophets championed and God demanded.[114]

Accurate scales and dry measures were to be used in buying, selling, and exchanging (vv. 10-11). The shekel was the unit of monetary ex-

---

[109] D. A. Hubbard, *Joel and Amos* (Downers Grove: InterVarsity, 1989), 220. See his discussion of Amos 8:4-7.

[110] See J. A. Motyer, *The Day of the Lion* (Leicester: InterVarsity, 1974), 181, for his discussion of the impact of covetousness on Israel.

[111] P. H. Kelley, *Amos: Prophet of Social Justice* (Grand Rapids: Baker, 1972), 116-17. See his discussion of dishonest practices in the marketplace.

[112] Craigie, *Ezekiel*, 301-2. See his discussion of vv. 10-12.

[113] Hals, *Ezekiel*, 324. See his discussion of 45:10-17, which he entitles "Proper Weights and Measures as the Basis for the Required Offerings."

[114] Cooke, *Ezekiel*, 497.

change, and a standard weight for the shekel was set (v. 12). Metal coins were handmade in molds and so were not of standard weight or size. In all buying and selling, money was weighed rather than counted. By shaving bits of metal off these nonstandard coins, unscrupulous merchants and customers could defraud each other especially if coins were counted. Consequently the coins had to be weighed. Merchants sometimes added lead to weights so that it took more shekels to balance their scales. Such falsification and dishonesty was an abomination to Yahweh.[115]

No standard conversion table has been established for the weights and measures named by Ezekiel. A *homer* was a dry measure of approximately five bushels. An *ephah* was one-tenth of a *homer,* making it about one-half bushel. A *bath* was a liquid measure of about five-and-one-half gallons.[116] The *shekel* weighed an average of about four-tenths of an ounce and equalled twenty-four *gerahs*. The *shekel* was one-fifth of a *mina*. Weights and measure were used to measure offerings of grain, commodities and money (vv. 11-12). Mention of this regulation first suggested that honesty, justice, and probity in the temple as well as in the marketplace were foremost with God.

Just dealings precede acceptable worship. God abhors false balances (Prov 11:1; Amos 8:5; Mic 6:11) because they represent injustice and deceit (Ezek 45:9-12). Jesus made this same connection between justice in our relationships and acceptable worship in the Sermon on the Mount (Matt 5:21-26).

---

**13**"'This is the special gift you are to offer: a sixth of an ephah from each homer of wheat and a sixth of an ephah from each homer of barley. **14**The prescribed portion of oil, measured by the bath, is a tenth of a bath from each cor (which consists of ten baths or one homer, for ten baths are equivalent to a homer). **15**Also one sheep is to be taken from every flock of two hundred from the well-watered pastures of Israel. These will be used for the grain offerings, burnt offerings and fellowship offerings to make atonement for the people, declares the Sovereign LORD. **16**All the people of the land will participate in this special gift for the use of the prince in Israel. **17**It will be the duty of the prince to provide the burnt offerings, grain offerings and drink offerings at the festivals, the New Moons and the Sabbaths—at all the appointed feasts of the house of Israel. He will provide the sin offerings, grain offerings, burnt offerings and fellowship offerings to make atonement for the house of Israel.

---

[115] Zimmerli, *Ezekiel 2,* 476. This demand for honesty in the marketplace goes back to the Holiness Code (Lev 19:30) to insure that the balances were not manipulated.

[116] Wevers, *Ezekiel,* 326; Bunn, "Ezekiel," 363; "Weights and Measures," *IDB* 3:1634-40; M. P. Matheney, "Weights and Measures," *HBD,* 1403-7.

*Offerings for the Prince (45:13-17).* **45:13-17** The people will provide for the operation of the temple by making an offering to the prince. This was not like the tithe but like the provision for the service of the tabernacle in Exod 30:11-16.[117] The required offering for grain will be one-sixth of all produce (v. 13). One percent of the oil will be given for use in the temple (v. 14) and one of every two hundred animals (v. 15). These commodities will be used in the feast days and festivals of the temple.[118]

Everyone will be required to participate in these offerings brought to the prince as the administrator of the temple stores and the Messiah's special representative (v. 16). Offered items will be used in the burnt offerings, grain offerings, drink offerings, New Moon or new month celebration, Sabbaths, all the feast days, general sin offerings, and fellowship offerings to make atonement for the people.

This system of offerings brought picture lessons of the need for personal cleansing from all sin. The sacrificial system was never intended to be a method for salvation. Rather, this system was designed to call attention to the need for personal redemption. No sacrifice was provided in the Mosaic system for sins committed deliberately and intentionally. The offerings, including the sin offering, were provided for sins committed unintentionally and unknowingly (see Lev 4:2,13,22,27; 5:3-4,15,18; Num 15:24-31). There was only one recourse for sins committed deliberately and knowingly. The sinners could humble themselves, entreat the grace of God and plead for his mercy. David is the example of one who appealed to God in this way because of his great sin of lust, adultery, and murder (2 Sam 12:13; Pss 32:1; 51:1).

It was precisely for this reason that Moses did not seek to offer a sacrifice for the people when they sinned by making the idol of the golden calf while he was away with God on Mount Sinai (Exod 32:1). Instead he appealed for mercy based on the character of God (Exod 34:6-7). The sacrifices were therefore never intended to be a means of salvation. They were a picture of the need for personal repentance and faith based on the mercy and grace of God. Also the system of offerings and sacrifices in the millennial temple will offer no alternative plan for salvation. They will picture the mercy and grace of God available through confession of sin, repentance of the sinner, and faith in Jesus the Messiah, who is the perfect sacrifice and all-sufficient offering (Heb 10:10).[119]

---

[117] Zimmerli, *Ezekiel 2,* 477. See his discussion of 48:13-15.

[118] Wevers, *Ezekiel,* 327. See his discussion of v. 17; cf. 45:22–46:15.

[119] Alexander, "Ezekiel," 983-84. See his discussion of the "practical lessons," which point to Jesus the Messiah.

The people were responsible to provide for the operation of the temple, its services, and the priests. Tithes and offerings have always been the acceptable means for funding God's work. Everyone was to participate in this, the only legitimate method for temple support. The sanctuary was never to be supported by merchandizing.

**[18]"'This is what the Sovereign LORD says: In the first month on the first day you are to take a young bull without defect and purify the sanctuary. [19]The priest is to take some of the blood of the sin offering and put it on the doorposts of the temple, on the four corners of the upper ledge of the altar and on the gateposts of the inner court. [20]You are to do the same on the seventh day of the month for anyone who sins unintentionally or through ignorance; so you are to make atonement for the temple.**

**[21]"'In the first month on the fourteenth day you are to observe the Passover, a feast lasting seven days, during which you shall eat bread made without yeast. [22]On that day the prince is to provide a bull as a sin offering for himself and for all the people of the land. [23]Every day during the seven days of the Feast he is to provide seven bulls and seven rams without defect as a burnt offering to the LORD, and a male goat for a sin offering. [24]He is to provide as a grain offering an ephah for each bull and an ephah for each ram, along with a hin of oil for each ephah.**

**[25]"'During the seven days of the Feast, which begins in the seventh month on the fifteenth day, he is to make the same provision for sin offerings, burnt offerings, grain offerings and oil.**

*Regulations for the Feasts (45:18-25).* **45:18-25** The first of the feast regulations described is an annual rite of purification for the temple (vv. 18-20). This rite is to be carried out on the first day of the first month, which would have been March or April each year.[120] The prince is to offer a bull as a sin offering and place the blood on the doorposts of the sanctuary, the four corners of the altar, and the gateposts of the inner court (v. 19). The same ceremony is to be repeated in the seventh month for anyone who had committed unknown or unintentional sins (v. 20; see discussion of vv. 13-17).[121]

The Passover observance followed by the Feast of Unleavened Bread is also the responsibility of the prince (v. 21; cf. Exod 12:1-2; Num 28:16-25). At Passover the prince will offer a sin offering for himself and the people. On the seven days of the Feast of Unleavened Bread that followed, the prince offered seven bulls, seven rams, and a male goat as a sin

---

[120] Wevers, *Ezekiel,* 329-30.
[121] Zimmerli, *Ezekiel 2,* 483. See his discussion of v. 20a.

offering each day (v. 23). Accompanying these sacrifices is to be an ephah of grain and one hin of oil, which was about twelve pints (v. 24).[122]

The feast of the seventh month is the Feast of Tabernacles. It is described in Lev 23:33-36 and Num 29:12-38. Since it too was a seventh-day feast, the same regulations applied (v. 25). Ezekiel saw these feast days as observances to be used by Israel in their millennial worship to celebrate the redemptive work of the Messiah.

[1]"'This is what the Sovereign LORD says: The gate of the inner court facing east is to be shut on the six working days, but on the Sabbath day and on the day of the New Moon it is to be opened. [2]The prince is to enter from the outside through the portico of the gateway and stand by the gatepost. The priests are to sacrifice his burnt offering and his fellowship offerings. He is to worship at the threshold of the gateway and then go out, but the gate will not be shut until evening. [3]On the Sabbaths and New Moons the people of the land are to worship in the presence of the LORD at the entrance to that gateway. [4]The burnt offering the prince brings to the LORD on the Sabbath day is to be six male lambs and a ram, all without defect. [5]The grain offering given with the ram is to be an ephah, and the grain offering with the lambs is to be as much as he pleases, along with a hin of oil for each ephah. [6]On the day of the New Moon he is to offer a young bull, six lambs and a ram, all without defect. [7]He is to provide as a grain offering one ephah with the bull, one ephah with the ram, and with the lambs as much as he wants to give, along with a hin of oil with each ephah. [8]When the prince enters, he is to go in through the portico of the gateway, and he is to come out the same way.

*Regulations for the Sabbath (46:1-8).* **46:1-8** The inner east gate of the sanctuary was closed for six days and opened on the Sabbath and New Moon, a special Sabbath celebrating the beginning of a new month (v. 1).[123] Sabbath observance in the millennial temple allowed the fulfillment of the typology of the Mosaic covenant foreshadowing Jesus the Messiah, our Sabbath rest.[124]

The inner east gate is the place from which the prince will carry out his ministry on Sabbath and feast days (v. 2).[125] He will not enter the inner court or take part in the sacrifices because he was not a priest. He remained inside the east gate of the inner court to perform his duties while the people were just outside the gate in the outer court (v. 3). This placed

---

[122] Alexander, "Ezekiel," 985-86; see his discussion of vv. 21-25.

[123] See Cooke, *Ezekiel,* 508, for his discussion of 46:1.

[124] Alexander, "Ezekiel," 986. The Mosaic covenant will find its fruition in the messianic kingdom; see also 37:15-28.

[125] Zimmerli, *Ezekiel 2,* 490. See Zimmerli's discussion of 46:2.

the prince in a mediatorial role between the priests of the inner court and the people of the outer court.

For each Sabbath observance the prince will bring six male lambs, one ram, plus a grain offering and a hin of oil for each ephah of grain (vv. 4-5). On the New Moon he will bring an offering consisting of a young bull, six lambs, a ram, a grain offering, and a hin of oil for each ephah of grain (vv. 6-7). The prince will perform his mediatorial duties entering the east gate by way of the porch (v. 8).[126]

Every aspect of worship is to be a celebration of the redemptive work that God has done in Jesus the Messiah. In the Old Testament believers looked forward to the coming Messiah. In the church age believers serve the resurrected Messiah. In the millennial kingdom Israel will observe the elements of their covenant in celebration of the salvation of Messiah in retrospect of his work (Ezek 45:17–46:8).

[9] " 'When the people of the land come before the LORD at the appointed feasts, whoever enters by the north gate to worship is to go out the south gate; and whoever enters by the south gate is to go out the north gate. No one is to return through the gate by which he entered, but each is to go out the opposite gate. [10]The prince is to be among them, going in when they go in and going out when they go out.

[11]" 'At the festivals and the appointed feasts, the grain offering is to be an ephah with a bull, an ephah with a ram, and with the lambs as much as one pleases, along with a hin of oil for each ephah. [12]When the prince provides a freewill offering to the LORD—whether a burnt offering or fellowship offerings—the gate facing east is to be opened for him. He shall offer his burnt offering or his fellowship offerings as he does on the Sabbath day. Then he shall go out, and after he has gone out, the gate will be shut.

[13]" 'Every day you are to provide a year-old lamb without defect for a burnt offering to the LORD; morning by morning you shall provide it. [14]You are also to provide with it morning by morning a grain offering, consisting of a sixth of an ephah with a third of a hin of oil to moisten the flour. The presenting of this grain offering to the LORD is a lasting ordinance. [15]So the lamb and the grain offering and the oil shall be provided morning by morning for a regular burnt offering.

*General Worship Regulations (46:9-15).*  **46:9-15**  General regulations for worship are described in this passage. First, in order to insure an orderly flow of people on worship days, the north gate is designated as the gate of entry (vv. 9-10). The prince accompanied the worshipers who en-

---

[126] Alexander, "Ezekiel," 986; Taylor, *Ezekiel,* 276.

tered the outer court by the north gate. The south gate is designated as the gate of exit. No one could leave by the gate of entry.[127]

Second, every animal of sacrifice brought by a worshiper was to be accompanied by an offering of one ephah of grain plus a hin of oil (v. 11). Third, any time the prince desired, he can offer a freewill offering. When he presents such an offering, the inner east gate is opened for him, and the regulation of 46:1 temporarily is set aside. (v. 12).[128] Fourth, daily sacrifices are to be offered consisting of a yearling lamb (v. 13). Accompanying the sacrifice is to be a grain offering of one-sixth an ephah of grain and one-third a hin of oil (vv. 14-15). Under the Mosaic system this offering was made each morning and each evening, but in the millennial temple it is offered only in the morning.[129]

All the details of worship are a reminder that God is a God of order, not chaos: "Everything should be done in a fitting and orderly way" (1 Cor 14:40). This is an appropriate prescription for worship at any time (Ezek 46:9-15).

**[16]"'This is what the Sovereign LORD says: If the prince makes a gift from his inheritance to one of his sons, it will also belong to his descendants; it is to be their property by inheritance. [17]If, however, he makes a gift from his inheritance to one of his servants, the servant may keep it until the year of freedom; then it will revert to the prince. His inheritance belongs to his sons only; it is theirs. [18]The prince must not take any of the inheritance of the people, driving them off their property. He is to give his sons their inheritance out of his own property, so that none of my people will be separated from his property.'"**

*Regulations concerning the Prince and His Property (46:16-18).* **46:16-18** The preexilic kings were able to increase the property holdings of the crown by purchasing available property (2 Sam 24:24; 1 Kgs 16:24). The prince will exercise the same right of purchase and will be able to increase his land holdings by purchase of available property (v. 16).[130] Inheritance and property rights were extremely important and carefully guarded by the Israelites. All property was to be returned to its original owner or family in the Year of Jubilee (Lev 25:10). The same regulation will apply in the millennial kingdom to all property given by the

---

[127] Cooke, *Ezekiel,* 509.

[128] Taylor, *Ezekiel,* 277.

[129] Alexander, "Ezekiel," 987; see his discussion of vv. 13-15.

[130] Zimmerli, *Ezekiel 2,* 496; see his discussion of vv. 16-18 and cf. 2 Sam 24:24; 1 Kgs 16:24; 21:1.

prince to a servant (v. 17). Any property given by the prince to one of his sons will be theirs in perpetuity. The prince specifically will be prohibited from taking the property of others and giving it to his sons but was free to give them his own (v. 18).[131] Materialism is always a barrier to effective worship. The regulations concerning property and ownership were designed to discourage covetousness and encourage recognition of God's ownership of all things (46:16-18).

**[19]Then the man brought me through the entrance at the side of the gate to the sacred rooms facing north, which belonged to the priests, and showed me a place at the western end. [20]He said to me, "This is the place where the priests will cook the guilt offering and the sin offering and bake the grain offering, to avoid bringing them into the outer court and consecrating the people."**

**[21]He then brought me to the outer court and led me around to its four corners, and I saw in each corner another court. [22]In the four corners of the outer court were enclosed courts, forty cubits long and thirty cubits wide; each of the courts in the four corners was the same size. [23]Around the inside of each of the four courts was a ledge of stone, with places for fire built all around under the ledge. [24]He said to me, "These are the kitchens where those who minister at the temple will cook the sacrifices of the people."**

*Regulations for Cooking in the Temple (46:19-24).* **46:19-24** Ezekiel was brought to the entrance of the priest's building in the inner court that was described in 42:1-14. In these rooms the priests will cook the animal offerings and bake the grain offerings to avoid defilement by contact with the people (v. 19; cf. 44:19).[132] In the four corners of the outer court were kitchens used to prepare sacrifices for the people (vv. 21-24). The temple will be a healthy fusion of spiritual worship and social interaction.[133] God provided for fellowship between himself and human beings. He also provided for interaction between humans and incorporated it as a vital part of worship.[134]

Proper worship includes good social interaction and interpersonal relationships as well as person-to-God relationships. The temple service in the millennium will allow one to eat of the good things of God and share

---

[131] Taylor, *Ezekiel,* 277; this was done to safeguard the prince's inheritance.

[132] Ibid., 277-78; Enns, *Ezekiel,* 194; Davidson, *Ezekiel,* 346-47; Cooke, *Ezekiel,* 513. The "consecration" of the people refers to setting them apart as holy unto the Lord.

[133] Taylor, *Ezekiel,* 278. This view of the temple prefigures the ideal spiritual-social interaction that also would characterize the church.

[134] Craigie, *Ezekiel,* 310; see his discussion of the "visionary" character of vv. 19-24 and its meaning for an interactive community of worshipers.

in a time of fellowship as well as worship (46:19-24).

### (4) Vision of the River Flowing from the Throne (47:1-12)

Before undertaking a discussion of this passage and its concomitant allusions to geographical changes in Jerusalem and its environs, some attention must be devoted to the geographical and topographical features of the city. Jerusalem is located thirty-four miles inland east of the Mediterranean coast nestled in an outcropping known as the Ophel-Moriah ridge. The elevation of this ridge averages 2,500 feet above sea level, varying from 2,080 feet on the southeast to 2,528 feet at Jaffa Gate. The city is located twenty-four miles west of the northern end of the Dead Sea, which is the lowest depression on the earth, 1,292 feet below sea level.

Valleys surround Jerusalem on three sides. The Hinnom Valley forms the western and southern boundaries of the city, and the Kidron forms the eastern boundary. One additional valley bisects the ridge from south to north on the eastern side of the mountain and just west of the temple mount. It was called the Tyropoeon Valley or Valley of the Cheesemakers. Across the Kidron Valley the eastern ridge of the Mount of Olives also connects with Mount Scopus and forms the closure of the Kidron Valley on the north by connecting with the Ophel-Moriah ridge. On the eastern side of Mount Scopus and the Mount of Olives, the elevation drops rapidly into the Jordan rift and down to the Dead Sea. All the mountains that surround the Ophel-Moriah ridge are higher in elevation than the ridge itself, including Mount Scopus (NE), the Mount of Olives (E), the Mount of Offense (SE), Hill of Evil Council (S), and the Western Hill (W).[135]

The city has no rivers or perennial streams, but it does have eight to ten springs and a system of cisterns, reservoirs, conduits, and aqueducts.

---

[135] Jerusalem boasts thirty centuries of recorded history. During those thirty centuries the catalog of its distresses is awesome. Twenty times the city was under siege, twenty times under tactical blockade, eighteen times destroyed and reconstructed, not to mention the perils of the twentieth century. The present old city wall is a remnant of the wall constructed by the Crusaders in the twelfth century A.D. This wall was partly destroyed and rebuilt by the Ottoman Turks in the fifteenth century A.D. The wall today with its eight gates and city perimeter was built under the supervision of Süleyman the Magnificent in A.D. 1527 when he rebuilt the city after his conquest over the Crusaders.

Nehemiah mentioned twelve gates in his survey of the city in preparation for reconstruction in the fifth century B.C. (Neh 3:1-32), but at least one gate he identified was an inner city gate. This means that the older city had at least eleven outer gates of entry to locations that are unknown today. The old city today is divided into four quarters along religious lines. These quarters are the Christian quarter (NW), the Armenian quarter (NE), the Muslim quarter (SE), and the Jewish quarter (SW).

Thus there has always been an ample supply of water so necessary for the stability and growth of cities in the Near East. Jerusalem also sits just east of the watershed that divides the Jordan rift and the Mediterranean Sea.

The old city of Jerusalem was located on a portion of the Ophel-Moriah ridge that has several subdivisions. The southeast spur was known as the hill Ophel and also as the City of David. Mount Moriah is the east-central promontory that became known as the Temple Mount. Bezetha Hill is the northwest corner of Mount Moriah and has been associated with Calvary or Golgotha. West of Ophel and Mount Moriah across the Tyropoeon Valley is the Western Hill that is also called Mount Zion. The highest elevation of the whole area is the upper western ridge that lies in the area of Jaffa Gate and to the immediate north of the gate. The northern plateau lies from the Wadi Joz on the northeast to the Hinnom Valley on the northwest.[136]

Some interpreters consider chaps. 47–48 to be wholly symbolic.[137] If this line of interpretation is adopted, the details of Ezekiel's descriptions take on a different significance, and the geographical features of the area are irrelevant. Those who follow this method consider the ideas behind the symbols to be the only aspects of the message that are of real value. Alexander takes the literal approach to the passage. This approach ignores the apocalyptic character of the passage and is concerned more with factual details while ignoring their deeper significance.[138]

The view taken here is that Ezekiel 47:1–48:35 is neither wholly symbolic nor wholly literal. The best approach, considering the apocalyptic character of the text, is to regard the chapters as both a literal description with accurate details but also as highly symbolic with deeper truths. This approach is adopted by Davidson and will be the one followed in the discussion of 47:1-12.[139]

Ezekiel 47:1-12 may be divided into four sections, each of which describes some aspect of the river that flowed from the temple: (1) the source of the

---

[136] See further in E. Orni and E. Efrat, *Geography of Israel* (Jerusalem: Israel Universities, 1976), 321-31; G. A. Smith, *Jerusalem*, vol. 1 (London: Hodder and Stoughton, 1907), 31-49; W. H. Mare, *The Archaeology of the Jerusalem Area* (Grand Rapids: Baker, 1987), 20-23; I. W. J. Hopkins, *Jerusalem: A Study in Urban Geography* (Grand Rapids: Baker, 1970), 28-44; M. Burrows, "Nehemiah 3:1-32 as a Source of the Topography of Ancient Jerusalem," *AASOR* 14 (1933-34): 120-21; J. R. Baskin, "Jerusalem," *HBD*, 765-73.

[137] J. B. Taylor (*Ezekiel*, TOTC [Downers Grove: InterVarsity, 1969], 278) dismisses the possibility of literal fulfillment of this passage.

[138] R. H. Alexander ("Ezekiel," EBC 6 [Grand Rapids: Zondervan, 1986], 990) notes that this river was expressly provided for the physical restoration of the land of Israel.

[139] A. B. Davidson, *The Book of the Prophet Ezekiel* (Cambridge: Cambridge University Press, 1892), 349-50.

river (vv. 1-2), (2) the size of the river (vv. 3-5), (3) the sufficiency of the river (vv. 6-8), and (4) the saving power of the river (vv. 9-12).

**¹The man brought me back to the entrance of the temple, and I saw water coming out from under the threshold of the temple toward the east (for the temple faced east). The water was coming down from under the south side of the temple, south of the altar. ²He then brought me out through the north gate and led me around the outside to the outer gate facing east, and the water was flowing from the south side.**

THE SOURCE OF THE RIVER (47:1-2). **47:1-2** The "man" who appears here is the angel-guide who had taken Ezekiel through his vision of the new temple in 40:3. He regularly appears in 40:1–46:24 to guide the prophet in his tour of the millennial temple. The "man" brought the prophet back to the entrance of the temple area, where he saw water coming from the threshold of the sanctuary. The "threshold" may refer to some architectural feature visible to Ezekiel from a vantage point outside the sanctuary.[140] If this threshold is like the one in 46:2, it probably was elevated. Perhaps the water flowed under it, or it may have had an outlet built in the threshold itself. The water that flowed from the threshold proceeded from the sanctuary on the east side and then flowed southeasterly past the altar on the south side, then to the south side of the eastern gate (v. 2).[141] From that point it became a stream that flowed into the Kidron Valley at first turning south, then continuing past the Hinnom Valley, and then taking a turn southeast.

This description of the flow of the water follows the contours of the present geographical and topographical features of the city of Jerusalem and its environs today. Ezekiel 47 hints at some possible major changes in the geography of the area. If changes do occur, then the flow of the water would follow the topography of the altered terrain on the eastern side of the old city.

Some physical transformation of the area just outside the eastern gate of the temple mount, the Kidron Valley, and the Mount of Olives was suggested in Ezekiel's previous messages 34:26-30; 36:8-12,30-36; 37:25-28. In addition to these hints, other prophets refer to a physical alteration of this area associated with the last days of history and the final judgment (see Joel 3:18; Zech 13:1; 14:4-8). A great cleavage in the Mount of Olives such as the one described in Zech 14:4 would allow the water to flow

---

[140] See W. Zimmerli, *Ezekiel 2,* Her (Philadelphia: Fortress, 1983), 511. He suggests that מִפְתַּן הַבַּיִת may refer to an architectural or structural feature of the temple complex.

[141] See S. Fisch (*Ezekiel* [London: Soncino, 1950], 323).

east from the temple area before turning southeast toward the Dead Sea. Although Ezekiel did not specifically mention such changes, his vision does not contradict anything revealed by these other prophets.

Zimmerli's discussion of the topography reveals that there are only two plausible options to understanding this passage. First, some would claim that the flow of the water from the temple mount follows the natural contours of the land. In this case the water would flow into the Kidron Valley, then southeastward to the point of intersection with the Hinnom Valley. It would then flow through the wadi En-nar, which finally turns eastward. This would be the route taken by one traveling from Jerusalem to Jericho. Second, based on the idea of dramatic geographical changes that will result in a cleavage in the Mount of Olives described in Zech 14:4, the water would flow unobstructed toward the Dead Sea.[142]

Zimmerli leaves the question open concerning whether the water flows by a more direct route and therefore through the cleavage suggested by Zech 14:4-8 or whether it follows the present natural contours of the land. While he takes no position, he implies in his discussions that the idea of a direct flow through a "miraculous cleavage" in the Mount of Olives probably was what Ezekiel described. His discussion does affirm that these are the only two plausible explanations based on what we know from Ezekiel.

The existence of available water sources in this area has been a matter of record since earliest times. David entered the city when he conquered it by coming up the "water shaft" (2 Sam 5:8), and Solomon was anointed king at the spring Gihon (1 Kgs 1:38), which Hezekiah connected by tunnel to the pool of Siloam (2 Kgs 20:20). Mention of a spring on the temple mount inside the enclosure of the temple area has been found in the Letter of Aristeas dated ca. 100 B.C. Other springs and reservoirs in the area as well may have been covered by earthquakes or destruction.[143] The idea of water flowing from the temple mount is therefore not unreasonable.

That the source of this river had its origin at the threshold of the sanctuary is a most significant fact. Symbolically it presents a beautiful picture of God as the Source of life for a world that thirsts for spiritual truth, including forgiveness and salvation (John 4:14; 7:37-38). The correspondence of language, symbols, and figures between Ezek 47:1-12 and Rev 22:1ff. is more than coincidental. The answer to this phenomenon is not to be found in borrowing but is evidence that there are two independent wit-

---

[142] See Zimmerli, *Ezekiel 2*, 513.

[143] G. A. Cooke, *The Book of Ezekiel*, ICC (Edinburgh: T & T Clark, 1986), 517-18; see also L. Ritmeyer, "Locating the Original Temple Mount," *BAR* 18 (1992): 34-36, where he shows the location of the reservoirs on the temple mount.

nesses each with its vision describing the same area. Ezekiel's vision has been a common source of rituals associated with Sukkoth among Jews and with water baptism among Christians.[144] The root meaning of these symbolic applications is expressed in the truth Ezekiel saw that God is the source of life-giving and healing waters, which flowed from his sanctuary (vv. 1-2).

God alone is the Source of life and provides the Word of life that is the life-giving water that quenches the thirst of the human heart for life, forgiveness, and salvation (47:1-2; John 4:14; Eph 5:26; Rev 7:17; 21:6; 22:1,17).

**³As the man went eastward with a measuring line in his hand, he measured off a thousand cubits and then led me through water that was ankle-deep. ⁴He measured off another thousand cubits and led me through water that was knee-deep. He measured off another thousand and led me through water that was up to the waist. ⁵He measured off another thousand, but now it was a river that I could not cross, because the water had risen and was deep enough to swim in—a river that no one could cross.**

THE DEPTH AND WIDTH OF THE RIVER (47:3-5). **47:3-5** The size of the river is described in a manner totally different from the process of measurement used on the temple complex in chaps. 40–42. Four identical thousand-cubit distances were measured by the angel-guide to suggest the increasing depth of the water.[145] At each thousand-cubit interval, he led Ezekiel into the water with him. The prophet reported the depth in increasing increments of "ankle deep" (v. 3), "knee deep" (v. 4), "waist deep" (v. 4), and "deep enough to swim in" (v. 5). Apparently there is no particular symbolic significance in this method of measuring the river. Ezekiel's comments do provide the reader with a personal frame of reference to judge the water depth and rapid rise of the river's flow.

When the prophet first saw the water, it was coming (lit. "trickling," v. 2) out of the threshold of the sanctuary. This trickle from the sanctuary soon became a flowing stream when it reached the south side of the eastern gate. The word in v. 2, *mĕpakkîm* ("flow"), was commonly used to describe liquid flowing from a bottle. It is a participle that suggests continuous flow.[146] By the time the fourth measurement of depth was tak-

---

[144] See Cooke, *Ezekiel*, 517.

[145] Zimmerli, *Ezekiel 2,* 512; see also table of measure for cubits in discussion of 40:5-16.

[146] Ibid., 511-12; both words מְפַכִּים, "flow," and יֹצְאִים, "coming out" (used in v. 1), are participles used to describe the continuous movement of the water.

en (v. 5), the flow had become a flood.

The river is like the blood of the Messiah from the cross of Calvary that began as a trickle (John 19:34). Finally, the blood, like the river, became a flood of redemption for all people (Rev 1:5). So the flow from Calvary became a fountain of redemption for all people including Israel (see Zech 13:1-6; Rev 1:5-6). Just so, the water of life that the prophet saw coming from the threshold came forth gently, then began to flow, and finally became a mighty river of life healing all in its wake. When God's Word is received, he transforms death into life and produces life in abundance springing up as life-giving water within every person. This abundant sustenance was made available to all people through Jesus Christ (John 4; 10:10).

**⁶He asked me, "Son of man, do you see this?"**

**Then he led me back to the bank of the river. ⁷When I arrived there, I saw a great number of trees on each side of the river. ⁸He said to me, "This water flows toward the eastern region and goes down into the Arabah, where it enters the Sea. When it empties into the Sea, the water there becomes fresh.**

**⁹Swarms of living creatures will live wherever the river flows. There will be large numbers of fish, because this water flows there and makes the salt water fresh; so where the river flows everything will live. ¹⁰Fishermen will stand along the shore; from En Gedi to En Eglaim there will be places for spreading nets. The fish will be of many kinds—like the fish of the Great Sea. ¹¹But the swamps and marshes will not become fresh; they will be left for salt.**

**¹²Fruit trees of all kinds will grow on both banks of the river. Their leaves will not wither, nor will their fruit fail. Every month they will bear, because the water from the sanctuary flows to them. Their fruit will serve for food and their leaves for healing."**

THE POWER OF THE RIVER (47:6-12). *The Restoring Power of the River (47:6-8,12).* **47:6-8,12** The sufficiency of this life-giving water from the throne of God is portrayed in language reminiscent of the garden of Eden and is similar to that of Rev 22:1-4. It also is another expression of the idea presented in 36:35 regarding the restoration of Eden (see "Restoration of Edenic Ideals," p. 349). As Ezekiel walked with the angel-guide along the banks of the river, the guide asked, "Do you see this?" (v. 6). Ezekiel saw numerous evergreens on both banks (v. 7) that bore fruit every month (v. 12). The fruit of the trees was good for food, and the leaves of the trees had healing properties. Thus both the elements of the tree of life concept from Gen 3:22 and the restoration of the tree of life with healing and salvation of John's vision in Revelation are found in

Ezekiel's vision of the healing waters of the river.[147]

The life-giving power of the water is presented in this vision of fruitfulness, food, and healing. The water of the river ultimately produced the fruitfulness of the trees because it brought life from the sanctuary of God (v. 12). The water continued its flow down to the Arabah (v. 8), a name that once applied to the whole lower Jordan River valley including the Dead Sea and south to the Gulf of Aqaba/Eilat. Today the name "Arabah" refers to the flat plain that continues south from the Dead Sea between the mountains of Transjordan on the east and the mountains of Judea on the west connecting the Dead Sea region with the Gulf of Aqaba/Eilat.[148] So the water will enter the Dead Sea, probably at the northern end near where the Jordan River empties into it today.

The "sea" of v. 8 is the Dead Sea that contains twenty-four to twenty-six percent minerals compared with normal sea water, which contains four to six percent.[149] Because of this extremely high mineral content, there are no fish or other aquatic life in the water, hence its name, the Dead Sea. The sufficiency of the water from the throne is portrayed in the miraculous transformation of everything that it touched. Ezekiel said the toxic water of the Dead Sea became "fresh" (v. 8). The sufficiency of the water of life from the throne of God is evidenced by the fact that no additional elements were needed to produce life, fruit, transformation, or healing. With the life-giving water from God the barren becomes fruitful, the dry becomes nourished, the empty becomes filled, the bitter becomes sweet, the unhealthy is healed, and the dead is made alive (vv. 6-8; Luke 7:21-22).

*The Healing and Saving Power of the River (47:9-11).*   **47:9-11**   The healing and saving power of this water is demonstrated by the revitalization of the Dead Sea. The water from the sanctuary descended from the temple area 2,430 feet above sea level to the surface of the Dead Sea 1,292 feet below sea level, a drop of over 3,700 feet. The combination of the living water from the sanctuary with the toxic water of the Dead Sea will heal the deadly properties of the poisonous water, and it will be filled with life (v. 9). The Dead Sea will become the "living sea," teaming with aquatic life and fish (vv. 9-10).

On the banks of the Dead Sea, fishermen seen in Ezekiel's vision will stretch their nets from En-Gedi to En-Eglaim. En-Gedi is located at the

---

[147] See Cooke, *Ezekiel,* 521-22.

[148] Ibid., 520; Fisch, *Ezekiel,* 325; J. W. Wevers, *Ezekiel,* NCB (Grand Rapids: Eerdmans, 1969), 335.

[149] See Cooke, *Ezekiel,* 520; Zimmerli, *Ezekiel 2,* 510.

midpoint of the west bank of the Dead Sea near Masada. En-Eglaim has been identified with Ein-Feska at the northwestern end of the Dead Sea near Qumran.[150] The fish the prophet saw in his vision were numerous in species as well as quantity, comparable to that of the Great Sea or Mediterranean (v. 10). The marshes and swampy areas around the Dead Sea will remain saline perhaps to provide a source of salt for domestic use (v. 11).

Everything in Ezekiel's description presents a picture of the life-giving, healing, and life-sustaining properties of the water from the sanctuary. Whatever the water touches from the parched earth in the Judean wilderness to the toxic mineral water of the Dead Sea is given life (v. 9). On its journey from Jerusalem the river nourishes the grove of trees that produces fruit every month (v. 12). The leaves of these trees will not wither but will be a valuable commodity providing healing herbal medicines. The water of life flows into what is today a dry desolate area, which the prophet in this vision saw restored to a fruitful habitat. He saw the final restoration of all things that in his earlier vision he had called the restoration of the garden of Eden (36:25)[151] Thus in both a literal and symbolic way he presented the salvific efficacy of the life that flows from the throne of God to transform everything and everyone who will receive it.

It is not surprising that these same figures appear in the vision of the apostle John in Rev 22. There he described the new Jerusalem in much the same words as Ezekiel used in 47:1-12. There, too, the water of life flows from the throne of God, and the fruitfulness of the trees provides sustenance and healing. In John 4:1-26 Jesus told the woman at the well that the healing waters of God could be an internal "spring of water welling up to eternal life" (John 4:14). Likewise, in John 7:37-38 streams of living water are presented as flowing from the body of believers, suggesting the life-giving flow that comes into a person's life through faith in God and Jesus Christ.

The early church spiritualized the visions of both Ezekiel and John. In these interpretations the river represented the increase in the number of believers; the fourfold measurement of the water represented the four Gospels with the deepest measurement depicting the Gospel of John, which was the "deepest"; and the river was a symbolic foregleam of baptism.[152] This symbolic approach to interpretation focused solely on spiri-

---

[150] Fisch, *Ezekiel,* 326; Taylor, *Ezekiel,* 280; Wevers, *Ezekiel,* 336; Zimmerli, *Ezekiel,* 513. Alexander ("Ezekiel," 991) says that the location of En-Eglaim is uncertain and may be located on the east bank of the Dead Sea, in which case fishermen would fish from both sides of the sea.

[151] See "Restoration of the Edenic Ideals," p. 349.

[152] See Zimmerli, *Ezekiel 2,* 515-16.

tual aspects of the vision of Ezekiel while ignoring any possible literal or physical truths. This illustration serves as a reminder of the consequences of taking an unbalanced approach to this passage. The passage is both symbolic and literal, and any interpretation should necessarily reflect both elements.

The vision of 47:1-12 is one of the most compelling expressions of hope for life in the Old Testament. The river Ezekiel saw was a real river with water that had life-giving and healing properties. But this real river also represents the spiritual life and healing that flows to the human family from the throne of God.

This picture of a healing stream, issuing from the temple, fertilizing the desert, and changing the bitter waters of the Dead Sea into sweet rests on some natural and some spiritual conceptions common in Ezekiel's time. There was a fountain connected with the temple-hill, the waters of which fell into the valley east of the city and made their way toward the sea. Such waters in the east are the source of every blessing. Yahweh himself is the giver of all such blessings that flow from his presence.

When the tabernacle of God is with his people, external nature also will be transfigured. Every good is to be enjoyed, and there will be no more curse. The desert will blossom like the rose. The barren land toward the east and the bitter waters of the sea were a contradiction to the ideal of an external nature subservient in all its parts to those in the fellowship of God. Therefore the desert will be fertilized and the waters of the sea healed.

It would be an error to regard this fertilizing, healing stream as a mere symbol of heaven. This would overstep the limits of the Old Testament since the Hebrews had no conception of a transcendent sphere of existence such as heaven. The final abode for humanity was considered to be still on earth. God came down and dwelt with humans; they were not translated to abide with God. However, God's presence with humans on earth did give to earth the attributes of heaven. In these blessings the Hebrews saw in the token and the sacraments God's favor and presence with them (cf. Ps 34: 9).[153]

The salvific power of the river of life is shown in the life it generated in everything it touched. God is the source of the river, but a world of lost people is its end (Ezek 47:9-12). Abundant blessings for the human family are a basis for praise and thanksgiving to the gracious Father who is their source. Praise God from whom all blessings flow! (Pss 146–150).

---

[153] See Davidson, *Ezekiel*, 349-50.

### (5) Vision of the New Boundaries (47:13–48:35)

The new kingdom envisioned by Ezekiel included a new temple, a new way of life, a new quality of life, and in this final vision a new land. This land is new not only in quality but also in the arrangement of the tribal units that occupy it. Seven tribes are located north of the temple area and city of Jerusalem. Five tribes are located south of the sacred district described in 45:1-8. The central sacred district contains carefully defined areas for the sanctuary, the city, the prince, the Zadokite priests, and the Levites. The sacred district is located in the geographical center of the land.

This final section of the book may be divided into seven parts: (1) the boundaries of the land (47:13-20); (2) the equitable allocations of the land (47:21-23); (3) the allotments of the seven northern tribes (48:1-7); (4) the allotments for the sanctuary, Zadokite priests, and Levites (48:8-20); (5) the allotment for the prince (48:21-23); (6) the allotments for the five southern tribes (48:23-29); and (7) a description of the Eternal city, "The Lord is There" (48:30-35; and see the map "Millennial Tribal Allotments," p. 428).

[13]**This is what the Sovereign LORD says: "These are the boundaries by which you are to divide the land for an inheritance among the twelve tribes of Israel, with two portions for Joseph.** [14]**You are to divide it equally among them. Because I swore with uplifted hand to give it to your forefathers, this land will become your inheritance.**

[15]**"This is to be the boundary of the land:**

**"On the north side it will run from the Great Sea by the Hethlon road past Lebo Hamath to Zedad,** [16]**Berothah and Sibraim (which lies on the border between Damascus and Hamath), as far as Hazer Hatticon, which is on the border of Hauran.** [17]**The boundary will extend from the sea to Hazar Enan, along the northern border of Damascus, with the border of Hamath to the north. This will be the north boundary.**

[18]**"On the east side the boundary will run between Hauran and Damascus, along the Jordan between Gilead and the land of Israel, to the eastern sea and as far as Tamar. This will be the east boundary.**

[19]**"On the south side it will run from Tamar as far as the waters of Meribah Kadesh, then along the Wadi [of Egypt] to the Great Sea. This will be the south boundary.**

[20]**"On the west side, the Great Sea will be the boundary to a point opposite Lebo Hamath. This will be the west boundary.**

THE BOUNDARIES OF THE LAND (47:13-20). **47:13-20** Beginning with an introductory statement in vv. 13-14, this passage describes the details of the new tribal allotments for the seven tribes located to the north of the sacred district. Four elements in these descriptions stand out. (1) God will make the allotments personally (v. 13) in contrast to the allotments of the conquest Joshua made and determined by casting sacred lots (Josh 14:1-5). (2) All allotments will be based on original tribal names, thus restoring tribal identity lost after the exile (v. 13).[154] (3) The allotments will be made in partial fulfillment of the promise of God to Abraham (Gen 12:1-3; 15:7-21; 17:1-14) and the promise of a double portion to Joseph (v. 14; Gen 48:5-6,22). (4) The tribal allotments will be of equal size (v. 14).[155]

The boundary descriptions are similar to those of Num 34:3-12 and will be determined by mention of border cities on the north (vv. 15-17), east (v. 18), south (v. 19), and west (v. 20). Exact identification of every place name cannot be given with certainty.[156] Several possible approaches for interpreting the parameters of the northern boundaries have been suggested by Zimmerli. First, Ezekiel's description could be an attempt to reconstruct an exact parallel to the elements of Num 34. Second, this passage could be an attempt to redefine the royal boundaries of the Davidic kingdom. Third, the passage may be an attempt to incorporate five conceptions of the boundaries of the "Land of Israel" that existed at various historical periods with its largest limits being from the Brook of Egypt to the Euphrates River. These five conceptions were: (1) Canaan of the Patriarchs, (2) the land of Moses' time, (3) the land of Joshua's time, (4) the land of Israel's settlement, and (5) the land of the kingdom of Israel. The first four of these boundary definitions were ethnographic while the last was imperialistic.[157]

In Ezekiel's description the northern border will extend east from the Mediterranean Sea to Hethlon, Zedad, Lebo-Hamath, Berothah, Sibraim near Damascus to Hazer-Hatticon on the border of Hauran.[158] These cities form a line east from the Mediterranean Sea toward Damascus ending at Hazar-enan, which has been identified as Baniyas (vv. 16-17).[159]

From that point the eastern boundary will extend southward to Hauran

---

[154] Zimmerli, *Ezekiel 2*, 527.

[155] Alexander, "Ezekiel," 991. אִישׁ כְּאָחִיו is literally "each one like his brother," meaning that the tribes will get an equal portion.

[156] Taylor, *Ezekiel*, 281; Zimmerli, *Ezekiel 2*, 528-29.

[157] See Zimmerli, *Ezekiel 2*, 529-30.

[158] Alexander, "Ezekiel," 980.

[159] See Taylor, *Ezekiel*, 281.

as far as Tamar near the southern end of the Dead Sea, narrowing at the southern end (v. 18). There the boundary will be traced from Tamar west to Meribah Kadesh continuing to the Wadi of Egypt, identified as the Wadi El-Arish (v. 19)[160] and ending at the Mediterranean Sea. The western boundary will be the sea from the Wadi of Egypt north to Lebo-Hamath (v. 20).

[21]"You are to distribute this land among yourselves according to the tribes of Israel. [22]You are to allot it as an inheritance for yourselves and for the aliens who have settled among you and who have children. You are to consider them as native-born Israelites; along with you they are to be allotted an inheritance among the tribes of Israel. [23]In whatever tribe the alien settles, there you are to give him his inheritance," declares the Sovereign LORD.

THE EQUITABLE ALLOCATION OF THE LAND (47:21-23). **47:21-23** The land will be distributed with equity. Each tribe will receive the same size portion of property in contrast to the allotments of various sizes in Josh 14:1-5. Provisions even will be made for aliens who settle in the land and who have children. They will be considered the same as native Israelites in the distribution of the land. These provisions are similar to those of Lev 19:34; 24:22; and Num 15:29 (vv. 22-23).[161] The resident aliens were those who had adopted the religion and law of the Hebrews. They were proselytes who were entitled to the same rights and privileges of native born Israelites (see Isa 56:3-8). Thus the new boundaries suggest that the new kingdom will preserve the laws of equity that eliminated discrimination against those residents who were proselytes or Jews by choice, making the new land a model for justice and righteousness.[162]

[1]"These are the tribes, listed by name: At the northern frontier, Dan will have one portion; it will follow the Hethlon road to Lebo Hamath; Hazar Enan and the northern border of Damascus next to Hamath will be part of its border from the east side to the west side.
[2]"Asher will have one portion; it will border the territory of Dan from east to west.
[3]"Naphtali will have one portion; it will border the territory of Asher from east to west.
[4]"Manasseh will have one portion; it will border the territory of Naphtali from east to west.

---

[160] See Wevers, *Ezekiel,* 338; Fisch, *Ezekiel,* 328.
[161] See Alexander, "Ezekiel," 992; Wevers, *Ezekiel,* 338.
[162] Taylor, *Ezekiel,* 282; Zimmerli, *Ezekiel 2,* 532.

⁵"Ephraim will have one portion; it will border the territory of Manasseh from east to west.
⁶"Reuben will have one portion; it will border the territory of Ephraim from east to west.
⁷"Judah will have one portion; it will border the territory of Reuben from east to west.

THE ALLOTMENTS OF THE SEVEN NORTHERN TRIBES (48:1-7). **48:1-7** The order for the allotments to the seven tribes located north of the sacred district does not follow any pattern found elsewhere in the Old Testament.[163] While the allotments will be of equal size, exact dimensions are not given (cf. 47:14). The seven tribes situated to the north were Dan, Asher, Naphtali, Manasseh, Ephraim, Reuben, and Judah. Dan, who at one point had been involved heavily in idolatry, will be located farther from the sanctuary (see Judg 18:31; 1 Kgs 12:29-30). Both Dan and Naphtali were sons of Jacob by Bilhah, a concubine and maid of Rachel. Asher, born to Jacob by Zilpah, also a concubine and maid of Leah, would occupy the allotment between Dan and Naphtali. These three northernmost tribes were descendants of concubines, which may account for their location farthest from the sanctuary (vv. 1-3). By contrast Judah, the tribe from whom the Messiah descended (Gen 49:8-12), will occupy the area bordering the sacred district and sanctuary (v. 8).[164]

The two tribes to be located below Naphtali are Ephraim and Manasseh, the sons of Joseph (vv. 4-5). There was never a tribe of Joseph, but instead he received a double portion for his role as deliverer of his family when he was a ruler in Egypt (Gen 4:5,22). Jacob blessed the two sons of Joseph by receiving them as his adopted sons, thus giving them equal status with his other sons (Gen 48:5). Then Jacob elevated the second-born son Ephraim over the firstborn Manasseh by blessing him with his right hand on his head and predicting the ascendancy of his descendants over that of his elder brother (Gen 48:8-22).

Reuben will receive the allotment of land below Ephraim (Ezek 48:6). He was the firstborn of Jacob, but like Manasseh he was supplanted by his younger brother Judah. Judah, the family from which the Messiah came (Gen 49:3-4,10-12), will receive the portion of land to the south of Reuben that bordered the sacred district (Ezek 48:7-8).

Each tribe will be given an equal portion of land based on the parameters of the border set forth in 47:13-23 with each tribal boundary parallel to the one to its north and/or south. No mention of specific measurements

---

[163] See Alexander, "Ezekiel," 993.
[164] Taylor, *Ezekiel,* 282-83.

of the width of these allotments from north to south are given, but the rabbis consider the width to be twenty-five thousand cubits.[165] No purpose is specified for the tribes in granting these allotments, but it is most likely based on two elements. First, the element of racial purity seems to be suggested. The tribes who are descended from concubines will be placed at the outer limits of the northern allotments, Dan, Asher, and Naphtali and in the southern allotments with Gad, who was a child of Jacob by Zilpah.[166] Second, those tribes with close ties to the line of Messiah, Judah and Benjamin, will be closest to the sanctuary and bordered on the sacred central district.

The return to the tribal league arrangement for the nation is significant. The reestablishment of these tribal identities suggests the importance of the family unit to God. These tribal units in the Old Testament were family groups united under a common family leader for purposes of worship, protection, education, and general well-being. It is the kind of family-community that has unfortunately been in decline in the last half of the twentieth century. Ezekiel saw a return to that kind of caring, loving family-community as part of the plan of God for his people in the end times and for his eternal kingdom as well. The reestablishment of tribal identities signals an eschatological emphasis on the restoration of tribal family units and inclusion in these family units not native-born Hebrews (48:1-7).

**8"Bordering the territory of Judah from east to west will be the portion you are to present as a special gift. It will be 25,000 cubits wide, and its length from east to west will equal one of the tribal portions; the sanctuary will be in the center of it.**

**9"The special portion you are to offer to the LORD will be 25,000 cubits long and 10,000 cubits wide. 10This will be the sacred portion for the priests. It will be 25,000 cubits long on the north side, 10,000 cubits wide on the west side, 10,000 cubits wide on the east side and 25,000 cubits long on the south side. In the center of it will be the sanctuary of the LORD. 11This will be for the consecrated priests, the Zadokites, who were faithful in serving me and did not go astray as the Levites did when the Israelites went astray. 17It will be a special gift to them from the sacred portion of the land, a most holy portion, bordering the territory of the Levites.**

**13"Alongside the territory of the priests, the Levites will have an allotment**

---

[165] Fisch (*Ezekiel,* 330) suggests that the rabbis used rods, but cubits is the most likely meaning. This was twenty-five thousand cubits measured by a six-cubit measuring rod; see discussion of 45:15-20.

[166] See Wevers, *Ezekiel,* 338-39.

25,000 cubits long and 10,000 cubits wide. Its total length will be 25,000 cubits and its width 10,000 cubits. [14]They must not sell or exchange any of it.
This is the best of the land and must not pass into other hands, because it is
holy to the LORD.
[15]"The remaining area, 5,000 cubits wide and 25,000 cubits long, will be
for the common use of the city, for houses and for pastureland. The city will
be in the center of it [16]and will have these measurements: the north side 4,500
cubits, the south side 4,500 cubits, the east side 4,500 cubits, and the west side
4,500 cubits. [17]The pastureland for the city will be 250 cubits on the north,
250 cubits on the south, 250 cubits on the east, and 250 cubits on the west.
[18]What remains of the area, bordering on the sacred portion and running the
length of it, will be 10,000 cubits on the east side and 10,000 cubits on the
west side. Its produce will supply food for the workers of the city. [19]The
workers from the city who farm it will come from all the tribes of Israel.
[20]The entire portion will be a square, 25,000 cubits on each side. As a special
gift you will set aside the sacred portion, along with the property of the city.

THE ALLOTMENTS FOR THE SANCTUARY, ZADOKITE PRIESTS, AND LEV-
ITES (48:8-20).   **48:8-20**   The sacred district at the geographical center
of the land will be reserved for the prince, the Zadokite priests, the Levites, and their families. This area is described in 45:1-8, which parallels
this passage. The sacred allotment has four divisions: (1) the allotment for
the caring priests including the sanctuary (vv. 9-12), (2) the allotment for
the Levites (vv. 13-14), (3) the allotment for the city (vv. 15-20), and (4)
the allotment for the prince (vv. 21-22).[167]

The sacred allotment will be twenty-five thousand cubits wide from
north to south, and it parallels the tribal allotments in size from east to
west following the parameters of the border established in 47:13-23 (v. 8).
A special twenty-five-thousand- by ten-thousand-cubit section in the center of the sacred district will have three subdivisions. This central section
is called "the special portion you are to offer to the LORD" (v. 9). It will be
set aside for the Zadokite priests who will minister in the sanctuary to be
located in the center of this section (vv. 10-11). This special position of
honor is a reward to the Zadokite priests for their faithfulness to the Lord
(see 44:15-31). They will be charged with the administration of this land
and the sanctuary (v. 12).[168]

Just north of the sacred district will be a portion of land the same size

---

[167] Alexander, "Ezekiel," 994.

[168] The word תְּרוּמָה (portion" v. 8) used in vv. 8,9,10,12,18,20. The word literally
means "contribution or offering" and is from the root רום ("be high"). Ezekiel used it to
designate an area of land that was considered the personal possession of Yahweh. He appointed the Zadokite priests to oversee this district; see Zimmerli, *Ezekiel 2,* 532-35.

as the allotment for the Zadokites. This allotment will be given to the
Levites (v. 13) in perpetuity. They will neither sell nor barter it (v. 14).

The central sacred district will be called "holy to the Lord" (48:14) and
will demonstrate the central place of worship in the new kingdom. Located at the geographical center of the land, all life will revolve around this
area for worship of God, whose dwelling will be in the midst of his people. No clearer picture may be found in Scripture of the central role worship should have in all human life (48:8-14).

To the south of the central division of the Zadokites will be a section
25,000 by 5,000 thousand cubits, which will be the allotment for the city
(v. 15). The city proper will occupy a section 4,500 by 4,500 cubits square
with a 250-cubit perimeter of pastureland on every side (v. 17). The remainder of this section will be agricultural and will be used to cultivate
food for the city. The entire sacred district will be 25,000 by 25,000 cubits
(v. 8) and will be sacred to Yahweh.

Ezekiel saw the new city of God, new Jerusalem (Rev 21:2,10-22).
This city will ever be the abode of the presence of God in the midst of his
people. Whereas cities have always been known as places of moral corruption and rebellion, this city will be a place of eternal rest, refuge, and
personal fellowship with others and God (48:8-20,30-35).

²¹"**What remains on both sides of the area formed by the sacred portion
and the city property will belong to the prince. It will extend eastward from
the 25,000 cubits of the sacred portion to the eastern border, and westward
from the 25,000 cubits to the western border. Both these areas running the
length of the tribal portions will belong to the prince, and the sacred portion
with the temple sanctuary will be in the center of them. ²²So the property of
the Levites and the property of the city will lie in the center of the area that
belongs to the prince. The area belonging to the prince will lie between the
border of Judah and the border of Benjamin.**

THE ALLOTMENT FOR THE PRINCE (48:21-22). **48:21-22** The two
remaining portions of land outside the central sacred district on the east
side and west side will be given to the prince and his family.[169] This area
will be bordered by the allotment for the tribe of Judah on the north and
Benjamin on the south (vv. 21-22). The divided allotment with the three
sacred areas between the eastern and western portions is most unusual.
The placement and significance of this segment of the land remains an
enigma.

At least three factors stand out regarding this allotment. (1) The territo-

---

[169] See "Millennial Tribal Allotments" map, p. 428.

ry for the prince is larger than that of either the Zadokite priests or the Levites. This fact is more impressive when you realize that this allotment was for one family in contrast to the others that were for tribal groups. (2) The proximity of the land allotted to the prince to that of the Zadokite priests, Levites, the sanctuary and the city corresponds to his probable role as the administrative representative of the Messiah (see 44:1-3). (3) The location of these two territories will make them the eastern and western boundaries of the sacred area twenty-five thousand cubits square and suggests a possible role for the prince and his family as guardian or protector.

Provision is made for anyone who responds by faith to join the family community. Resident aliens will be adopted into a family tribal unit if they have children and if they become committed by faith to God and his word. By adopting the covenant, they also will commit themselves to live and rear their families under the authority of the Word (47:22).

[23]"As for the rest of the tribes: Benjamin will have one portion; it will extend from the east side to the west side.
[24]"Simeon will have one portion; it will border the territory of Benjamin from east to west.
[25]"Issachar will have one portion; it will border the territory of Simeon from east to west.
[26]"Zebulun will have one portion; it will border the territory of Issachar from east to west.
[27]"Gad will have one portion; it will border the territory of Zebulun from east to west.
[28]"The southern boundary of Gad will run south from Tamar to the waters of Meribah Kadesh, then along the Wadi [of Egypt] to the Great Sea.
[29]"This is the land you are to allot as an inheritance to the tribes of Israel, and these will be their portions," declares the Sovereign LORD.

THE ALLOTMENTS FOR THE FIVE SOUTHERN TRIBES (48:23-29). **48:23-29** These verses explain the details of tribal allotments south of the sacred district where five tribes will be located. As noted earlier, Benjamin will border the sacred area on the south. No particular reason for this apparent position of honor is evident. Benjamin was the youngest son of Jacob born to him by Rachel (Gen 35:18). He was a source of comfort to his father after the death of Rachel and the loss of Joseph, the other son of Rachel. The descendants of Benjamin provided Israel with their first king, Saul (1 Sam 9:1-17). Perhaps the fact that people of Benjamin being the first to affirm David's leadership as king after he returned from fleeing the revolt of Absalom was in some way connected with their privileged position in this tribal allotment (2 Sam 19:16-17).

South of Benjamin will be Simeon (v. 24), then Issachar (v. 25), Zebulun (v. 26), and Gad (v. 27). The southern boundary of Gad's allotment will form the southern boundary of the new kingdom as described in 47:19. Three of the tribes to the south were Leah's children, Simeon, Issachar, and Zebulun; one tribe, Gad, was Jacob's son by Leah's handmaid, Zilpah. None of the tribes north or south of the sacred district seem to receive allotments that show any regard for their former position assigned after the conquest in Josh 14–22.[170]

[30]"These will be the exits of the city: Beginning on the north side, which is 4,500 cubits long, [31]the gates of the city will be named after the tribes of Israel. The three gates on the north side will be the gate of Reuben, the gate of Judah and the gate of Levi.

[32]"On the east side, which is 4,500 cubits long, will be three gates: the gate of Joseph, the gate of Benjamin and the gate of Dan.

[33]"On the south side, which measures 4,500 cubits, will be three gates: the gate of Simeon, the gate of Issachar and the gate of Zebulun.

[34]"On the west side, which is 4,500 cubits long, will be three gates: the gate of Gad, the gate of Asher and the gate of Naphtali.

[35]"The distance all around will be 18,000 cubits.

"And the name of the city from that time on will be:

THE LORD IS THERE."

DESCRIPTION OF THE ETERNAL CITY (48:30-35). **48:30-35** These final verses of the book focus on the city that will lie foursquare in the southern sector of the sacred district. It is somewhat of a surprise to learn that the final abode of God with human beings will be a city. Cities were notorious seats of moral corruption and rebellion against God in the Old Testament. The first city named in the Bible was born in rebellion. This city, named "Enoch," was built by Cain in defiance of God's curse and directive that he would be a vagabond or nomad all the days of his life (Gen 4:12,14). Nimrod built a city and a tower and called all people to join him in rebellion against God. He sponsored the construction of a city and a tower to enable people to become masters of their own fate (Gen 10:9-12; 11:1-9).

Sodom and Gomorrah were cities notorious for their moral depravity (Gen 13:13; 19:1-29). Abraham specifically chose not to dwell in these cities of the plain. The consequences of dwelling there are illustrated in the choice made by Lot's two daughters to have a child by their father

---

[170] Taylor, *Ezekiel*, 284.

(Gen 19:30-38). The sons born of these immoral plans were the progenitors of nations who became the bitterest enemies of God's people (see discussion of Ammon (Ezek 25:1-7) and Moab (Ezek 25:8-11).

The concept of "city" received a more respectable showing when forty-eight Levitical cities were established upon settling the land (Num 35:6-8). These centers of worship were to permeate the land with truth, justice, and righteousness. Of these forty-eight cities six were set aside as cities of refuge. They were to be special centers of justice and mercy. In any circumstance that involved loss of human life, the person causing the death, whether willfully or unintentionally, was liable to punishment by death. The cities of refuge allowed a person a safe haven where the priest acted as judge, heard the case, and decided the fate of the refugee. Thus provision was made to insure justice and to provide pardon for the innocent.

The choice of forty-eight cities was not arbitrary. The number forty-eight (four times twelve) symbolized a new kingdom. Those forty-eight Levitical cities are represented in one final form of the new kingdom of God seen by Ezekiel. The six Levitical cities that were cities of refuge anticipated a seventh. Six is one short of the number of fullness or perfection. One might have expected there would be seven cities of refuge since seven is the number of completeness, but why six? Those six cities of refuge were reminders of the imperfection of justice in the old kingdom and anticipated a new kingdom with a seventh city of refuge. The city that Ezekiel saw was that seventh and final city of refuge, the new Jerusalem that was to be an eternal and perfect city of refuge, rest, and justice. This was the dwelling place anticipated and sought by Abraham, who looked for a city "with foundations, whose architect and builder is God" (Heb 11:10,16).

While the specific name of the city that Ezekiel saw is never mentioned, clearly the "city" is the new Jerusalem.[171] The wall of this city will have twelve gates, three to be located on each side. Each gate will be named after one of the twelve tribes with one exception. There is a Joseph gate instead of two gates called Ephraim and Manasseh.[172] This suggests that the double portion applied only to territorial allotment whereas the gates preserve the son/tribe identity of Gen 46:8-28.[173]

---

[171] Zimmerli, *Ezekiel 2,* 538.

[172] Taylor, *Ezekiel,* 284-85. The replacement of the name of Joseph in the tribal list does not mean different authorship of this passage, but it does point to the intricate detail of the plan Ezekiel envisioned.

[173] Ezekiel used an unusual word for "gate" in referring to these; he called them תוֹצְאֹת ("exits," or "going out places") in v. 30 as opposed to שְׁעָרִים ("gates"), which he used in vv. 31-34; see Zimmerli, *Ezekiel 2,* 546.

Three gates will be located on the north side of the city and probably are named from east to west: Reuben, Judah, and Levi (Ezek 48:31). On the east the three gates probably are listed from north to south and are Joseph, Benjamin, and Dan (v. 32). From east to west on the south side of the city are the gates of Simeon, Issachar, and Zebulun (v. 33). On the west side are the gates of Gad, Asher, and Naphtali (v. 34). The total circumference of the city will be eighteen thousand cubits, which is nearly six miles, making it approximately one and a half miles on each side.[174]

Ezekiel's description is similar to John's vision in Rev 21, especially the twelve gates (Rev 21:12-14). Ezekiel specified the name of the tribe assigned to each gate, while John simply stated that the gates will be named for the twelve tribes of Israel (Rev 21:12). The tribe of Levi received no territorial allotment in the division under Joshua (Josh 18:7), but they will have a gate in the new city.

The existence of twelve gates into the city places an emphasis on accessibility. Each gate will be named for one of the sons of Jacob who were the progenitors of the twelve tribes of Israel. That the tribal identity is superseded in the names of the gates by the personal names of the ancestral heads of the tribes is a reminder that access to God always is based on personal response, not corporate identity. God has always stressed the necessity for personal response to him in matters of fellowship and salvation (48:30-35).

The city, which is the new Jerusalem, also is given a new name (v. 35). This new name takes its significance from Ezekiel's earlier visions. He had witnessed the departure of Yahweh from the sanctuary and temple area (10:1–11:25) and then his return (43:1-5). In his final vision the prophet received a promise of Yahweh's eternal presence. The name of the city will be *Yahweh-Shammah* in Hebrew, which means, "The Lord is There!" This name embodies the idea of the eternal residence of God with his people and the assurance that he will never again depart. Also his presence will no longer be confined to the holy of holies in the sanctuary, but he will dwell in the city whose name preserved the promise, "The Lord is There!"

Ezekiel's ministry began with the vision of the storm that represented the destruction of his nation and the exile in Babylon. His final vision closes with the calm, confident words of the promise contained in the name "The Lord Is There," the new capital of the new kingdom. The apostle John also saw this city, which he described in Rev 21:1-4 (cf. 7:13-17). Especially significant is 21:3, "I heard a loud voice from the

---

[174] See Wevers, *Ezekiel*, 343.

throne saying, 'Now the dwelling of God is with men, and he will live with them. They will be his people, and God himself will be with them and be their God.'" Thus the new name of the city represents the permanence of the divine presence as well as the availability of God to his people. This revelation to Ezekiel of the name of the city is the greatest gem of this passage, if not the entire book. This revelation of love, fellowship, and salvation is a grand and glorious future prospect.

John witnessed a partial fulfillment of Ezekiel's promise when Jesus came, the Messiah, who was called Immanuel by Isaiah (Isa 7:14, Heb. "God with us"). The apostle also envisioned the millennial city and its transformation into the eternal city of God's presence.[175] The name suggests the grand finale to the twenty-five year ministry and the forty-eight chapters of messages in which Ezekiel saw God withdraw from the temple. In this grand finale he not only sees God return but hears the new name that presents the idea that God's return is permanent. Ezekiel, like John, had this grand climax to his visions in which he saw the restoration he had first envisioned, recorded in chaps. 33–37.

The new boundaries, new tribal alignments, and new city will be physical manifestations of the new kingdom, which Ezekiel saw. Although the word "new" is not used in association with the kingdom or any of its descriptions, clearly Ezekiel saw the arrival of a totally new order. This, after all, is the whole point of chaps. 40–48. The arrival of a new order is the logical conclusion of the earlier promise of a "new heart" and a "new spirit" that God pledged to Israel (see Ezek 11:19; 18:31; 36:26). It also anticipated the new creature and new creation that every person can become through faith in the Messiah, Jesus Christ (2 Cor 5:17). Finally, it anticipates the "new heaven" and "new earth" described as part of the coming new kingdom in Rev 21:1–22:21.

Ezekiel saw five elements of the new kingdom that revealed the restoration would be permanent. First, the new temple will be dedicated to and indwelt by the one true God, Yahweh (40:1–43:12). He will finally and eternally be accessible to his people. Second, the new order of worship (43:12–46:24) will be designed to confirm the new covenant of Israel and commemorate the work of Christ. Third, the new quality of life (47:1–48:29) will be filled with material fruitfulness and spiritual fulfillment. Fourth, the new city (48:30-34) will be a symbol of the new unity and oneness of Israel and God. Fifth, the new name of the city will be *Yahweh Shammah*, "The Lord is There!" (48:35), as a testimony of God's eternal presence among his people.

---

[175] Taylor, *Ezekiel*, 285.

"And the name of the city from that time on will be THE LORD IS THERE!"

"JEHOVAH-SHAMMAH"<br>THE LORD IS THERE

One of the names of the Lord our God,
   Which speaks of His love and His care,
Is called in the Hebrew — "Jehovah-Shammah"
   And it means that "The Lord is there."

In your hours of sorrow and your times of grief,
   When your soul seems so filled with despair,
Reflect on the words of "Jehovah-Shammah"
   And know in your heart — "He is there."

When you're flat on your back or you're suffering pain
   And you're feeling that life is not fair,
Start counting your blessings from "Jehovah-Shammah";
   Just think on His love — "He is there."

When your plans go awry or your dreams fall apart,
   When your burdens are heavy to bear,
Lean hard on the promise of "Jehovah-Shammah";
   You are never alone — "He is there."

When the devil's temptations press hard on your soul,
   And he deviously seeks to ensnare,
Run quickly to Jesus, your "Jehovah-Shammah";
   Then your battle is won — "He is there."

When your heart overflows with thanksgiving and praise,
   And you pour out yourμ love in your prayer,
There's rejoicing in heaven by "Jehovah-Shammah";
   For He hears and we know — "He is there."[176]

—Margaret Elaine Harlan

"THE LORD IS THERE!" (Ezek 48:35).
"Never will I leave you; never will I forsake you" (Heb.13:5).

---

[176] This poem is used by permission of the author, Ms. Margaret Elaine Harlan of Dallas, Texas. It was written after she attended a session taught by this writer on Ezekiel 48 and captures the spirit and message of the chapter.

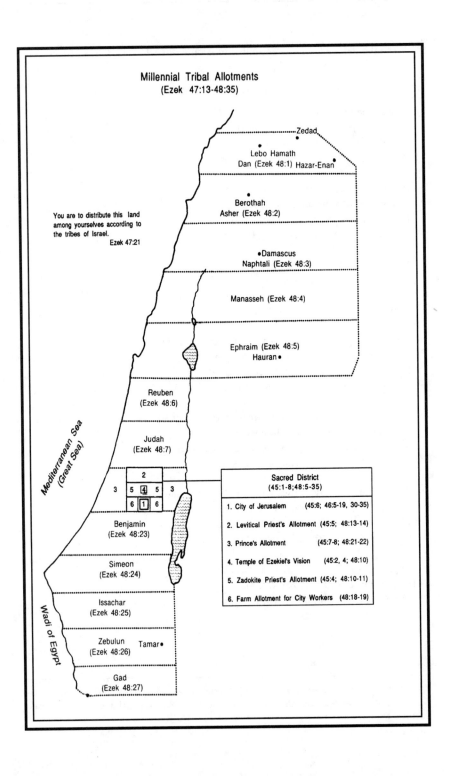

Millennial Tribal Allotments
(Ezek 47:13-48:35)

Zedad

Lebo Hamath
Dan (Ezek 48:1) Hazar-Enan

Berothah
Asher (Ezek 48:2)

You are to distribute this land
among yourselves according to
the tribes of Israel.
Ezek 47:21

•Damascus
Naphtali (Ezek 48:3)

Manasseh (Ezek 48:4)

Ephraim (Ezek 48:5)
Hauran •

Reuben
(Ezek 48:6)

Judah
(Ezek 48:7)

Mediterranean Sea
(Great Sea)

2

3   5  4  5   3
     6  1  6

Benjamin
(Ezek 48:23)

Simeon
(Ezek 48:24)

Issachar
(Ezek 48:25)

Zebulun    Tamar •
(Ezek 48:26)

Wadi of Egypt

Gad
(Ezek 48:27)

Sacred District
(45:1-8;48:5-35)

1. City of Jerusalem        (45:6; 46:5-19, 30-35)

2. Levitical Priest's Allotment (45:5; 48:13-14)

3. Prince's Allotment        (45:7-8; 48:21-22)

4. Temple of Ezekiel's Vision   (45:2, 4; 48:10)

5. Zadokite Priest's Allotment (45:4; 48:10-11)

6. Farm Allotment for City Workers  (48:18-19)

# Selected Subject Index

# Person Index

# Selected Scripture Index